THE INTERNATIONAL ENCYCLOPEDIA OF SECRET SOCIETIES AND FRATERNAL ORDERS

THE INTERNATIONAL
ENCYCLOPEDIA OF
SECRET SOCIETIES AND
FRATERNAL ORDERS

ALAN AXELROD

Checkmark Books™

An imprint of Facts On File, Inc.

The International Encyclopedia of Secret Societies and Fraternal Orders

Checkmark Books
An imprint of Facts On File, Inc.
11 Penn Plaza
New York NY 10001

Library of Congress Cataloging-in-Publication Data

Axelrod, Alan, 1952–
The international encyclopedia of secret societies and fraternal
orders / Alan Axelrod.
p.   cm.
Includes bibliographical references and index.
ISBN 0-8160-2307-7 (hc)
ISBN 0-8160-3871-6 (pb)
1. Secret societies—Encyclopedias. I. Title.
HS119.A94   1996
366'.03—dc20   95-45819

Contents

Introduction

There is but one absolute truth concerning secret societies: There are no absolutes. Secret societies change with time, with geography, and with personal inclination. However, the vast majority of fraternal orders and secret societies have two prominent features in common: secrecy and initiation. The organizations in this book have—or, at least, at one time had—some sort of ritual that separates the member of the society from the nonmember. Complex though a given ritual may be, its essence is summed up in a single question: "Can you keep a secret?"

If few people are able to recall the first time they were asked this question, all remember what the secret conferred: a sense of belonging. Those who know the secret are the insiders, "us." Those who do not know the secret are the outsiders, "them." Learning a "secret" with awful (but often unspecified) penalties for disclosing it to outsiders bound us to our childhood playmates. Much the same principle operates, for adults, in secret societies. Indeed, most often, the nature of the secret is relatively unimportant. It is the *sharing* of the secret that really matters.

Sometimes, of course, the secrecy is something more than a survival of childlike impulse. For example, both the Freemasons and the Mafia are secret societies, in that both have initiations and oaths kept secret from outsiders. Both have meeting places, or lodges, where members gather. The difference is that Freemasons are (relatively) open about it all, while the Mafia maintains an altogether lower profile, assuring secrecy through the *omerta,* or code of silence, which is enforced by tradition as well as very real and fatal consequences if violated.

A useful distinction is between *secret* societies and *clandestine* societies. The Freemasons are secret, but not clandestine. They meet openly, and the Masonic Lodge is something of a landmark in many cities. The Mafia, in contrast, are both secret and clandestine. This does not mean that the Mafia should be excluded from a study of secret societies. It does not even mean that the *form* of a local Mafia chapter is much different from the *form* of a Freemason's Lodge. Both exclude outsiders by means of recognition signals, which are conveyed during initiations, and both have their hierarchies and degrees, their *Capos* and Past Grand Masters. They differ principally in their ends; and this is the handiest, perhaps most meaningful way to go about classifying and differentiating secret societies.

It must be noted that a few organizations covered in this book are neither initiatory nor oath-bound. They are here for one of two reasons. Either they were once initiatory or oath-bound but have subsequently dropped the requirement as an anachronism, or they are (or have been) perceived or feared as secret societies, perhaps because they share certain other characteristics with secret societies, such as meeting in lodges and having their own jargon.

The Evolution of Secret Societies

Secret societies are probably as old as anything else recognizable as human culture. A primitive secret society is the equivalent of an extended—and idealized—family. Just as we can trust family members, so we can trust people who are members of our own totem, sodality, blood brotherhood, or clan-by-marriage. The very earliest secret societies, therefore, were social/benevolent/

mystical/political. They may also have had trade aspects (a clan of flint-knappers, a clan of skin-curers, a sodality of shamans), but crime was still a concept of the future. Together with the tribe, which is based on an uneasy mixture of family relationships and brute force, the initiatory secret society *was* society. The large entry on West African secret societies in this volume reflects this.

As other political units coalesced—the city-state, the petty kingdom, the alliance—the trade aspect of the secret society gained in importance; trade skills became the "mystery" around which societies were organized. Members learned two things. One was the set of skills on which the group depended, skills that were unknown (or imperfectly known) to outsiders. The other was a system of symbols by which other members may be recognized. This is almost certainly the origin of the Freemasons, the Compagnonnage, and a limited number of other secret societies.

Then, as the division of labor became still more marked, it was no longer possible for one person to master the whole "mystery" of, say, masonry. From being a trade association, the guild (if it survived) became increasingly a social organization. Almost certainly, this is the way in which "accepted masonry" evolved: Social, or "accepted," members joined the trade, or "operative," members of the craft. At this point, the mystical aspect of the organization could take any direction that the fancy of the new, "accepted" members might choose. This is probably the origin of the wild proliferation of rites and lodges that bedevil Freemasonry to this day: the Ancient and Accepted Rite, the Scottish Rite (the same thing in most jurisdictions), the York or American Rite, and so forth.

During this evolutionary stage, the individual lodge (or the Grand Lodge, if it purports to rule over several lodges) was also likely to start taking its benevolent aspects to greater lengths. Instead of the informal hat-passing for widows and orphans, there might appear a formalized system of benefits; and instead of being totally inward-looking, the emphasis might shift to general philanthropic works instead of supporting only members or their widows and orphans. (The members themselves are almost certain to be male, a point that will be discussed shortly.)

At this juncture in a secret society's evolution, there are two possibilities: materialism or decadence. If the society chooses the path of materialism, it becomes more and more a benevolent and welfare organization. If it chooses decadence, whether deliberately or accidentally, the last remnants of the "mysteries" will be reduced to meaninglessness or near-meaninglessness. The latter course is epitomized by the Freemasons.

Perhaps surprisingly, it is in this senescent stage of materialism or decadence that the society is most likely to be emulated. The myriad "secret societies" that sprang up in the United States in the latter part of the 19th century were almost all materialist; the "mysteries" and initiations were mere window dressing tacked on to what were effectively insurance societies. A few purely social societies emerged, such as the Concatenated Order of Hoo-Hoo or E Clampus Vitus, but they were very much in the minority. In Europe, and especially in France, there have been many more "mystical" secret societies, some of them founded in the last few decades, but few of them have grown very large.

Finally, the society reaches a stage where the imperative is compelling: Change or die, because current conditions bear no resemblance to the way that things were when the society was founded. Benevolence is rendered all but unnecessary by the rise of the welfare state and corporately supported insurance programs. At the same time, social ties are loosened by the advent of alternative amusements, most notably video and television, which isolates people in their own homes.

This is only one model of the rise and fall of secret societies. The role of the political secret society has not been touched upon, and the changes that secret societies undergo have been presented as logical and as partaking of an almost Marxist historical inevitability: There is more to it than this. Even an "evolved" secret society may change, and at any stage, a secret society may mutate from one form to another. The mutation may be temporary or permanent; it may herald a rebirth or a final decline; but the possibility is always there.

After the first stage, the primitive tribal secret society, evolution into a trade society is by no means the only available option. Almost equally important, at least for a few centuries, was the mystical or religious society. In ancient Egypt and in Greece, there were the "Mystery Schools," which remain the prototype of modern mystical secret societies. The trade society may also be emulated, appearing without any direct antecedent. A trade union is perhaps the most obvious version of such an emulation, though the Compagnonnage (of less skilled workers than Master Masons) is arguably an emulation of Freemasonry. Thereafter, almost anything is possible. Political secret societies adopt the forms of older societies. The Carbonari owed a great deal to Freemasonry and to the Illuminati, but in the final analysis they and their kin used the older societies as models, rather than being derived from them. Alternatively, existing societies may be hijacked for political ends: George Washington and his colleagues plotted revolution in Masonic lodges. And mystical societies of all kinds may arise at any time. The Hermetic Order of the Golden Dawn, the Thule Gesellschaft, and so on claim remote and arcane ancestry, even if they were invented in Chicago in the 1880s or Milan in the 1920s.

Secret societies are presently in general decline (a topic more fully covered toward the end of this introduction), and of the relatively few that are in a good state of health at present, most are either social or ethnic/benevolent in orientation. This notwithstanding, as of the close of the 20th century, there appears to be a renewed interest in mystical societies such as the Rosicrucians (an organization of the late 19th century, though it claims a more remote ancestry), and it may be that if secret societies have a future, this type of association is it.

The Names and Supposed Antiquity of Secret Societies

Secret societies invent wonderful names for themselves, often laying claim to great antiquity. Moreover, one soon discovers that the resonance and magnificence of a name, or claims to a history measured in centuries and even millennia, have nothing to do with the size or "real world" power of the organization. In 1995, for example, the Ancient Order of Foresters of the Pacific Coast Jurisdiction boasted some 200 members, while the Ancient Mystic Order of Samaritans could muster just under 4,000; but the prosaic-sounding Catholic Daughters of the Americas numbered 160,000.

The two phenomena—high-falutin' names and fanciful history—are closely related. Secret societies have always attracted a certain number of distinguished individuals (Goethes, Washingtons, Franklins and the like), but they have also appealed to people whose lives are so unremarkable that they feel the need for artificial stimulation and exaltation. Such rank-and-file members crave high-sounding titles and bogus historics.

Women and Secret Societies

Women have mostly played a very small role in secret societies. The vast majority of secret societies and fraternal orders have either been all-male or have admitted women only as secondary members. Typically, women must have a male relative who is a member of an organization before they can be admitted to an "auxiliary" organization, the activities of which are often subordinate to those of the main male order.

On those rare occasions when women have founded secret societies (such as P.E.O.) or where they have transformed a women's auxiliary into a society in its own right, they have frequently shown a steadfastness of purpose, a degree of financial and organizational acumen, and a lack of interest in petty squabbles, which male organizations would do well to emulate.

(Because fraternal orders and secret societies are such male-dominated activities, we have used the masculine pronoun throughout this book, except where it is patently inappropriate.)

Schisms and Splinter Groups

One last point to make, before going on to discuss the different types of secret societies, is that a great many societies have focused as much on dissent as they have on fraternal amity. Three separate tendencies can be seen: schism, splinter, and reinvention.

Many organizations seem to have been founded by near-megalomaniacs or, at the very least, by men suffering from delusions of grandeur. Initially, these individuals often attracted others with a similarly tenuous grasp on reality, and there were three scenarios played out again and again. One was that the organization collapsed, never to be heard of any more. The second was that it collapsed, but before it had disappeared entirely, someone managed to salvage the wreckage. The third was that the wilder excesses of the founder or founders gradually died away, and the organization drifted into the mainstream.

If there was a *schism*, as there frequently was, both branches would then vociferously claim to be the only true representatives of the original society, so that there are often two organizations with the same name—though, sometimes, one of them may adopt the epithet "Improved" to denote the split. At this point, one (or both) of the schismatic branches might die off or decline into insignificance; both branches might continue to flourish, perhaps giving rise to further schisms; or, surprisingly often, there might later be a reunification.

Splinters are slightly different from schisms in that they do not seek to overthrow or replace the original organization; they merely want a change of emphasis, which they do not feel will be possible within the parent organization, so they set up in business for themselves, usually under a different name. Magical secret societies are peculiarly prone to splintering, as a brief study of the Hermetic Order of the Golden Dawn shows.

Other splinter groups arise as a result of national differences; the American Masonic lodges, for example, refuse to acknowledge the authority of the Grand Lodge of England, under whose aegis they were originally set up.

No matter what the cause of the splintering, the prognoses are much the same as for schisms. The splinter may die; may flourish, sometimes even to the extent of supplanting the parent; or (very rarely) may reunite with the parent.

Reinventions are perhaps the most confusing of all. Often passed off as revivals of dormant groups, they use some of the jargon and structure of an earlier society, but may well have completely different aims and constituencies. Frequently, the societies that were "revived" turn out never to have existed; the "reinvented" society has composed a fanciful history for itself. In the most confusing cases, however, there is just enough relationship between the "revival" and one or more previous societies to make it impossible to guess what is "revived," what is borrowed from elsewhere, and what is cut from the whole cloth. One other form of reinvention is the foundation of a "new" secret society with a cheerful disregard for the possibility that anyone else might have used the same name; or, for that matter, that they might still be using it.

The net result of schism, splinter and reinvention is that there are certain concepts or pretended histories amounting almost to "catch-phrases," which are adopted by all manner of secret societies. For example, there are more than a dozen different varieties of Forester; Rosicrucianism is a hopeless tangle; as Umberto Eco pointed out in his novel *Foucault's Pendulum*, sooner or later the lunatics will always bring up the Templars; and the intertwinings of Theosophy and Anthroposophy must tax even the devotees of both.

Types of Secret Societies

Endless divisions and subdivisions could be created, but broadly, the aims or ambitions of all secret societies and fraternal orders fall more or less into one of seven groups

1. social
2. benevolent (or service)
3. ethnic
4. trade
5. mystical (or religious)
6. political
7. criminal

It is comparatively rare for a society to fall neatly under a single heading. Even the Mafia, which most people would unhesitatingly characterize as purely criminal, has its other aspects. Mafiosi meet for social gatherings, look after widows and orphans (for whose children they may, after all, be responsible), and lobby politicians either formally or informally. They are commonly regarded as being Italian (or, even more specifically, Sicilian), which would tend to make them, as much as anything else, an ethnic organization. In fact, the Mafia is ethnically varied. The Jews and, to a considerably lesser extent, the Irish were coopted into the Mafia as representing previous generation of criminals in the United States, and

at least one leading Mafioso was Welsh: Murray "The Camel" Humphries. It is true, however, that the higher levels of Mafia membership are reserved not merely for Italians, but for Sicilians. The mystical aspect of Mafia life is negligible, but it is not nonexistent: Oaths may be sworn on the Bible, and there is a certain amount of mystical mumbo-jumbo associated with the initiation. And, of course, while their trade is crime, they may also be involved in other businesses, perfectly legal, if often morally disputable.

Other societies will be found in these pages that are (for example) mystical/criminal, or social/political/ethnic, or trade/benevolent/social, or almost any other combination of the various possibilities listed above. But at least the categories allow us to bring some order to the welter of organizations that exist.

1. Social Societies

For most of the 19th and 20th centuries, social societies (almost a tautology) have been the most important type of secret society.

In the 18th century, even under the Regency at the beginning of the 19th century, they might accurately have been categorized as drinking clubs, where people went to enjoy a drink (and more) in the company of like-minded people. The City of Lushington is a fine example, and there are 19th- and even 20th-century survivals such as the "Clampers" (E Clampus Vitus). To this day, a companionable drink is one of the most important aspects of a lodge meeting for hundreds of thousands of adherents of secret societies. There are, however, nondrinking social clubs, especially in the United States. It is almost incredible to many Europeans that an American Masonic lodge is "dry" and that the main reason for going seems to be the perpetuation of ritual. It is impossible to believe that the earliest "accepted Masons" were averse to a drink, the more so in view of the fact that Masonic gatherings in the 18th century were normally held in taverns.

Examples of social societies include the Freemasons, the Odd Fellows, the various "ungulates" and "ruminants" (Buffalo, Moose, Elks), and such secondary organizations as the Shriners and the Bagmen of Bagdad. The ways in which the different clubs enjoy themselves is varied. Some are relatively quiet and restrained and may even be given to intellectual discussion, while others are based on "letting off steam" and may be boisterous in the extreme.

A subdivision of social societies is Orders of Knighthood. Most of the great chivalric orders (the Garter, the Golden Fleece, etc.) functioned as social clubs for the aristocracy, usually along with a benevolent or service aspect such as "reclaiming" the Holy Land for Christianity, protecting the virtue of high-born maidens, and so forth.

2. Benevolent or Service Societies

A benevolent or service society is set up to do good, rather than merely to be enjoyable. Some people distinguish between societies that help only their own members (benevolent or friendly societies) and societies that help other people (charitable or service societies), but this is not a very helpful distinction. Many societies support local or other charities, even when the main thrust of their work is directed toward looking after their own. Equally, societies that pride themselves on charitable work (such as the Lions or the Rotary Club) would hardly be human if they did not help one another out in time of trouble.

In the 19th century, countless benevolent societies were set up as a form of proto-welfare state, to provide a cushion against accident, old age and even in some cases unemployment. They were particularly common in the United States, where recent immigrants could rarely rely on an established network of family, friends, and (as a last resort) the parish to help them. In some cases, older-established social clubs also took on benevolent aspects. With the rise of the welfare state in the 20th century, this sort of society became less and less relevant. Some disappeared entirely; some rethought their aims (for instance, placing more emphasis on ethnic ties than on financial support); and some began to function, in effect, as insurance companies on the same sort of commercial footing as a regular business, though usually without making profits. In the last type, premium proceeds were normally ploughed back into the organization, thereby keeping premiums lower, or were applied to charitable works. Many examples of this sort of society will be found in this book.

Some chivalric orders fall (or originally fell) into this category. The service in question was normally rugged, romantic, and dramatic, as in the case of the Templars, and the transition of the Hospitallers of St. John of Jerusalem into, first, a fighting order and then a naval order (all the while remaining hospitallers) is a fascinating history of a service organization.

3. Ethnic and Cultural Societies

It might be more accurate to call these "exile societies," because people rarely feel the need to band together with their countrymen when they are in their own country. Logically, therefore, the United States is the great home of ethnic societies. Just about every ethnic group that emigrated into the United States has (or has had) its own ethnic society.

Typically, the ethnic society provides three things. One is a chance to reminisce and exchange news about "the old country." The second is a way to try to preserve the culture of "the old country" in the new generation. The third is an insurance/benevolent aspect, a formalization of helping one another out.

There are forms of this sort of society that do exist inside their own cultural milieu and function to reinforce the culture. Certain political organizations serve such a purpose, and in tribal African societies there are secret societies whose function it is to preserve the culture of their forebears. These African secret societies may partake of almost all of the other kinds of activity described under the seven headings here; some are even trade societies, limited to certain callings such as blacksmithing.

4. Trade Societies

In the 20th century, trade unions and trade fraternal benevolent organizations (such as the Fraternal Order of Police) are the most important manifestations of trade societies. In earlier days, there were associations of craftsmen (Freemasons, the Compagnonnage); of less skilled trades (for example, charcoal burners); of merchants and artisans (guilds); and of others.

Comparatively few genuine trade organizations are covered in this book. There are, however, many other organizations that either drew from genuine trade associations (Freemasonry, since the 18th century) or purported to be modeled on trade associations (the Carbonari, for example).

5. Mystical and Religious Societies

Mystical societies are at once the most obvious and the least obvious of secret societies. They are the most obvious, because everyone can name a few—the Mystery Schools of ancient Greece, the Hermetic Order of the Golden Dawn—but they are also the least obvious, because there is a thread of mysticism interwoven with almost all secret societies and because there are surprisingly many mystical societies that are not very well known—Les Hommes de L'Intelligence, for example.

These societies are easier to understand if they are divided into three subclasses: mystical, religious, and magical.

Mystical societies may in some cases by indistinguishable from religious societies, but most of them share one characteristic: ultimate incomprehensibility. For the adherent of a mystical secret society, belief alone is rarely enough. There must also be a massive and complex edifice of thought, preferably supported by a massive and opaque canon of mystical literature. Often, mystical societies are infuriatingly vague and elusive to outsiders. It is, for example, next to impossible for a non-Theosophist to grasp the meaning of Theosophy.

Religious societies are usually (though not invariably) more straightforward. The adherent is given something to believe in, and he or she had better believe in it. The minutiae and regulations of a religious secret society may constitute altogether as massive a canon as the writings that underpin a mystical secret society, but the focus is usually much clearer. It is also usually Christian, although there are pagan religious societies, principally in Europe but also the United States.

Magical societies typically differ from both mystical and religious societies in their goals. They are much more concerned with achieving results (such as the conjuration of demons or the transmutation of metals) than with undefined personal improvement. Once again, this is not true of all magical societies, but it is fairly typical. Another characteristic of magical societies is that they typically emphasize the variations in individual potential and stress the importance of individual practice in achieving one's goals. They may demand obedience to a Magus or Master, but this is normally a purely personal one-to-one relationship with a living person, rather than accepting a general creed. A Christian might say that he has a one-to-one relationship with Christ, but no one expects him to be a slave to his parish priest in order to pursue his chosen path.

6. Political Societies

In a reasonably free democracy, such as exists in Western Europe or the United States, the only reason for a political secret society to exist is because its views are so far out of the mainstream that it cannot attract mass support. Essentially, a political secret society in a free country must either subscribe to a species of paranoia (as have some of the American nativist or anti-Semitic organizations of the 19th and 20th centuries) or must advocate illegal means or ends: the use of terror as a political weapon, or the violent overthrow of a generally tolerated government.

Not all societies are free, of course, and this was even more commonly the case in the past. As early as the end of the 15th century, there were associations like the Poor Conrads in Germany that sought a better deal from life. In the 18th century, secret societies were undoubtedly associated with the American and the French revolutions. By the early 19th century, secret societies were working toward freedom for Greece. Then there were the Decembrists and, later, the Nihilists in Russia, the Omladina and other organizations working in the Balkans, usually against the interests of Austria-Hungary (this was what precipitated World War I); and in the 1920s and 1930s, there were anti-fascist and anti-communist secret societies, especially in Germany.

As the 20th century draws to a close, political secret societies are much less widespread than they have been at other times. This is partly because democracy (or a facsimile thereof) is more widespread than ever before, and partly because a political secret society now has far less need to work *inside* the country against whose gov-ernment it is plotting. The leaders of an antigovernment movement can normally rely on finding sanctuary in another country, and modern telecommunications and transport mean that only a relatively few members of any organization have to work "underground" in the country whose politics they are trying to undermine.

7. Criminal Societies

The Mafia is so well known as to need very little introduction here, and it serves as a paradigm case for other criminal societies. There are (or have been) a number of other criminal societies, with a greater or lesser degree of criminality, and they are also covered in this book. Examples include the Camorra (the Neapolitan equivalent of the Mafia) and the Garduna in Spain. Of course, whether a society is "political" or "criminal" often depends on the political orientation of the commentator, and if the remove in time is great enough, it may be impossible to distinguish clearly between the two.

Societies Sui Generis

Having said that there are seven categories, it may seem unreasonable to introduce a residual category. The point is that there are some societies that resist categorization. Certainly, the Vehmgericht could be categorized as a service organization or an ethnic or cultural association, or a political organization, or possibly even as a criminal organization; but in each case, it would be a matter of forcing a square peg into a round hole. The Vehmgericht partook of all of these definitions, and more besides. For example, it functioned as an extralegal police and judiciary. How do you classify such an organization?

Reasons for Joining Secret Societies

Regardless of the type of society, the next question must be why people join secret societies. The reasons depend both on the organization and on the person joining. Some people seem to be joiners by nature; others are not.

Generally, however, reasons for joining an organization fall into nine categories, even if the distinctions between the categories are often blurred.

1. Business

Some organizations are better known than others for favoring "brothers" when it comes to awarding contracts and other business favors. To some extent, such favoritism is inevitable, because most people would rather deal with someone they know rather than with a complete stranger. In other cases, there may be an aggressive policy of dealing only with "brothers," whether you know them personally or not, as in the second heyday of the Ku Klux Klan, just after World War I.

In some organizations, furthering business contacts during formal meetings is expressly forbidden, which leads to the suspicion that the temptation, and perhaps the habit, was once so widespread that it needed to be suppressed.

2. Desire to Be "Different"

The vast majority of the people who join secret societies know that their impact on the world will be negligible. They will leave no great books, no great business dynasties, no magnificent works of art behind them. In life, they are at the mercy of overseers: foremen, bosses, superintendents. They shop at anonymous stores; they are not recognized, even by many of the people they see daily.

In the lodge, by contrast, they are someone special. They are automatically among friends; they are privy to "secrets" other people do not know; they may be elected to some post within the lodge, with a wonderfully exalted title, and wear resplendent robes and weighty badges of office. Their names will be entered in weighty tomes. In order to achieve this exalted state, they do not have to do anything particularly demanding or remarkable.

3. Desire for Knowledge

Many organizations promise secret knowledge and arcane teachings, though, in most cases, the promise far exceeds the value of what is actually delivered.

4. Fear

A number of groups attract members who are afraid either that a comfortable *status quo* will be upset, or that their own relative position in society will decline still further unless they band together against some other group of people. In other words, the motivation is negative; they are against something, rather than for anything (though they may twist the language to make it appear otherwise). Racist, anti-Semitic, anti-Catholic, and anti-immigration societies (often calling themselves "patriotic") are good examples.

5. Good Fellowship

Even where the purpose of a society is ostensibly something other than good fellowship, many people would not join (or at least would not stay) unless they enjoyed themselves.

6. Habit

"My father was a Mason" (or an Odd Fellow, or an Elk, or whatever) is still a common reason for joining a secret society.

In some cases, the person who joins for such a reason will go on to enjoy the benefits of belonging to the organization; in other cases, he will merely go through the motions.

7. Mutual Aid

In the days before the government assumed a large part of the responsibility for sick pay, accident insurance, old age pensions, and so forth, mutual benefit societies were the only way for most working people to protect themselves from many of life's misfortunes. During the 19th century, vast numbers of mutual benefit associations were formed, usually with strong fraternal trappings. It is likely that the fraternal aspect of the association removed any stigma that might be attached to accepting charity.

The other aspect of "mutual aid" is that a stranger in a new town will have his integration into the community eased if he belongs to an organization that already exists there. This is one of the reasons why the lodge was such an important feature of so many towns on the American frontier, or in the rootless gold-mining country of the American Far West, where the Odd Fellows flourished particularly.

8. Special Benefits

The Elks were originally founded to circumvent a New York law that forbade saloons to open on a Sunday. Getting around liquor laws is a common example of a "special benefit" conferred by a club.

On a more exalted level, the Odd Fellows and some other organizations were especially strong on education and offered assistance and scholarships to members and their sons (but rarely daughters).

9. Status

In some communities, merely belonging to the "right" club or clubs is essential to social and commercial prominence. It is by no means unknown for membership in a given organization to be an unwritten qualification for participation in local government.

Another way in which membership of a society can convey status is via its offices and degrees. A Master Mason can feel superior to an Entered Apprentice, while a Mason of the Thirty-third Degree can feel superior to a mere Master. And, of course, election to a post in the lodge can bring respect from fellow lodge members.

The Decline of Secret Societies

Even while this book was in preparation, any number of secret societies apparently disappeared—though it is difficult to be sure that a society has vanished, since there are rarely newspaper announcements of such events. Even where a society declines almost to nothing, the operative word remains "almost." There is also the question of what constitutes "deceased." It is, after all, quite open to anyone to say that they belong to any secret society, and if there is no one to argue, who is to say that they do not?

All of this notwithstanding, the decline in reported numbers and membership figures has been inexorable for most secret societies. The *Encyclopedia of Associations,* a standard reference, which solicits information directly from associations, tells the story year by year. Annual declines of 5 to 10 percent are commonplace. Taking a longer view reveals even more spectacular declines. The Order of Owls had 600,000 members in the early 1920s (an era when many fraternal orders peaked); about 200,000 in the late 1950s; about 40,000 in 1979; and only about 5,000 a decade later. Only a few organizations have prospered or even remained stable. What, then, were the processes at work behind this decline? And what enabled a few organizations to buck the trend?

The most obvious reason for the decline of so many organizations can be summed up briefly: choice, together with the atomization of society.

Choice is the more obvious of the two reasons. A hundred years ago, the "Lodge Night" was something to look forward to. Today, there is the ubiquitous television (rendered still more attractive by the advent of the videocassette recorder and the satellite dish); there are movies; there are compact discs and tapes and more; there are floodlit night-time sports; there are automobiles to be driven and motorcycles to be ridden; there are restaurants (if our ancestors could afford to eat out, there was rarely anywhere they would want to do so for pleasure); there is late-night shopping. The range of leisure activity is enormous. Also, a vast increase in relative affluence means that comparatively expensive hobbies can be undertaken with impunity—and switched at will. In contrast, when you committed yourself to the Freemasons, or the Odd Fellows, or whoever, you were making a relatively modest financial commitment but you were signing up for life.

The second point, *atomization,* is summed up by the now-venerable hippie dictum, "do your own thing." Today, you are *forced* to do your own thing. There is no one to share it with. Television isolates us in our living rooms and separates us from the promenade, the public concert, the neighborly visit. Automobiles isolate us from public transportation and even the walk to work. And even when we do walk, the personal stereo isolates us from our surroundings. Soon, the increase in "telecommuting," working entirely from the home, linked to a "virtual office" by computer modem may cut us off from person-to-person contact in the workplace. We have

become increasingly self-centered (if decreasingly self-sufficient), and joining a club seems quite simply foreign and irrelevant.

One specific historic factor has also contributed to the general decline. The Great Depression of the 1930s put a large dent in the membership of secret societies. Even the comparatively modest sums needed for lodge dues proved too much for many. Others were simply too busy working to take time to go to their lodges. During the 1930s, all manner of organizations lost people in droves. Some societies went under; others started to recover as the money started to flow again later in the decade, though few regained their former glory.

Criteria for Inclusion of Entries

It is impossible for any guide to fraternal, secret, and similar societies to be entirely comprehensive. There is always just one more obscure secret society that pops up, even in a field that had seemed fully gleaned. The general criteria for inclusion in this book follow, but it is important first to emphasize that a number of organizations that do *not* meet these criteria have also been included, provided they have either regarded themselves as secret societies or have been treated as secret societies by others. In particular, many sects and religions have been perceived or castigated as secret. In general, though, these criteria have been follows:

1. The organization must not be avowedly open to the general public. In other words, you must make a conscious effort to join.
2. There must be, or must have been, some rite or oath of initiation; merely paying a subscription is not enough, nor is it sufficient to join a common-interest society.
3. There must be, or must have been, a declared intention to do one or more of the following:
   (a) Transfer some secret or "Great Teaching"
   (b) Behave fraternally or benevolently toward others
   (c) Support one another against others

Entries Other Than Organizations

There are several entries that do not describe organizations. In general, these fall into two groups.

First, there are *concepts* that appear frequently in other entries and that can, for the sake of convenience, be discussed in a single entry. For example, "degrees" or grades are a common feature of secret societies, so they have their own entry. Likewise, there are entries on magic, on lodges, on tantra, and so on.

Second, there are *individuals* who are important in the world of fraternal orders and secret societies. Some of these are treated in their own entries.

Abecedairiens

Little is known about the Abecedairiens or Abecedarians, which one French authority describes only as "une petite secte peu connue" (a small, little-known sect). The society opposed what it saw as the excesses of printing, believing it to be a medium for the dissemination of false knowledge. For Abecedairiens, the only knowledge of value came directly from the Holy Spirit

This society seems to have developed within a few years of Johannes Gutenberg's introduction of movable type in 1456. However, the Abecedairiens did not long endure.

Abelites

Originated as an obscure Christian sect in Hippo, North Africa, during the fourth century. Abelites reemerged in the mid-17th century as a German society of persons who professed to imitate Abel in all his virtues. Their principal meetings were held at Griefswald, near Stralsund. It has been reported that the Abelites amused themselves more with moral and literary debating than with earnest imitation of Abel's virtue.

Aborigines

The Aborigines was a short-lived English secret society, founded in 1783, that cashed in on the craze for secret societies of the time. The most entertaining feature of the society was the way in which candidates (on being made an "Original") swore their OATHS upon a fine collection of sartorial symbolism, viz. the Cap of Honour, the Collar of Freedom, the Coat of Honesty, the Jacket of Sincerity, the Shirt of Prudence, the Breeches of Modesty, the Garters of Reputation, and the Stockings of Sobriety. The secret password of the order was "Eden," which symbolized the garden where Adam, the great aboriginal, was formed.

Acacia Fraternity

3901 West 86th Street, Suite 430
Indianapolis, IN 46268
(317) 872-8210

The Acacia Fraternity was founded in 1904 as a college fraternity for FREEMASONS, though it soon also admitted the sons of Freemasons. The fraternity publishes the *Triad,* semiannually. There were 44,000 members in 1993.

In Masonic lore, the acacia is almost overloaded with symbolism and hidden meanings, which makes it a logical choice for the symbol of a Masonic college fraternity. The symbolism of the acacia is tripartite, signifying the immortality of the soul, innocence and purity, and the process of initiation. It is the acacia that is rendered as "shittim wood" in many biblical passages, and commended as the material for various sacred objects (Exodus 25–27).

The first chapter of the Acacia Fraternity was founded in 1904 by 14 Master Masons at the University of Michigan. At first, membership was open only to Master Masons, but in 1933 it was opened to the sons and brothers of Freemasons and even to men who could obtain the sponsorship or recommendation of two Master Masons, though in the latter case at least one of the sponsors had himself to be an Acacian.

In addition to the normal activities of a college fraternity, Acacians receive instruction in the ideals and culture of Freemasonry. They also support the Shriners' Burns Unit for Children.

While Acacians may dispute that they are "part" of Freemasonry, the ties seem undeniable, and indeed the prohibitions by the Catholic Church and others against Masonic organizations extend to Acacia. To pledge is therefore to subject oneself to automatic excommunication.

See COLLEGE FRATERNITIES AND SORORITIES.

Academy of the Ancients

Nothing is known of this organization beyond what Heckethorn notes in his *Secret Societies of All Ages and Countries:* "It was founded at Warsaw by Colonel Toux de Salverte, in imitation of a similar society, and with the same name, founded in Rome towards the beginning of the 18th century. The object of its secret meetings was the cultivation of the occult sciences."

See HECKETHORN, CHARLES WILLIAM.

Academy of Sublime Masters of the Luminous Ring

The Academy was a blend of the teachings of FREEMASONS and PYTHAGOREANS, founded in France in 1780 by Baron Blaerfindy, who was a Grand Officer of the Philosophic Scotch Rite. Blaerfindy apparently believed that Freemasonry was a lineal descendant of Pythagorean teachings, and indeed that Pythagoras himself founded the craft. The first and second DEGREES were Masonic, and the third Pythagorean. There is nothing to indicate that the order was long-lived.

Accoltellatori

The Accoltellatori was a non-political Italian criminal secret society in Ravenna, the existence of which was unmasked (and ended) when most of the members were brought to trial in 1874. This situation came about only because a member turned informant. Outsiders who tried to alert authorities to the activities of the organization suffered swift retribution. Those who witnessed crimes committed by the Accoltellatori invariably remained silent, lest they forfeit their lives.

Adoptive Freemasonry

In Adoptive Freemasonry, a female lodge is "adopted" by a male lodge but otherwise works much like any other lodge. Traditional Grand Lodge of England (GLE) Freemasonry, the one from which almost all other lodges ultimately derive their authority, does not recognize and has never recognized women FREEMASONS. There are, however, two traditions of female Masonry: Adoptive Freemasonry, most popular today in the United States, and Androgynous Freemasonry, that is, Lodges admitting both men and women.

Women's lodges existed as early as the 18th century, apparently coexisting with men's lodges. When the Duchess of Bourbon was appointed Grand Mistress of Adoptive Masonry in France in 1775, the order worked the four DEGREES of Apprentice, Companion, Mistress and Perfect Mistress. These adoptive lodges were so called because they were "adopted" by conventional masculine lodges.

Whether such organizations as the Order of the EASTERN STAR are genuine adoptive lodges or not is disputable, but a Master Mason serves as patron of each Eastern Star lodge, and he must be present for initiations.

American Adoptive Freemasonry in particular seems to place a great deal more emphasis on Christianity and Christian symbolism than masculine Freemasonry. Instead of taking RITUALS AND CEREMONIES from Egyptian sources, adoptive lodges are much more likely to turn to the Bible.

It is important to distinguish between Adoptive Freemasonry, as just described, and Speculative Freemasonry, in which people who are not practicing or "operative" Masons are "accepted" into a Masonic lodge.

See also RAINBOW FOR GIRLS, ORDER OF; CRUSADERS.

Adorateurs de l'Oignon

The Adorateurs de l'Oignon ("Worshippers of the Onion") are less risibly known as the Association Apostolique ("Apostolic Association"). They were founded in 1929 by François Thomas as a magical/spiritualist group advocating sexual abstinence. The significance of the onion, summarizing from Brother Thomas's own *Little Book of Wisdom* (*Petit Livre de la Sagesse*) is that even after the stalk has been broken in order to promote ripening, the mystical vegetable renews itself asexually, year after year, in a better body than it had the previous year (*dans un corps meilleur que celui qu'il avait l'an passé*).

Aetherius Society

6202 Afton Place
Hollywood, CA 90028
(213) 465-9652

Founded in 1955 by George King, who reported contact with an extraterrestrial—specifically, Venusian—being called Aetherius, the organization exists to "spread the teachings of the Master Aetherius . . . the Master Jesus and other Cosmic Masters; organize the Society so as to create favorable conditions for closer contact and, ultimately, meetings with People from other Planets; tune in and radiate Spiritual Power transmitted during a Holy

Time or Spiritual Push in order to enhance all Spiritual practices . . . ; form a Brotherhood based on the teachings and knowledge of the Cosmic Masters; spread the spiritual mission known as Operation Starlight known throughout the World as directed by the Cosmic Masters; perform and support the spiritual missions known as Operation Sunbeam and Operation Prayer Power; observe annually July 8 and other holy days as directed by the Cosmic Masters; design and construct five Shape Power Temples as directed by the Cosmic Masters; to research and build specialized equipment to manipulate spiritual energies."

Aetherius Society members perform and support "spiritual missions" aimed at promoting ecological balance and the spiritual progress of mankind. They form study and prayer groups with the object of furthering world peace and enlightenment. They endeavor to promote the scientific study of the power of prayer and of "Shape Power." The organization maintains a library and publishes the bi-monthly *Cosmic Voice,* as well as a small number of books on spiritual subjects.

African Architects, Order of

The Order of African Architects (*Architects de l'Afrique, Afrikanisches Bauherren*) was an early order akin to Freemasonry. The Architects appeared in two incarnations. The first order was established in Germany in 1756 but was short lived. Eleven years later, in 1767, another order was founded that probably had no real connection with Freemasonry but that was a much greater ornament to the Craft inasmuch as new members were admitted on the basis of intellectual ability, rather than mere wealth or social standing. The African Architects sought to rescue Masonry from the charlatanry into which it was in danger of falling. By modern standards, the order was not really Masonic at all, but should be called quasi-Masonic. In the light of other Masonic rites and orders, this looks to an outsider like a piece of Masonic theological quibbling. Unfortunately, we do not know what the African Architects actually *did,* and their supposed intellectual excellence may have been something that was perceptible only to a student of the Craft.

Only the first three DEGREES (in the "First Temple") were conventionally Masonic. The other eight degrees were a part of the "Second Temple" and were as follows:

4. Architect, or Apprentice of Egyptian Secrets (or Bosonien)
5. Initiate into Egyptian Secrets (or Alethopilote)
6. Cosmopolitan Brother
7. Christian Philosopher
8. Master of Egyptian Secrets
9. Squire of the Order
10. Soldier of the Order
11. Knight of the Order

The last three degrees were culled "superior degrees" and were conferred with great discrimination.

There were also 12 splendidly-named officers, as follows:

1. Grand Master
2. Deputy Grand Master
3. Senior Grand Master
4. Junior Grand Warden
5. Drapier [sic]
6. Almoner
7. Tripcoplerius, or Treasurer
8. Graphiarius, or Secretary
9. Seneschal
10. Standard-Bearer
11. Marshal
12. Conductor

African Legion

The African Legion was a paramilitary organization founded by Jamaican-born African-American nationalist leader Marcus Garvey. It is unclear precisely when the legion was established and how many members it mustered. However, Garvey had founded the Universal Negro Improvement Association in Jamaica in 1914. Two years later, he arrived in the United States to establish a branch, and by 1919 there were 30 branches. In 1920, the UNIA held a national convention in New York City, which was attended by some 50,000 blacks from 25 countries. It was probably at this time that the African Legion was formed, along with the Universal Black Cross Nurses, the Universal African Motor Corps, the Black Star Steamship Line, and the Black Eagle Flying Corps. In 1921, Garvey organized the Empire of Africa, declaring himself provisional president. He appealed—without success—to the League of Nations for permission to settle a colony in Africa. In 1923, Garvey was arrested for mail fraud in connection with the Black Star Steamship project. Convicted, he was sentenced to five years in prison. After serving two years, Garvey was released when President Calvin Coolidge commuted his sentence to deportation as an undesirable alien. Little if anything ever came of the African Legion. Garvey himself failed to revive interest in the UNIA, and he died in relative obscurity in 1940.

African National People's Empire Re-established

c/o William Bert Johnson 18900 Schoolcraft Detroit, MI 48223

The African National People's Empire Re-established was founded in 1951 as a fraternal and patriotic society for Americans of African heritage and natives of Africa. There were over 351,642 members in 1994, and the

Empire published the bimonthly *AFANPERA Bulletin* and the quarterly *AFANPERA Newsletter*. The organization promotes the health, education, and welfare of African people and conducts a specialized education program.

Agrippa von Nettesheim, Heinrich Cornelius

Like Dee, the Bacons and various others, Heinrich Cornelius Agrippa von (of) Nettesheim is one of those shadowy figures who is claimed as an initiate by an extraordinary number of secret societies. All references to him include the fact that he founded several secret societies on his own account, though details are hard to come by: It is all but impossible to find a description of the man and his activities that contains more facts than accusations or fantasies. For example, he is frequently accused of exploiting the members of the societies he founded; this may be true, or it may simply be that he was not inherently dishonest but was unable to separate their funds from his—the latter normally being much smaller, as he was more or less permanently in financial straits. He has been more intensively studied in France than in England, where for many years the authoritative biography was the *Life of H. C. Agrippa,* by H. Morley (London, 1856).

Briefly, the details of his life are as follows. He was a noted magician who was born in Köln in 1486 and died (almost certainly at Grenoble) in 1535. His best-known book is *De Occulta Philosophia* ("On Hidden Philosophy"), which was probably written around 1510 but which was not published until 1531. In it, he espoused the "Solomonic" theory that man is a microcosm of the universe, in accordance with the Emerald Key of Hermes Trismegistus, "*Est quod inferior est quod superior*"—"That which is below is that which is above is that which is below . . . " The Inquisition did not consider him entirely sound.

His career was, to say the least, checkered: He served Maximilian I of Germany, William VI of Monferrato, Charles III of Savoy, and the Archbishop of Köln; was a university lecturer at Pavia; was town orator at Metz; practiced medicine in Köln, Geneva, Freiburg, and Lyons; and was jailed for debt in Brussels. His early death (at the age of 49) was probably a result of ill treatment received while imprisoned by Francis I of France for a real or fancied disparagement of the Queen Mother. His other books included *De incertitudine et vanitate scientarum et artium atque excellentia Verbi Dei declamatio* (Antwerp, 1531), an argument concerning (in the words of the title) "the uncertainties and vanities of science, as compared with the certainty of the Word of God," and *De matrimonii sacramento* (*On the Sacrament of Marriage*).

De incertitudine outraged France's Charles V (to whom he was court secretary), and Agrippa was branded a heretic. Actually, in rejecting every type of scientific and magical knowledge, Agrippa turned to the Bible for solace. He spent his last years in seclusion with his Bible.

His reputation remains to this day controversial. At the least informed level, he lives on as one of the icons of magic, a legend among the better-educated followers of the New Age. At a slightly more informed level, he is dismissed as a charlatan and a mountebank. Then, at a more informed level again, he is seen in the context of his time: a flawed polymath, but still a man who was sufficiently highly regarded by a number of princes that he served them in many capacities.

See BACON, FRANCIS; BACON, ROGER; DEE, JOHN.

AHEPA, Order of (American Hellenic Educational Progressive Association)

1707 L Street, NW, Suite 200
Washington, DC 20036
(202) 785-9284; fax: (202) 785-9820

The Order of AHEPA was founded in 1922 at Atlanta, Georgia, as a fraternal, national, and patriotic society for men of Greek extraction: The order operates in the United States, Canada, Australia, and Greece. There were 60,000 members in 1989, including the auxiliaries: the Daughters of Penelope (women), Maids of Athena (young women), and Sons of Pericles (young men). The organization publishes *The Ahepa,* a magazine.

AHEPA was originally founded of six Americans of Greek ancestry to help Greek immigrants assimilate into American society—meetings have always been held in English—while keeping alive Greek ethnic awareness and supporting the country of origin. During the 1920s, the United States was in the throes of one of its periodic fits of xenophobia, and Greeks were frequently targeted for discrimination. One of the main initial functions of the Order of AHEPA was to overcome this prejudice:

> To advance and promote pure and undefiled Americanism among the Greeks of the United States . . .
> To educate the Greeks in the matter of democracy, and in the matter of the government of the United States.
> To instill the deepest loyalty to the United States.
> To promote fraternal sociability.
> To practice benevolent aid among this nationality.

Within a few days of the order's being founded, non-Greeks were also declared eligible for admission. Among the more famous of these were Franklin D. Roosevelt (who was initiated when governor of New York) and Harry S Truman. In 1989, about 5 percent of the membership was of non-Greek descent.

Since its founding, the order has expanded into Canada and Australia, with additional chapters in the Bahamas and Greece, and has made appropriate modifications to the objectives, as can be seen in its 1989 fact sheet, which lists the following "Objects and Principles":

To promote and encourage loyalty in its members to the country of which they are citizens;

To instruct its members in the tenets and fundamental principles of government;

To encourage interest and active participation in the political, civic, social, and commercial fields of human endeavor;

To pledge its members to oppose political corruption and tyranny;

To promote a better and more comprehensive understanding of the attributes and ideals of Hellenism and Hellenic culture;

To promote good fellowship, and endow its members with a spirit of altruism, common understanding, mutual benevolence and helpfulness to their fellow man;

To endow its members with the perfection of the moral sense;

To promote education and maintain new channels for disseminating the fields of culture and learning . . .

The order has the trappings of a secret society on the Masonic model, with RITUALS AND CEREMONIES and a vow of secrecy and signs, but is essentially a benevolent, civic-minded fraternal aid association.

The DEGREES are the same as the elective offices—Officer of the Local Lodge, Officer of the State Lodge, and Officer of the Supreme Lodge—and these are also the three levels of organization, on the usual Masonic plan, though in addition to Supreme Lodge officers (elected for one year) there is also a Board of Directors, who are again elected but who hold office for three years. Surprisingly for a Greek organization, the regalia consists of Turkish-looking fezzes and white trousers.

Although it maintains that it is a nonpolitical and nonsectarian organization, AHEPA maintains a pro-Greek stance on Cyprus. Apart from that, the order has organized programs for disaster relief in the United States, Greece, and even Turkey. It has funded schools in the United States and Greece, and provided a surprising amount of civic statuary.

The sums of money it raises have been impressive: During World War II the order sold $500 million in U.S. war bonds as an official issuing agency and, more recently, it contributed $100,000 toward the restoration of the Statue of Liberty. In an average year, the order contributes "$250,000 to various charities; $400,000 to scholarships and other educational activities; $300,000 to cultural activities; $150,000 to athletic programs; $200,000 to civic programs; $900,000 to support local Greek communities and the Church; and, $100,000 to patriotic activities." It also gives the Socratic, Aristotelian, Pericles, and Solon Awards to people in many areas of public life.

In a world where fraternal orders are almost every-

where in decline, the Order of AHEPA is remarkable for having more than doubled its membership between 1978 and 1989, as well as for raising an average of more than $35 a head, every year, toward the various causes it supports.

Aid Association for Lutherans

4321 N. Ballard
Appleton, WI 54919
(414) 734-5721

The Aid Association for Lutherans (A.A.L.) was chartered in 1902 as a fraternal benefit insurance society for Lutherans and their families in the United States. There were 1,433,900 members in 1988. It publishes *Who's Who* (monthly); *Branching Out* (bimonthly); and *Correspondent* (bimonthly).

The main reason for the existence of the A.A.L. is the unwillingness of the founders to take the type of oaths normally associated with regular secret societies and lodges. From an initial, informal basis in 1899, the association was chartered as a fraternal benefit society in the state of Wisconsin in 1902 and went on to become a very large mutual life insurance company. It was, however, some years before it admitted to being in the life insurance business; Martin Luther had condemned such enterprises as they betrayed insufficient faith in Providence. Taking money and investing it could also be interpreted as usury.

Initially, like so many other fraternal mutual benefit insurance societies, the A.A.L. was actuarially unsound, but after the state of Wisconsin pointed this out to it in 1905, the organization took steps to remedy it and was operating on a full legal reserve basis by 1911. Until 1927, the A.A.L. reflected its heavily Teutonic origins by habitually conducting its business in German.

In addition to its insurance activities, the A.A.L. maintains a fair-sized library (12,000 books) on business management, fraternalism, and life and health insurance.

Aissaoua

See ISAWA.

Albertus Magnus

Albertus Magnus, or Albert of Cologne, is one of those mysterious and magical characters claimed by an extraordinary range of secret societies as one of the "Hidden Masters" in their past. Born in 1205 or 1206 in Lauingen, Swabia, he was described by Roger Bacon in the late 1240s as "the most noted of Christian scholars." He was also an intimate of Thomas Aquinas, but because of his wide-ranging interests (especially in the experimental sciences), he was popularly regarded as a magician.

The historical Albertus was the son of a German

nobleman who was educated at the University of Padua. Against the wishes of his family, he joined the Dominican order in 1223, and sometime before 1245 he was sent to the Dominican convent of Saint-Jacques at the University of Paris. There he undertook nothing less than the presentation of the entire corpus of knowledge his times possessed, creating over the next 20 years a vast body of learned works.

Albertus Magnus was canonized on December 16, 1931, and in 1941 he was declared the patron saint of all who cultivate knowledge.

Certain historians of Freemasonry lay claim to Albertus Magnus as one of their own, but there is no historical substance to this—any more than there is truth to the similar claims of numerous other secret societies.

See BACON, ROGER.

Alfredians, Order of

A beneficiary fraternal order based in Boston, Providence, and elsewhere in New England, it flourished about 1880. The organization commemorated April 23 as the date of Alfred's A.D. 871 accession to the throne of England, and also as Shakespeare's birthday (they called the Bard "the embalmer of the Anglo-Saxon tongue"). The order was described as "dormant" in 1907, and there is no evidence that it has since been revived.

Alhambra, International Order of the

4200 Leeds Avenue
Baltimore, MD 21229
(301) 242-0611

The International Order of the Alhambra was founded in 1904, in Brooklyn, New York, as the recreational wing of the KNIGHTS OF COLUMBUS, though it also dedicates itself to the preservation of Roman Catholic historical sites and to charitable works. It exists in the United States, Canada, Mexico, Japan, and the West Indies. Members must be Third- and Fourth-Degree members of the Knights of Columbus, which is to say that they must also be male, Catholic, and over 18. Membership is by invitation only, and there were 9,500 members in 1989.

The International Order of the Alhambra was founded by a small group of Catholic men in Brooklyn and is to the Knights of Columbus what the SHRINERS are to the FREEMASONS, though it has never been formally recognized by the Knights of Columbus.

Despite the lack of recognition, many princes of the Church are or have been members, including Pope Paul VI and Pope John Paul II. Even with such patronage, membership has declined, from over 13,000 in the 1960s, to about 11,000 in 1978, and under 10,000 by the early 1990s.

The three major purposes of the order are

To promote social and fraternal association among its members,

To commemorate Catholic historic places, persons or events of international significance,

And to assist and provide means to further the cause of the handicapped and mentally retarded.

The order's initiation rite is based on the Christian reconquest of Spain, and it takes its name from Alhambra, the surrender of which in 1492 marked the end of the Moorish occupation, which had begun in 711. This is the only one of the DEGREES that is worked, but it is very elaborate; only the larger "caravans" (lodges) are likely to have all the paraphernalia and costumes required, though the Baltimore headquarters will rent initiation equipment to smaller caravans who wish to carry out an initiation.

The regalia is based on that of the Shriners; in parades, Alhambra members (Sir Nobles) wear colorful pseudo-Moorish dress and are traditionally accompanied by camels. Most caravans have names derived from Moorish Spain, including Salamanca, Algeciras, Guzera, and Zamora; the first caravan, which is still in existence, was called Abd er Rahman. In 1990 there were about 200 caravans, which are largely autonomous; the ruling body of a caravan is an elected Grand Divan headed by a Grand Commander. Overall administration is carried out by a 15-member Council of Viziers (the Supreme Divan) elected at a biennial convention.

The international constitution and by-laws is called Al-Sunna and consists of a mixture of general regulations and lofty aspirations. (The use of the term "Al-Sunna" could be deeply offensive to a devout Moslem. Al-Sunna [literally "the form" or "the way"] is an adjunct to al-Quran [the Koran] based on traditions of the words and deeds of the Prophet and forms the basis of Islamic law for the Sunni tradition.)

The organization has contributed handsomely to programs for the mentally retarded and the physically handicapped, often with special emphasis on the needs of children; again like the Shriners, it provides an opportunity for its members to engage in often boisterous jollifications while contributing to and raising money for good works.

All-American Association

The All-American Association was a genuinely PATRIOTIC ORGANIZATION, not an anti-immigration, anti-Catholic movement. Its aims included the (literal) unmasking of "hooded and masked bands, mobs and other similar organizations," especially the KU KLUX KLAN and similar organizations. The organization resolved to demonstrate by example the virtues of good citizenship and to oppose "by moral suasion . . . the self-asserted right of any organization or clan to set themselves up as censors of the conduct and arbiters of the rights and liberties of the people."

The association was incorporated in Tennessee in 1923, but may have disappeared at about the same time as the second manifestation of the Klan, during the late 1920s.

Alliance of Poles in America

6966 Broadway
Cleveland, OH 44105
(216) 883-3131

The Alliance of Poles was founded in Ohio in 1895 as a fraternal benefit life insurance organization for Poles and those of Polish extraction. The alliance also tries to keep alive a Polish pride without infringing on the primary American loyalties of its members. There were 20,000 members in 1994.

Alliance of Socialist Democracy

The Alliance of Socialist Democracy was an anarchist secret society founded in Geneva in 1868 by Mikhail Bakunin (1814–1876) after he had been expelled from the First International (the proto-communist trade union), and after he had been accused by no less a person than Karl Marx of stealing party funds.

Followers joined from Switzerland, France, Belgium, Spain, Russia, and Italy. Under Bakunin's direction, the alliance plotted a revolution in Italy, but nothing actually came of the plans. Likewise, planned actions in Switzerland and France also failed to materialize. The order probably died before Bakunin, and certainly did not outlive him.

Alliance of Transylvanian Saxons

5393 Pearl Road
Cleveland, OH 44129
(216) 842-8422

The Alliance of Transylvanian Saxons was founded in 1902 as a fraternal and insurance organization for persons of "Transylvanian Saxon birth or descendant thereof, or married to a Saxon or descendant thereof, or of German birth or a descendant thereof," aged 16 to 60, of high moral caliber, and able to pass a medical examination for insurance purposes. There were 8,892 members in 1989.

The *Siebenburger Bund* was founded on July 1902. On August 31 of the same year, it became the *Central Verband der Siebenburger Sachsen,* by which title it continued to be known until 1965, when it changed its name to the Alliance of Transylvanian Saxons. It offered a death benefit from the very start, initially on a flat ASSESSMENT system; then from 1913 to 1924 on a graded assessment system; and thereafter on a sound actuarial basis.

In addition to this, the organization seeks to preserve Saxon culture and has done a good deal of philanthropic work among Saxons in Saxony and elsewhere. In order to hold the interest of Saxon youth, there are a number of (mostly sporting) programs for the Transylvanian Saxon Junior Association. The alliance is not, however, a classic "secret society" or ritualistic fraternal organization: there is no RITUALS AND CEREMONIES, merely local installation procedures, and members promise to uphold the organization's constitutions.

The alliance has remained roughly constant in size for many years, with nine to 10,000 members.

Allied Masonic Degrees of the United States, Grand Council of

The Grand Council of the Allied Masonic Degrees of the United States was formed in 1932 in Salisbury, North Carolina, as a supervising body for the DEGREES listed below.

Royal Ark Mariner
Secret Monitor
Knight of Constantinople
Saint Lawrence of the Martyr
Architect
Grand Superintendent
Grand Tyler of Solomon
Superintendent
Master of Tyre
Excellent Master
Installed Sovereign Master
Installed Commander Noah
Red Branch of Erin

Membership is by invitation, and invitations are extended only to Royal Arch Masons of the YORK RITE.

Alligator Societies

These were—or are—secret criminal societies active between the Sierra Leone and the Volta rivers in West Africa. As late as 1911, four members of an Alligator Society in the Tonko Limba chiefdom of the Karene district of Sierra Leone were sentenced to death for having murdered a boy. In 1916, in the Barri chiefdom, Alligators were convicted of having used a young member for criminal purposes. The single largest Alligator Society was headquartered in the Bassam district of the Ivory Coast and boasted an association with criminal organizations in the American South.

The Alligator Societies generally used a model of an alligator or an alligator skin in their ceremonies. In the Gambia, observers reported an Alligator Society ceremony in which a boy donned an oiled alligator skin and danced. A society in Sierra Leone used a model of an alligator made of two large dug-out canoes, with the head carved in the shape of an alligator and two glass windows serving as its eyes. It was widely reported and believed that this vessel was actually an operational four- to six-man submarine used in the capture of victims.

Reports that the Alligator Societies practiced cannibalism were frequent.

Aloyau, Société de l'

La Société de l'Aloyau translates as "The Society of the Sirloin," a curious name for an organization that existed in prerevolutionary France and professed not only to possess many documents pertaining to the TEMPLARS but also to be the successors of that order. They were dispersed by the French Revolution.

Alpha Galates

Alpha Galates was a French secret society founded (or at least registered, according to the society's own records) just before World War II, in December 1937. It stressed the importance of the traditions of chivalry, though it had no pretensions to being a true chivalric order. In its journal, *Vaincre,* it promulgated a melange of apparently pro-Vichy French nationalism, a "United States of the West," mythology, and chivalry.

The reservation that it was "apparently" pro-Vichy must be made because there is the possibility that it concealed something deeper; perhaps its anti-Semitism was only a mask for messages to the French Resistance, evidence for which may be seen in the fact that it was attacked by the virulently pro-Nazi *Au Pilori* in 1942.

Amaranth, Supreme Council Order of the

2303 Murdoch Avenue
Parkersburg, WV 26101
(304) 485-0423

The Supreme Order of the Amaranth was founded in 1873 in New York City as a fraternal order for Master Masons and wives and female relations (either blood or adopted) of Master Masons. There were 59,000 members in 1993.

The Order of the Amaranth is an example of ADOPTIVE MASONRY, the system whereby women are not allowed to become "real" FREEMASONS but are permitted to organize and run subordinate lodges, provided they can secure the patronage of a (male) Master Mason.

It is also an illustration of the capacity for schism that is exhibited by so many fraternal orders: It was originally intended as the third of the DEGREES in the Order of the EASTERN STAR, but was rejected by that order and therefore set up on its own account in June 1873. Until 1921, applicants for the order had to be members of the Eastern Star, but, since then, Masonic connections have been enough.

The order has little or no connection with the Royal and Exalted Order of the Amaranth, allegedly founded by Queen Christina of Sweden in 1653, nor with the short-lived Order of Amaranth founded in New York City on June 14, 1873, by J. B. Taylor.

As with many female AUXILIARIES, especially in the United States, there is a stronger Christian flavor to the ritual than is to be found in the parent organization, which subscribes essentially to DEISM. In addition to Christian hymns, the initiation involves singing a verse of "Home, Sweet Home." As is usual in adoptive masonry, a Master Mason must be in attendance at initiations, where the candidate is given bread and salt, crowned with a wreath, and tapped on both shoulders with a wreath, somewhat after the fashion of a knightly investiture.

The order seems to be in decline. In the 1960s, there were more than 85,000 adherents; by the middle of the 1970s, they were down to 83,000; in 1988, only 75,000; and a year later, just 70,000.

Amazons, Order of the

The Order of the Amazons was an androgynous branch of the FREEMASONS reported to have existed in North America in the middle of the 18th century. With the rise of Masonic orthodoxy, it probably disappeared before the 19th century. No further information is available.

American Brotherhood

There have been at least three societies bearing the title American Brotherhood. The first was an American nativist secret society founded in New York City in 1844. The second American Brotherhood was also founded in New York City, in 1847, and was apparently a standard fraternal secret society in the tradition of Freemasonry and the ODD FELLOWS. It is extinct. The third American Brotherhood was founded in 1915 as a fraternal benefit society, open only to American citizens, and with a generally patriotic subsidiary mission. Like its predecessors, it is extinct.

An American Brotherhood U.S.A. was also founded in 1915, and may well be the same as the third American brotherhood, above. Its ostensible purpose was to "Americanize Americans" (as the organization's Supreme Supervisor put it in 1923) as well as providing insurance benefits; members could join either as beneficiary or nonbeneficiary (social) adherents. Membership was limited to American citizens; the RITUALS AND CEREMONIES were based upon episodes from American history; the three DEGREES were Unity, Service, and Attainment. The brotherhood is either extinct or maintains a very low profile.

American Fraternal Benefit Societies

The number of minor American fraternal benefit societies of the late 19th and early 20th centuries is legion, and to provide individual entries on each would require another book. Only the more important ones are therefore treated individually; many of the others will be found below.

Aegis, Order of

The Order of Aegis was a fraternal graded ASSESSMENT organization founded in 1892 in Baltimore, Maryland. The Order of Aegis wrote insurance certificates for $500, $1,000, $2,000 and $3,000 and provided sick insurance for white men and women aged 16 to 55. Its emblem was a shield bearing the Stars and Stripes surrounded by a scroll, which read, "Fraternity, Equality, Protection and Security."

Its principal aim was insurance: The "secrets" of the order were reduced to those serving to identify members.

At the beginning of the 20th century it boasted about 6,500 members, but by about 1920, the organization was probably extinct.

Ahvas Israel

Ahvas (or Ahavas) Israel was a Jewish fraternal benefit society founded in New York City in 1890 by a number of habitual "joiners" who belonged to one or more of the FREEMASONS, the Independent Order of ODD FELLOWS, the Sons of Benjamin (see below) and the Independent Order BRITH ABRAHAM. By the turn of the century, its membership was about 3,000, but it never prospered greatly and apparently disappeared a few years later.

American Benefit Association of New York

Little is known about this tiny association except that it had 939 members at the end of 1922.

American Benefit Society

The American Benefit Society was founded as an insurance society in 1893. Thirty years later, it boasted 44 lodges and 1,390 benefit members, with a Supreme Lodge in Boston. It admitted both men and women, aged 18 to 45, provided they were "socially acceptable," able to earn a living, and believed in a supreme being. The society seems either to have disappeared or to have merged with (or turned into) a conventional insurance company.

American Benevolent Association

The American Benevolent Association was founded in St. Louis, Missouri, in 1894 with a single degree. It is apparently extinct. (See DEGREES.)

American Benevolent Legion

The American Benevolent Legion was a mutual assessment beneficiary society, originally organized in San Francisco some time around 1900 but apparently extinct a couple of decades later.

American Fraternal Circle, Order of

The American Fraternal Circle was a short-lived Baltimore mutual assessment organization, founded prior to 1889 and dead by 1894.

American Fraternal Insurance Union

Organized in Batavia, New York about 1890, this was a beneficiary and social association for men and women. Its lodges were scattered throughout western New York. It is presumed extinct.

American Home Watchmen

The American Home Watchmen was incorporated in Pennsylvania in 1909 as a strongly moralistic whites-only fraternal benefit order. The founder was a Presbyterian clergyman, Moore Sanborn. The order seems to be long extinct.

American Star Order

The American Star Order was a Rumanian Jewish charitable and benevolent association organized in New York City in 1884. It is long extinct.

American Workmen

The American Workmen had a ritual and no fewer than six DEGREES, and was founded a little later than most benefit societies, 1908, in Washington, D.C. The order appears to be long extinct, but in the early 1920s there were 14,629 members in 208 lodges. (See RITUALS AND CEREMONIES, LODGE.)

Americans, Ancient Order of Loyal

The Ancient Order of Loyal Americans was founded in Guthrie, Oklahoma, in the first decade of the 20th century and was reported as extinct some 15 years later. It was a patriotic, social, and fraternal organization, but appears to have had no particular links with any other organization.

Americus, Order of

The Order of Americus was founded in 1897 in Pennsylvania. It adopted graded assessments from the first, and women were admitted on the same terms as men. Apart from these progressive traits, it seems to have been quite unremarkable and is now apparently extinct.

American Stars of Equity

The American Stars of Equity, open to both sexes, was founded in 1903 in Illinois. It was extinct a decade or so later.

Amitie, Order of

The (American) Order of Amitie was a short-lived Philadelphia mutual assessment society that died in 1894.

Atlantic Self-Endowment Association of America

The Atlantic Self-Endowment Association of America was a short-lived mutual assessment organization, founded in 1886 and apparently dead less than two decades later.

Big Four Fraternal Life Association

The association was organized in Denver, Colorado, to pay sick and death benefits by means of mutual assessments. It no longer exists.

Brotherhood of America

The Brotherhood of America was founded in 1890 in Philadelphia, admitting men and women on the same terms. By the 1920s, almost four-fifths of the 14,000 or so members were "social" (uninsured), and in the middle of the Depression, in 1935, the society quietly merged with the MACCABEES.

Brotherhood of American Workmen

The Brotherhood of American Workmen was a small (now probably extinct) organization that claimed to furnish "not Cheap insurance, but Good insurance cheaply."

Chaldeans, Modern Order of

The Modern Order of Chaldeans was founded in Brownsburg, Indiana, in 1888 and disappeared about 20 years later. It was slightly unusual in that it was a working-class society.

Chevaliers of Pythias

The only resemblance between the Chevaliers of Pythias and the KNIGHTS OF PYTHIAS was that neither of them could spell "Phintias." The Chevaliers was established in Boston in 1888 as a charitable and beneficiary secret society and took its name (and presumably some of its ritual) from the older organization. They are defunct.

Colonials, Fraternal Order of

The Fraternal Order of Colonials was organized in 1903 and licensed to do business by the Insurance Department of Missouri. Little has been heard of it since.

Colored Brotherhood and Sisterhood of Honor

The Colored Brotherhood and Sisterhood of Honor was an African-American social and beneficial fraternity organized in Franklin, Kentucky, in 1886. The society apparently became extinct early in the 20th century.

Columbian Circle

The Columbian Circle was a fraternal beneficiary insurance society organized in 1895; it was a typical organization of the time, effectively a mutual insurance company with a veneer of fraternalism. In 1918 it absorbed the Catholic Knights and Ladies of America. It has probably metamorphosed into a nonfraternal company since.

Columbian Fraternal Association

The Columbian Fraternal Association was a fraternal death, accident, and sick benefit society founded in 1910. Although there were almost 7,000 members in the early 1920s, the Association is probably extinct now.

Columbian League

The Columbian League was founded in 1896 as a splinter group of the Ancient Order of United Workmen. The founders believed that changes were needed to ensure the survival of the United Workmen, but the new organization expired about 10 years later. See UNITED WORKMEN, ANCIENT ORDER OF.

Columbian Mutual Life Assurance Society

The Columbian Mutual Life Assurance Society was founded as the Columbian Woodmen in 1903. It admitted both men and women, and paid sick and death benefits. Although it does not appear in the modern ENCYCLOPEDIA OF ASSOCIATIONS, it may have made the transition from a fraternal organization to a life insurance company.

Continental Fraternal Union, Order of the

The Continental Fraternal Union was organized in Richmond, Indiana, in 1890 and lasted less than two decades. Like so many other failed fraternal benefit societies, it was founded by an assembly of "joiners"—adherents of the FREEMASONS, the Ancient Order of United Workmen, the ODD FELLOWS, and KNIGHTS OF THE YORK CROSS HONOUR—to provide the financial support that these societies either lacked or did not administer to the liking of the founders of the new organization. See UNITED WORKMEN, ANCIENT ORDER OF.

Cowboy Rangers, National Order of

The Cowboy Rangers based their RITUALS AND CEREMONIES on the myths and realities of the Old West. Apart from this and its late founding date, there was nothing remarkable about this now-extinct organization.

Daughters of Hope

The Daughters of Hope were reported by the 1890 U.S. census to exist in Olneyville, Rhode Island, but by the early years of the 20th century, the organization was dead.

Eclectic Assembly

The Eclectic Assembly was a mutual ASSESSMENT beneficiary fraternity founded in 1893 with the purpose of issuing short-term or endowment policies—always a recipe for financial disaster. The RITUALS AND CEREMONIES were based on undefined mythology, and the signs of the order referred to "God's covenant with man." The Eclectic Assembly presumably died in the early 1920s.

Empire Knights of Relief

The Empire Knights of Relief was organized in Buffalo, New York, in 1899. As so often, the founders belonged to a wide range of other secret societies, including the United Workmen, the ROYAL ARCANUM, the FREEMASONS, and the ODD FELLOWS. It was also unable to decide whether it really was a secret society or not, another commonplace feature among such groups. Its published announcements said that it had "no secrets or ironclad oaths," but the Supreme Secretary said "it is called a secret society, and properly, too." The organization probably disappeared by the 1920s. See UNITED WORKMEN, ANCIENT ORDER OF.

Equitable League of America

The Equitable League of America was a mutual ASSESSMENT insurance society organized in the 1880s and dead by 1894.

Equity, Order of

The Order of Equity was founded in 1889, with a ritual that referred to the parable of the Good Samaritan and the healing of the lepers. It was never large or particularly successful, numbering some 4,000 members. In 1897, the society went into receivership.

Fraternal Aid Union

The Fraternal Aid Union was originally organized as the Fraternal Aid Association in 1890 in Lawrence, Kansas, but the name was changed some time after 1900. It was a typical fraternal benefit society. In 1917 the union merged with the Improved Order of HEPTASOPHS.

Fraternal Brotherhood

Apart from being a tribute to the potential for redundancy of the English language (it is hard to see how a "brotherhood" could *not* be "fraternal"), the Fraternal Brotherhood was a secret fraternal beneficiary society for

both sexes, organized in Los Angeles, California, in 1896. As usual, it was a mutual insurance society with a fraternal overlay, including passwords, rituals, and LODGES. It is unclear whether it died or metamorphosed into a modern insurance company.

Fraternal Guild

The Fraternal Guild was a short-term (and short-lived) endowment order founded in San Francisco in 1889 and almost certainly extinct two or three decades later.

Fraternal Home Insurance Society

The Fraternal Home Insurance Society was organized in Columbus, Ohio, in 1885 as the Supreme Ruling of the Fraternal Mystic Legion. Membership was limited to white persons aged between 16 and 55 at the nearest birthday. By the early 1920s, the headquarters were in Philadelphia. It is unclear whether the society eventually died or metamorphosed into a conventional insurance company.

Fraternal Legion

The Fraternal Legion was a short-lived but otherwise typical fraternal benefit society of the late 19th century. Founded in Baltimore, Maryland, in 1881, it was apparently extinct 15 years later.

Fraternal Mystic Legion

The Fraternal Mystic Legion was formed on December 9, 1884, for professional and business people; President McKinley was a member. The circumstances surrounding its decline and disappearance are unclear, but it is long gone now.

Fraternal Reserve Association

The Fraternal Reserve Association was established in Oshkosh, Wisconsin, in 1902 as a whole-family fraternal beneficiary society with no more than the thinnest veneer of fraternal trappings. The society seems eventually to have turned into a conventional insurance society.

Fraternal Tributes

The Fraternal Tributes, organized in Rock Island, Illinois, in 1897, lasted for about 20 years.

Fraternal Union of America

The Fraternal Union of America was formed in Denver, Colorado in the 1890s, strutted its brief hour, and disappeared by 1923.

Friendly Fellows, Fraternity of

The Fraternity of Friendly Fellows was founded in New York in 1885 and survived until at least 1890, but was gone by 1896.

Golden Links, Order of

The Order of Golden Links was founded in 1905 in Wheeling, West Virginia, and admitted both men and women. It was never large, and in 1922 it merged with the American Insurance Union, losing its fraternal character. This order bore no relation to the Knights of Golden Links of the World, another, even more obscure mutual sick and benefit society based in Nashville.

Golden Rod, Order of the

The Order of the Golden Rod was founded by members of various other societies, as a vehicle for providing insurance, in Detroit, Michigan, in 1894. It seems to have disappeared before World War I. The insurance basis was a little eccentric: The ASSESSMENT was $0.25 per $250, and all members held at least two certificates. On the death of a member, his heirs had the option of continuing to pay the assessment until the certificate fell due, or of withdrawing the accumulated sum plus interest at 7 percent. The society is long extinct.

Golden Rule Alliance

The Golden Rule Alliance was organized in Boston prior to 1889 as a mutual assessment beneficiary society, and is now extinct.

Golden Seal Assurance Society

The Golden Seal Assurance Society was founded as the Order of the Golden Seal, but changed its name in 1919, when it switched to an actuarially sound mortality system. There were under 10,000 members in 1921, and despite a recommendation in 1923 from the Committee on Secret Work that the RITUALS AND CEREMONIES be revised, it seems likely that the society is no more.

Golden Star Fraternity

The Golden Star Fraternity was small and limited to the area in which it operated: New York, New Jersey, and Connecticut. Founded in 1881, it seems to have been a typical fraternal benefit society, admitting both men and women. It is long gone; even at the beginning of the 20th century, it could boast only about 2,200 members, and was almost certainly extinct by the end of World War I.

Good Fellows, Royal Society of

The Royal Society of Good Fellows, now long extinct, was organized by members of the ROYAL ARCANUM, the FREEMASONS, KNIGHTS AND LADIES OF HONOR, ODD FELLOWS and others in Rhode Island in 1882, and admitted both men and women.

Grand Fraternity

The Grand Fraternity was incorporated under the laws of Indiana in 1885, then reincorporated in Pennsylvania in 1893. It was a secret beneficiary society, founded by the usual mixture of FREEMASONS, members of the ROYAL ARCANUM, and so forth, but with a bare minimum of RITUALS AND CEREMONIES. Any "acceptable" white person over 16 years of age could join. It was based in Philadelphia early in the 20th century, but is now probably extinct.

Heralds of Liberty

The Heralds of Liberty existed in two separate incarnations. The first Heralds of Liberty society was founded in Philadelphia in 1900, and the second (for which no date of foundation is available) was based on Huntsville, Alabama. Both are probably long extinct.

Home Builders, Order of

The Orders of Home Builders or Homebuilders was founded in 1890 in Pennsylvania as a typical fraternal benefit society that also operated a savings department. It is long gone.

Home Circle, The

The Home Circle was founded in Boston in 1879 with the intention of making fraternal benefit insurance available to women; at that time, only men were usually insured. As a secondary aim, it was a refuge for enthusiastic fraternalists. Founders included members of the ROYAL ARCANUM, FREEMASONS, ODD FELLOWS, KNIGHTS AND LADIES OF HONOR, and Ancient Order of United Workmen. The four DEGREES were remarkably practical; members could join any of them at initiation, and they corresponded to insurance benefits of $500, $1000, $2000 and $3,500. The order is long extinct. See UNITED WORKMEN, ANCIENT ORDER OF.

Home Forum Benefit Society

The Home Forum Benefit Society was founded in Illinois in 1892; the RITUALS AND CEREMONIES were based on the Roman forum, at which the learned and noble met to discuss the issues of the day. It apparently lasted little beyond the turn of the century.

Home Palladium, The

The Home Palladium was founded in Kansas City, Missouri, in 1891 and had more than 2,000 members by the 1920s. Unless it has become a conventional insurance society, it is extinct.

Imperial Mystic Legion

This was a very short-lived fraternal benefit society founded in Lincoln, Nebraska, in 1896 and apparently extinct by 1905.

Independent Sons and Daughters of Purity, Grand United Order

The Grand United Order of the Independent Sons and Daughters of Liberty was established in Harrisburg, Virginia, prior to 1890, when it first appeared on the census. It was probably extinct by the beginning of the 20th century.

International Geneva Association

The International Geneva Association was a fraternal benefit society set up in 1904 to provide insurance for workers in the hotel and catering trades. It is unclear whether it still exists, at least under the original name.

Iowa Legion of Honor

The Iowa Legion of Honor was organized in Iowa in 1879 and was extinct before World War I. It was apparently a schismatic offshoot of the AMERICAN LEGION OF HONOR.

Keystone Guard

The Keystone Guard flourished just before World War I. In July 1923, the postmaster of Athens, Pennsylvania (where the Guard had been headquartered), returned a letter to it marked "Out of business long ago."

Knights and Ladies of Azar

The Knights of Azar were organized in Chicago in 1893 and had 300 members in 1897, when it decided to admit women as well. They are long gone, and the meaning of the word *Azar* has vanished with them.

Knights and Ladies of Security

The Knights and Ladies of Security was incorporated in 1892 in the state of Kansas and was well-run from the start; it was one of the first societies to have a legal reserve fund. Around the end of World War I, the order changed its name to the Security Benefit Association and ceased to be a secret society.

Knights and Ladies of the Golden Precept

The founders of this 1896 Iowa fraternal beneficial society contemplated establishing lodges throughout the Union. From the lack of subsequent information, it appears that they did not get much beyond the stage of contemplation.

Knights and Ladies of the Golden Star

The Knights and Ladies of the Golden Star was organized in Newark, New Jersey, in 1884. The organization was unique in that the *whole family* of a member was admitted and insured—by no means a bad idea. It also

paid annuities to members over 50 who had been in the order for 21 years. Its founders were members of the Royal Templars of Temperance (a total abstinence society; see TEMPERANCE SOCIETIES), and saloonkeepers and bartenders were therefore refused admission. The order has been defunct since the first decade of the 20th century.

Knights of Friendship

The Knights of Friendship was founded in 1859, long before insurance became fashionable. The order worked three DEGREES: Knight Junior, Knight Bachelor, and Knight Errant. In 1920 there were 20,000 members, but the order is long gone now.

Knights of Honor

The Knights of Honor was organized in 1873 in Louisville, Kentucky, and was slightly unusual in that membership required no formal oath—merely a promise, which was presumably less binding. The events of 1875–77, when a ladies' auxiliary degree (see AUXILIARIES) was first authorized, and then rescinded, led to the formation of the Order of Protection of KNIGHTS AND LADIES OF HONOR.

The dissolution of the Knights of Honor in 1916 was a consequence of their inability or refusal to accept sound actuarial methods for their insurance.

Knights of Jerusalem, Ancient Order of

The Ancient Order of Knights of Jerusalem was a small beneficiary society paying death and funeral benefits. The founding date is unknown, and the order was defunct by 1923. The female auxiliary or sister organization (see AUXILIARIES) was the Ancient Order of Daughters of Jerusalem. Both the parent order and the auxiliary had their headquarters in Washington, D.C.

Knights of the Blue Cross of the World

The Knights of the Blue Cross of the World was a short-lived fraternal benefit society founded in 1888 in Homer, Michigan. Members were paid weekly sick benefits, and death benefits were also paid as a pension instead of as a lump sum.

Knights of the Golden Eagle

The Knights of the Golden Eagle was founded in Baltimore in 1872. The order had a militaristic and Christian slant to its RITUALS AND CEREMONIES, which were based on events and legends from the Crusades and worked three DEGREES. The organization disappeared in the late 1960s or early 1970s. The auxiliary was the Ladies of the Golden Eagle. See AUXILIARIES.

Knights of the Golden Rule

The Knights of the Golden Rule was organized (perhaps with a touch of gallows humor) by survivors of the yellow fever epidemic of 1878, which had caused the demise of the Order of Mutual Aid (see Mutual Protection, Order of, below). Shortly after its foundation, ladies were also admitted, and the organization became the Knights and Ladies of the Golden Rule. Like so many similar societies, it disappeared in the first decade of the 20th century, despite its graded ASSESSMENT plan adopted in 1892.

Knights of the Loyal Guard

The Knights of the Loyal Guard were founded in Flint, Michigan, in 1895 and are now long extinct.

Knights of the Red Cross

The Order of the Red Cross and Knights of the Red Cross (to give it its full title) was founded in 1879 by members of the Ancient Order of United Workmen, with a gloss of Christianity and Freemasonry. The order is defunct. See UNITED WORKMEN, ANCIENT ORDER OF.

Loyal American Life Association

This group was founded in 1896 in Illinois, and was apparently dead before World War II.

Loyal Knights and Ladies

The Loyal Knights and Ladies was an offshoot of the Knights and Ladies of Honor (see Knights of Honor, above). It was founded in 1881 in Boston and is long gone.

Loyal Mystic Legion of America

The Loyal Mystic Legion of America was founded in 1892 and was extinct by about 1920. The headquarters were in Hastings, Nebraska.

Mechanics, Independent Order of

Among the Independent Order of Mechanics, the word *mechanics* was used in its old sense of men who worked at trades, rather than in the professions or business. It was founded in Baltimore in 1868, surviving for perhaps 30 years.

Modern American Fraternal Order

The Modern American Fraternal Order was founded in Effingham, Illinois, in 1896 as a mutual assessment fund. It is apparently long extinct.

Modern Brotherhood of America

The Modern Brotherhood of America, established in Tipton, Iowa, in 1897, was fairly typical except that it offered a "duofold protection" plan, which covered life insurance and provided a modest savings plan for old age. It apparently lasted less than a decade.

Modern Knights Fidelity League

The Modern Knights Fidelity League was founded in Kansas in 1891. The RITUALS AND CEREMONIES were based on the story of Don Quixote and Sancho Panza and involved three DEGREES. It shares with the BEN HUR LIFE ASSOCIATION, the VRIL SOCIETY, and a few other organizations the dubious distinction of being a secret society founded on a novel.

Modern Romans

The Modern Romans was organized in Michigan in 1904 and seem to have disappeared before World War II. The order's actuarial mathematics were interesting: All policyholders were divided into 10-year "classes," each of which had to take care of its own losses until the class size fell below 1,000, at which point it was amalgamated with the next succeeding class. The name "Modern Romans" was apparently chosen because the ancient Romans had well represented permanency and fidelity.

Modern Samaritans

The Modern Samaritans, since 1936 the Samaritan Life Association (a conventional insurance company), started out as a typical fraternal benefit society founded in 1897 in Minnesota.

Mosaic Templars of America

The Mosaic Templars of America was an African-American fraternal benefit society set up in Little Rock, Arkansas, in 1883. The order apparently disappeared some time before World War II.

Mutual Protection, Order of

The Order of Mutual Protection was founded in St. Louis in 1878. At this distance, it is impossible to see what prompted the founders to break away from their predecessors, the Order of Mutual Aid, to found a new society. The organization has been defunct since about 1930.

"Mutual Protection Society" was also one of the many names for organizations related to the KNIGHTS OF THE GOLDEN CIRCLE. It is unrelated to the Order of Mutual Protection.

Mystic Brothers, Independent Order of

This was a very short-lived but otherwise typical fraternal benefit society founded in Boston in 1882 and gone by the late 1890s.

Mystic Workers of the World

The Mystic Workers of the World united at Fulton, Illinois, in 1892. The founders were FREEMASONS, ODD FELLOWS, WOODMEN, KNIGHTS OF PYTHIAS and others. The RITUALS AND CEREMONIES centered around charity. Since 1930, the organization has been known less mystically as Fidelity Life Assurance.

National Benevolent Society

The National Benevolent Society was founded in Kansas City, Missouri, in 1894 and is no longer extant. In 1921, the society was licensed to do business in 26 states and the District of Columbia, but could muster only 5,558 members. It may be assumed that the organization went under during the Depression.

National Fraternal League

The National Fraternal League was founded in Green Bay, Wisconsin, in 1902 on the typical actuarially unstable assumptions. After changes to the ASSESSMENT schemes in 1906 and 1913, it was actuarially sound, and by 1919 it had improved sufficiently to merge with the NATIONAL MUTUAL BENEFIT (see also BEAVERS).

National Fraternal Union

The National Fraternal Union was, despite its grandiloquent title, a typical, modestly sized, short-lived fraternal benefit society. It was founded in 1889 and gone some 20 years later. It worked three DEGREES and was founded by the usual coterie of professional joiners, including representatives of the FREEMASONS, the ODD FELLOWS and the KNIGHTS OF PYTHIAS.

National Fraternity

The National Fraternity was founded in Philadelphia in 1893 by members of the Ancient United Order of Workmen (see UNITED WORKMEN, ANCIENT ORDER OF.) The RITUALS AND CEREMONIES were based on the history of the United States, and the governors of the LODGES were "Sections" under the direction of a "Board of Control," stunningly pedestrian terms in the generally overblown world of fraternalism. The organization died long before World War I.

National Home Guards

The National Home Guards was organized in 1907 in Pennsylvania. Never very large, it had only 1,249 members in 1921, when many other such organizations were at their height. It is defunct.

National Protective Life Association

The National Protective Life Association was founded in 1891 and was slightly unusual only in that it was open both to men and women. It was originally founded as the National Protective Legion by a group of FREEMASONS in New York state and is now extinct.

New England Order of Protection

The New England Order of Protection was founded in 1887 as an offshoot of the Knights and Ladies of Honor (see Knights of Honor, above). Founders included FREEMASONS, KNIGHTS OF PYTHIAS, members of the ROYAL ARCANUM, and others. It presumably died in the Depression.

New Era Association

The New Era Association was established in 1897 and found its membership in Michigan and Illinois. It appears to have placed more emphasis on practical help than on secrecy of ritual. Defunct now, it had nearly 36,000 members at the end of 1922.

North Star Benefit Association

The North Star Benefit Association, founded in 1899 and based in Moline, Illinois, offered disability, accident, and old-age benefits. The head officer was called the "Chief Astronomer." It is defunct.

Northwest Legion of Honor

The Northwest Legion of Honor was founded in Iowa in 1884 and derived from the AMERICAN LEGION OF HONOR. It used graded ASSESSMENT but, despite this actuarial prudence, it appears to be long extinct.

Occidental Mutual Benefit Association

This association was founded in 1896 with headquarters in Salinas, Kansas, and was disbanded in the mid 1920s.

Pente, Order of

The long-extinct Order of Pente was founded in 1888 in Philadelphia, Pennsylvania, and took its name from the five-year certificates that were a feature of the society's insurance plan. The SEXENNIAL LEAGUE was formed in the same city in the same year, with a similar plan, though obviously on a six-year basis.

Pilgrim Fathers, United Order of

The Pilgrim Fathers was founded in 1878 with a graded ASSESSMENT plan and is long gone. Its LODGES were called "Colonies."

Pioneer Fraternal Organization

The Pioneer Fraternal Organization, which in 1972 merged with the Wawanesa Mutual Life Insurance Company of Manitoba, Canada, was founded in the same city in 1892. By the 1960s membership of the Pioneers had dropped to 1,600.

Praetorians, Modern Order of

The Modern Order of Praetorians was a typical late 19th-, early 20th-century fraternal benefit society, resembling the modern WOODMEN of America. In 1957 it converted to a regular, commercial mutual life insurance company.

Protected Home Circle

The Protected Home Circle was organized in 1886 in Sharon, Pennsylvania, admitting men and women (the latter a better actuarial risk) on equal terms. The RITUALS AND CEREMONIES were Christian in orientation: In addition to the Initiatory degree, the society also worked the Kibosh degree, which was intended to accent the lighter side of life. In 1964 it converted to a mutual life insurance society.

Protestant Knights of America

The Protestant Knights of America managed to unite a feudal, Catholic, royalist concept—knighthood—with a Reformed religion in a republican country. It was founded by some of the leading lights of St. Louis in 1895 and disappeared a decade or two later.

Puritans, Independent Order of

The Independent Order of Puritans appears to be defunct and was short-lived at that. The date of foundation is unknown, but the order claimed to be the first fraternal beneficiary organization to pay monthly annuities.

Pyramids, Ancient Order of

One authority described this order as "a new fraternal, beneficiary society, organized at Cairo, Mich.," while another, reporting it "extinct" a few years later, puts its place of origin in Topeka, Kansas. Both agree that the order was founded in 1905.

Red Cross, Legion of the

The Legion of the Red Cross—which apparently bore no relationship to the well-known medical relief agency or even to the FREEMASONS (which has its own "Red Cross of Constantine")—nor yet to the Knights of the Red Cross, above, was founded in 1885 in Maryland by some members of the Knights of the Golden Eagle (see also above). The ritual was based on events and legends of the Crusades. The organization was never large, with 3,100 members in 1905 and 2,300 in 1910. By 1915, the order had disappeared.

Royal Benefit Society

The Royal Benefit Society, now apparently extinct, was founded in New York in 1893 as a fraternal benefit insurance society with a minimal ritual.

Royal Highlanders

The Royal Highlanders, founded in 1896 as a fraternal benefit society open to men and women on equal terms, was the forerunner of the Lincoln Mutual Life Insurance Company (1946), though it had already reincorporated as a life insurance company in 1937. The RITUALS AND CEREMONIES were based on Scottish history.

Shepherds, Independent Order of

The Independent Order of Shepherds was established in Toledo, Ohio, in 1917, but was probably defunct by the early 1920s.

Shepherds of Bethlehem, Order of

This society was open to both sexes but is now apparently long defunct. It was founded in Trenton, New Jersey, in 1896, though the authors of the original literature published by the order claim origins shortly after the birth of Christ, in the Holy Land.

Shield of Honor, Order of

This group was founded in Baltimore in 1877, with the customary white, male-only membership. It prospered briefly, but began to decline even before World War I, and it appears to have died by 1930. The ritual involved swords and a bow and arrow resting on an open Bible.

Sons and Daughters of Protection

The Sons and Daughters of Protection was founded in 1896 and lasted for about a decade thereafter.

Sons of Abraham, Independent Order of

This organization was founded in 1892 for the Jews of Manhattan and Brooklyn, and seems to be long extinct.

Sons of Benjamin, Independent Order of

This was a short-lived society for the Jews of New York City, founded in 1877.

Sparta, Order of

The Order of Sparta was an offshoot of the Ancient Order of United Workmen (see UNITED WORKMEN, ANCIENT ORDER OF), founded in 1879 as a mutual assessment benefit society with a one-dollar assessment. The ritual was based on stories of ancient Sparta. The order flourished for a while, but died many years ago.

Supreme Mechanical Order of the Sun, League of Friendship of the

This improbably named organization was intended to provide fraternal benefits for blue-collar workers; in 1868, when the league was founded, the term "mechanic" had a wider meaning than today. The order did not outlast the century.

True Reformers, Grand United Order of

The Grand United Order of True Reformers was founded in Richmond, Virginia, in 1881. At one time it was very successful, with 70,000 members, but it appears no longer to exist.

United Friends of Michigan

The United Friends of Michigan was formed in 1889 as a result of a schism in the Order of Chosen Friends. It disappeared some 30 or 40 years later. See CHOSEN FRIENDS, ORDER OF.

Unity, Order of

The Order of Unity was founded in 1889 and dissolved in the early 20th century.

Western Samaritans

The chief feature that distinguished the Western Samaritans was their late date of foundation, namely 1922. The society was for white adults of both sexes, but apparently lasted little more than a decade.

American Fraternal Union

111 Fourth Avenue South
Ely, MN 55731
(218) 365-3143

The American Fraternal Union was founded in 1898 as a fraternal benefit life insurance society. Present eligibility is open, up to 80 years of age, and there were 22,846 members in 1993. The Union publishes *New Era* monthly.

The American Fraternal Union is a typical fraternal benefit society in slow decline, despite having changed its name from the South Slavonic Catholic Union in 1941 and having thereafter opened its doors to all, regardless of race or religion, provided they are under 80. The loss of membership has slowed of late (there were 24,000 members in 1979, 28,000 in 1968), and it is not impossible that the union will metamorphose into a successful mutual insurance society. Meanwhile, it supports charitable works (directed mostly at ongoing problems such as illiteracy and malnutrition in the United States) and supports mass-interest sports events such as baseball, bowling, and golf.

American Freemen

The original Order of American Freemen was a "nativist" (i.e., xenophobic and anti-immigration) group, which was a manifestation of the thought of KNOW-NOTHINGS in the mid-19th century.

In its second incarnation, the Order of American Freemen was a patriotic (i.e., xenophobic and anti-immigration) and anti-Catholic secret society founded in Pennsylvania in 1884 by members of 13 seceding lodges of the AMERICAN PROTESTANT ASSOCIATION. In this latter manifestation, it was almost certainly gone by the end of World War I. See PATRIOTIC ORGANIZATIONS.

American Hunters

The American Hunters (*Cacciatori Americani*) was an Italian secret society and offshoot of the CARBONARI, founded at Ravenna in 1818. The British poet Lord Byron, who was captain of the *Turba* or "mob" section of the Ravenna carbonari, financed and armed the American Hunters and was their honorary leader during this period of nationalistic fervor in Italy.

Small as the society was, it apparently spawned the following, all with the same purpose, namely Italian independence from Austria:

Sons of Mars
Defenders of the Country
Artists' Brethren
Friends of Duty

American Insurance Union

The American Insurance Union, established in 1884 in Columbus, Ohio, was founded by members of a splinter group from the Fraternal Mystic Circle, who were aided and abetted by various other fraternalists. The FREEMASONS, KNIGHTS OF PYTHIAS, and ODD FELLOWS did not, however, succeed in burying the organization under a welter of ritual. By means of a cautious admissions policy (men and women, aged 15 to 49, living in the more "healthful" areas of the United States), and by means of sound management, the union prospered to the point that, in 1923, it was able to build a new $5 million headquarters in its home town. In 1931 it effectively forswore fraternalism and reincorporated as the American Insurance Union, Inc. This is not uncommon for well-run fraternal benefit organizations.

Accepting only members from "healthful" regions of the United States was not unusual among Northern insurance societies. The "malarial" south and the "pestilential" large cities were commonly excluded.

American Knights of Protection

The American Knights of Protection had some very typical features, as well as others that were most unusual, for an organization of its time (it was founded in 1894 in Baltimore).

The typical features were that it was founded by a crowd of "joiners" (from the KNIGHTS OF PYTHIAS, Knights of the Golden Chain, JUNIOR ORDER OF UNITED AMERICAN MECHANICS and others) and that it was in favor of public schools and the "American Way."

On the unusual side, it offered both beneficial and social membership, and it offered them to whites and African Americans alike. It appears to have been a genuinely pro-American organization, standing up for the American ideals of freedom, equality, and justice for all. This is a welcome change from most organizations claiming the same ideals. As often as not, the word *American* in the title of an organization meant that it was anti-immigration (and frequently anti-Catholic), and supported liberty only for those who had already immigrated, urging the exclusion of all others. Unfortunately, the American Knights of Protection seems to have survived no better than most others; it apparently disbanded by the 1920s.

American Krusaders

As is suggested by the spelling, this was a clone—or klone—of the KU KLUX KLAN. Its principal activities were whipping up hysteria, together with a small but unpleasant degree of intimidation and violence.

It was founded in Arkansas in 1923, during the resurgence of Klan sentiment, but did not long survive. It apparently incorporated an even less-known Klan-type group, the Riders of the Red Robe. Membership was open to "male white persons of good health."

American Legion

700 N. Pennsylvania Street
Indianapolis, IN 46204
(317) 635-8411

First and foremost an association for United States exservicemen, the American Legion was founded in Paris in 1919. As of 1993, there were 3,025,927 members.

The American Legion is not a secret society in the classic sense, but it has had elements of RITUALS AND CEREMONIES and also a strong political agenda. Moreover, in some localities, American Legion membership consists entirely of Freemasons.

By the 1920s, the Legion began to assume semiofficial status in the federal government, which gave it certain surplus military equipment and granted it tax exemption on its building in Washington, D.C. The Legion has historically exerted influence on local, state, and federal legislators and was instrumental in securing GI and veterans' benefits. At many times, however, its right-wing orientation motivated agitation for such intolerant legislative measures as a ban on citizenship for foreign-born Japanese (1920) and a push for legislation requiring all foreign-language newspapers to file translations with the U.S. Postmaster General.

The American Legion Auxiliary is the ladies' branch of the organization and works in support of veterans' rights and welfare, especially for the wounded and the elderly.

American Legion of Honor

The American Legion of Honor was founded in 1878 as a fraternal, social, and beneficial secret society for men and women aged 18 to 50. Despite a membership of 62,457 in 1889, it is now extinct.

Unlike the better-known French *Legion D'Honneur*, the American version was primarily an insurance organization; even the initiation could be replaced by a "formal obligation" at any convenient time and place.

By the end of the century in which it was founded, it was still one of the larger and more popular societies, but it was already on the way down; there were just over 36,000 members at the end of 1896, which in itself was a drop of some 15,000 since the previous year. The losses were for familiar reasons: a lack of actuarial soundness, leading to a run on claims, combined with hard times, poor capital management, and a reduced influx of new, young, healthy members. The Legion went into receivership in 1904.

An interesting sidelight is that in 1894, approximately one member in eight was a woman. Other American "Legion of Honor" organizations, apparently related to this one, were the Iowa Legion of Honor (1879) and the Northwestern Legion of Honor (1884). The latter was incorporated for business in Iowa, Nebraska, Kansas, Minnesota, and the Dakotas.

American Order of Clansmen

The American Order of Clansmen was founded at San Francisco in 1915 and might as well have spelled "Clan" with a "K"; it was for loyal, white American citizens who wanted to counteract the influence of those of the white race who refused an undivided allegiance to America and the American flag. In 1919 it was reorganized as a beneficiary order, which paid an $8 a week sick benefit and a $125 funeral benefit—to men. Women were admitted as associate members, but got no sickness benefit and only a $50 funeral allowance. The order is apparently long defunct.

American Order of the Square

This patriotic, protective, and philanthropic fraternal order, which paid sick benefits, was founded in 1921 in Rochester, New York. A Masonic influence is indicated by the name; "on the square," like "on the level," is a Masonic phrase meaning "all right" or "one of us." The order probably disappeared during the Depression.

American Order of United Catholics

The American Order of United Catholics was founded in 1896 in New York City, largely in self-defense against nativist American PATRIOTIC ORGANIZATIONS. Although it was a secret society, in deference to Catholic teaching, there were no OATHS. The order is defunct.

American Protective Association

The American Protective Association was one of the so-called PATRIOTIC (i.e., anti-immigrant) ORGANIZATIONS. It was founded in 1887 in Clinton, Iowa, by Henry F. Bowers. It enjoyed meteoric growth, with more than 2 million members in 1900, but its decline was equally rapid, and it disappeared by 1911.

The A.P.A. (as it was generally known) was a late flowering of the principles of KNOW-NOTHINGS. Its members were virulently anti-Catholic, and the organization was in favor of putting "the subjects of the Pope" into ghettos in major cities.

Until about 1890, the A.P.A. was mostly a local movement, with chapters all over the United States, but by 1896 the chapters had coalesced, and the overall organization boasted over 2 million members, many absorbed from older "patriotic" organizations and left-overs of the Know-Nothing movement. The RITUALS AND CEREMONIES of the A.P.A. were published in the *Congressional Record* as early as October 1, 1893.

The caliber of the A.P.A. can be judged from its argument that the American Civil War was "instigated by the Roman Hierarchy" and from its totally fabricated lists of desertion statistics for the War Between the States:

Natives of the United States: 5 percent desertions from 1,625,267 enlistments (45 percent of those deserting were Roman Catholics)
Germans: 10 percent desertions from 180,817 enlistments
Irish: 72 percent desertions from 144,241 enlistments
British: 7 percent desertions from 90,000 enlistments
Other foreigners: 7 percent desertions from 87,855 enlistments

There are no systematic records of the nationalities of the men who enlisted to fight in the war, and no records at all of the nationalities of those who deserted.

Like so many organizations calling themselves "patriotic," the A.P.A. pledged allegiance not to a United States that was the world's beacon of freedom and opportunity, but to a bigoted land with restricted immigration and a "thought police" atmosphere.

The A.P.A. floated candidates for the election of 1896. After 1896, the A.P.A. struggled on for a few years, but the 2 million membership figure of 1900 probably involved a good deal of double-counting and wishful thinking. When a *real* crisis came along, in the shape of World War I, the people of the United States turned out to have more sense than to listen to what the A.P.A. purveyed, and the organization was probably dead by the time the Treaty of Versailles was signed. The predictably named junior branch, the Junior American Protective Association, for those aged 14–21, died with them.

American Protestant Association

The American Protestant Association was a manifestation of the nativist movement of mid-19th-century America, the same movement that spawned the KNOW-NOTHINGS. It was founded in about 1849 on an anti-immigration, anti-Catholic platform, and was the forerunner of the AMERICAN PROTECTIVE ASSOCIATION (see previous entry); it was typical of the so-called PATRIOTIC ORGANIZATIONS, which have soiled the word "American" by using it in their titles.

The association favored slamming the door of immigration and keeping "America for Americans."

The RITUALS AND CEREMONIES were akin to that of the ORANGEMEN. There were originally five DEGREES. When two of these were dropped in 1884, it prompted a schism, which led to the Order of AMERICAN FREEMEN. There was also a branch that seceded in 1878, retaining the original name, but made up largely, probably exclusively, of African Americans. The threefold LODGE hierarchy was the Subordinate Lodge, the State Lodge, and the Right Worthy Lodge of the United States.

The Junior American Protestant Association was founded as the junior branch of the main association in 1864, but in 1890 it declared independence from the parent order and changed its name to Loyal Knights of America.

American Turnerbund

The American Turnerbund was a group of small German-speaking societies. One source lists 172 such societies in the United States during the early 20th century, with a total membership of 30,843 or an average of 180 members each. The groups were dedicated to physical education and rationalistic thought. In its heyday, American Turnerbund was notorious for its militant rationalism and its attacks on the Catholic Church. The society ran a teacher training college in the 1920s. Neither that institution nor the Turnerbund exists today.

Amicists, Society of

The Amicists was a students' secret society, allegedly established in Paris at the College of Clermont and widespread in Germany during the 18th century, though presumably suppressed prior to 1799, as the principal book on the subject appears to be *Der Mosellaner — oder Amicisten — Orden nach seiner Entstehung, innern Verfassung und Verbeitung auf den deutschen Universitaten, usw* (F.C. Laukhard, Halle, 1799). The title translates as "The Mosella-ners—or Amicists—the Order from their Founding, Inner Constitution and Prohibition at the German Universities, and so forth." See also MOSEL CLUB, which may well be the same thing.

Amis Réunis, Loge de

The Loge des Amis Réunis ("United Friends' Lodge") was founded in Paris in 1771 and attempted in 1785 to disentangle the "old" FREEMASONS from a welter of "new rites and new degrees." After the death of Savalette de Langes, a leading light of the lodge, the United Friends dissolved and its library was scattered.

Anchor, Order of Knights and Ladies of the

The Order of Knights and Ladies of the Anchor was a short-lived system of androgynous FREEMASONS, arising in France out of the Order of Felicity in 1745. Neither the Anchor nor the order from which it split lasted long. (See FELICIDADE, ORDEM DE.)

Ancient Oaks, Order of

The Ancient Oaks was unusual in being a "vegetable" fraternity instead of an "animal" fraternity (like the Elks, for example). The order was an offshoot of the Order of OWLS. The reason that the "Local Nest" of the Owls at Grand Rapids, Michigan, split on August 9, 1912, was that the "Order of Owls is governed by one John W. Talbot and four associates . . . who run things to suit themselves and give no account of the moneys received. The Order has no legal standing anywhere in the U.S. and is careless in admitting new members."

Ankh

The ankh or Crux Ansata has been used as the symbol of a number of mystical organizations since its origination in ancient Egypt. The classical Greeks in particular imported Egyptian "mysteries" with the same kind of enthusiasm as "New Age" Californians.

The ankh resembles a Christian cross (which it antedates by many centuries) with the part above the cross-arm in the form of an open oval resembling a horse collar. There are various interpretations of its significance: The most conventional is that it symbolizes the masculine and feminine principles, from a resemblance to the sexual organs.

Wearing an ankh on a chain or thong around the neck has for some time been *de rigeur* among ROSICRUCIANS, but it has also attracted the attention of the fringes of the born-again Christian movement, to whom it is apparently a satanic symbol.

Annunciation, Supreme Order of the Most Holy

The Supreme Order of the Most Holy Annunciation is the premier of the Italian DYNASTIC ORDERS OF CHIVALRY, founded in 1362 by Amadeus IV, Count of Savoy, as the Order of the Collar. Originally comprising 15 knights, the order was expanded to 20 in 1434 and was renamed—with its present title—in 1518 by Duke Charles III. It may be awarded by the royal house of Savoy, the former kings of Italy. The Italian republic moved to suppress it by Law 178 on March 20, 1951, but it has been questioned by lawyers specializing in this arcane field whether the government had the power to do this.

Anonymous Society

The only reference to this society is found in Heckethorn, who reports that it "existed for some time in Germany, with a grand master resident in Spain, occupied itself with alchemy." No date of founding or flourishing is given, and no other reference to the society can be found.

Anthroposophical Society in America

529 W. Grant Pl.
Chicago, IL 60614
(312) 248-5606

Established in 1923, the Society had 3,000 members in 1994 and is dedicated to fostering "the lives of the soul and the spirit in individuals and society." The group promotes the "spiritual science" of anthroposophy, which was founded by Rudolf Steiner (1861–1925), an Austrian philosopher. The Society periodically publishes the *Directory of Anthroposophical Initiatives* and the semiannual *Journal for Anthroposophy*.

Steiner was long associated with the THEOSOPHICAL SOCIETY in Austria, but broke with that body in 1912 over a dispute with its president, Annie Besant, who claimed that Jiddu Krishnamurti was Christ reincarnated. After breaking with the Theosophists, Steiner founded the Anthroposophical Society.

The belief system of the Anthroposophists is certainly obscure to outsiders, and the sheer magnitude of Steiner's literary output (some 350 volumes of writings, including many collected lectures) is daunting. However, Steiner himself set out the clearest summary of his "spiritual science" in *Anthroposophical Leading Thoughts*, which he wrote shortly before he died:

1. Anthroposophy is a path of knowledge, to guide the Spiritual in the human being to the Spiritual in the universe. It arises in man as a need of the heart, of the life of feeling; and it can be justified only inasmuch as it can satisfy this inner need.

2. Anthroposophy communicates knowledge that is gained in a spiritual way. . . . For at the very frontier where the knowledge derived from sense-perception

ceases, there is opened through the human soul itself the further outlook into the spiritual world.

The Anthroposophical Society promotes the study and practice of methods to develop the spiritual communion defined above. These include the study of the natural sciences, projective geometry, sculpture, painting, speech formation, interpersonal relationships, and eurythmic dance. Anthroposophy has given rise, importantly, to the Waldorf School movement, the largest nonsectarian independent school system in the world. The Camp Hill movement, also a development of Anthroposophy, is a system of villages for children and adults with special needs. Although Steiner clearly intended Anthroposophy to supersede conventional religion, he worked with various Protestant groups and individual clergymen to develop the Christian Community, a modern church that is not formally connected with the Anthroposophical Society, but which is allied to it in spiritual orientation.

Anti-Masons

The Anti-Masons had nothing to do with the later American Anti-Masonic political party formed in the wake of the MORGAN AFFAIR, or with the French *Ligue Anti-Maçonnique.* Instead, it was a secret society founded in County Down, Ireland, in 1811, with the purpose of expelling FREEMASONS from Ireland; the Catholic church has never taken kindly to Freemasons.

Anti-Poke-Noses, Order of

The Order of Anti-Poke-Noses commendably eschewed euphemism when they banded together to fight the resurgent KU KLUX KLAN in 1923. Founded in Searcy County, Arkansas, their stated aim, in the preamble to their constitution, was to oppose "any organization that attends to everyone's business but their own." They are long extinct.

Antoinism

Antoiniste
49 Rue du Président-Gervais
75019 Paris

Antoinism is a quasireligious sect founded in 1905 by Antoine Louis (1846–1912), a former Belgian miner; its basic tenet is that faith alone is all that is required for perfect health. M. Louis was convicted in 1911 of practicing medicine without a license, and died just after his 66th birthday. His widow continued the sect, and after her death in 1941 his nephew took over. From an all-time high of maybe half a million members, his order *Les Vignerons du Seigneur* ("The Vineyard Workers of the Lord") had dropped to maybe 150,000 adherents in the late 1980s.

Arcana Workshops

P.O. Box 605
Manhattan Beach, CA 90210
(213) 379-9990 or (213) 540-8689

The Arcana Workshops teach enlightenment by correspondence course from their Los Angeles area headquarters. Like the ROSICRUCIANS, they believe in human perfectibility, basing their teachings on the work of the theosophist Alice A. Bailey. They also hold meetings at full moon in the months corresponding to Aries, Taurus, and Gemini, and publish a monthly magazine, *Thoughtline.*

Archangel Michael, Legion of

See IRON GUARD.

Arctic Brotherhood, The

The Arctic Brotherhood was apparently formed aboard ship by would-be prospectors on their way to the Klondike in 1899; it certainly survived until sometime after 1923 when President Warren G. Harding was made a member, but is now defunct.

Next to nothing is known of this order, except that it required kindness to horses and dogs.

Areoiti

This is (or was) a Tahitian secret society, with a religious basis. Their MYSTERIES have the usual connections to DEATH AND RESURRECTION but also refer to "the generative power of nature," presumably a fertility cult. This is given added credence by the fact that one authority, Heckethorn, refers to their "disgusting and immoral" rituals, though he does admit that there is "a foundation of noble ideas." Initiates of the various DEGREES (seven or 12 in number, depending on the authority) were tattooed in different ways.

The Areoiti maintain their own genealogy, hierarchy, and traditions, believing themselves to be descended from the god Oro-Tetifa. The society forms—or formed—an institution of priests, although laymen may also be admitted. Membership was traditionally coveted, since members enjoyed great consideration and privilege, being revered as wise men and judges, whose counsel was sought to mediate disputes. See HECKETHORN, CHARLES WILLIAM.

Argonauts, Order of

According to one authority, this order was formed in Germany in 1775 by some brethren of the Rite of Strict Observance (see STRICT OBSERVANCE, CLERKS OF THE), admitting both men and women, but veering a long way from the FREEMASONS; for example, the head of the LODGE (which was supposed to represent the deck of a ship) was called the Grand Admiral. Another writer records that it was founded by one Konrad von Rhetz of Riddagshausen near Brunswick, who built the lodge on an island that was part of his estate. The order was something of a good-time club, as suggested by its motto, *Es Lebe die Freude,* which might best be rendered "Joy Forever!"

The order probably disappeared about 1787, which was the year of Konrad von Rhetz's death.

Armenenschaft

A German mystical secret society founded in the mid-to-late 19th century by an Austrian called Guido von List, an enthusiastic scholar of Germanic folklore. The RIT-UALS AND CEREMONIES were based on Nordic or Teutonic mythology, with special reference to Odin or Wotan and the significance of runes — though the DEGREES were simply lifted from the three degrees of the FREEMASONS.

Von List was politically on the extreme right and believed that, when the Christian church had suppressed the OLD RELIGION, the Templars and the Rosicrucians had inherited guardianship of the ancient spiritual and aristocratic traditions, while the Freemasons became guardians of the democratic tradition.

The Armenen were well known to the early members of the Nazi party, and the swastika was an important symbol for the sect. Moreover, there is evidence that List's Armenen theories, which included a vision of the ideal German state, inspired early Nazi thinking. Some scholars have seen Armenenschaft as a prototype of the Third Reich.

The ORDO TEMPLI ORIENTIS apparently derived from the Armenenschaft.

Artisans' Order of Mutual Protection

2233 Spring Garden Street
Philadelphia, PA 19130
(215) 561-5720

The Artisans' Order of Mutual Protection was founded in 1873 as a fraternal benefit life insurance society for men in the United States. It publishes *The Artisan* six times a year and published the centennial *A Century of Fraternalism: 1873-1973.*

The Artisans' Order of Mutual Protection is an absolutely typical American fraternal benefit society. It was first conceived in the late 1860s as a means of providing better beneficial protection for artisans, but, apparently unwilling simply to start a mutual insurance society, the founders devised elaborate RITUALS AND CEREMONIES based largely on the FREEMASONS. Despite the "artisans'" label, the leading light among the founders was a doctor — and Freemason, also involved in the Ancient Order of United Workmen — named James Bunn.

Even for the time when the order was founded, the ritual was too long, too tedious, and too blatantly a Masonic knock-off to suit the majority of its members.

Accordingly, it was simplified within a short time. There was no women's department until 1955, although a junior department was founded in 1933, for males aged 30 days to 18 years. It was in the 1950s that the order reached its all-time high of 36,000 members, but has declined since then. There were 32,000 members in 1967; under 26,000 in 1978; and only 18,000 or so a decade later. The noninsurance activities of the society include scholarships and children's programs, as well as the usual charitable projects.

Armenian Secret Societies

There have been Armenian political secret societies, striving for the freedom of their country, for centuries. With the collapse of the Soviet Union, they are no less active. Historically, Armenia has been divided between the Turks and the Russians, and governed (mostly very badly) by both. Turkish as well as Russian authorities killed many thousands of Armenians. The single worst massacre came in 1915, when the Ottoman government ordered the deportation of 1,750,000 Armenians to Syria and Mesopotamia, an action that resulted in the deaths of some 600,000.

Little specific information exists concerning individual Armenian secret societies. In Russia, it is known, Armenians formed a secret society in 1888. By the turn of the century, Armenians organized against their Turkish overlords in societies that resembled the CARBONARI of pre-independence Italy. Five separate committees were organized, each with two hundred members, and all coordinated by a central committee. However, the members of one committee were unknown to the others. The committees each had a name: Frochak (Flag), Abdag (Bellows), Gaizag (Thunderbolt), Huntchak (Alarm), and Votchintchak (Destruction). The committees were responsible for various assaults upon Ottoman official installations, including the Ottoman Bank in 1895. Members were sworn to absolute allegiance and pledged to die before revealing any of the society's secrets.

Asanteman Association

The New York Times of May 25, 1987, reported the existence of this group, which maintained a network of "Chiefs" to help members of the 21 Asante (also spelled "Ashanti" or "Ashantee") communities then extant in the United States. The Asante are a Ghanaian tribal people, and the Asanteman Association rendered help with immigration and education, and operated a mutual assistance program. As reported in *The New York Times,* the organization was led by a King, at the time Nana Kwabena Oppong. The *Encyclopedia of Associations* reports that the order's address is "unknown since 1989 edition."

Ashmole, Elias

Elias Ashmole (1617-1692) is best remembered as the founder of what became the Ashmolean Museum at

Oxford University, but to FREEMASONS he is noted for his diary entry of October 16, 1646, in which he recounts his making as a Mason—one of the earliest noteworthy Accepted Masons, as distinct from Operative or stone-working masons. Perhaps inevitably, he has also been claimed by the ROSICRUCIANS and as a member of the ILLUMINATI.

The truth is that he was a polymath of his time and that his interests were wide-ranging. His *Theatrum Chymicum Brittanicus* (1642) was a leading treatise on chemistry/alchemy (the two were just beginning to separate). He was also a leading astrologer and an antiquarian—his passion for which eventually eclipsed his other pursuits.

Asia, Initiated Knights and Brothers of

The Initiated Knights and Brothers of Asia were a short-lived and very eclectic German society, borrowing elements of Christian, Jewish, and Islamic ceremonies under a Rosicrucian banner. They were founded either in Berlin or Vienna in about 1780.

The object of the order was the study of the natural sciences and a search for a panacea to prolong human life. Some authorities identify the order with alchemical traditions, while others take pains to differentiate the order from alchemical pursuits; for example, some authorities claim that the order pursued methods of transmuting base metals into gold, while others state that the order explicitly proscribed such pursuits. To further confuse matters, some authorities underscore the order's relation to Rosicrucianism, while others state that members did not profess Rosicrucian beliefs.

Asia, Perfect Initiates of

The RITUALS AND CEREMONIES of the Perfect Initiates of Asia (apparently an offshoot of the FREEMASONS) was described at length in a bulky manuscript bought by a M. Bailleul in 1821 and sold to a M. Ragon, who promptly shortened and modified it. There is no record of its ever actually having been worked.

One authority, Heckethorn, does refer to the *Initiated Brethren of Asia* (which may or may not be the same thing) as an early form of Freemasonry founded in Vienna and concerned with mystical and alchemical practices "in opposition to the ROSICRUCIANS." This society spread to Italy in the early 19th century. The Perfect Initiates were founded at Lyons, and consisted of seven degrees. It was never of more than minor importance in Freemasonry.

Asiatic Brethren

The Asiatic Brethren were an offshoot of the ROSICRUCIANS and probably originated in Italy about 1780, whence they spread to Russia. (Another authority gives a founding date of 1786 in Schleswig and Hamburg.) Their

full title was "The Order of the Knights and Brethren of St. John the Evangelist from Asia in Europe."

The catholicity of the organization was remarkable. The LODGES were called Melchisedeck Lodges, and masters were titled Worshipful Chiefs of the Seven Churches of Asia—not an unreasonable claim in a society that admitted Jews, Turks, Persians, and Armenians, among others.

The Brethren claimed interests in the KABBALAH and alchemy, and worked five DEGREES. The two lesser degrees were Seeker and Sufferer, while the three chief degrees were Knights and Brother-Initiates from Asia in Europe; Wise Masters; and Royal Masters, also known as True Rosicrucians, or Initiates of the Degree of Melchisideck.

The Grand Lodge, or Sanhedrim, ruled the whole thing—and to some profit. Each lodge had plenty of officers, and (for example) the franchise fee to found a Master Lodge was seven ducats, plus two ducats for the carpet, and a General Chapter was 50 ducats. In 1787, a sometime member published the secrets of the order, which, however, does not seem to have been long-lived.

Assassins

The original secret society of the Assassins was founded as a religious/political order in the late 11th century in the near east. It has been extinct for centuries.

Hassan-i-Sabbah, whom the crusaders called the Old Man of the Mountains, seized the castle of Alamut in northern Persia in A.D. 1090, and from there he directed his Isma'ili sect until his death in 1124 at the age of about 90. By this time he had amassed many more castles and fortresses, mostly in remote and inaccessible areas.

His successors were Kia Burzugumid (reigned 1124–38); Mohammed (1138–62); and Hasan ala Dhik-rihi 's-Salam (1162–66), who proclaimed himself the first of a new line of "open" imans, represented today by the Aga Khan.

In the mid-13th century, the Assassins' castles in Persia began to fall; Alamut itself was taken in 1256. The decline of the order in Syria was not long behind; the last stronghold there, Kahf, fell in 1273. This marked the effective end of the Assassins as a closed order, though some suggest that THUGGEE was the invention of Assassins who escaped to India; and no doubt an interesting story could be woven about Assassins who escaped to Europe.

The Assassins are most famous for their use of murder to further political ends. The word *assassin* was first used in the sense of "a political murderer" by Dante in the early 14th century. The interrelationship between politics and religion among the Isma'ilis remains so close as to be inseparable, though they seem to have forsworn assassination for centuries. The current Aga Khan, head of the sect, is known as a peacemaker.

It has been suggested that the Assassins took hashish in order to steel themselves for their grisly task, and that "Assassin" derives from "Hashish" rather than from "Hassan." Whether or not they took the drug, and whether or not they experienced visions of paradise as a result, is disputable. Marco Polo was responsible for the traditional tale concerning the Assassins; it was he who said that initiates were taken to a secret valley where they were entertained with hashish, wine (forbidden to the faithful in this lifetime, but permitted in paradise) and earthly houris. The idea was to give them a foretaste of the life to come, so that thereafter death would seem a welcome release from the trials of the world, but it is likely that this is only a traveler's tale.

From the middle of the 12th century, when the Assassins were at their height, the TEMPLARS were their close neighbors. The Christian order seems to have held the Islamic order in its sway. For many years, the Templars collected an annual tribute of 2,000 gold pieces from the Assassins. It is from this close relationship that many of the charges laid against the Templars were derived, along with all sorts of conspiracy theories and other fringe ideas.

Assessment

An assessment is a means of raising money from a fraternal or mutual aid organization. It differs from a membership fee in that it is much closer to an insurance premium; that is, it is a sum paid in expectation of financial return. This return may be in the form of a death benefit, or a sickness benefit, or an old-age pension, or some other form of support.

There have been various different kinds of assessment, as described below. In many organizations, each has been tried in turn, but for all except the smallest benefits, the only assessment system feasible in the long run is the last, the regular graded assessment with actuarially sound reserves.

Ad hoc Assessment: This was one of the earliest forms of assessment and is an institutionalized version of the "whip-round" or "passing the hat." On the death of a member, or in other times of need, everyone contributes a modest sum. While this is perfectly satisfactory for a small organization, in which everyone knows everyone else, and where the actual sums involved are quite small anyway, the administrative problems of extracting (say) a dime each from 50,000 or 60,000 members would be nightmarish.

Irregular Assessment with Reserves: A rather easier system than the *ad hoc* assessment creates a general fund from a one-time assessment and pays money out of the general fund. When the reserve begins to run low, the members of the organization are assessed again. The main drawbacks to this system are that a run of bad luck can wipe out the kitty, which can discourage members, while a run of good luck

can lead to carelessness and to an unwillingness to replenish the reserves to adequate levels.

Regular Ungraded Assessment: Administratively, the regular ungraded assessment system is the easiest of all. Everyone pays the same weekly, monthly, or annual amount, which is applied to the reserve. If money is paid out faster than it comes in, the assessment may be increased or benefits may be reduced in scope or amount.

The lack of "grading" is, however, a major drawback. In the late 19th and early 20th century, many societies had problems with members who joined when in a very poor state of health and promptly died. This destabilized the reserves and led to the next system.

Regular Graded Assessment: Here, the assessment paid by each member depends on his or her age and health; older members pay less than younger ones, and members who are unable to pass a physical examination are not admitted as beneficiary members, though they may be admitted as social ones. The only flaw in this system lies in balancing the assessment against the benefits. Even graded assessment plans went broke with depressing frequency, often as the result of an epidemic, but sometimes simply as the consequence of an aging membership. Too many elderly members died, and not enough new dues were coming in to replenish the reserves.

Regular Graded Assessment with Actuarial Reserves: This is the system on which all modern, licensed insurance companies operate. The system pegs premiums to age, while maintaining a reserve fund based on the proportion of younger and older members. It was the difficulty of establishing adequate reserves that led to the decline of most fraternal orders, while others set up special insurance divisions that might or might not require membership in the fraternal organization. Some large modern insurance companies that operate on a mutual benefit basis started out as fraternal organizations, but gradually lost their RITUALS AND CEREMONIES and other paraphernalia as insurance became the main reason for their existence.

Associated Fraternities of America

The Associated Fraternities of America was (as its name suggests) an association of different fraternal organizations. It was founded in 1901 as a protest against the workings of another association of fraternal organizations, the National Fraternal Congress. In 1903, however, the two merged to form the NATIONAL FRATERNAL CONGRESS OF AMERICA, which still exists.

Associated Patriots

The Associated Patriots was a reaction to the restoration of the Bourbon monarchy in France in 1814. The so-called "White Terror" of Royalist vengeance on the perpetrators of the Glorious Revolution was Draconian in the extreme, and many wished for a return to Republican days. The Associated Patriots sought to foment a revolution toward this end.

The Associated Patriots, however, was a doubly shadowy association, because many of those arrested on account of supposed membership were not in fact members, while many of the leading lights of the Patriots were never touched because the government could not gather sufficient evidence against them.

The true members almost certainly included the Marquis de Lafayette and his friends Manuel and Argenson, together with many who had held office under, or served in the armies of, the republic and the empire.

Those who were arrested were mostly pulled in as a result of the work of *agents provocateurs* who circulated in cheap taverns, buying rounds of drinks and leading the patrons in singing patriotic songs that might, among the less circumspect revelers, lead to revelations of republican sympathies. They would then be drawn into "conspiracies," which did not exist outside the French secret police.

Little more was heard of the Associated Patriots after convictions resulted in three peculiarly barbaric executions prior to 1820. Three leaders—one Pleignier, a writing master; Carbonneau, a leather cutter; and Tolleron, an engraver—were treated as parricides, who had acted against their "father," the king. Their heads were veiled, their right hands severed, and then they were finally decapitated.

Astrum Argentinum

Astrum Argentinum, the "Silver Star," was founded in 1905 by occultist Aleister Crowley (see CROWLEY, ALEISTER) as an offshoot of the Hermetic Order of the Golden Dawn (see GOLDEN DAWN, HERMETIC ORDER OF). Crowley intended it as a "school for initiates." He adopted the "three dots" style of abbreviation, so the organization is often known as A.˙.A.˙.

The grades were Probationer, Neophytus, Zelator, Practicus (or "Praeticus"), Philosophus, and Dominus Luminis ("Master of Light"). The only copy of the RITUALS AND CEREMONIES that was at hand during the present compilation was in French, and has a distinctly culinary air: *"Le mage avec la baguette. Sur l'Autel sont placés l'Encens, le Feu, le Pain, le Vin, la Chaine, le Fouet, le Poignard et l'Huile."* ("The magician with the wand [or 'stick of bread']. On the altar are placed the Incense, the Fire, the Bread, the Wine, the Chain, the Birch-rod [whip of chastisement], the Dagger and the Oil.") In the names of some of the subsequent AWARENESS BEINGS in this ritual, such as Hoor-Apep, the hand of the THEOSOPHICAL SOCIETY seems apparent.

The order soon succumbed to the same misfortunes as

the Golden Dawn; the adepts mutually excommunicated one another.

Athene, Order of

The Order of Athene was, according to one authority, a "society of those who believe in the Good" and in the "Association of the Elect." Its members assiduously cultivated a taste for the fine arts, and their official organ, edited by one George L. Thompson in Keene, New Hampshire, was called *The Machete*. Although active in the nineteen-teens, the society was almost certainly extinct by the early 1920s.

Athenian Secret and Fraternal Societies

In ancient Athens around 500 B.C., fraternal obligations of many kinds flourished. The *gene* (families who all claimed descent from a common ancestor; singular *genos*) provided the first line of fraternal aid, but if the *genos* failed there was the *phratry* (network of related families), the *deme* (tribe or neighborhood), and the *polis* (state).

Outside blood (birth or marriage) relationships, there were various other fraternal or similar mutual-benefit organizations. Of these, the *eranos* and the *hetairia* come closest to modern fraternal orders.

Eranos is described by Homer as a meal to which all contributed, a cross between LUNCHEON CLUBS and a potluck supper, though "eranos" also came to mean "subscription," as people paid money instead of bringing food. It seems very likely that the *eranos* functioned as a social and drinking club, much like early Accepted FREEMASONS.

Hetairiai bore a still closer resemblance to modern fraternal orders, though they were mainly confined to the most affluent members of the city-states. Many were political; in the hothouse atmosphere of Athenian society, some of them gave rise to scandals resembling those surrounding the Italian *Propaganda Due* lodge of the 1970s and 1980s (see "P2"). Others were merely drinking clubs, while yet others pandered (quite literally) to baser tastes: Pretty slave boys and girls were furnished for the members. Many people belonged to several *hetairiai* and were duly reprimanded by contemporary writers.

The Ancient Greeks also had *thiasoi*, *emperoi*, and *naukleroi*. *Thiasoi* were voluntary religious organizations of various kinds, while *emperoi* and *naukleroi* were associations of traders and shipowners, respectively. Both *emperoi* and *naukleroi* rather resembled modern Chambers of Commerce, Employers' Associations, and even TRADE UNIONS. City-states other than Athens had organizations similar to all of the above.

Atlantis

30, rue de la Marseillaise
94300 Vicennes, France

"Atlantis" was founded in 1926 by Paul Le Cour, with the avowed intention of rediscovering the symbolism and traditions of the fabled lost continent of Atlantis, both by traditional archaeological and scientific methods and by the "law of analogy," which is considerably less rigorous. The society organizes numerous meetings, conferences, study voyages, etc., and publishes the bimonthly *Atlantis*.

Auxiliaries

Fraternal organizations are overwhelmingly a masculine invention, though there have been a number of fully independent and very successful women's organizations (see P.E.O. SISTERHOOD, for example). Many men's organizations will, however, have a "Ladies' Auxiliary," which seems to serve two principal functions. The first is to remove some of the objections raised by women, namely that they are excluded from their husbands' lodge activities. Second, it provides a large pool of free labor for fêtes and fund-raising; it is rarely the men who make the sandwiches and clear up afterwards at such gatherings. In a few cases, ladies' auxiliaries have detached themselves to a greater or lesser extent from the founding men's organization. Almost invariably, the RITUALS AND CEREMONIES of ladies' auxiliaries are much more conventionally Christian in their orientation than the ritual of the parent organization.

Awareness Beings

"Awareness beings" is a more accurate term for the "gods" of Buddhism and some other religions, including various religions embraced or founded by *aficionados* of secret societies. Contrary to Christian beliefs, these gods are not worshiped as externally existing beings. Rather, they are the personification of spiritual qualities. For example, Avalokitesvara (Chenrezigs) is the Buddha of Compassion and is often represented with a thousand arms; the symbolism is that every one of those thousand arms is waiting to reach out and help. This is much easier to understand than abstract "compassion."

In Christianity, there are, in fact, different representations of Christ that are useful when meditating upon different aspects of the Redeemer. There is a Christ of Compassion (the Sacred Heart), a Christ of Salvation (Christ the Redeemer), and even a wrathful Christ driving the money lenders from the temple.

The saints of the Christian calendar also represent different character traits, usually those deserving of emulation, as do the various heroes of initiation rituals (see RITUALS AND CEREMONIES). For example, HIRAM ABIF provides FREEMASONS with an awareness being whose life and actions teach lessons deemed worthy of propagation.

Babende

Babende is or was a West African secret society among the Bangongo of Zaire. The legend of its founding is extraordinarily down-to-earth, and even explains the masks worn by the members. Long ago, there was a chief who wanted to catch a criminal, but he was too old and stiff, while the malefactor was young and active. The old chief therefore chose a number of young men to help him. After accomplish the current mission, they agreed to band together whenever necessity called again. In order to avoid revenge from the criminals and their associates, the young men wore masks.

The OFFICERS consist or consisted of four judges, four court officers, four messengers and four policemen. The Head, called Elder Babende, carries an official staff, and ordinary members wear conical hats. A cylindrical drum — of ancient origin — is (or was) ritually played at meetings.

Babiism

Mirza 'Ali Mohammad of Shiraz (1819 or 1820-50), born to a merchant, claimed to be the Bab, or gateway, to the hidden *imam,* the perfect embodiment of the Islamic faith. In 1844, after spontaneously composing a commentary on the *surah* (chapter) of Joseph from the Koran, 'Ali Mohammad assembled 18 disciples, who became apostles of a new faith in Persia.

The Bab was accused by political and religious leaders alike of fomenting rebellion — indeed, the growing legions of his followers did engage in bloody uprisings — and he was imprisoned in 1847 and again in 1848, until he was executed on July 9, 1850.

His followers, the Babis, made a formal break with Islam and worked to overthrow the Shah's despotic regional governors. After 1863, the Babis became less a political organization and more a religious one, splitting into the short-lived Ezelis and the influential Baha'ai, who survive as an international religious sect today.

Orthodox Islam regards the Babis as heretics because they believe in continuous revelation rather than in the finality of revelation as made by the Prophet Mohammad.

Bacon, Francis

Francis Bacon, Baron Verulam, Viscount St. Albans (1561-1626) is one of a number of figures who are claimed as past members by an extraordinary number of secret societies, especially FREEMASONS and ROSICRUCIANS. Others include ALBERTUS MAGNUS, Count Cagliostro (see CAGLIOSTRO, ALESSANDRO) and Roger Bacon (see BACON, ROGER) who is often confused with the later Baron Verulam.

A polymath who excelled in law and philosophy and was well versed in natural science (including some of the earliest attempts to systematize psychology), Francis Bacon was also a politician and the author of numerous books, including an influential "philosophical romance" entitled *The New Atlantis.* It is not hard to see, therefore, why Bacon might be claimed by the various organizations; however, it seems likely that he was merely the inspirer of a large number of DEGREES, RITUALS AND CEREMONIES, and so forth, rather than an actual initiate into them.

Bacon, Roger

Not only is Roger Bacon (c. 1214–94) gleefully claimed by the ROSICRUCIANS and an impressive number of other organizations, the more eclectic of them also manage to confuse him with Francis Bacon (see BACON, FRANCIS), who was no relative, and who was born some two and three-quarter centuries after Roger's death.

A man whose inventiveness was comparable to Leonardo da Vinci's (witness his work on gunpowder or spectacle lenses, or his predictions concerning flying machines or circumnavigating the globe), Roger Bacon was also a man of strong opinions who, for example, described St. Thomas as a teacher yet unschooled, whose works were full of puerile vanity and voluminous superfluity. In short, Bacon was a man either to love or hate, and he received his share of both emotions.

Scholarly accounts of Bacon make no mention of Rosicrucianism, largely because (claims to the contrary notwithstanding) he had nothing to do with it, since it had not been invented yet.

Bagmen of Bagdad, Ancient Mystic Order of

c/o Jack Mills
4798 Brook Ridge Road
Roanoake, VA 24014
(703) 344-0368

The Ancient Mystic Order of the Bagmen of Bagdad (AMOBB) was founded in 1895 in Ohio as the "fun" and burial insurance arm of the Order of United Commercial Travelers of America (see UNITED COMMERCIAL TRAVELERS, ORDER OF). There were 6,000 Bagmen in 1994.

Today, the Ancient Mystic Order of Bagmen of Bagdad is variously seen as a "fun" organization and as the "inner circle" of the Order of United Commercial Travelers of America (O.U.C.T.A.). Members dress up in pseudo-Arab costume and fezzes for parades (though they do not parade very much, anymore), but the organization also provides the more sober service of funding burial of deceased members.

At one time, there were RITUALS AND CEREMONIES, which may have been in use into the 1970s. Membership has fluctuated through the years: about 4,000 in the mid-1960s, about 6,600 in the mid-1970s, and about 6,000 a decade later. The parent organization, OUCTA, had 175,000 members in 1988.

Bamileke Secret Societies

The Bamileke secret societies of Cameroon are of Sudanese origin and include the following groups:

Mankui — For young men; a "farm" organization for *Mandjong* (below).
Mandjong — Young warriors' association.
Makam — "Farm" or preparatory order for *Kaa* (below).
Kaa — School for learning tribal costumes and traditions.
Meke — For "courtiers" to the chief.
Tingop — "Police" organization; always masked.
Nie — Association of parents of chiefs, responsible for dances and orchestras.
Foufou — "Hit men" who execute sentences of death; always masked.
Koundji — Association of "under-chiefs."
Mansou — Association of the best (women) cultivators.
N'Dakoum — "Hit men" responsible for carrying out minor punishments determined by the chief.
N'Sop — Association of captives and strangers.
Panyop — Council of elders and judges.
Quitong — As *Panyop,* above.
Quo Si — Religious association of elders.

Bananas, Order of

Apparently a deliberate satire on the fondness of Americans for fraternal orders, the organization initiated 110 members at a session in the New York Athletic Club early in November 1923, the branch being called "Banana Bunch No. 1, New York Plantation." The order was also reported to be nonsectarian and to have high ideals. The original Bananas no longer seem to exist, at least in any organized form. There is, however, an International Banana Club, founded (according to its own leaflets) by "Top Banana" Ken Bannister in 1972 as a worldwide "fun" club. To get "planted" (*sic*) in the Banana Club in 1991, applicants had to "Send $10 and your NAME, ADDRESS, PHONE, DESIRED TITLE and any COMMENTS to International Banana Club Headquarters, 2524 N. El Molino Avenue, Altadena, California 91001 AND YOU WILL IMMEDIATELY 'HARVEST' A 1-1/2″ BANANA CLUB MEMBERSHIP PIN" plus a membership diploma and "Your own BANANA CLUB BUSINESS CARD." The promotional literature observes that bananas are shaped like a smile, have no bones, contain no cholesterol, don't leak, have no seeds, and come in their own wrappers. There are no DEGREES in the conventional sense (though members can acquire degrees of Master of Bananistry or Ph. B.). The literature asserts: "We have one major rule: there are NO RULES AND REGULATIONS in this bunch!" Nevertheless, there is a password ("WODDIS") and a hand signal. There is also a Banana Museum at the Altadena Headquarters.

Baphomet

"Baphomet" is a corruption of "Mohammed" in the Provençal dialect. The TEMPLARS were accused of worshipping Baphomet, among other idols and false gods. The name was also adopted by occultist Aleister Crowley (see CROWLEY, ALEISTER) for one of his "magickal" names in the Hermetic Order of the Golden Dawn (see GOLDEN DAWN, HERMETIC ORDER OF).

Baptist Life Association

8555 Main Street
Buffalo, NY 14221
(716) 633-4393

The Baptist Life Association was founded in the state of New York in 1884 as a fraternal benefit life insurance society for Baptists. Membership is now open. The association publishes the *Baptist Life Association News and Views* quarterly. There were 12,703 members in 1994.

The German Baptist Life Association was founded with a strongly Christian bias, which remains to this day; the word "German," however, was dropped in 1934. This is a typical religious fraternal benefit society, with social and religious events, scholarships for qualifying members, and a range of insurance benefits, including annuities for old age. The membership has not varied by more than a few hundred for decades, remaining in the 12,000 to 13,000 range.

Barbati Fratres

Historians of the FREEMASONS identify the Barbati Fratres ("Bearded Brothers") as among the ancestors of the Craft; they were the builders of Catholic convents, active beginning in the year 851 at the Abbey of Corbey (or Corbie, or Corbeia) in northern France, near Amiens.

While there were Barbati Fratres at Corbey—religious converts who led a quasimonastic life, but were not fully monks—the term *fratres barbati* was generally applied to nontonsured (but necessarily "bearded") individuals who took only a vow of obedience rather than the full monastic vows. These persons were also called *conversi*. The particular Barbati Fratres group at Corbey in the ninth through 13th centuries were practical masons who specialized in the construction of convents. They are celebrated in Masonic histories for their refusal to bow to a decree of William Abbott of Premontré to shave their long, flowing beards. Indeed, the group vowed to "fire every cloister and cathedral" in France, if the decree were enforced. The decree was withdrawn.

Bastards, International Brotherhood of Old

2330 S. Brentwood Boulevard, Suite 666
St. Louis, MO 63144-2096
(800) 424-9090 and (314) 961-2300 ext. 69

The International Brotherhood of Old Bastards (I.B.O.B.) was founded in 1813 (but see below) to give members "The opportunity to prove you're a real bas-

tard." It is a worldwide brotherhood, open to both sexes, and there were 1,742,968 members in 1990. The Brotherhood publishes *Ye Olde Bastards Bulletin*.

The true extent of the International Brotherhood of Old Bastards is a matter of some conjecture. A letter to the Supreme Archbastard resulted in the arrival of a very impressive membership pack, including even an I.B.O.B. Hertz Discount Card.

Although the organization undoubtedly exists, what follows is unavoidably a mixture of fact and fiction; as such, it has been officially endorsed by the Supreme Archbastard.

The date of 1813, given above, is the date of foundation of American Formal Bastardy by Bro. Cozen P. Bantling in a house of ill repute in Boston. The original foundation of the I.B.O.B. traces its history, formally and informally, to at least the 14th century (according to some sources, the early 15th century in Spain), when the organization was given its current name by William the Bastard. The original order had expired before the 16th century, but was revived in the late 18th century as a part of the general mania for secret societies; another name for the ILLUMINATI was the Illuminated Bastards, and there are many signs of Bastard ritual among the FREEMASONS.

Some Old Bastards claim roots that extend back at least to the Hittites, and possibly still further; Petra, the "rose-red city, half as old as time," is held to be particularly important. Such claims to extreme antiquity are at least as justifiable as those of many other organizations described in this encyclopedia.

The RITUALS AND CEREMONIES are of such antiquity that they are now lost almost entirely; most of them centered around agriculture, particularly the cultivation and subsequent preparation of grapes and barley, with unexplained interpolations from weaving and brasswork. The revised ritual, prepared by the Reverend Archer in 1867, is now recognized as spurious. There are said to be no fewer than 63 DEGREES (or 138 according to the Mali Rite), divided into four Temples: Outer Pronathaon, Cullicule, Initiated, and Templar.

Informal initiations, as well as elevations to the higher degrees, can be performed by almost any Archbastard and, indeed, are likely to be if you buy him a drink. Depending on the capacity of the officiating Archbastard, it is possible to advance by any number of degrees in a single evening, sometimes repeatedly, depending on who is counting. There are no LODGES—Bastards meet informally—but there is a Staff Chapel. The organization is ruled from the office of the Supreme Archbastard.

The oath (see OATHS) is unusual in that it contains absolutely no penalties, except the possibility of being forgotten by the Supreme Archbastard if you do not send him a prepaid Christmas card. It does, however, carry the implication that far from seeking to conceal the organization, the initiate will do his best to disseminate an artful mixture of fact and fiction about it.

According to the *Encyclopedia of Organizations,* the I.B.O.B. absorbed the *Inter-Faith Bastards and Politicians Sodality* and the *Blessed Order of Mercenary Missionaries,* as well as other organizations. Schisms leading to the formation of splinter organizations have, however, resulted in the following:

Ancient and Original Brotherhood of Old Bastards
Catholic Brotherhood of Old Bastards
Free and Accepted Bastardy, York Right [*sic*]
Grand Independent Lodge, Brotherhood of Old Bastards
Improved Order, Brotherhood of Old Bastards
Independent Brotherhood of Old Bastards of North and South America, Europe, and Africa
Royal and Ancient Brotherhood of Old Bastards
United Order, Brotherhood of Old Bastards

Other organizations claiming to be descended from the original Williamine Order include the Illuminated Bastards, already mentioned, and the Bastards of the Temple of the Rosy Cross.

Bavarian National Association of North America

The Bavarian National Association of North America was a typical ethnic fraternal benefit society, organized in 1884 by Bavarian immigrants to the United States. In 1934 the Bavarian National Association merged with the Unity Life and Accident Insurance Association.

Bavarian Orders of Knighthood

The premier order of the House of Bavaria (Wittelsbach) was the Order of St. Hubert, founded in 1444 to commemorate the Bavarian victory over Arnold of Egmont on St. Hubert's Day. It was revived and confirmed by the Elector Maximilian Joseph in 1800.

The Order of St. George, Defender of the Faith in the Immaculate Conception was the second highest order. It was allegedly founded during the Crusades, but effectively dated from 1729, when it was reestablished by Maximilian Emmanual, Elector of Bavaria.

Bayard, Jean-Pierre

Jean-Pierre Bayard wrote *Le Guide des Sociétés Secrètes* (Phillipe Lebaud, Paris, 1989), as well as a number of other books dealing with legends, the VEHMGERICHT, FREEMASONS, the ROSICRUCIANS, the COMPAGNONNAGE and more.

Le Guide is an excellent book, though one may occasionally question its author's choice of categories and organizations. In particular, many of the "clubs" he lists are more usually considered as religious organizations rather than secret societies. It is also concerned almost exclusively with current organizations; there is very little history. A number of important American organizations, such as the Moose, the Elks, and the Eagles, are either excluded altogether or mentioned only in passing.

Bears, Fraternal Order of

The Fraternal Order of Bears seems to be one of many failed "animal" fraternities; it was founded in 1911, but was almost certainly extinct a decade and a half later. Nothing is known of their aims, RITUALS AND CEREMONIES, or anything else.

Beati Paoli

The Beati Paoli or "Blessed Pauls" was a shadowy Sicilian and Calabrian society, akin to the better-documented VEHMGERICHT in their activities. It is of uncertain date; a Sicilian writing in 1840 placed its origins in the 12th century. It received mixed press; some accused it of being no more than a criminal society, while others saw it as a defender of the common man. Probably it was both—possibly even at the same time. The Beati Paoli was opposed to the arrogance of baronial and kingly power and to the corruption of the clergy. Indeed, the order may be seen as a product of the spiritual movement that produced the Albigenses and other radical religious reform groups. The Beati Paoli was said to have preferred the *Evangelium Aeternum,* a cabalistic and Gnostic text by John of Parma, to the Old and New Testaments. This document nurtured the Beati's tenet that God is dualistic, the creator of good as well as evil.

The Beati Paoli met at night, by candlelight, and the sect was regarded with great suspicion by authorities. Members may have seen themselves as Robin Hood figures, committing any crime deemed to promote the "public good."

The derivation of the name of the order, Blessed Pauls, is unknown.

Beavers

There seem to have been three varieties of "Beavers," which are dealt with alphabetically below. The appeal of the animal is clear; it is celebrated for industriousness and (presumed) foresight.

Fraternal Order of Beavers

The Fraternal Order of Beavers was, like a number of other "animal" fraternities, founded just before World War I, an attempt to cash in on the success of the ELKS, the Moose (see MOOSE, INTERNATIONAL), and, to a lesser extent, the EAGLES. Actually, the order was founded before the war, in 1911, but effectively refounded afterwards and substantially reorganized in 1919. Its headquarters were in Pennsylvania.

It is not clear when the Beavers disbanded, but it was years ago.

Beavers National Mutual Benefit

It is likely that the Beavers National Mutual Benefit was related to the Beavers Reserve Fund Fraternity, founded about a decade and a half earlier in the same state and with headquarters in the same city (Madison, Wisconsin). Unfortunately, there are conflicting accounts of the intertwined Beaver associations.

Like a number of other successful fraternal insurance organizations, the Beavers National Mutual Benefit eventually dropped its ritual (in 1931), when it decided to concentrate on insurance. At the same time, it changed its name to National Mutual Benefit, which still exists in Madison, Wisconsin, and claims the Beavers Reserve Fund Fraternity as its origin.

Beavers Reserve Fund Fraternity

The Beavers Reserve Fund Fraternity, organized in 1902, is the oldest of the three "Beaver" organizations; it flourished and then, probably in the 1930s, died in Wisconsin.

Ben Hur Life Association

P.O. Box 312
Crawfordsville, IN 47933
(317) 362-4500

The Ben Hur Life Association was founded in 1894 in Crawfordsville, Indiana, as a fraternal insurance group for persons of both sexes over the age of 18. There were 15,000 members in 1989.

Founded as the Tribe of Ben Hur by Lew Wallace, Civil War general, politician, and author of the novel *Ben Hur*, the Ben Hur Life Association adopted its current name in 1930. It therefore has the unusual distinction of having its ritual based on a work of fiction. More importantly, it was an early graded ASSESSMENT mutual insurance organization—although instead of having a fixed benefit with a variable assessment, it had a fixed assessment with a variable benefit. The assessment was always $1 per certificate per month, but the value of the certificate dropped according to the age at which you joined. It was $3,000 for those joining between 18 and 23, but for those who failed to join before the age of 54 (the maximum age for joining was 65), it was a mere $500. There were also half certificates and double certificates, but although men and women were admitted "upon absolute equality," no man's life could be insured for more than a double certificate while no woman's life could be insured for more than one certificate.

The LODGE structure was Court, possibly Tribe (it is no longer clear), and Supreme Tribe. The number of DEGREES is also unclear today, but the RITUALS AND CEREMONIES stressed morality, religion, and patriotism.

The main emphasis is and always has been on life insurance, but by 1920 the Tribe was also awarding annual $500 free scholarships to suitable members, a tradition that continued for many years. As with many other such organizations, members may be either beneficial (insured) or social. Interestingly, not all candidates are required to swear an oath upon initiation (see OATHS).

Regardless of their flexibility, the organization has suffered the fate of many others and has withered considerably, from well over 100,000 in 1910 to about 31,000 in 1979 and about 15,000 in 1990.

Besant, Annie

The name of Annie Besant (1847–1933) appears repeatedly in literature related to secret societies and fringe movements. At the age of 20 she married the Reverend Frank Besant (her maiden name was Wood), but she obtained a legal separation in 1873. She was a prominent Freethinker and socialist, the latter to an increasingly revolutionary degree. In 1889, she joined the Theosophical Movement (see THEOSOPHICAL SOCIETY) and became a disciple of Helena Blavatsky (see BLAVATSKY, HELENA). Thereafter, she divided her time between Theosophy and Indian politics (she was President of the Indian National Congress in 1917, at the age of 70), as well as promoting J. Krishnamurti as the New Messiah (after about 1910). Her *Autobiography* was published in 1893.

Bibliotheca Esoterica

Subtitled *Catalogue Annoté et Illustré de 6707 Ouvrages Anciens et Modernes qui traitent des Sciences Occultes . . . comme aussi des Sociétés Secrètes . . . en vente a Librarie Dorbon-Aine*, this bookseller's catalog is a singular repository of improbable tomes useful to the researcher into secret societies—*if* he or she can find the works referred to, many of which are unique manuscripts. The catalog itself was reprinted in 1975 by Editions du Vexin Français, Brueil-en-Vexin, Yvlines.

Big Dogs, Exalted Order of

The Exalted Order of Big Dogs, an association of musicians, was affiliated with the American Federation of Musicians. It flourished in the second decade of the 20th century, with LODGES called "Kennels" and an oath defined as an "oath of fealty" (see OATHS). The order no longer exists.

Bilderburg Group

The Bilderburg Group is one of many modern political secret societies described by Michael Howard in *The Occult Conspiracy*. It is (he says) dedicated to one-world-government.

The group took its name from the Bilderburg Hotel in Osterbeck, Holland, where it held its first meeting in May 1954 under the leadership of Prince Bernhard of the Netherlands, who presided until 1976, when Sir Alec Douglas-Hume took over. Howard reports that no official membership list exists, but that once or twice a year "eighty to a hundred people drawn from the political, financial and media spheres" hold secret talks, the nature and content of which "few" are willing to divulge.

According to Robert Eringer—author of *The Global Manipulators* (Bristol, 1980)—the group was founded by Dr. Joseph Retinger, "reputed to be the top agent for international Freemasonry" and banned from Downing Street when he accused Lady Asquith of being a lesbian. Retinger reportedly foiled a scheme hatched by Texas oilmen to foment a second Mexican-American war in the middle of World War I; made special missions for the Vatican in the 1920s; parachuted into occupied Poland with the S.O.E. in the 1940s; and, in the 1950s, succeeded in linking the C.I.A. to his own "American Committee for a United Europe," which was reportedly "running" the future Pope Paul VI as its main agent in the Vatican. The Bilderburg Group is described as yet another front for the ILLUMINATI, as evidenced by its 39-member steering committee (13 + 13 + 13). In the usual Illuminatist fashion, it is both right-wing and left-wing; in 1976, 15 representatives from the Soviet Union attended a Bilderburg Group meeting in Arizona. Howard also links the organization with the ROUND TABLE, the Institute for International Affairs, the TRILATERAL COMMISSION, and the COUNCIL FOR FOREIGN RELATIONS.

The *Encyclopaedia Britannica* provides a more neutral description of the Bilderburg Conference, observing only that it is an annual three-day conference attended by about 100 of Europe's and North America's most influential economists, bankers, politicians, and government leaders. Held in a different Western nation each year, the conference is always cloaked in an "atmosphere of rigid security." Delegates are chosen by an international steering committee, which meets in the organization's small secretariat located in The Hague.

Blackball

The traditional way of voting on whether or not to admit a candidate to a club is by giving each member two balls, one black and one white. Each member casts one ball into a vase or other container, white for, black against. If a candidate attracts too many black balls (one failed candidate was told that his admission ballot was "pure caviar"), he is refused admission. No explanation is usually required, and the ballot is customarily secret.

In some clubs and individual lodges, a candidate can be "blackballed" by a single vote, though at least three against is the normal minimum. Other clubs require a percentage of votes cast, or of the membership; 10 percent of votes cast is one limit, a third is another, while some organizations work on a simple majority.

Black Brothers, Order of the

The Black Brothers (Schwarze Brüder) were one of many college societies that formed during the late 18th century in German universities. However, members claimed an origin of 1675. The order was reportedly founded in Giessen and Marburg, but by 1783 was headquartered in Frankfurt. The order may have given rise to the Black Legion, a political society active in Germany during the late Napoleonic era.

Black Front

The Black Front was an anti-Nazi society founded in 1930 by dissident Nazis, notably Otto Strasser and Walter Stennes, who tried to live up to the "Socialist" part of "National Socialism." Strasser and Stennes had been expelled from the Nationalsocialistische Arbeiterpartei (Nazi Party). They set up headquarters in Prague and led the activities of Nazi emigrés against Hitler, but with no success. Strasser's brother Gregor was killed in a 1934 purge, and Otto Strasser fled to Canada.

Black Hand

The Black Hand is almost certainly an extortion racket rather than an organized club or gang, but because there are so many references to a criminal "Black Hand Gang" it warrants inclusion here.

The *modus operandi* is simple: The victim is sent a demand for money or goods, signed either with the print of a hand dipped in black ink, or with a crudely drawn black hand.

On those rare occasions when the victim has gone to the police and the police have been able to apprehend the extortionist (as in the case of threats against Enrico Caruso, the famous singer), the offender has almost invariably been a free-lance petty criminal or a member of a street gang with no connection to a secret society. At most, a "Black Hand Gang" is a small-time, *ad hoc* affair.

Various suggestions have been made about the origin of the Black Hand, many of them tracing it back either to Sicily or to Naples. Certainly, Italian immigrants were favored targets for the Black Hand in the United States in the late 19th and early 20th centuries; but Irish gangs had been in exactly the same line of business in New York—albeit without the theatrical addition of the black hand—in the 1850s.

It has been suggested that the first criminal society to use the "Black Hand" or *Mana Negra,* sobriquet was started in the south of Spain in 1835. If there has ever been a genuine Black Hand criminal secret society (which is by no means certain), it seems that it relies on a frightened community of peasants or recent immigrants who dare not seek the protection of the law, or who do not believe that the law can (or will) help them.

Black Hand (Serbia)

The Serbian Black Hand descended directly from the OMLANDINA, consisted of young army officers, and was run by a former high officer of that organization, Colonel Dragutin Dmitrievich, better known as Apis, "the Bull." Riddled with bullets and left for dead after the 1903 assassination of King Alexander Obrenovič and Queen Draga of Serbia, Apis recovered to fight another day.

A macabre aspect of the Black Hand was its choice of tubercular students, who might be expected to die shortly in any case, as assassins. The attempt on the life of the Emperor of Austria in 1911 was made by a tubercular youth called Jovanovic, and the three "hit men" who targeted Archduke Francis Ferdinand and his wife Sophie in Sarajevo were also consumptive: Gavrilo Princip (or Prinzip, or Prinzep), Nejelko Tchabrinovich, and a boy called Grabezh. All were under 20. The 1914 assassination, for which Princip was tried and convicted, touched off World War I.

Apis served as Chief of Staff of the Third Serbian Army, with some distinction, but was executed in 1917 at the behest of Serbian premier Nikola Pašič after a show trial. In his last will and testament, he declared, "I die innocent of the crime with which I am charged, and convinced that my death is necessary for reasons of high state policy." The Black Hand was largely suppressed after this, but continued in deepest secrecy, headquartered at the farm of Yanka Pusta in Hungary, and was responsible for the assassination of Serbian King Alexander I in Marseilles. This had the desired effect of moving Yugoslavia from the French sphere of influence into the Italian/Axis sphere, and played a minor role in fomenting World War II. Thus the Black Hand played a part in the genesis of two world wars in a quarter of a century.

Black Legion

Some authorities report that the Black Legion developed from a small self-help social club organized by marginally employed, unskilled factory workers in Detroit during the early 1930s. Others hold that it was founded in Ohio in 1931 by a former KU KLUX KLAN member, Virgil Effinger. Whatever its precise origins, the order's members were, for the most part, whites who had migrated from the hill country of Mississippi, Kentucky, and Tennessee, and whatever its founding motives, the organization soon turned to racial violence. Many of its members were former Klansmen, and some historians believe that only former Klansmen were accepted for membership.

Lodges spread from Detroit to industrial centers in Ohio and Indiana. Members signed an oath in blood, vowing that "Before violating a single clause or implied pledge of this, my obligation, I will pray to an avenging god or an unmerciful devil to tear out my heart and roast it over flames of sulphur." By the mid-1930s, the movement was large, counting among its 40,000 members public employees and small-time politicians in addition to factory workers. Anti-black, anti-Catholic, anti-Jew, and anti-immigrant, it was courted by the Silver Shirts, an American Nazi organization. The order's political influence was decidedly on the rise when a WPA worker named Charles Poole was found murdered, execution style, on a suburban road near Detroit on May 13, 1936. That fall, 11 Black Legionnaires were convicted of the killing, and other members were exposed, resulting in the dismissal of almost 100 Oakland County, Michigan, public employees. Following the revelation of the murder, the Black Legion effectively ceased to exist.

The Ku Klux Klan, quick to distance itself from an order with which it apparently had so much in common, called for punishment of the Legion as a whole. When Hollywood made a Humphrey Bogart movie loosely based on the order and entitled *The Black Legion,* featuring scenes that showed the KKK's copyrighted insignia on the hooded robes of Legion members, the Klan sued Warner Bros. for libel.

Black Shirts (or Blackshirts)

There were three Black Shirt groups: One was a Nazi corps of the German SS and, therefore, a military organization rather than a secret society. The two other groups, the Italian *Camicie Nere* ("Black Shirts"), organized by Benito Mussolini, and the English Black Shirts, organized by the British politician and member of Parliament Sir Oswald Mosley, did have the trappings of a secret society. Both groups wore black shirts as part of their uniforms.

The Italian Black Shirts were organized in March 1919 to counter Socialist organizations and individuals. Organized into Squadri d'Azione (Action Squads), they were violent thugs responsible for hundreds of deaths. Following the Black Shirts' "March on Rome" in the fall of 1922, Mussolini was catapulted to power, and on February 1, 1923, the Black Shirts became an official national militia. The Black Shirts dissolved in 1943, after Mussolini fell from power.

The English Black Shirts were founded, on Mussolini's model, in 1932 by Sir Oswald Mosley, who had entered Parliament as a Conservative, then became a Labourite, and finally founded his "New Party," the British Union of Fascists (B.U.F.)—the Black Shirts. The B.U.F. published a journal called *Blackshirt,* in which Mosley railed against the parliamentary system, aired his anti-Semitism (his own wife, who died in 1933, was half Jewish), and railed against the Bolsheviks. The B.U.F. was prohibited after the outbreak of World War II, and Mosley was detained from 1940 to 1943. He resurfaced politically in 1948 with the radical right-wing Union Movement.

Blavatsky, Helena Petrovna

Born Helena Hahn on August 12, 1831, in Yekaterinoslav, Ukraine, Madame Blavatsky was an immensely popular writer on spiritualist topics and cofounder of the THEOSOPHICAL SOCIETY. When she was 17, she married General Nikifor V. Blavatsky, a provincial vice governor, many years her senior. After a few months, the couple separated, and Madame Blavatsky became absorbed in the study of psychic phenomena, occultism, and spiritualism.

She traveled throughout Asia and Europe, settling briefly in the United States in 1873, where she engaged in the exposure of various spiritual and psychic frauds — so-called "table rappers" — who were in vogue during the late 19th century. In New York, she became associated with H. S. Olcott, with whom she founded the Theosophical Society in 1875.

Her first book, *Isis Unveiled,* published in 1877, was an indictment of contemporary Western religion as spiritually bankrupt. Despite the popular success of *Isis Unveiled,* interest in the Theosophical Society faltered, and Blavatsky and Olcott moved to India, where they reestablished the organization's headquarters in Adyar, near Madras. Madame Blavatsky began publication of a journal, *The Theosophist,* and the society soon attracted some 100,000 members.

Madame Blavatsky toured Europe, broadcasting to great adulation what she claimed to be extraordinary psychic powers. In 1884, however, the Indian press branded her a fraud, and the following year she was the subject of an investigation by the London Society for Psychical Research. That body likewise concluded that her claims were without basis. Following this, Madame Blavatsky left India and withdrew from the public eye, living quietly in Germany, Belgium, and then London. Her health deteriorating, she wrote two books now regarded as classics of spiritualism, *Key to Theosophy* (1888) and *The Voice of Silence* (1889). She died in London on May 8, 1891. Her collected works, published in a uniform edition almost a century after her death, fill 14 volumes.

Blazing Star, Order of the

The Order of the Blazing Star was a short-lived order of the FREEMASONS, founded in Paris in 1766 by a Baron Tschoudy, author of a book entitled *The Blazing Star.* The Blazing Star itself is an important symbol of Freemasonry, meaning almost anything, according to the taste of the Masonic encyclopedist. At different times, the symbol has signified Divine Providence, the Star of Bethlehem, Prudence, Bounty, or, simply, the Sun. The order, which never assumed prominence in Freemasonry, consisted of degrees of chivalry ascending to the Crusades and following the system of the TEMPLARS.

Blue Friars, Society of the

The Society of the Blue Friars is part of the FREEMASONS and exists for the sole purpose of honoring Masonic authors, one of whom is appointed a "Blue Friar" every year. The society was founded in 1932 and is headed by a "Grand Abbot."

Blue Goose, Ancient and Honorable Order of the

12940 Walnut Road
Elm Grove, WI 53122
(414) 782-7658

The Ancient and Honorable Order of the Blue Goose was founded in 1906 as a "fun" and social organization for fire insurance men (now "property and casualty insurance men"), but has since metamorphosed into an insurance society for the same people. There were 10,000 members in 1989. There was a modest amount of humor in the names of the Nest or Pond (i.e., LODGE) officers: The president was the Most Loyal Gander; the vice president, the Supervisor of the Flock; the warden, Custodian of the Goslings; the secretary, Wielder of the Goose Quill; and the treasurer, Keeper of the Golden Goose Egg. The order publishes the *Grand Nest Bulletin* annually and the *President's Bulletin* three or four times a year.

Blue Lodge

The "Blue Lodge" or "Symbolic Lodge" is the basic LODGE of the FREEMASONS, in which are performed the initiations for the three basic DEGREES of Entered Apprentice, Fellow Craft, and Master Mason. The "blue" is said to symbolize the blue sky under which the original Operative Masons worked when they were building cathedrals and the like.

To become and remain a member of any higher degree or to join any SIDE DEGREE ("fun" organization) such as the SHRINERS, a Master Mason must retain membership of his Blue Lodge. This is a matter merely of paying dues, not of physical attendance, so Blue Lodge attendance may well be as low as 10 percent of lodge membership.

Blue Shirts

BLACK SHIRTS and BROWN SHIRTS were familiar fascist movements/secret societies. Less familiar are the Blue Shirt groups, which appeared in at least three unrelated varieties in three different nations during the 1930s.

In Ireland, the Blueshirts (one word) was the name popularly bestowed upon the Army Comrades Association, led by Edmund Cronin and, as of April 1933, uniformed in blue shirts. By July, 1933, leadership fell to Eoin Duffy, an opponent of the government of Eamon de Valera. Duffy officially renamed the group the National Guard. The Blueshirts were fascists, whose basic philosophy was based on the papal encyclical *Quadragesimo Anno* and Benito Mussolini's theory of the corporate state. The Blueshirts supported Francisco Franco in the Spanish Civil War, sending a brigade to fight in Spain in 1936–37.

In China, the Blue Shirt Society was a secret organization within the Chinese Nationalist Party (Kuomintang, or KMT) and was active from 1932–38. It was founded in Nanking on March 1, 1932, by a group of 20 men dedicated to "saving the nation" after the Japanese invasion of Manchuria. At its height, the Blue Shirt Society consisted of 100,000 members directed by an inner circle of 300 individuals. Although outsiders saw the society as a fascist organization, the members regarded themselves as participants in the Chinese Renaissance Movement dedicated to modernizing China through a particularly aggressive application of the ideology of KMT leader Sun Yat-sen. The group advocated radical land reform, including collectivization, and industrialization financed through a mix of private funding and state capital. Although the Blue Shirts favored democratic government in China, they believed that a temporary dictatorship was necessary to create the stability to establish democracy.

As the Renaissance Movement, the Blue Shirt Society was successful in instituting four mass campaigns during the 1930s: the New Life Movement, the National Voluntary Labor Movement, the National Economic Reconstruction Movement, and the National Military Education Movement. Despite this success, an Extraordinary National Conference of the KMT in March 1938 dissolved the Blue Shirts, whose members became part of the Three People's Principles Youth Corps.

Finally, in the United States, there have been at least two Blue Shirt groups, both active in the 1930s. The National Blue Shirt Minute Men were an antifascist organization with an estimated membership of 10,000 in 1937. Their only moment of public prominence seems to have come in 1936, when they stormed a pro-Hitler meeting in Brooklyn, New York, burning *Der Führer* in effigy, hurling epithets at the American Nazis, and charging police lines four times.

Another anti-Nazi group, the Blue Shirts of Loyalty, was formed in Indianapolis and later changed its name to the Sons of Loyalty. Announcing an initiation fee of $3 until the first 2,000 members were recruited, after which initiation would cost $5 a member, and assessing monthly dues of 50 cents, the Blue Shirts of Loyalty was governed by a Grand Council, which used the funds collected to mount a publicity campaign against Naziism. After the group became the Sons of Loyalty, all fees were dropped,

and the order was funded by donations from Richard S. Kaplan, a Gary, Indiana, attorney, and others. As the Sons of Loyalty, the group claimed to have suppressed pro-Nazi radio programs and the publication of fascist pamphlets.

B'nai B'rith International

1640 Rhode Island Ave., NW
Washington, D.C. 20036
(202) 857-6600

The Independent Order, B'nai B'rith (literally, "Brotherhood of the Covenant") was founded in New York City in 1843 as a fraternal, charitable, and benevolent Jewish association. The order soon spread to Germany and several other countries.

The smaller "Improved Order" was founded as a splinter group in Baltimore in 1887, and is American only.

Today, B'nai B'rith is not so much a fraternal order as a vast charitable and benevolent foundation, often the recipient and donor of very generous gifts. It has funded libraries, schools, and much more. One of its major achievements in the United States has been in reducing tension between Orthodox, Conservative, Reformed, and Progressive Jews. Through its Anti-Defamation league, B'nai B'rith has also sought to expose and combat anti-Semitism.

B'nai B'rith was founded in part because Jews were not admitted to Freemasonry.

B'nai Zion

136 East 39th Street
New York, NY 10016
(212) 725-1211

B'nai Zion is a fraternal benefit life insurance society founded (as the Order of the Sons of Zion) for Jews in 1908; the name was changed to the present style in 1945. Apart from its size (34,000 members in 1989), it is a standard ethnic fraternal insurance society, promoting Jewish causes as well as providing insurance. In 1981, it absorbed BRITH ABRAHAM. The organization publishes the quarterly *B'nai Zion Voice*.

Boxers

The "Boxers" was the name British imperialists gave to the I-ho ch'uan ("Righteous and Harmonious Fists"), a secret Chinese revolutionary society that flourished at the turn of the century and fomented the so-called Boxer Rebellion of 1899–1901, a violent nationalist movement to expel foreigners from China. The society practiced sacred boxing and calisthenic techniques, which they believed would render them impervious to bullets and other injuries.

An offshoot of the Eight Trigrams Society (Pakua chiao), which had spearheaded rebellions against the

Ch'ing Dynasty during the late 18th and early 19th centuries, the Boxers gained official sanction in 1898, when conservative forces—led by the resolutely anti-Western Empress Dowager—came to power in the Chinese government. Enrolled into a semiofficial "Righteous and Harmonious Militia," the Boxers attacked Chinese Christians and Western missionaries and also burned down churches and the homes of Westerners during 1899. Finally, Boxers in Peking (Beijing) killed the German foreign minister and laid siege to other diplomats and their families, who took refuge in the capital's Roman Catholic cathedral.

The siege was broken and the rebellion ended on August 14, 1900, when an international force (including a substantial contingent of U.S. Marines) captured—and looted—Peking. An official protocol was concluded in September 1901, which exacted harshly punitive reparations from the Chinese, weakening the government and paving the way for revolution.

Brethren, The

1 Widcombe Crescent
Bath, Avon BA2 6AQ England
0225-310893; Fax 0225-480134

Often called (though not among themselves) the Plymouth Brethren, this secret society may be considered a Protestant religious denomination. It was founded about 1825 by a group of young Irishmen in Dublin as an alternative to "High Church" Anglicanism. Three years after its founding, John Nelson Darby (1800–82), godson of Admiral Nelson, popularized the movement throughout Ireland and Great Britain. As a result, the Brethren's evangelical Protestantism, resembling Puritan belief, came to be called Darbyism.

In 1848, the Brethren split into the Exclusive Brethren, who accepted what some deemed the "High Church" authoritarianism of Darby, and the Open Brethren, who rejected Darby's authority and held to the autonomy of local congregations. Neither the Exclusive nor Open Brethren have any ordained ministry, nor do the Open Brethren have a central body to coordinate local churches. Indeed, local congregations often join other religious groups and denominations for such purposes as Bible study. There is a regular program of foreign ministry work, which is administered by a committee comprised of the editors of the monthly periodical *Echoes of Service,* based in Bath, England.

Brith Abraham

Literally "the covenant of Abraham," Brith (or B'rith) Abraham is a classic example of a schismatic offspring outstripping the parent order. The original order was founded in 1859; the split came in 1887; the original order went under in 1927; and the Improved Order finally merged with B'NAI ZION in 1981.

Order of Brith Abraham

The Order of Brith Abraham was founded in 1859 in New York City as a male-only fraternal and insurance order, taking as its models the Independent Order B'NAI B'RITH, the Independent Order FREE SONS OF ISRAEL, and a certain amount of the FREEMASONS.

Originally appealing mainly to German and Hungarian Reformed Jews, it later broadened its scope as Russian and Polish Jews swelled its ranks. Its objectives were:

1. To aid members in financial need
2. To give medical assistance to sick members
3. To bury deceased members in accordance with Jewish religious law
4. To provide for the families of deceased members
5. To assist members in becoming good American citizens

It was never a stable organization. The schism of 1887 has already been mentioned, and in 1905, when the District Deputy attended the Paterson, New Jersey, LODGE to install new officers, "he was publicly insulted, his deputy's commission was torn in pieces, and he was ordered to get out of the lodge." Fifty-two members of the New Haven chapter thought to secede in 1907, taking with them part of the funds of the lodge. Membership declined steadily after 1909 (largely to the benefit of the Improved Order, see below) and in 1927 the organization had to declare that it was no longer able to meet its financial obligations. There were barely 8,000 members left when the New York Commissioner of Insurance took over.

Improved Order of Brith Abraham

The Improved Order seems for once to have been exactly what its name stated: an improved version of the original, no more, no less. It admitted women, and was far more smoothly run. By 1917, when the order reached its peak, there were 206,000 members, and in 1924 the order reversed the normal sequence by adding a social (noninsurance) class of membership to what was essentially an insurance order. Usually, insurance was added to an existing fraternal organization.

During the Depression, membership plummeted. By the eve of World War II, there were about 50,000 members. Thereafter, the decline was long and steady. A name change in 1968 to just "Brith Abraham" made no difference; in 1981, the order merged with B'nai Zion.

Brith Sholom

3939 Conshohocken Avenue
Philadelphia, PA 19131
(215) 878-5696

Brith Sholom was founded in 1905 as a fraternal assistance society for Jews, but after World War II, membership was opened to all over 16 years of age. It operates in the United States and Israel, had 6,000 members in 1988, and publishes the *News* weekly and the *Digest* periodically.

The Independent Order of Brith Sholom ("Covenant of Peace") was originally founded to assist Jewish immigrants when they arrived in the United States, teaching them about their opportunities and responsibilities and functioning as a mutual help organization. As the flood of Jewish immigrants declined, it shifted its ground to a human-rights organization; after World War II (during which it rescued a number of children from death at Nazi hands), it ceased to limit membership to Jews, though its Zionist tendencies are likely to render it unattractive to those who are not profoundly sympathetic to the cause of Jewry.

It is not an insurance organization. Instead, it claimed at one time to have the largest fraternal sports program in America (a claim which may no longer be true in view of the drop in numbers, down from 20,000 in 1979), and it promotes Jewish causes and awareness as well as raising truly spectacular sums of money for good causes, such as the Albert Einstein College of Medicine at Yeshiva University, New York; a senior citizens' home in Philadelphia; and a rehabilitation center for disabled Israeli soldiers in Haifa.

Brotherhood of American Yeomen

The Brotherhood of American Yeomen was a secret fraternal benefit society organized in 1897, with RITUALS AND CEREMONIES based (somewhat improbably) on Sir Walter Scott's novel *Ivanhoe*. In the initiation ceremony, chivalry and yeomanry were described as synonymous terms, which suggests that the founders were willing to take liberties with historical concepts. Although there were well over 200,000 members in the early 1920s, the order does not appear in the modern *Encyclopedia of Associations*.

Brotherhood of the New Life

The Brotherhood of the New Life was a mystical, religious, communal society in which groups of three or four persons were formed in the Brotherhood, but if affection resulted, the group was broken up. Parents were separated from children, and husbands from wives.

Although at the beginning of the 20th century some members of the Brotherhood were reported still to live in California and some in Nebraska, it seems likely that the organization is now as extinct in those states as it is in North Carolina, where it was first founded in 1851, or in New York, where it was refounded in 1858.

Brotherhood of the Union

There have been at least two Brotherhoods of the Union in the United States.

The first believed in anything *but* brotherhood and unity. It was one of the many intolerant and xenophobic know-nothing organizations of the mid-19th century (see KNOW-NOTHINGS) and was born in Philadelphia (the "City of Brotherly Love") in 1850. The only entertaining thing about this repellant organization was that its chief officers were called Supreme Washington, Supreme Jefferson, and Supreme Franklin. The RITUALS AND CEREMONIES were allegedly inspired by "the Gospel of Nazareth and the Declaration of Independence." LODGEs were called Circles, with State Councils and the Supreme Circle at the top. The female auxiliary (see AUXILIARIES) was called the Home Communion.

The second manifestation was more palatable than the first, but not a great deal more successful. It was a mutual assessment beneficiary fraternal society, which could muster 12,666 members in 1897, but which had apparently disappeared 10 years later.

Brotherhood of the West Gate

The Brotherhood of the West Gate was clear proof that the people of the 1890s were as susceptible to lightly sketched "secrets of the universe" as the people of the 1990s. It was a brotherhood seeking to solve "the esoteric mysteries of the microcosm," and to restore "inner harmony." The Brotherhood's organ was *The Oracle*, published at Bridgeton, Maine. The organization is almost certainly defunct.

Brown Shirts

The Brown Shirts was a typical post–World War I "Shirt" movement that took its name from the colored shirts members wore to proclaim their allegiance to fascism. They functioned as Adolf Hitler's private army, also known in the late 1920s and early 1930s as the SA or *Sturmabteilung*, and they greatly assisted the Führer-to-be in his rise to power. Unfortunately for them, once their usefulness was over large numbers were slaughtered in the notorious "Night of the Long Knives" purge, when the power of the Nazi Party was consolidated. Those who had known Hitler when he was just another minor-league fascist were eliminated. See also BLACK SHIRTS; FASCIST ORGANIZATIONS.

Buffalo, Royal Antediluvian Order of

Founded in 1822 as a social order, the Royal Antediluvian Order of Buffalo was open to any male. It operated in Great Britain, with some overseas chapters.

Despite the "Antediluvian" part of its name, there is absolutely no evidence that the R.A.O.B. dates from before the Flood described in the book of Genesis, chapter 6. In fact, there is no evidence that it existed before 1822. The Buffalo do, however, furnish an interesting and well-documented example of the transition from a drinking club to a full-blown secret society with

RITUALS AND CEREMONIES, Good Works, and so on. The group is also interesting in that it antedates by many decades both of the well-known American ruminant orders, the ELKS and the Moose (see MOOSE, INTERNATIONAL), both of which seem to have borrowed from the older English order.

The Buffalo themselves borrowed in turn from the Masons, as did just about every other secret society of the 19th and 20th centuries.

Originally, the Buffalo formed in a pub in London. To this day, the British TAVERNS AND PUBS, inns, or boozers retain elements of the social stratification and differentiation that was far more marked two centuries ago. There are still folk music pubs, motorcyclists' pubs, theatrical pubs, poetry pubs, pubs catering to nearby businesses (financial pubs, dockyard laborers' pubs, journalists' pubs), and many more. Mensa normally meets in pubs in Britain.

Initially, therefore, a drinking club may form as much by accident and aggregation as by design; then some wag or would-be organizers gives the club a name, and the secret society is born. At first, the RITUALS AND CEREMONIES are not standardized, but depend on the whim of the members present, and how well lubricated they are; but over the years, not least as founder members seek to recapture their lost youth, the rituals are ossified. The 1828 account by Pierce Egan ("Finish to the Adventures of Tom, Jerry and Logic") of the foundation of the Buffalo is an excellent eyewitness account of the early days of a society:

At the Harp, in Great Russell Street, opposite Drury Lane Theatre, the BUFFALO SOCIETY was first established, in August 1822, by an eccentric young man of the name of Joseph Lisle, an artist, in conjunction with Mr. W. Sinnett, a comedian, to perpetuate, according to their ideas upon the subject, "that hitherto neglected ballad of 'We'll chase the BUFFALO!' "

The Harp was also the meeting place of the CITY OF LUSHINGTON, which some historians have attempted to link to the Buffalo, though the City of Lushington probably antedated the Buffalo by about 40 years. To return to Pierce Egan, we have an account of the making of the Buffalo, as follows:

He is seated on a chair in the middle of the room, with a bandage placed over his eyes. The initiated BUFFALOES are waiting outside the door; the orator being decorated with a wig for the occasion. On a given signal, they all enter the room, with what they call the Kangaroo Leap, and jump around the chair of the "degraded wretch," (as the victim is termed) [and sing the following]:

Come all you young fellows who's a mind for to range
Unto some foreign country, your station for to change.
Your station for to change, away from here to go.
Thro' the wide woods we'll wander to chase the Buffalo.

Chorus

We'll lay down on the banks of the pleasant, shady Wo,
Thro' the wide woods we'll wander to chase the BUFFALO

There are (or were) many more verses, each succeeded by the chorus, though the full song was not normally sung until the end of the ceremony. Pierce Egan continues:

This is succeeded by a solemn march, and the following chant; the BUFFALOES carrying brooms, shovels, mops and a large kettle by the way of a kettle drum—

Bloody-head and raw-bones!
Bloody-head and raw-bones!
Be not perplex'd'
This is the text,
Bloody-head and raw-bones!

The charge is then given to the "victim" by the Primo Buffalo, accompanied by the most extravagant and ridiculous gestures:—

"Degraded wretch!—Miserable Ashantee!—Unfortunate individual!—At least you were so, a quarter of an hour since. You are now entitled to divers privileges; you may masticate, denticate, chump, grind, swallow, and devour, in all turnip fields, meadows and pastures; and moreover, you have the special privilege of grazing in Hyde Park:—Think of that, my Buffalo! You may also drink at all the lakes, rivers, canals and ponds; not forgetting the Fleet and lower ditches. You are entitled to partake of all public dinners (upon your paying for the same). Such are the advantages you will enjoy: but you must promise to gore and toss all enemies to BUFFALO-ISM."

To summarize the next page or two, there are some awful puns (such as promising to go to Hornsey Wood, and proving oneself an Hornament), followed by the removal of the blindfold, a repeat of the chorus of "Chase the Buffalo," initiation into the SIGNS, and some more songs. The new-made Buffalo "is then called on for the customary fees for liquor, and a small compliment for the Buffalo in waiting: the expenses are in proportion to the means or inclination of the newly-made member." As for the reference about drinking from the Fleet, it is worth noting that in those days, the Fleet or Flete River was a notorious sewer.

Originally, the Buffalo were just that—Buffalo—with no "Royal" or "Antediluvian" ornaments. The addition of "Loyal" probably came very quickly, because in the early 19th century, secret societies were looked upon as potentially dangerous and subversive. When the Buffalo were founded, the French Revolution and the Terror were little more than a quarter of a century old. By the time the first Constitution of the Grand Primo LODGE of England was drawn up in 1866, the term "Royal" had been adopted, apparently without justification or permission; this appears to have happened in the late 1840s. The adoption of "Antediluvian" is also of uncertain date, but again seems to have come into general use in the 1850s.

The spread of the Buffalo, as with so many similar organizations, appears to have been carried out mostly by traveling theater companies; Manchester was the first hotbed of the new order, after London, with the Shakespeare Lodge, then the Boston (Lincolnshire) Lodge followed in about 1848.

The officers of the lodge took some time to standardize their titles: The Primo Buffalo might also be a Royal Primo or a Sitting Primo, but an 1848 rule book from Boston offers the following:

OFFICERS DUTIES

Aldermen   To keep the Kangaroos in the different Wards in order, and see they want for nothing.

City Taster   *To taste the gatter [sic]*, and if it is not good to have the Landlord, if a Buff, brought to trial.

City Constable   Not to deliver a summons without being paid for it, and if required, to put an unruly Brother out of the Lodge.

City Scavenger   To keep the room in good order, and to sweep for the new made Brother to kneel down.

City Waiter   To furnish the lodge with all Pipes, Tobacco, and whatever call'd for by the Primo.

City Doctor   To look to those who are to be made and see that they are in good health.

Secretary   To keep the Books, and keep account of all monies received and expended.

Primo Buffalo   To see that all is kept in good order

Host   To have a good fire, and plenty of candles in the room if required.

The "Kangaroos" referred to at the beginning are the regular or garden-variety Buffalos. Other early Buffalo literature refers to the numerous famous people who were Buffalo: Noah, Solomon, Sampson, Brutus, William the Conqueror, Richard I, Sir John Falstaff, General Tom Thumb, Shakespeare, George IV, Richard Brinsley Sheridan, and others. The only "Buffaloess" was Elizabeth I; as the Boston brothers said in their ritual of 1848:

Solomon . . . had one thousand, seven hundred and four wives, and three thousand and two concubines, most Buffaloes are fond of women, but here I must caution you how you trust them, as we never admit them to our councils.

From the very beginning, the occasional "whip-round" for a brother in trouble must have been natural; but essentially, the Buffalo was a drinking club that usually met on Sunday evenings, the actor's day off. There was also a card issued to members who were "on the road," which "enabled them to call at lodges en route and collect enough to permit them to starve gracefully."

During the 1860s, though, a distressing air of moral worthiness seems to have blown through the comfortably beer-laden lodges. Not only was the whole of Buffaloism systematized, but terms such as *Goodness* started to be bandied about. The Constitution of the Grand Primo Lodge of England was signed by representatives of all lesser lodges on May 18, 1866, with delegates from the following lodges: Grand Surrey, Britannia, Bloomsbury, Walworth, Beehive, York Minster, Flowers of the Forest, Sampson, and Shapespeare. In the same document, we find that officers are now as follows:

Grand Primo of England
Deputy-Grand Primo of England
Grand Tyler [patently a Masonic borrowing]
Grand Constable
Grand Physician
Grand Barber
Grand Minstrel
Alderman of Juniper
Alderman of Poverty
Secretary

For the origins of "Juniper" and "Poverty," see CITY OF LUSHINGTON.

Predictably, with this new tide of order, there were dissents; and the Grand Surrey Lodge set up business in competition with the Grand Primo Lodge in 1867. On the positive side, a sick fund was established at around the same time; but the Buffalo never became a friendly society (see FRIENDLY SOCIETIES) or insurance society, though the Royal Antediluvian Order of Buffalo Sick and Funeral Fund ran for many years, and only dissolved when it became clear that there was absolutely no actuarial soundness in its running.

A second Degree was added in 1874, a Third Degree a little later, and a Fourth Degree in about 1886 (see DEGREE). By now, there were KNIGHTS OF THE GOLDEN HORN, Companions of the Ark, and all kinds of Past Masters, Past Primos, and the like.

In May 1888 the Buffalo held the first Convention of the lodges, and Buffaloism was becoming thoroughly respectable. Before the end of the century, work was in hand to raise funds for an orphanage. The foundation stone was laid on October 3, 1903, and the building was opened on May 30th, 1904. In the course of the next 40 years or so, the whole orphanage question was a matter of bitter and political dispute, and the order finally got out of the orphanage business in 1945.

In 1906, an organization-within-an-organization came to light, the Chapters (Lodges) of Knights. This time, it was also being organized and formalized, with such success that the Knights Militant wound itself up in 1915. The Knights of the Golden Horn, another subgroup of the Buffalo, was founded in about 1872 and seceded from the parent organization in 1925.

Come World War I, the Buffalo bought (and drove) ambulances for the war effort. The ambulances were actually lettered R.A.O.B., and were apparently well received.

In 1910, a committee to look into convalescent homes had been authorized, and in 1924 the order bought "Elsinore" in Scarborough, on the northeast coast of Yorkshire. In the next decade two more followed, one at Weston-super-Mare (at the mouth of the Bristol Channel), and the other at Southport, in 1945 (it was sold in 1972). The Old York Hotel in Weston-super-Mare entered service in 1963. As the Buffalo aged, they felt the need to be put out to pasture—a far cry from the original drinking club.

Two unrelated "Buffalo" organizations were established in the United States. The Benevolent Order of Buffaloes was founded in New York in 1881 and became extinct by the early 1900s. The Loyal Order of Buffaloes was set up in Newark, New Jersey, in 1911. It was a fraternal benevolent association, providing family physician services as well as death, sickness, accident, and disability benefits—all for a $6 initiation fee and 75-cent monthly dues. Its Newark headquarters was called the "Home Range." It no longer exists.

Bugs, Order of

The Bugs are unfortunate proof that humor alone cannot sustain an organization. No more do loyal Bugs meet in Bughouses, or pay homage to the Supreme Exalted Bugaboo. Nor have they done so for many years—probably not since about 1912, when the order was supposed to have been founded in Massachusetts.

Builders, New Order of

The New Order of Builders was not a part of the FREEMASONS, as the name might suggest, but rather an order founded in New York City in 1879 as a primitive socialist fraternal benevolent club based on labor, not capital. According to Stevens, on page 338 of the *Cyclopaedia of Fraternities,* members were required to perform "public service" for six hours a day, five days a week, 20 days a month, and 10 months a year, for 29 years; after which they would be "permitted the enjoyment of life, liberty, culture, and happiness thereafter 'without money and without price.' "

It was a wonderful idea, but it had no hope of succeeding. Without incentives to work any harder than was strictly necessary, with an essentially backward-looking, agrarian premise, and with the usual drawbacks of all utopian schemes, it was doomed. The New Commonwealth, Columbia (where it was all supposed to happen), did not long outlive the founder, William H. Von Swarworst.

Builders of the Adytum

5105 N. Figueroa Street
Los Angeles, CA 90024

The American-based Builders of the Adytum was founded by Paul F. Case in 1922 and is one of those numerous orders that defy easy categorization. One authority classifies it under the FREEMASONS, but also makes it clear that it derives from the Hermetic Order of the Golden Dawn (see GOLDEN DAWN, HERMETIC ORDER OF) via the short-lived (1922–24) *School of Ageless Wisdom.*

The course of study begins with the Tarot, in the Golden Dawn pack (presumably the Crowley pack; see CROWLEY, ALEISTER), and then progresses through the Tree of Life, alchemy, and spiritual evolution. The basic degree, which is initiatory, is "Companion Builder." The further DEGREES are not clear.

There are apparently "Anglo-Saxon," Australian, Spanish, and French branches, with the French having responsibility for the entire Francophone world.

The word "Adytum" is defined in the *Oxford English Dictionary* as the inmost part of a temple, typically where the oracles are delivered.

The organization publishes *The Open Door,* monthly.

Builders, Order of the

The Order of the Builders is (or was—it may no longer exist) a "farm" organization for FREEMASONS, rather like the Order of De Molay (see DE MOLAY, ORDER OF). It was founded in Chicago, Illinois, in 1921.

Bulwer-Lytton, Lord Edward

Lord Edward Bulwer-Lytton (1803–73) is remembered chiefly (insofar as he is remembered at all today) as a writer of occult and Gothic novels, chiefly *Zanoni,* though *The Coming Race* and *The Last Days of Pompeii* are also highly regarded by his devotees.

During his lifetime, Bulwer-Lytton was known as an authority on occult matters, though it is less clear whether he was actually (as has been claimed by some ROSICRUCIANS and others) a practicing Rosicrucian and possibly a sometime Grand Master, or for that matter whether he really practiced the ritual magic of which he sometimes wrote (see MAGIC AND SECRETS). He is claimed as a member of several occult groups. His membership of the SOCIETAS ROSICRUCIANA IN ANGLIA (which is not disputed) may well have been honorary, purely in acknowledgment of his knowledge of Rosicrucian and Kaballistic (see KABBALAH) matters as expressed in his novels.

His *The Coming Race* shares with *Ben Hur, Ivanhoe,* and a few other works of fiction the distinction of being a novel on which a secret society was based. See the VRIL SOCIETY.

Bundschuh

The Bundschuh or Sandal Society was a German political society of peasants in the late 15th and early 16th centuries; it was among the fomenters of the Peasants' War of 1524–25, a mostly abortive and generally unsuccessful uprising among German peasants who wanted to attain the freedoms and privileges enjoyed by their Swiss counterparts.

Butt-Thompson, Captain F. W.

Captain F. W. Butt-Thompson was the author of *West African Secret Societies* (London, 1929). This is an estimable book, to which the present *Encyclopedia* owes a great deal in the entries on the secret societies of that area.

Some readers may find it hard to believe Butt-Thompson's accounts of some of the things he witnessed, but anyone who has traveled in the remoter parts of the world can tell stories of "magical" events that defy any modern explanation; and the age in which Butt-Thompson was traveling on the "Dark Continent"—the last quarter of the 19th century and the first quarter of the 20th—was considerably more magical than our own, at least in those areas. He came admirably close to his stated aim, which was "to record something of the old tribal discipline and society organization of West Africa, now slowly but surely passing, and to do this as far as possible without an attempt 'to point a moral or adorn a tale.' "

Cagliostro, Alessandro

"Count" Alessandro Cagliostro—his real name was Giuseppe Balsamo—was born in Palermo in 1743 and was one of the most preposterous and (it must be said) entertaining charlatans of all time. He adopted the title by which he is commonly known in about 1765–70, when he first appeared in European society after having studied alchemy and allied subjects throughout the near East; his career prior to that time included what the *Encyclopaedia Britannica* calls "a series of ingenious crimes" in Sicily.

He claimed to have mastered the transmutation of metals and the secret of eternal youth; to be able to manufacture and administer love philtres, and potions for making ugly women beautiful; and much, much more. He was imprisoned at various times in the Bastille in Paris; in the Fleet Prison in London; and (finally and fatally) in San Leo in Italy, to which he was condemned by the Pope for heresy in 1789. His original sentence was death, but this was "mercifully" commuted to imprisonment in a doorless room, into which he was admitted via trapdoor in the ceiling, never to leave it alive. He died in 1795.

His main relevance to the present encyclopedia is that his name appears in association with almost every secret society of the time, especially the FREEMASONS. Anywhere that there was a chance of bilking the gullible—and in 18th-century secret societies there were plenty of chances to do exactly that—he would do his best.

The most entertaining account of Cagliostro's life is to be found in the *Memoires pour servir a l'histoire du comte de Cagliostro,* published in 1786, but unfortunately these *Memoires* are almost entirely fictional. This does not stop them from being quoted as gospel by a wide range of writers. Carlyle's *Miscellanies* is alleged to be the most reliable account, though Carlyle was not a contemporary of Balsamo.

Cagoule

The Cagoule (*La Cagoule,* "The Hood") was the popular name for the ultranationalist, anticommunist French political and militant secret society formed in autumn 1936 by Eugene Deloncle; more officially, the society was known as the O.S.A.R.N. (*Organisation Secrète d'Action Révolutionnaire National*) or the C.S.A.R. (*Comité Secret d'Action Révolutionnaire*).

With remarkable cynicism, the Cagoulards launched a terror campaign against precisely those bourgeois who were their constituents, confident that the outrages would be interpreted as the work of communists. Members were disguised by hoods, resembling those of the American KU KLUX KLAN. On September 11, 1937, they bombed buildings belonging to the *Groupe des Industries Métalliques* and the *Confédération Genérale du Patronat Français.* Unfortunately for them, the police were more efficient than they expected; while on the trail of the communists, they discovered the real authors of the attacks. The Cagoulards also suffered a blow when one of their explosive stores went up in Villejuif. They imported their arsenal, including machine guns and dynamite, from Germany, Spain, Belgium, and Italy.

There was a good deal of public hysteria; the press

created the impression that the Cagoulards were everywhere, and that what appeared to be the case (that the whole plot had been nipped in the bud) was not so. The affair was reported as if only the "front men" had been arrested, while the manipulators behind the scenes were still free.

During World War II, various Cagoulards and Cagoulard sympathizers apparently worked well against the Germans, but in 1948 the trials of the survivors (which had been started in 1937–38, but were interrupted by the war) were finally completed and the organization faded away.

Calderai del Contrapeso

The Calderai del Contrapeso was a short-lived secret society founded in Italy in January 1816 to oppose the CARBONARI, allegedly under the patronage of the Archbishop of Naples, Cardinal Ruffo. The name literally means "The Braziers of the Counterweight [or Counterbalance]," and "Calderai" is sometimes rendered "Calderari."

Count Orloff, in his *Memoirs of the King of Naples,* records the Calderai oath as given below. It gives a fair idea of their aims and ambitions, as well as a breathtaking demonstration of the manifold possibilities of subordinate clauses.

I, [Name], promise and swear upon the Trinity, as supreme director of the universe, upon this cross, and on this steel, the avenging instrument of the perjured, to live and die in the Roman Catholic and Apostolic Faith, and to defend with my blood this religion, and the Society of True Friendship, the Calderari, to which I am about to belong. I swear never to offend in honour, life or property the Children of True Friendship; I promise and swear to all the Knights True Friends all possible succour that shall depend on me.

I swear to initiate no person into the Society before I arrive at the Fourth Rank.

I swear eternal hatred to all Masonry, and to its atrocious protectors; as well as to Jansenists, Materialists, Economists and Illuminati. I swear as I value my life never to admit any of them into the Society of Friendship.

Lastly I swear that if, through wickedness or levity, I suffer myself to be perjured, I submit to the loss of life as the punishment of my error, and then to be burnt: and may my ashes, scattered to the wind, serve as an example to the Children of Friendship throughout the whole world. And so help me God, for the happiness of my soul and the repose of my conscience.

As might be expected of a group that so clearly displays tolerance, Christian fellowship, and goodwill to all men, the Calderai proved to be a bigger danger to the state than the Carbonari. They were suppressed by royal decree, apparently successfully (for they were devoted royalists), in the same year that they were founded. See also DECISI and FILADELFI.

Camels, Order of

The Order of Camels was founded in 1920. It was open to men over 22, and is probably now extinct. The Camels took a single oath, to oppose prohibition.

Camorra

The Camorra was a Neapolitan criminal secret society founded some time between 1810 and 1820; like the MAFIA, it was also exported, most successfully to the United States. It is now probably extinct.

Sometimes known as the "Neapolitan Mafia," the Camorra was initially a rather different society from both the Mafia and from what it later became. "Camorra" in Spanish means a quarrel, and similar criminal fraternities are known to have existed in Spain long before the second decade of the 19th century, which is when the Italian society first became known.

If it was not founded in the prisons of Naples, it certainly flourished there. It was a fraternal, social society of many kinds of prisoners, though most were common criminals. After about 1830, it began to function in the city as a criminal guild. It also had political aspects—the Bourbon rulers of Naples commanded no respect, nor did their police—and was a leader in free-trading (smuggling). As in other places where the legitimacy of customs dues were disputed, many legitimate businessmen and even nobles both secular and spiritual connived at freetrading. Like the modern Mafia, it also liked to keep its turf exclusive; free-lance villainy was quickly and permanently eradicated.

Especially after 1848, the Camorra began to run Naples in the same way that Al Capone ran Chicago with the Mafia. The Camorra survived a major government crackdown in 1877, when 57 leading *camorristi* were arrested simultaneously. After a political scandal in 1900, the candidates of the Camorra were defeated in 1901 by the Honest Government League. The Camorra was seriously damaged in Italy in 1911 by the Cuocolo trial. Some say it was broken by it, but it did not disappear completely, because Benito Mussolini promised in the 1920s to combat the Camorra just as he promised to combat the Mafia.

Whatever its career in Italy, the Camorra had successfully begun to operate in the United States by the 19th century. Until prohibition welded the big gangs together into the modern form of organized crime, there were some cities where the Camorra and the Mafia ran neck and neck. The two most important were New Orleans, where a bloody gang war ended in Mafia ascendancy by about 1919, and New York.

The end of Camorra power in New York came about because the Mafia was more feared. Although in 1916 the Brooklyn Camorra under Don Pelligrino Morano murdered Nicholas Morello of the Manhattan Morello Mafia, the hit backfired when federal authorities successfully prosecuted the hit squad. Morano himself went down for conspiracy; several trigger men went to the chair; and what was left of the Camorra thrashed about in a bloody death spasm for two or three years, after which any survivors seem to have gone over to the Mafia.

Canadian Fraternal Association

The Canadian Fraternal Association is the voluntary regulatory body for Canadian fraternal life insurance, founded in 1891. When it was founded, about one-quarter of all life insurance in Canada was sold by fraternal organizations, a proportion that has decreased more than tenfold in the years since.

Canters

The Canters or Muckers were a short-lived German secret society of the late 17th century. One authority, Heckethorn (see HECKETHORN, CHARLES WILLIAM) accuses them of "immoral practices" and "debaucheries of the most revolting description," and rages against "the cruel and hideous precautions" that were taken to prevent the birth of children in the community—"precautions we are not allowed to describe." Further details are not forthcoming, and it is not clear whether the adherents are involved in sexual magic or whether they were in it for the sex alone.

Carbonari

The name *Carbonari*, "charcoal burners," has been applied to several political, revolutionary secret societies. Properly, the word is Italian and applies to the Italian organization or organizations of that name, but there are enough references to the "French Carbonari" and the "Spanish Carbonari" to warrant covering them here; the *Totenbund* may have been the "German Carbonari" (see below).

The Italian Carbonari

The Italian Carbonari was founded at the beginning of the 19th century as a political secret society, probably for men only, dedicated to the unification of a free Italy. It is now extinct.

The exact date of the foundation of the Carbonari is no longer known, but the organization was first noticed in Naples early in the reign of Joachim Murat, which was from 1808–15, and the *Alta Vendita* (principal lodge) was based in that city. The Carbonari have some organizational similarities with the French FENDEURS, though the earlier organization seems not to have been political at all.

There are also clear influences from the FREEMASONS, though this is true of almost any secret society formed at any time, and especially of European secret societies formed in the late 18th or early 19th centuries.

Despite being officially suppressed in September 1813, the Carbonari were not destroyed; on the restoration of the Bourbons in 1815, Italy was fairly alive with them. They were probably at their peak in the 1820s, and indeed their banner (red, blue, and black) was the flag of Italian unification until superseded in the 1830s by the flag of Young Italy. The earliest accounts of the Carbonari date from the 1820s; after that, although they may have survived for many decades, they were effectively usurped by Mazzini's Young Italy (see YOUNG EUROPE).

The "legend" on which they were founded is apparently the work of an ill-educated Gaul. In Scotland, during the reign of one Queen Isabella, the disaffected masqueraded as charcoal-burners, carrying dissent along with the charcoal; but when they providentially met the King of France, Francis I (1494–1547), who had been hunting along the Franco-Scottish border [*sic*] and was lost in the forest, they were taken under his protection. Thereafter they flourished and spread through Germany and England.

The 10 articles of the Carbonari were as follows:

1. Good Counsinship is mainly founded on religion and virtue.
2. The place of meeting is called the Baracca; the place surrounding it, the Forest; the interior of the lodge, the Vendita.
3. The members are called Good Cousins, and are divided into Apprentices and Masters.
4. Tried virtue and purity of morals are qualifications for membership.
5. Six months must pass before an Apprentice can become a Master.
6. It is forbidden to argue directly or indirectly against religion.
7. All conversation on religion in general and against good morals is prohibited.
8. Secrecy is to be preserved concerning the mysteries of the order.
9. What takes place within a Vendita is not to be disclosed to members of another Vendita, much less to the uninitiated.
10. The greatest reserve is recommended to all persons with whom members are not well acquainted, but more especially in the bosoms of their own families.

The officers were the Master, the Secretary, the Orator, and the Master's First and Second Assistants. Backless Benches ran parallel to the long side of the LODGE, which was supposed to be wainscoted with wood and paved with brick. The Master's desk at the top. On the Master's right sat the lesser Masters (with their hats), and on his left sat the Apprentices (bare-headed).

The influence of Freemasonry is seen not only in the use of such terms as "Grand Master of the Universe" for God (and "Honorary Grand Master" for Christ), but also in its array of symbols. For example, the Master's desk in the lodge was supposed to be a rough block of wood decorated with the following in a line: cloth; water; salt; a cross; leaves of certain trees; sticks; fire; earth; a crown of white thorns; a ladder; a ball of thread; and three ribbons, one each of blue, red, and black. Behind the desk was an irradiated triangle with the initials of the password of the Master's degree, flanked on the left with a triangle painted with the arms of the vendita and on the right with three triangles bearing the initials of the sacred words of the apprentice.

This was only a beginning; there was so much secret society baggage that it is a wonder that they had any time for political activity. Indeed, Young Italy, with more political action and less ritual, rapidly eclipsed the Carbonari in the 1830s.

For the Apprentice degree (see DEGREES), the candidate was blindfolded or hoodwinked, then swore upon an axe to preserve the secrets of the order and to help fellow Good Cousins. For the Master's degree, the presiding officer was addressed as Pilate, while his assistants were Caiaphas and Herod. The candidate took the part of Christ. Other degrees are mentioned by various writers.

In the melee of 19th-century Italian politics, the Carbonari were anti-Napoleonic and favored a united Italy under constitutional monarchy, whether Murat or Bourbon. Everyone seems to have tried to use the Carbonari for their own ends: Murat favored them at first, then tried to exterminate them in September 1815, then after the Hundred Days (Napoleon's return from Elba) and the Bourbon restoration, King Ferdinand tried to do the same thing. From early 1816, the Carbonari were also opposed by the CALDERAI DEL CONTRAPESO, while the DECISI also threw their weight into the Italian political struggle by bypassing the middleman; instead of supporting any political party, they preferred to go directly into the robbery and murder business for themselves.

The Carbonari promoted the Neapolitan revolution of 1820, which met with partial success—the king actually agreed to constitutional government—but their success was reversed shortly afterward by government forces, including 50,000 Austrian troops imported to help King Ferdinand break his oath. In 1831 they rose against the Papal States and met with great success in Romagna and the Marches; while rulers of Parma and Modena were also expelled by Carbonarist uprisings. Once again, Austria intervened, and the Carbonari seem to have taken the hint. Little is heard of them again, but the more energetic among the members must have joined Young Italy in droves.

The *Latini* were reported by Heckethorn (see HECKETHORN, CHARLES WILLIAM) to be an inner lodge of the Carbonari. The *Litterateurs* were a small society that probably merged with the Carbonari; their arms were the same, and they first appeared in Palermo in 1832.

French Carbonari

The Charbonniers existed in at least two incarnations. The first was effectively indistinguishable from the FENDEURS; the DEGREES were Apprentice, Master, and Hewer, and the five degrees of the Fendeurs (which means "Hewers") appear to have been superimposed on the third degree of the original Charbonniers.

About 1820, a new version of the Charbonniers arose out of the Fendeurs, apparently from the upper ranks once more. By 1822, there may have been as many as 60,000 French Carbonari. They apparently operated along much the same lines as their Italian model, and they were believed to be behind the uprisings of 1821 at Belfort, Thouars, La Rochelle, and elsewhere; and again in 1822 at Saumur, Lyons, and Marseilles. With the revolution of July 1830, the Charbonniers seem to have assimilated easily enough into the mainstream, supporting the government of Louis Phillipe, though individual members may well have joined other revolutionary secret societies when the French Carbonari disintegrated in the mid-1830s.

Spanish Carbonari

Italian exiles founded the Spanish Carbonari in 1821, and in 1822 attempted to foment revolution in Spain by enlisting French Carbonari in the regiments poised for the invasion of Spain. They attempted to make common cause with the COMUNEROS and Freemasons, who had hitherto been untied in opposing them; predictably, internal bickering and fundamental differences of opinion about the future of Spain doomed their efforts from the start.

German Carbonari

The *Totenbund,* or "Band of Death," was a German offshoot of the Italian Carbonari who took a solemn oath to rid the world of all tyrants.

Cardinale, Hyginus Eugene

Cardinale's *Orders of Knighthood, Awards and the Holy See* (Gerrard's Cross, U.K., 1985) is the definitive work on Catholic chivalry. It is also very well illustrated with the insignia of the various orders. There are excellent entries on the significance of the various saints, and on the many orders dedicated to them.

Carnes, Mark

Mark C. Carnes is the author of *Secret Ritual and Manhood in Victorian America* (New Haven, Conn.: Yale University

Press, 1989), an extremely interesting book about the purpose and nature of RITUALS AND CEREMONIES, often written in the style of a novel.

Carrefour de l'Amitié

7 rue de Saulnier
75009 Paris

The *Carrefour de l'Amitié* or "Crossroads of Friendship" is a fraternal derivative of FREEMASONS open to prominent politicians, whether Masons or not; membership is by invitation.

Catholic Daughters of the Americas

10 West 71st Street
New York, NY 10023
(212) 887-3401

The Catholic Daughters of the Americas was founded in 1903 as a fraternal service organization. It operates in the United States, Dominican Republic, Guam, Mexico, Saipan, and the Virgin Islands. Catholic women over the age of 18 are eligible to join. In 1994 there were 160,000 members. The Daughters publishes *Share* magazine, four times a year.

The organization was originally founded as the National Order of the Daughters of Isabella; the name was changed in 1921. The founders were members of the Utica, New York, branch of the KNIGHTS OF COLUMBUS, another prominent Catholic organization.

The first national officers, elected on June 18, 1903, were mostly men. John E. Carberry was the Supreme Regent; the National Secretary, National Treasurer, and National Advocate were all men. The Supreme Vice Regent was, however, a Miss Mary L. McKernan. The Board of Directors included three men and three women. After John Carberry's death in August 1906, McKernan took over as Supreme Regent.

The order's ritual, also devised by the Knights of Columbus, was (and is) predictably Roman Catholic in orientation. There is now only a single degree (see DEGREES), though there were once more. The objectives, as listed in the original articles of incorporation, were:

1. To promote the social and intellectual standing of members
2. To achieve literary goals
3. To render aid and assistance among its members as shall be desirable and proper, by such lawful means they deem best

In practice, the organization concentrated principally on the third goal, though as early as 1913 it was able to buy a large, impressive building from Utica Council No. 189 of the Knights of Columbus, borrowing $10,000 (at 5 percent interest) to finance the purchase.

From the start, aid and assistance were not restricted to members. Members were very active during World War I as nurses and clerks, and as hostesses for parties given to honor servicemen; they also conducted sewing and knitting classes for the Red Cross. In the civilian field, members contributed to Braille translations and other work for the blind; clothing for the needy; and a great deal of fund raising for the Church.

After the war, the Catholic Daughters helped with veterans' organizations as well as continuing their civilian and religious work. At the 1919 Biennial Convention the order decided to sponsor a junior program for girls aged 12–18.

In 1923, shortly before her death, Genevieve Walsh, who had succeeded Mary McKernan, relinquished the leadership to Mary Duffy, who was to lead the Catholic Daughters for 27 years. Under her direction, membership grew steadily: There were 170,000 members by 1928, and in World War II the Catholic Daughters once again did sterling volunteer work: 8,314 members served as Red Cross instructors; 72,147 completed Red Cross courses; 7,468 were blood donors; 15,061 members made 4 million surgical dressings; and some 50,000 members sewed and knitted 1 million articles of clothing. In addition to purchase by members of $4.7 million worth of war bonds, the Courts purchased another $1.6 million worth and sold $3 million worth.

Since then, the order has raised immense amounts of money, hitting the million-dollar-a-year mark as early as the 1960s, dividing donations between temporal and spiritual causes. Their aid to physically and mentally handicapped children is extensive. Other causes espoused include opposition to abortion, and support for efforts "to counteract the growing menace of obscenity and pornography in all forms of the communications media."

Membership reached its highest point (over 215,000) in the late 1960s, but slipped back to 174,000 by the late 1970s, at which level it remained more or less constant for a number of years. Even so, it is a healthy organization by any standards: 170,000 members at the *beginning* of a membership drive in the late 1980s makes it still the largest organization of Catholic women in the world.

The Junior Catholic Daughters of the Americas was founded in 1925 and is apparently divided to match the American school system: Juniorettes, aged 6–10; Juniors, aged 11–14; and Teens, aged 15–18.

Catholic Knights Insurance Society

1100 W. Wells
Milwaukee, WI 53233
(414) 273-6266

The Catholic Knights Insurance Society was founded for fraternal, religious, and insurance purposes in 1885, in the United States. In 1989, membership stood at 82,000. The Knights publish *The Catholic Knight,* quarterly.

The Catholic Knights of Wisconsin, who became the Catholic Knights Insurance Society, was an off-shoot of the CATHOLIC KNIGHTS OF AMERICA, which went in for insurance in a big way, becoming the largest Catholic fraternal insurance society in Wisconsin.

In addition to its insurance arm, local branches carry out educational and social programs, and support various "Catholic Action" activities.

Catholic Knights of America

3525 Hampton Avenue
St. Louis, MO 63139

The Catholic Knights of America was founded in Nashville, Tennessee, in 1877 as a fraternal and insurance organization. Membership is open to any Catholic man over 18. In 1995 the membership of the organization stood at 17,000. It publishes *The CKA Journal* monthly.

The Catholic Knights of America was formed on April 23, 1873, though the name was not finally chosen until June 19 of that year. The Catholic Knights very nearly came to an end a decade later when the treasurer absconded with the funds, but sterling work by the other officials kept it afloat, and a good proportion of the money was even recovered.

Like many other Catholic fraternal organizations, it was founded to provide Catholics with the fraternal and insurance benefits denied them because good Catholics may not join the FREEMASONS or many other societies. A ladies' auxiliary (see AUXILIARIES) was founded on the same graded ASSESSMENT insurance basis as that governing the men. The insurance remains important to this day (see CATHOLIC KNIGHTS INSURANCE SOCIETY).

A "hard-line" Roman Catholic organization, completely faithful to the Church, the Knights are not afraid to espouse causes that follow from this commitment, such as a stance against abortion. Specifically religious activities include masses for the souls of dead members, $1,000-a-year scholarships for four years to seminarians, and distribution of both rosaries and the *Good News New Testament*. Secular programs include life, annuity, and other forms of insurance and fraternal orphans' benefits; high school scholarships; a Law Enforcement Recognition Program; and various contests (photo, essay, and poster) for young members. In those areas where the Knights owns its own hall, it is built close to a Roman Catholic church and is made available to the church. Otherwise, meetings are held in church halls or in the church itself.

Since 1893 there has been a Uniform Rank. Company A (for men) wears paramilitary uniforms, while Company C (the ladies' company) wears white skirts and dark blazers.

Membership has fluctuated over the years, with about 21,000 in the late 1960s; 25,000 in the late 1970s; and over 17,000 in the late 1980s.

Catholic Knights of Ohio

The Catholic Knights of Ohio was founded in 1891 in Hamilton, Ohio, as a fraternal benefit society with membership open to Catholics of both sexes over the age of 16; there were 18,000 members in 1979. Information about the Knights after 1979 was not found during preparation of this work.

The Catholic Knights of Ohio are—or were—a typical religious fraternal benefit society, supporting principally Catholic causes in addition to good works, organizing athletic events, and, of course, providing insurance. There are—or were—two DEGREES, though not very secret, as this would be contrary to Catholic teachings.

Catholic Knights of St. George

The Catholic Knights of St. George was founded in 1881 as a fraternal benefit insurance society, operating primarily in the eastern United States. It was organized from among the German Catholics who fled their native land after the Franco-Prussian War of 1870–71. The order was a typical ethnic/religious fraternal benefit society, with strong emphasis on Catholic causes (including opposition to legal abortion), an old people's home (founded in 1923), youth programs, and more. It is not clear when the organization became defunct.

Catholic Workman

P.O. Box 47
New Prague, MN 56071
(612) 758-2229

The Catholic Workman is a fraternal insurance society founded in St. Paul, Minnesota, in 1891. In 1993 there were 15,000 members in the United States. It publishes the *Catholic Workman* monthly.

Founded as the *Katolicy Delnick* in 1891 by a group of Czech Catholics under Father John Rynda, Catholic Workman was apparently modeled on the CATHOLIC KNIGHTS OF AMERICA. The decline in numbers is modest compared to similar organizations. In 1965, Catholic Workman had 19,000 members in 16 states, mostly in Czech parishes; the organization lost less than 25 percent in a quarter of a century.

Celtic Church

The Celtic Church—closer in doctrine and in its RITUALS AND CEREMONIES to Syria than to Rome—still exists. Although it is not a secret society, it may be regarded as such by many western Christians because of the infusion of pre-Christian and non-Christian Celtic beliefs.

As with many of the secular groups in the present book, the Celtic Church is not in fact a true survival, but a restoration. The French Dominican Jules Ferette was consecrated bishop of Iona in 1866, and he in turn consecrated Richard William Morgan, of the Church of England, as the British patriarch in 1874.

The Archbishop of Dol and the Celts is of still more recent origin, dating from 1952 and related directly to the Syrian Patriarchate of Antioch; the other branch derives from the Jacobite Patriarch of Antioch.

Cercle de Paris

Tour Tokyo
20 Avenue d'Ivry
75645 Paris Cedex 13

The Cercle de Paris, or "Circle of Paris," is a Masonic association that gives dinners for prominent persons active in promoting republican and humanist ideals.

Chauffeurs

The Chauffeurs or "Warmers" was a French criminal society that existed from about the 14th century to the end of the 18th century. Theft from outsiders—"the profane"—was acceptable and even praiseworthy, but theft from brethren brought heavy penalties, and repeated offenses merited death. The group's name was taken from its habit of lighting a fire to burn the feet of persons suspected of concealing the whereabouts of their wealth. It reached its peak during the Reign of Terror, and, indeed, it may be that prior to the French Revolution it was a much less influential group, who seized its opportunity when law and order was destroyed.

The Chauffeurs was effectively annihilated in 1799 after its chief hiding place was discovered by an infiltrator. A small band survived to maraud on the other side of the Rhine until 1803, when it, too, was brought to justice.

Chesneaux, Jean

In 1970, Jean Chesneaux edited *Mouvements populaires et sociétés secrètes en Chine aux XIXᵉ et XXᵉ siècles* (Paris: Maspero, 1970). In 1972, Stanford University Press published *Popular Movements and Secret Societies in China 1840–1950,* unfortunately without nine of the original papers (including Feiling Davis's *Le Rôle économique et sociale des sociétés secrètes*), but with the addition of one previously unpublished paper.

Chinese Secret Societies

There is in China a tradition of secret societies that stretches back for centuries and even millennia.

At first sight, the tradition of the East is quite unlike that of the West. Instead of being primarily associations of the bourgeoisie, the Chinese organizations have a strong *demimondaine* bias: part political "fringe" movement, part appeal to the downtrodden masses, and part straightforward banditry and organized crime ("protection money" and the like). Running through all of this,

there is also a strong thread of mutual assistance and fraternal benefit.

The difference is, however, more apparent than real. Arguably, the traditional Chinese secret society was the manifestation of a nascent bourgeoisie, unable to metamorphose into a true middle class because of the rigorous Confucian control exercised by the aristocracy of the Mandarins who ran the Celestial Empire.

Because of the nature of Chinese secret societies—complex, interwoven, poorly understood by westerners, and of limited interest to most readers—there are very few individual entries in this encyclopedia, though some (such as the BOXERS) are included separately.

Historically, Chinese secret societies were affiliated with or descended from one of two great groups: the White Lotus group of northern China, or the Triads of southern China. Individual gangs or groups might be more or less clearly related to one or the other, but an understanding of the twin origin of the societies helps one to understand the nature of all Chinese secret societies.

The White Lotus Group

The White Lotus group, as the name implies, took much of its belief system from Buddhism, albeit in a form so distorted as to be barely recognizable as originating in the teachings of the Enlightened One. The group was essentially millennialist, believing in the third *kalpa*, or "age of the world," in which the Buddha Maitreya will complete the teachings of Buddhism. We are currently living in the Red Sun age of Gautama Siddartha, the Buddha Sakyamuni.

The overlays and underpinnings are, however, enormously complex. There is a doctrine of an Eternal Mother, either antedating or coeval with the Old Buddha of the Celestial Reality of the Unexcellable who came forth from the True Void; there are strong elements of Manichaeism (see HERETICS); there is a current of Taoism; and Maitreya himself seems to be confounded with the "Buddha" (more properly "awareness being"; see AWARENESS BEINGS) Amitabha, the Buddha of Limitless Light. There are even calculations of the 9.6 million "Original Sons" who are to be saved in the Boats of the Law. At this point, the theology becomes so complicated as to defy further explanation.

Although the Buddha himself urged his followers not to take anything on faith, but to "test it as a goldsmith tests gold," the majority of White Lotus secret societies seem to have operated more on a very fixed belief system, which they "bought" as a package.

The White Lotus secret societies often had a strong political element; the group was concerned that the rulers of the Middle Kingdom should both hold and be subject to the Mandate of Heaven, which (if withdrawn) meant that the dynasty was not legal and could—or, indeed, should—be overthrown. In this sense, they were faintly akin to numerous other political groups in other countries throughout the world, though their mish-mash of religious beliefs lent them an internal coherency that greatly exceeded that of the factious (often factitious) and schismatic humanists of 18th-, 19th-, and 20th-century Europe. In many ways, they were more akin to the political arm of a movement that somewhat resembled the Reformation in Europe.

Leading White Lotus secret societies included the following:

Eight Trigrams Sect (Pa-kua Chiao)
Celestial Order Sect (T'ien-l Chiao)
Observance Sect (Tsai-li Chiao)
Abstinence Sect (Chai Chiao)
Boxers (I-ho Ch'uan, "Fists of Righteous Harmony")

The Triads

The Triad societies were less avowedly political than the White Lotus societies and more given to adventurism and (frequently illegal) entrepreneurism. The growth of foreign and internal trade loosened social ties in the 18th century, which greatly expanded the role of Triad-style organizations: The rootless beneficiaries or victims of the changing times formed all sorts of guilds, mutual assistance groups, clubs, and more. Unlike the White Lotus, which in its very nature kept a watchful eye on the government and the social order, the Triads sought always to make an accommodation with the existing establishment. A parallel might be drawn with some of the more corrupt American big cities of the 1920s and 1930s, where organized crime and the "party machine" were frequently indistinguishable from one another. The Triads would get involved in political action only if there was a probability of personal profit.

The relationship between members of different organizations within *Hung Men*, "the Vast Gate," was flexible. Like the members of the European rogues' and beggars' societies (see MERCELOTS), they could count on hospitality in a strange area. Recognition signals might include a particular way of positioning one's tea cup or fingering one's lapels. They might also be recruited into whatever local villainy was afoot, or recruit local villains for purposes of their own. On the other hand, the individual members were just that—individual—and there was no hierarchy headed by a Godfather or a Fu Manchu; at most, there might be local gang bosses who resembled the Al Capones and Legs Diamonds of Chicago between the world wars.

Also, some of the Triads were genuine, open, straightforward benevolent associations, though this was more often a result of evolution than of deliberate planning. There were also times when Triad organizations effectively *were* the local government. At the fall of the Ching dynasty, the Red Spears must have operated in somewhat

the same way as the VEHMGERICHT, a *de facto* source of rule and rough justice. In such cases, law-abiding citizens might join a criminal or semicriminal society, possibly transforming it or absorbing it into village life as they did so.

Because of their nature, Triad societies rose and fell faster than White Lotus societies, and went under far more names, many of them fairly dramatic.

Leading Triad groups included the following:

1. Red Spears (Hung-ch'iang Hui)
2. Elder Brothers (Ko-lao Hui; these were courted by no less a person than Mao Tse-tung, illustrating a clear link with a "party machine")
3. Three Harmonies society (San-ho Hui)
4. Green Gang (Ch'ing Pang)
5. Red Gang (Hung Pang)
6. Three Dots Society (San-tien Hui)
7. Golden Coin Society (Chin-ch'ien Hui)
8. Double Dragon Society (Shuang-lung Hui)
9. Crouching Tiger Society (Fu-hu Hui)
10. Dragon Flower Society (Lung-hua Hui)

Chinese Secret Societies Outside China

Although the "dreaded Tong" was a staple of Victorian thriller writers, and despite such events as the Tong Wars at Chinese Camp in California in the later 19th century, Chinese secret societies seem always to have continued partly as organized crime and partly as benevolent societies, mostly deriving from the Triad tradition.

In London, even in the 1980s, there were periodic accounts of Chinese restaurants being smashed up (and the occasional person killed) by sword-wielding Tong Gangs, and there are Chinese gangs in other cities that have substantial Chinatowns. In the sleepy town of Guadalupe, on California's central coast, the Hop Sing Tong Benevolent Association announces its presence with a carved lintel stone, which would hardly be practical if the organization were anything other than the benevolent association it purports to be.

Chosen Friends, Order of

The Order of Chosen Friends lasted only from 1879 (when it was founded in Indianapolis, Indiana) to the first decade of the 20th century, but it provides a microcosm—almost a parody—of the history of a typical fraternal benefit society.

Prominent among the founders were FREEMASONS and ODD FELLOWS, who wanted a fraternal benefit society that would pay disability and old age benefits. To their credit, they founded the first fraternal benefit society to admit women. The elaborate RITUALS AND CEREMONIES were written by a Methodist clergyman who was also an Odd Fellow and a Freemason. And there were no fewer than five schisms in the order, resulting in the spawning of the

Order of United Friends (New York, 1881); the Independent Order of Chosen Friends (California, 1881); the United Friends of Michigan (1889); the Canadian Order of Chosen Friends (1892); and the United League of America (1895). All of these schisms were the result of personal squabbles and exercises in fraternal politicking; and, as might be expected, none of the orders (original or schismatic) prospered.

Christian Democrats

As well as being the name of a European political movement that survives and, indeed, flourishes in many countries to this day, there was also a band of so-called Christian Democrats who were an anti-Semitic political secret society in Dallas, Texas, before World War II.

Christian Knights and Heroines of Ethiopia of the East and West Hemispheres

This African-American order was formed in Alabama in 1915 and is now probably extinct. Its purpose is unclear at this time, but it was probably a fraternal benefit society with strong religious overtones.

Christian Cynosure

The *Christian Cynosure* was a monthly magazine published by the National Christian Association, which was organized in 1868 as the National Association of Christians Opposed to Secret Societies. The title of the association is self-explanatory; its avowed intent was to "expose, withstand and remove secret societies." The *Christian Cynosure* also printed a 300-page book called *Modern Secret Societies* in 1903, which had been through six editions by the early 1920s, though unfortunately a copy eluded the compiler of this work. It is not clear when the *Christian Cynosure* ceased publication.

As might be guessed, it is far from an unbiased publication, and there is a tendency to take offense where none could reasonably be taken and to find fault where none could reasonably be found.

Although the Association was nominally nondenominational, it drew most, if not all, of its supporters from what might be called the "Hot Gospel" or "Hellfire-and-Damnation" school of Christianity—though there were apparently Catholic adherents as well.

Christian Protective League

As in many other organizations, the word "Christian" was a front for anti-Semitism. This political secret society was based in Alabama.

Cincinnati, Order of the (Society of the)

The original Order of the Cincinnati was founded by George Washington (see WASHINGTON, GEORGE) and other officers of the Continental Army. It was established on May 17, 1783, as an American hereditary order, but faded in a few decades. It was then revived as the Society of the Cincinnati in 1893. It is the early history that is most interesting.

Lucius Quintus Cincinnatus (born ca. 519 B.C.) was a hero to the patricians of Rome. According to Livy, he strongly opposed the phebians and resisted the attempts by Terentilius Arsa to draw up a code of laws that were equally applicable to patricians and plebians alike, but what really endeared him to the ruling classes was the story of his leaving his modest farm to assume the Dictatorship of Rome at public (i.e., patrician) request, winning a battle against the Aequians in a single day, taking his Triumph in Rome, with great spoils, and then returning to his modest life on the farm, his public duty done.

The Order of the Cincinnati admired the "gentleman-farmer-turned-warrior" story, and saw this as a model for their new republic; this is, after all, the sort of life that many of them had led, and no less than Lord Byron called Washington the Cincinnatus of the West.

It is interesting that these revolutionary worthies wanted to establish what amounted to an Order of KNIGHTHOOD, which would effectively ennoble those families whose patriarchs had fought against their king. The eldest son of each member of the order had the right of succession to his father's place. True, the several states could nominate talented or patriotic citizens to the society, but these new members would receive only limited membership. The American people soon saw through this scheme; or if they did not see right through it, they were deeply suspicious of it. "Melt down your eagles!" was their cry; the emblem of the order was a golden eagle, much as it was for several of the royal families of Europe.

For these reasons, and possibly because the concept of hereditary *noblesse oblige* was not a part of American society, the original order never exercised as much influence as its founders may have envisioned—though George Washington, who was a great "joiner," was elected President-General in 1787 and was thereafter reelected until his death. The order was still sufficiently highly regarded in 1885 that the Congressional Order of Precedence of that year placed officers of the Order of Cincinnati after state governors, no mean rank.

In 1893, the Society of the Cincinnati was revived as a watered-down and nonhereditary version of the old order.

The Daughters of the Cincinnati were founded, without the permission of the Cincinnati proper, in 1894. Membership was open to women descended from members of the original Cincinnati or of officers of the Revolutionary army or navy who had died in the service of their country.

City of Lushington

The City of Lushington was founded in about 1760 in London as a social club and became extinct in the last third of the 19th century, after more than a hundred years of existence. Its title allegedly came from "Lush," an 18th-century term for beer or liquor. The criteria for eligibility are no longer clear. The club operated in the Drury Lane area of London and was based at the Harp Tavern on Great Russell Street.

The members of the club originally consisted of "theatricals, singers, literary men, jovial tradesmen, and well-to-do mechanics," and they called themselves "Citizens of the Ancient and Honorable City of Lushington." The presiding officer, addressed as My Lord Mayor, wore mayoral robes and was assisted by four Aldermen, each responsible for one corner or "Ward" of the "City" — the room in which they met.

To envision the wards, imagine that you are entering a room via a door in one wall, and that there is more of the room to your right than to your left as you enter. On your immediate left is "Poverty Ward," nearest the door, so that those who are shabbily dressed or who cannot stand their round may slip out easily. On your immediate right is "Suicide Ward," apparently so named for those who had taken a solemn oath that while they might lay violent hands on their glasses, they would never lay violent hands upon their own lives.

"Juniper Ward" is on the far left; juniper is, of course, the chief flavoring constituent of gin. On the far right, there is "Lunatic Ward"; and it is worth knowing that to this day, strong drink (especially strong beer) is sometimes referred to as "lunatic broth" in England.

"Elections" were frequently held, with wild promises of what the candidates would do if elected. The oath (see OATHS), required before voting, ran roughly as follows:

I, [Name], do swear that I have been an inhabitant of the City of Lushington for _____ years, and that I have taken within its walls _____ pots of porter, _____ glasses of *jackey*, and smoked _____ pipes.

That is to say one pot of heavy wet, one glass of juniper and one loading of weed, at least annually; have been the cause of such acts in others, or have been present when such acts were performed, and that I have not polled at this election.

During the Election, the Constables of the City guarded the doors, bearing staves surmounted with quartern pots. The successful candidate would buy drinks for all and sundry, and the unsuccessful candidates would thank their supporters in the same manner. All in all, the City was a fairly typical Tavern Club of the period (see TAVERNS AND CLUBS).

Civil Club, The

The Civil Club was probably the earliest of the LUNCHEON CLUBS. It was founded in London in 1669 with the intention that "members should give preference to one another in their respective callings." In the same year, the

order apparently added public service to that intention, not least as a result of public criticism. The Civil Club met at the Mermaid Tavern and the Old Cheshire Cheese in London.

Clan-na-Gael

Clan-na-Gael was founded in the United States in 1869 to promote Irish independence; by 1873 it claimed to have absorbed almost all other similar societies in the United States. In 1881 a schism occurred with more than usual violence: One of the leading lights, Dr. P. H. Cronin, of Chicago, was assassinated.

There are still Americans who call themselves supporters of Clan-na-Gael, but it is hard to tell whether the order still exists, or whether its supporters are following the fine Celtic tradition of living in the past.

Clavel, Abbé F. T. Begue

The Abbé Clavel was the author of the *Histoire Pittoresque de la Franc-Maçonnerie et des Sociétés Secrètes Anciennes et Modernes* ("Quaint History of Freemasonry and Secret Societies Old and New"), published in 1842. His historical impartiality is, to say the very least, questionable, but this did not stop other Masonic authors from quoting Clavel as if he were gospel, and thereby lending extra credence to his fantasies. See PLATONIC ACADEMY.

Clermont, Chapter of

The Chapter of Clermont seems to have been an early part founded in 1754, of the FREEMASONS. The group worked six DEGREES, the extra ones being Knight of the Eagle, Illustrious Knight or Templar, and Sublime Illustrious Knight. Many more degrees were subsequently invented. The Chapter of Clermont was apparently the inspiration for the Rite of Strict Observance (see STRICT OBSERVANCE, CLERKS OF).

Clover Leaves, Fraternal Order of

It is strange that there have not been more vegetable (as distinct from animal) fraternal groups. This one was a fraternal benefit society founded in 1911 and probably went under during the Great Depression. It enjoyed a period of very modest success in the mid to late 1920s, when there were only a few hundred members.

College Fraternities and Sororities

More than any other type of organization covered in this book, college fraternities illustrate fundamental differences between the United States and the United Kingdom (and indeed the rest of the world). In Britain, there is nothing that remotely resembles the American college fraternity or sorority.

Fraternities and sororities are often known as "Greek

Societies" or simply as "Greeks" from the custom of using Greek letters as a means of identification. The National Panhellenic Conference, founded in 1902, is an organization of sororities that derives its name from this custom; the fraternal equivalent is the National Interfraternity Council (1909).

At their simplest, fraternities are university social clubs. Freshmen were not traditionally eligible for membership—sophomores, juniors, and seniors made up the fraternities—though today it is normally possible for a "pledge," or provisional member, to become a full member in his or her second semester.

"Rushing" is the process by which members are recruited. At the more exclusive and self-important fraternities, prospective members are invited to parties to be scrutinized; at others, the "smokers," or rush parties, are open. The criteria for admission vary: Some sororities in particular are notorious for preferring appearance to intellect, while others are based on money or social standing.

Once someone has met the often arbitrary requirements of the local fraternity or sorority chapter, he or she is invited to become a "pledge"—a novice with preliminary vows. If he or she is offered more than one pledge, he or she will have to choose between them; no one may belong to more than one fraternity, though membership of professional fraternities (for example, for lawyers) and HONOR SOCIETIES (for the scholastically inclined) is allowed.

Because fraternities and sororities offer no reasons for acceptance or rejection, they can easily ignore modern views on "affirmative action." Thus, there tend to be black fraternities, Jewish fraternities, and WASP fraternities. There is even a Masonic fraternity (see ACACIA).

After a probationary period, the "pledge" undergoes a secret initiation; in many fraternities, this seems to involve a great deal of beer. The initiation commonly has all the trappings of a secret society, with oaths, passwords, and ritual; but most (perhaps all) work only a single degree (see DEGREES). The most normal forms of initiation are loosely based on Masonic Rituals, either going back to the Masonic root or deriving from other organizations that had borrowed from the Masons. There may also be a considerable degree of rough-housing and even sexual immorality. In the heyday of the fraternities, which was probably the 1920s and 1930s, "hazing"—rough-housing—became so severe that a number of students were badly injured or even killed. At Duke University, for example, a boy was covered with shellac; the intention was to touch him with an ice cube to give him the impression he had been set on fire. Unfortunately, the match that was struck to lend verisimilitude to the proceedings was waved too close to the victim; he really was set afire. Other stories include young men choking to death while being forced to swallow live goldfish, or dying of alcoholic poisoning after being forced to chug large quantities of hard liquor.

The initiation is one of the major factors distinguishing a fraternity house from a private hall of residence. While such halls are quite common in Britain, they expect far less commitment from their members—certainly, no secret oaths or formal initiations, though buying a round of drinks never goes amiss.

Each fraternity maintains a number of chapter houses, one at each college where the fraternity is represented. Members of the fraternity eat, sleep, and study in the chapter house attached to their college, which may well be of princely size and appointments. Between them, the various fraternities own many millions of dollars' worth of property, much of the money for which comes from successful alumni. Originally, however, the money for these houses came from the undergraduates themselves.

The national headquarters of each fraternity or sorority oversees the whole thing, publishing a magazine and directories of members, and often a songbook.

Many colleges disapprove strenuously of the fraternity system. On a number of campuses, fraternities and sororities are banned altogether. Criticism centers on drinking, on rough-house initiations, and on lack of supervision. At other colleges, the vast majority of students belong. (American politicians seem almost always to have been fraternity men.)

At Harvard, the national fraternities are generally agreed to be less important than the local societies; and at Princeton, there are only local social clubs without Greek-letter names. The famous "Skull and Bones" is an interfraternal society at Yale for senior men; this and similar societies are more important than the fraternities themselves. At Cornell, about 30 percent of the female undergraduates belonged to sororities in 1989.

History of Fraternities

The first fraternity known to have been organized in the United States was Phi Beta Kappa, founded at the College of William and Mary on December 5, 1776. William and Mary closed in 1781 as a result of the American Revolution, but in 1779 Elisha Parmele (a member) was empowered to establish other "meetings," or chapters, which he did in 1780 at Yale and, in 1781, at Harvard. Other chapters followed, but in 1826 Phi Beta Kappa changed from being a secret fraternity to an open honor society (see HONOR SOCIETIES). Since 1875, women have also been admitted. Four out of the next five fraternities were founded at the same college, Union College in Schenectady, New York. They were Kappa Alpha (1825), Delta Phi and Sigma Phi (both 1827), and Psi Upsilon (1833).

Sigma Phi organized a branch at Hamilton College in 1831, and in 1832, Alpha Delta Phi was founded at the same college. Alpha Delta Phi moved into Miami University of Ohio, and once again the idea fell on fertile ground; Beta Theta Phi, the first "western" fraternity, was founded there in 1839. A hundred years later, there were more than five dozen major fraternities in the United States, a number that has declined only slightly since then.

Sororities were slower off the mark, beginning with L. C. Sororis (Monmouth College, 1867), which changed its name to Pi Beta Phi in 1870, the same year that Kappa Alpha Theta was founded at De Pauw. African-American fraternities made their appearance in 1906.

Although fraternities remain strong, their influence was much diminished in the second half of the 20th century. Many people found the whole rigmarole childish, and membership can be expensive: In addition to the obvious expense of fraternal dues, some fraternities and many sororities dress to the nines. On the other hand, the benefits remain compelling also: The advantages in later life of belonging to the "right" fraternity are akin to having gone to the "right" school or the "right" Oxford college in England.

Fraternities have also given rise to some of the most extraordinary examples of hyperbole ever to be uttered in the New World, some of which border on blasphemy. Bishop Huntingdon's "Next to God, I love dear old Psi U" is extraordinary enough, but what is one to make of the Beta Theta Pi assertion that the pirating of their ritual constituted "perfidy unexampled since the apostasy of Judas Iscariot"?

Coming Men of America
The Coming Men of America was founded in 1892 for boys and young men aged 14–21, ostensibly as a club for schoolchildren and students. It seems, however, to have been heavily influenced by FREEMASONS. One of the main founders was a 32nd-degree Freemason, a member of the ODD FELLOWS, and a member of several other secret societies, and it was the Masons who loaned their halls as a place for the society to meet. In 1905 there were over 20,000 members, but it was probably defunct by the 1920s.

Comitadjes
The Comitadjes of Macedonia was a partly political, partly criminal society existing between 1893 and 1934, initially to free Macedonia from the Turks and subsequently to pursue self-determination.

Groups or chapters consisted of men, often led by Orthodox priests and schoolteachers. The society was originally formed with the typical "Liberty or Death!" watchword, but the sheer brutality of Turkish retaliation against Macedonian activists led to an understandable desire for vengeance — which is where some of the "criminality" may have come in. It is also likely that the Turks

deliberately attempted to smear the Comitadjes by referring to them and treating them as garden-variety bandits. It is even possible that the Turks actively encouraged some bandits to prey upon villagers and travelers, promising freedom from prosecution if the bandits let it be known that they were of the Comitadjes. The Chinese attempted to pull a similar trick in Tibet in the 1950s and 1960s.

After World War I, the Macedonians still found themselves saddled with unwelcome leaders; Yugoslavia was the new target of their ire. In due course (exactly when it happened is unclear), the Comitadjes metamorphosed into the Orim.

Community of Jesus
The Community of Jesus was a shadowy secret religious brotherhood that existed in 1913 and had its headquarters at San Francisco. Beyond this, no information concerning the organization seems to exist.

Compagnonnage
The Compagnonnage was a French fraternal trade organization of stone-masons, unrelated to the FREEMASONS. It was almost certainly medieval, with an origin prior to 1655, and is now extinct.

What if the Masons had admitted *only* "operative" (working) masons instead of "accepted" masons from other walks of life? This is the question that is answered, to some extent, by the Compagnonnage.

Its origins are unclear. The very first French trade guilds may have begun where their Roman predecessors left off. The Compagnonnage itself traced its origins back into medieval times, though without any great diligence; as an organization of working men, it was more concerned with the present than with the past. It was, however, a secret society very much like the Masons, with passwords, initiations and the legends to support them.

The first crafts to join the Compagnonnage were reputedly stone-cutters, carpenters, joiners, and locksmiths. The last two were normally considered together, resulting in three divisions. Other trades joined later, though from the legend (described below), it seems that hatters and wheelwrights were also in at the beginning.

The Compagnons were *not* master craftsmen in the medieval sense, nor had they any internal structure that could raise them to Master status. Under French law, until after the Revolution, a Master could take as many Servants (employees) as he liked, provided he did not reveal to them the mysteries of the craft; but the employment and treatment of Apprentices, to whom mysteries were revealed, was much more closely controlled. The Compagnons were unapprenticed servants, but they were also journeymen craftsmen in their own right (in the modern sense), so it is not surprising that they organized their own "guild."

In every town, there existed a branch of the Compagnons. The officers were the *Premier-en-ville,* the *Second-en-ville* (the "First-in-town" and the "Second-in-town"), and the *Rouleur* or agent, who found work for the itinerant Compagnons. Itinerant they were, too, for the Compagnonnage administered the *Tour-de-France,* a circuit of major cities, which the Compagnons had to complete to be full members. The scope of the Tour almost certainly varied over the centuries, but at the beginning of the 19th century the full circuit was about 1,500 miles, and it had to be made on foot. At each city, the Compagnon would be found lodging with a *Mère* (mother), and the Compagnonnage would make sure that he had settled his obligations to her before allowing him to move on. The time taken to make the Tour was up to the individual. It was not unheard of for him to take four years or more.

The Compagnonnage was founded, according to legend, by King Solomon, Maitre Jacques, and Père Soubise. King Solomon needs little introduction, but the others are less well known.

Maitre Jacques was a Frenchman, born in what is now Saint-Romili in the south of France, but which was then Carte in Gaul. By the age of 26, he had reached Jerusalem, where he worked on the Temple and carved two pillars so exquisitely that he was received Master. There, he met Maitre Soubise (Père Soubise). They returned to Gaul together, the best of friends, but had differences of opinion and went their separate ways with their separate disciplines. Maitre Jacques was assassinated by disciples of Maitre Soubise, but with his dying words he told his disciples to found the Compagnonnage. He was eventually buried, with a great deal of circumstantial description that was no doubt useful in establishing passwords, at the spot where he was assassinated. His hat went to the hat makers, his tunic to the stone cutters, his cloak to the joiners, his sandals to the locksmiths, his girdle to the carpenters, and his pilgrim's staff to the wheelwrights.

According to a legend of more recent times (and probably better founded), there was a great split in the Compagnonnage in 1401, during the building of the cathedral at Orleans, which resulted in murder, mayhem, and imprisonment for many. Jacques Moler of Orleans and one Soubise (again) of Nogent-sous-Paris led the winning fraction, and their adherents became known as Compagnons Passants. The interesting thing here is not just that one of the characters was called Soubise, but that "Moler" is pronounced in much the same way as "Molay," and this calls to mind the noble de Molay of TEMPLARS fame.

There were originally three DEGREES, the *Attendant* (aspirant), the *Compagnon Reçu* (received journeyman), and the *Compagnon Achévé* or *Compagnon Fini* ("achieved" or "finished"). Only the highest rank could hold office. In about 1803, an additional degree of *Initié* (initiated) was invented, which seems to have been principally a reaction to the plethora of degrees invented by the Freemasons; in 1843, the new degree was suppressed at a general assembly of the Compagnonnage.

The RITUALS AND CEREMONIES, which seem to be correctly reported (what follows is taken from voluntary disclosures made by the various trades after 1651 in response to criticism from the Church) varied from trade to trade, but had a heavy Christian influence. Curiously, though, the rituals themselves could be viewed as blasphemous. The Hatters' ritual, for example, was based on the crucifixion, with the candidate on the cross; and most rituals involved a new "baptism," during which the Compagnon took a new name, and swore on bread and wine to uphold the Compagnonnage. There were also rituals that have no apparent significance to the outsider: The Cutlers took candidates into the countryside (a good way to avoid eavesdroppers), showed them the signs, and so on, of a passed Compagnon, had then told them to place one unshod foot on a cloak on the ground and walk around it so that the shod foot walked on the grass and the unshod foot walked on the cloak.

The regalia consisted of a heavy cane about 5 feet long, presumably symbolic of the pilgrim's staff, to which were attached colored ribbons; ribbons were also worn on the hat and clothes. The positioning of the ribbons denoted the status of the wearer—a preliterate equivalent of diplomas and degree certificates. There were apparently frequent arguments about who was entitled to wear what ribbons, and how. The sign of recognition (also used at funerals and convocations) was known as the *Guibrette* or *Accolade.* The canes were laid crosswise on the ground, and each Compagnon placed a foot in one of the four quadrants. They then turned inward, placing their right feet in the opposite quadrants, grasped each other's right hand, and kissed before exchanging whispered passwords.

By the end of the 19th century, the Compagnonnage was dead. However, modern revivals do exist: Fédération Compagnonnique des Métiers du Bâtiment «Les Devoirs» (161 avenue Jean-Jaurès, 75019 Paris); Association Ouvrière des Compagnons du Devoir du Tour de France (82 rue de l'Hôtel-de-Ville, 75004 Paris); and Union Compagnonnique (Compagnons du Tour de France des Devoirs Unis [15 rue Champ-Lagarde, 78000 Versailles]).

Comuneros

The Confederation of the Comuneros was a Spanish political secret society formed in 1821. They were modeled on the FREEMASONS, which had been active in Cadiz as early as 1812, but this was a special Spanish model of the Craft. The restoration of Ferdinand VII in 1814 led to a reestablishment of the Spanish Inquisition, which set about suppressing the Freemasons with great enthusiasm. This politicized the Freemasons, who were the guiding force behind the revolution of 1820 that curbed Ferdinand's worst excesses.

Once they were in power, the Freemasons split into two camps, the Constitutionalists, who wanted no more than a curb on despotism, and the Liberals, who wanted a wider-ranging interpretation of freedom for all. The most radical among the Liberals founded the Comuneros, commemorating the revolt of the *comunidades* of Castile against Charles V, 300 years previously.

The order was open to both sexes and soon gathered 60,000 members. LODGES of seven to 50 members were called *Torres* (towers); smaller lodges were forts. The combined lodges of each province constituted a *Comunidad*. At the top of the whole organization, there was a Supreme Assembly with a Commander, Lieutenant Commander, Alcalde (Mayor), Treasurer, and four Secretaries.

Admission was by ballot; the RITUALS AND CEREMONIES were more in the nature of a political oath than an initiation into a mystery.

In 1822, the Freemasons and the Spanish CARBONARI joined with the Comuneros, but in early 1823 the Comuneros either double-crossed the others or (possibly) told the truth, that the Freemasons wished to proclaim a regency and expel the King from the country instead of keeping him on as a puppet. Predictably, Ferdinand recast his government to include more Comuneros. The French sent a peace-keeping force in April 1823 and restored Ferdinand's absolute monarchy; whereupon the monarch celebrated by massacring all those who had opposed him or who had upheld the Constitution of 1814. Ferdinand was a sufficiently loathsome character that the Duke of Angouleme, who had led the French armies, refused to accept any Spanish military decorations and honors for his part in restoring the power of the Spanish monarch.

The "Sons of Padilla" seems simply to have been another name for the Comuneros; the name comes from Juan de Padilla, who led the Castilians against King Charles V.

Concordists

Little is known about the Concordists beyond the fact that they were a secret order established in Prussia by one M. Lang, on the remnants of the "Tugendverein," which had been founded in 1790 as a successor to the Illuminati. The Tugendverein was suppressed in 1812 by the Prussian government. For information on the Tugendverein, see TUGENBUND.

Confraternite du Grand Chêne Celte

This very small neopagan group conducts its business in the French language (as distinct from the Breton tinge of the H.T.D., a similar-looking organization to the outsider). Astrology, the conjuration of spirits, and automatic writing are (or were) apparently its main interests.

Confrérie du Krääm

Michel Monereau
BP 13
95509 Gonesse Cedex, France

The *Confrérie du Krääm* or "Brotherhood of Krääm" was based on the Tantric cult of ecstasy and on a sexual vision of the cosmos. Its adherents develop the *Kundalini,* the serpent power in the *chakra* (energy center) at the base of the spine.

Consistorials

A Roman Catholic society that wanted Italian independence but not unification. The group wanted the Austrians out, and Italy divided among the existing Italian princelings and the Pope. Consistorials were contemporary with, but opposed to, the early 19th-century CARBONARI.

Constitutional Society of European Patriots

A short-lived political secret society, founded in about 1820, along the lines of the (earlier) CARBONARI or the (later) YOUNG EUROPE movement. It was founded in Madrid by General Pepe—formerly of the Carbonari and by then in exile—"to open a communication between the most enlightened patriots of the different cities in Europe." It was dedicated (as the name suggests) to the promotion of constitutional rule in Europe generally and in Spain especially. It was effectively ended by the French invasion of Spain of 1823. See COMUNEROS.

Conway, David

Author of *Secret Wisdom: The Occult Universe Explored* (London: Jonathan Cape, 1985), which was described by Colin Wilson as "One of the best books on magic ever written."

It is a book that makes very great demands upon the reader. On the Dedication page, there are words in what look like Welsh, which are presumably a quotation or motto of some kind; Wales figures largely in the book. Thereafter, Mr. Conway cheerfully pulls together ancient Greek mystical and philosophical traditions; Hindu and possibly Buddhist teachings; modern subatomic physics; and much, much more. To be *au fait* with everything in these pages would require very considerable scholarship indeed.

It would be churlish to suggest that Mr. Conway might himself be unequal to the demands that he makes upon his readers, and *Secret Wisdom* possesses an internal consistency that can make a book truly riveting, once the reader has gotten into it. What is more, it reads more as the journal of an explorer than as the gospel of a crank.

Although some secret societies are mentioned in passing, such as the Hermetic Order of the Golden Dawn (see GOLDEN DAWN, HERMETIC ORDER OF), this book is more of a survey of the raw material from which mystically and magically oriented secret societies are formed, rather than a treatise on the societies themselves.

Corks, Ye Ancient Order of

The Ancient Order of Corks purports to descend from the Jolly Corks, who later became the ELKS; but as this Ancient Order of Corks is a Masonic organization, and as in the finest traditions of American FREEMASONS it is impossible to distinguish between fact and fantasy, the kindest that can be said is that there is no *clear* link. The Masonic organization was founded in 1933, well after the Jolly Corks grew antlers.

Cornet of Horse

This obscure secret society was one of several (the names of most of the others have been lost to history) involved in a Polish revolt of 1830 against the rule of Russian Czar Nicholas I. The order—probably with other secret societies—was plotting rebellion when a rumor was spread that the czar was about to lead a Russian and Polish army into France and Belgium to crush the revolutions that had broken out there. Accordingly, on November 29, 1830, the Cornet of Horse started a revolution. It was short-lived. The order seems to have been destroyed by Russian forces at the Battle of Ostrolenka on May 31, 1831.

The derivation of the name of the society is rather obscure. *Cornet* is a cavalry unit (also the officer who leads that unit), and most likely this is the sense of the term the members of the order intended.

Cosmic Movement

The "Cosmic Movement" had a great influence in Western Europe and especially in France between World War I and World War II, with the *avant-garde* and the Jews particularly active.

Originally of Southern Tunisian inspiration, the movement was masterminded by one "Themanlys," who received messages from "Aya Aziz." The movement's publication, *La Revue Cosmique* ("Cosmic Review"), was a mish-mash of Gnosticism, DEISM (God was the "Cause without Cause"), and sheer incomprehensibility. For example, love of light for the sake of life was labeled "involution," while love of life for the sake of light was called "evolution." There were seven "states of matter," and the "cosmic texts" frequently quoted biblical passages, but placed upon them an interpretation that was far from the conventional. It is unclear whether the Nazis suppressed the society or whether it died of its own accord—or whether, for that matter, it yet survives.

Cougourde

This was an association of liberals during the Bourbon restoration in France. It arose at Aix, in Provence, and spread to various parts of France, but its existence was ephemeral. *Cougourde* is French for the calabash gourd. It does not seem to have been related to any other society, nor is it clear why the society took the name it did.

Council for Foreign Relations

One of several bodies allegedly promoting one world government described in Howard's *The Occult Conspiracy*. Perhaps inevitably derived from an equally shadowy earlier group, the ROUND TABLE, it seems to have been formed in 1919 or thereabouts as the American counterpart of the Institute for International Affairs.

Before World War II it was apparently criticized as an elitist, right-wing pressure group, while after the war it magically changed its complexion to become an advocate of international socialism, working through the United Nations. As a "front group" for latter-day ILLUMINATI, it has been accused by paranoiacs of almost every political kidney of "reversing the democratic process which instigated the 1776 American Revolution," and integrating both capitalism and communism in a new world state.

To quote Howard once again, "The CFR's apparent contradictory political ideals are said to be typical of modern Illuminati front groups," who are equally at home with the ideologies of the Right and the Left, so long as they further the Illuminatist cause which "transcends conventional politics." The CFR does, however, form a part of the explanation why the United Nations is regarded with such suspicion by latter-day Know-Nothings with a weakness for conspiracy theories.

Council of the Trinity

The Council of the Trinity confers the following (Christian) Masonic DEGREES:

> Knight of the Christian Mark and Guard of the Conclave
> Knight of the Holy Sepulchre
> Holy and Thrice Illustrious Order of the Cross

Needless to say, these degrees bear no relation to true orders of chivalry, and their acceptability to many Christians is doubtful.

Court of Honor

The Court of Honor followed a pattern fairly typical among successful fraternal benefit insurance societies—that is, among societies that did not actually collapse through mismanagement or unrealistically starry-eyed actuarial assumptions.

The Court of Honor was organized in Springfield, Illinois, in 1895, with an elaborate ritual. It prospered principally as an insurance company (in 1920 there were over 75,000 benefit members and only 2,300 social members), and then transformed itself into a regular life insurance company. In the early 1920s it changed its name to the Court of Honor Life Association, and in 1924 it reincorporated simply as Springfield Life Insurance, after its headquarters city. In 1934, it merged with Abraham Lincoln Life, and in 1935 it was reinsured with Illinois Bankers Life.

Cowan

The word *cowan* appears in the *Oxford English Dictionary* as "one who builds dry-stone walls; applied derogatorily to one who does the work of a mason, but has not been regularly apprenticed or bred to the trade . . . Hence, one uninitiated in the secrets of Freemasonry." In the former sense, it first appeared in 1598; in the latter, 1707. The derivation was unknown, even to the compilers of the *Oxford English Dictionary*. FREEMASONS love the word and have exerted themselves mightily over its derivation.

Crescents

This obscure American patriotic secret society originated in California after the Civil War and was quite active in San Francisco at the time, then quickly faded.

Croatian Catholic Union of the United States of America and Canada

One West, Old Ridge Road
Hobart, IN 46342
(219) 942-1191

A fraternal benefit life insurance society for Croatians and other Roman and Greek Catholics in the United States and Canada. In 1988 there were 13,000 members. The Union publishes *Nasa Nada* ("Our Hope") monthly.

The only remarkable thing about this typical ethnic fraternal benefit society is the late date of founding— 1921—otherwise, its activities are predictable, though no less valuable for that. They include insurance; assistance to the Catholic Church, including support for theological students; scholarships; and disaster relief. The numbers show a very slight decline, from 13,772 in 1965, to 13,500 in 1978, to the present 13,000; but basically, this is a small, sound, life insurance organization.

Croatian Fraternal Union of America

100 Delaney Drive
Pittsburgh, PA 15235
(412) 351-3909

The Croatian Fraternal Union of America was formed in 1924 by the merger of earlier fraternal benefit insurance societies for persons of Croatian or Slavic descent and their relatives. There were 90,000 members in 1988. The Union publishes *Zajednicar*, weekly.

The National Croatian Society of the United States of America, the forerunner of the Croatian Fraternal Union of America, was founded in 1894 as a typical ethnic fraternal benefit society; the present title was adopted in the mid-1920s, at about the same time that the National Croatian Society merged with the Croatian League of Illinois. The Slovanic Croatian Union also joined the fold in 1939.

Its activities are exactly what would be expected. In addition to the obvious insurance aspect, there are good works, mostly directed at care of the old, and scholarships for qualified members; and there are youth programs, especially "Junior Tamburitza Groups," which keep alive Croatian folk dances. Membership is in a slow decline, with a loss of about 10 percent per decade between 1970 and 1990.

Croix Blanche Universelle

The *Croix Blanche Universelle*, the "Universal White Cross," is a "chivalric" Christian brotherhood founded in or before 1950 by André Karquel. Some idea of its orientation may be gathered from its first tenet, *"Jésus m'est tout"* ("Jesus is everything to me"). Its aim is internal transformation, to achieve such worthy goals as respecting everyone, regardless of their origins. It seems to be so diffuse, both in its aims and in its membership, as scarcely to make it possible to differentiate members from other well-intentioned people.

Crowley, Aleister

Aleister Crowley was the most celebrated—or reviled—self-proclaimed magician and Satanist of modern times. He was born Edward Alexander Crowley in Leamington Spa, Warwickshire, England, on October 12, 1875, the son of fundamentalist adherents to the Plymouth Brethren sect. His upbringing, accordingly, was strict and dogmatic, and Crowley himself later claimed that his fascination with black magic and Satanism began as a reaction against the oppressive faith of his parents. Crowley's mother, often exasperated at her rebellious child, called him "the Beast," an allusion to Beast 666 in the Book of Revelation. Crowley subsequently adopted this as his emblem.

Obnoxious as it may have been to him, Crowley's childhood was economically privileged (his father was a prominent brewer of ale), and the boy was given an excellent education at Malvern and Tonbridge schools, followed by Trinity College, Cambridge. It was there that he encountered the mystical writings of Carl von Eckartshausen, in particular *The Cloud Upon the Sanctuary*. By 1898, he had joined the Hermetic Order of the Golden Dawn (see GOLDEN DAWN, HERMETIC ORDER OF) and was an avid student of the Kabbalah. Crowley was later expelled from the Golden Dawn because of his persistent disputation with its organizer, Samuel Liddell Mathers.

In addition to his early interest in the occult, Crowley was an avid chess player, writer of pornographic verse, and (by all accounts) prolific fornicator. He also claimed to possess a faculty for conjuring up spirits—for better or worse, most of them evil spirits—and sometime after 1903, following his marriage to Rose Kelly, the daughter of a prominent portraitist, he evoked a spirit he called Aiwass, who dictated to him a work called the *Liber Legis* (Book of the Law), which (according to Crowley) proclaimed a new magical era in the history of the world. In truth, the law was reducible to a single precept: the "Law of Thelema," which was simply "Do what thou wilt shall be the whole of the Law."

Following this revelation—sincere or manufactured— Crowley devoted himself to the study of mythology and what he called "magick," evolving a confused and confusing mythology and living the most intensely dissipated of lives, centered on obtaining sexual gratification from a series of women and men. At about the time he established a homosexual relationship with the mystical poet Victor Neuburg in 1909, Crowley became head of the English branch of the ORDO TEMPLI ORIENTIS (or O.T.O.). Crowley left England for the United States during World War I, acquiring a stable of "Scarlet Women" (an allusion to the "Scarlet Woman" who rides upon the Beast in *Revelation*), upon whom he practiced the sexual secrets of Tantric yoga, which he had begun studying.

Crowley left the United States in 1919, leaving as his legacy the inspiration for subsequent occult and Satanist groups, most of which were or are based in California. In 1920, Crowley founded the Abbey of Thelema at Cefalu, Sicily, a commune composed of two mistresses and a group of the devoted. With his most famous "Scarlet Woman," Leah Hirsig, Crowley performed a ritual by which (he said) he had achieved Ipissimus, becoming a god. Whatever spiritual effect this may have had on him, it made him intolerable to Hirsig, whom Crowley threw over for a new "Scarlet Woman," Dorothy Olsen. As far as can be determined, life at Cefalu was an indulgence in drugs and sex punctuated by study of the occult. It ended in 1923, after the death (probably due to food poisoning) of a follower named Raoul Loveday. Loveday's demise resulted in an investigation and the expulsion of Crowley from Sicily. After living for a time in Tunisia and France, suffering from an addiction to heroin, he returned to England, where—incredibly enough—he sued the sculptor Nina Hammett for libel. She had written in her 1932 autobiography, *Laughing Torso*, that Crowley was a practitioner of black magic, an assertion to which the magician inexplicably took exception. The result was a sensational public revelation of his lifestyle, which earned him the popular title of the "wickedest man in the world."

The closing decade of Crowley's life was marked by illness, drug addiction, and bankruptcy. Given his many exertions, he was a fairly prolific author, producing verse, fiction, mystical writings, a study of the Tarot system (*Magick in Theory and Practice*, published in 1919 and still considered valuable), and several volumes of autobiography. He died in 1947. To his detractors, he was a vicious, self-absorbed sexual miscreant. To his admirers, he was not only a spiritual and philosophical inspiration, but a hero of social protest, in whose life may be seen a foreshadow of the hippie movement of the 1960s and early 1970s.

Crowned Republic

Some authorities believe this was an actual utopian fraternity organized by a Dr. Marsh of Boston in 1860 and elaborated in 1879. It aimed at social reorganization with a view to secure personal freedom, social unity, and universal wealth. Others believe that the Crowned Republic never existed as anything more than a plan for a utopian secret society. If it did ever exist, it has vanished without a trace.

Crusaders

The Crusaders are a female auxiliary of the Knights TEMPLARS of Free and Accepted Ancient York FREEMASONS, though separate membership figures from that order were not readily available.

What little information is given below is gleaned from the RITUALS AND CEREMONIES as published by the indefatigable EZRA A. COOK PUBLICATIONS. "There was," according to this pamphlet, "between Freemasonry and the Crusaders a much more intimate relation than has been generally supposed." Indeed, general supposition outside the Craft is still that there was little or no formal connection between Craft Masonry and the Crusaders, and that accepted Masonry did not then exist.

The legend, however, is as follows. St. Helena, mother of Constantine the Great, searched in the Holy Land in A.D. 296 for the True Cross. She found three crosses, and Pope Marcellimus discovered the true one by touching each in turn to a dying woman. The True Cross, of course, restored her instantly to perfect health.

The ritual, executed by women, involves many Christian trappings, including the Lord's Prayer. The officers of the first degree (see DEGREES) are the Priestess, who plays St. Helena; the second and third priestesses, who take over if a higher-numbered priestess is unavailable; a Verger; two Guards, one for the Outer Sanctuary and one for the inner Sanctuary; a Secretary; and a Treasurer.

The oath (see OATHS) is unusually bloodthirsty for a women's organization:

That for the violation of the least particle of any of the here taken oath, I become the silent and mute subject of this Order, and have the power and wrath turned upon my head to my destruction and dishonor, which like the nail of Joael may be the sure end of an unworthy wretch, by piercing my temple with a true sense of ingratitude and for a breach of silence in case of such an unhappy event I shall die the infamous death of a traitor, by having a spear or sharp weapon like as my Lord, thrust in my left side, bearing testimony even in death to the power of Mark of the Illustrious Cross. Amen.

The costume is a "white skirt and white waist, white cape interlined with red," with one corner thrown or pinned back to reveal the lining, and a red fez with a yellow tassel. There is an extraordinarily militaristic drill, beginning, "Madam Crusaders, fall in," and continuing with dressing from the right, numbering, and so on.

In the second degree ("Invincible Crusaders No. 2"), there are a Most Illustrious Priestess, a Senior Priestess, a Junior Priestess, and so forth, while the Crusade of Syria is the third degree and is headed by the Most Invicible Priestess.

CSA Fraternal Life

2701 South Harlem Avenue
Berwyn, IL 60402
(708) 795-5800

Founded in 1854, and operating in the United States, CSA Fraternal Life is a fraternal benefit insurance society, open to both sexes, 18-65 years old. It had 30,000 members in 1990. It publishes the *CSA Journal,* monthly.

The Bohemian Slavonic Union, founded in St. Louis, was the antecedent of this typical fraternal benefit society, known for most of its career (until 1982) as the Czechoslovak Society of America. The only remarkable thing about the organization is the very early date of foundation; it may well be the oldest ethnic fraternal group still active in the United States.

It is, however, in decline. It absorbed the Society of Taborites in 1933 and the Unity of Czech Ladies and Men in 1977, but the membership figure given above is significantly less than the 1979 figure of 50,000, which itself was a small decline from the 52,000 of the late 1960s. About two-thirds of the members carry insurance; this explains an apparent leap in membership in the late 1980s, because until about 1990, only insured members were listed as "members" in publications such as the ENCYCLOPEDIA OF ASSOCIATIONS.

Part of the decline may be attributed to an unusually high regard for RITUALS AND CEREMONIES, which apparently survived far longer and far more strongly in the CSA than in many comparable societies. Schmidt, in *Fraternal Organizations* (see SCHMIDT, ALVIN J.), also refers to "ritual or degree teams" who put on "meaningful and inspiring exhibitions" at lodge meetings and public functions. These were still in operation in 1990, though in the words of the society's public relations office, "the ritual isn't as dark and gloomy as it used to be; the degree teams install officers, run child-naming ceremonies, and so forth."

The activities of the organization are absolutely typical: In addition to the insurance, they sponsor various competitions (though some are a little unusual—photographic and poster competition and a Miss CSA competition), award scholarships, and maintain archives, which include Czech books dating back to the 1860s. Their charitable work generally focuses on a different project each year, with the head office matching local lodges' contributions dollar for dollar.

Cubs

This is a fraternal and benevolent society organized at the San Francisco Exposition, in 1915, and now extinct.

Czech Catholic Union

5349 Doloff Road
Cleveland, OH 44127
(216) 341-0444

The Czech Catholic Union was founded as a fraternal benefit life insurance society for Catholics of both sexes in the United States. The Union publishes *Posel* ("Messenger") monthly. In 1995 there were 5,000 members.

The Czech Roman Catholic Central Union of Women was formed in 1879 by the alliance of two older altar and rosary societies, St. Ann Society No. 1 (1867) and St. Ludnila Society No. 2, of the parish of St. Wenceslaus in Cleveland, Ohio. The name was changed to the present style in 1938.

It is a typical ethnic/religious fraternal benefit society, providing a seminary scholarship at St. Procopius Abbey and supporting Czech Benedictines in various countries, supporting various charities at a local level, organizing youth programs, and of course providing insurance for its members. It is much reduced in numbers from its glory days: In World War II, for example, the society bought a bomber to assist the war effort, and local Cleveland groups bought an ambulance for the Red Cross. The present figure of over 5,000 is a marked decline from the almost 10,000 members a decade previously, though times have been hard before: In 1967, there were only 6,600 members.

Dames of Malta

Like so many other organizations, the Dames of Malta claimed descent from the Poor Knights of the Hospital of Saint John in Jerusalem, which was itself founded in 1099.

Again like so many other organizations, the operative word is "claimed." The Dames of Malta seem to have been a purely American invention. The order was actually founded as the Ladies of Malta in 1896, but upon the merger with the Daughters of Malta in 1902, the new name was adopted. It was apparently the ladies' auxiliary of the Ancient and Illustrious Knights of Malta, and functioned as a charitable and benevolent organization.

Originally, the eligibility requirements were for white "Female Protestants, over sixteen years of age, competent to pursue some useful occupation; a believer in the doctrines of the Holy Trinity as expressed in the Apostles' Creed," and while one may assume that the color bar was eventually dropped, it gives a fair idea of the nature of the organization. Members had also to be "A true Protestant, not married to a Roman Catholic, physically able to give the unwritten work correctly, able to read, write, and speak the English language." Knights of Malta in good standing in their own Commanderies were also admitted.

The RITUALS AND CEREMONIES were highly secret and were based on the "glorious past, the deep religious significance of its institution and the fact that it is the only Knightly Order having one Universal Passwort [sic] that admits to all council chambers around the world." As late as 1978, the group's brochures still stated that it was "destined to play an important part in the history of America's progress." They used to publish a thrice-yearly magazine called *Malta Chat*.

LODGES were called Commanderies, with a governing council called the Zenodacia, which in turn was subject to the Supreme Commandery of the Ancient and Illustrious Knights of Malta.

The organization apparently no longer exists: The ENCYCLOPEDIA OF ASSOCIATIONS noted that the address had remained unknown to it since 1982, though it was formerly based in Pittsburgh, Pennsylvania. There were 28,000 members in the 1920s, but only 5,000 or so in the late 1970s.

Darbyism

See BRETHREN, THE.

Daughters of America

A female auxiliary (see AUXILIARIES) to the JUNIOR ORDER OF UNITED AMERICAN MECHANICS, founded in Bennet, Pennsylvania, in 1891, the order appears no longer to exist. In its heyday, it combined a poisonous brand of the KNOW-NOTHINGS' anti-immigration sentiment with advocacy of Bible reading in the public schools.

The Daughters' first object was "to promote and maintain the interests of Americans, and shield them from the depressing effects of unrestricted immigration." It also sought "to maintain the Public School System of the United States of America, and to prevent interference therewith, and uphold the reading of the Holy Bible therein," but "to oppose sectarian influence with State and National affairs."

Daughters of Isabella

375 Whitney Avenue
New Haven, CT 06511
(203) 865-2570

The Daughters of Isabella, named for Queen St. Isabella of Portugal, is a female auxiliary (see AUXILIARIES) to the KNIGHTS OF COLUMBUS. It was founded in 1897 and had 100,000 members in 1994.

Much of the work of the Daughters of Isabella is praiseworthy—work with the Red Cross, blood banks, and so on—while some is a matter of opinion (they are strongly opposed to legal abortion) and some is engagingly eccentric, such as a prolonged campaign to have the birthday of Queen St. Isabella (April 22) proclaimed an American national holiday.

As an organization, it has several unusual qualities. It is not like most auxiliaries, because women (aged 16–59) are admitted in their own right instead of as appendages to their menfolk, who belong to a male-only organization. There is no life insurance, only a funeral benefit fund, and perhaps most surprisingly, there are genuine RITUALS AND CEREMONIES, with quarterly passwords and more—a most un-Catholic undertaking.

Daughters of Isis

This female auxiliary (see AUXILIARIES) to African-American SHRINERS, founded in 1910. Somewhat unusually, there is a shred of originality in the RITUALS AND CEREMONIES, which are loosely based on the legends of the Egyptian goddess after whom the order is named, instead of being the usual milk-and-water Christianized version of a male ritual. The oath (see OATHS), in which the postulant agrees to a penalty of having her body sliced in 14 parts and thrown into a river, is also unusual in a women's organization.

There is still the usual religious aspects of ritual, in which the candidate kisses the Bible three times, Al-Quran once, and a red stone once.

In 1979 there were 12,000 members in 184 "Courts" (LODGES—the national lodge is the "Imperial Court"). Current membership figures were not available at the time of writing.

Daughters of Rebekah

422 N. Trade
Winston, NC 27101
(919) 725-6037

The International Association of Rebekah Assemblies is the governing body of the Daughters of Rebekah, which was founded in 1851 in South Bend, Indiana, as a female auxiliary of ODD FELLOWS. The Daughters accept women of good moral character over 18. They publish the *Fraternal Publication* nine times per year and an annual *Journal*.

Schuyler Colefax—an Odd Fellow and, later, vice-president of the United States—founded the Daughters of Rebekah in 1851, after receiving permission to do so from the Grand Lodge of Odd Fellows in 1850.

The ritual for the one degree ("Assembly") was Christian; Deist rituals seem always to have been considered excessively strong meat for women's auxiliaries (see DEGREES; DEISM; RITUALS AND CEREMONIES). Equally predictably, the ritual was based upon self-effacement, humility, and the like; while men were imitating warlike Red Indians, beleaguered settlers, and so forth, their womenfolk were subjected to rituals like this, where (in the organization's own words) Rebekah's kindness and hospitality to a humble unknown servant portrays the grandeur of her character.

The Rebekah Assemblies declined less rapidly than the Odd Fellows. Membership was 331,844 in 1977; the present figure is 215,000.

The Educational Foundation provides loans to members to help them study, and there are annual scholarships to deserving students. The World Eye Bank benefits from assistance from the Rebekah Assemblies, which also sponsor youth pilgrimages.

The Daughters Militant are (or were) an organization within the Daughters of Rebekah, while the Theta Rho Clubs were the junior order of the Daughters of Rebekah; the name was presumably chosen to make them sound like a college fraternity (see COLLEGE FRATERNITIES AND SORORITIES).

Daughters of Scotland

The Daughters of Scotland were brought together in Ohio and incorporated in 1899 as a fraternal group for those of Scottish blood. The society appears to be extinct.

Daughters of the Eastern Star

The Daughters of the Eastern Star was founded in New York on October 15, 1925, for girls aged 14–20, whose parents were members of the EASTERN STAR. The governing body was the Grand Chapter of the Eastern Star, and although the ostensible purpose was to influence young girls to become ideal American women, it is hard to believe that the main purpose was not to create a "farm" organization for the Eastern Star proper. The order seems to be extinct.

There were three DEGREES: Initiatory, Honorary Majority, and Public. The Honorary degree was automatically conferred when a "Daughter" reached the age of 21. The LODGES were called Triangles and appear to have been directly under the supervision of the Eastern Star in New York, outside of which the organization seems never to have spread.

Death and Resurrection

A fundamental part of many RITUALS AND CEREMONIES is the theme of death and resurrection.

The Christian parallels are obvious, but it is worth remembering that many other pre-Christian and non-Christian deities are also represented as dying and being reborn — Mithras is one of the best-known examples (see MITHRAISM), while the story of Osiris is much the same — and that some legends seem almost willfully non-Christian, such as the slaying of Hiram Abif in the ritual of the FREEMASONS. In fact, the theme of death and rebirth is fundamental in many (if not all) human societies at some stage in their evolution. The shamans whose rituals predate all organized religions frequently spoke (and still speak) of dying or at least of wrestling with death as a part of the "dream-quest" they undertake as a part of becoming a shaman. Going further back still, there is the archaeological evidence of the "fat goddesses" or "earth mother" figurines as found in many places, especially Malta. These figures seem to indicate that the very earliest religious or belief systems were based on fertility, which is usually identified both with the female principle and with the cycle of the seasons: The death of winter and the rebirth of spring. These beliefs survived into historical times (albeit *remote* historical times), as evidenced by the MYSTERIES of ELEUSIS and elsewhere.

It may smack of popular psychology to identify these ancient beliefs with, say, the initiation ceremonies of the ELKS or EAGLES; but it is also hard to escape the conclusion that both serve a similar psychological need.

Quite apart from this, it is also hard to avoid the suspicion that the whole panoply of coffins and skeletons and bones and everything else associated with death, which is so commonly found in rituals, is in large part juvenile play-acting.

Decisi

A short-lived secret society, formed in Naples in 1807 to oppose the French and dedicated to the use of assassination as a means of furthering their ends. The LODGEs were called *Decisione* — "Decisions" — and officers included the Director of Funeral Ceremonies and the Registrar of the Dead, as well as the usual Grand Master.

As one might expect of a Neapolitan secret society of the period, the Decisi were not averse to a little private gain as well: "Contributions" were solicited by the Grand Master, who might reinforce his request by placing four dots after the name of the person approached. Without the dots, the penalty for non-compliance might have been as mild as slaughtering cattle or burning a house. With the dots, it was death.

Dee, John

John Dee (1527–1608), like Cornelius Agrippa, ALBERTUS MAGNUS and the two Bacons (see AGRIPPA VON NETTISHEIM, HEINRICH CORNELIUS; BACON, FRANCIS; BACON, ROGER), is one of the "adepts" who is claimed as a member by an inordinate number of secret societies. As so often, most accounts of his life seem to have been written by those with an axe to grind: He is painted either as the most shameless charlatan (Samuel Butler parodied him mercilessly in *Hudibras*) or as one of the greatest men of all time, comparable with Leonardo da Vinci. The truth lies somewhere between.

In 1546, at the age of 19, he was made Under-Reader of Greek at Trinity College, Cambridge, then newly founded; shortly afterward, he was made a Fellow of the new college. In 1547 he befriended the cartographer Mercator in Louvain, learning all he could about navigation for the greater magnification of England. He also studied logic, mathematics, astronomy, and optics.

He also took an interest in what would today be called "parapsychology," including telepathy, natural magic, and astrology. He was appointed Astrologer Royal to Queen Elizabeth, though it may well be that a great deal of his "astrological" work (especially when he was traveling on the continent) was a cover for espionage. Certainly, his interest in Trithemius's *Steganographia* and the accelerated completion of his own *Monas Hieroglyphia* seem not to have been entirely mystical and magical. The latter work, with its strong elements of cryptography and encipherment, was described by Sir William Cecil as being of the utmost value for the security of the realm. His work on SCRYING, on the other hand, seems to have been entirely magical.

During an absence from England in 1583–89 (he was in Poland with Count Adalbert Laski), a mob broke into Dee's house and destroyed his books and instruments; his notoriety as a magician was already widespread. On his return, he was well received by the queen but never gained the preferment he sought. He was Warden of Christ's College, Manchester, from 1595–1605, retiring to Mortlake in 1605 and dying there three years later at the age of almost 80. For a fully biography, see *John Dee,* by Richard Deacon (London: Muller, 1968).

Deer, Improved Order of

The original Order of Deer, on which the new order purported to be an improvement, has vanished without trace; and the Improved Order, founded in 1913, seems now to have vanished almost as completely, despite a membership of 500,000 in 1920. The other venison-yielding fraternities — ELKS and MOOSE INTERNATIONAL — seem to have cornered the ungulate market.

Defenders

The Defenders was one of the many manifestations of the Irish independence movement and was founded about 1784 in County Armagh. At first it was a Catholic society and then, by the 1790s, it was a pan-Irish interdenominational movement.

Its original purpose was literally to defend itself and its property against the excesses of English overlordship, but after 1792 it was more political and apparently merged more and more with the UNITED IRISHMEN. It was a grassroots organization of working men. In the words of their chronicler Richard Robert Madden (*United Irishmen*, second series, London: 1843), "They had no persons in their body of the upper or even middling class in life." By 1794, the group had expanded its scope beyond Ireland to "quell all nations, dethrone all kings, and plant the true religion that was lost at the Reformation." Its radicalism was too powerful for the Catholic church, however, and some Catholic politicians denounced the order as a mere collection of "unthinking oppressed people." It ceased to exist as a separate body (from the United Irishmen) during the late 1790s.

Degree of Honor Protective Association

325 Cedar Street
St. Paul, MN 55101
(612) 224-7436

The Degree of Honor Protective Association was founded in 1910 as a fraternal, insurance, and patriotic organization for "any person of good moral character and a believer in the existence of a Supreme Being, who is between the ages of sixteen (16) and sixty-five (65) years." It had 73,223 members in 1988. The Association publishes *The Degree of Honor Review* bimonthly.

The Degree of Honor Protective Association is in considerably better shape than the Ancient Order of United Workmen (see UNITED WORKMEN, ANCIENT ORDER OF), from which it sprang. Originally, the Degree of Honor was founded in 1873 as a female auxiliary to the United Workmen. In 1882, the Degree of Honor added an insurance option, and in 1896 a Superior Lodge was formed. Finally, in 1910, the Degree of Honor Protective Association came into being.

From its inception, the insurance was on a legal reserve basis and the ritual was strongly Christian; both characteristics continue. There are two classes of members, Insured and Social. As far as can be discovered, it works only one degree, though there is also a burial service.

The watchwords are Constancy, Honor, and Purity, and the motto is *Talitha Cumi*, or "Maiden, Arise" (Mark 5:46). As with so many fraternal secret societies working rituals, membership has declined steadily: 120,000 in 1967, 86,000 in 1979, and a little more than 70,000 in 1990.

Men were admitted in the late 1920s, though women remained in control of the organization. In addition to the insurance side of things, the Degree of Honor promotes social, patriotic, and civic events and holds adult and junior meetings.

Degrees

Many fraternal orders and secret societies have different ranks or grades of membership, and these are normally called "degrees." Originally, these degrees may have corresponded to simple promotion; this still happens in some organizations, such as the Order of AHEPA (see AHEPA, ORDER OF). In other cases, they may have corresponded to ever-greater levels of admission into the secrets of the organization; a period of probation would be followed by full admission, full admission by elevation to the degree of Master, and so forth. Again, this still happens, but its significance is now minimal. The main requirement for a superior degree in most lodges is mere time-serving. Sometimes, the two approaches are combined: One has to have been a member for a certain length of time, or to have held some sort of office in the LODGE, before proceeding (or being elected) to a higher degree. The usual way to refer to these degrees is to say that an organization "works" a certain number of degrees.

Particularly in the 19th century, large numbers of degrees were invented apparently *ex nihilo* to satisfy a love of pomp and rigmarole. Today, many organizations (especially FREEMASONS) work an extraordinary number of degrees, and the differences between the various degrees are not always clear to the members, let alone to outsiders.

Nor are these degrees always progressive. While the SCOTTISH RITE of Freemasons works 32 degrees (the 33rd is honorary), often with minimal delays between each degree, there are also SIDE DEGREES. These either are not recognized by the main body, and represent more or less unofficial branches of the organization, or involve initiation into "fun" organizations like the SHRINERS or the GROTTO.

Ngakpa Choegyam, an initiate of a number of Tantric Mysteries and a Doctor of TANTRA as well as the author of several books on mystic enlightenment, suggests that many people do not even know how many degrees their organization works: "If they refer to the Thirty-Eighth Degree, and you ask them about the Forty-First Degree, the chances are that they will look at you with new respect, because you know something they don't. If they start questioning you, just look mysterious. Or look guilty, and tell them no, you were mistaken—in a way that leaves them in no doubt that you weren't."

Deism

Deism, or belief in a Supreme Being, is central to many, perhaps most, fraternal orders and secret societies in the western world.

To some extent, the substitution of deist beliefs for

Christianity seems to have arisen from the Masonic traditions, which purportedly antedate Christianity—Christian rituals would be hard to square with a pre-Christian organization—but, much more importantly, it owes its origin to the fact that there was a craze for joining the FREEMASONS and other secret societies in the so-called Age of Reason. Not only did rationalists of the 18th century have difficulty in believing in the more extreme and dogmatic versions of God, they were also trying to break down the barriers between different Christian sects and even (though more rarely) the barriers between Christianity and Judaism. By leaving their God undifferentiated, they hoped to avoid conflict. The legacy of this semiopenmindedness has, however, been twofold.

First, while many groups profess deism, they are in fact basically Christian; or at most, they fall into the Near Eastern Judaeo-Christian-Islamic tradition of deism. Many, while professing to make no inquiry into a member's belief, even use the Bible as a central part of their RITUALS AND CEREMONIES. Requiring belief in a supreme being necessarily excludes agnostics, atheists, most Buddhists, and members of a number of other Far Eastern religions.

Second, because their God does not necessarily mesh with the God of a particular sect, oaths sworn as part of the initiation ceremonies are deemed irreligious and even blasphemous by some sects. Catholics who belong to some organizations are excommunicated; other organizations do not warrant excommunication, but members of them may be denied the sacraments.

There has also been a modest, but consistent, neo-pagan streak. This is especially true in German societies (see EDELWEISS, THULE GESSELSCHAFT), who have a weakness for Norse and Old German gods, while the French are more catholic (with a small "c") in their tastes and have been known to haul the Roman and Greek deities in. There are also Druidic (or pseudo-Druidic) deities (see DRUIDS), and the Horned God and the Earth Mother have enjoyed one of their periodical revivals during the 1990s.

Many of the American "fun" societies, such as the SHRINERS, are given to taking the name of Allah in vain, together with a casual abuse of al-Quran (the Koran). In Islamic eyes, the degree of blasphemy that is perpetrated by such orders is unbelievable, and any element of deviation from Christian orthodoxy is normally as naught by comparison; the nearest parallel might be with holding a black mass as a joke (which has been done; see HELL FIRE CLUB).

Delphic Priesthood

The Delphic Priesthood was an Italian secret society of the first part of the 19th century, dedicated to freedom for Italy. Their RITUALS AND CEREMONIES were nautical: The LODGE was a "Ship," and the Master of the Lodge a "Pilot." The order hoped for help from America, unlike the INDEPENDENCE, who favored Russia. Elements from among them probably merged with the CARBONARI.

De Molay, Order of

10200 N. Executive Hills Boulevard
Kansas City, MO 64190
(816) 891-8333

The Order of De Molay was founded in 1919 in Kansas City, Missouri, for young men aged 13–21. There were 60,000 members in 1988, principally in North America. They publish a magazine, the *De Molay Councilor*.

The Order of De Molay was founded by a far-sighted member of the FREEMASONS named Frank S. Land, ostensibly to encourage and develop good citizenship and sound character among youth. In reality, it is a "farm club" from which future Masons might be drawn; perhaps two-thirds of the membership goes on to become Masons.

There were nine founder members in 1919. Originally, De Molay admitted only the sons of Master Masons, but the rules were changed to admit any male relative aged 14–21 of a Mason, or anyone of the same age with a "Masonic background." The lower age limit was dropped to 13 in the 1980s, but enrollment continues to fall rapidly; the 1988 total was 40,000 fewer than only a decade previously, and over 100,000 lower than in the mid-1960s.

The organization takes its name from Jacques de Molay, last head of the TEMPLARS, who was imprisoned for seven years, grievously tortured, and finally burned at the stake on March 14, 1314, by King Philip IV of France with the connivance of Pope Clement V.

The order works two DEGREES, namely Initiation and the Degree of De Molay. Both were devised by Frank Marshall, a newspaperman in Kansas City. The first is a heavily Christian ceremony in which the candidates kisses the Bible; it also reflects 19th-century values with its concentration on the six jewels of the crown of youth: cleanliness, comradeship, courtesy, filial love, patriotism, and reverence for sacred things. The De Molay degree dramatizes the trial and execution of its unfortunate namesake.

Upon achieving the age of 21, a member may no longer attend De Molay meetings unless he becomes a Master Mason; any Master Mason may attend.

It is very much a junior Masons' fraternal club. Apart from its fraternal, social activities and the Leadership Conferences it organizes, it also raises money for humanitarian charities and operates the De Molay Dream Factory, making the wishes of chronically ill children come true by organizing trips for them. It had begun to play down the anti-Communist programs it sponsored in the 1960s, even before the collapse of the Soviet Union in the late 1980s.

The Order of De Molay is also known as DeMolay International.

Deprogramming

"Deprogramming" adherents of various sects is a minor industry; the main targets are young people who join the "Moonies" (the Unification Church), the Hare Krishna movement, and the Scientologists.

Although it is not difficult to sympathize with the parents of young people who turn aside from their parents' wishes, it is also not difficult to suspect that "reprogramming" might be a more accurate name.

Desoms

The odd title is an acronym for *Deaf Sons of Master Masons*; the organization was founded in the state of Washington in 1946. It confers a single initiatory side degree on deaf males of good moral character who are closely related to a Master Mason (see SIDE DEGREES).

Deutsche Union

The Deutsche Union, or German Union, also known as the Two-and-Twenty from the number of its members, was apparently an attempt to cash in on the passion for secret societies, which blossomed in the late 18th century. It was founded by Charles Frederick Bahrdt (1741–92), and although Vivian (upon whose *Secret Societies Old and New* this account is chiefly based; see VIVIAN, HERBERT) gives no dates, Mackey says that it was founded at Halle in 1787 and that several of the early members were FREEMASONS (see MACKEY, ALBERT G.).

Avowedly dedicated to the enlightenment of mankind and the dethroning of superstition and fanaticism, with a bit of benevolence and philanthropy thrown in, its aims were commendable but hardly modest: "To diffuse intellectual light, to annihilate superstition, and to perfect the human race."

The actual aims of the society seem more to have been concerned with the personal enrichment of Herr Bahrdt, in which it was but briefly successful. In 1790, he was convicted of conspiracy (Vivian) or libel (Mackey), though apparently not of bilking the public, which then as now was a much lesser crime. Regardless of his offense, he was thereupon cast into prison, where he died.

De Witt, Jean

Jean De Witt was the pen name of Herr A. Buloz, born in Altona, Germany, in 1800. He was the author of *Les Sociétés Secrètes de France et d'Italie* (Paris, 1830).

He joined the Black Knights (see SCHWARZER RITTER, DEUTCHER ORDEN) in his teens, and as a result had to flee to England in 1818; in 1821, he joined the CARBONARI in Geneva, for which he was imprisoned. After escaping, he married an heiress and settled down to grow old comfort-

ably. In *Les Sociétés Secrètes* (one of many French books bearing much the same title), he deals with the above secret societies, especially the Carbonari, as well as the Società della Santa Fe, the Society of European Regeneration, and the Council of Sublime Perfected Masters.

Dragon Society

The only conveniently accessible account of the Dragon Society is given in Howard's *The Occult Conspiracy*, where the ideas expressed are attributed to "the American writer Andrew E. Rothovius," whose books do not seem to be listed in the bibliography and who does not appear in the mammoth bibliography at the end of Manly P. Hall's *Secret Teachings of All Ages*.

According to Howard, the Dragon Society was an English group of the late 16th and early 17th century dedicated to the return of the OLD RELIGION, which (in this version) involved key lines (invisible lines that link magical sites) and sacred power centers. Politically, they hoped that James VI of Scotland/James I of England would abdicate in favor of his son Henry, Prince of Wales, who would then rule over a spiritually regenerated kingdom. Henry's death in 1612 dashed their hopes and caused many of them to set sail for the New World; Henry Adams, founder of the noted American political dynasty, was one of them.

Assuming that the society existed, the political aspect seems more credible than the religious. The Dragon of Wales as a political rallying point is at least as potent an explanation for the title of the society as any concern with ley lines might be.

Drinking Clubs

Drinking clubs are normally of two kinds. One kind has its origin in a need to circumvent laws restricting the sale of liquor: The ELKS originally arose in this way, and the American speakeasies of the Prohibition period are well known.

Even after England's relaxation of liquor licensing laws in the late 1980s, clubs where one could legally drink after hours continued to flourish. They are legal because they are not open to the general public; typically, 24 hours must elapse between joining the club and buying a drink. In the United States, "dry" counties may permit liquor sales only to members of clubs, though there is often no waiting period. This sort of "club" is only secret where it is perforce also clandestine, as in Islamic states such as Saudi Arabia, where the consumption of alcohol is interdicted.

The second kind of drinking club is typified by the German *Stammtisch*. This was originally a trade, student, or business fraternity, which met at a drinking house; one of the earliest was for the sailing masters of Königsberg in Prussia (now Kaliningrad). A *Stammtisch* is often nothing more than a group of like-minded friends who gather for a friendly drink together, usually once a week. Although these organizations are far from formal, and dues are rarely charged, "membership" is usually by invitation only, "initiation" will almost certainly involve buying a round of drinks, and at least in Germany the "club-house" table is typically marked by the landlord with a pennant and defended against strangers. Some such organizations are very old. One fraternity in Freiburg, Baden-Württemberg, claims an unbroken tradition stretching back more than six centuries. It is by no means inconceivable that the first Accepted Masons were joining the equivalent of the local *Stammtisch*.

For an account of an English drinking club that has now sadly disappeared, see CITY OF LUSHINGTON.

Droit Humain

"Droit Humain" ("Human Rights"), founded in 1894, was a form of FREEMASONS admitting both men and women. It arose from the admission of a woman to a French lodge in 1882, and in early 1914 spawned the short-lived *Grande Loge Mixte*. It appears to be extinct.

Druids

It is from Gaius Julius Caesar that we learn most about the original Druids, the priest-administrators of Gaul. They were known and apparently respected internationally as philosophers in the time of Sotion of Alexandria (about 200 B.C.), according to Diogenes Laertius; and as a supratribal organization with judicial and educational functions, they were very powerful. They taught the transmigration of souls; held mistletoe sacred; and apparently practiced human sacrifice, usually using criminals. The Druids of ancient Britain (and especially Celtic Druids) seem to have been more mystical and less worldly.

There are two strains of modern Druidism. One is (or purports to be a) continuation of the old Druidic ways: Its principal bodies are the *Gorsedd Beirdd Ynys Brydain* (the Bardic Assembly of the Isle of Britain, essentially a Welsh body), the *Breuriez Barzed Breiz* (the equivalent Breton organization, founded 1855) and the *Gorseth Kernow* (the Cornish version, founded as recently as 1928). All three are essentially pseudo-Bardic "revivals" of a culture which never really existed in the form in which it was resuscitated, though they are good clean fun.

Currently active organizations include:

Gorseth Kernow (P.G. Laws, 2 Donnington Road, Penzance, Cornwall).

Gorsedd de Bretagne (*Fraternité des Druides Bardes et Ovates de Bretagne*), established at Gwencamp in 1900. The "Bretagne" in this case is Brittany, and the Gorsedd partakes strongly of Breton nationalism; initiates are given Breton names. Female initiates form the

Korriganed, a separate division. Since 1900, this order has been affiliated to the HTD (Ker Henri Saint-Thurien, 29114 Bannalec).

Collège Bardique des Gaules, founded in 1933. These Druids conduct their business in French (6 rue des Petits-Champs, 75002 Paris).

Collège Druidique des Galles, founded in 1942, the result of a schism from the above-mentioned order. This college is interested in astrology and magic and is not recognized by other orders (René Bouchet, 40 rue du Colonel-Fabien, 93700 Drancy).

Collège Druidique Traditionel or *Collège des Druides Gaulois,* founded in 1979 by a retired magistrate living in Corsica. The founder, Jérôme Piétri, has written books and articles on reincarnation, Druids and magic in the 21st century, and more.

Confraternité de Druides et Femmes consacrées de la nation Picarde, working three DEGREES separately for men and women (Claude Bruillon, 9 Rue Latour, 80000 Amiens).

Confraternité Philosophique des Druides, another schismatic order from the College of Druids, Bards and Ovates of Brittany, above, founded in 1975. There are three degrees (bards, *ovates, aweniz*) for men, and three parallel degrees in the *Korriganed* or female auxiliary (*ettanerz, galloudegez, kellenerez;* see AUXILIARIES). The beliefs are further out than usual: The Grand Druid wrote a book called *Les Celtes et les Extra-Terrestres* (Eds. Marabout, 1973), in which he canvassed the extraterrestrial origins of Druidism, some 8,000 to 12,000 years ago (Grand Druide, 24 rue Copernic, 44000 Nantes).

Confrérie des Druides de Provence. The founders of this branch believe that the Provençal *menhirs* (standing stones) were put in place by Atlanteans using levitation. (Syndicat d'Initiative, place de Verdun, 83340 Luc-en-Provence).

Druides des Celtes de Normandie, founded in 1979, concerned principally with philosophy and poetry (Michel Velmans, BP 129, 50400 Granville).

Fraternité des Druides d'Occident, founded in 1974 with the intention of restoring the Druidic priesthood (Jacques Dubreuil, Kerdivuzit en Lothey, 29190 Pleyben).

Fraternité Interceltique du Grande Espace, founded in 1982 to revive Druidical religion (4 impasse du Capitaine-Lescpt, 35400 Saint-Malo).

Fraternité Universelle des Druides, founded in 1976 and headed by a Grand Druidess (8 rue Montcalm, 34000 Montpelier).

La Grande Chêne Celte, College Celtique, founded (or "reactivated") in 1960. A *chêne* is an oak (10 rue Denoyez, 75020 Paris).

Grand Collège Celtique. This appears to be similar to many primitive secret societies, specializing in RITES

OF PASSAGE. Babies can be *consacré* (dedicated or consecrated or "baptized") within seven days of birth, and at seven they become *abvaven,* at 14 *gwalenn,* at 15 *kenehen* and at 21 *diskibl.* They can then become Bards or Ovates but cannot be made Druids until they are 42 (Ker Sklerijenn, La Ville Lesne, 35290 Saint-Onen-la-Chapelle).

Grande Collège Druidique de Bibracte, founded in 1981. This order is concerned with ancient Irish texts transcribed by Christian monks (Julien Jallois, BP 364, 58008 Nevers Cedex).

Grande Mère des Celtes, an initiatory group affiliated to the Grand Chêne (see above).

The other kind of modern Druid is part of a secret society—or rather, a tangle of secret societies—which seems for the most part to have a strong flavor of FREEMASONS and often makes no real attempt at continuing Druidical traditions.

The first of the modern Orders seems to have been the Druid Order, founded by John Toland on September 21, 1717, at the Apple-Tree Tavern in London. The date is suspiciously close to the promulgation of the first written material on modern Freemasonry. Next came the Ancient Order of Druids in 1781. Subsequent schisms led to the United Ancient Order of Druids, the American United Ancient Order of Druids, the Loyal Order of Druids, and (another) Order of Druids (1858). Resembling the ODD FELLOWS in many ways, the Druids spread to the United States (1839), Australia, Germany, and possibly elsewhere.

Unlike the vast majority of fraternal orders, the Druids' form of DEISM is not primarily Christian; rather, it hews to the pre-Christian Druid religion.

American Order of Druids

This was a short-lived fraternal benefit society, chartered on May 17, 1888, in Massachusetts, which was open both to men and women.

Ancient Order of Druids

This is the one that was founded in London in 1781 and has links with "le do" and with Royal Arch masonry (see ROYAL ARCHMASONS, GENERAL GRAND CHAPTER OF) (Grand Imperial Secretary, 67 Saxondale Avenue, Birmingham B26 1LP).

United Ancient Order of Druids

The British headquarters of the U.A.O.D. is as follows: Druids Hall, 8 Perry Road, Bristol BS1 5BQ. It seems to be a friendly society (see FRIENDLY SOCIETIES) that has far fallen from its previous popularity.

The U.A.O.D. in its American avatar was (it *may* still exist) a fraternal benefit society, which in its later days offered insurance. Basing its teachings on seven precepts allegedly propounded by Merlin the magician, it exhorts (or exhorted) members to:

> Labor diligently to acquire knowledge for it is power
> When in authority decide reasonably, for thine authority may cease
> Bear with fortitude the ills of life, remembering that no mortal sorrow is perpetual
> Love virtue—for it bringeth peace
> Abhor vice—for it bringeth evil upon all
> Cultivate the social virtues, so shalt thou be beloved by all men

The structure was as follows: the lodge was called a "Grove," after the oak groves in which the original Druids reputedly met; the district lodge was called a Grand Grove; and there were (or are) Supreme Groves in the United States and some other countries. Women were eligible for a parallel order called a Circle, though male Druids might also join the Circle. The Chapter was the "fun" side of Druidism.

The U.A.O.D. worked three DEGREES, Ovate, Bard, and Druid. The RITUALS AND CEREMONIES were based very loosely (and without human sacrifice) on ancient Druidic myths.

It was never a very large organization: 17,000 members in 1896 and 35,000 in 1923, while by 1965 the *California Druid* magazine of San Francisco had a circulation of 6,000 copies. Schmidt (see SCHMIDT, ALVIN J.), in his *Fraternal Organizations,* believed it extinct in 1979, and the ENCYCLOPEDIA OF ASSOCIATIONS said that the address of the Supreme Grove was "unknown since 1972," but the 1989 San Francisco telephone directory listed two numbers, neither of which has proven reachable.

Druid Order

This is the Druid group that holds the summer solstice festivals at Stonehenge, and is therefore much more concerned with the traditions of Druidism than most of the other British societies. Contact persons are: Christopher Sullivan, 161 Auckland Road, London SE1 92H, and Dr. Thomas Haugham, 77 Carlton Avenue, Dulwich, London SE21.

Universal Druidic Order

This was formed (or "revived and regrouped") in 1966 by one Desmond Bourke, from the Ancient and Archaeological Order of Druids and the Literary and Archaeological Order of Druids. In order to be admitted to the former, one had to be a Freemason (22 Broad Walk, Blackheath, London SE3 8NB).

Duk-Duk

This is an obscure secret society on the islands of New Pomerania, formerly New Britain, whose hideously masked or chalk-painted members execute justice and collect fines. They are allowed great latitude in carrying out punishment, including arson and murder. They recognize one another by secret signs, and their festivals are strictly closed—on pain of death—to the uninitiated.

Dynastic Orders of Chivalry

A dynastic order of chivalry is one that lies in the personal gift of an individual, usually a sovereign or the descendant of a royal family, even if that family no longer has a kingdom. Dynastic orders are often of considerable antiquity—some are alleged to antedate the Crusades—and the right to ennoble people under a dynastic order may be transferred in much the same way as real property; the Sacred and Military Constantinian Order of St. George affords an excellent example (see ST. GEORGE, SACRED AND MILITARY CONSTANTINE ORDER OF).

Because a dynastic order is hereditary, the head of any family with the gift enjoys the *ius collationis* (the right to confer), and this right continues despite political change, republicanism, and even purported abolition.

The right by which dynastic orders were founded, though, appears on close examination to be little greater than the right by which the members of the PETER PAN CLUB appoint their Lord High Poobah. Age and (in some cases) political or Papal recognition are all that add legitimacy to these orders, which are rooted (if anywhere) in the Divine Right of Kings.

Cardinale (see CARDINALE, HYGINUS EUGENE), in *Orders of Knighthood, Awards and the Holy See,* covers a good number of dynastic orders including the following:

Noble Order of the Golden Fleece (Austria)
Noble Order of the Golden Fleece (Spain)
Noble Order of the Seraphim (Sweden)
Order of St. Joseph (Habsburg-Lorraine)
Order of St. Michael of France (Bourbon-Orléans)
Order of St. Stephen (Habsburg-Lorraine)
Order of the Dames of the Starry Cross (Habsburg-Lorraine)
Order of the Holy Ghost (Bourbon-Orléans)
Royal and Military Order of St. Louis (Bourbon-Orléans)
Royal Order of Maria Louise (Spain)
Royal Victorian Chain (Great Britain)
Royal Victorian Order (Great Britain)

Eastern Star, Order of the

The Order of the Eastern Star has a tangled history. Originally conceived as an American form of ADOPTIVE MASONRY as early as the 1840s, it took until 1876 for the General Grand Chapter, Order of the Eastern Star, to be formed; and there are at least two separate organizations that both say that they are dedicated to the unification of all Eastern Stars, but which lead a separate existence from the General Grand Chapter and were founded in 1947 and 1962 respectively. There is also an African-American organization, dating from the days when American Masons officially barred blacks from membership.

General Grand Chapter, Order of the Eastern Star

1618 New Hampshire Avenue, N.W., Washington, DC 20009, (202) 667-4737

The General Grand Chapter of the Order of the Eastern Star was founded in 1876. It currently extends worldwide, in association (where appropriate) with the Supreme Grand Chapter of Scotland. It is open to Master Masons in good standing, and their female relatives over the age of 18 years. There were 2,087,063 members in 1994.

Robert Morris, Master Mason, schoolteacher and poet, first attempted in the 1840s to establish Adoptive Masonry in the United States, using a ritual of his own devising. At first reviled by fellow Masons for betraying Masonic secrets, he nevertheless persisted and throughout the 1850s conferred various DEGREES on female relatives of Master Masons, with varying levels of cooperation from other Master Masons. His Families of the Eastern Star dated from 1857.

Real acceptance was slow in coming, and it was not until Morris's rituals were revised by the Masonic publisher Robert Macoy in 1866 that any greater success came. Macoy added the degrees of Queen of the South, Past Matron's Degree and the Amaranth Degree. Even then, it was 10 years before the Central Grand Chapter was organized, and the Grand Lodge of England still does not admit that the Eastern Star has anything to do with Freemasonry. Indeed, the G.L.E. has in the past threatened with expulsion any Master Mason who receives any O.E.S. Degree or serves as Worthy Patron.

The order as now constituted works five degrees, based on the story of five women in the Bible—an example of the way in which organizations adhering to DEISM have become progressively more Christian in the United States, especially where women are involved. The slogan of the order is, "We have seen His star in the East, and are come to worship Him." The order even awards scholarships to those involved in religious training.

The ritual also illustrates powerful patriarchal values, and, of course, the degrees must be conferred by a (male) Master Mason. The degrees are

1. Obedience, symbolized by Adah daughter of Jepthah (daughter)
2. Devotion to religious values, symbolized by Ruth (widow)
3. Fidelity, exemplified by Esther (wife)

4. Faith in the Redeemer, symbolized by Martha sister of Lazarus (sister)
5. Charity, symbolized by Electa, identified as the "Elect Lady" in the second epistle of St. John (mother)

The initial choice of characters certainly seems strange to an outsider, as Adah was a human sacrifice, and Jepthah the Gileadite appears from the description in Judges 11 to have been an outstandingly unattractive and inflexible fellow. In return for being allowed to win a battle against the "children of Ammon," he promised Jehovah to slaughter as an offering the first thing that came to greet him when he returned home (verses 30–31). He was apparently expecting his daughter's pet lamb, but the daughter beat the lamb to the portals. He was, therefore, convinced he ought to kill her.

Equally strangely, she wished to go to the mountains to bewail her virginity (verses 37–38), which he permitted; and when she came back two months later, not having had the sense to stay away, he killed her. It is one of the most unedifying passages in Holy Writ.

Much the same form of ceremony is used for all five degrees, which are very milk-and-water compared with the Masonic originals: no swords pointed at bared breasts, no tongues torn out and bodies buried at the tide-line. A further degree, Queen of the South, is honorary.

According to the Eastern Star Ritual as published by EZRA A. COOK PUBLICATIONS—

When a lady claims to have taken these degrees, and has given one or more of the SIGNS, a Mason may examine her in the following manner:
Question: "Are you a sister of the Eastern Star?"
Answer: "We have seen his star in the East."
Question: "For what came you here?"
Answer: "We came here to worship him."
Question: "Have you the cabalistic word?"
Answer: "I have."
Question: "Will you give it to me?"
Answer: "I will, with your assistance."
Question: "Begin."
Answer: "No, you begin."
Question: "Begin you."
Answer: "F."
Question: "A."
Answer: "T."
Question: "A."
Answer: "L."
Question: "Has that word any signification?"
Answer: "It has, two. First, that it would be fatal to the character of any lady for truth who should disclose the secrets of these degrees unlawfully. Second, each of the letters of this word stands for one or more words, which words make the cabalistic motto."

Question: "Have you the Cabalistic motto?"
Answer: "I have."
Question: "Will you give it to me?"
Answer: "I will, with your assistance."
Question: "Begin."
Answer: "No, you begin."
Question: "Begin you."
Answer: "Fairest."
Question: "Among."
Answer: "Ten thousand."
Question: "Altogether."
Answer: "Lovely. Fairest—among—ten thousand—altogether lovely.

Note that it is the Mason who interrogates the woman, reinforcing her position of inferiority. It is not hard to sympathize with the G.L.E. in its disdain for the order.

Functionally, the Order of the Eastern Star is something between a female version of Masonry in its own right, and an organization riding on the shirt-tails of Masonry; one cannot help wondering how many women would join without the prompting of husbands, fathers, and other male relatives.

Charitable giving includes scholarships for students in religious training, and more.

Another branch or sect of the Eastern Star is the Federation of Eastern Stars, founded in 1962 and purportedly dedicated to the unification of Eastern Star orders worldwide. It had 105,000 members in 1994 and was a female auxiliary of Federation of Masons of the World.

The Federation of Eastern Stars of the World was founded 15 years earlier, in 1947, and is also purportedly dedicated to the unification of Eastern Star orders worldwide. It had 57,000 members in 1994.

With such a strong fraternal spirit—two separate organizations dedicated to unity (but not with each other) and both separate from the main body, to say nothing of excluding the Prince Hall (Black) Order—it is not surprising that the Eastern Star is in decline. The total membership given above is under 2.6 million, which is less than the membership of the General Grand Chapter alone in the 1970s.

The Order of the Constellation of the Junior Stars is the juvenile arm of the Eastern Star.

E Clampus Vitus

E Clampus Vitus was formed as a "fun" organization, probably in Mokelumne Hill, California, in 1849. It lapsed, and was revived as a fun-cum-historical society. In 1991 there were approximately 50,000 members in 62 LODGES, but there was no settled head office.

E Clampus Vitus (sometimes E Clampsus Vitus) is an example of a fun-loving society that eventually came to take itself too seriously, evolving from pure burlesque and serious drinking, it turned into a worthy organization with a penchant for local history.

In its original form, it was not very attractive—there was a great deal of rowdyism and horseplay—but at least it lived up to its original mission, which was to parody the FREEMASONS and other organizations that took themselves too seriously.

Although Lois Rather (in *Men Will Be Boys* [Oakland, California, 1980]) traces the history of the "Clampers" to unspecified southern states before 1849, it is widely accepted in California that E. Clampus Vitus is a native California organization founded in Mokelumne Hill in the Gold Country by Joseph H. Zumwalt during the Gold Rush year. The SONS OF MALTA may, however, be an ancestor of the original Clampers.

E Clampus Vitus originally seems to have existed for one simple reasons: to initiate new members, partly for the malicious pleasure of humiliating them, and more importantly because a new member had to buy drinks all round for existing members. When a new "mark" was spotted by a Clamper—maybe a new businessman in town, maybe even an unfortunate traveling salesman—he would be fed the line that in order to do business in the area, he had better join E Clampus Vitus. More often than not, especially if other Clampers joined the conspiracy and told him the same story, he would accede.

The "initiation" took several forms, including pushing the candidate backwards into a pile of cow manure, hoisting him in the air and leaving him there, or dumping him in a vat of water; but the most usual form seems to have been the "ride on the rocky road," in which the candidate was placed in a wheelbarrow and pushed along a ladder laid flat on the floor. Sometimes, the wheelbarrow would be lined with wet sponges. Before or after all this, the unfortunate candidate would also be subjected to a barrage of personal questions, often accompanied by jeers and catcalls. The only incentive to remain in the organization, once one had been tricked into joining, was that one could join the tormentors of the next candidate.

The RITUALS AND CEREMONIES, such as they were, seem to have been horseplay tempered with parodies of FREE-MASONS, ODD FELLOWS, and other fraternal orders; the head of the order is to this day the Sublime Noble Grand Humbug, and there were other ranks (applied without excessive regard for detail or consistency), such as the Clampatriarch. An early head of the Clampers, Ephraim Bee, was known as the Grand Gyascutis and later as the Grand Lama.

At least one LODGE also had higher DEGREES, but no one took them very seriously. It has long been said within the organization that, traditionally, no one was in a fit state to record what went on at the meetings, and the morning after, no one could remember.

The move toward greater seriousness set in around the time of the Civil War, when the date of the Clampers parade was changed from the first Saturday after the snows to the Fourth of July—a reprehensibly sensible act suggesting that E Clampus Vitus was beginning to lose touch with its burlesque roots.

Like many other organizations, the present-day E Clampus Vitus is a revival of the original. The old E Clampus ran out of steam in the late 19th century, but was revived about 1930 by a lawyer named Carl Irving Wheat. Wheat was deeply interested in California history, and under his guidance the revived organization devoted itself to that subject. Clamper commemorative plaques of bronze or stone are to be found on many "historical" California buildings, some of which antedate the 20th century. Typically, these plaques give a brief history of the building.

Wheat was not entirely given to seriousness, however, and most Clampers remained thirsty men. He (and they) also had a weakness for misleading histories of the order, such as *Adam Was a Clamper, An Abridged History of Clamperdom from the Garden of Eden to Hangtown and the Founding of Platrix Chapter No. 2* (1979, by Don Louis Perceval, Montrose, California).

When Wheat died in 1967, the soberer elements of the organization took over—or attempted to do so. *The Clamper,* the official organ of the order since 1961, railed in December 1974 against the "grotesque antics, obscenities, vulgar displays and graceless manners" of some Clampers. Worse still, it attacked the holy institution of drinking. Then again, there *were* problems: Many Clampers regarded a six-gun as a part of the regalia (along with blue jeans and red braces, or "suspenders"), and the combination of guns and alcohol can become excessively interesting. In 1967, one man was accidentally shot dead at a party in Columbia near Sonora.

To this day, though, Clampers retain the image (where they are known, which is principally in the Gold Country of northern California) of being fond of a dram. For example, the Women's Christian Temperance Union (W.C.T.U.) visited Petaluma in 1979 to read the inscription on the water fountain they had installed a century earlier in 1879: "TOTAL ABSTINENCE IS THE WAY TO HANDLE THE ALCOHOL PROBLEM." They then went on to attempt to evangelize nearby Andresen's Tavern. There they found a sign that read, "NEVER TRUST A MAN WHO DOESN'T DRINK" and a bunch of Clampers in fancy costumes and military outfits. These worthies encouraged the ladies to move on, in no uncertain manner.

Needless to say, the name means nothing, and has been variously rendered as E Clampus Vitus, E Clampsus Vitus, E Clampsus Vitae, "Clampers" (also used as the name for members), and E.C.V. The Clampers appear to be in good order: There were 20 chapters in 1970, 32 in 1979, and over 50 in 1991.

Eco, Umberto

Umberto Eco's novel *Foucault's Pendulum* (Gruppo Editoriale Fabbri Bompiani, Milan, 1988; English-language edition by Picador/Pan, 1990) should be read by anyone who is interested in secret societies. Not only is it a spectacular (yet surprisingly unobtrusive) display of scholarship and an extremely entertaining book, it also illustrates brilliantly the mechanism by which conspiracy theories arise, and the way in which correlations both genuine and specious can be made between a very wide range of secret societies. The fascinating thing is that Umberto Eco (born 1932) brings to bear two qualities markedly lacking in the vast majority of books on similar subjects: a very fair idea of what he is taking about, and a magnificent sense of playfulness. The book abounds with penetrating observations on the nature of secret societies and on the nature of those who believe in them.

Edelweiss

Edelweiss (also called Edelweiss-Pirates) was a movement that existed between World War I and World War II, with the aim of reconstructing the cultural and ethnic patrimony of the ancient Nordic races. It was as happy with myth as with history; the Hyperborean city of Thule (also highly regarded by the THULE GESELLSCHAFT) was central to its beliefs (see HYPERBOREA).

Hermann Goering was initiated into the society in the 1920s after meeting Count Eric von Rosen, a leading light of the society, in northern Sweden; Goering also married von Rosen's sister-in-law, Karin von Kantzow. Despite the early presence of a man who would rise to the top of the Nazi hierarchy, and despite the Nordic mythological orientation of the order, Edelweiss resisted the Nazi drive toward total conformity. Indeed, the "edelweiss" emblem connoted purity and aloofness, and Edelweiss members often wore motley clothing to contrast themselves with the uniformed Hitler youth, who referred to their unsightly clothing as "Räuberzivil," or "robber's mufti."

Egbo

The Egbo is a West African secret society derived from SI'MO and especially from Oro. Its main sphere of influence is (or was) in southern Nigeria, especially among the Efik, Ekoi, and Ibanan peoples. Among the Efik, it gave rise to the EKKPE, and among the Ekoi, to the Ngbe.

In addition to its mystical aspects—which are mainly of a phallic/fertility cult nature, with a generous lacing of supernatural powers—it exercises (or at least exercised) many more mundane, but arguably more immediately useful functions such as "collecting debts for its members, providing police services, and safeguarding members' property from robbery and fires." According to Butt-Thompson (see BUTT-THOMPSON, CAPT. F. N.),

A member of *Egbo* with a grievance has only to rush into the street, look out for a gentleman connected with the society, slap him on the waistcoat place, and that gentleman has then and there to drop any private matter of his own he may be engaged in, call together the grade he belongs to, and go into the case. Or, if an *Egbo* gentleman is not immediately get-at-able, the complainant has only to rush to the *Egbo* house, and beat the *Egbo* Drum, and out come the *Egbo* Officials to his assistance.

Butt-Thompson also asserts that they have even taken credit for stopping small wars.

The High Egbo presides over many officials, some of whom rank as priests, and some of whom belong to DEGREES, which evolved effectively into secret societies in their own right. There seems to be a parallel here with some of the Masonic Side Degrees and other organizations. The first degree after initiation is *Ekpiri Ngbe* ("Little Egbo"), and others include *Ebu Nko, Nbawkaw, Ndibu* (the "Mother of Degrees"), *Oku Akama, Eturi, Nkanda,* and *Idion*. Membership is limited to males, and Europeans have been admitted to the order's minor grades as honorary members. See also WEST AFRICAN SECRET SOCIETIES.

Ekkpe

Ekkpe is (or was) a West African protective secret society among the Efik and other peoples of Nigeria. Purporting to be the original EGBO, the organization at one time boasted the following resounding and heterogenous titles:

Yor Olulo	Head man
Osun	Deputy head man
Opiapalabo	Champion
Okonalabo	Singer
Ogbogrualabo	Judge
Okurubenkerebiobele	Executioner
Oyemobinalabo	Jailer
Osi	Policeman
Oduminawoi	Horn-blower

Admission is or was limited to males, at puberty. See also WEST AFRICAN SECRET SOCIETIES.

Elect

The word "elect" comes from the Latin *eligere,* to choose; "electum" is the past participle. In the adjectival sense of "chosen" it is popular among secret societies, either as part (or all) of the name of some DEGREES, or as part of the name of the society itself. Mackey (see MACKEY, ALBERT G.) lists the following "Elects" in his *Encyclopedia of Freemasonry,* and he is concerned *only* with FREEMASONS!

Depositary Elect
Elect Brother
Elect Cohens, Order of
Elect Commander
Elect Master

Elect of Fifteen
Elect of London
Elect of Nine
Elect of Nine and Fifteen
Elect of Perignan
Elect of the New Jerusalem
Elect of the Twelve Tribes
Elect of Truth, Rite of
Elect of Twelve
Elect Philosopher
Elect Secret, Severe Inspector
Grand Elect
Grand Prince of the Three Elect
Irish Elect
Sublime Elect Lady
Little English Elect
Perfect Elect
Perfect and Sublime Mason Elect
Sovereign Elect
Sublime Elect
Supreme Elect
Symbolical Elect

Elect Cohens

The Elect (or Chosen or Select) Cohens—*Cohens Elus*—was a short-lived French variant of FREEMASONS, founded by Martines de Pasqually (1727–74) in 1754–67 (it took him some time to work out the details and gather in the faithful). The slightly improbable use of "Cohen" in this context is explained by the fact that the Cohens were the priestly caste of the Jews.

In addition to the traditional grades (Entered Apprentice, Companion, Master Mason), there were whole extra levels. The next level up was Apprentice Cohen, Companion Cohen, Master Cohen; then came Chosen Master Cohen (or Grand Architect) and Commander of the Orient (or Grand Elect of Zerubabel); and finally, in the fourth level, the Rose-Cross.

The original *Ordre des Chevaliers Maçons Elus Cohens de L'Univers* ("Order of Knights Masons Elect Cohens of the Universe") disappeared in 1780, but their heavily Christian doctrine influenced the Revised SCOTTISH RITE. In 1942, the order was reconstituted by Robert Ambelain as the *Ordre Martiniste des Elus Cohens* or "Martinist Order of Elect Cohens." See also MARTINISM.

Eleusis

The religious MYSTERIES of Eleusis probably appeared in Greece in the sixth or seventh century B.C., possibly from Egyptian sources. The mysteries have been lost for many centuries.

The Eleusian Mysteries demonstrate the links among religion, magic, and secret societies, which continue to this day. The origins seem to lie in the RITES OF PASSAGE of

Eleusis, a city of Classical Greece about 14 miles west of Athens. The Athenians adopted the rites after conquering Eleusis, extended them through the area under Athenian hegemony, extended them again to barbarians (non-Greeks), and preserved them even after the advent of Christianity. They were finally suppressed during the reign of Theodosius the Great (d. A.D. 395), and the sacred buildings were destroyed by Alaric the Goth in A.D. 396.

The *mysta* (candidate) received the Lesser Mysteries in the spring at Athens; six months later, he or she could receive the Greater Mysteries at Eleusis during the month of Boedromion, roughly equivalent to September. The significance of the timing of the Mysteries, at spring and harvest time, reflects the fertility-cult basis of the Mysteries. A further degree, *epopt,* was available at least a year after receiving the Greater Mysteries, but the number of epopts was always very small.

The principal officers were the Hierophant; the Dadoukos or torch-bearer; the Hierokux or Sacred Herald; and the Priestess of Demeter. The last shows the character of the Mysteries, which were based on DEATH AND RESURRECTION as symbolized by the cycle of the seasons and by a fertility cult. The mysteries of Eleusis were much involved with the generative principle, and women were prominent in them—perhaps a relic of matriarchal days when the magical strength of women was more highly prized than in historical times.

Clement of Alexandria (d. A.D. 220) devotes a long passage in the *Proreptikos* to a very jaundiced account of the Eleusian Mysteries; of Demeter who was raped (or seduced) by her son Jupiter, and who then gave birth to Kore, who also lay with Jupiter; and of the relationship of the ORPHIC MYSTERIES to those of Eleusis. He describes the heart of the mystery of the Corybantes—also related to Eleusis—in these words: "This is the whole mystery: an assassination and a burial!"

With the very minimum of scholarship, and with much less effort than is often expended, all manner of parallels between these Mysteries and others can be discovered. For a second example, the origin of the Eleusian mysteries lies in Demeter's resting at Eleusis in her search for Kore. Weary, she sits by a well, and Baubo, one of the original inhabitants of Eleusis, invites her into her house and offers cyceon, a drink compounded of water, meal, honey, wine, and cheese flavored with wild mint. Demeter cannot at first be tempted; but when Baubo raises her skirt in front of the goddess to expose her nudity, Demeter is moved to laughter and her sorrow lessens. This can be taken as a parable of the revelation of agriculture to mankind, but it also calls to mind the behavior of King David as recounted in the second book of Samuel, 6:16–20.

A considerably more interesting reference is to the serpentine form of Jupiter in his union with Kore. The serpent, the God Who Passes Through the Body (*ho dia kolpon theos*), immediately calls to mind the Kundalini or Serpent Power mysteries of Hinduism—a parallel made all the stronger by the traditional conclusion to the Eleusian mysteries, *Kogx Om Pax,* or *Canscha Om Pacsha* as it is still recited to this day. This is a Sanskrit mantra signifying in the first word the fulfillment of desire; in the second, the cosmic syllable (compare "Om mani padme hum"); and in the third, the following of the ever-changing path of unchanging duty.

The actual initiation into the Greater Mysteries seems to have consisted of a ritual purification, including sexual abstinence for nine days; a ceremonial meal; and the presentation of a sacred drama, which may or may not have involved simulated (or even actual) sexual intercourse between the Hierophant and the Priestess. The last was probably a relic of a much earlier King/Earth-Mother coupling, such as is recorded among the Ancient Britons and others. The ceremonial or sacramental meal seems to have centered around cyceon (see above), and sacred cakes of wheaten and sesame flour. The latter can be seen reflected in the Christian host or in the *tormas* of Tibetan Buddhism. The Lesser Mysteries were concerned more with Kore, and may well be separate (and Athenian rather than Eleusian) in origin—the Mystery of a lesser goddess subsumed into a greater Mystery.

Sacred symbols of the various traditions included celery (alleged to have sprung from the blood of Corybant); pomegranate seeds, derived from the blood of Dionysius; and all manner of rustic symbols of fertility and plenty, such as pastry, piglets, serpents, and representations of the vulva. The mystery of the epopt centered around the symbolism of a single ear of corn, reaped in perfect silence.

Disclosure of the Mysteries was punishable in the same way as treason. At some time around 429–23 B.C., a philosopher called Diagoras of Melos spoke against the Mysteries (it is believed by some that Clement of Alexandria was quoting Diagoras in his diatribe, mentioned above), and escaped trial only by fleeing; a bounty of a talent of gold was set on his head. Even discussion of the Mysteries was risky: Aristotle was forced into exile for revealing a part, and Aeschylus escaped punishment for the same offense only by proving that he had never actually been initiated.

With any society that is rooted in such remote antiquity, and which was substantially destroyed more than one and a half millennia ago, it is hard to draw many conclusions or even to quote accurate facts—the more so as most of the available information comes either from apostates or Christians, neither of whom could be expected to be entirely accurate or unbiased reporters. Much of what is to be found even in respectable works of scholarship is blatantly anti-Eleusian, and a great deal of Foucault's speculation has been dismissed by many (but

not all) subsequent scholars. Even so, the parallels with modern secret societies are hard to ignore:

1. The "secrets" were open to all who underwent the initiation
2. They were open to all ranks and conditions, at least in theory, and involved the barest minimum of moral inquiry into the character of the candidate
3. In Aristotle's words, "the initiated do not so much learn anything as feel certain emotions, and are put in a certain frame of mind"; or as the Homeric hymns put it, they saw something that comforted their souls, rather than learning anything of great importance. The Freemasons, the Elks and many other secret societies, might well be described the same way.

Eliphas Levi

"Eliphas Levi" is a name commonly encountered by students of the occult; he seems to have taught or inspired innumerable founders and members of the more magically inclined secret societies and is almost always quoted with approval as an authority and a scholar.

In fact, his scholarship was weak, as was his flesh. Born in 1810, he was christened Alphonse-Charles Constant, attended the seminary at Issy, and was ordained deacon in 1835. At this point he fell for a girl called Adèle and left the seminary before he was appointed priest; his mother killed herself in despair.

He was imprisoned for 11 months for sedition; in 1846, at the age of 36, he married a girl half his age who then went off to become a sculptress in her own right and to be the mistress of sculptor James Pradier, though the marriage was annulled in 1865 (he was a Catholic *abbé,* after all). He read widely, but not terribly wisely, in all manner of occult subjects, and he wrote *Dogme et rituel de haute magie* ("Dogma and Ritual of High Magic") and more. Levi influenced BULWER-LYTTON (see also VRIL SOCIETY) and many others. He died in 1875, aged 65. In France, there is to this day a *Cercle Eliphas Levi* (Moulin de la Petite Reine, 78580 Maule).

Elks

The Elks are the oldest and largest of the "Big Three" orders that name themselves after assorted wildlife; the other two are the Moose (see MOOSE, INTERNATIONAL) and the EAGLES. In addition to the main order, there is an African-American order, and there was once an insurance arm. There are also various related female organizations, not always auxiliaries.

Benevolent and Protective Order Of Elks of America

2750 Lake View Avenue, Chicago, IL 60614, (312) 477-2750

The B.P.O.E. was founded in 1868 in New York as a drinking club (see DRINKING CLUBS), but later broadened drinking club (see DRINKING CLUBS), but later broadened into a fraternal, charitable, and service organization. It is open to male U.S. citizens over 21, of whom some 1,500,000 were Elks in 1994.

According to the organization's *What It Means to Be an Elk,* "the animal from which the Order took its name was chosen because a number of its attributes were deemed typical of those to be cultivated by members of the fraternity. The Elk is distinctively an American animal. It habitually lives in herds. The largest of our native quadrupeds, it is yet fleet of foot and graceful in movement. It is quick and keen of perception; and while it is usually gentle and even timorous, it is strong and valiant in defense of its own."

The origin of the B.P.O.E. lay in an informal drinking society called the Jolly Corks, formed in 1866 to circumvent a New York law that closed saloons on Sundays.

The founders were a group of actors who rented a room first on 14th Street and then on the Bowery, where they could drink in peace of a Sabbath evening. Members carried a cork; failure to do so meant having to buy a round of drinks. Their leader, the aggressive American nationalism of modern Elks notwithstanding, was an English actor called Charles Algernon S. Vivian. It seems likely that he borrowed at least some of the paraphernalia of the Elks from the Royal Antediluvian Order of Buffalo (see BUFFALO, ROYAL ANTEDILUVIAN ORDER OF).

As the drinking club grew in size and popularity, the name (if not the intent) was made more sober; the change was apparently inspired by a stuffed elk's head on display at Phineas T. Barnum's museum. According to some accounts, it may actually have been the head of a moose. (The founders were after all actors, not taxonomists.)

By the Elks' own reckoning, the organization was founded on February 16, 1868, and its aims are the four cardinal virtues of charity, justice, brotherly love, and fidelity; the promotion of the welfare and happiness of their members; the fostering of patriotism; and the cultivation of good fellowship.

To this day, good fellowship ranks very high. Elks Lodges sell good liquor at very reasonable prices, and their breakfasts are an excellent value, if somewhat out of step with a cholesterol-conscious world. If an Elks Lodge is in session at 11:00 P.M., they drink a toast to absent brothers. *What It Means to Be an Elk* says that the fraternity "seeks to draw into its fraternal circle only those who delight in wholesome associations with congenial companions."

The organization provides very well for Elks fallen on hard times, and for the families of dead brethren. The Elks also contribute a great deal to military veterans' hospitals, and they are rightly renowned for this and for other charitable works. The Elks National Foundation—the charitable and humanitarian wing—was founded in 1928.

The Elks are also very strong on patriotism. More than 70,000 Elks fought in World War I, and "over one thousand of them made the last supreme sacrifice in that service." In World War II, on Pearl Harbor Day itself, the Grand Exalted Ruler "telegraphed the President of the United States, placing at the latter's disposal the full strength of the Order." In due course, "The Adjutant General asked the Elks for 45,000 recruits; through the efforts of the Lodges 97,000 men were enlisted in record time."

The Elks who remained at home shipped vast quantities of cigarettes and tobacco to the fighting forces, and for those who came back, their work with veterans (especially wounded and disabled veterans) has always been extensive and enthusiastic. They have also taken pains to look after soldiers' families; for example, in the summer of 1918, they built a 72-room structure for the families of the 40,000 soldiers stationed at Camp Sherman, Ohio.

The Elks National Memorial Building is a magnificent edifice dedicated on July 14, 1926 and rededicated on September 8, 1946, to take account of World War II. It has subsequently been rededicated again to include "the American patriots of Korea and Vietnam."

When the organization changed from the Jolly Corks to the B.P.O.E., it borrowed a certain amount from the Masons, including aprons and such terms as "Tyler" for the guardian of a lodge, and "Lodge of Sorrow" (a funeral service for a dead Elk). It also established a governmental structure "Following the general plan of our Federal government," dividing the organization into Legislative, Executive, and Judicial branches.

Although local LODGEs each raise large sums of money every year, there is also a central fund called the Elks National Foundation, which was established in Miami in 1928, "by amendment of the Constitution of the Grand Lodge," which immediately donated $100,000 as the nucleus of the fund. This Foundation is charged with furthering the charitable, educational, patriotic, and benevolent activities of the order. It is extremely wealthy.

The Elks National Home, for elderly Elks, was established at Bedford, Virginia, in 1902; it was later rebuilt and dedicated anew on July 8, 1916. The main building (which still stands) is very impressive; there have been a number of additions since.

Membership was for many years limited to "white male citizens of the United States, not under twenty-one years of age, who believe in the existence of God" and who are not "directly or indirectly a member of or in any way connected or affiliated with the Communist party, or who believe in the overthrow of our Government by force." As long as election to a lodge was still carried out by the old BLACKBALL system, entrance to the B.P.O.E. remained subject to these requirements regardless of legislation and public outcry to the contrary, but in 1989 the Grand Lodge changed the rules so that a simple two-thirds majority vote in favor of a candidate was sufficient to ensure admission.

The structure of the B.P.O.E. consists of a Grand Lodge and Subordinate Lodges. A Subordinate Lodge may be established only in a United States city, which has within its corporate limits not less than 5,000 inhabitants; many small cities have taken advantage of this. In larger cities, there may be one Elks lodge for every 500,000 people or substantial fraction thereof, in the absence of special dispensation from the Supreme Lodge. In 1900 there were over 1.5 million members.

Elks can also get plenty of committee experience at the local lodge. Committees include:

Auditing and Accounting Committee
Visiting Committee (visiting the sick)
Relief Committee (aid or relief)
Social and Community Welfare Committee
Lapsation Committee (dues-chasing)
Youth Activities Committee
Committee on Indoctrination (prior to initiation)
Americanism Committee ("implementing . . . patriotic activities")
Membership Committee
Memorial Day Committee
Flag Day Committee
National Service Committee
Government Relations Committee
Public Relations Committee
Investigating Committee (examine applicants)
National Foundation Committee
House Committee (club house)
and Special Committees as necessary

Although the Elks in their own literature say that "The Order questions no man's religion; nor bars him on account of his creed," there is a strongly Christian bias, despite the fact that no prayers may be offered in the name of Christ. This slant is made clear during the initiation into the single degree of the B.P.O.E., that of Loyal Knight. In this, the Esquire places a Bible on the altar (which is decorated with an American flag), while the organist plays "Nearer, My God, to Thee." He declares, "This is the Bible, the Book of the Law, upon which is founded Justice," and the members sing,

Great Ruler of the Universe
All-seeing and benign
Look down upon and bless our work
And be all glory Thine

May Charity as taught us here
Be ever born in mind
The Golden Rule our motto true
For days of Auld Lang Syne

"Auld Lang Syne" is effectively the fraternal anthem of the Elks.

The oath that follows includes secrecy (not revealing "the confidential matters of the Order"), obedience to the Elks' rules, a promise to uphold the Constitution of the United States, never to reveal the name of anyone who has received help from the lodge, and so forth. It is also forbidden to use membership of the lodge for business purposes, or to introduce politics or religion into the lodge meetings. "If I break this oath, may I wander through the world forsaken; may I be pointed out as a being bereft of decency and manhood, unfit to hold communion with true and upright men. And may God help me, and keep me steadfast in this my solemn and binding obligation in the Benevolent and Protective Order of Elks in the United States of America. Amen."

The official Christian reaction to all this varies with the sect. The Catholics leave it up to individual conscience, while some Lutheran and other sects specifically proscribe membership.

Improved Benevolent and Protective Order of Elks

P.O. Box 159, Winston, NC 27986

The I.B.P.O.E. was founded in 1897 in Cincinnati, Ohio, in response to the refusal of the established order to admit African Americans.

The Elks were never strong on radical harmony in their early days. In 1912, the (white) Elks even went so far as to seek and obtain an injunction in New York state barring the (black) Improved Elks from using the name. The judge opined that they could choose from "a long list of beasts, birds and fishes which have not yet been appropriated for such a purpose." The judgment has been ignored.

As well as the obvious fraternal aims lifted from the Elks (whence they also borrowed their RITUALS AND CEREMONIES and DEGREES), the I.B.P.O.E. also proposed "the expression of ideals, services and leadership in the black struggle for freedom and opportunity"; and in 1926, at the National Convention, it formed a Civil Liberties Department, which the very next year was opposing the segregation of high schools in Gary, Indiana.

Thus provided with clear ideals as well as an agreeable fraternal structure, the I.B.P.O.E. has held its ground as others have declined: 300,000 members in the 1960s and about 450,000 from the late '70s to the '90s.

The Daughters of the Independent, Benevolent, Protective Order of Elks of the World is the auxiliary, and (unlike its white counterparts) is recognized as such by its menfolk. It has been very active in civil rights as well as in patriotism and good works.

Antlers

The Antlers was a junior division of the B.P.O.E., who, despite its refusal to countenance official female auxiliaries, seemed happy enough to approve (in the Grand Lodge session of 1927) "organizations of young men under 21 years of age in the manner prescribed by statute." In fact, the San Francisco Lodge No. 3 had organized a prototypical Antlers lodge as early as 1922.

In 1946, after the Antlers had virtually disappeared as a result of enlistment for World War II, the Grand Lodge Session repealed all references to the Antlers in the *Constitution and Statutes,* and such isolated Antlers lodges as may remain are in much the same position as the Benevolent and Protective Order of Does (below), a sort of semiofficial affiliate in a state of limbo.

Does, Benevolent and Protective Order of the

It is not clear whether this attempted auxiliary antedated the prohibition in 1907 by the Elks of all degrees, auxiliaries and insurance aspects. All that can be said is that the Does still exists, apparently without any centralized authority and even without any fixed ritual, though Schmidt (in *Fraternal Organizations*) says that Corinthians I:xiij is important in at least one version of their ritual, just as it is to the *Daughters of the Improved Benevolent and Protective Order of Elks,* who *are* a recognized auxiliary of the African-American Elks.

Lady Elks

The Lady Elks operate only at a local level, doing good works and providing fraternal support for one another despite the official indifference or even hostility of some of their menfolk.

Royal Purple

In Canada, where the writ against auxiliaries apparently does not run, there is a female auxiliary called the Order of the Royal Purple. It is open to women above 18 who have a close male relative who is an Elk. The ritual is Christian-influenced. An interesting aside is that, traditionally, admission was by BLACKBALL, but the "balls" were cubes.

Elks Mutual Benefit Association

The Elks Mutual Benefit Association was a short-lived insurance branch of the Elks, founded in 1878, but finally crushed by the resolution of 1907, which also banned degrees and auxiliaries.

See also EMBLEM CLUB OF THE UNITED STATES OF AMERICA.

Emblem Club of the United States of America

5516 King Arthur Court, Ste. 16
Westmont, IL 60559
(312) 969-8689

The Emblem Club of the United States of America was founded in 1926 as a social and fraternal club for female

relatives of ELKS, aged 18 and over. There were 41,000 members in 1989. It publishes *Emblem Topics* 10 times a year.

The Emblem Club is effectively (though not officially) a female auxiliary (see AUXILIARIES) of the Benevolent and Protective Order of Elks. Its origins lay in World War I, when a group of Elks' wives used to meet regularly to roll bandages; they incorporated themselves (in the State of Rhode Island) as the Emblem Club in 1926.

Like their husbands and fathers, the members of the Emblem Clubs are fiercely American and strongly conformist. There are committees on Americanism, Color Guard, and the like. Despite this, there is a ban on discussing religion or politics at Emblem Club meetings.

The good works included a national disaster fund, set up in 1964 after the Alaskan earthquake of that year.

Membership has remained more or less constant for many years. It grew very slightly (by about 2.5 percent) in the 1980s. The RITUALS AND CEREMONIES were written by Elks and includes a nondemoninational prayer and a salute to the American flag.

Emeth-Achavah, Ancient Order of

The Ancient Order of Emeth-Achavah is sufficiently ancient to be dead, though it was founded only in 1898 in Denver, Colorado, by one Franklin P. White. The order's organ was called *The Light of Kosmon.* Little beyond this is known about the organization. It was extinct by the early 1920s.

Emperors of the East and West, Council of

The Council of the Emperors of the East and West was one of the many manifestations of early FREEMASONS in France. It was established in Paris in 1758, and involved the following magnificent titles (among others):

Grand Patriarchs Noachite
Sovereign Prince Masons
Substitutes General of the Royal Art
Grand Superintendents and Officers of the Grand and
    Sovereign Lodge of St. John of Jerusalem

It had no significant links with the HOSPITALLERS, or with anything else much, and was absorbed into the Grant Orient (the governing body of French Freemasonry) in 1781.

Encyclopedia of Associations

This is a massive work, published annually by Gale Research (Detroit, Michigan) and available in most libraries. It is invaluable for checking the current membership, address, president or other contact person, and other "vital statistics" of a vast number of organizations.

Each organization is described briefly—typically in 50–100 words—but organizations no longer functioning are omitted.

Endowment Fraternal Organizations

In the late 19th century, a number of short-term endowment orders appeared in the United States, typically based on a five-, six-, or seven-year term. Most were actuarially unsound and soon disappeared; many may only have been reported in obscure local newspapers. A sample of those whose existence was noted (though little more is known about them, in some cases) follows:

American Benevolent Union
Industrial Benefit Order
Industrial Order of America
National Dotare
Order of Pente
Order of Solon
Order of the Benevolent Union
Order of the Royal Ark
Order of the Solid Rock
Order of the World (of Boston)
Order of Vesta
People's Favorite Order
People's Five-Year Benefit Order
SEXENNIAL LEAGUE
Sons and Daughters of America
Union Endowment
United Endowment League
United Order of Equity

See also AMERICAN FRATERNAL BENEVOLENT SOCIETIES.

Eon, Chevalier d'

The Chevalier D'Eon (1728–1810) is one of those mysterious persons who are enthusiastically claimed by a number of secret societies: a swordsman who killed several men in duels, an undercover agent for Louis XIV, and even a lady in waiting to various princesses and queens.

He (or she) seems to have been a genuine hermaphrodite and to have enjoyed *affaires* with members of both sexes. A committee of matrons called upon to determine Eon's sex returned a verdict of "undecided," though at his death the priest declared him a man. He was certainly a member of the HELL FIRE CLUB and may also have joined the FREEMASONS.

Equitable Aid Union of America

The Equitable Aid Union of America was a typical fraternal benefit society founded in 1879 in Columbus, Pennsylvania, by FREEMASONS and others. Although it had 30,000 members in 1896, it failed (like so many others) in the great recession of the late 1890s and went into receivership in 1897. This can have been no great surprise. The death rate had risen from 12.2 per 1,000 per year in 1981 to 17.4 per 1,000 per year in 1895, in which year disbursements were $801,435 and income was $792,895.

Equitable Fraternal Union

P.O. Box 448
Neenah, WI 53215
(414) 722-1574

The Equitable Fraternal Union was incorporated in 1897 as a typical insurance organization with a thin veneer of fraternalism, which later changed to a conventional insurance company.

The veneer of fraternalism adopted by this association was too thick for the *Christian Cynosure* of March 1919, which "proved" that the union had a religious ceremonial in conflict with the belief of a consistent Christian. Eventually, in 1930, the order merged with the Fraternal Reserve Association of Oshkosh, Wisconsin (founded in 1902), and changed its name to the Equitable Reserve Association, otherwise known as the Equitable League of America, under which title it still exists. Then, but without changing the name, the Germania Mutual Life Assurance of Wisconsin was absorbed in 1949, followed by the Royal League of Berwyn, Illinois.

There were 29,733 members in 1993, an improvement on the 29,310 reported in the early 1920s, but some 12,500 less than a decade earlier. The activities of the association are exactly what would be expected: sports for the young, scholarships, social events, and insurance.

Erigen

Erigen (Johannes Scotus Erigena, ca. 815–ca. 877) was a scientist and theologian of the Dark Ages who has been credited with elaborating the first complete synthesis of the Middle Ages. He is believed to have been either Scottish or Irish.

Erigen's reasoning is dense but intriguing and attracted suspicion from more orthodox theologians as early as the 850s. To put it crudely, he seems to have specialized in believing six impossible things before breakfast. For example, the world was both eternal and had been created, the former for logical reasons and the latter for theological reasons. The difference was, he maintained, apparent rather than real.

Although this makes sense to a Buddhist (it is all a part of *Maya,* the World of Illusion), it had the potential for shaking up Christians quite a bit. Such flexibility of mind is also useful to devotees of the more outlandish secret societies, which means that Erigen has been claimed by a variety of erudite if eccentric pseudohistorians to have been a member of a wide variety of secret societies—at the very least, of the GREAT WHITE LODGE.

Esoteric Fraternity

P.O. Box 37
Applegate, CA 95703

The Esoteric Fraternity was founded in 1887 in Boston by Hiram Erastus Butler, a former sawmill operator, who, after losing several fingers in a mill accident, had lived as a hermit in a New England forest for 14 years. During this period, he received revelations from the Lord. Gradually, Butler spoke these revelations to others and, in so doing, found himself gathering a small following. Some dozen men and women pooled their funds and moved to Applegate, California, where they established a quasimonastic commune.

The central tenet of the Fraternity's lifestyle is celibacy, and the population of the original commune, which still exists today, never rose above 40 and, according to at least one source, numbered only three individuals at the beginning of the 1980s. However, the Esoteric Fraternity claims some two thousand "followers" worldwide. In addition to celibacy (which the order believes is a prerequisite to belief in God), the Esoteric Fraternity teaches Esoteric Christianity and a belief in reincarnation — the continual rebirth of old souls. They believe that they are the chosen people, the Order of Melchizedek mentioned in *Revelation*. They believe that their numbers will swell to 144,000 and at that they will come to rule the earth.

Upon his death in 1916, Butler was succeeded by Enoch Penn, who edited the journal *Esoteric Christian*. The periodical ceased publication on Penn's death in 1943. He was succeeded by Lena Crow, who died in 1953, and William Corcco (died 1972). The most recent president of the organization is Fred Peterson, a convert from Mormonism. The Esoteric Fraternity publishes and sells the religious works of Hiram Butler and Enoch Penn.

E-Soter-Ists of the West

Little is known of this order beyond its name and the fact that the word *west* refers to the Americas. The division of the word *Esoterists* must have had some significance. The order flourished in the United States during the late 19th century and is probably now long extinct.

Essenes

The Essenes were a Jewish religious secret society of the pre-Christian era. They would not be particularly important to the present work if they were not the darlings of the proponents of some sorts of conspiracy theories.

The facts (insofar as they are known) are these. The Essenes supported themselves by manual labor, rejected slavery, refused to make or use weapons of war, held all property in common, and lived a communal, monastic sort of life. Nothing is known of their origins, though Josephus suggested that they were very ancient and derived from the Egyptians. Little is known of their RITUALS AND CEREMONIES, and no one ever set down the secrets they actually possessed. They were highly regarded by their contemporaries for their honesty, steadfastness, and refusal to do anything that they knew to be wrong.

The Essenes worked four DEGREES, which were based on the strictness with which they adhered to their beliefs: The stricter the regimen, the higher the degree. The beliefs themselves seem to have been orthodox Jewish for the period. The Essenes were probably all but extinct by the time of Christ.

So much for fact. Speculation is altogether more entertaining. The FREEMASONS claim the Essenes for their own. Some say that Jesus was an Essene, quoting his moral probity as "proof." Others confuse the Essenes with the SICARII, a much more radical sect. Typically, all sorts of pietist historians and conspiracy theorists interweave their own fantasies with quotes from the writers of antiquity, usually without making much attempt to evaluate them or even to verify the sources.

Eternal and Universal Brotherhood of Mystics

The Eternal and Universal Brotherhood of Mystics fell far short of both eternity and universality. It was active in the nineteen-teens, but disappeared without trace by the early 1920s. It used to publish a magazine called *The Mystic Magazine* in Boston, but copies have proved impossible to find. The order's goals were to lead men to a superior and more progressive life, to a life of peace, power, and abundance, to inculcate the oneness of all life and to defend whatever is true, pure, elevated, useful, and practical, no matter what its source.

Ethnic Organizations

Many nationalities have established fraternal or other mutual-support groups in the United States; some of these groups are of considerable antiquity, going back into the 18th century, while others are constantly being formed.

Typically, they were, and are, founded to assist new immigrants and to keep alive the culture and traditions of the old country, and often to educate the children of immigrants (many give scholarships). Some, marked with an asterick in the following list, are in the "old country" and promote cultural exchange. Yet others, marked with a dagger, are fraternal benefit life insurance companies. Many fraternal benefit life insurance groups no longer limit membership to the original ethnic group.

Approximately 200 organizations follow; all are currently active major groups. All are listed in the ENCYCLOPEDIA OF ASSOCIATIONS unless otherwise noted. The figures in brackets are the date of foundation and the membership as of 1994. Groups with fewer than 500 members are not listed here unless they are of unusual antiquity. Associations with their names in small capitals are covered in individual entries.

(Albanian) Free Albania Organization (1940/1,000)

Arab Americans, National Association of (1972/not available)

Armenian General Benevolent Union (1906/22,000)

Armenian Students Association of America (1910/1,500)

Armenian Women's Welfare Association (1921/500)

*(Austrian) Osterreichisch-Amerikanische Gesellschaft (1945/5,000)

Australian-New Zealand Society of New York (1939/2,500)

Baltic Women's Council (1947/not available)

(Baltic) United Baltic Appeal (1966/1,200)

Belarusan-American Association in the USA (1949/2,000)

*Belgian-American Association (1945/4,000)

Byelorussian-American Youth Organization (1950/600)

(Coptic) American Coptic Association (1974/not available)

(Cossack) World Federation of the Cossack National Liberation Movement of Cossakia (1972/9,762)

Croatian Catholic Union of the USA (1921/13,000)

†Croatian Fraternal Union of America (1924/90,000)

Croatian National Congress (1974/6,000)

Croatian Peasant Party (1918/2,500)

Croatian Workers Association of America (1978/4,780)

†Czech Catholic Union (1879/5,323)

Czech Heritage Foundation (1974/1,200)

†(Czech) CSA Fraternal Life (1854/31,235)

(Czech) National Alliance of Czech Catholics (1917/not available)

Danish Brotherhood in America (1882/8,605)

(Danish) Supreme Lodge of the Danish Sisterhood of America (1883/4,000)

Estonian Educational Society (1929/900)

(Estonian) World Federation of Estonian Women's Clubs in Exile (1966/1,000)

Ethiopian Community Mutual Association (1981/500)

(European) National European American Society (1990/740)

Finlandia Foundation (1953/3,000)

*(Finnish) League of Finnish-American Societies (1943/50,000)

(French) Assemblée Nationale des Franco-Americains/National Association of Franco-Americans (1977/7,000)

†(French) Association Canado Américaine (1896/39,000)

*(French) Association France-Etats-Unis (1945/4,000)

(French) Committee of French-Speaking Societies (1927/1,500)

(French) Federation of French American Women (1951/8,000)

†(French) Union Saint-Jean-Baptiste (1900/40,000)

German-American National Congress (1958/30,000)

German Society of the City of New York (1784/600)

German Society of Pennsylvania (1764/1,000)

Germans-from-Russian Heritage Society (1971/2,200)

(German) American Council on Germany (1952/700)

(German) American Historical Society of Germans from Russia (1968/6,000)

(German) Schlaraffia Nordamerika (1939/919)

(German) Steuben Society of America (1919/not available)

Greek Catholic Union of the USA (1892/52,000)

(Greek) American Hellenic Alliance (1983/1,200)

(Greek) American Hellenic Educational Progressive Association (1922/50,000)

(Greek) Chian Federation of America (1974/3,000)

(Greek) Daughters of Evrytania (1948/600)

(Greek) Daughters of Penelope (1929/12,000)

(Greek) Evrytanian Association of America (1944/850)

(Greek) Maids of Athena (1930/1,500)

(Greek) Order of Ahepa (1922/50,000)

(Greek) Panarcadian Federation of America (1931/5,000)

(Greek) Panepirotic Federation of America, Canada, and Australia (1942/55,000)

(Greek) Society of Kastorians "Omonoia" (1910/750)

(Greek) Sons of Pericles (1926/2,000)

(Greek) United Hellenic Voters of America (1974/17,000)

(Greek) see also Macedonian, below

(Hispanic) American GI Forum of United States (1948/20,000)

(Hispanic) American GI Forum Women (1948/6,000)

(Hispanic) League of United Latin American Citizens (1929/110,000)

Hungarian Catholic League of America (1943/not available)

Hungarian Congress (1960/500)

†Hungarian Reformed Federation of America (1896/18,433)

(Hungarian) American Hungarian Federation (1906/not available)

(Indian) Association of Asian Indians in America (1967/1,000)

(Indian) Association of Indian Muslims of America (1985/600)

(Indian) Friends of India Society International (1976/3,000)

(Indian) India-Net (1992/1,700)

(Indian) National Association of Americans of Asian Indian Descent (1980/12,000)

(Indian) see also Native American, below.

†(Irish) Ancient Order of Hibernians in America (1836/191,000)

(Irish) Knights of Equity (1895/10,000)

(Irish) Society of the Friendly Sons of St. Patrick in the City of New York (1784/1,500)

Israeli Students' Organization in the U.S.A. and Canada (1950/2,300)

Italian-American Cultural Society (1957/2,500)

Italian Catholic Federation Central Council (1924/25,000)

Italian Sons and Daughters of America Fraternal Association (1895/5,000)

(Italian) American Committee on Italian Migration (1952/10,000)

(Italian) American Italian Congress (1949/700)

(Italian) National Council of Columbia Associations in Civil Service (1938/105,000)

(Italian) National Organization of Italian-American Women (1980/800)

(Italian) Order Sons of Italy in America (1905/500,000)

(Italian) Unico National (1922/8,000)

Japanese American Citizens League (1929/28,000)

(Japanese) National Association of Japan-America Societies (1979/not available)

(Japanese) Nippon Club (1905/2,600)

Jewish Cultural Clubs and Societies (1953/12,000)

(Jewish) American Federation of Polish Jews (1960/600)

†(Jewish) B'NAI ZION (1908/34,000)

(Jewish) BRITH SHOLOM (1905/6,000)

(Jewish) Free Sons of Israel (1849/5,000)

(Jewish) Labor Zionist Alliance (1972/7,000)

(Jewish) United Order True Sisters (1846/12,000)

†(Jewish) Workmen's Circle (1900/37,000)

(Latvian) American Latvian Association in the United States (1951/10,000)

(Latvian) World Federation of Free Latvians (1960/150,000)

Lithuanian Alliance of America (1886/4,000)

Lithuanian American Roman Catholic Women's Alliance (1914/900)

Lithuanian Catholic Alliance (1886/3,069)

Lithuanian Catholic Students' Association "Ateitis" (1910/500)

Lithuanian Regeneration Association (1948/19,000)

Lithuanian Roman Catholic Federation of America (1906/300,000)

(Lithuanian) Aetetis Association of Lithuanian Catholic Alumni (1920/1,100)

(Lithuanian) Association of Lithuanian Workers (1930/1,600)

(Lithuanian) Knights of Lithuania (1913/4,600)

(Lithuanian) National Lithuanian Society of America

(1949/750)

(Lithuanian) United Lithuanian Relief Fund of America (1944/2,000)

Macedonian Patriotic Organization of U.S. and Canada (1922/not available)

(Macedonian) Pan-Macedonian Association (1947/6,000)

(Manx) North American Manx Association (1928/920)

(Native American) American Indian Heritage Foundation (1973/16,000)

(Native American) American Indian Liberation Crusade (1952/4,000)

(Native American) American Indian Movement (1968/5,000)

(Native American) Arrow, Inc. (1949/2,305)

(Native American) Association on American Indian Affairs (1923/40,000)

(Native American) Council for Native American Indians (1974/843)

(Native American) Manilaq Association (1966/6,500)

(Native American) National Congress of American Indians (1944/2,155)

(Native American) National Indian Youth Council (1961/12,000)

(Native American) National Urban Indian Council (1977/500)

(Native American) Pan-American Indian Association (1984/3,200)

(Native American) Survival of American Indians Association (1964/500)

(Native American) United Native Americans (1968/12,000)

Netherlands Club of New York (1903/1,000)

Nigerian Students Union in the Americas (1962/25,000)

(Nigerian) Organization of Nigerian Citizens (1986/700)

(Norwegian) Norway-America Association (1919/815)

(Norwegian) Sons of Norway (1895/90,000)

(Philippine) Legionarios del Trabajo in America (1924/1,200)

Polish American Congress (1944/3,000)

Polish Beneficial Association (1900/16,246)

Polish Falcons of America (1887/30,000)

†Polish National Alliance of the United States of America (1880/256,997)

†Polish National Union of America (1908/30,000)

†Polish Roman Catholic Union of America (1873/90,000)

†Polish Union of America (1890/9,000)

†Polish Union of the United States of North America (1890/11,698)

†Polish Women's Alliance of America (1898/65,000)

†(Polish) Alliance of Poles in America (1895/18,000)

(Polish) American Federation of Polish Jews

(1960/800)

†(Polish) Association of the Sons of Poland (1903/7,000)

(Polish) Mutual Aid Association of the New Polish Immigration (1949/800)

†(Polish) Northern Fraternal Life Insurance (1895/6,543)

(Polish) Union of Poles in America (1894/7,000)

Portuguese Continental Union of the United States of America (1925/8,688)

Portuguese Society Queen St. Isabel (1898/12,000)

†(Portuguese) Luso-American Fraternal Federation (1957/15,000)

†(Portuguese) Luso-American Life Insurance Society (1957/15,000)

(Romanian) Union and League of Romanian Societies of America (n.d./4,992)

Russian Brotherhood Organization of the U.S.A. (1900/7,832)

†Russian Independent Mutual Aid Society (1931/825)

†Russian Orthodox Catholic Mutual Aid Society of U.S.A. (1895/1,510)

Russian Orthodox Catholic Women's Mutual Aid Society (1907/1,789)

†Russian Orthodox Fraternity Lubov (1912/1,080)

(Russian) Carpatho-Russian Benevolent Association Liberty (1918/800)

(Russian) Congress of Russian Americans (1972/3,000)

(Russian) Fund for the Relief of Russian Writers and Scientists in Exile (1920/517)

(Russian) Lemko Association of U.S. and Canada (1929/1,100)

†(Russian) Orthodox Society of America (1915/2,183)

Saxons see Transylvania, below

(Scandinavian) Independent Order of Svithiod (1880/2,000)

(Scandinavian) Fraternity of America (1915/2,500)

Scottish Heritage U.S.A. (1965/3,000)

(Scottish) American Scottish Foundation (1956/3,000)

(Scottish) Council of Scottish Clans and Associations (1974/450)

(Scottish) Daughters of Scotia (1895/4,000)

(Scottish) St. Andrew's Society of the State of New York (1756/1,000)

(Scottish) Sons of Scotland Benevolent Association (1876/not available)

Serb National Federation (1901/15,200)

(Silesian) World Association of Upper Silesians (1948/not available)

(Slavic) National Slavic Convention (1973/120,000)

†Slavonic Benevolent Order of the State of Texas (1897/60,000)

†(Slavonic) Sloga Fraternal Life Insurance Society (1908/2,247)

†(Slavonic) WSA Fraternal Life (1908/9,500)

Slovak-American National Council (1982/500,000)

Slovak Catholic Sokol (1905/50,000)

†(Slovak) First Catholic Ladies Slovak Association (1892/87,000)

†(Slovak) First Catholic Slovak Union of the U.S.A. and Canada (1890/80,000)

†(Slovak) National Slovak Society of the United States of America (1890/18,000)

†(Slovak) Sokol U.S.A. (1896/12,000)

†Slovene National Benefit Society (1904/47,764)

Slovenian Women's Union (1926/10,000)

†(Slovenian) American Mutual Life Association (1910/16,805)

Spain see Hispanic, above

(Sri Lankan) Association of Sri Lankans in America (1978/2,500)

(Sri Lankan) Eelam Tamils Association of America (1979/800)

Swedish Women's Educational Association (1979/5,300)

(Swedish) United Swedish Societies (1903/4,800)

(Swedish) Vasa Order of America (1896/35,000)

Swiss Benevolent Society of New York (1846/800)

†(Swiss) North American Swiss Alliance (1865/3,350)

(Taiwanese) World Federation of Taiwanese Associations (1974/200,000)

†(Transylvania) Alliance of Transylvania Saxons (1902/8,892)

Turkish-American Associations (1965/15,000)

(Turkish) Assembly of Turkish American Associations (1979/10,050)

Ukrainian Catholic Soyuz of Brotherhoods and Sisterhoods (1976/750)

†Ukrainian Fraternal Association (1910/20,000)

Ukrainian Gold Cross (1931/700)

†Ukrainian National Aid Association of America (1914/8,710)

†Ukrainian National Association (1894/69,000)

Ukrainian National Women's League of America (1925/5,000)

(Ukrainian) Association of American Youth of Ukrainian Descent (1950/1,025)

(Ukrainian) League of Ukrainian Catholics of America (1933/700)

(Ukrainian) Plast, Ukrainian Youth Organization (1911/3,000)

†(Ukrainian) Providence Association of Ukrainian Catholics in America (1912/17,927)

(Ukrainian) Selfreliance Association of American Ukrainians (1947/14,900)

(Ukrainian) United Ukrainian American Relief Committee (1944/1,500)

Welsh National Gymanfa Ganu Association (1929/2,000)

The American Nationalites Council, Americans by Choice, and the Federation of American Cultural and Language Communities are all dedicated to the diverse national and ethnic groups of America.

Eudiaque, Ordre

The Ordre Eudiaque or Eudiacal Order is (or was) a mixture of vague religiosity (including vegetarianism and yoga) and 19th-century hierarchical initiation. The order refused to be bound by dogmas, but apparently had little trouble in being bound by the following DEGREES:

Of the Lesser Mysteries:
    Dociste (Novice)
    Stomatische (Mastery of the physical body)
    Dianoïste (Mastery of autosuggestion and hetero-suggestion)
    Pneumatiste (Who has received the Divine Breath)
Of the Greater Mysteries:
    Prothyme (Novice)
    Grammate (Receiving the gift of writing for the good of all)
    Logiste (Sacred Orator)

From the ranks of the Logistes were chosen the 12 members of the Synedre, or Supreme Council. The aim of all of this activity was (or is) to achieve "Eudia" or serenity.

The society seems to have been invented by a Frenchman, Henri Durville, in the 1890s, though it may have been invented by his father Hector. The order became dormant some time in the 20th century, but may have revived during the early 1970s. It is unclear whether it is active at all today.

Eulis Brotherhood

The Eulis Brotherhood was a splinter group from the HERMETIC BROTHERHOOD OF LUXOR, founded by the tireless Paschal Beverly Randolph (see RANDOLPH, P. B.) in 1868. It drew upon TANTRA, predictably concentrating on the sexual aspect. Randolph believed that sex was the principal dynamic force in nature and was the author of a number of erotic novels. He said that man is the positive pole of manifestation, while woman is the negative. To make life more interesting, the phallus is positive, while the masculine brain is negative, and the polarities are proportionately reversed in women. Randolph advised copulating with a "beloved companion" rather than with a whore, an ignorant virgin, or an adultress, since choosing the right person would result in union with God.

The Brotherhood may have been active after a period of dormancy in the early 1970s, though some authorities insist that this was not the case.

Ezra A. Cook Publications

P.O. Box 796
Chicago, IL 60690
(312) 685-1101

Many of the manuals, written rituals, and so on, of the various secret societies have been "pirated" at various times, and one of the very best sources for copies of them is Ezra A. Cook Publications. This publishing house puts out facsimiles of original material—much of it copyrighted just before World War I—and is an invaluable source of material for the student of secret societies.

It seems that the original intention of the publisher was to expose the wicked ways of the various organizations. The faithfulness of the rendition of the rituals—and the fact that they were very much cheaper than "official" copies in many cases—led, however, to the paradoxical result that the "pirated" manuals are often used by the very members of the society Cook set out to expose.

Several pamphlet-style catalogs, each dealing with a different area of interest, are available from the publisher.

Fabre D'Olivet, Antoine

Antoine Fabre D'Olivet (1768–1825) studied the ILLUMINATI, the PYTHAGOREANS, the Egyptian MYSTERIES, and more. He is most closely associated with the theory of "correspondences" between heaven and earth, the perceived and the unperceived, the sensible and the imperceptible. The upshot was a pseudo-Pythagorean form of FREEMASONS with an agricultural bent. The three DEGREES became Aspirant, Laborer, and Cultivator. He also synthesized several religious traditions, at least to his own satisfaction.

Families, Society of

The *Société des Famillies* commenced, like some Irish secret societies such as the UNITED IRISHMEN, as a legitimate and open society that was suppressed and then refounded as a secret society. Its forebear was the *Société des Droits de l'Homme* ("Society of the Rights of Man"), which had become illegal as a result of French laws prohibiting the formation of a society of more than 20 people without government permission.

Although the older, legal society mustered about 3,500 members at the time of its closure, the newer society had probably reached a maximum of 1,200 members when it was raided (and its gunpowder factory was closed) in 1836. It then changed its name to *Les Saisons* ("The Seasons") and eventually instigated an armed revolt on May 12, 1839. When this failed, the organization struggled along and even survived a schism in 1846, which gave rise to a new group, the Dissidents. They were in the forefront of the Revolution of 1848, leading the attack on the Foreign Ministry, but after the establishment of the new Republic, their love of intrigue overcame their political acumen, and they plotted against the new provisional government just as they had plotted against the monarchy before.

The accession of Napoleon III as emperor on December 2, 1850, marked the end of Families, Seasons and Dissidents alike.

Fascist Organizations

Fascism is easier to recognize than to define, and, besides, one man's fascism is another man's conservatism. Also, a purist might argue that the only true Fascist Party was Mussolini's in Italy. The word may, however, be used to group together a number of right-wing political parties, particularly of the 1920s and 1930s, many of which spawned secret societies.

The word *fascist* comes from the Latin *fasces,* a bundle of sticks symbolic of the Roman Senate, and is used as a symbol of how a single stick may be broken, but a bundle will endure. The archetypal fascist was Hitler, an evil genius who saw that by carefully slanting his appeal to the working class and lower middle class, he could achieve immense popular support for even the most repulsive strategies. Whereas communism has historically been most successful in developing countries, where it promises a better future than has ever existed (the exact opposite of Marx's own predictions), fascism has historically been more successful when coupled with nationalism in a country that seeks to regain past glories—whether real or imagined.

American Fascist Societies

Americans are understandably loath to label any home-grown organizations as "fascist," though outsiders have been less kind. Many self-styled PATRIOTIC ORGANIZATIONS sail very close to fascism, while Lantoine (*Les Sociétés Secrètes Actuelles en Europe et en Amérique,* page 129) lists the New York-based American Christian Defenders as an anti-Semitic political secret society in the United States in the 1930s. Lantoine also offers the Christian American Crusade of Los Angeles (page 125), the Christian Democrats of Dallas (page 129), the Christian Protective League of Mobile, Alabama, the Constitutional Christian Party of San Francisco, the National Gentile League (founded and headed by Donald Shea), the American Gentile Protective Association, and the American Gentile Youth Movement (which believed that "for peace and prosperity, each nation must exterminate its own Jews") (the last three on pp. 128–29).

British Fascist Societies

See BLACKSHIRTS.

French Fascist Societies

Following World War I, the French left-wing and Communist parties were grouped together as the "Popular Front" and were opposed by an equally broad right wing, including *Action Francaise; Croix de Feu,* formed in the late 1930s; and *Volontaires Nationaux,* again from the late 1930s.

German Fascist Societies

Germany's N.D.S.A.P., "Nazi" or National Socialist Workers' Party, is the best known of all fascist parties, but when it began it was only one of many. Some joined forces with the Nazis more or less gracefully; others fought the Nazis and lost. Other German fascist societies between the world wars included the following:

1. Black Reichswehr—a heavily militaristic *Freikorps* (independent army)
2. *League of Patriotic Combat*—an amalgamation of militaristic or merely thuggish groups, including the Oberland Union (see below), the Reichsflagge (see below) and more; they took part in Hitler's "beer-hall *Putsch*" in 1923
3. *Monarchists Steel Helmets*—nominally dedicated to the restoration of the kaiser, the Monarchists Steel Helmets were ready to throw in their lot with other right-wing organizations as long as they opposed the Weimar Republic

4. *Oberland Union*—these were another of the constituents of the League of Patriotic Combat (see above)
5. *Reichsbanner Schwarz-Rot-Gold*—seems to have been a precursor of or rival to the Nazi Party
6. *Reichsflagge*—one of the groups that joined the League of Patriotic Combat (see above)
7. *Stahlhelm*—probably identical to the "Monarchists Steel Helmets," above; if they were not identical, they were hard for an outsider to tell apart
8. *Unterland*—another group that joined the League of Patriotic Combat (see above)
9. *Werewolves*—the werewolf (*Werwolf*) was a popular symbol with the neopagan German right, and it is not surprising that the name was adopted by a fascist group in the 1920s.

Federal Life Insurance of America

2335 South 13th Street
Milwaukee, WI 53215
(414) 645-2407

The Federation Life Insurance of American was formed in 1911 as a fraternal benefit life insurance society for Poles or Americans of Polish descent. There were 4,476 members in 1994.

It owes its origins to the Federation of Polish Catholic Laymen, founded in Milwaukee, Wisconsin, and was originally a Polish "pressure group." It asked for the appointment of Polish bishops, demanded a more equitable distribution of wealth among parishes, and elected lay officials to administer parish funds.

In 1913, the organization incorporated and began to offer fraternal insurance, shortly thereafter changing its name to the Federation of Poles in America. In 1924, it changed its name again, to the present form; in 1940 it set up a women's branch.

With this history aside, it is a fairly typical small fraternal benefit society, involved in good works and social events (with a Polish ethnic slant) as well as selling insurance.

Federation of Masons of the World

1017 East 11th Street
Austin, TX 78702
(512) 477-5380

As with so many organizations within FREEMASONS, the Federation of Masons of the World can be dealt with only briefly, lest the Craft dominate the book.

The federation purports to be dedicated to unifying all established Masonic jurisdictions, regardless of their origin. As is common in the Craft, however, this statement is not in one-to-one correspondence with verifiable fact. A brief telephone call to the headquarters elicited a very cold "No" in response to the question, "Does this [dedication to unification] include Prince Hall [African

American] Masonry?" A further call to a past senior officer of Prince Hall Masonry confirmed that this is so.

Felicidade, Ordem de

The Ordem de Felicidade (Order of Felicity or Happiness) is a secret society of navigators or sailors founded in Paris in 1742. It was initially allied with FREEMASONS and worked four DEGREES: Cabin-boy, Captain, Chief of Squadron, and Rear-Admiral. The LODGE was called a Squadron, a lodge meeting was a Voyage, and so forth.

Originally limited to persons of elevated character, good humor, and knowledge of the ways of the sea, in later years it first became recreational and androgynous, then admitted people of all sorts. Shortly thereafter, probably still in the 18th century, it dissolved.

Fendeurs

The Fendeurs ("Hewers") was founded in Paris on August 17, 1747, as a social fraternal order open to both sexes, but disappeared after a few decades. The Fendeurs was certainly extinct by about 1850.

The organization was founded by the Chevalier Beauchaine, a prominent French member of the FREEMASONS and the Master of the Golden Sun LODGE in Paris. The order purported to be based on the "Good Cousins" of the forests of the Jura and the Bourbonnais region, and made the usual protestations of equality and brotherhood. From the way it was accepted in fashionable Paris, though, it seems to have had more to do with pastoral fantasies and *divertissement* than with the honest wood cutters to whom, for example, the Abbé Barruel believed it could be traced.

Forest Masonry consisted effectively of two DEGREES, namely Fendeur (also known as *Charbonnier* or "Charcoal burner") and "Prodigal Converted." Higher degrees may have once existed, but, if so, they early fell into disuse. These obsolete orders were *Scieur* ("Sawyer") and *Charpentier* ("Carpenter").

Apolitical almost to the extent of being antipolitical, the Hewers seem to have been given to good fellowship and an earthy good humor. Their lodge was in the open air and was known as a *Chantier* (wood yard), while the Master was known as the *Père Maître* or Father Master. In the four huts on the east side of the *Chantier* were Cousin Hermit, Cousin Winedresser, Mother Cateau, and the Bear. Cousin Hermit and Mother Cateau tipped water over the candidate, the latter's offering being soapy; Cousin Winedresser presided over a barrel of wine, and his hut was marked by a stick with a cabbage impaled on it; and the Bear wrestled with the candidate, though the horseplay does not seem to have been particularly violent. Other officers took the names of trees: Cousin Oak, Cousin Elm, and so on.

The male oath (see OATHS) was as follows (version of 1788):

I promise and swear on my word of honor, on the bread and wine of hospitality, and in the presence of the Father Master and the worthy Cousins of this Wood-yard, never to betray in any inn the secrets of the worthy Cousins, Comrades Hewers. I promise never to try to oust any cousin, also never to change the felling of the woods arranged by the worthy Cousins. I swear never to have carnal intercourse with the wife of a Cousin, unless she asks me three times. I swear to defend, help and aid Cousins, and to put them back on their path if they stray; and to lodge them in my hut; or if I fail in my oath, I consent to have my head severed from my body by all the axes of the Wood-Yard, and to be exposed in the depths of the forest to be there devoured by wild beasts.

There was a certain disregard for bourgeois convention, and a determination to enjoy oneself come what may; the line "unless she asks me three times" is quite magnificent, and traditionally Gallic. The women's oath was shorter, its obligations, if anything, even less onerous:

I promise and swear on my word of honor, on the symbol of cleanliness, in the presence of the Father Master and the worthy Cousins of this Wood-yard, never to betray the secrets of the worthy Cousins, worthy Companions Hewers, and if I fail in my promise, I consent to be soaked, beaten, and twisted like a bundle of dirty linen. Then to be cast to the bottom of the vat of the worthy and benevolent Cousin Cateau, then to be exposed for forty days in the deepest Forest to live only on acorns like a sow, and to be devoured by wild beasts.

The PASSWORDS, countersigns, and catechisms indicate a similar disinclination to take the secret society fad too seriously:

"How old art thou?"
"As old as pleasure."
"Why?"
"Because pleasure is of every age."

Or:

"What is the best wine one can drink?"
"That which you drink in your neighbor's house, because as a rule, it costs you nothing."

It is a sobering thought that many of those who disported themselves in the *Chantiers* probably went to the guillotine a few decades later; but their attitude tells us a good deal about pre-Revolutionary French society.

Ferguson, Charles W.

Charles W. Ferguson wrote *Fifty Million Brothers: A Panorama of American Lodges and Clubs* (New York: Farrar and Rinehart, Inc., 1937), easily the most entertaining of all the standard American works on secret societies and fraternal orders.

The book has, however, a number of significant flaws for the modern reader. First, it is of course considerably out of date. Second, it is by no means comprehensive. Third, it is not invariably accurate: Dates and details are sometimes treated in a rather cavalier fashion. Fourth, it is extremely American-oriented, with considerably less treatment than is appropriate of parent orders in Britain and elsewhere.

Fifth Order of Melchizedek and Egyptian Sphinx

This secret society, open to men and women, was known also as the Solar Spiritual Progressive Order of the Silver Head and Golden Star. Members claimed it had been founded several thousand years "A.M.," which means "ante-Melchizedek" or "after Melchizedek." The last appearance of this order was in Boston, in 1894.

For further information on Melchizedek himself, see Genesis 14:18-20, and the beginning of Chapter VII of the Epistle to the Hebrews. By the conventional reckoning of Bishop Usher, this King of Salem would have reigned in about 1900 B.C.

Filadelfi

The Filadelfi (as in "Philadelphia") was one of the many Italian political secret societies of 1815-25 or thereabouts. It was militaristic in character and dedicated to a free Italy. Its seal was a figure of Liberty wearing a Phrygian cap and bearing a *fasces*.

Fils d'Adam

The Fils d'Adam is a shadowy group, which is apparently still active in France. Reportedly, its members include necrophiles, who hire young prostitutes to make themselves up as corpses, and individuals who stage—or have staged in the past—attempted sexual unions between a woman and a snake in order to atone for Original sin. The only location ever reported for the society—or its activities—was a villa in Villacoublay.

If the Fils d'Adam is a group of individuals with a taste for socially questionable or repugnant sexual activity, it is possible that it uses various cover names in order to evade the authorities. Certainly, the Fils d'Adam is entirely unrelated to the SONS OF ADAM founded in Kansas in 1879. Nor is it as sensational as the 15th-century European order known as the Adamites or Adamiani, who were accused of child murder and nocturnal orgies.

First Catholic Slovak Ladies Association

24950 Chagrin Boulevard
Beachwood, OH 44122
(216) 464-88015

A fraternal benefit life insurance society founded in 1892. Membership is now open to all, but it retains a strong Catholic Slovak appeal. It publishes *Fraternally Yours*, monthly. There were 87,000 members in 1994.

The First Catholic Slovak Ladies Association (originally "Union" rather than "Association") is a typical fraternal benefit society, of a fair size but declining (there were 95,000 members in 1979 and 102,000 in 1965). Programs provide strong support for the Catholic church, nursing and other scholarships, social events with a Slovak slant, youth programs, and a home for the aged. Despite the name, membership is open to both men and women.

First Catholic Slovak Union of the United States of America and Canada

6611 Rockside Road
Independence, OH 44131
(216) 642-9406

A fraternal benefit life insurance society for Catholic Americans of Slovak descent, founded in 1890. It publishes *Jednota Newspaper,* weekly, and *Furdek* and *Kalendar,* annually. There were 80,000 members in 1993.

The *Prva Katolicka Slovenska Jednota* is a typical ethnic fraternal benefit society with insurance features, larger than most (though considerably smaller than a decade earlier, when it stood at 105,000), and with the range of activities that one might expect from the name of the organization: support for the Catholic church (each LODGE is affiliated with a Catholic parish), scholarships, summer camp, sporting activities, events promoting Slovak culture, and so forth. Surprisingly, in view of its Catholic nature, the Union has an oath (see OATHS). It also has most of the other paraphernalia of a secret society, including a plethora of officers.

Flamel, Nicolas

Nicolas Flamel (1330-1417) was the most noted French alchemist of the Middle Ages, allegedly a Hermetic adept. He is therefore claimed as a member of innumerable French secret societies, much as Roger Bacon (see BACON, ROGER) is claimed in the English-speaking world.

Flamel claimed to have mastered the transmutation of metals, but in 1380 fell afoul of a French royal edict banning all such research and ordering the destruction of all alchemical laboratories. His life seems to have been reasonably comfortable, and several books attributed to him have appeared since his death.

Fleas, Royal and Exalted Order of

The Royal and Exalted Order of Fleas was mentioned in the *Colorado Citizen,* published (somewhat improbably) at Columbus, Texas, on June 27, 1923. Nothing more is known of it.

Fludd, Robert

Robert Fludd, or Robertus de Fluctibus, as he preferred to be known, lived from 1574-1637 and actually *was* a member of the ROSICRUCIANS, unlike many whose names are claimed by the adherents of the Rosy Cross. He was a strange combination of mystic, philosopher, and natural scientist, and painted with a broad brush: His most famous (and certainly widest-ranging) work was *Summum bonum, quod est verum magiae, cabaael, alchymiae, fratrum Rosae Crucis verorum verae subiectum* — "The Utmost Good, which is True Magic, the Cabbala, Alchemy, the Brotherhood of the Rosy Cross, Made Known." As the *Encyclopaedia Britannica* put it, "The opinions of Fludd had the honour of being refuted by J. Kepler, P. Gassendi and M. Mersenne . . . Thomas de Quincy considered him to have been the immediate . . . father of Freemasonry."

Pietists among the FREEMASONS have mixed feelings about him; as a genuine historical figure who really did take an interest in the undifferentiated slurry of proto-Masonry, he is valuable, but to attribute too much to him would be to throw away almost five millennia of more or less carefully contrived history and legend.

Foresters

According to its own legends, the Foresters began in medieval times in the royal forests of England, and admitted men of other professions as early as 1840. This looks, however, very like a pietist attempt to claim parity with the FREEMASONS. In any case, the suppression of many secret societies in England in the wake of the French Revolution means that such claims cannot easily be checked. There are still several varieties of Foresters today, but there were many, many more in the past. Their talent for schism amounted almost to genius.

Ancient Order of Foresters

c/o Paul Perry, 182 Kulana Street, Hilo, HI 96720, (808) 935-2351

This was the first schismatic order, derived from the Royal Order of Foresters (below) in 1832. It came to the United States in 1864, but in 1874 the parent lodge refused to grant autonomy to the American order, and in 1879 the Independent Order of Foresters (see below) was formed and promptly shifted its headquarters to Canada. The Ancient Order is reputed to survive to this day in Britain, but in the United States it is on its last legs and is represented by yet another semischismatic order, the Ancient Order of Foresters of the Pacific Jurisdiction, based in Hilo, Hawaii. According to the ENCYCLOPEDIA OF ASSOCIATIONS, the rolls were quoted as 300 for 1994; this was down from 336 a decade earlier. In 1896, the order counted 119,000 members.

Canadian Foresters Life Insurance Society

P.O. Box 850, Brantford, ON, Canada N3T 5S3, (519) 753-3461

This was founded in 1879 as the Canadian Order of Foresters, by secession from the Canadian branch of the Independent Order of Foresters (see below). It survives to this day, and boasted 21,000 members in 1994. The society publishes *The Canadian Forester*, quarterly.

Catholic Association of Foresters

347 Commonwealth Avenue, Boston, MA 02115, (617) 536-8221

Founded in 1879, this fraternal benefit society was formerly called the Massachusetts Catholic Order of Foresters. In 1994, it had 12,000 members.

Catholic Order of Foresters

This is one of the larger branches and appears not to be schismatic. It was formed to provide Foresters' benefits for Catholics who might otherwise have difficulty with the "secret society" aspect of other orders. It was founded in 1879 and is open to Catholics of both sexes, over the age of 16. It had 145,000 members in 1994.

Founded in 1883 as the Illinois Catholic Order of Foresters, this order changed its name to the present form in 1887; women have been eligible for membership since 1952. Boys and girls up to the age of six may be enrolled as Rangers; those from seven to 15½ as Forest Rangers; and thereafter as Foresters.

There are three administrative levels: the Subordinate Court, the State or Provincial Court, and the High Court. The three DEGREES are the Degree of Protection, the Exalted Degree, and the Legion of Honor Degree. The order follows the best traditions of friendly societies by visiting the sick and awarding college scholarships, but it is also a legal reserve fraternal life insurance society.

In 1965, the Catholic Order of Foresters absorbed the Catholic Central Union (1877), a society for Catholics of Czech ancestry; in that year, there were 191,000 members in almost 1,300 courts, 1,170 in the United States and 101 in Canada.

Companions of the Forest of America

250 West 57th Street, Room 209, New York, NY 10107-0208, (212) 246-1330

The Companions of the Forest of America was founded in 1885 as a fraternal order and mustered only 3,000 members in 1994.

Foresters of America

The Foresters of America was originally founded in 1889 as the Ancient Order of Foresters of America, when it broke away from the Ancient Order of Foresters, who still owed allegiance to a subsidiary lodge nominally under the jurisdiction of the Ancient Order of Foresters in England. The Knights of the Sherwood Forest were an appendant order. The Ancient Order of Foresters of America changed its name to the style given above in 1895, but the order appears no longer to exist.

Independent Order of Foresters

789 Don Mills Road, Don Mills, ON, Canada M3C 1T9, (416) 429-3000

The Independent Order of Foresters (I.O.F.) was the result of a schism from the Ancient Order of Foresters in 1879. It functions as a fraternal benefit insurance society in Canada, the United Kingdom, and the United States, and admits adults of both sexes. There were approximately 1.4 million members in 1994.

The I.O.F. is the biggest Foresters organization and claims direct ancestry from the original orders. It now functions principally as an insurance mutual benefit society, though orphans of Foresters and old and indigent Foresters are cared for by the order.

There are no fixed lower age limits for initiation, and there is only one degree. Members are required to believe in God (see DEISM), but the order is nonsectarian.

The I.O.F. has the customary plethora of officers, including (at Local Court level) the Chief Ranger; Court Deputy; Past Chief Range; Vice Chief Ranger; Recording Secretary; Financial Secretary; Treasurer; Public Relations Officer; Orator; Promoters; Senior Woodward; Junior Woodward; Senior Beadle; Junior Beadle; Trustees; Financial Committee; and Organist. The last is expected to "conduct the musical exercises and services of the Court, thereby adding to the effectiveness and pleasure of the meetings."

In addition to the insurance aspect, for those who like traditional fraternalism there are social occasions arranged by the Local Courts, which also raise money for (or volunteer time to help) many charitable organizations. Three charities mentioned in *The Independent Order of Foresters — What Does It Mean?* are Big Brothers, Prevention of Child Abuse, and Spina Bifida.

The *Robin Hood Band* is the junior boys' order, and the IOF also absorbed the *Royal Templars of Temperance* in 1931; the *Modern Brotherhood of America* in the same year; the *Catholic Mutual Benefit Association* in 1952; and the *Order of Scottish Clans* in 1972.

Independent Order of Foresters of Illinois

This was a secession from the Massachusetts Catholic Order of Foresters (below), and was founded in Chicago in 1879. In its turn, in 1883, it gave rise to the Catholic Order of Foresters (above).

Irish National Order of Foresters

The Irish National Order of Foresters seems to have been founded independently (i.e., not schismatically) in Dublin in 1876, as a beneficiary fraternal order. By the end of the 19th century, it was operating also in Australia, Canada, the United Kingdom, and the United States. It is unclear whether it still exists, and if so, in what form.

Junior Foresters of America

The Juvenile Foresters was an English junior auxiliary, though it is not clear of which branch of forestry (it was probably the Ancient Order). The Junior Foresters of America was the junior branch (12–18 years of age) of the Foresters of America, above.

Massachusetts Catholic Order of Foresters

This order was founded in Boston in 1879, partly in the interests of self-government (as distinct from remaining subordinate to England) and partly to remove Catholic objections to oaths and other trappings of more traditional secret societies. The Knights of St. Rose were the second degree of this order, which seems to be extinct.

National Catholic Society of Foresters

446 East Ontario Street, Suite 900, Chicago, IL 60611, (312) 266-6250

The National Catholic Society of Foresters was founded in 1891 as the Women's Catholic Order of Foresters and changed its name in 1966. It is effectively an insurance company, admitting Catholics of all ages and both sexes. The society publishes *Junior Junction,* bimonthly, and *National Catholic Forester,* quarterly. There were 59,100 members in 1994.

Pennsylvania Order of Foresters

This was a short-lived schism, apparently from the Foresters of America (see above).

Royal Order of Foresters

The Royal Order of Foresters was the first to be legally constituted, in 1813. An intriguing aspect of their early RITUALS AND CEREMONIES was initiation by combat with cudgels, which was apparently abandoned in about 1843. After the schism of 1832, which gave rise to the Ancient Order of Foresters (above), the Royal Order apparently lost most of its members (including whole Courts) to the newer organization.

United Order of Foresters

The United Order of Foresters existed in two forms. One was the American rump of the (Canadian) Independent Order of Foresters, which resulted from the schism of 1879 and changed its name in 1881; it soon disappeared. The second avatar was organized in 1894 by members of various other Foresters groups, and appears also to be extinct today.

Frankists

The Frankists are one of the schools of Kabbalists (see KABBALAH), following the teachings of Jakob Frank

(Yankieve Leibowitz, 1720–91), a Galacian Jew who was the most notorious of the false messiahs.

In his travels through the Balkans, Frank met followers of Shabbetai Tzevi (1626–76) and claimed to be the reincarnation of that messianic leader. In 1751, Frank claimed to be the messiah himself and, four years later, in Poland, formed the sect that bears his name. The Frankists abandoned traditional Judaism, claiming that, as followers of the Zohar, the most important work in the Kabbala, they were above moral law. Because of their belief in the Zohar, they were often called Zoharists.

Frankist practices included organistic sexual rites, which became so odious that the Jewish community branded the group as heretics in 1756. This act was sufficient to earn the Frankists the protection of Roman Catholic authorities, who saw the order as a means of promoting dissension among the Jews. As to Frank himself, he converted to Catholicism and publicly committed his followers to baptism. No less a figure than Augustus III, king of Poland, stood godfather to Frank at his baptism. Despite this, the insincerity of Frank's conversation soon became apparent, and he was imprisoned by the Inquisition in 1760. Frank was freed 13 years later by invading Russians, and he settled in Offenbach, where he proclaimed himself a baron and lived in a magnificence financed by his followers.

The sect survived its founder's death in 1791, as Frank's daughter Eve took up the reins of leadership. She quickly ran the order into bankruptcy, however, and following her death in 1816, the Frankists disintegrated, its baptized adherents being absorbed by the Catholic church.

Franks, Order of Regenerated

The Order of Regenerated Franks was a political brotherhood founded in France in 1815. It imitated the ceremonies of the Masons. Not to be confused with the FRANKISTS.

Fraternal Monitor

520 North Dearborn Street
Chicago, IL 60610-4901
(312) 836-4400

The Fraternal Monitor, established in 1890, is published monthly and is devoted to the financial and social aspects of fraternalism. It is edited by James A. Bullew.

Fraternal Patriotic Order of Americans

A group founded in 1913 with the classic (and quite contradictory) goals of KNOW-NOTHINGS: the first, separating church and state, and second, promoting the reading of the Bible in public schools.

Fraternitus Saturni

The Fraternitus Saturni (Brotherhood of Saturn) was founded in Sweden and Denmark in the 17th century and had lodges in Poland also. It was revived by one Gregory Gregorius, who founded the Pansophic ("All Wisdom") LODGE in Berlin in 1921; Aleister Crowley (see CROWLEY, ALEISTER) was one of those who attended the opening. The Nazis banned the order, along with others of the same kind, in 1933, and some of its leading lights were apparently imprisoned. After the war, it was reconstituted again, as a German neo-Rosicrucian order (see ROSICRUCIANS). For once, it does not seem to have been an organization devoted to one world government, but its prewar members may have been involved in intelligence work, principally for the Allies.

Freemasons

Just about everything concerning Freemasonry is shrouded in mystery or in the even more impenetrable *Nacht und Nebel* of Masonic pietism. "Operative" (stone-working) masons banded together in the 14th century or earlier, while "Accepted" Masonry began in about 1600 and became important about a century later. Today, there are probably 10 million adherents worldwide.

Freemasonry is unquestionably the largest, oldest, and most influential of all secret societies. As such, it warrants the longest single entry in this work, as well as a number of subsidiary entries.

Precisely because it is so large, so old, and so influential, Freemasonry is also the best documented of all secret societies. In many libraries, there are more books dedicated to "the Craft" (as Masons call it) than there are on all other secret societies put together. Accordingly, the difficulty in compiling a brief outline of Freemasonry lies more in deciding what to omit than in trying to discover more about the Brotherhood. "Brotherhood," like "John's Brothers" and "Brethren of the Mystic Tie," is one of several names under which Freemasonry may go.

Sources of Information

There are said to be more than 50,000 books on the Craft, and not one of them tells the whole story. The vast majority of accounts, verbal or written, can be divided into two effectively opposing camps. On the one hand, there are the Masons themselves, whose enthusiasm for their organization is understandable and often praiseworthy. On the other hand, there are those who, for various reasons, want to do Masonry down: the apostates, the sensationalists, the conspiracy theorists, those with tender religious sensibilities, and others. Even when an author purports to be impartial, it is rare for him to remain entirely dispassionate through his account. In light of this, the following *caveats* should be entered:

1. Any generalization about the Craft, based upon the experience of individual Masons or groups of Masons,

is necessarily imperfect. Freemasonry changes to suit the times, but its individual members and lodges may change or deviate from the mainstream still more—and they cannot know what other Masons are doing.

2. One gets from the Craft what one brings to it. For self-seekers, it is an excellent tool for advancement. For the clubbable, it is a first-class club. For the mystic, there is a fine range of mysticism. And for the little boy who loves dressing up and pretending to be important, it is the ultimate little boys' club.

3. The Craft in Britain is very different from the Craft in the United States, and both are different from the Craft in Europe or in South America. This argument is enlarged below.

4. In order to be initiated, one must take oaths and make affirmations, which may offend the religious sensibilities of many. Again, this point is enlarged below.

The Origins of Freemasonry

The masons who worked on the great medieval cathedrals (and to a lesser extent, on palaces, bridges, and other public works) were necessarily itinerant; they typically ranged all over Europe. Neither noble nor serf, they were not bound to any one place; they were truly free masons.

Wherever they gathered to work, they established LODGES. At first, they probably rented rooms at an inn, or rented a house, though in the larger cities where there was plenty of work, they might eventually buy property or presumably even build a lodge. These original lodges served two purposes. One literally was to provide somewhere to stay, a lodging place. The other was to provide a meeting place and headquarters for masons, where a Master Mason (who had served his apprenticeship and was almost as much architect as stone-cutter) might be recognized and distinguished from impostors. In this sense, they functioned as a combination TRADE UNION and Better Business Bureau. The easiest way to distinguish Master Masons in an age that was commonly both lawless and illiterate was by secret GRIPS and PASSWORDS.

The Secrets of Freemasonry

The original secrets of the Freemasons were almost certainly trade secrets, probably combined with mutual assistance in the form of names of contacts and so forth, though a panoply of ritual and ornament had grown up as early as the 14th century and was consolidated in the 15th. A text of 1425 that names Euclid as the founder of Masonry and traces the Craft back to the Tower of Babel and the Temple of Solomon must owe at least part of its content to wishful thinking. This text is a part of the "Old Charges," a collection of over 100 documents that are regarded by modern Masons as the main guide to the precepts of Masonry. The history of the Old Charges is by no means clear, and there is not even any firm

agreement on how many there are, but a popular figure is 115.

The modern secrets are either very secret indeed or substantially nonexistent. According to Masonic pietists, the innermost secrets were conveyed to Adam by God; were concealed and preserved during the Flood in a cave dug by Enoch; and were codified in the Temple of Solomon. The tradition of the transmission of these secrets is of course Masonic; there seem to be no non-Masonic corroborations of their nature of existence.

Masonic Calendars

Masonic calendars are an excellent example of Masonic thinking. Master Masons traditionally date their calendar from the creation of the world (*Anno Lucis*), calculated by the simple expedient of adding 4,000 to the common Christian calendar, which is probably a convenient rounding from Bishop Usher's traditional calculation of the creation at 4004 B.C.

Royal Arch Masons are slightly more intrepid mathematicians, and add 530 years to the common Christian calendar. This *Anno Inventionis* is said to commemorate the date of the commencement of the Second Temple in Jerusalem, by Zerubbabel.

Other choices include adding 1,913 to the common calendar to get *Anno Benefacio,* dating from the blessing of Abraham by the High Priest Melchisedek, who is presumably to be confused with King Melchizedek; this is the Calendar of the Order of High Priesthood. Then the Cryptic Masons add a straight 1,000 years, ostensibly dating their *Anno Depositionis* from the foundation of the Temple of Solomon. Knights Templar (the Masonic variety, not the originals) use the year of the foundation of the Templars as their starting point, choosing 1118 as being as good a year as any. And Scottish Rite Masons, the most intrepid mathematicians of all, add 3,760 to the common era up to September in each year, and 3,761 from September to December inclusive: this is the *Anno Mundi,* or "Year of the World."

Speculative Masonry

Although the original Freemasons were actual workers in stone, honorary membership is recorded as early as 1600 in the Edinburgh Lodge. The 17th century saw a considerable growth in "speculative" Masonry, the Masonic term for the admission of members who were not stone workers or "operative" masons. In 1619, the London Masons' Company founded the "Acception" in about 1619 for speculative Masons; "Accepted" or "Gentlemen" Masons were not a part of the company, but they were admitted to the lodge on payment of twice an operative mason's dues. Elias Ashmole (1617–92, of Ashmolean Museum fame) became a Mason in 1646; Sir Christopher Wren (1632–1723) was also said to have joined, though conclusive evidence is impossible to find.

The reasons for the development of speculative Masonry are unclear, but four causes seem like:

The first is a genuine interest in the world at large, and especially in building and architecture. This was the time when the Grand Tour began to gain in popularity among young gentlemen wishing to broaden their education.

The second is mystical. John Bunyan's *Solomon's Temple Spiritualized* was an allegory that drew parallels between the builder's craft and the process of spiritual development. The same process of allegory can be seen in the "conceits" of the Metaphysical poets of the previous (16th) century. The study of these allegories was not, however, dogmatic; it was more in the nature of free-thinking inquiry, for this was the dawn of the Age of Reason.

The third is that by the beginning of the 17th century, operative Freemasonry was dead on its feet. The last great Gothic building in England was arguably the Chapel of King's College in Cambridge, which was completed in about 1512. No doubt Freemasons worked on baroque buildings, but the age of the architect was arriving. It is interesting to speculate upon the extent to which Freemasonry was responsible for the appearance of architects. Regardless of that, the Acception enabled traditionally minded operative Masons to keep their lodges alive, which might otherwise have lapsed entirely.

The fourth and final reason is that in all probability, Masonic lodges functioned as agreeable clubs where one could meet like-minded people in interesting and convivial surroundings. The gentleman of the Acception might feel that operative masons were below him socially, but he no doubt regarded them (with or without being patronizing) as the "salt of the earth." And if he did not care for their conversation, why, there were always the other gentlemen to talk to.

Throughout the 17th century, and even into the early 18th century, the individual lodge was very much the basis of the Craft—a logical consequence of the original purpose of Freemasonry. As the number of speculative Masons grew, though, so did the pressures for a more formal organization.

Masonry in the 18th Century

In 1717, four London lodges united to form the United Grand Lodge, and their authority rapidly spread throughout England and into the colonies. Scotland and Ireland retained their own Grand Lodges, however. In 1722–23, the *Book of Constitutions* was drawn up by Dr. James Anderson, a minister of the Church of Scotland, at the request of the United Grand Lodge.

The *Book of Constitutions* formalized Masonic ritual and (in all probability) added a few new ideas of its own. The legend of HIRAM ABIF (King Solomon's Master Mason) dates from this period, as does the representation of the Craft as a pyramid, with the Grand Master at the apex; this symbol is still seen on U.S. currency.

Among Anderson's innovations were attempts to formalize the Landmarks and Charges of Masonry. There is still dispute about these, and even about their precise number—there was a further revision of Masonic doctrine as early as 1738—but the Landmarks are aspects of Masonry that may not be changed, and the Charges are guidelines to Masonic behavior.

Twenty-five major Landmarks, widely though not universally agreed upon, are summarized below. Those in quotation marks are taken directly from Mackey's *Encyclopaedia of Freemasonry;* they are quoted verbatim because understanding their full meaning requires Masonic exegesis. Masons are highly enthusiastic, though not always highly competent, symbolists, interpreters, and exegetes.

1. Recognition of a Brother Mason
2. Division of Symbolic Masonry into three Degrees
3. The Legend of the Third Degree [Hiram Abif]
4. The election by the Craft of the Grand Master
5. The prerogative of the Grand Master to preside over any assemblage of the Craft in his jurisdiction
6. The prerogative of the Grand Master to grant dispensations for conferring degrees other than at regular initiations
7. The prerogative of the Grand Master to give dispensations for opening and holding lodges
8. The prerogative of the Grand Master to make Masons at sight
9. The necessity for Masons to congregate in lodges
10. The government of a lodge by a Master and two Wardens
11. The necessity that a lodge, when congregate, shall be guarded ("tiled," in Masonic parlance)
12. The right of every Mason to be represented in all meetings of the Craft
13. The right of appeal to the Grand Lodge against any decision made in a local lodge
14. The right to visit and sit in every convened lodge
15. Exclusion of unknown visitors without "strict trial and due examination"
16. Autonomy of local lodges and lack of mutual jurisdiction
17. "Masons are amenable to the laws and regulations of the Masonic jurisdiction in which they reside"
18. Masons must be male, free-born, unmutilated, and legally adult
19. Belief in the existence of a Supreme Being
20. Belief in the existence of a life after death
21. Displaying the Book of Law within the lodge [the Bible in Christian countries, the "book of faith" in other countries]
22. Equality within the lodge
23. Secrecy

24. "The foundation of a speculative science using an operative art is used in Masonry for the purpose of religious or moral teaching"
25. The immutability of Landmarks

In practice, Masons can accept or reject any of these Landmarks, but if they do, they may be shunned or declared "clandestine" (see below) by other Masons. The Charges are more widely agreed on. The wording of each Charge varies greatly, but the following heads are standard:

1. Of God and Religion
2. Of the Civil Magistrate supreme and subordinate
3. Of Lodges
4. Of Masters, Wardens, Fellows, and Apprentices
5. Of the management of the Craft in working
6. Of behavior:

> In the Lodge while constituted
> After the Lodge is over and the Brethren not gone
> When Brethren meet without strangers, but not in Lodge
> In the presence of strangers not Masons
> At home and in the neighborhood
> Toward a strange Brother

Schism and Reunification

The authority of the United Grand Lodge and the *Book of Constitutions* was not universally recognized in the early 18th century, and in 1751 there came a schism.

Understandably, as befitted a body of medieval worthies who found much of their work in building cathedrals, operative Masons had mostly been strongly Christian, and their ritual reflected this; prayers were said in the name of Jesus Christ, and Christianity was taken for granted.

The more radically minded gentlemen of the Acception, though, were imbued with the modern ideas of DEISM. They wanted the Christian part of the Craft downplayed considerably and were uncomfortable with the old order. The Reverend Anderson himself, in the *Constitutions,* said, " 'Tis now thought more expedient only to oblige them to that religion to which all men agree, leaving their particular opinions to themselves." To be charitable, this may be interpreted as an exhortation for Catholics and Protestants to work together, though in the light of subsequent developments it is impossible to guess the intentions of anyone.

Another faction of the Acception, composed mostly of lodges that had not joined the 1717 Grand Lodge, was keen on expanding the DEGREES to include the Holy Royal Arch (see ROYAL ARCH MASONS, GENERAL GRAND CHAPTER OF), to which a Master Mason (formerly the highest degree) might be "exalted." Given that Masonry was originally a craft guild, and that the vast majority of guilds have by tradition recognized only Apprentice (Entered Apprentice), Journeyman (Fellow Mason), and Master, many Masons saw the Royal Arch as an unnecessary complication.

In 1751, because of these differences of opinion, the "Antients" formed their own Grand Lodge: They were pro-Christian and worked the Royal Arch, while the 1717 Grand Lodge leaned toward deism and refused to recognize the new degree.

The two Grand Lodges reunited in 1813 when two brothers, the Duke of Sussex and the Duke of Kent, were the two Grand Masters. The Antients dropped their objection to the watering down of Christianity, while in a remarkable form of words the 1717 Grand Lodge declared that the Royal Arch did not constitute a new degree, but was merely a culmination of the other three degrees and completed the making of a Master Mason.

The Royal Arch was not, however, ruled by the Grand Lodge but rather by a Grand Chapter (with subordinate chapters), and to a large extent there remained two overlapping organizations. Today, perhaps one Master Mason in five in Britain is also a member of the Royal Arch.

Despite these and other doctrinal quarrels, speculative Freemasonry was exported from Britain almost from its inception. Throughout the 18th century it boomed, especially in Protestant lands. Lodges sprang up like mushrooms: Frederick the Great of Prussian (1740–86) is credited with introducing the Craft into his country, and was Grand Master. Many other pre-Unification German princes and princelings were Masons, too, including Frances I of Austria (1708–65).

A lodge was formed in Paris in 1725 by expatriate Englishmen, and although it was officially discouraged by Louis XV in 1737, it was often tolerated, at least unofficially. The rival lodges of the Grand Orient and the Grand Lodge were united in 1773. A similar "blind eye" treatment existed in Spain and the various Italian states, though the Swiss and some other Protestant states actually imposed bans: the Netherlands in 1735, Sweden and Geneva in 1738, Zurich in 1740, and Berne in 1745.

The credentials of some of these lodges were dubious. Liberal admixtures of ROSICRUCIANS and their attendant Egyptian (or pseudo-Egyptian) rites made their way into the Craft, and the famous and influential Count Cagliostro (1743–93; see CAGLIOSTRO, ALLESANDRO) was to a large extent a charlatan, despite the influence he wielded among German and Russian Masons; among his innovations were women's lodges under a "Queen of Sheba." He finally lost considerable credibility by attaining a life span some 5,505 years shorter than the 5,557 years he claimed to be possible.

During the 18th century, there were heavy political overtones in many lodges. Scottish Freemasons, seeking a Jacobite restoration, used the Craft as a political tool.

There was a temporary alliance between them and Rome (especially the JESUITS) to try to secure the return of a Catholic monarch. This was the era of Michael Ramsay ("the Chevalier Ramsey") and the Kilwinning Lodge. By 1738, though, the Pope had had enough, and Clement XII issued a bull forbidding Catholics to join or support Freemasonry on pain of excommunication.

This was in itself probably a political move, designed to reinforce the temporal authority of the papacy, and it was widely ignored, though Freemasons were, in fact, imprisoned and tortured in Spain and Portugal, and it was unwise to profess Freemasonry in Poland. Papal hostility was reiterated frequently; Benedict XIV issues a reaffirming bull in 1751, and between 1821 and 1902 there were no fewer than 10 more encyclicals denouncing the Craft and reaffirming the bull of Clement XII. The encyclical of Leo XVIII (promulgated in 1884) is particularly strongly worded.

In Britain's American colonies, prominent Freemasons included Benjamin Franklin, George Washington, Alexander Hamilton, the Marquis de Lafayette, Paul Revere, and John Paul Jones. The first American lodge was founded as early as April 13, 1733, and many more followed. No less than treason was plotted in the lodges. It was from the Green Dragon, the meeting place of St. Andrew Lodge in Boston, that the instigators of the Boston Tea Party set out. Both the Declaration of Independence and the American Constitution are prime examples of the kind of rationalism (with mystical/deist overtones) that characterized the Craft in the Age of Reason, and American paper currency is to this day fairly awash with Masonic symbolism.

According to Ferguson (*Fifty Million Brothers*), who described Washington's Continental Army as "a Masonic convention," both sides maintained and scrupulously respected one another's "field lodges." The Patriots even went so far as to return under guard of honor Masonic emblems and other materials abandoned during a hasty retreat. The same source alleges that after the recapture of Philadelphia in 1778, Washington donned full Masonic regalia and marched in the company of 300 fellow Masons to a Masonic service.

On the other side of the Atlantic, Freemasons initially supported the French Revolution as a reaction against the oppression of the *ancien régime;* but during the Terror, when the Jacobins came to the fore, the voice of reason — or of the middle and aristocratic classes — was no longer welcome. Freemasonry was banned in France in 1792, and the former Grand Master, the Duc d'Orléans, went to the guillotine in 1793. The Craft was legalized again in 1798.

Masonry in the 19th Century

The tradition of political activism behind lodge doors continued unbroken from the 18th century to the 19th. At the very end of the 18th century, in 1796, there were strong Masonic components in the UNITED IRISHMEN and in the "Conspiracy of Equals," a French movement of 1796 holding that the original ideals of the Revolution had been compromised. The Philhellenic Movement, dedicated to Greek freedom, culminated in the establishment of a semi-independent Greece in the 1820s, while the Decembrists were less lucky in their uprising against the Tsar in 1825. In Italy, there were the CARBONARI.

Unsurprisingly, such political activity made the Freemasons unpopular in many quarters, and populist anti-Masonic movements were often violent. This was true for the first third or even the first half of the nineteenth century, and was world wide; see, for example, ANTI-MASONS and the MORGAN AFFAIR.

Despite such setbacks, the Craft recovered and steadily increased in both numbers and complexity throughout the latter part of the 19th century. Some offshoots went on to a separate existence of their own, such as the Carbonari and the (modern) ILLUMINATI, while others remained within Masonry.

It is also worth noting that while American Freemasonry remained for the most part relentlessly committed to excluding African Americans (see Black Freemasonry, below), the Grand Lodge of England continued to show itself willing to induct non-whites. In India, Parsees were admitted as early as about 1860, followed by both Hindus and Moslems.

20th-Century Masonry (General)

In the 20th century, the relationship among church, state, and the Craft remained uneasy. Masons in many continental European countries have traditionally been strongly anti-Catholic — this is especially true in Belgium, Italy, Portugal, and Spain — and Latin America suffers the same sort of strain. In Scandinavia, by contrast, the nobility and even the monarchy are traditionally Masonic and may hold the highest officers. The same is true to a very large extent in England.

Freemasonry did not do very well under either communism or fascism, though. In Soviet Russia, it was banned in 1922; Franco closed all Masonic lodges in Spain after the Civil War (the Masons were avowedly Loyalist); and by 1935, German Freemasons were about as well regarded by Hitler as were Jews, Gypsies, and homosexuals. Lodges were closed, paraphernalia destroyed, and members sent to concentration camps. For the rest of the century, Freemasonry would also be banned by other dictatorships of the left and the right, including that of Fidel Castro in Cuba.

The proliferation of degrees of initiation, which had begun in the early 18th century and continued apace, was so complex by the late 20th century as to defy analysis even by a Freemason. Different lodges recognize different authorities and are on varying terms with one another, while different individual Masons follow different paths within the Craft.

Furthermore, the origins of many degrees is pure fantasy, such as the supposed links between the Kilwinning Lodge and the Knights Hospitalers, or the Templar connections. Because each State Grand Lodge is independent, variety is inevitable; and it seems that ever since the *Book of Constitutions* was written in 1722–23 and then revised in 1738, there has been a constant tendency to "improve" the rituals. The description of the ritual that follows is, therefore, a guide to general practice only; individual lodges may have ceremonies that are very different. Even so, the general form of modern initiations is so well reported in so many books that a brief description of the ceremony of the first degree (that of "Entered Apprentice") will suffice here.

Admission and Ritual

To begin with, the candidate must request admission. Traditionally, Masons never recruit anyone, though they have been known to inform people that if they were to apply, they would likely be well received.

The minimum age for admission varies, typically from 18 to 25, but it is 21 in most jurisdictions. It may be reduced if the candidate's father is a Mason.

The candidate must profess belief in a supreme being (though not necessarily in a Christian God) and must be sound in mind *and body;* theoretically, anyone who is maimed in any way is excluded. After scrutiny by an admissions committee, the candidate is put up for admission by general ballot by BLACKBALL. This must be unanimous, but the candidate gets two chances; one black ball in the first ballot is said to "cloud" the vote, which is then retaken.

The lodge room of the BLUE LODGE is traditionally on the second or third floor, to discourage eavesdroppers. There is an altar in the center of the room. On it rests a Bible, and the square and compasses. Around this burn three tapers. Over the Master's chair is a large "G": some say for God, some say for Geometry.

The candidate is divested of his coat and trousers, and goes barefoot; he slips off the left sleeve of his shirt to expose his left breast. One theory holds that this is to demonstrate that he is not a woman in disguise.

On his right foot, the candidate is "slipshod," or wears a slipper; in most lodges he is given a pair of trousers to wear, though in the days of long-tailed shirts, this was by no means always the case. All metal objects, such as coins, watch, or tie pin, are taken away from him. A noose, often of blue silk, is put about his neck. He is "hoodwinked," or blindfolded.

The symbolism of all this is to remind him that he was accepted penniless, directionless, and partially clad, and that he should in the future help fellow Masons who may be so distressed.

After a formal request for admission, and a question-and-answer session regarding his intentions, he is admitted to the Lodge Chamber, where the point of a sword or dagger (or of a pair of compasses) is pressed against his left breast. This is the "Shock of Entrance" and is accompanied by the homily:

> Mr. [Name], on entering this Lodge for the first time, I receive you on the point of a sharp instrument pressing your naked left breast, which is to teach you, as this is an instrument of torture to your flesh, so should the recollection of it ever be to your mind and conscience, should you attempt to reveal the secrets of Masonry unlawfully.

After the reading of biblical passages and the kissing of the Bible, the candidate swears the well-known oath, in which he pledges secrecy on peril of

> having my throat cut across, my tongue torn out by the root, and buried in the sand of the sea at low water mark, or a cable's length from shore, where the tide regularly ebbs and flows twice in twenty-four hours.

There is no record of this penalty ever having been enforced, and some lodges weaken it greatly by continuing:

> . . . or the more effective punishment of being branded as a willfully perjured individual, void of all moral worth, and totally unfit to be received into this worshipful Lodge.

The noose (or "cable tow") is removed, and when the Master asks the candidate what he desires most at this time, he gives the answer—as he has been advised to do— "Light," whereupon the hoodwink is removed.

He is presented with a 24-inch gauge, representing the 24 hours of the day; a mallet, representing the forces of conscience; and a chisel, representing the sharpness of conscience. Explanations of these "Mysteries" are given, and at the end of the ceremony, he is said to have "worked the first degree."

For the Fellow Craft degree, there are more sartorial indignities, this time with the slipper on the left foot and the right breast bared. The tools of this degree are the plumb, square, and level, and the oath involves "having my left breast torn open, my heart and vitals taken hence and given as prey to the beasts of the field and the vultures of the air." There is no record of this penalty having been exacted, either.

To become a Master Mason, the initiate bares his breast on both sides, rolls up his trouser legs, and volunteers to keep his secrets "under no less penalty than that of having my body severed in two, my bowels taken from thence and burned to ashes, the ashes scattered before the four winds of heaven."

Once again, there seem to be no reliable records of this ever being done. It is also unclear whether the oath concerning chastity that was quoted by Captain

Morgan—"I do promise and swear that I will not violate the chastidy of a Master Mason's wife, mother, sister or daughter, I knowing them to be such."—is still administered—or indeed, whether it was ever widely administered.

On top of these three original degrees, there are innumerable others, including Cryptic Degrees, the Thirty-Three Degrees of the Scottish Rite, the innumerable degrees of the ORIENTAL RITE OF MEMPHIS AND MISRAIM, and more. Degrees were still being invented well into the 20th century, where the focus of inventiveness shifted from France to the United States in the mid to late 19th century.

In practice, modern Freemasonry is as far divorced from the revolutionaries of the 18th and early 19th centuries as it is from the mystics of the 17th century and the actual stonemasons of the 13th century. There are now effectively two branches, the United States and the rest of the world.

20th-Century Masonry: Outside the United States

England, the home of speculative Freemasonry, remains strongly Masonic. In his book *The Brotherhood* (London, 1984), Steven Knight paints a somewhat chilling picture of the power of the Craft, with special reference to the law and politics.

The royal family is heavily (though not necessarily enthusiastically) involved in Freemasonry. Queen Elizabeth is Grand Patroness, though Prince Philip is reputed to be an indifferent Mason, who has never troubled to rise above the rank of Entered Apprentice. He apparently joined at the insistence of King George VI, more or less as a condition of receiving his consent to marry the Princess Elizabeth. The Prince of Wales and Heir Apparent has expressed an aversion to joining.

As already mentioned, the Royal Arch is worked by perhaps 20 percent of all British Master Masons, and there are many who (like Prince Philip) never even feel the need to become Master Masons. The Thirty-Third Degree is not the everyday ambition in the U.K. that it appears to be in the United States. This is not to say that Freemasonry is less important in Britain than in the United States; rather, it is lower-key, a part of an Establishment that is vastly stronger (and more flexible and more permeable) than any in the United States.

As in the United States, being a Mason is only a part of joining this Establishment, membership in which is reinforced by having gone to the "right sort" of school and to the "right" university, as well as coming from the "right sort" of family. The more traditionally minded Briton's chauvinism on this last point is impossible for many Americans to grasp.

As befits a traditionally minded organization, British Freemasonry has no truck with such innovations as the SHRINERS, and indeed had offered suspension or expulsion to any British Mason who becomes involved with such frivolites. On the other hand, it cannot be denied that the apparently unshakable self-confidence of the Grand Lodge of England (G.L.E.) has enabled it to admit individuals and even to charter whole lodges with an openhandedness that would never be acceptable to many American Masons.

In the rest of Europe, Freemasonry is, if anything, even more Establishment-minded than it is in Britain. Its power is extremely hard to gauge, but, as already indicated, it enjoys royal and noble patronage in many northern European countries. Even in Italy, the *Propaganda Due* (see P2) lodge was the center of a major government scandal in the 1980s. Masons and non-Masons alike have alleged that one reason why the Catholic Church has been so anti-Masonic is that even princes of the Church have been attracted to it, and that, as a result, the Holy Father himself fears its power.

20th-Century Masonry: In the United States

In the United States, social class is largely defined first by what you earn, and then by what you do. This means that Freemasonry is both more, and less, homogenous than in Europe.

It is more homogeneous because the appeal of the Craft is mostly to the professions and would-be professions. It is less homogenous because success in a profession cuts across social classes to a far greater extent than it does in Europe.

In the United States, there is much more emphasis on money, not merely as a qualification for membership, but also for spending on initiations and charities. As already mentioned, many more Americans than Europeans go in for the Royal Arch and other higher and side degrees, and this costs money.

Another major difference is the prevalence in the United States of "fun" organizations such as the TALL CEDARS OF LEBANON OF NORTH AMERICA, the Shriners, and so forth. As already mentioned, these are beneath the dignity of the Grand Lodge of England, but the reason for their prevalence in the United States is not hard to see. Most or all American lodges prohibit the consumption of alcohol on lodge premises, and there are even some that take a dim view of brethren who are engaged in the sale of wines, beers, and spirits. By contrast, G.L.E. lodges are rarely if ever "dry." This lingering nod to Prohibition could well explain why American Masons need "fun" organizations.

All in all, the influence of Freemasonry in the United States is probably a great deal patchier than it is in Europe. In some areas—especially in small towns, where the judge and the sheriff are elected and might well be part of a Masonic clique—there may well be more abuse of the Mystic Tie than in Europe. The same might also be true at the highest levels of government, given the number of presidents who have been claimed as Masons. But by and large, because there is no single, dominant American "Establishment" in the European sense, the overall impact of the Craft on the body politic is probably a good deal less than on the other side of the Atlantic. Strong evidence of this is that each American state operates its own Grand Lodge, which it takes to be at least equal in standing with the original Grand Lodge of England.

Black Freemasonry

In what was formerly the British Empire, Masonic lodges varied in their attitude toward admitting nonwhites, but by the dissolution of the Empire there were many mixed lodges, many of which survive to this day. As already mentioned, India led the way.

Until recently, few American Masonic lodges even made the pretence of being open to African Americans; though, ironically, black Freemasonry in the United States dates back to the time of the Revolution. Prince Hall and 14 other gentlemen of color were probably initiated as early as 1775 into Military Lodge No. 441 under the jurisdiction of the Grand Lodge of Ireland, and after obtaining a charter from the Grand Lodge of England in 1784, Prince Hall founded African Lodge No. 459 in 1787. This was the first of many thousand African-American lodges, generally known as Prince Hall lodges.

For many years, American Masons refused to acknowledge the existence of these lodges; or worse, they condemned them as "clandestine" (see False Freemasonry, below). The Grand Lodge of New York went so far in 1851 as to declare that African and Native Americans were "unfit" for the Craft. Other white Grand Lodges have had an on-again, off-again relationship with Prince Hall Masonry, beginning with the Grand Lodge of Washington in 1897. The usual pattern was that a white state lodge agreed to recognize Prince Hall Masonry, other lodges served their connection with the white lodge, and finally recanted its heresy.

Although Prince Hall lodges freely admit whites, and although Prince Hall Masons are admitted to white lodges outside the United States, the venom of some white lodges has in the past been extraordinary. There are tales of white Masons being suspended or expelled for acting as pall bearers at the funeral of a black brother.

False Freemasonry

The attractions of Freemasonry have always been such that many people, denied admission for one reason or another to the orthodox lodges, have either set up "clandestine" lodges or have been gulled by lodges that are entirely fraudulent. Of course, the authority to set up a lodge has never been clearly defined or universally agreed upon, so lodges that are "clandestine" in that they do not operate with the approval of one Grand Lodge may be quite legitimate in the eyes of another. A lodge may also be declared clandestine, even if it has hitherto been legitimate, if it offends against the Landmarks (see above).

A fraudulent lodge, on the other hand, normally sets up in business with an impressive sounding name and then proceeds to part as many fools as possible from as much money as may be extracted in as short a time as possible; the money comes from the sale of initiations into a wide range of degrees. Some are of genuine origins, or pirated, and others are cut from the whole cloth. Ferguson, in *Fifty Million Brothers*, quotes the National Grand Lodge of the Independent Order of Freemasons of the United States of America, Inc., which parted many would-be Masons from their money "until the courts intervened" in about 1935 or 1936.

Freemasonry and Mormonism

A number of writers have seen so many points of resemblance between the Church of Jesus Christ of Latter Day Saints (MORMONS) and Freemasonry that it has been alleged that Mormonism was lifted wholesale from the earlier organization. Others have been less able to see the connection, except insofar as both have rituals, passwords, and patriarchal temples.

Freemen's Protective Silver Association

The Freemen's Protective Silver Association was bizarre even by the standards of secret societies. It was established in Spokane, Washington, in 1894 "to unite the friends of silver under one banner to battle for the white metal and to wage war against the gold monopoly." Bankers and lawyers were not eligible to join.

The association has to be seen in the context of the "sound money" presidential election of 1896, when advocates of a gold standard were pitted against those who wanted a silver standard and against "bimetallists," who wanted silver coined at one-sixteenth the value, weight for weight, of gold. The political ramifications were clear enough — "silver" states and mining interests against "gold" states and mining interests, and the West trying its strength against the East, where the gold was stored and where the bankers were. It is no clear, however, why a legal and essentially political organization should wish to manifest as a secret society, complete with RITUALS AND CEREMONIES.

It is by no means inconceivable that the "sound money" issue was a carefully orchestrated attempt to divert attention from the real problems of the United States, which were being raised by the Populist Party, itself an outgrowth of the Knights of Labor and the GRANGE. The Populists were essentially a grassroots reaction to the Robber Barons of the Gilded Age and advocated nationalization of railroads and telegraphs as well as a graduated income tax. Their defeat in the 1892 elections marked the effective disappearance of socialist ideals in the United States for a decade or more, though they made some gains in the midterm elections of 1894 and can be credited with taming the worst excesses of the Gilded Age. Without the secret trappings of movements like the Freemen's Protective Silver Association, the Populists might well have amounted to something more significant.

By the time of the 1896 election, the association had spread throughout the Pacific Coast states and as far as Missouri and boasted some 800,000 members—almost a manifestation of mob hysteria. After the election, the whole issue just fizzled out, and the association declined rapidly in importance, together with the SILVER KNIGHTS OF AMERICA and the Patriots of America, who pursued the same ideas east of the Mississippi.

Freesmiths, Ancient Order of

Der Alte Orden der Freischmiede is alleged to descend from the VEHMGERICHT, but its first appearance in the United States was in Baltimore in 1865. LODGES were called "smithies," and the officers were the Sun (chief officer), the Moon (deputy chief) and so on through the firmament. There were six lower degrees, and three higher: Grand Marshal, Grand Master, and Cavalier. There were fraternal benefit aspects: $5 a week sick pay, $125 on the death of a brother's wife, $500 to the heirs of a brother. The Freesmiths are extinct today.

Free Sons of Israel

250 Fifth Avenue, Suite 201
New York, NY 10001
(212) 725-3690

The Free Sons of Israel were founded in 1873 in New York City as a fraternal benefit society, with insurance, for Jews. The organization now admits both sexes, aged 18 or older and publishes the *Reporter* three times per year. There were 8,000 members in 1994.

Originally founded as the Independent Order of Free Sons of Israel, this is a typical ethnic fraternal benefit society remarkable only for its antiquity—1849 is a much earlier founding date than most such societies can boast—and for the fact that membership has been remarkably constant at around the 10,000 mark for several decades, although it has fallen off recently. As usual, there are insurance and fraternal divisions; social programs; an emphasis on the cultural and religious heritage of the members; scholarships and sports for younger members; and help for the aged.

French Rite

The French (or Modern) Rite is, with the SCOTTISH RITE and YORK RITE, one of the three main rites of modern FREEMASONS. It was invented by the Grand Orient of France in 1786, with the usual nods toward antiquity, and works the following DEGREES:

1. Apprentice
2. Fellow-Craft
3. Master
4. Elect
5. Scotch Master
6. Knight of the East
7. Rose Croix

This rite is practiced in France, Brazil, and Louisiana. It is often referred to by its French name, *Rite Français ou Moderne*.

Friendly Societies

Friendly societies (the term is British) are essentially *financial* mutual aid associations; that is, they collect money from their members in times of health and disburse it in times of sickness or infirmity and (usually) for funeral expenses. Other benefits may also be payable: sums on the birth of children, or (under the Friendly Societies Act of 1896) the relief or payment of members when on travel in search of employment, or in case of shipwreck or damage to boats or nets, or insurance against loss by fire of the tools of one's trade.

Friendly societies may or may not have the trappings of fraternal RITUALS AND CEREMONIES. In England, the earlier friendly societies often were ritualistic, but later ones were not; and of those that survive, ritualism is both increasingly rarely encountered, and of declining importance where it is found.

The historical evolution of friendly societies is interesting, in that although such things have always existed in every civilized society, they have changed their form in order to meet changing social circumstances. As the *Encyclopaedia Britannica* points out, "no definite historical links" have been traced between the medieval guilds and modern friendly societies, though some of the friendly societies that existed in England in the 20th century were founded before the end of the 17th century.

The mid to late 18th century was the first period of major expansion, specifically of the ritualistic groups. The ODD FELLOWS were in existence by 1745; the Independent United Order of Mechanics was founded in 1757; the United Ancient Order of DRUIDS came in 1781. According to Sr. F. M. Eden's treatise of 1801, *Observations on Friendly Societies for Maintenance of the Industrious Classes during Sickness, Infirmity, Old Age and other Exigencies*, there were at the turn of the century some 7,200 friendly societies, many of them financially unsound.

Parliament first took note of the burgeoning movement in 1793, but seems to have been as concerned with controlling potentially subversive societies (remember, this was in the wake of the rebellion of the American colonies and of the French Revolution) as with making sure that the societies were financially sound and treated their members equitably.

Then, in the mid to late 19th century, ritual played a much smaller part in the workings of such organizations as the *Hearts of Oak Benefit Society* (founded in 1842) and the *National Deposit Friendly Society* (founded in 1868).

Under the National Insurance Act of 1911, the friendly society movement was drawn into association with the national health scheme. Under the arrangements of this act, a friendly society could become an "approved society" for National Insurance purposes, while still carrying on its wholly voluntary operations as a friendly society. This arrangement lasted until 1948, when the National Insurance Act of 1946 came into effect, severing the connection between friendly societies and National Insurance. This was done partly in ideological grounds—the New Jerusalem leftists were very much in the ascendant, and were interested principally in centralized socialism—and partly as a genuine streamlining operation.

Since then, and with the growth of the "welfare net," the importance of friendly societies has waned in Britain; although many still exist, they have (like American benefit societies) either declined or changed their base to provide a wider range of insurance services.

Friends of Greece

The Friends of Greece was a Sicilian secret society founded in 1821 and dedicated to seeking Italian independence from Austria. Their name is a reference to the contemporary Greek struggle for independence from Turkey. The Friends of Greece may also have served as a vigilante group patrolling the bandit-plagued roads of 19th-century Sicily.

Friends of Truth

The Friends of Truth were an antiroyalist secret society recruited in Paris, along Masonic lines, among students, artists, tradesmen, and denizens of the Latin quarter in about 1820. They were seen as successors of the ASSOCIATED PATRIOTS and, like them, agitated to restore the Republic. The French police quietly suppressed them.

Galilean Fishermen, Grand Order of

The Grand Order of Galilean Fishermen was a beneficiary society for African Americans of both sexes, founded in 1856 in Washington, D.C., by one Anthony S. Perpener. It displayed great eclecticism in its choice of symbols, claiming descent from FREEMASONS and using the fish (*ichtheus*), the passion cross, the rose, and the letters INRI—which most people would associate with the Passion of Christ, but which Masons identify with the 18th degree of the Ancient Accepted SCOTTISH RITE.

Sick and death benefits were paid, and its early date of founding makes it one of the first organized fraternal societies in the United States. It claimed 56,000 members in 1897, in lodges scattered from New England to the Gulf of Mexico. It was active as late as 1980, but is now apparently defunct.

Garduna

The Garduna, a Spanish criminal secret society, owed its foundation to Ferdinand V of Castile and Leon (1452–1516), also known as Ferdinand the Catholic. Ferdinand's greed was tempered only by a self-preserving cunning, which stopped him from going too far. He founded the precursors of the Garduna, using brigands as a means to harass Moors, Jews, and heretics. It was a straightforward program of royally sponsored robbery and murder.

When the brigands refused to give a large enough share of their booty to the crown, Ferdinand retaliated by invoking the law. At this, the brigands united as the Garduna, a criminal secret society, which centralized and formalized the preexisting situation of an extralegal, criminal society.

There were nine DEGREES, in groups of three, together with signs and passwords, and there was a record book that detailed the dealings of the Garduna with the Inquisition between 1520 and 1667. In effect, the Garduna became an unofficial weapon of the Inquisition. This was discovered during a Government raid in 1821, after which the society's Big Brother (*Hermano Mayor*) or Grand Master and 16 others were hanged in 1822. The Garduna was reputedly reorganized in South America, where it may yet flourish to this day.

Gentlemen's Clubs

The London gentleman's club has undergone many changes; has been savagely lampooned for centuries, often by its own members; has not infrequently gone bankrupt (there are far fewer traditional gentlemen's clubs today than there were on the eve of World War II); is a byword for living in the past; and yet survives.

The original gentlemen's clubs were mostly coffee houses, though some were taverns. They served two main functions: as a place to talk, and as a place to gamble. Throughout the late 17th century, the whole of the 18th century, and the years of the Regency, they differentiated themselves increasingly from their origins until they became, in effect, homes away from home, catering to what might broadly be called the Establishment. In the Victorian and Edwardian eras, many newer clubs were opened in frank imitation of the older ones. Between the two world wars, they declined slowly; several lost their premises to bombs during World War II; and since then, their decline has been all but precipitate.

Traditionally, each club catered to a different clientele. The Rag (the Army and Navy Club) was for junior officers in the armed services; the United Service Club catered to senior officers; the Athenaeum (in the happy phrase of Anthony Lejeune) "has a formidable reputation for intellectuality, gravity, deep respectability and episcopacy"; the National Liberal Club, as the name might suggest, traditionally let anyone in; and so forth. Also, some clubs are considered more socially acceptable than others. For example, the "Chauffeurs' Arms," otherwise known as the Royal Automobile Club, may have attracted noble automobilists and even royal patronage, but it would be extremely bourgeois to belong only to the R.A.C. and to no other clubs.

Even among the greatly reduced ranks of London gentlemen's clubs in the late 20th century, these distinctions still hold true. Those who wish for an excellent and competently illustrated history are referred to *The Gentlemen's Clubs of London*, written by Anthony Lejeune and illustrated with photographs by Malcolm Lewis (Dorset Press, 1984). The clubs covered are as follows:

The American Club
The Army and Navy Club
The Arts Club
The Antenaeum
The Bath Club
The Beefsteak
Boodle's
Brooks's
Buck's
The Caledonian Club
The Canning Club
The Carlton Club
The Cavalry Club
The City of London Club
The City University Club
The City Livery Club
The Devonshire Club
The East India and Sports Club
The Garrick Club
The Gresham Club
The Guards' Club
The Hurlingham Club
The Junior Carlton Club
The Lansdown Club
The M.C.C.
The National Liberal Club
The Naval and Military Club
The Number Ten Club
The Oriental Club

The Oxford and Cambridge Club
Pratt's Club
The Press Club
The Public Schools Club
The Reform Club
The Roehampton Club
The Royal Automobile Club
The Royal Air Force Club
The Royal Thames Yacht Club
The St. James's Club
The St. Stephen's Club
The Savage Club
The Savile Club
The Travellers' Club
The Turf Club
The United Service Club
The United University Club
White's Club

A few of these clubs—notably the Beefsteak, in its original form—had initiations and RITUALS AND CEREMONIES, but these were mostly lighthearted things (reminiscent of the CITY OF LUSHINGTON), which disappeared in due course. Admission was traditionally determined by the old BLACKBALL system, and if one's candidate were blackballed, the decent thing used to be to resign. Today, membership is usually handled by a membership committee. The ordinary members have a say only if they feel strongly that a particular person should not be admitted, though members will usually be "sounded out" by the committee.

The most remarkable thing about many London clubs is that they are the precise opposite of what most people would expect a club to be; that is, they are not places for socializing, but places for *getting away from* other people. One may (or may not) have a few friends whom one meets at the club, but one does *not* go to a club to mingle, as one might at an ELKS lodge or a SHRINERS convention. Even at those clubs where one is expected to talk to people without being introduced, such as the Beefsteak, the membership is small and changes but slowly. Only a very few clubs operate on a really large membership base.

The decline of the clubs is the result of a number of different causes, most notably the following:

The decreasing gap between rich and poor. In the days when a club servant was paid £60 a year and a club member might spend £10,000 a year without blinking (plenty spent five or 10 times as much), it was obviously easier to maintain premises and servants. Today, *after taxes* (and there were no income taxes in the days just described), a club servant would consider himself poorly paid at £10,000, while a club member might consider himself comfortably off with an annual income of as "little" as £50,000.

The rise of the "week-end." When one lived in 19th-century London, or if one left one's country estate for "the season," the club was a popular place of resort on a Saturday evening. If one were in the professions or in trade, one would normally work on Saturday mornings, and the whole of Saturday afternoon might also be spent at the club. Since the 1920s, it has, however, become increasingly usual for Londoners to go to the country for the weekend, and for provincials to come to London for the weekend.

Uxoriousness. The modern pattern of husbands and wives spending time together was unknown to the well-to-do in the heyday of London's clubs. It was by no means unusual for a man to dine at his club, while his wife dined at home. Only the poor spent as much time together as is today considered normal.

German Freedom Society

The German Freedom Society was a specifically anti-Nazi political secret society, which flourished in Germany in the 1930s. It placed great faith in the written word; besides publishing *Neuer Vorwarts, Neue Front,* and *Das Banner,* it also produced books or pamphlets that, at first sight, looked like (for example) cook books or volumes of poetry, but which after a few pages turned into political tracts. The German Freedom Society also pulled off some very stylish *coups,* such as deluging a Gestapo ball in Graz with leaflets when the lights went down for a waltz.

Gist, Noel P.

Noel P. Gist, Ph.D., wrote *Secret Societies: A Cultural Study of Fraternalism in the United States,* published as a part of the University of Missouri Studies, Volume XV, No. 4, October 1, 1940.

While the nonsociologist might easily be deterred at first, especially by Chapter I ("The Concept of Culture Pattern"), this is a remarkably readable book with a great deal of information. Dr. Gist backed up his arguments with a vast amount of solid information on the history, constitution, and nature of the societies he studied, often accompanying his observations with hard-to-find details on such topics as PASSWORDS, symbols and so forth.

Inevitably, some of the information is dated, but the rate at which secret societies have changed their rituals and the like since the 1930s has mostly been very slow. Gist's outlook is remarkably sober and free from the levity that characterizes other works.

Gleaners, Ancient Order of

5200 West U.S. 223, P.O. Box 1894
Adrian, MI 49221
(517) 263-2244 or (800) 992-1894

The Gleaners was founded in 1894 in Cairo, Michigan, as a fraternal insurance society for men and women over

16 "of good moral character . . . who furnish satisfactory evidence of insurability" and who "believe in the existence of a Supreme Being, the Creator and Preserver of the Universe." The organization publishes *Arbor News* (monthly) and *The National Gleaner Forum* (quarterly). There were 43,000 members in what is now the Gleaner Life Insurance Society in 1994.

The Gleaners took its name from the biblical book of Ruth and was at first militantly committed to the values of rural and small-town America. It would admit only people who were actively engaged in farming, gardening, or like activities, or who lived in towns of under 3,000 people. It later changed its rules, though, to admit anyone as defined above. Admission was by the BLACKBALL system.

There are three classes of membership: Beneficiary, Junior and Cooperative. Juniors can graduate automatically to Beneficiary membership by staying in the organization for a certain period. "Cooperative" membership is social membership, without financial benefits, but with fraternal participation.

Although it has always been a beneficiary society, its RITUALS AND CEREMONIES involved the following DEGREES: Introductory, Adoption, Ruth, and Dramatic. The outsider figure played by the candidate for admission is a "Moabitish stranger." There are also ceremonies for installation and funerals. The symbols draw on obvious sources; the emblems of the first degree are the sheaf, sickle, and hourglass. LODGES are called Arbors; there appears to be only two tiers, with the Supreme Arbor above the local lodge.

The Gleaners is very strong on the family, and, indeed, its emblem shows an "ideal family" of father, mother, son, and daughter, with the parent holding stalks of grain across which are the words *"Prudens Futuri,"* which might best be translated as "thought for the morrow."

The Gleaners is not particularly involved in charitable works. The Gleaner blood bank operates at local Arbor level "as a health guard to Gleaner members," and the organization stresses such all-American activities as bowling, baseball, and square dancing. There are also "great Gleaner picnics." The Gleaners provides for the orphans of deceased fellows and also provides a number of college scholarships and loans. It encourages its employees to study, reimbursing expenses to them.

Gnosticism

Gnosis means knowledge or knowing; gnostic religions are therefore disciplined to accept the word of others (especially the orthodox) as being above their own personal experience of God.

This notwithstanding, Gnostic Christians (of whom the term "Gnosis" is most frequently used) had a number of apparently shared beliefs that were very different from the mainstream. Their canon was different, including gospels not accepted by the modern church (such as the Gospel of Mary Magdalene), and they believed that all of visible creation was the work of a "demiurge" or emanation of God. This view is not much removed from the KABBALAH, and closely related to the dualism of Zoroastrianism. Many Gnostic sects were based on revelations that were not made to (or not accepted by) other branches of Christianity. It is in this last characteristic that Gnosticism has some slight relevance to some modern secret societies, which claim mystical knowledge of great antiquity.

By the time of the Nicaean Council in A.D. 325 (which ostensibly met to discuss Arianism), Gnosis was so far out of the mainstream that it could hardly be considered a part of Christianity, but it never entirely vanished. There were always gnostic overtones in all sorts of cults and societies—see, for example, les HOMMES DE L'INTELLIGENCE—and in the 19th century the rise of biblical scholarship brought to the fore the question of Gnosticism.

Since then, such discoveries as the Dead Sea Scrolls or the Nag Hammadi library have revived an interest that is both scholarly and (on occasion) mystical. There is, for example, a Gnostic Church (*Eglise Gnostique*), which meets at the Librairie du Merveilleux, 29 rue de Trévise, 75009 Paris. It was founded by Jules Doinel, a young philosopher and bookstore owner of Orléans, who worked out the principles of his church in 1889, appointed several bishops in 1894, and left the church in 1895 to publish *Lucifer démasqué* ("Lucifer Unmasked") under the pseudonym of Jean Kotska. His bishops were interesting, in that they constituted an abbreviated roll call of leading French mystics of the period: Papus (Toulouse), Sédir (Concorygo), and Guénon (Alexandria); Victor-Emile Michelet may also have been a member. The Gnostic Church (at least in France) draws its recruits from MARTINISM and from the Egyptian Rite of Memphis-Mizraim.

Goats

The original Society of Goats (or just "the Goats") appeared in Limburg in about 1770. It was an antifeudal peasants' political secret society with overtones of satanism: The symbolism of the goat is often satanic, and the RITUALS AND CEREMONIES were apparently designed to foster an affinity with the Prince of Darkness. Members wore goatlike masks as they terrorized the bourgeoisie and aristocracy, sacking churches, burning castles and manors, and killing their occupants. Robbery was rampant and one frequent heard the terrified cry, "The Goats are coming!"

At their height, the Goats were so numerous that it was assumed they were in league with the devil, who transported them from place to place. Devilish, certainly, was the order's initiation ritual, which consisted of getting the candidate drunk, putting him astride a wooden goat hung on pivots, then swinging him around at high velocity. He was convinced that he had been riding through space on the devil's crupper.

The movement was well supported. From 1772–74 alone, the tribunal of Foquement condemned 400 Goats to be hanged or quartered, and it was not until about 1780 that the Goats were finally suppressed.

Golden Chain, Order of the

584 Bloomfield Avenue, Apartment 10-B
West Caldwell, NJ 07006
(201) 226-8555

This is the name of two unrelated organizations. The first was a mutual assessment beneficiary society organized in Baltimore in 1881 by members of the Knights of Honor, the Royal Arcanum, the American League of Honor, as well as Freemasons. It provided life insurance, sick pay, and disability benefits and was defunct by the early 20th century.

The second organization was founded in 1929 by a group of Master Masons in Asbury Park, New Jersey, solely for "fraternal purposes"—although it soon also sponsored a number of philanthropic programs, including a 138-acre summer camp in Blairstown, New Jersey, established in 1950 for underprivileged and handicapped children.

The order's secret ritual echoes Masonic tradition, and its insignia is a chain of six oblong links formed into a hexagon surrounding six shields. At the center of the insignia are the initials OGC. The order now consists exclusively of female relatives of Masons and Master Masons. OGC "Links" (chapters) are in Connecticut, Massachusetts, New Jersey, New York, Pennsylvania, Delaware, and Michigan, and the Grand Link (national headquarters) is located in New Jersey. In 1994, there were 2,000 members.

Golden Circle, Order of

The Golden Circle is a women's auxiliary (see AUXILIARIES) to African-American Masons of the 32nd and 33rd degrees in the United Supreme Council, Ancient and Accepted Scottish Rite-Prince Hall Affiliate. Organized in 1908, the O.G.C. is supervised by a male, known as the Illustrious Deputy. The order works only one degree, that of Loyal Lady.

O.G.C. supports national African-American organizations, including the N.A.A.C.P. and the United Urban League.

Golden Cross, United Order of the

A teetotaling fraternal benefit organization for men and women, the United Order of the Golden Cross was founded by a group of FREEMASONS in 1876. It prospered on the graded ASSESSMENT plan and finally merged in 1962 with the WOODMEN of the world Life Insurance Society.

Golden Dawn, Hermetic Order of the

The Hermetic Order of the Golden Dawn was founded in England in 1887 as a secret society dedicated to magic and mysticism. Membership was open, subject to acceptance.

The Hermetic Order of the Golden Dawn has achieved nearly legendary status, for a number of reasons. The most important is probably the notoriety (now much diminished, but considerable even as late as the 1950s and 1960s) of Aleister Crowley (see CROWLEY, ALEISTER), the self-proclaimed "wickedest man in the world." Crowley was only one of the well-known figures of the movement, which also included the poet William Butler Yeats, the novelist Arthur Machen, and others. Another reason for the order's fame is the remarkable synthesis of a large number of magical traditions, which was accomplished by the founders of the G∴D∴—the arrangement of dots is traditionally used when writing of the Golden Dawn, but may be Masonic in origin; God or the Great Architect is sometimes written G∴. Yet a third major reason is the extraordinarily convoluted and jargon-ridden structure of the organization: It really sounds like a secret society ought to sound, with wondrous titles such as "Ipsissimus." This word (insofar as it has any meaning) may be translated as "most completely himself" or "utterly self-possessed"; *ipse* is the Latin pronoun for "himself" or "itself," and the *-issimus* suffix is the superlative form of an adjective.

The G∴D∴ warrants an extended entry as a rare example of a secret society that was (pretty much) *sui generis,* and that really was centered around "secret knowledge," which arguably could confer real power upon the holder. It borrowed heavily from all kinds of other societies, it is true, and especially from the ROSICRUCIANS; but much of the content, and almost all of the way in which the content was put together, make the G∴D∴ a special case. Also, it attracted numerous literate and critical adherents, some of whom turned apostate, some of whom founded their own versions of the order, and some of whom "developed" the concept within the mainstream. For this reason, for its notoriety, for the fact that the order epitomized a great deal about late 19th-century secret societies, and for the relatively short and therefore easily studied life of the original order (1887–1923, approximately), the G∴D∴ is the subject of a very large body of literature. It is also a particularly interesting study in that it all happened in recent historical times.

The Origins of the G∴D∴

The G∴D∴ was founded by Dr. William Wynn Westcott, Samuel Liddell McGregor Mathers, and Dr. A.F.A. Woodward upon an extremely flimsy basis. In 1887, Dr. Westcott ac-

quired an old manuscript, perhaps from a Reverend Woodford (the number of similar names, all beginning with "W," is fruit for a conspiracy theory all on its own). This manuscript contained the outline of a magical ritual. Although commonly referred to as "ancient," the manuscript is in fact on paper bearing an 1809 watermark, and it is possible—though not likely—that it was a fabrication by the founders of the G∴D∴, written on some old paper.

The manuscript may not have been complete, and the ritual most certainly was not, so Dr. Westcott—a respected London coroner, but also a devotee of ritual and a student of the occult—called on his friend Mathers to flesh it out.

Mathers was well described by Yeats as a man of "much learning but little scholarship, much imagination but imperfect taste." His critical faculties were not well developed, and his enthusiasms were unpredictable, but he studied magic with great eclecticism. He was able to enlarge the "cipher manuscript" (it is in a Hermetic cipher of the Middle Ages) without difficulty, drawing heavily on the work of ELIPHAS LEVI, who is not highly regarded among scholars.

The cipher manuscript may have been a draft of a secret society ritual by some other person, now unknown, or it may have been notes on a ritual that someone had seen or read about, but when Mathers had finished with it, the result was a glorious hodgepodge. For example, where the original manuscript reads, "H. recites prayer of gnomes" ("H" being the "hierophant" or priest), Mathers translated the *Oraison des Sylphes* from Levi's *Dogme et Rituel,* and inserted that wholesale, instead.

The source of the manuscript may be doubtful, but, on balance, it does not seem to have been a deliberate fabrication by anyone involved with the Golden Dawn; with the accretions that Mathers added, it did not need to be. There is a much more doubtful provenance, though, for the letters Dr. Westcott produced in an attempt to build a history for his new organization. The so-called Sprengel letters were supposed to have come from a German Rosicrucian initiate who chartered the G∴D∴ and legitimated much of its ritual. Ellis Howe, in his *Magicians of the Golden Dawn* (London, 1972), makes an extremely strong case that the letters were spurious, written by Westcott himself, and this is only the earliest taint on the organization. The arguments against the authenticity of the letters are lengthy, but a telling component is that they all read as if they were written by an English-speaking person whose command of German was imperfect.

Be that as it may, the three chiefs plunged ahead with their new group. Five DEGREES were mentioned in the cipher manuscript, and four of them bore the same names as the first four grades of the SOCIETAS ROSICRUC-

IANA IN ANGLIA (a Masonic derivation on the Rosicrucians), but with different numbers. To satisfy his love of degrees and ritual, Westcott appears to have continued the system, using the next two "orders" of Rosicrucianism and then creating the grade of Ipsissimus from the whole cloth. The five manuscript grades are astericked in the following list:

SOCIETAS ROSICRUCIANA IN ANGLIA	HERMETIC ORDER OF THE GOLDEN DAWN
	0° = 0 = Neophyte*
First Order	
1° Zelator	1° = 1° Zelator*
2° Theoricus	2° = 9° Theoricus*
3° Practicus	3° = 8° Practicus*
4° Philosophus	4° = 7° Philosophus*
Second Order	
5° Adeptus Minor	5° = 6° Adeptus Minor
6° Adeptus Major	6° = 5° Adeptus Major
7° Adeptus Exemptus	7° = 4° Adeptus Exemptus
Third Order	
8• Magister Templi	8° = 3° Magister Templi
9• Magus	9° = 1° Magus
	10° = 0° Ipsissimus

As is clear from many other examples in this book, degrees were dear to our Victorian forebears, and the G∴D∴ started out with plenty. Perhaps modestly, the chiefs reckoned themselves only 7° = 4°; the Third Order was originally available only to inhabitants of the Astral Plane.

The Initial Recruitment

Unlike their predecessors and perhaps rivals, the members of the THEOSOPHICAL SOCIETY, the G∴D∴ next decided to make entry into their new club difficult. The way the G∴D∴ was initially promoted shows a systematization of the way in which many other secret societies must have grown: by personal invitation and by carefully fostered repute. Recruits were sought among many Master FREEMASONS, and the earliest initiations were held at a Masonic hall. At this point, the "black magic" aspect of the society was negligible; it was promoted as a group for research into Hermetic traditions.

The Golden Dawn fostered its reputation through the pages of publications appealing to occultists and by a well orchestrated whispering campaign. The chiefs created a "controversy" about the legitimacy of various organizations that claimed Hermetic knowledge. At least one of these organizations may never even have existed, at least not as described, but was a fabrication by G∴D∴ members, who created it in order to denounce it. There were also disingenuous letters in the same papers asking whether a society that matched the description of the G∴D∴, and that had formerly existed in Paris and elsewhere, was still in existence; and replies that confirmed that is was. Those who were *au fait* with the surprisingly extensive British

occult "scene" of the late 19th century used such phrases as "abuzz with talk about" and "everyone had heard of."

Leads that made it easy for prospective members to find the organization were deliberately left open, and the G∴D∴ netted some surprising fish; for instance, the eminent physicist William Crookes (later Sir William Crookes) joined in June 1890, though he allowed his connection with the society to lapse a few months later. He was already a member of the Society for Psychical Research.

The Heyday, 1890–1900

The G∴D∴ flourished in the last decade of the 19th century as a fairly exclusive club with a great deal of mumbo-jumbo ritual and a pseudoscientific attitude toward the investigation and practice of magic. It may have been the purported rigor of its approach that initially attracted the likes of Crookes. The ritual was focused on a fairly standard darkness-into-light theme, which is not surprising given the Masonic antecedents of Westcott and his associates from the Rosicrucians. But it was spectacularly ornamented by Mather's eclectic elaborations.

The Golden Dawn also purported to give genuine instruction on the practice of ritual magic. There were instructions for the consecration of "lotus wands" and for the drawing and consecration of pentacles, the use of arcane symbols and symbolic colors, and much more. At this stage, though, everything was still fairly genteel. There was nothing that could frighten even a Victorian maiden lady. The idea seems to have been that the initiate learned the theory, but abstained from the practice. There may, however, have been a more sinister "inner circle" of magical initiates, though it is still important to distinguish between the kind of ritual magic that they practiced, and satanism.

Ritual magicians may well work within the framework of Christianity. Though most sects frown upon it, magic is not necessarily incompatible with the Christian religion, and some of the most prominent Victorian occultists were clergymen, usually of the Church of England. More often, though, ritual magic regards Christianity as of minor relevance. Satanism, by contrast, *needs* Christianity. It is a reaction *against* the Christian religion, which it deliberately parodies and blasphemes. Most ritual magicians regard satanism as the poor relation of ritual magic. Satanic rituals may or may not work, and if they do work, they are rarely controllable, depending on raw energy (mostly hate, with a good dose of sexual frenzy in some cases) rather than controlled forces.

Decline and Fall, 1900 Onward

As early as 1892–93, the difficult personality of Mathers was leading to friction and dissent within the G∴D∴

Some of the other members were treating the order with less respect than the chiefs thought proper, and there were expulsions and resignations. Around 1900, shortly after the raising of Frater Perdurabo (Aleister Crowley) to 5° = 6° by Mathers in Paris, that matters really came to a head. By then, relationships between Mathers, who had taken up residence in Paris, and the English side of the G∴D∴ had grown so bad that the Britons refused to acknowledge Crowley's exaltation. Crowley entered the order on November 18, 1898, and reached Philosophus 4° = 7° in May 1899. Later in that same year, he had moved to Boleskine, Scotland, as a suitable location for his "Abra-Melin Operation," a fearsome scheme of practical magic.

Crowley's "magick" (as he spelled it) was excessively strong meat for the rest of the G∴D∴, with the exception of Mathers, and he was denied access to the Second Order (which the attentive reader will recall begins at 5° = 6°, Adeptus Minor) in London; whereupon, he journeyed to Paris to be initiated by Mathers. After a battle that included an invasion of the London "Vault" by Crowley as an emissary of Mathers, Mathers was thrown out, and W. B. Yeats was elected Imperator of the Isis-Urania Temple on April 27, 1900.

From then on, great squabbling broke out over the "secret groups" (inner organizations, with their own magical theories), but this was of far less interest to the outside world than the Horos trial.

Mr. and Mrs. Horos were shadowy figures whose orbits had intersected with those of the G∴D∴ on several occasions. They were a mixture of adept and charlatan, with more emphasis on the latter. Early in 1900, they had first ingratiated themselves with Mathers, then stole a copy of the G∴D∴ from him, after which they seem to have set themselves up as unauthorized G∴D∴ operators. They had left Cape Town in mid to late 1900, with the South African police snapping at their heels, and they arrived in London toward the end of the year. In September 1901, Mr. Horos was tried for the rape of a young girl called Daisy Adams, and his wife (a.k.a. Swami Vive Ananda) was tried for aiding and abetting him in the offense. He was sentenced to 15 years of penal servitude, while his wife drew seven years' detention.

The problem for the G∴D∴ was that the stolen ritual surfaced, and was simultaneously denounced as blasphemous (by the judge in the case and others) and ridiculed. There was wholesale panic within the order. Faction fought faction. The existing rituals were denounced (by A. E. Waite) as "spurious archaisms with the worst style of journalistic English," though his proposal to bring the rituals "back as closely as possible to the original cypher manuscript in order to shorten and improve the working" argues that he was not familiar with the cipher manuscript, nor yet with the fact that most of the ritual was

Mather's invention. Howe (in *Magicians of the Golden Dawn*) sums up the factionalism. One group, headed by Waite, "wanted to throw overboard the old 'Magical' tradition . . . and be free to pontificate about the Graces of the Spirit"; the Brodie-Innes faction wanted to restore and preserve "Mather's authoritarian concept of the order"; while Dr. Felkin actually wanted to find the Secret Chiefs, "and continue from that point."

Thereafter, the G∴D∴ seems to have been dominated by very sincere would-be ritual magicians, each of whom pursued his or her particular version of the Truth (and especially of the Golden Dawn) with greater tenacity than reason.

Mathers died in 1918, while Westcott survived the closure of that last relic of the original schisms, the Stella Matutina Lodge (which lasted from about 1901–23), dying in 1925. Crowley went on to pursue his own spectacular career, not dying until 1947. An Israel Regardie Foundation in the United States flourished in the early to mid-1980s, but it was a "New Age" version of the G∴D∴ as a "loving and growth-oriented system."

Golden Fleece, Noble Order of the

The Noble Order of the Golden Fleece was founded on January 10, 1430, at Bruges, originally as a religious order. Since then, it has enjoyed a chequered career. It survives in Spain, Austria, and elsewhere, but its size is no longer clear.

The Noble Order of the Golden Fleece (*Toison d'Or*) furnishes a fine example of the evolution and fragmentation of a traditional Order of Knighthood, which seems to have been founded in much the same spirit as the ELKS or Moose (see MOOSE, INTERNATIONAL), albeit with more fanfare. It was founded by Philip the Good, Duke of Burgundy, to mark his marriage to the Infanta (Princess) of Portugal, Isabella. Among the first 15 knights elected (by Philip the Good) were Edward IV of England, Ferdinand I of Naples, and John II of Sicily. It was to be above all other orders, including that of the Garter, and to be a "Company of Friends."

On the death of Philip the Good in 1477, Archduke (later Emperor) Maximilian of Austria became the Head and Sovereign of the order, which would otherwise have devolved upon his wife Marie de Bourgogne (daughter of Charles the Bold), who could not head the order in her own right because of her sex. This was a fair model for the way that leadership of the order moved around in the centuries that followed. In 1701, two separate monarchs were claiming the order for their own, both with supportable cases, and in 1809 Napolean added another version. He pointed out that his eagles had vanquished the Golden Fleece of the Kings of Spain and the Golden Fleece of the Emperors of Germany, and so he proposed to found the Military Imperial Order of the Three Golden Fleeces, incorporating the two already extinct and the one that he proposed to found.

Napoleon's order never amounted to anything, but the Spanish branch continues as an ordinary civil award, which can be made to almost anyone, including non-Catholics, while the Austrian branch is bestowed only upon members of royal families, or the highest nobility, who are also professed Catholics.

Golden Key, Order of the

If the Order of the Golden Key still exists (which is by no means certain), it is yet another subdivision of the FREEMASONS. Founded at the Beta Chapter of Sigma Mu fraternity at the University of Oklahoma at Norman in 1925, the order aims (or aimed) "to establish and perpetuate a University to include an entire community and a Center of Learning based on Masonic philosophy."

A "Sovereign Preceptory" (national organization) was established in Joliet, Illinois. Membership in the Order of the Golden Key was open to those belonging to the Knights Templar. The order worked two degrees, the Pledge or Chief Craftsman and the Initiatory or Knight of the Golden Key. In 1978, the Masonic Service Association responded to a researcher that it did not have an address for the organization.

Good Samaritans and Daughters of Samaria, Independent Order of

The Independent Order of the Good Samaritans and Daughters of Samaria was an African-American fraternal benefit society. It was also a total abstinence (or "temperance") society, which helps to account for the unusually early date of founding for such an organization—September 14, 1847—and its watchwords, "Love, Purity, and Truth." It was founded in New York City, with the backing of the (white) Grand Lodge of the Grand United Order of Good Samaritans. Both men and women were admitted. Like the paternal order, it has ceased to exist.

It is worth noting that the *state* lodges of the white parent organization wielded authority over the *local* lodges of the African-American order. The Good Samaritans and Daughters of Samaria had no state lodges of its own, only strictly local lodges.

Good Templars, International Organization of

Good Templar Center
2926 Cedar Avenue South
Minneapolis, MN 55407
(612) 721-7606

The Good Templars was founded in 1851 in Utica, New York, as a fraternal temperance society for teetotalers of either sex. It has since spread worldwide and publishes the *National Good Templar* 10 times a year. In 1994, there were 5,000 members in the United States alone.

The Good Templars promotes total abstinence from alcohol. The founder, Daniel Cady, had been a member of the Sons of Temperance (founded 1842), which had assumed a number of fraternal and benevolent characteristics while trying to reform drunks and keep them reformed. His *Knights of Jericho* (1850) soon metamorphosed into the Good Templars in 1851, survived schism and reunification the following year (the short-lived *Independent Order of Good Templars*) and went on to prosper. It always admitted women on the same basis as men, and has, according to its own literature, always been racially mixed. In 1868 the organization spread to England.

At the turn of the century, the Good Templars in the United States boasted about 350,000 members. It has shrunk drastically since then, but seems to be on the rebound from the low of 2,000 quoted by Schmidt in his *Fraternal Organizations* in 1979.

Its greatest strength is to be found outside the United States, especially in Sweden. Lodges also exist in Austria, Canada, Denmark, England, Finland, France, Germany, Greece, Iceland, India, Ireland, Japan, Liberia, the Netherlands, Nigeria, Norway, Scotland, Switzerland, Turkey, Wales, and elsewhere. Membership worldwide is probably between half a million and a million.

Originally, the Good Templars worked three DEGREES, namely Heart, Charity, and Royal Virtue. The RITUALS AND CEREMONIES and regalia were much diminished in the 1970s as the organization tried to make itself more modern and relevant. Now, the initiatory degree of Justice is the only one worked. Initiates are requested to promise to do all in their power "to promote total abstinence of intoxicating beverages both through the enforcement of laws and through [their] own way of life."

Gormogons, Ancient (or August) and Noble Order of

The Ancient (or August) and Noble Order of Gormogons was announced to the public on September 3, 1724, in the London *Daily Post,* wherein it was declared that this society was of Chinese origin, founded in remotest antiquity. FREEMASONS were not to be admitted until they renounced Freemasonry and burned their Masonic paraphernalia. Beyond this, little is known about the society, which disappeared in 1738 (the year of the Papal Bull *In eminenti apostolatus specula*), but it may have been a Catholic-inspired secret society intended to offset the growing popularity of Freemasonry. Alternatively, it may have been a simple test of the gullibility of Freemasons and others.

This essentially Jacobite Masonic society may be related to the Harodim (see HARODIM, GRAND CHAPTER OF THE ANCIENT AND VENERABLE ORDER OF).

Grail Movement

c/o Grailville
932 O'Bannonville Road
Loveland, OH 45140
(513) 683-2340

Founded in 1940 as the U.S. branch of the International Grail Movement, this is a Christian women's movement that works for human liberation through personal renewal, community development, religious search, education, medical-social agencies, and the arts. It is primarily ecofeminist in philosophy and conducts educational programs on women's issues, social justice, spirituality, and the environment. In addition to its Loveland, Ohio, headquarters, it maintains offices in Cornwall-on-Hudson, New York, and San Jose, California.

The organization is also known simply as The Grail and is unrelated to the Movement of the Grail (see GRAIL, MOVEMENT OF THE) or to the Holy Grail Foundation, a Spiritualistic church founded in the 1940s by Rev. Leona Richards.

Grail, Movement of the

22 rue Colbert
93100 Montreuil-sous-Bois or
3 rue de Chevreuil
67000 Strasbourg, France
U.S. Address: 2081 Partridge Lane
Binghamton, NY 13903
(607) 723-4501

The *Mouvement du Graal* is reported to have 15,000 adherents worldwide, with about 1,000 of them in France. The thesis of the movement is that, by the grace of the Holy Grail, man can become free. The founder was a German, Oskar Ernst Bernhardt, but he took the name Abd-Ru-Shin and moved to Austria.

The Grail Movement of America was founded in the 1930s to perpetuate Bernhardt's teachings.

See also GRAIL MOVEMENT.

Grand College of Rites of the United States of America

This is one of the countless subdivisions of the FREEMASONS, with the stated purpose of studying the history of Masonic RITUALS AND CEREMONIES and weeding out unauthorized rites—though in the absence of international agreement on what is "authorized" and who has the authority to authorize it, this seems a hopeless task. It was founded in 1932 in Washington, D.C.

Grange

1616 H Street NW
Washington, D.C. 20006
(202) 628-3507; Fax: (202) 737-5163

The Order of the Patrons of Husbandry, better known as the Grange or the Grangers, was founded in 1867 as a fraternal trade society for small farmers and their families in the United States. Those from 5 to 14 years of age could join the Junior Grange. The organization publishes *National Grange—Washington Update* (weekly), *Grange Newsletter* (monthly), and *View from the Hill* (monthly). There were 325,000 members in 1994.

The National Grange of the Order of the Patrons of Husbandry was founded in Fredonia, New York, by a member of the FREEMASONS called Oliver Hudson Kelley. Allegedly, the Grange (as it has been known ever since) was designed to help the South to recover from the Civil War. It was a new secret society, arranged on more or less Masonic lines, dedicated to promoting rural life. In practice, the location of the first Grange—as a lodge is called—and the way in which urbanites flocked to the organization leads to the suspicion that Kelley just wanted to found another secret society. In New York City, for example, the Grange consisted of 45 people engaged in the indisputably nonrural activities of wholesale merchandising and sewing-machine manufacture.

The Grange RITUALS AND CEREMONIES, as Kelley devised them, consisted of no fewer than seven DEGREES, as follows:

Degree	Male	Joint	Female
First	Laborer		Maid
Second	Cultivator		Shepherdess
Third	Harvester		Gleaner
Fourth	Husband		Matron
Fifth		Pomona	
Sixth		Flora	
Seventh		Ceres	

Full membership in the Grange comes from working the fourth degree; those who have taken only the first degree are known as provisional members. As for the symbolism of the three higher degrees, all are the names of Roman or Italian deities of considerable antiquity. Pomona was a goddess of fruit and gardens, her priest at Rome was the *Flamen Pomonalis,* and the Pomonal sacred grove was near Ostia. Flora was the goddess of flowers, whose Floralia was celebrated in late April and early May with theatrical performances noted for their sexual license. Ceres was the goddess of food plants, whose *Ludi Ceriales* were celebrated in mid-April. An order within the seventh degree, the Order of Demeter or the Priests of Demeter, controls the secret work. Demeter was, of course, a Greek goddess of agriculture, central to the Eleusian Mysteries (see ELEUSIS).

The ritual of the degrees clearly borrows heavily from Freemasonry, as do most secret societies. The altar in the lodge room bears an open Bible, and various agricultural impediments, such as the pruning hook and the shepherd's crook, decorate the place. An American flag is prominently displayed.

As usual, a blindfold symbolizes the passage from outer darkness to inner light, and all manner of trade implements are invested with mystical and symbolic meaning. The tools of the first degree, for example, are the axe, the plough, the harrow, and the spade, and the chaplain explains that agriculture is the noblest of occupations, as it was instituted by God in the Garden of Eden.

Part of the oath involves promising to obey the laws of the state and the nation, as well as the orders of Grange superiors. The deist approach (see DEISM) is very strongly Christian, and has apparently never been proscribed by religious organizations, though the Lutherans have apparently objected to some aspects of the work.

The fact that the Grange admitted women as well as men from the very start may have contributed to the almost exponential growth of the early Granger movement. Although it was slow at first—it took almost seven years from the original founding to break the quarter-million barrier during 1874—in only another 18 months or so it had soared above the three-quarter-million level, hitting 860,000 in 1875.

Like many mushrooming organizations, though, the Grange was overcome by its own self-image: Grange-funded factories and cooperatives sprang up, and rapidly collapsed when the requisite business skills were found lacking. By 1880, members had fallen away in droves, and membership was about 124,000. The process of rebuilding was slower.

Despite what might be seen as Kelley's excessive concern with ritual, it cannot be denied that the Grange also had a powerful educational and self-help component. It also had great political significance. Grangers were instrumental in founding the Populist Party (see FREEMEN'S PROTECTIVE SILVER ASSOCIATION). Not only did the Grange lobby for the establishment of a secretary of agriculture (before 1889, there was no such post), but when a secretary of agriculture was finally appointed, he was a member of the Grange. Since then, the Grange has promoted agricultural colleges, agricultural research stations, and the expansion of the rural free delivery network operated by the U.S. Postal Service.

The structure of the organization begins with the Subordinate Granges, numbered in the thousands, and the Pomona Granges, which are district or country associations of Granges and are numbered in the hundreds. Both Subordinate and Pomona Granges send delegates to the State Granges (not found in every state), and the State Granges in turn send delegates to the National Grange in Washington, D.C. The first four degrees are conferred by the Subordinate Granges; the fifth, appropriately enough, by the Pomona Granges; the sixth by the State Granges; and the seventh by the National Grange.

Great White Lodge

The Great White Lodge is less frequently mentioned than it used to be, but it is still encountered in the writings and preachings of those who believe in conspiracy theories and among the maunderings of the older mystical secret societies.

The date of foundation is as far back as the imagination can conveniently stretch. The Ancient Egyptians are widely favored as the founders, though there are those who maintain that it was really founded by Atlanteans, Hyperboreans (see HYPERBOREA), citizens of Mu, and possibly even the denizens of Cthulu. No one seems to accept anything more recent than the Himalayas in the seventh or eighth century A.D., or less exotic than the more romantic-sounding areas of the Near East.

The founders may, according to the taste of the believer, have been Egyptian (or Atlantean, Hyperborean, and so on) priests or priest-kings, or Hindu sages, or Tibetans, or Native Americans, or members of any or all of the Tribes of Israel. Great Masters of the Lodge have purportedly included Krishna, the Buddha, Ahura Mazda, Christ, the Prophet Mohammed, Guru Rinpoche, Roger Bacon (see BACON, ROGER), Jacques de Molay, and the Dalai Lama.

The Great White Lodge has been preserved in the various MYSTERIES of the ancient world, the TEMPLARS, the Cathars and other Christian HERETICS, the FREEMASONS, the ILLUMINATI, the ROSICRUCIANS, members of the THEOSOPHICAL SOCIETY, the Hermetic Order of the Golden Dawn (see GOLDEN DAWN, HERMETIC ORDER OF), and numerous other secret and nonsecret societies of varying repute.

As to what the Great White Lodge actually *does*, there are three schools of thought.

One says that it doesn't actually *do* anything, but merely acts as an inspiration to those who run the Templars, Freemasons, Illuminati, Rosicrucians, and so on.

The second says that it "directs" the people who run all these orders, according to some plan that is beyond the understanding of everyday mortals. Its methods of direction seem to be somewhat indirect; at best, it delivers "spirit messages."

The third view is the hardest to grasp, because its adherents insist that the Masters of the Universe construct and execute a Galactic Plan.

Inherently, the idea of a Great White Lodge of benevolent Masters who keep an eye on the world is an attractive one, but no one has ever encountered a member of the lodge, and no established religion has had much time for such a concept. The Great White Lodge is essentially a 19th-century mixture of heterodox Christianity and Hinduism, the ancient Egyptian pantheon, Buddhism, and Mithraism, Wicca, and more.

Greek Catholic Union of the USA

5400 Tuscarawas Road
Beaver, PA 15009
(412) 495-3400

The Greek Catholic Union of the United States of America was founded in 1892 as a fraternal benefit life insurance society for Catholics (Greek or Roman rite) of Russian or Slavic origin, and their spouses. It publishes the *Messenger* bimonthly. There were 52,000 members in 1994.

This is a typical ethnic fraternal benefit society with a strong religious slant and (presumably in deference to the Catholic church) no RITUALS AND CEREMONIES. In addition to the insurance and religious activities, there are social benefits and an unusually attractive-sounding retirement complex.

Green Island

Formed in Vienna in 1855, Green Island was a revival of the Order of Knights (see KNIGHTS, ORDER OF), which had been founded in Wetzlar in 1771. Like that earlier organization, Green Island was a parodic spoof of "knightly" activity and existed purely for amusement. It counted among its members many literary men of note—though it is no longer recorded just who these were.

Gregorians

This order was established early in the 18th century in England to ridicule and generally oppose the Freemasons. It is known that the organization lasted at least until 1797, because a sermon of that year, preached before their members, survives. However, by the later 18th century, the Gregorians seem to have reconciled with Freemasonry, as evidenced by the membership of some prominent Freemasons during that period.

Grips

Secret handshakes or "grips" feature in the ritual of many secret societies. Their original function was to enable members of an organization to recognize one another (see also PASSWORDS and SIGNS) or to confirm recognition; this was particularly important in a preliterate society.

The best-known handshake, and one that can apparently still open a number of doors, is the basic grip of the FREEMASONS: a regular handshake, except that the thumb is used to press on the first protruding knuckles of the other person's hand. It has the great advantage of being unobtrusive both to bystanders and (if he does not know the grip) to the person whose hand is shaken.

Many organizations have different grips for different DEGREES: one for the Apprentice, one for the Fellow, one for the Master, and so forth. The drawback to this is that there are only so many ways in which one can shake hands and still appear natural. For example, the Revised

ODD FELLOWS manual gives no fewer than seven grips. For the initiatory grip: "With the first two fingers of the right hand seize and link with the first two fingers of the brother's right hand; with the thumb (your own) touch each of the two fingers (your own) and thus form the grip. No shaking hands in making the grip." This echoes the linked chain of the Odd Fellows' symbol.

For the grip of the Golden Rule Degree: "With the index finger of the right hand form a link at the second joint; and with the ball of the thumb press between the knuckle and second joint, the back of the index finger of the Patriarch forming the link with you. No shaking hands in making the grip."

For the Royal Purple Degree: "Each Patriarch will grip the index finger of the other's right hand, the ball of the thumb being on the knuckle joint. No shaking hands in making the grip."

Grotto

1696 Brice Road
Reynoldsburg, OH 43068
(614) 860-9193
Daughters of Mokanna:
4240 Vernon, NW
Canton, OH 44709
(216) 492-4484

"Grotto" is the common name for the Mystic Order of Veiled Prophets of the Enchanted Realm, which was founded in 1890 in Hamilton, New York, as a "fun" organization for Master Masons. There were 39,000 members in 1994.

The Fairchild Deviltry Committee, to give it its original name of 1889 or 1890, became the "Supreme Council of the Mystic Order of Veiled Prophets of the Enchanted Realm" on June 13, 1890. It has generally been known as the Grotto ever since, after the name adopted for the LODGES.

The ritual is a standard Islamic-parody model, allegedly derived from a secret manuscript discovered in a vault in Teheran, but nevertheless revised in 1940. Like the SHRINERS, the Grotto is a reaction to dry, pseudoscholastic FREEMASONS. It is commonly known as the Blue Lodge Shrine because any Master Mason in good standing in his own BLUE LODGE may join; that is, membership is not restricted to those with higher DEGREES.

The Grotto is noted for its support of cerebral palsy research and dentistry for the handicapped.

The Daughters of Mokanna are the female auxiliary (see AUXILIARIES) of the Grotto. The order was founded in 1919.

Unlike many other Masonic subdivisions, the membership of the Daughters seems to be falling rapidly: There were only 4,822 members in 1994, a drop of over 1,000 since 1988, and there were about 8,000 in the late 1960s.

The nomenclature within the Daughters needs little comment: The local lodges are called "Caldrons," the national lodge is the "Supreme Caldron," and the chief national officer is the "Supreme Mighty Chosen One." Their good works are directed at victims of cerebral palsy and at dentistry for the handicapped.

Another female auxiliary of the Grotto is the Mysterious Order of the Witches of Salem, about which no information is available.

Guardians of Liberty

The name "Guardians of Liberty" will provoke suspicion among students of secret societies; more often than not, any organization with "Liberty" in the title is dedicated to the opposite of liberty, namely a blind obedience to a narrow-minded cause.

The Guardians of Liberty were an anti-Catholic society, which urged its adherents to vote against *any* candidate who was a Catholic, regardless of his personal qualities or of the merit of his adversary. Astonishingly, the Guardians were founded as late as 1911, but, unsurprisingly, the organization soon ran into internal intolerance. A group calling itself the P's or Pathfinders seceded from the Guardians, which they perceived as insufficiently vicious. It seems that both these pernicious incarnations of the KNOW-NOTHINGS are now extinct.

Guelphic Knights

The Guelphs or Guelphic Knights was a high *vendita* or LODGE of the CARBONARI. Founded in about 1816, it held its chief lodge in Bologna, with inferior lodges in other Italian cities.

The original Guelphs was a German alliance, party, or faction of the 12th century, which owed allegiance to the dukes of Saxony and Bavaria (its rival was the Ghibellines, which supported the lords of Hohenstaufen), but by the 13th century the Guelphs were supporters of the Pope against the Holy Roman Empire. The term "Guelph" and "Ghibellines" remained for centuries as terms in Italian politics, though often without much reference to historical relevance.

Guilds

It is earlier to recognize a guild than to define one. The word *gild* appears in *Danegild* (protection money paid to the Vikings by those who would otherwise be ravaged by them) and *Wergild* or *Weregild,* the money paid as compensation to the victim's relatives by a killer or his relatives. The word's cognate, *geld,* survives as "money" in German and Yiddish. Despite all these financial connotations, *gild* also meant sacrifice, worship, and banquet. Historically, guilds can be classified as religious or benevolent, merchant, and craft. All three have many similarities with modern secret societies or fraternal orders, and with antecedent Roman secret societies and pagan blood brotherhood ceremonies, including PASSWORDS, OATHS, and even RITUALS AND CEREMONIES.

All three types of guild also seem to have had a common sociological reason for existence. Old ties based on kinship and the settlement were weakening, largely because of increasing population, but the state did not yet exist in any way that could enforce a new order; and so the guilds came about as a means of self-help and self-government, probably the closest thing that there has ever been to a true social contract.

Religious and Benevolent Guilds

Guilds of the Holy Roman Empire are mentioned in the Carolingian capitularies of A.D. 779 and 789, and increasingly often thereafter. They had no doubt existed for decades, and possibly for centuries, before this first documentary notice was taken of them. In Norway they appear in the records of the 11th century; in Denmark, in the 12th; and in Sweden, in the 13th. In Britain, there are unusually comprehensive guild records from the first half of the 11th century, relating to brotherhoods in Abbotsbury, Cambridge, and Exeter.

They were all sworn brotherhoods, but the ways in which they helped one another varied. The thanes of Cambridge not only contributed money to help pay *wergild,* they also afforded practical assistance in settling blood feuds. The Exeter group offered help when a member's property was destroyed by fire. Both Exeter and Abbotsbury also provided for holy masses for the salvation of deceased brothers' souls.

By 1388, English guilds were important enough that Parliament required what we would now call a census. Sheriffs were to request details of foundation, ordinances, and property from the masters and wardens of the various guilds.

The range of activities undertaken by the guilds was extraordinarily wide. They were oath-bound mutual-assistance societies like the FREEMASONS; they were charities; they were civic service groups, in the manner of modern LIONS or Rotary Clubs (see ROTARY INTERNATIONAL); and they were religious, like the KNIGHTS OF COLUMBUS. They even had overtones of a modern political "party machine," though this was no more than a reflection of the fact that those same local worthies who might be expected to be interested in government were also likely to be members of the local guild. Much the same phenomenon can be seen in the United States today.

Their income derived from admission fees, annual dues, and gifts and bequests, and their expenditure can be divided into four main groups, though not all guilds would be active in all four areas. The areas were:

1. Assistance to members. Financial and practical help might be given to the old, the sick, the impoverished,

and to those who had suffered losses from such causes as robbery, shipwreck or fire

2. Assistance to nonmembers. Charitable help might be given to the old, the poor, and the sick, even if they were not members of the guild dispensing the largess

3. Religion. Lights might be supported at certain altars; brethren might be given a Christian burial, with masses for their souls thereafter; and feasts and processions might be sponsored

4. Civic. Schools, roads, bridges, and town walls might all be "adopted" (or even built and maintained) by guilds

In England, the Guilds were suppressed in 1547 by one of the first acts of Parliament of the reign of Edward VI, but they had already outlived a part of their usefulness. In the future, many of their functions would be more closely (or at least more officially) integrated with local or national government of the nation-state.

Merchant Guilds

Historians' views of the purpose of the merchant guilds, which seem to have originated in England just after the Norman invasion of 1066, will be seen to differ in tune with the historians' political sympathies. At their best, the merchant guilds enforced trading and quality standards. At their worst, they were the means of perpetuating the privileges of an expanding bourgeoisie, and a convenient way of fixing prices to the advantage of the seller rather than the buyer.

Either way, they illustrate the truth of the maxim that each class acts in its own interest. They had the right to trade freely in their native boroughs—they were limited by *area,* not by *trade* or *craft*—and they had the right to tax and to regulate or prohibit those who were not members of the guild but still wished to trade in their area. During fairs, or at duly constituted markets, greater freedom of trade was permitted; and the guilds always exercised far more control over retail selling than over wholesale.

In addition, they also functioned (to varying degrees) in the same way as the religious or benevolent guilds already described. Merchant guilds were much more important in some cities than in others. In a big city, where businesses came and went in much the same way as they do today, their influence was much smaller than in primarily agricultural boroughs, where competition was weaker and where they survived longest. Both the importance and the membership of merchant guilds diminished as craft guilds (see below) became more and more important in the 13th and 14th centuries.

Craft Guilds

Craft guilds are the "misteries" described in the entry entitled MYSTERIES; they were also known as companies. The distinction between craft and merchant guilds is hazy, and has always been so. Historically, artisans were often admitted to merchant guilds because, after all, they were also merchants. In the case of, say, a goldsmith who sells his own wares, the distinction between craftsman and merchant is almost impossible to draw; the same is substantially true of, for example, the cord-wainers or the wheel-wrights. Even so, the craft guilds began to overhaul the merchant guilds in both number and influence as early as the 13th century. This was mainly a result of an increase in the division of labor. Much the same process can be seen at work today in demarcation disputes between TRADE UNIONS, where the installation of an automatic glass door might be expected to require the attentions of a carpenter, a glazier, and an electrician.

As with the merchant guild, though arguably more vehemently, the craft guilds sought to protect their own monopolies, but they also served useful purposes: Apprenticeships were regulated, standards set, and "cowboy" operators (as they would now be called) were prevented from working.

Usually, there were two DEGREES: Apprentice and Master. Apprentices were typically bound for three to seven years, depending on the craft and the location, and served as low-paid labor as well as learning the craft. Traditionally, the parent or guardian of the apprentice paid the master for accepting the boy, and at the end of his apprenticeship the apprentice was expected to produce a "masterpiece," a piece of work that demonstrated that he was now a master craftsman.

Masters could take apprentices, though the number of apprentices they could take and the terms by which they could teach them and exploit them were strictly regulated by the guild. There might also be state regulation, as evidenced in England by acts of Parliament from as early as the beginning of the 16th century.

Higher degrees than Master referred to offices within the guild: Master of the Lodge, for example, or (in due course thereafter) Past Master.

The Journeyman

The Journeyman was outside the sort of guild just described, being a trained but nonapprenticed craftsman with a status of his own, but no hope of ever aspiring to become a Master. In self-defense against the Master/ Apprentice system, Journeymen formed their own organizations or guilds in about the 14th century. Journeymen could work anywhere at their craft, but could not take apprentices. In many trades, they were required to work in a variety of places before they could settle down, produce their "masterpiece," and be accepted the equivalent of a master.

The Decline of the Guilds

The craft significance of guilds declined steadily from a high point in about the 15th century, aided (once again)

The Decline of the Guilds

The craft significance of guilds declined steadily from a high point in about the 15th century, aided (once again) by the rise of the nation-state with its weakness for legal regulation in place of a "social contract." By the end of the 18th century the older guilds were dying, though the apprenticeship system survived into the 20th century. Time-served master craftsmen are still highly respected and valued in England and other European countries.

The Political Power of Guilds

On the European mainland, guilds were perpetuated in another manner. These essentially bourgeois organizations attained considerable political power from the 13th century onward, at the expense of the nobility, by demanding or arrogating to themselves more and more rights and privileges. In those cases where they were not squeezed out by the newcomers, the older merchant guilds did much the same, and new merchant guilds, which specialized in a specific *commodity* rather than a specific *area,* were also founded and came in on the act.

As early as the 14th century, Dutch and other guilds began to amalgamate, effectively becoming "party machines." The term "Guild Hall" for the City Hall or *Rathaus* is no coincidence. In Britain, where industry was more developed and where democracy was more apparent, this trend was much less obvious.

Gurdjieff, George Ivanovitch

Born George S. Georgiades, probably in 1872 in Alexandropol, Armenia, Gurdjieff spent his youth in northeast Africa, the Middle East, India, and Central Asia, imbibing the spiritual traditions of these regions. Returning to Moscow in 1913, he became a teacher there as well as in Petrograd (subsequently called Leningrad and today St. Petersburg), where he gathered a following of students interested in his spiritual teachings.

Gurdjieff fled to the Caucasus during the Russian Revolution, then established the Institute for the Harmonious Development of Man in 1919 at Tiflis (present-day Tbilisi), Georgia. In 1922, the Institute moved to Fontainebleu, France.

Gurdjieff's followers at the Institute led Spartan, even monastic, lives, punctuated by philosophical-spiritual dialogues and readings from Gurdjieff's books, many of which are still highly regarded and widely reprinted (especially *Beelzebub's Tales to His Grandson* and *Meetings with Remarkable Men*). Gurdjieff also formulated a program of ritual exercise and dance, performed to music of his own composition.

In 1923, a disciple named P. D. Ouspensky introduced Gurdjieff's teachings to a wide audience in the west. Indeed, it is largely through the work of Ouspensky, a writer as lucid as Gurdjieff was obscure, that the former's philosophy was transmitted and survives. Gurdjieff's basic tenet was that human beings lived in a kind of perpetual sleep state. The great task of an enlightened life was to transcend that state and reach new levels of vitality and awareness.

Gurdjieff's Institute for Harmonious Development closed at Fontainebleu in 1933, though Gurdjieff himself continued to teach in Paris until his death on October 29, 1949.

Harodim, Grand Chapter of the Ancient and Venerable Order of

The order was established in London in 1787 by the celebrated Masonic lecturer William Preston, who intended it to "represent the art of Masonry in a finished and complete form."

The Harodim consisted of five grades, equivalent to Masonic degrees and including the standard three of the Craft as it existed at the time, in addition to Past Master and Royal Arch. The name "Harodim" was in vogue masonically during the 1780s and was meant to evoke an association with the builders of King Solomon's Temple.

Preston's new order was never wholly accepted by the Grand Lodge, and while many Masons admired the system he had created, the Harodim eventually disappeared.

Harugari, German Order of

c/o Max Math, Executive Officer
7625 Hooker Street
Westminster, CO 80030
(303) 428-1500

The improbably named German Order of Harugari was organized in New York in 1847 or 1848 for mutual assistance and the celebration of German culture. The word *Harugari* was alleged to derive from a society of the same name among the ancient Cimbri, the tribe best known for defeating Gnaeus Papirius Carbo in 113 B.C. and Marcus Junius Silanus in 109 B.C., before their own final defeat near Vercellae in 101 B.C.

The newer order, also known as the *Deutscher Orden der Harugari,* worked five DEGREES with the motto "Friendship, Love, and Humanity." Some religious groups objected to the *absence* of religion in their LODGES.

There was a temporary schism from 1860–69, and there was also an Illinois order. At one time, there were 20,000 members in the Harugari Singing Society alone, but in 1994 there were only 90 members in all.

Haymakers

This name has been applied to two organizations, the National Haymakers' Association and the Ancient and Honorable Order of Haymakers.

The first-named group was organized in 1879 as the "fun" or "friendship" society of the Improved Order of RED MEN. In 1980, the organization had 10,000 members and was headquartered in New Eagle, Pennsylvania. It is not listed in more recent editions of the ENCYCLOPEDIA OF ASSOCIATIONS and is most likely defunct.

The N.H.A. had the familiar trappings of a fraternal organization. Local meeting places were called Haylofts, and officers bore such titles as Collector of Straws (secretary) and Keeper of Bundles (treasurer), and there were also a Guard of the Hayloft and a Guard of the Barndoor. The initiation rite was heavily influenced by the FREEMASONS.

The second-named organization, the Ancient and Honorable Order of Haymakers, was fictitious—nothing more than a made-up example in a June 5, 1923, speech by President Warren G. Harding, but mistaken by some historians of secret societies as a reference to an actual organization.

Hearts of Steel (a/k/a Steelboys)

The Hearts of Steel was an Irish political and militaristic secret society founded in 1769, formed largely, but not exclusively, from tenants evicted by the Marquis of Donegal. On Christmas Eve, 1770, 1,200 farmers calling themselves "Hearts of Steel" marched on Belfast to protest the evictions. The military opened fire on them, killing several. Unrest spread and was met by an act of 1772 to repress the Steelboys. The order was largely Presbyterian.

Heckethorn, Charles William

Charles William Heckethorn was born in about 1826, probably in Switzerland, but came to England at an early age. He died in his adopted land in 1902. He is known to have written six works of nonfiction, one novel, one volume of poetry, two translations of foreign works, and *The Secret Societies of All Ages and Countries, Embracing the Mysteries of Ancient India, China, Japan, Egypt, Mexico, Peru, Greece and Scandinavia, the Cabalists, Early Christians, Heretics, Assassins, Thugs, Templars, the Vehm and Inquisition, Mystics, Rosicrucians, Illuminati, Freemasons, Skopzi, Camorristi, Carbonari, Nihilists and other Sects*.

The first edition was published in 1875, but the second edition of 1897 was so massively revised—the fruit of more than two decades' additional research—that it was effectively a new book.

Hell Fire Club

The Friars of St. Francis of Wycombe, to give the Hell Fire Club the name under which it was organized, was founded by Sir Francis Dashwood in 1746 and constituted a fascinating mid to late 18th-century club of rakes. The club is long extinct, but the notoriety of its members comes from their involvement in three areas: sex, black magic, and politics.

For the first, they were typical bucks of the day; the following gives a fair idea of their interests and preferences: teenage virgins, courtesans of outstanding beauty, and public performances. They were able to indulge their wildest fantasies because they were all quite wealthy.

For the second ground of notoriety, black magic, they seem to have been concerned principally with ridiculing the Catholic faith. This was a perfectly acceptable attitude of the day. This was before Catholics had had their civil rights returned to them, and the Gordon Riots of 1780 showed the depth of anti-Catholic feeling that existed well after the Hell Fire Club was formed. They do not seem to have been Satanists in the modern sense. Even so, the established church still wielded plenty of

power, and their magical practices were much more frowned upon than their whoring. When their opponents wished to attack them, it was on the grounds of blasphemy rather than their sex lives.

For the third head, politics, they numbered among their members some of the leading political figures of the day, whether noble or commoner. The Earl of Bute, arguably the one man most responsible for the loss of the American colonies, was a member; so was George Wilkes, the political polemicist; and "Hell-Fire Francis," Sir Francis Dashwood, was the second baronet of the line. America's Ben Franklin was also a member.

Hell-Fire Francis was born in 1708 and was an enthusiast in both the 18th-century and 20th-century senses of the word. He had a tremendous sense of beauty, and spiritually typified the Age of Reason with a personal philosophy that sought understanding but was overshadowed by an almost medieval regard for the church. On his Grand Tour, commencing in 1729, he visited Russia (where he is alleged to have slept with Empress Anne), Turkey, and Italy. It was in Italy that his love-hate affair with the Catholic church was most clearly visible. His behavior in chastising the papists was counterbalanced by tearful sessions at the altar rail, begging for a sign "that he might believe."

One evening, all but dead drunk, he believed that he had been threatened by a screaming four-eyed devil and saved by an angel in a white robe. What he actually saw and heard was two cats mating on his window-sill and being frightened off by his tutor in a nightshirt. His tutor unfortunately did not disabuse his charge of the mistaken impression, and for a while Francis was mightily pro-Catholic; but when his erstwhile tutor's tongue was loosened by liquor by some other young rakes in London, the true story came out, and the order was born in reaction.

Initial meetings were held in 1746 at the George and Vulture in the City, home of a former Hell Fire Club (which was where the name came from), but later transferred to Medmenham Abbey in 1752. Francis was now in his early 40s, so the popular image of young rakes was not strictly accurate. Thomas Potter, son of the Archbishop of Canterbury, was 33 in 1852, and he seems to have been one of the younger "Monks."

There were two grades, Superior and Inferior; the Superiors consisting of Sir Francis and 12 others, and the Inferiors (from whom new Superiors could be created on the occurrence of a vacancy), who might have numbered as many as 40 or 50 at the club's height. All could bring guests, of either sex. The monks were attended by nuns, some of whom were professional prostitutes, either at the beginning or at the height of their careers, and others who might be "dollymops"—amateurs—or even women of respectable status.

Despite some attempts to ascribe enormous political

power to the Medmenhamites, it seems that the Friars generally separated business and pleasure.

The club seems to have withered away at around the time of the Gordon Riots, in 1780.

Heptasophs

The original Order of Heptasophs was founded in 1852 as a fraternal order apparently modeled on FREEMASONS, open to white men of good moral character, over 18, believers in a supreme being, possessed of some known reputable means of support, free from any mental and physical infirmity, and having sufficient education to sign their own applications for membership. It later started to offer insurance, as did the schismatic Improved Order. The original order is now extinct, and the Improved Order is a part of an insurance company.

"Heptasoph" does not appear in the *Oxford English Dictionary*, but its root is clear enough: *hepta-* from "seven" and *-soph* from "sophos," wise. The Order of the Seven Wise Men is one of the older secret societies, though now extinct.

Although the order was founded on April 6, 1852, in New Orleans, it may go back further, to the MYSTICAL SEVEN or Rainbow Society founded in Oxford, Mississippi, in 1848, as a branch of an organization of the same name first founded in 1837. The Mystical Seven was actually a college fraternity (see COLLEGE FRATERNITIES AND SORORITIES), part of which subsequently became a part of Beta Theta Pi, and other parts of which may have pursued other destinies. Graduate or other members of this fraternity may have been responsible for the Heptasophs.

Of course, such a modest time scale was not sufficient for the pietists of the organization, who purported to trace their lineage back to 1104 B.C. and Zoroaster, who was allegedly head of the Persian Magi at that time. Subsequent Magi, including the Three Wise Men who attended the infant Jesus, were of course in on the act as well.

In practice, the RITUALS AND CEREMONIES seem to have been a Hellenized version of Freemasonry. Little can be discovered about it now, though it was reportedly elaborate and exceptionally beautiful, based on ancient mysticism. It was essentially Deist (see DEISM)—reference was made to the "Supreme Archon of the Universe," and although "archon" is a perfectly defensible word, it does sound very like the Masonic term "architect." The primary meaning ("chief magistrate") and secondary meaning ("ruler or president") given in the *Oxford English Dictionary* are perhaps more appropriate than the third: "A power subordinate to the Deity, held by some of the Gnostics to have made the world."

There were four ritual DEGREES, though an insurance (beneficiary) degree and a uniformed degree were also available. The structure consisted of Conclave, Grand Conclave (on a state level), and Supreme Conclave.

The Civil War made a serious dent in the membership, after which recovery was slow, and after the schism of 1878 many potential members joined the rival Improved Order. In the 1870s, the question of insurance became increasingly widely debated. From 1872, local lodges (Subordinate Conclaves) could pay benefits "at option," but by the middle of the decade some members wanted formal insurance while others did not; and when the order did not move fast enough, a schism led to the formation of the Improved Order of Heptasophs on August 10, 1878. The meeting that led to the schism was held at the Baltimore Odd Fellows Hall.

Shortly after this, the original order also entered the insurance market. Membership of this new "degree" was subject to medical examination, and the amount paid to life insurance beneficiaries on death of a member was $300. The Heptasophian Mutual Benefit Fund, maintained by a 25¢ ASSESSMENT, paid $500 to "widows, heirs or assignees of decreased members." Wives of members were also eligible. There was never a women's auxiliary.

Although animosity between the old and new orders died down after a relatively brief period—perhaps six years—the Order of Heptasophs was never large. As its high point in 1906, it had 4,000 members, 1,000 of whom were in the life insurance branch. It apparently died before the Improved Order.

Improved Order of Heptasophs

The birth of the Improved Order of Heptasophs in 1878 has already been mentioned, and while the new order kept much of the old ritual—many of its members seceded *en masse* from the original order—it was always more interested in insurance than in fraternalism. Given the choice, it seems that most people preferred cash benefits to mysticism; there were 35,000 members at the beginning of the 20th century and 676,887 members in 1915, when the organization was at its peak.

Insurance benefits were also vastly larger than those offered by the parent order: $1,000 to $5,000 as opposed to $300.

The Improved Order always worked closely with state insurance regulatory bodies, placing its schemes under the regulation of each state as soon as such a body was set up. Despite this apparently hard-headed business approach, and despite the fact that the Improved Order dropped the "Grand Conclave" level of organization early in its history in favor of a two-tier structure, there were still those who remained committed to the old fraternal ways, and Zeta Conclave of Baltimore (which initiated the schism) and the Grand Conclave of Easton, Pennsylvania, both built handsome temples dedicated "to the principles of the Fraternity." The Zeta Temple cost $40,000 at the turn of the century.

The Improved Order of Heptasophs merged with the Fraternal Aid Union in May 1917; the Fraternal Aid

Union in turn became the Standard Life Association in 1933.

Hereditary Societies

Hereditary societies differ from ETHNIC ORGANIZATIONS in that the emphasis is normally on history rather than on ethnicity. The reason for including them here is that many of them insist (or used to insist) on some sort of initiation, and also, even where they are not oath-bound, they still commonly exhibit a great deal of fraternal spirit.

There are very large numbers of these groups: the 50 or so listed below appear in the ENCYCLOPEDIA OF ASSOCIATIONS unless otherwise noted. Those with separate entries in this encyclopedia are marked with small capitals in the usual way. Numbers in brackets refer to the date of foundation and the number of members in 1994: for example "Californianos, Los (1969/700)" means that Los Californianos were founded in 1969 and had 700 members in 1994.

Organizations with fewer than 500 members are omitted, though many exist. Unfortunately, this excludes such intriguing organizations as the Descendants of the Illegitimate Sons and Daughters of the Kings of Britain (1950/260). Also omitted are those societies open to the public—that is, without proof of relevant ancestry—though some organizations inquire more deeply into ancestry than others.

Organizations having their roots in the Civil War are under "(Civil War)," while organizations whose origins are not clear, even to the historian, are given a few words of explanation.

America, Colonial Dames of (1890/2,000)
America, National Society Daughters of Founders and Patriots of (1898/2,250)
America, Order of the Founders and Patriots of (1896/1,200)
American Colonists, National Society, Daughters of the (1921/10,700)
American Revolution, National Society of the Children of (1895/10,000)
American Revolution, National Society, Daughters of the (1890/204,000)
American Revolution, National Society, Sons of the (1889/27,000)
Ancient and Honorable Artillery Company, National Society, Women Descendants of the (1927/1,150)
California Pioneers, Society of (1850/1,200)
Californianos, Los (1969/700)
Confederacy, Children of the (1954/3,926)
Confederacy, United Daughters of the (1894/25,000)
Cincinnati, Daughters of the (1894/550)
CINCINNATI, ORDER OF THE (SOCIETY OF THE) (1783/3,500)
Civil War, Auxiliary to Sons of Union Veterans of the (1883/3,172)

Civil War, Daughters of Union Veterans of the (1885/6,000)
(Civil War) Hood's Texas Brigade Association (1966/1,000)
(Civil War) Ladies of the Grand Army of the Republic (1885/2,000)
(Civil War) Military Order of the Loyal Legion of the United States (1865/950)
(Civil War) Military Order of the Stars and Bars (1938/1,270)
(Civil War) National Woman's Relief Corps, Auxiliary to the Grand Army of the Republic (1883/12,000)
(Civil War) Sons of Confederate Veterans (1896/12,500)
(Civil War) Sons of Sherman's March to the Sea (1966/745)
(Civil War) Sons of Union Veterans of the Civil War (1881/2,500)
Colonial Clergy, Society of the Descendants of the (1933/1,400)
Colonial Wars, General Society of (1892/4,250)
Declaration of Independence, Descendants of the Signers of the (1907/911)
Descendants of Colonial Governors, Hereditary Order of the Descendants of (1896/750)
Flagon and Trencher (1962/800)—pre-Revolutionary tavern keepers
Holland Society of New York (1885/1,000)—Dutch Colonial
Huguenot Society, National (1951/5,000)
Indiana Pioneers, Society of (1916/1,650)
Jamestowne Society (1936/2,900)
Mayflower Descendants, General Society of (1897/22,000)
New England Women, National Society of (1895/2,500)
New Jersey Settlers, Descendants of the (1940/500)
New York, St. Nicholas Society of the City of (1835/600)
Old Plymouth Colony Descendants, National Society of (1910/1,000)
Oregon Pioneers, Sons and Daughters of (1901/800)
Pioneer Rivermen, Sons and Daughters of (1939/2,000)
Piscataqua Pioneers (1905/700)
Republic of Texas, Daughters of (1891/6,500)
Revolution, General Society, Sons of the (1876/6,600)
United States Daughters of 1812, National Society (1892/4,600)
Utah Pioneers, National Society of the Sons of (1933/2,400)
Utah Pioneers, National Society, Daughters of (1901/24,000)
War of 1812, General Society of the (1814/1,500)

Washington's Army at Valley Forge, Society of the Descendants of (1976/900)

Numerous general and local genealogical associations, and groups open to people without ancestral qualifications, are also listed in the *Encyclopedia of Associations*.

Heretics

Heresy is the rejection of religious orthodoxy and dogma. Throughout history, even today, such an attitude has invited persecution, sometimes to the utmost degree, so it is not surprising that many heretical movements have effectively functioned as secret societies, with signs, passwords, and initiation rituals.

Christianity was once such a society. The heresy of the Christians arose not in their choice of deity or their form of worship, but from their intolerance of all other deities and their consequent refusal to make what might be called "social" obeisances and sacrifices. The civil authorities saw this rejection of civil (Roman) values as a symbol of subversion or incipient rebellion, and therefore took the appropriate steps to suppress the new secret society. To this day, some Christians still carry one of the symbols from this time: the fish, which by a Greek word (*ichtheus*) proclaims their faith in Jesus Christ as the Son of God.

This shows clearly how "heresy" is a matter of political definition, not inherent merit or worth. It is quite possible for a heretic to be morally or intellectually superior (or both) to those whose teachings are rejected.

Inevitably, heretics have been accused of all kinds of things that they do not do. The *osculum infame* (kissing the devil's backside) and infanticide are two of the hoarier accusations, the latter being hurled at the Christians with the same abandon as the Christians would later exhibit in accusing others.

As with other secret societies, it is difficult to get an accurate account of what heretical groups really believed or did, but a brief survey of major Christian heresies is still useful, because so many heretics were branded as secret societies.

Adoptionism: A school founded in Rome in about A.D. 185, holding that Jesus was a man who was adopted by God and thereby became perfect. It had a number of adherents until the early to mid-ninth century, but thereafter became mainly a subject of theological dispute.

Albigenses: A heresy that first appeared in the south of France in about A.D. 1012 to 1020, theologically related to the earlier *Bogomils* and contemporary *Cathari,* below. The Albigenses are chiefly noteworthy because of the Albigensian Crusade, effectively a crusade by northern France against southern France between 1209 and 1229 (the year of the Treaty of Paris), though this did not actually exterminate the Albigenses, and persecution continued. On a single day in 1245, for example, 200 heretics were burned in Montségur. Montségur remains a center of attraction for French mystics, much as Glastonbury is for their English counterparts; see the societies listed under Cathars, later in this entry. Massacres like the one at Montségur, under the ever-watchful eye of the Inquisition and with the backing of such papal bulls as *Ad extirpanda* (1252), led to the dissipation of the Albigenses by the early 14th century.

Beguines and Beghards: The Beguines was founded in about 1170 by Lambert le Begue, who wanted to create a community of women devoted to the religious life but without monastic vows. He had already done much good work in establishing (mostly at his own expense) the hospital of St. Christopher, for the widows and children of crusaders.

The idea spread rapidly, and the Beguine cities-within-cities were run by women, for women — though by the 14th and 15th centuries, they had become mere almshouses instead of religious cooperatives. Where the endowment was not sufficient to keep the members of a Beguine in contemplation, the Beguines would work; for they believed *Laborare est Orare* ("To Work is to Pray"). There are still Beguine communities to this day, especially in the Netherlands and Germany, where they work with the sick and the poor.

The Beghards, their male counterparts, were first recorded in Louvain in 1220, initially living by the *Laborare est Orare* rule, but later transferring their affections to begging; this may be the origin of the word *beggar.* Some were "poor Christians" like the *Fraticelli* (below), but others were summed up by the Synod of Trier (1310), which referred to those "who under a pretext of feigned religion call themselves Beghards." They were all equally accused of promoting heresy and duly persecuted to extinction, primarily under Pope John XXII. The female Beguines were also persecuted, but much less. Even John XXII directed that they be left alone.

Bogomils: The Slavic roots of the word *Bogomil* mean "God-Loving." The heresy was of Bulgarian origin and was sufficiently well-rooted there by 970 that a priest called Cosmas wrote a treatise against the organization in that year. It flourished for some time, despite persecution, while moving steadily westward; the Bosnian Church was effectively an institutionalized Bogomilism, which was not dissolved until the mid-15th century.

Some of its views seem unexceptionable. It abhorred wealth and corruption in the clergy; infant baptism was seen as meaningless — only adults could understand what was happening — and baptism itself was not by water but by prayer, reflection, and chanting. Other ideas could raise some problems: Jesus was not divinely born, his miracles were to be interpreted spiritually or allegorically rather than as historical accounts, and sacraments and ceremonies were irrelevant. Teachers were elected from among the congregation, who were known as the Elect and who had the potential to realize their own Christ-nature. Meetings were held in private houses, not in churches.

Where members' beliefs became really interesting, though, was in the doctrine of God's two children, Satanail the elder (who rebelled) and Michael the younger, who became the Christ and broke the power of Satanail, depriving him of the divine suffix "-il" and transforming him to Satan—a clear indication of the Manichaean origins of the heresy (see below).

Cataphrygianism: See Montanism, below.

Cathari: The Cathars, or "Pure Ones," seem first to have appeared as the *pauperes Christi,* the Poor Ones of Christ, at a trial of heretics in Cologne in 1143. The term *Cathari* did not surface until about 20 years later, when the movement gathered strength, especially in southern France.

The Cathari were essentially Manichaean (see below). This world, and all in it, they believed, are a creation of Satan (who also inspired the malevolent parts of the Old Testament), and is therefore both purgatory and hell combined. Unless humans can achieve realization through Christ, they may be reborn in either the human or the animal realms. *Perfecti* had achieved realization, acted as priests, and were entitled to use the Lord's Prayer. *Credentes* were not yet Sons of God, and therefore had to work through the intercession of saints instead of appealing directly to their Holy Father.

The *perfecti* were completely antisex: no marriage, and not even eggs or dairy products, which are corollaries of sexual reproduction. For this reason, many Cathari remained *credentes* until late in life, or even on the death bed. Even for the credentes, marriage was a civil matter, not a sacrament.

Initiation was performed via the *consolumentum,* administered by a *perfectus.* The candidate, addressed as Peter, renounced the harlot church and the cross, was baptized by the laying-on of hands, and became perfect. The rite, reputed to have come down in a straight teaching lineage from Christ himself, removed original sin and realized the god-head within the candidate. The story of the end of the Cathari is told under the heading of Albigenses, above. A number of cathar societies exist today, including:

Société du Souvenir et des Etudes cathares, founded in 1950 to cultivate the memory of the Cathars and to carry out research into them. One of the leading lights apparently combined anthroposophy (see ANTHROPOLOGICAL SOCIETY IN AMERICA) with "a Freemason/ Cathar affiliation" (Lucienne Julien, Honorary Secretary-General, 23 Avenue du Président-Kennedy, 11100 Narbonne).

Institut d'Etudes Cathares, more historical in orientation than the above society (Centre René Nelli [CNEC] Hôtel du Département, 11600 Villegly).

Groupe de Recherches archéologiques de Montségur et des environs (GRAME) (Mairie de Montségur, 09150 Belesta).

Les Amis de Montségur (no address).

Le Groupe Néo-Cathare (apparently operating from the homes of its founders).

Le Cercle Cathar et Gnostique, a small society (BP 16, 60 rue Charles-Gounond, 34502 Béziers).

La Roise-Croix de Harlem, dedicated to "primordial teaching" and emitting Christic rays. This group has its own theories about the GREAT WHITE LODGE, based in the Gobi Desert. The headquarters is in Holland (Rozekruis-Pers, communauté religieuse, Baké Nessergracht 11-13, Haarlem).

La Flamme Cathare, founded in 1984. One of its activities is lighting a flame at Montségur, then carrying it to Toulouse, where the organization is based. The group also arranges fairs, rites, festivals, and more (Espace Saint-Cyprien, 1 rue Jacques-Darré, 31300 Toulouse).

Les Chevaliers de la Flamme Cathare are related to the society above (36 chemin de Narrade, 31400 Toulouse).

Docetae: The Docetae believed that Christ's body was not real, but only apparent—an exceptionally fine theological point that turns on the question of when something is (or is not) what it gives every appearance of being. The heresy flourished and died in the first two or three centuries after Christ's death.

Donatists: A North African sect originating at the beginning of the fourth century, the Donatists held that the Church must necessarily exclude all those who have committed mortal sin. On close examination, it appears that the birth of the heresy was as much political as moral; two rival groups wanted their respective candidates to succeed to the throne of Bishop of Carthage. But the sect struggled on until about the seventh century, albeit in very small numbers.

Ebionites: The Ebionites was a second-century sect who adhered more closely to Judaism than most Christians, even down to rejecting the apostle Paul on the grounds of his apostasy from Jewry. It held that Christ was man, rather than God, though divinely endowed. By the third century, its members had apparently drifted into other sects, including orthodox Christianity.

Fraticelli: Pope John XXII first used the term "Fraticelli" (little brothers) to describe Minorite (see below) heretics in 1317. They believed that the way for the true church lay in abandoning all worldly goods, as they maintained Christ had done—in opposition to a decretal issued by John XXII. The Fraticelli were enthusiastically persecuted for centuries, especially by order of Martin V in 1426, despite (or perhaps because of) their personal asceticism and holiness. They were finally suppressed in about 1466–67 after a renewed campaign of persecution under Paul II.

Hussites: John Huss (1369–1415), a reformer from Bohemia in what is now the Czech Republic, was a follower of John Wycliffe (see Lollards, below). He preached against clerical abuse of power, false miracles, and the like, and was burned alive (he was arrested after being granted a safe conduct) for his preaching. After his death, his followers took a political stance against the Holy Roman Empire; battles were fought from 1419–36, and the Church of Bohemia remained essentially Hussite until its traditions merged with the others of the Reformation.

Lollards: The Lollards (from the same root as lullaby; the "soft singers") were the English followers of John Wycliffe (ca. 1380–84), whose teachings inspired John Huss (see Hussites, above).

Wycliffe was capable of extremely fine and subtle argument. To simplify his views, he was against temporal wealth for the church; denied that the priesthood in Rome had lived up to its professed apostolic succession; opposed idolatry, which he saw not merely in altars, plaster saints, and so on, but also in the doctrine of transubstantiation (which he branded a false miracle); denounced auricular confession as one of the main roots of the arrogance of the clergy; denied that any war could be just; and argued that vows of chastity led to unnatural vice among men and child murder among women. He died of a stroke on New Year's Eve 1384–85. In 1428, his remains were dug up and burned as those of a heretic.

The Lollards were persecuted as late as the reign of Henry VIII and were a major tributary in the broad stream of the Reformation.

Manichaeism: Manichaeism is a religion in its own right, some two centuries newer than Christianity, which influenced its rival and gave its name to a whole school of heresies.

Mani was born in Persia in A.D. 215 or 216 (the 527th year of the Astronomers of Babylon) and, according to tradition, began to preach his new religion some 25 years later. The fundamental premise of the Manichaean religion is that the world is both the creation and the battleground of two entirely separate deities: the force of Light and the force of Darkness. Man was created by the force of Darkness, but incorporates all that part of the spirit of Light that had been stolen by Darkness. Morality (and religion) are the quest to use that internal Light to overcome Darkness both internal and external.

Manichaeans were divided into *electi* or *perfectes* and *catchumemi* or *auditores.* While the ultimate goal of the religion was perfection, it was a realistic and flexible system, which favored working toward perfection with the materials at hand (the imperfect self) rather than making a quantum jump toward an unknowable perfection. The "pure" Manichaeism of North Africa appears to

have died out in the seventh century after the invasion of the Vandals, but it influenced Christianity almost from its inception, and the Manichaean tradition survived well into the Middle Ages in several of the heresies described above and below.

Marcionite Churches: In Rome, in the second century, Marcion preached a version of Christianity based on the pure and uncorrupted gospel of Christ, the corruptions having been removed by Marcion, working along the lines of St. Paul. He was unusual, to say the least, in postulating a Just God (the Creator of the world and God of the Jews) and a Good God, superior to the Just God and the father of Christ. This dualism led to some extremely interesting theology, and was also the destruction of the Marcionite way, because it made Marcionism an easy target for Manichaean (see above) infiltration in the fourth century. Marcionism seems to have vanished around the seventh century, but there are more than traces of it in the Bogomil and Cathari teachings (see both, above).

Minorites: The Minorites or "Little Brothers" show how close an orthodox group can come to heresy. St. Francis of Assisi called his brethren "Minorites," but lively dissent soon arose between those who wanted to continue their founder's tradition of owning no property (the so-called Zealots), those who advocated the moderate use of property (the Moderates), and a small group that was quite at home with property (the "progressive" branch); this happened in the first third of the 13th century. Those of the Zealots who could not accept Moderate tenets soon splintered further into the Fraticelli (above) and into another movement akin to Montanism (below). These were effectively Minorite heresies.

Monarchianism: At the end of the second century and the beginning of the third, the Monarchians believed *either* that Christ was a man raised to the Son of God by being greatly filled with divine wisdom *or* that he contained the fullness of Godhead but was not separate from the indivisible deity.

Monophysites: Monophysites, in the Eastern Roman Empire, believed that Christ's dual nature as God and Man was inseparable, and that he had but one nature composed of both aspects. The group was first suppressed by the Eastern emperor Justin II (ruled A.D. 565–78) and disappeared in the following century or so.

Monothelites: Closely related in theology to the Monophysites (above), the Monothelites held that Christ had a single will, as distinct from a single nature. Pope Agatho pointed out in 679 that if there are two natures (as was already dogma), there must be two wills, but the human must conform perfectly to the divine.

Montanism: Montanism takes its name from Montanus, who appeared on the Phrygian border in the second half of the second century (hence the alternative name for the heresy, Cataphrygianism). He and his two female companions were, they maintained, the bearers of the spirit of truth (*Paraclete*), which Jesus promised in the Gospel of St. John; and their presence continued the revelation of the Holy Spirit.

This was clearly threatening to the Catholic church, which was coalescing into a power base and elevating past revelations to the status of dogma. The Montanists could not be forgiven, despite the admission (which even the orthodox made) that they were not truly divergent from Christ's teachings. When Montanism was banned by a decree of Justinian, the Phrygians closed themselves in their churches and burned them down about their own ears, but other Montanist churches appear to have survived in places—notably Spain—as late as the fourth century A.D. Montanist or neo-Montanist echoes can be detected in many places, from the Minorites (above) to the MORMONS.

Nestorianism: Nestorius, who died in about A.D. 451, was a Syrian who abhorred the custom of calling the Blessed Virgin the Mother of God, because (he argued) it was impossible that God be born of a human woman. To the accompaniment of some very political-looking finagling, the otherwise ultraorthodox Nestorius was replaced as Patriarch of Constantinople in A.D. 431. Nestorian churches survive in the Near East and Asia to this day, especially in the form of the Syriac Church.

Paulicianism: The Paulicians were named after Paul of Samosata and flourished in Asian Minor and Armenia from about the fifth century onward. They apparently still existed in the 19th century. They were part Manichaean (above) and part Marcionite (above), and, like the Druses, they saw no great difficulty in appearing to be of the dominant church that surrounded them.

Waldenses: The Waldenses were a part of the Manichaean-Bogomil-Cathari-Albigensian tradition (see all of these, above). They first came to prominence in the south of France in the late 12th century, denying that the Catholic Church is the Church of Christ and asserting the right of the layman to perform the rites of the sacrament, something the Hussites (above) also advocated. The Waldenses of Lombardy also maintained (with the Donatists, above) that no one in mortal sin could consecrate the sacrament.

They suffered the usual persecution, especially at the hands of the Dominicans, and there was a special attempt at extermination in 1487 (under a Bull of Innocent VIII). As a result of a synod of 1532, they joined with Swiss Protestantism and were by then known as Vaudois, a description of a Protestant sect still to be found in Switzerland and the valleys of southern France. But their troubles were not over. In 1655, for example, they were the targets of appalling persecution at the hands of Catholic armies (including specially imported Irish troops). The revocation of the Edict of Nantes in 1685 launched a new pogrom, and for much of the 17th century their clergy depended on handouts from Protestant England. Effectively, the Vaudois have now been subsumed into generic Protestantism.

The word "voodoo" (referring to Haitian-African animism) is widely believed (without any believable shred of theological or other evidence) to derive from the Creole *vaudoux,* in its turn a corruption of *Vaudois.*

Hermandad

Hermandad (Spanish for "brotherhood") is a term applied to any number of unions of municipalities organized throughout medieval Castile for specific purposes—usually as common police forces or as forces for defense against the strongarm tactics of various magnates.

The most famous *hermandades* were those of Toledo, Talavera, and Villa Real, whose mounted constables (called *caudrilleros*) apprehended, tried, convicted, and executed—all in summary fashion—rural bandits.

During the 12th century, when the *hermandades* first began to appear, they were feared and distrusted by the Castillian crown. But Henry II officially recognized them by a royal decree of 1370. However, by the 15th century, the *hermandades* had begun to decline, and the brotherhoods were officially suppressed by royal decree in 1476. In that year, a new, highly organized constabulary system was established in Castile, which was dubbed the Santa Hermandad. The formally constituted body practiced a form of justice as swift and summary as that introduced by the vigilante version of the *hermandad,* but the new organization created much dissatisfaction among the nonnoble subjects whose taxes were required to support it, and the Catholic Monarchs acted to reduce its funding, prestige, and authority in 1498. Nevertheless, the Santa Hermandad survived in hobbled and inefficient fashion as a rural constabulary well into the 18th century.

Hermanos Penitentes

The *Orden de Los Hermanos Penitentes* was a secret sect, closely allied to the *Flagellantes* of the Middle Ages. Members indulge in self-flagellation and commemorate Holy Week by crucifying one of their number, who is tied to the cross until he is near death. The order, which survives today in the southwestern United States, may be descended from the *Confradia del Tercer Orden de Franciscanos,* established in New Mexico between 1682 and 1685.

Members of the Penitentes are divided into two classes: La Luz (the Light), which consists of the Hermano Mayor (Chief Brother) and other titled individuals, and De las Tinieblas (Of the Darkness), consisting of common brothers. Meetings are held in the Morada, or private meeting hall, and public processions take place every Friday during Lent and on the last three days of Holy Week. Methods of public flagellation include scourging with rough pads or prickly pear cactus, rubbing the skin with flint to draw blood, and actually lashing the flesh.

Officially, the Catholic Church considered the Hermanos Penitentes practitioners of "criminal extravagances," and the archbishop responsible for New Mexico caused the excommunication of entire Moradas during the mid-19th century. Still, the practice survived, flourished, and continues today.

Hermes Trismegistus

Hermes Trismegistus, Thrice Great Hermes, is also known in late hieroglyphic forms as "Twice Very Great Hermes" and in the demotic as "Five Times Very Great Hermes."

He is the Egyptian Hermes, not the cadaceus-bearing Greek used as a symbol of the medical profession. He is a manifestation of Thoth, the scribe of the Egyptian gods, though he is also persistently identified with Anubis.

A large number of syncretic religious writings have been attributed to him. The so-called *Corpus Hermeticum* (the "Body of Hermetic Work") is a compilation of remarkable eclecticism, which probably dates from post-classical times. If there is anything in the teachings, it has unquestionably been entangled with enormous quantities of superfluous material from the earliest times, and the maunderings of most subsequent writers such as ELIPHAS LEVI have added little or nothing. Nevertheless, the sonorous sound of the name and the millennia-old tradition of magic that surrounds it mean that the writings attributed to Hermes Trismegistus are widely studied by anyone with pretensions to mysticism.

Hermetic Brotherhood of Luxor

The Hermetic Brotherhood of Luxor was founded in Boston in the middle of the 19th century. The first Secretary-General was a Scot named T. H. Burgoyne, and the first (visible) Grand Master was an American called Peter Davidson. They combined hermetic philosophy (see HERMES TRISMEGISTUS) with a 19th-century mechanistic view of the perfectibility of man, pointing out that, while a coconut can become a palm tree and a puppy can become a dog, a palm tree cannot become a coconut nor a dog return to puppyhood. By a shaky analogy with a shady philosophical question (Does not a tree "become" its fruit?), they argued that man must always progress—and they professed to have the key to that progress.

They postulated three immutable occult laws, of Form, of Activity, and of Affinity. The society may still exist, based in Zurich. One of the main works of the organization, *Traité méthodique des sciences occultes* ("Meth-

odological Treatise on Occult Sciences"), was reissued in Paris in 1967.

Hermetic Fraternity

The Hermetic Fraternity was organized in Chicago in about 1884 for the study of "Hermetic Philosophy" and was responsible for the publication of several books. The fraternity appears to have vanished in 1904 when its leading light, Dr. W.P. Phelon, died.

Hermine d'argent, Ordre Hermetique de l'

8 rue Roger-Coumaillaud
17100 Saintes, France
(at last report)

The Hermetic Order of the Silver Ermine (or Silver Stoat) is a French order based on teachings contained in the Book of Nabelkos, which was apparently written by Gwenaël d'Echebrune at the inspiration of the Number of the Beast mentioned in Revelation, 666. The order practices a type of TANTRA, together with sublimination of sexual energy.

Heroines of Jericho

The Heroines of Jericho are part of ADOPTIVE MASONRY and come (or came) in two colors, black and white. The black order appears to be the older, dating from just after the foundation (in 1775) of Prince Hall Freemasonry, while the white order was allegedly founded in France in 1790 and came to the United States just after the War of 1812.

A religiously oriented order, its ritual requires the services of a lodge chaplain. Membership is also open to male members of Royal Arch Masonry (see ROYAL ARCH MASONS, GENERAL GRANDE CHAPTER OF), who are called Knights of Jericho. Currently, no headquarter address for this organization is known.

Hetaira

The Hetaira, from the Greek "Union of Friends," was a shadowy secret society, or possibly a sequence of secret societies, dedicated to the liberation of Greece from Turkish rule. The earliest date mentioned for its foundation is 1796, though it does not seem to have gotten properly under way until the first decade of the 19th century. Emissaries called Apostles tied to garner support in Greece as well as abroad. From about 1816, when Anthymos Gazi launched a new propaganda movement in Greece, the movement gathered strength among a wider and wider range of people. After the Revolution of 1822, it petered out and probably expired in 1827 when Great Britain, France, and Russia agreed to guarantee the existence of a semi-independent Greece.

The foundation of the Hetaira is ascribed to various people, and its initial location to various places, including

Vienna, Odessa, and Moscow. Most of the high officials were noble and well-educated Greeks in exile. As a cover, it used *Heterai Philomuse,* an organization dedicated to the preservation of Greek art and culture during Turkish occupation.

Hibernians

"Hibernia" is the classical name for Ireland (from the Greek). The origin of the secret society known as the Hibernians is hazy, and even the date is unclear, varying from 1565 to the 1690s. The Ancient Order of Hibernians in America (the paradigm entry here) was founded on May 4, 1836.

Prior to 1836, the Ribbonmen (a late 18th-century anti-Protestant Irish society) and their successors, the Ancient Order of Hibernians (A.O.H.), may (or may not) have protected outlawed Catholic priests; acted as a terrorist-*cum*-vigilante group against English landlords; rallied to Wolf Tone's Irish uprising of 1798; and generally fought for Ireland. Stevens suggests that whatever happened before 1836, the A.O.H. adopted the form of a fraternal secret society after it had arrived in the United States, borrowing its structure and its ritual from other groups such as the Odd Fellows.

Ancient Order of Hibernians in America

31 Logan Street, Auburn, NY 13021; (315) 252-3895

The American Ancient Order was founded in 1836 in New York City as a religious, political, fraternal society, which later offered insurance. It was open to Catholic men of Irish descent aged 16–45, and there were 191,000 members in 1994. The Daughters of Erin are their female auxiliary (see AUXILIARIES).

Even since its appearance in the United States in 1836, the A.O.H. has been through a number of revisions. It was always an example of "muscular Christianity," and in the 1840s and 1850s it was called upon to combat the so-called "nativist" parties epitomized by the KNOW-NOTHINGS, who detested immigration and Catholicism about equally. In 1853, members were sufficiently numerous to muster 12,000 for the annual St. Patrick's Day Parade, which in the political atmosphere of the day must have come close to incitement to riot.

In the 1860s and 1870s, it provided the structure for the "Molly Maguires" labor movement, described below. Only in the 1880s did it begin to resemble its present form, and even then, there was a brief schism between the A.O.H. proper and the A.O.H. Board of Erin (1884–98). Since then, it has continued to support the Catholic faction in Ireland, even since the partition into Eire and the Six Counties.

Molly Maguire was a widow who was ejected from her poor cottage in Ireland by a heartless landlord, and in the vigilante days of the Ribbonmen (above), her name was frequently signed to notes warning other landlords not to overstep their bounds. She may or may not have actually existed.

In American usage, the Molly Maguires were Pennsylvania coal miners who formed a union against mine owners. Going beyond ordinary trade union practice, the Mollies probably engaged in arson, sabotage, intimidation, and murder. Whether they did or not, 19 of them were hanged for such offenses.

The A.O.H. provided the structure, passwords, and meeting places for the Mollies, though the Mollies could be seen more as an organization that exploited the A.O.H. than as part of it—except, of course, that pro-Molly feeling generally ran strong in the relevant lodges. Their actions were repudiated at the 1876 National Convention, at around the same time that the Mollies themselves were penetrated and broken by agents of the Pinkerton Detective Agency.

The basic unit of the A.O.H. is the Division (lodge); the next layer seems to be the biennial national convention. The RITUALS AND CEREMONIES are not easily discovered, nor the number of DEGREES, but the lodge emblems are (predictably) the harp and shamrock as well as the three links and the clasped hands. Each Division used to be substantially autonomous, setting dues and benefits, but since the insurance has had to conform to relevant federal and state law, greater uniformity has become the norm.

On a charitable level, the A.O.H. has supported Catholic educational charities and Catholic missions overseas. They also award the John F. Kennedy Memorial Medal biennially (he joined in 1947).

Membership was given as 125,000 in 1897 (plus 40,000 in the schismatic A.O.H./B.O.E.); 181,000 in 1965; 191,000 in 1978; and 191,000 again in 1994.

High Twelve International

11155 S. Towne Sq. #B2
St. Louis, MO 63123
(314) 487-3387

High Twelve International, founded in 1921, is one of the Masonic LUNCHEON CLUBS; it is open to Master Masons and is almost exclusively American. The club publishes the *High Twelvian* bimonthly. There were 25,000 members in 1994.

"High Twelve" is a Masonic term meaning noon. It appears in some ancient Masonic texts and is by tradition the hour at which Operative Masons (see FREEMASONS) eat. The High Twelve luncheon club was founded on May 17, 1921 by the Reverend E. C. Wolcott, a Congregational minister as well as a Freemason.

Its stated purpose is to "inculcate the ideals taught in Masonry by uniting in the happy bonds of a fraternal hour," those ideals being the strengthening of Masonic ties, participation in community activities, and the furtherance of the American public school system.

High Twelve International goes to great pains to emphasize the fact that it is not a civic luncheon club, but to an outsider, the differences are not easy to see—except, of course, that those attending must be Masons. In fact, they must be Masons "of a recognized Lodge," which excludes Prince Hall (black) Masons in many states.

There are no DEGREES, for the organization is open only to Master Masons, and no RITUALS AND CEREMONIES, as lunch meetings are held once a week at noon. "Music, speaking, high-class entertaining and social hour are featured."

It is not merely a social and Masonic organization, however; funds raised by the Wolcott Foundation (established in 1952) are used to cover one-year scholarships for those working on masters' degrees at the School of Government and Business Administration or the School of Public and International Affairs at George Washington University in Washington, D.C. Other funds are contributed to Masonic youth organizations, such as the Order of De Molay, Job's Daughters, and the Order of Rainbow for Girls, and to Masonic old people's homes. (See DE MOLAY, ORDER OF; JOB'S DAUGHTERS, INTERNATIONAL ORDER OF, RAINBOW FOR GIRLS, ORDER OF.)

Although it calls itself "International," the vast majority of support for High Twelve is within the United States. There are subordinate state organizations and below them, local organizations. The officers at each level consist of a president, three vice presidents, the immediate past president, a secretary, a treasurer and a general counselor.

Hiram; or, The Grand Master-Key

The full title of this estimable work, a thick pamphlet of fewer than eighty pages, published in London in 1766, is in full: HIRAM: or, the GRAND MASTER-KEY To the Door of both ANTIENT AND MODERN FREEMASONRY. Written by "A Member of Royal Arch" (possibly S. Gosnell), it provides an excellent insight into the early stages of Freemasonry.

Hiram Abif

Hiram Abif was, in the traditions of the FREEMASONS, the chief architect of the Temple of Solomon, on which most Masonic RITUALS AND CEREMONIES and legend is based; his name may also be rendered Chiram, being spelled *cheth, resh, mem* in Hebrew.

Most or all of the legend of Hiram Abif is made up. His name is mentioned only in I Kings vii:13–14, though II Chronicles ii:13–14 may reasonably be taken to refer to the same man. Everything else comes from the Masonic Book of Constitutions, or from even less historically verifiable sources. The Book of Constitutions says:

This inspired master was, without question, the most cunning, skillful, and curious workman that ever lived; whose abilities were not confined to building only, but extended to all kinds of work, whether in gold, silver, brass or iron; whether in linen, tapestry or embroidery; whether considered as architect, statuary, founder or designer, separately or together, he excelled.

He is supposed to have died seven years after starting work on the Temple. The legend is one of the "secrets" of Freemasonry, which most Masons will do their best to avoid recounting. It is, however, well documented, as follows.

Every noon—High Twelve, in Masonic parlance—Hiram Abif went into the temple to pray. Three Fellow-Craftsmen, not yet Master Masons, determined to wait for him as he came out and to force him to give them the secret word of recognition of the Master Mason. Their names were Jubela, Jubelo, and Jubelum. These are the Ruffians of Masonic tradition; the Masonic group called the Ruffians is sometimes taken as another, independent secret society, but this does not seem to be the case.

Jubela was at the south gate, where the Master went first. When Abif refused to divulge the word, Jubela struck him in the throat with a 24-inch rule. The Master hastened for the west gate, where Jubelo demanded the word; when it was refused, Abif was struck on the chest with Jubelo's square. Finally, at the east gate, a blow between the eyes from Jubelum's mallet completed the job. Abif fell dead, still having refused to disclose the word—or, as Masons have it, the Word or the *Word*.

The murderers buried their victim over the brow of Mount Moriah and placed a sprig of acacia on the grave. The murderers were rapidly discovered (before the body was found!) as they tried to escape to Ethiopia. A search party sent out by no less a person than King Solomon (in Masonic tradition, a chum of the builder) soon found the grave, marked by the evergreen sprig. Then, after the Entered Apprentices and the Fellow-Craftsmen had failed to resurrect their Master, he was raised by the Master Mason with the "strong grip of a lion's paw."

Hoffmansche Bund

The Hoffmansche Bund was a German secret society, named after the lawyer who founded it. It had as its object the universal distribution of arms throughout Prussia and the establishment of a vast citizen army trained through a system of gymnasiums. It was founded in about 1813 and finally dissolved on October 18, 1915.

Holy Sepulchre of Jerusalem, Equestrian Order of the

Church and Monastery of St. Onofrio
Vatican City

The Equestrian Order of the Holy Sepulchre of Jerusalem was founded as a religious/military order, but is now purely religious. It operates worldwide as an award for Catholics, though non-Catholics may receive the Cross of Merit. There were over 10,000 members in the mid-1980s, about a quarter of them in the United States.

The Equestrian Order of the Holy Sepulchre of Jerusalem is not as well known as some of the other military orders of great antiquity, such as the Knights HOSPITALLERS, but it still survives with an unbroken lineage. It was founded as the Sacred and Military Order of the Holy Sepulchre of Jerusalem in about 1099 A.D. by Godfrey de Bouillon, leader of the First Crusade. Its purpose was to protect the sacred sites of the Holy Land and the pilgrims who went to visit them. Most notably, the order was to protect the Holy Sepulchre itself. The new order was approved by Callistus II in 1122, and fought in all major battles in the Holy Land until the fall of Acre in 1291.

From then until 1847, the Guardian or Custodian of Mount Sion (a Franciscan) was empowered to dub knights in the Basilica of the Holy Sepulchre, though for practical reasons the order was mostly dispersed in its European priories. Twice in the next 200 years, the order nearly met with the same fate as the TEMPLARS—suppression—and in 1489 it was provisionally united with the Hospitallers by Innocent VIII. It was reconfirmed as an independent order by Alexander VI in 1496. It remained on shaky ground, though, as the Reformation challenged its religious foundation, and the growing power of the nation-state challenged its temporal wealth. In addition, a crusading order without a crusade must necessarily be somewhat directionless.

In 1847, following an agreement with the Turkish empire, Pius IX reinstated the Latin Patriarchate of Jerusalem and made the Patriarch the Grand Master of the order. This new leader expanded the order greatly by delegating to other knights the power to dub further knights in any country.

Until 1868, there had been but a single degree (see DEGREES) of Knight below that of Grand Master, but in that year Pope Pius IX added two more degrees, Knights Commander and Knights Grand Cross. Later, the degree of Knights Commander with Star (or Grand Officers) also made its appearance. Yet another rank was established in 1949 under Pius XII, that of Knight of the Collar. Furthermore, women were admitted as early as 1871 (the Countess Mary Frances Lomas was the first), a practice regularized by Leo XIII in 1888. Their degrees are Dames, Dames Commander, and so on.

From 1907–28, control reverted to the papacy, but then it re-reverted to the Patriarch of Jerusalem. In 1931, the name of the order was changed to its present form, and in 1945 the seat of the order was moved to Rome. In 1949, it became a legal corporation under canon law. In 1962, John XXIII authorized modernization and, in 1977, Paul VI approved the new constitutions.

The objects of the Order are set forth in the current constitutions as follows:

1. The practice of the Christian life in filial love toward the papacy and the Church
2. The conservation and propagation of the faith in the Holy Land
3. The protection and upholding in the holy places of the sacred, indefeasible rights of the Catholic Church

The order also plays an important part in charitable work of all kinds. For non-Catholics who help the order in its works, there is a Cross of Merit awarded in the same degrees as the Catholic foundation.

Homesteaders

The Homesteaders was founded in 1906 as a fraternal insurance society for men and women in the United States and Canada who were "first-class risks, physically and morally." The society is now extinct, and has no connection with a 1978 "back-to-the-earth" movement of the same name.

The BROTHERHOOD OF AMERICAN YEOMEN used the word "Homesteads" for its LODGES. In 1906, two officers of the American Yeomen (John E. Paul and Clarence B. Paul) were forced to resign their posts. They took from their former employers the word "homestead," a certain number of RITUALS AND CEREMONIES, and a fair number of members. Although the organization is now extinct, the ritual is interesting.

Both men and women were admitted from the start, and the organization prospered. By 1920, it had 30,000 members in 23 states, plus Canada. In 1923, however, the group decided to change its fraternal ways and became a nonfraternal insurance organization under the name of The Homesteader's Life Association. The changeover is described in the *Fraternal Monitor* for November 1923. In 1932 it merged with the Golden West Life Insurance Association, formerly the Fraternal Brotherhood, and in 1948 it changed its name again to become the Homesteader's Life Company—the standard progression for a financially well-run mutual insurance company.

The organization was on the usual three-tier system, with Grand Homesteads and a Supreme Homestead; the latter met quadrennially.

The ritual was based on a dramatization of life in a pioneer village. The candidate was seized as a spy by the somewhat paranoid pioneers, who would then suggest that he be "bound to the back of a wild horse and burning brands attached to its heels, then turn them loose to wander upon the plains until he be dragged to the death befitting a spy."

Momentarily recoiling from such equine incendiarism, they would then decide to give him a chance to prove himself by rescuing the wife and daughter of a pioneer who is long overdue from the East. After a sequence of Indian attacks and so on, he would rescue the two ladies, though the missing pioneer dies on a stretcher as he is being carried back to the "barricade"—an interesting variation on the usual death theme, with skeletons and coffins. There was also a strong patriotic element, with an annual flag day.

Hommes de l'Intelligence

Les Hommes de l'Intelligence, the "Men of Intelligence," was a short-lived group of HERETICS from 1398–1410—or, at least, it was regarded as such. In practice, it seems to have been fond of both DEISM and sex, and to have had very little in common with the Christianity of its time. It is much more reminiscent of such 20th-century groups as the ORDO TEMPLI ORIENTIS or even the Process (see PROCESS, THE).

It was founded by Gilles de Leeuwe, called Gilles-le-Chantre. After an association with the Frères du Bien Mourir, Gilles took to public exhibitions of nudity in the streets of Brussels (as a symbol of childlike innocence), claiming direct inspiration from the Holy Spirit. He founded the Men of Intelligence in 1398.

The underlying principles of the organization were, first, the identity of God and Man and, second, "direct rule" by the Holy Spirit without intercession. The order denied the Final Resurrection, saying that Christ was already resurrected in all mankind. Members also believed in three Ages: the Mosaic Age or Age of the Law, the New Age or Age of Jesus, and the Age of Eli or Age of the Holy Spirit. The third Age, they maintained, was dawning; so the "New Age" was already old by 1398. The Man of Intelligence (or Woman; Gilles seems to have attracted a number of female followers) was free of all laws and conscience.

Astonishingly, the order escaped serious censure from the Inquisition. Gilles-le-Chantre died before any proceedings were instituted, and when in 1410 the Bishop of Cambrai ordered an inquiry, his successor Guillaume d'Hildernasse managed to fudge the issue so well that even when he was condemned as the follower of Gilles-le-Chantre, his punishment was a triple abjuration at the episcopal palace of Cambrai and three years incarceration there. In 1423 he returned to the Carmelite convent at Brussels as a *lecteur*, apparently little worse for his experiences. The remaining followers seem to have gone underground and to have escaped punishment.

Honor Societies

Honor societies are best considered as COLLEGE FRATERNITIES AND SORORITIES with the benefit of an education. They bear Greek letter names, just like fraternities and sororities, but are open only to those who maintain high academic standards. Their origins were the same as other fraternities—either social clubs, or in frank imitation of existing organizations.

They are private clubs (that is, they are not run by the universities at which they have chapters), and admission is by invitation. The admission RITUALS AND CEREMONIES typically follow the pattern of other secret societies. Phi Delta Gamma, for example, uses a Bible, a yellow rose, and other symbols. The societies may organize speakers, publish journals, and function as "old boys' clubs" (and old girls' clubs), much in the manner of FREEMASONS.

Hooded Ladies of the Mystic Den

The Hooded Ladies of the Mystic Den were an auxiliary (see AUXILIARIES) of the KU KLUX KLAN, founded in Baltimore, Maryland, in 1923. Members were predictably anti-black, anti-Catholic and pro-Bible, especially when it came to putting their brand of Christianity into the public schools as an antidote to "imported evils," by which they meant Catholicism.

The order advocated stringent immigration laws and legislation to promote the exclusive use of the English language in all institutions, public or private.

Hoo-Hoo, International Order of

P.O. Box 118, 207 Main Street
Gurdon, AR 71743
(501) 353-4997

The Concatenated Order of Hoo-Hoo was founded as a "fun" fraternal society for men involved in the lumber industry. Called today the "International Order," it is principally American and publishes the *Hoo-Hoo Log and Tally Magazine* quarterly. There were 7,300 members in 1994.

The Concatenated Order of Hoo-Hoo was founded on January 21, 1892, in Gurdon, Arkansas, to which its headquarters had returned at the time of this writing. In the intervening years, it has moved a long way from its intention, which was to fight superstition and conventionalism, and became a parody of established secret societies. It started out with the intention of having nothing that other orders possess. Originally, there were no lodge rooms. Meetings, or "concatenations," were held in hotels, the first being at the St. Charles Hotel in New Orleans on February 18, 1892. Even the name is unique. "Hoo-hoo" is not some arcane lumberman's distress call, but a word coined by one of the founders, Bolling Arthur Johnson, about a month before the order was founded. He used it to describe a lonesome tuft of hair on the head of one Charles H. McCarer. "Concatenated" referred both to the cat, which was chosen as the symbol, and to "concatenation," or "linking together in a chain."

The founding members were not just lumbermen. They also included railroad men (who transport lumber) and newspaper men (who cover it with print). The organization chose as its emblem a black cat, to show its disdain for superstition, and based much of its RITUALS AND CEREMONIES on the cat's nine lives. Their officers were the Supreme Nine, made up of the Snark, the Senior Hoo-Hoo, the Junior Hoo-Hoo, the Bojum or Boojum, the Scrivenotor, the Jabberwock, the Cuctocacian, the Arcanoper, and the Gurdon. The overall leader was the Snark of the Universe. One of the high points of the ritual was the Embalming of the Snark, by which process he passed into the House of Ancients.

The theme of nines was continued. In 1937, initiation cost was $9.99; annual dues were $0.99, and the constitution originally limited membership to 9,999, though that was subsequently changed to 99,999. There are also nine Ethical Principles, though it is not clear whether these were a part of the original conception or a subsequent addition as the order matured into respectability.

In 1909 (appropriate enough), it started down the slippery slope to seriousness with a funeral fund (raised by a $2 ASSESSMENT against 3,000 members), which was fraught with actuarial loopholes. The relatives of deceased members were paid $250, which was no mean sum in 1909, and when the reserves fell too low, there would be another assessment.

In the absence of medical examinations and age limits, the Concatenated Order was playing actuarial Russian Roulette. The next change, therefore, was a requirement that no death benefits payable for the first 60 days of membership.

By 1921, it was calling itself "a living, moving, inspiring Force! A force for good! A force for fellowship! A force for welding all lumbermen into a compact, humanitarian body for SERVICE [their capitals] to God, Family and Country." It described itself at this time as "the Pioneer Business Fraternal Order of the World" and "the Largest Business Fraternal Order of the World." It even put out such messages as "Radical and Bolshevist attacks on the organized business and personal property rights of America call for a sharp class association in every department of business life."

In 1965, it threw out the "Concatenated" part of the title as being outdated. By the 1980s, it had so far forgotten itself as to dedicate itself to the promotion of lumber in many ways: by sponsoring exhibits at state and county fairs, paying lecturers, giving scholarships, giving awards for carpentry in vocational schools, and sponsoring tree-planting projects.

Horrible Conspiration Club

The Horrible Conspiration Club is included chiefly for its delightful name; it was (and may still be) a small club of FREEMASONS belonging to the Mystic Lodge of Pittsfield, Massachusetts. It was founded in 1913 and was limited to the "sacred" number of 27 members (perhaps 3 × 3 × 3?).

Hospitallers

The Order of the Hospital of St. John the Baptist in Jerusalem was founded in about A.D. 1050 as a religious/military order to serve pilgrims going to the Holy Land. The main order survives, in very small numbers, in Rome; but countless other organizations claim to be descended from it.

The Knights Hospitallers was one of the three great military orders. Although it was founded 50 years before the First Crusade, it was during the Crusades that it rose to eminence—though many would say that its finest hour was at the Siege of Malta in 1565. A number of societies more or less descended from the original Knights Hospitaller still exist and are listed in the subheadings under this entry.

The original foundation was exactly what its name suggested, a hospital in Jerusalem for the benefit of Christian pilgrims. It was funded by merchants from Amalfi (near Naples), and was attached to a Benedictine monastery. At first under the auspices of St. John the Almoner, it was later dedicated to St. John the Baptist.

At the very end of the 11th century, during the Siege of Jerusalem, the Rector of the Hospital was Peter Gerard. According to legend, he threw down loaves of bread to his fellow Christians outside the walls—the besiegers were as hungry as the besieged—but when he was hauled before the Moslem governor and accused of treachery, he stuck to his story that he had been bombarding them with stones. When the loaves were produced in evidence, it was found that the loaves had turned to stone, and he was acquitted.

After the fall of Jerusalem in 1099, many Crusaders rewarded the Hospital with gifts of land and money. Godfrey de Bouillon himself, the first Christian ruler of the Holy City, gave it his own Manor of Montboise in Brabant in return for services done to les povres foybles et malades ("the poor feeble and sick"). Soon, the Hospital was wealthier than the Benedictine monastery to which it was attached, and Gerard sought and received papal permission to found a new order. The original aim of the order was the succor of the sick, together with the traditional monastic vows of poverty, chastity, and obedience.

After Gerard's death in 1118, Raymond du Puy became the new rector. Finding that many of his brethren were military men of noble birth, he added (with papal sanction) a further vow, that of fighting the enemies of the faith. This the order did with enthusiasm, and although it retained its medical mission and its monastic vows, it now functioned primarily as a military organization. The "Rule of Raymond," as summarized in a Bull of Boniface VIII, runs:

I, Raymond, the servant of Christ's poor, and Master of the Hospital of Jerusalem, desire that all those Brethren who here dedicate themselves to the service of the poor shall, with Christ's assistance, maintain inviolate the three promises which they have made to Him—namely, chastity; obedience, which is to be understood to include whatever may be commanded by the Master; and to live without any property of their own; because the fulfillment of these three vows will be required of them by God at the last judgment. Let them not seek for or claim as due to them more bread and water or raiment, which things are promised them, and let their raiment be humble, because our master, the poor, whose servants we profess to be, appears scantily and meanly clad, and it is not right that the servant should be proudly arrayed whilst the master is humble

Under Raymond, the order was divided into classes. Knights of Justice had to be of noble birth and to have received their knighthoods already from secular hands. Conventual Chaplains and the Priests of Obedience formed the purely ecclesiastical arm, the former in Jerusalem and the latter at the various stations of the order in Europe. The Serving Brothers came from humbler ranks of society.

The order was by now extremely rich, and the hierarchy ran upward from the Knight Commander to a Prior, a Grand Prior, and then to the Grand Master. The basic unit of the order was the Preceptory or Commandery; a group of these formed a Priory; and the Priories of a country constituted a Grand Priory.

In 1259, Pope Alexander IV decreed in a letter to the Master of the Hospital that the costume of the order should be "black mantles, that they may be distinguished from others; but in campaigns and in battles they shall wear surcoats and other military decorations of a red color, on which there shall be a cross of white, like that on your standard." The cross on the standard was, of course, the eight-pointed cross now known as the Maltese Cross.

The fall of Acre in 1291 marked the end of Christian power in Palestine, and the Knights Hospitaller under its 21st Grand Master, John de Villers, retired to Cyprus. From there, in 1310, the order captured Rhodes under the leadership of Fulk de Villaret, the 24th Grand Master, and moved its headquarters there.

In a third transformation, the order then became a naval power. It established a fleet of galleys to protect Christian commerce from Levantine and African corsairs—and to harry the Infidel. Hospitallers were to remain on the island for more than two centuries, during which time they prospered still further, established themselves as front-line fighters for Christendom, and proved a perpetual thorn in the side of the Ottoman Empire.

While they were in Rhodes, the Hospitallers also reorganized themselves into Langues, or national groups, while still retaining the old threefold division into Knights of Justice, Conventual Chaplains and Priests of Obedience, and Serving Brothers. There were originally seven Langues: Provence, Auvergne, France, Italy, Aragon, England, and Germany. Castile was added later. Each Langue supplied one officer to the government of the Order: the Grand Commander from Auvergne, the Turcopolier (Commander of the Light Horse) from England, and so forth. These officers were called Conventual Bailiffs.

So great an irritation were the Knights Hospitallers to the Grand Turk, that in 1522 Suleiman the Lawgiver (Suleiman the Magnificent) mounted a gigantic attack on the island: 400 ships and an army of 140,000 Turks, together with 60,000 Wallachian and Bosnian peasants for siege works. The Knights under Philip de L'Isle Adam commanded 600 Brethren and 4,500 troops, so the odds against the order were almost 20 to one. After a great siege, of which Charles V of Spain said in praise of its defenders, "Nothing was so well lost in the world as Rhodes," the Knights left Rhodes on January 1, 1523. The Knights would not have another permanent home for seven more years, despite an offer (ironic in the light of later developments) of 20,000 crowns in gold from Henry VIII of England—an offer later made good in the form of artillery.

In 1530, Grand Master de L'Isle Adam accepted (somewhat ungraciously) the islands of Malta and Gozo, together with Tripoli. The feudal dues payable to the liege lord, Charles V, was a falcon annually—the original Maltese Falcon.

Between 1530 and 1565, the English Langue was dissolved by Henry VIII, but the order continued to harry the Grand Turk, fortifying Malta against the invasion they knew would come. It lost Tripoli in 1551. In 1565, Suleiman the Lawgiver dispatched another great fleet of 130 galleys and 50 transports, with perhaps 40,000 men. The order faced them with 474 knights and an army of perhaps 9,000, mostly Maltese volunteers.

It was a Jihad, a holy war, for both sides. The Pope granted plenary indulgence to anyone who fell fighting the Turk. Fort St. Elmo, the smallest fort, was garrisoned with 100 knights and a few hundred soldiers, though reinforcements were periodically carried in by boat, which also carried away the sick. To reduce that one outpost, before starting on the main fortifications of St. Angelo, cost Suleiman's army 8,000 men. About 1,500 Christians fell in all.

On the day St. Elmo was to fall, June 24, the noble knights De Guaras and Miranda were too weak to stand and fight. Both had been terribly wounded. They therefore ordered that they be strapped in chairs in the breach, where they knew the attack would come. Each had his great two-handed sword by his side. Both fell in the first wave, lost under a sea of white-robed attackers.

Against such resistance, the Turks might take one small fort, but they could not in the end prevail. They turned their attention to the Birgu, the main fortified part of the Knights' enclave. The fight was desperate. The 70-year-old Grand Master, Jean Parisot de la Valette, personally led a countercharge when the walls were breached. Maltese volunteers swam out to plant stakes in the seabed to prevent attacks by galleys, and fought with knives against Turkish swimmers, who were sent against them. The Maltese won. Miners and counterminers fought underground. At last, after the tardy arrival of the Viceroy's fleet from Sicily, the Grand Turk left on September 8, 1565. The Ottomans left behind 25,000 dead, over half their army.

Only six years later, in 1571, Ottoman sea power was finally crushed at Lepanto. This was the last great battle of galleys, and the Knights Hospitaller was prominent in the fight. Thereafter, its decline as a military order was rapid. Although its success during the siege brought them vast wealth in thanks offerings and conscience money (for many European princes had believed that Malta could not stand), it was spent in keeping the order in luxury and splendor. Valetta, "the city built by gentlemen, for gentlemen" and named after la Valette, stands as testament to this. The order sent ambassadors to all the Catholic courts, and the Grand Master was habitually addressed as "His Serene Highness" and "Prince of Malta."

The Rebellion of the Priests, the Quarrel with the Venetians, the Expulsion of the Jesuits — all were symptoms of dissension within the order, which, as a powerful pan-national Catholic organization owing allegiance only to the Pope, was increasingly anachronistic. But still, the order maintained the great Hospital that it had built, and its medicine was always up to date by the standards of the day.

The effective end of the order in its old form came when Paul I, tsar of all the Russias, offered to form an Orthodox Langue and to throw his weight behind the order on the condition he was made Grand Master. The order split. Some moved to Russia, and others stayed in Malta. Napoleon occupied the island briefly in 1798, only to be thrown out by the British in 1800. The Knights was expelled under the French occupation.

Members of the Knights who went to Russia elected the tsar as their Grand Master on the resignation of the 69th Grand Master, Ferdinant von Hompesch, but they requested the Pope to nominate his successor when the occasion arose. Pius VII declined to do this, and it was not until 1877 that Leo XIII appointed a new Grand Master. The headquarters of the order moved to Rome, and it is from the Palazzo di Malta on the Via Condotti, 68 Roma, that the present establishment of the original order is ruled.

The Sovereign Order Today

The present constitutional charter was approved by H. H. John XXIII on June 24, 1961. Members must be Catholics, and are divided into Knights of Justice and professed Conventual Chaplains; Knights of Obedience and Donats; lay members and honorary chaplains; Knights and Dames of Honour and Devotion, Knights and Dames of Grace and Devotion (who do not have to meet such rigorous standards in proving nobility of birth); Magistral Chaplains; Knights and Dames of Magistral Grace; and Donats of Devotion.

An Order of Merit may be bestowed upon Catholics and non-Catholics alike, but does not imply full membership. It exists in both civil and military wings, and consists of the Collar (a single rank, normally reserved for heads of state), the Cross with five ranks (Grand Cross of Merit, Grand Officer, Commander, Officer, and Cross of Merit, all with female equivalents), and the Grand Cross and Cross *pro piis meritis* (both reserved for the clergy).

Alliance des Ordres de Chevalerie des Hospitaliers de Saint-Jean-de-Jérusalem

There are Scandinavian, German, Dutch, and British national orders of St. John of Jerusalem, of which the Grand Masters are national sovereigns or pretenders. The seat of the alliance is in Berne, Switzerland.

As an example, the St. John's Ambulance Brigade in England is the leading volunteer paramedical organization. The Maltese Cross is a familiar sight on its ambulances at sporting events, fairs, and other occasions. This Protestant order was incorporated in the 19th century with the blessing of Queen Victoria; in 1963 it signed a joint statement with the Sovereign Military Order emphasizing the importance of charity to the sick.

Chevaliers Hospitaliers de l'Ordre Souverain et Militaire de Saint-Jean-de-Jérusalem (Chevaliers du Chypre, de Rhode et de Malte)

This group is based in Belgium (rue de la Reine 19, B-5200 Huy).

Knights of St. John

General Thomas Graziano, Supreme President
2206 Pinnacle Drive, Utica, NY 13501; (315) 724-9238

The Knights of St. John is a fraternal and religious order founded in the United States in 1879. It is open to "any practical Catholic gentleman," aged 16–55 — though social members may be over 55. The order operates in the United States, Africa, and the West Indies. There were 7,211 members in 1989. The order publishes the *Knight of St. John* magazine, the September 1978 issue of which contains a history of the order.

The connection between this and the original order is tenuous. It takes inspiration from the Hospitallers rather than claiming ancestry from them. It was founded in the United States in 1879, though the order says that "a number of individual commanderies were organized prior to that date in various parts of the country." Its original name was "The Roman Catholic Union of the Knights of St. John," which was later shortened to its present form.

Its members wear a pseudomilitary uniform: "a chapeau, double breasted coat, trousers, sword, belt and necessary trimmings," though "a marching uniform patterned after a naval officer's uniform is also acceptable." It describes itself as "the most prominent semi-military Catholic organization" in the United States. Members wear their uniforms when participating in church parades or parish events, and for such occasions as "First Communions, Confirmation, First Masses, Anniversaries, Forty Hours, Holy Thursday, Good Friday, Palm Sunday, etc." Sometimes, they guard the Blessed Sacrament in procession. "No greater honor can be accorded a layman than to stand guard beside his Eucharistic God in the uniform of a Knight. The mind cannot comprehend the blessings bestowed upon him for that simple, humble act of worship."

The order's stated objective is to "strive to capture men's hearts and minds for God by promoting among its members a filial devotion to Holy Mother, the Church and a respect for her authority."

The "many benefits" quoted in the brochure include:

An affiliation with the church in a very particular manner
An opportunity to wear the uniform of a Catholic organization
The practice of Catholic action by a public profession of faith
Parish involvement
Mission work
Fraternity
Social benefits
Benevolence
Sports program
Good fellowship

The order's mission work is carried out by sponsoring the erection of chapels through the Catholic Extension Society, to whom the order made a commitment in 1956.

The main sport of the order appears to be bowling: "The National Sports Committee through their Bowlers Mission Penny Program contribute to the chapel fund and to the National Apostolate for the Mentally Retarded as do many commanderies individually." Softball and golf are also played.

Lodges are called Commamderies; regional groups are ruled over by Grand Commanderies; the head office is the Supreme Commandery. Not all lodges offer sick benefits, though a "modest" death benefit is apparently available to all members of the order. There are fraternal rituals, though the use of the password was discontinued

in 1977 as having "no appreciable organizational value." The order appears to work only a single degree. Cadet commanderies are open to any Catholic boy who is eight years old and has received his first communion, and there is a ladies' auxiliary (see AUXILIARIES).

Oeuvres Hospitalières françaises de l'ordre de Malte

32 rue de Ranelagh, 75016 Paris

This order is reported to have about half a million members worldwide, about a quarter of a million of whom are in France. Its aims appear to be close to the original order in the 11th century, as the order dedicates itself to hospital work. In 1968 this order gave birth to Aide internationale de l'ordre de Malte (22 rue Dulurbe, 33000 Bordeaux) and to La Tradition chevaleresque (4 Avenue Marceau, 75008 Paris).

Sovereign Hospitaller Order of St. John

Villa Anneslie, 529 Dunkirk Road, Anneslie, MD 21212

The Sovereign Hospitaller Order was founded in 1960 as a charitable and social society for "Christians" (gender and age unspecified). The size is not known.

Known from 1960–76 as the Grand Priory of Poland-Lithuania, this derivative of the Knights Hospitaller sponsors seminars and training programs and conducts an annual fundraising social event for a selected charity or orphanage. It maintains St. John's Hospice in the United States. Practicing Christians of any ethnic background, not just Polish and Lithuanian, are eligible for membership.

Sovereign Order of St. John of Jerusalem (U.S.A.)

Information on the Sovereign Order of St. John of Jerusalem is derived from a leaflet, apparently current in the 1970s, originating from Shickshinny, Pennsylvania: "All other groups parading under different settings of the same words are simply provincial imitations, and as such, do not deserve any recognition." Any Christian who is willing to make a "substantial voluntary contribution or gift" to the headquarters is eligible to be considered for membership.

The order was small in the late 1970s, advocated the harnessing of cosmic energy for weather control, and published *The Maltese Cross,* a periodical.

Other Manifestations

In Malta, the order runs the biggest blood bank on the island. There are many other would-be orders, some of which appear in this encyclopedia, which also claim descent from the original order. Very few can make out a good case.

Houn' Dawgs, Order of

There is apparently no level of self-abnegation to which secret societies have not fallen in their choice of names. The Order of Houn' Dawgs was founded in Cabool, Missouri, in 1912, with "Kennels" for LODGES. It was probably extinct by the early 1920s.

H.T.D.

Revue Ogam: 2 rue Leonard-de-Vinci
Rennes
Revue Kad: 3 rue de Clisson
Rennes

The Henvreudeuriezh Tud an Derv ("Ancient Fraternity of Men of the Dog") is hardly ancient, having been founded in 1936 as a society espousing both Celtic paganism and Breton nationalism. Morvan Marchal, one of the founders, also founded Breiz Atao in 1919, and others may have been associated with Gwenn ha Du ("Black and White," the Breton colors), which Mariel (in his *Dictionnaire des Sociétés Secrètes*), describes as a terrorist organization (see MARIEL, PIERRE).

The RITUALS AND CEREMONIES were strongly based on the FREEMASONS. The noted Breton poet Gw. B. Kervezhiou (d. 1951) was a prominent member, who did much to encourage the use of Celtic imagery.

The Kredenn Geltiek is the ritual and religious manifestation of the H.T.D., though the name of the group's publication seems to argue the existence of a militant strain: It is called *Kad*, or "Combat." Other publications are *Ogam*, a periodical, and *Nemedon*, a review.

Human Leopards

Few West African secret societies have received much notoriety, but the Human Leopards was an exception. Ranging throughout Sierra Leone, the Leopard's principal activity was cannibalism. Reportedly, members purchased young boys, fattened them up, then killed, baked, and devoured them. They were also notorious for attacking travelers. They dressed in leopard skins, hid in the bush, then fell upon their victim, bringing him or her back to the other members of the order for a cannibal feast.

Membership in a Leopard society conferred privileges and power. The initiation ordeal was costly. Each prospective member was required to produce a teenage girl of his own or his wife's blood for sacrifice. On the night before the night of this sacrifice, a cannibal meal was consumed, and the candidate and four companions wandered through the forest, roaring like leopards. On the sacrifice night, all Leopard society members in the region gathered, wearing leopard masks and armed with "leopard knives" — pronged, clawlike weapons with double-edged blades. One member was nominated as "executioner," and, clad in a full leopard skin, he crouched by a trail along which, by prearrangement, the young victim was sent on her way by a parent or guardian. The executioner leaped from his hiding place and attacked the girl, slicing her throat with the leopard knife. The body was carried to a secret meeting place, where it was dissected and the internal organs studied with intense fascination. The flesh was then cut up and distributed to all members — as well as the child's parents (as a token of atonement in order to forestall a blood feud as a result of the "sacrifice").

The purpose of the Leopard's gory rituals was to create powerful medicine, not only to strengthen members of the order, but the tribe as a whole. It is unclear when the Human Leopards ceased to exist, if, indeed, they are entirely extinct as an order. Three members of the Human Leopards were hanged by British authorities in the Imperi country on August 5, 1895, for murdering and devouring a traveler. One of those executed had been a Sunday School teacher.

Hungarian Reformed Federation of America

2001 Massachusetts Avenue N.W.
Washington, DC 20036
(302) 328-2630

The Hungarian Reformed Federation of America was founded in 1896 as a fraternal benefit insurance society. Membership is open, with an understandably strong Hungarian appeal. The order publishes *Fraternity-Testveriseg* quarterly. There were 18,433 members in 1994.

The Hungarian Reformed Federation of America is a typical fraternal benefit society, declining steadily in numbers (from 28,000 in 1979 and 37,000 in 1965) and offering, in addition to the customary fraternal benefits, the usual run of competitions, scholarships, museums, archives, and the like.

Hunters

The Hunters, or Hunters Lodges, in a Canadian incarnation, was a militaristic political secret society formed early in 1838 after the Canadian insurrection of 1837, with the intention of bringing about another insurrection. It may have been backed by interests in the United States. There were four DEGREES: the Hunter, the Racket, the Beaver, and the Eagle, which roughly corresponded to private, sergeant, captain, and colonel. The society lasted only two years, but was militarily very active. Individuals from U.S. border states joined and, at its height, membership reached 40,000 to perhaps 60,000.

The Hunters planned (but failed to execute) an invasion of Upper Canada on July 4, 1838, and was unsuccessful in other incursions at Napierville, Lacolle, and Odelltown (all Lower Canada). It engaged in a number of border provocations intended to foment war between

Britain and the United States. U.S. President John Tyler warned it to disband—and, surprisingly, it did, by 1841.

Hyperborea

Hyperborea—the country beyond the wind—has been a legend for something like 28 centuries: Herodotus assures us that the Hyperboreans were mentioned by Hesiod, though they do not appear in Homer. The name Hyperborea is probably formed from the name of the Hyperborean people, "those who carry over," and is connected with the legend of how Delian devotees of Apollo used to get their offerings to the Hyperboreans, by passing them to the nearest nation with a request that they be passed on.

Hyperboreans lived for 1,000 years: Their longevity, together with the legendary remoteness of their home, has made them a fruitful source for speculation.

Iatric Masonry

A little-known branch of FREEMASONS that occupied itself in Germany in the 18th century with a search for the Universal Medicine. It was apparently a Hermetic Rite, and only one degree is known to have been associated with it: the "Oracle of Cos"—Cos being the birthplace of Hippocrates, father of medicine. Neither the order nor the rite exist any longer.

Illuminated Theosophists

This was a modification of the Masonic Rite of Pernetty. It was introduced into England in 1767 by a French surgeon named Benedict Chastanier and originally worked nine degrees. However, the order subsequently abandoned Masonic forms and became a Swedenborgian sect of the Theosophists. By 1784, the Illuminated Theosophists were no longer a Masonic lodge at all, but a society that met on Sundays and Thursdays at chambers in New Court, Middle Temple, London, to discuss Swedenborg's writings.

As originally conceived in Masonic terms, the nine degrees of the Illuminated Theosophists were: 1, 2, and 3, Symbolic degrees; 4, 5, and 6, Theosophic Apprentice, Fellow-Craft, and Master; 7, Sublime Scottish Mason, or Celestial Jerusalem; 8, Blue Brother; and 9, Red Brother.

Illuminati

The original Illuminati was founded in Bavaria on May Day 1776 as a club of freethinkers (and arguably of evolutionary anarchists). The original order is now extinct.

The organization that was founded in 1776 by Adam Weishaupt, Professor of Canon Law at Ingolstadt in Bavaria, is the best-known group of "Illuminati." It is, however, only one of many groups calling themselves or known as "Illuminati."

The word itself comes from the Latin, meaning "illuminated" or "enlightened," and there are two separate strands of Illuminist development. One is essentially a Protestant/Gnostic form of Christianity (see GNOSTICISM), and the other (to which Weishaupt adhered) is a free-thinking and often atheistic (or at least non-Christian) belief in the perfectibility of mankind; the chosen name of Weishaupt's Illuminati was *Perfektilibilisten,* the "perfectible ones."

The Christian strand was based on direct knowledge of the divine, in the Gnostic tradition; several adherents claimed direct contact with God and the Blessed Virgin.

The Spanish terms *aluminados* ("illuminati") or *alumbrados* ("out of the shadows") date back to at least the 15th century, and in 1511 a laborer's daughter known as La Beata de Piedrahita, who claimed to speak with God and the Virgin Mary, was investigated by the Inquisition; only the intervention of powerful friends halted the investigation. Even Ignatius Loyola, the founder of the JESUITS, was admonished by an ecclesiastical commission for his alleged sympathies with the *alumbrados* in 1527. By about 1623 the movement had spread to France and gained some influence in 1634 when Pierre Guérin, the *curé* of Saint-Georges de Roye, joined them. His followers, the Guerinets, were suppressed in 1635. Subsequent illuminati of this tradition have had little historical significance.

The other, non-Christian, strand is more complex. The ROSICRUCIANS are often held up as the leading perfectibilist Illuminati, but they claim their own history. The indisputable facts about Weishaupt's organization are the date of its foundation; the name of its founder; and the date of its suppression. The names of a number of eminent members are also known, including Johann Wolfgang Goethe, but it probably never numbered more than about 2,000 members between its foundation in 1776 and its suppression in 1785.

Weishaupt's Illuminati were interested in democracy, freedom, and reform of all kinds, which they apparently believed were historically inevitable. Such faith was a product of the Age of Reason, and the Illuminati were great believers in progress and improvement, which would eventually lead to a free society of equals. They saw themselves as being in the vanguard of this movement.

They had, however, a heavy mystical overlay. The lowest of their three classes included "novices," "minervals," and "lesser illuminati"; the second included "Freemasons," "Ordinaries," and "Scottish Knights"; and the third included "Priest," "Regent," "Magus," and "King."

Their link with the FREEMASONS is hazy. The clandestine nature of the meetings of both organizations made them good places to discuss dangerous ideas—ideas that would attract unwelcome attention from the established government and the established church if they were aired too publicly. Weishaupt made a deliberate effort to infiltrate the Freemasons, or at least to establish contacts through them. It was fear of new ideas, let alone of new ideas discussed in secret, that led the Bavarian government to suppress both the Illuminati and the Freemasons in 1785.

The Illuminati also seem to have borrowed from the florid imaginings of contemporary continental Freemasonry, where DEGREES multiplied like rabbits. There were three separate sets of degrees, and four or five degrees within each set, as follows:

NURSERY		1. Preparation
		2. Novice
		3. Minerval
		4. Illuminatus Minor
MASONRY	(SYMBOLIC)	1. Apprentice
		2. Fellow-Craft
		3. Master
	(SCOTCH)	4. Illuminatus Major or Scotch Novice
		5. Illuminatus Dirigens or Scotch Knight
MYSTERIES	LESSER	1. Prebyter or Priest
		2. Prince or Regent
GREATER		3. Magus
		4. Rex

The RITUALS AND CEREMONIES were apparently a mixture of Freemasonry and revolutionary politics, though the latter did not become particularly evident until the Illuminatus Dirigens rank, when the initiate was warned of the wiles of princes both temporal and spiritual. The aim of the order seems to have been a rational, atheist government.

The Illuminati would probably be forgotten now if they had not become the center of one of the greatest conspiracy theories of history. Although they were not a revolutionary organization, they almost certainly had a number of revolutionary members and they lived in revolutionary times. When the French Revolution took place in 1789, some people linked the Illuminati with it; the leading conspiracy theorist was the Abbé Augustin de Barruel, who traced the Freemasons and the Illuminati back to the Manichaean heretics of the third century A.D.

Barruel's works were taken up with enthusiasm by many subsequent generations of writers, including in particular Nesta Webster, whose *Secret Societies and Subversive Movements* (1924, and republished frequently since) tied the Illuminati and the Masons in with Lenin, the Irish Republican Army and international Jewry. Webster wrote several other books with the same theme.

Much as been published about the Illuminati, but little is actually known about them. They are second only to the TEMPLARS as a focus of fantasies.

Illuminati, Society of the

The (American) Society of the Illuminati was a schismatic Mormon secret society who borrowed the name of Weishaupt's order without any clear idea of the tradition to which it laid claim. The order was formed in about 1850 by James G. Strang. In traditional Mormon fashion, it admitted only men, though there was an auxiliary called The Covenant, which admitted both sexes. Little is known about the main order, but the Covenant took a somewhat muscular or militant view of Mormonism and swore on oath to defend the church even to the point of spilling blood.

Strang was an enthusiastic polygamist, and apparently an admirer of bloomers; he was shot and killed by one of his followers, who had been publicly whipped for refusing to compel his own wife to wear the garments. On his death, the tabernacle on Beaver Island in northern Lake Michigan (headquarters of both organizations) was destroyed by the fishermen who lived on the island, and the remaining adherents dissipated rapidly.

Immaculates of the United States of America, Independent Order of

The Immaculates, an African-American fraternal order, took its name from a previous organization, the Young

Men's Immaculate Association, but differed in offering beneficial insurance and admitting both men and women. The society was founded in Nashville, Tennessee, by W. A. Hadley on June 23, 1872, and has been extinct for many years. At the beginning of the 20th century, it had about 5,000 members.

IMRO (Internal Macedonian Revolutionary Organization)

IMRO was founded in November 1893 by Damyan Gruev, Gotse Delchev, and Yane Sandanski under the slogan "Macedonia for the Macedonians." It was a political secret society dedicated to the subversion and overthrow of Macedonia's Ottoman Turkish overlords. (In Macedonian, it was called VMRO, for Vatreshna Makedonska-Revolutsionna Organizatsiya).

Working covertly, IMRO swiftly gained popular support and staged major anti-Turkish revolts in 1897 and 1903, both of which were supported by a parallel pro-Bulgarian organization. These revolts failed. During the Balkan Wars of 1912–13, IMRO effectively became a covert arm of Bulgarian foreign policy; Bulgaria sought to wrest Macedonia from Serbian and Greek domination. During World War I, IMRO terrorism became uncontrolled, alienating supporters in Bulgaria as well as Macedonia. Nevertheless, IMRO survived the war and during the 1920s became a covert terrorist force in Balkan politics. Members of IMRO assassinated the Bulgarian prime minister Aleksandur Stamboliyski, beating him to death in the streets of Sofiya in June 1923. The organization seized control of the Macedonian district of Bulgaria and, clandestinely supported by elements of the Bulgarian war ministry and the Italian government, committed terrorist violence in Bulgaria and Yugoslavia through the 1920s and early 1930s.

The assassination of IMRO leader Todor Aleksandrov in 1924 split the organization into two rival factions, which devoted as much energy to gunning one another down as they did to practicing terrorism against others. When Kimon Georgiev seized the government of Bulgaria in 1934, assuming dictatorial powers, he ordered the suppression of IMRO once and for all, imprisoning its leaders and disarming the rank and file.

Independents

The Independents were an Italian secret society, dedicated to freedom for their country, founded in the first or second decade of the 19th century. They were alleged to have had particularly strong links to Russian secret agents, who had been present in Italy since 1815. The Independents reportedly also proposed offering the Italian crown to the Duke of Wellington, the hero of Waterloo.

International Alliance of Catholic Knights

The International Alliance of Catholic Knights is an umbrella organization of Catholic fraternal orders recognized by the Holy See as "knightly" but not pretending to be true Orders of KNIGHTHOOD. The groups include:

KNIGHTS OF COLUMBUS
Knights of St. Columbanus
Knights of the Southern Cross (Australia)
Knights of the Southern Cross (New Zealand)
Knights of St. Columba
Knights of Da Gama

Invisibles

Very little is known about this possibly fictitious order, which is supposed to have existed in 18th-century Italy. It is said to have advocated atheism and suicide. Presumably, the order if it ever existed at all, was short-lived.

Irish Republican Brotherhood

The Irish Republican Brotherhood was a political organization, founded about 1835 and operating in both Ireland and the United States. Membership was open to men only.

The Irish Republican Brotherhood was a part of the old American tradition of supporting Irish (Fenian) separatist groups on a freelance, local-fund-raising basis. The order arose out of Young Ireland, modeled on the YOUNG EUROPE plan, which had been at the forefront of the abortive Irish uprising of 1848. Unlike Young Ireland, which was mainly devoted to writing and oratory, the Fenian brotherhood was more militant, as evidenced by the oath (see OATHS):

> I, [Name], in the presence of Almighty God, do solemnly swear allegiance to the Irish Republic, now virtually established; and that I will do my very utmost, while life lasts, to defend its independence and integrity; and, finally, that I will yield implicit obedience in all things, not contrary to the laws of God, to the commands of my superior officers. So help me God. Amen.

It was founded by two exmembers of Young Ireland, John O'Mahoney and James Stephens, who left exile in Paris in 1853 to relight the flame of the Irish rebellion—O'Mahoney to New York and Stevens to Dublin.

O'Mahoney found the Emmet Monument Association in New York to be very receptive to his ideas—they were already intent on causing an Irish revolution, but had not actually done very much about it—while Stephens investigated the situation in Ireland. Building on the Emmet Monument Association, O'Mahoney appointed two secretaries and treasurers, but left other offices to be filled by democratic election.

In March 1858, supported with American money, Stephens swore in his first recruit in Ireland; thereafter, the order grew rapidly through the medium of pyramid selling. Stephens was the Chief Organizer of the Irish Republican Brotherhood (COIRB) and had four Vice Organizers or *V*s. Each *V* would appoint a number of Colonels or *A*s; each *A* would recruit nine *B*s or Captains; the *B*s, in turn, were each to recruit nine *C*s or Sergeants; and inevitably, each *C* was expected to recruit nine *D*s or Privates. The whole unit, from *A* to *D,* was known as a "Centre," and Centres were rapidly formed not only in Ireland, but in those parts of England and Scotland with large Irish populations—Glasgow, London, Sheffield, and the like. Later in 1858, Stephens sailed for America. As early as December of that year, a complete Centre of Fenians was arrested in County Cork for illegal military drilling.

Unfortunately for the Fenians, this was not its only setback. The American Civil War soaked up many of the troops who were supposed to be training to fight in Ireland, and the same conflict also stopped much money being sent back to the Emerald Isle. The total sent back from 1858 to 1867 was about £25,000, rather over $100,000 at the exchange rates then prevailing—a great deal of money for the time, but hardly enough to fund a revolution.

To make matters worse, the Catholic Church was opposed to the Fenians, as to all oath-bound societies, so Fenians mostly had divided loyalties.

The story thereafter is almost familiar. The Americans, wondering where their money was going, wanted the Irish to rise immediately. The Irish did not have enough money, and were in any case under surveillance by the English. In 1865, Stephens and others were arrested in Ireland, though Stephens escaped through the help of a warder who was sworn into the brotherhood. In 1866, habeus corpus was suspended in Ireland, and many more Fenians were collected. In 1867, the weakened brotherhood made a desperate attempt at a rebellion and, predictably, failed.

Meanwhile, in the United States, the organization had been quarreling among itself. It divided into two branches in January 1866, and thereafter divided into several more, all of which were thoroughly infiltrated by British spies. It also took part in paramilitary actions— apparently aimed at gathering arms—in the United States and Canada. These were uniformly unsuccessful and cannot have garnered support for the movement among non-Irish.

In late 1869, some 300 members of the Brian Boru circle of the Irish Republican Brotherhood in New York City seceded to join another organization, which had grown up within the Fenians, the Knights of the Inner Circle. This was the origin of Clan-na-Gael. The Irish Republican Brotherhood in the United States rapidly withered and became irrelevant as the newer organization gained importance.

In Ireland, the Irish Republican Brotherhood remained in existence, but passively so. There were occasional, sporadic flare-ups, but nothing much happened until 1899, when a Welshman—Arthur Griffiths, editor of the *United Irishman* in Dublin—proposed a campaign of passive resistance, which eventually grew into Sinn Fein ("We ourselves" or "Ourselves Alone"). This policy was adopted both by the I.R.B. and Clan-na-Gael, then abandoned in 1917, when Sinn Fein became a political party dedicated to the overthrow of British rule by whatever means available, including violence.

Iron Guard

This Romanian nationalist and fascist-sympathizing order was founded by Corneliu Codreanu, who was inspired by the anti-Semitic teachings of A. C. Cuza, a professor at the University of Jassy (Iasi). It developed from a number of nationalistic leagues founded in Romania during the 1920s, chief among which was the National Christian Anti-Semitic League, organized in 1923 in response to the government's having extended citizenship to Jews. The league perpetrated terrorist acts against Jews while preaching a campaign of "moral restoration."

Codreanu left the league in 1927 to found the Legion of the Archangel Michael, which exalted manual labor and comradeship and, like the National Christian Anti-Semitic League, called for moral regeneration. The legion was usually referred to as the "Iron Guard" by 1932 and placed four deputies in Parliament and built a substantial constituency among Moldavian peasants as a result of a public works program. The Iron Guard—or Legion of the Archangel Michael—became sufficiently threatening to the status quo that, in December 1933, Liberal premier Son Duca ordered it dissolved. Three weeks later, he was assassinated, and Guard/Legion members were arrested. Codreanu was released, however, and quickly set up a Legion Labor Corps, forging the All-for-the-Fatherland Party out of the Iron Guard. In 1937, the new party obtained 16 percent of the vote and placed 66 deputies in parliament.

During 1937–38, King Carol II established a royal dictatorship in Romania and cracked down on the Iron Guard, either murdering or arresting its leading members. When Iron Guards assassinated the minister of the interior, Carol ordered the execution of hundreds of imprisoned Iron Guard members, including Codreanu. Surviving members fomented a general uprising in response to this, forcing the abdication of Carol and elevating General Ion Antonescu, an ardent Iron Guard, to the position of dictator, with the commander of the Guard/Legion, Horia Sima, as vice premier.

In January 1941, elements of the Iron Guard came into conflict with the army and attempted a coup that quickly degenerated into a violent insurrection in which Iron Guards went on a rampage, murdering thousands of

Jews and others perceived as enemies. Guards captured and held the Bucharest radio statio for four days, broadcasting the slogan, "Long Live Death." Combined German and Romanian forces put down the insurrection within less than a week, killing or imprisoning Iron Guard leaders. A small core of Iron Guards survived and were released from prison in 1944 by the Germans as the Soviet army overran Romania. These Iron Guards set up a short-lived fascist government-in-exile in Vienna that died with the end of the fall of Nazi Germany in World War II.

Iron Hall, Order of

The Order of the Iron Hall, which lasted less than a decade and a half, was a fairly typical fraternal benefit society founded in Indianapolis, Indiana, in 1881. The career of the order was meteoric—there were 125,000 members at one point—but this was mostly due to the unusual financial basis of the order, which depended on two premises: first, an increase in funds from the paid-in but unclaimed dues of lapsed members, and second, a "chain-letter" form of accounting in which members were urged to recruit four more members, whose dues would support them.

Iroquois, Order of

The Order of Iroquois was a presumptuous attempt to perpetuate (or cash in on) the fame of the original NATIVE AMERICAN IROQUOIS CONFEDERATION in Indiana. It was founded in Buffalo, New York, in 1896 and disappeared in 1922 when it was absorbed by Fraternal Home Insurance of Philadelphia, Pennsylvania.

Isawa

The Isawa came to the attention of the West as a secret society that fought against French colonial domination in Algeria, Tunisia, and Morocco during the early 20th century. Calling itself the "Army of God," it employed assassination as its chief political weapon. The roots of the Isawa reach back to the beginning of the 16th century, when the order, whose name denotes "path," was founded by Shaykh Muhammad (born Isa al-Sufyani al-Mukhtari), a gifted and charismatic mystic. Although the founder seems to have taken no part in resisting the various Christian invaders of this region during this period, the order soon developed into a religious and political force that played an important role in fighting various colonial powers over the centuries, most notably the Portuguese and the French.

As a secret society, the Isawa employ an initiation ritual, which begins with a clasping of hands, and women are admitted to membership equally with men. Beyond this, however, the order is divided into several "clans," each of which is named after an animal, and members are admitted to only one clan. Part of the initiation ritual is to imitate the characteristic action of the animal emblematic of the clan. This could be quite dramatic. For example, those admitted to clans symbolized by animals who tear and devour their prey—jackals, cats, dogs, leopards, lions—participate in a ceremony that begins with the beating of tom-toms, playing of pipes, and a kind of monotonous dance. Following all of this, a live sheep is thrown into the middle of a square, initiates fall upon the animal, tear it limb from limb, and devour it raw.

Other rituals include ecstatic dancing and displays of fakirism, including such feats as walking on hot coals, taking burning brands between the lips, and swallowing broken glass. Members practice various forms of magic, especially conjuration and exorcism. Members are identified by the wearing of the *gattaya*, a mat of plaited hair, worn very long, and grown only from the top of the cranium.

The Isawa were active as late as the 1950s and, at their modern height in the late 1920s, seem to have numbered about 4,000, concentrated mainly in Morocco.

Note that al-Isawiyya was a Jewish sect active in the 10th century and unrelated to the Isawa.

Isis

The MYSTERIES of Egypt centered upon Isis and are probably the prototype of the mysteries of ELEUSIS. Several parts of the legend, such as Isis sitting wearily on the side of a well during her search for Osiris, are to be found in both traditions. There is a great deal about Egyptian theology in the *Chapter of Coming Forth by Day*, better known as the Egyptian Book of the Dead. According to tradition, this was written by Thoth, the Scribe of the Gods, and it centers around Osiris and Isis.

Osiris was murdered by Typhon, and his body torn into 14 parts, which were scattered all over Egypt. Isis sought each part and gave it a burial wherever it had fallen; the only part she could not find was the phallus, which fell into the Nile and was eaten by pike and sea bream, so she set up effigies instead. After all this, Osiris returned from the underworld, so there is a myth of DEATH AND RESURRECTION behind the Mysteries.

The drama of the Mysteries centered around the search for the body of Osiris, and involves a great range of symbolism. For example, the *sistrum* or sacred rattle used in the Mysteries contained four "things that are shaken," symbolizing the four elements of earth, water, fire, and air. Both Plutarch and Apuleius describe some aspects of the Mysteries of Isis, though often obliquely or in passing.

Italian Sons and Daughters of America Fraternal Association

419 Wood Street
Pittsburgh, PA 15222
(412) 261-3550

The Italo-American National Union was founded in 1895 as a fraternal benefit life insurance society for "Americans of Italian origin and their friends," and in 1991 it was absorbed by the Italian Sons and Daughters of America Fraternal Association. It operates only in the United States; there were 5,000 members in 1994, distributed among 34 local groups. The order publishes a monthly newsletter.

It is a typical ethnic fraternal benefit society, financing scholarships, good works, homes for the elderly, and cultural events in addition to furnishing insurance. The order confers Man of the Year, Michelangelo, Renaissance, and Leonardo da Vinci awards annually.

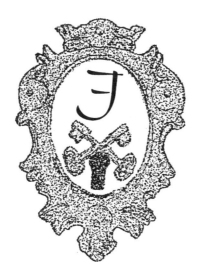

Javia Kartas

Javia Kartas is said to have been founded by Al-Kahina or Al-Qahina, Queen of one of the Berber tribes (the Djeraous of the Aures Mountains). She opposed both the Arab invasion and the spread of Islam during the first expansion of that religion in the seventh century; she and her tribe had apparently embraced Judaism. Her greatest success was against the 40,000 men of Hasan bin Numan in A.D. 696, but she was at the last betrayed by her adopted son, a boy she had saved in battle. She died fighting.

Despite all its feminist antecedents and the sad end of its leader, Javia Kartas became (and may still exist as) a masculine Islamic secret society with a membership policy described as "very exclusive." It is or was active among the Berbers of Morocco.

Jehu, Society of

This society was formed in France during the Revolution, to avenge revolutionary terror, but was itself extremely violent. Established in Lyons, it took its name from the king who was consecrated by Elisha to punish the sins of the house of Ahab and to slay the priests of Baal—that is, those associated with the Terror. The order was sometimes confused with the JESUITS, the Society of Jesus.

Jehu disappeared under the Consulate and the Empire, but reappeared in 1814–15 as the Knights of Maria Theresa, or Knights of the Sun. How long these two new orders lasted is unknown.

Jesuits

The Company of Jesus, *Societas Jesu*, is a mendicant Catholic religious order founded in 1540. It deserves a place in this book partly because of the way in which it has operated in the past and partly because of the rumors about the order that have been circulating almost since its foundation. The more lurid rumors—of human sacrifice and the like—are baseless, but there is little doubt that the S.J. has had an enormous effect upon the politics and attitudes of many nations, and it has surprisingly often been suppressed in the same way as other politically dangerous secret societies.

To a large extent, its influence (and its unpopularity) are due to the rigorous honesty, high standards, and formidable intellectual training historically associated with the society. The "secrecy" of the Jesuits is to a large extent a myth, but arises from a combination of envy and frustration.

St. Ignatius and the Foundation of the Society

At the age of 30 in 1521, at the defense of Navarre, Inigo Lopez de Loyola was struck by a French cannon ball at Pampeluna. While recuperating, the noble soldier turned to religion.

After years of study, during which time he visited Paris, Bruges, London, and many other cities, and after gathering about him the nucleus of what would become the S.J. in 1534–36, he was ordained in Venice in June 1537. In 1539 he submitted a request to the Pope to form a new order. On September 27, 1540, Pope Paul III signed *Regimini militantis Ecclesiae,* establishing the new order with a limit of 60 members. In April 1541, Ignatius was unanimously elected General, and from that time until his death in Rome on July 31, 1556, he worked to build the new company.

The cornerstones of *Societas Jesu* were and are rigorous self examination and meditation, with analytical testing of emotions as well as arguments. Loyola's *Book of Spiritual Exercises* (completed in about 1548) and the *Constitutions* (still not fully complete at his death) show his blend of tradition and rationalism. He was beatified in 1609 by Pope Paul V and canonized in 1622 by Pope Gregory XV.

Jesuit Training

After a brief "first probation," designed to acquaint the would-be Jesuit with the order, two years of novitiate follow. Upon acceptance and the taking of vows, the novice becomes a scholastic, which typically marks the beginning of a nine-year period of learning and teaching. Subjects studied include sciences, logic, literature, and philosophy as well as theology; it is during this time that the intellectual foundations are firmly laid.

He is next ordained, and spends a year of tertianship before being admitted to the Profession. Professed Jesuits represent the highest degree of the society (see DEGREES) and alone are eligible for the highest office. They make a vow of personal obedience to the Pope in addition to their usual priestly vows, and promise neither to desire nor to seek any dignity inside or outside the society. Those who are not professed are admitted as "formed spiritual coadjutors."

Civil Conflict

The rigor with which members of the S.J. examined themselves, their motives, and their theology could be applied to other aspects of life, sometimes leading to conflicts with orthodoxy. A classic example is that of Juan de Mariana, a Jesuit historian, who addressed the rule of tyrants in his *De Rege et Regis Institutione* ("On Kings and the Institution of Kings," 1599), concluding that an unjust ruler might legitimately be overthrown.

Conflict with both Protestants and Jansenists was another major feature of the society in the 16th and 17th centuries. The Counter-Reformation was to a large extent led by Jesuits, whose personal example as well as intellectual arguments stemmed the Protestant flood in a number of European countries. The conflict with the Jansenists was subtler, however.

Jansenists were named after their leader, Cornelius Jansen (1585–1638), Bishop of Ypres, who attacked Scholastic theology as irrelevant to the common man, devotional pietism as valueless without right mindfulness, and the growing spirit of DEISM as anti-Christian. His principal objections to the Jesuits, insofar as they can be understood by a nontheologian, seem to have been that they gave dispositions too easily, and relied too much on sacramental grace. The fact that the Jesuits also had a theological school at Louvain, where he held the Regius Chair of Scriptural Interpretation, may also have had something to do with it; clerics are far from immune from professional jealousy and the urge to empire building.

Even within the orthodox Catholic church and its loyal countries, the Jesuits still had their problems. Because of their spiritual and intellectual preeminence, royal confessors were often Jesuits, leading to claims of undue influence. Also, because of their special relationship with the Holy Father, they were seen as having a loyalty that went beyond the country of their birth or abode. Hard though it may be to understand today, the Jesuits were also seen as being insufficiently orthodox and rigorous in their Christianity, and they were assailed by the Jansenists on one side and the rationalists on the other, especially in France. This was the beginning of the Age of Reason.

At that time, religion was of course on the cutting edge of politics; these were the days of the Inquisition, the burning of heretics, and kings who insisted that their subjects follow the royal religion. It could therefore be argued that no matter what they did, the Jesuits were bound to find themselves embroiled in controversy. Most of the time, they were highly regarded teachers and missionaries.

Expulsion, Suppression and Re-Foundation

In the second half of the 18th century, anti-Jesuit feeling grew increasingly strong. The Jesuits were expelled from Portugal and Brazil in 1759; from France in 1764; and from the Empire of Spain and from Naples in 1767. An increasing number of ambassadors to the Vatican urged suppression of the order, the Spanish envoy even threatening schism.

In 1773, Pope Clement XIV gave in to the pressure, and the brief *Dominus ac Redemptor Noster* formally dissolved the Society, though two monarchs (Frederick II of Prussia and Catherine the Great of Russia) refused to promulgate the brief, and the Holy Father made no attempt to enforce it; indeed, his reply to the request of the Russian Empress to sanction the continued existence of the order in White Russia was masterly silence. The Fathers of the Sacred Heart, formed in Belgium in 1794, were ex-Jesuits, and so were the Fathers of the Faith, another contemporary order.

By the turn of the century, papal attitudes were softening. In 1801, the brief *Catholiae Fidei* condoned the existence of the society, and the bull *Sollicitudo Omnium Ecclesarium* of August 7, 1814, restored it—just in time, it seemed, for less than two years later the society was banned from St. Petersburg and then in 1820 from all the Russias, where, in the opinion of Tsar Alexander I, they had been winning too many converts from Russian Orthodoxy.

By this time, though, civil strife occurred only rarely between rival religious factions, as it had in the *Ancien*

Regime. Instead, Rationalist and antimonarchical forces were at work—and the Church in general, and the Jesuits in particular, were usually seen as representatives of the old order. Although the Church had now recognized the order once again, the Jesuits were in purely secular trouble, and they were thrown out of a number of countries—sometimes repeatedly. Some of the expulsions included:

1820	Russia, Spain
1830	France
1834	Portugal
1835	Spain
1845	France
1847	Switzerland
1848	Austria and Poland
1854	Spain
1872	Germany
1880	France
1901	France
1910	Portugal
1931	Spain

These were in addition to expulsions from Mexico and various South American and Central American countries. As may be seen by the number of times they were expelled from France, for example, it is clear that they were not always very good at leaving; often, they just "went underground."

This tenacity, plus their rigorous obedience to the dictates of an informed conscience, is what has always made them unpopular with demagogues both secular and religious.

Jews and Freemasons

"The Jewish-Masonic Conspiracy" is familiar to any student of World War II, but the phrase and the concept were far from original with Adolf Hitler. At first sight, the very concept is all but incredible; many lodges traditionally refused to admit Jews, and it is difficult to see what the common interests might be of Jews and Freemasons.

The answer, it soon turns out, is based on extreme nationalist politics. From a sufficiently paranoid viewpoint, both Freemasons and Jews are seen as having loyalties that transcend national barriers. From here it is but a short step to arguing that they are actively opposed to the state in which they find themselves, and this makes them easy and convenient targets for ultranationalist demagogues. In the less tolerant Protestant countries, or among certain groups in countries with a Protestant ideology, the same depth of feeling is from time to time summoned against Catholics; see the AMERICAN PROTECTIVE ASSOCIATION and AMERICAN PROTESTANT ASSOCIATION, for example.

An excellent survey of the whole subject is to be found in *Jews and Freemasons,* by Jakob Katz (trans. Leonard Oschry, Howard University Press, 1970).

Job's Daughters, International Order of

Supreme Guardian Council, I.O.J.D.
233 West 6th Street
Papilion, NE 68046-2210
(402) 592-7987

The International Order of Job's Daughters (I.O.J.D.) was founded in 1921 in Omaha, Nebraska, as a "farm" for the EASTERN STAR. Open to girls aged 11–20 who are related to Master Masons, it operates internationally, though mostly in the United States. In 1994, there were 24,000 members in the United States alone. The order publishes the monthly *News Exchange.*

The International Order of Job's Daughters was founded by Mrs. Ethel T. W. Mick, a member of the Eastern Star, using rituals written by LeRoy T. Wilcox of the FREEMASONS. As is usual with American Freemasonry, especially American ADOPTIVE MASONRY, there is a Christian bias. The title comes from Job XLII:xl: "And in all the land there were no women so fair as the Daughters of Job."

The avowed intentions of the order are to inculcate in young girls a "love of home and country and reverence for the teachings of the Bible," and to promote spiritual and character development.

The basic unit is the "Bethel," which consists of a minimum of 20 girls, 19 of whom are elected or appointed officers. The officers wear pseudo-Grecian white robes with white or purple cinctures. Only members, their parents or guardians, and duly qualified Master Masons or members of the Eastern Star may be present at meetings.

The Bethel layout is basically Masonic, though the emblems of the order are the white dove, the cornucopia, and an urn of incense. The flowers are lilies of the valley.

In the ritual, which is Masonic at heart, the Honored Queen takes the place of the Master, and the more bloodthirsty aspects of the penalties for oath-breaking are omitted.

Johannites

This Masonic sect was established in Paris, in 1814, by one Fabré-Paliprat (also spelled Palaprat), and attached to the so-called Order of the Temple, of which he was the Grand Master.

Fabré-Paliprat drew the order's liturgy from the Levitikon, a spurious gospel of St. John. The related Order of the Temple was founded by Fabré-Paliprat as a pseudo-revival of the TEMPLARS in 1804. The invention of the Johannite ritual in 1814 led to a schism in this order, though it seems the Johannites later re-merged with the Order of the Temple.

John Birch Society

P.O. Box 8084
Appleton, WI 54913-8040
(414) 749-3780

The John Birch Society was founded in December 1958 as an American patriotic and political society; it is open to U.S. citizens. There were 50,000 members in 1994.

The society is named after Captain John Birch, a Baptist missionary/soldier who was killed by Chinese communists in August 1945. It was founded by Robert Welch, a Massachusetts-based businessman, as a "pro-American, anti-Communist educational organization."

While the philosophy of the society does contain a number of libertarian elements—for example, they advocate withdrawal of the United States from the United Nations—the John Birch Society is basically right-wing and authoritarian. For example, it refers to the "adamant refusal" of the Surgeon General "to realize that explicit instruction about sexuality leads to rising promiscuity." It traditionally saw attempts to increase understanding between the United States and the Soviet Union as instances of "Soviet educators . . . writing courses to 'teach' American children." And it opposes "secular humanists, who deny God's existence, condemn belief in an afterlife, attack religion as a 'disservice to the human species,' call on all to establish their own systems of ethics, seek a socialized economy and an end to independent nations, and strive to establish an atheistic world government. Communists agree."

Local John Birch Society chapters participate in conservative advocacy programs, including letter-writing and petition campaigns devoted to specific issues. They sponsor Support Your Local Police Committees and an organization called Tax Reform Immediately. The organization maintains a speakers' bureau, biographical archives, summer youth camps, and seminar programs.

Jünglingsbund

The Jünglingsbund, or "Youngsters' Band," was a German students' secret society founded in Jena in 1821 and dedicated to freeing Prussia from French influence and to securing a representative government. The Jünglingsbund was an early manifestation of the Junges Deutschland (Young Germany) movement, which flourished from 1830–50, agitating not only for political reform, but for aesthetic revolution, ushering in an age of "dramatic realism" in German literature and art. Ironically, the revolutionary movement that swept Europe during 1848–49 led to the movement's decline.

Junior Order of United American Mechanics

The Junior Order of United American Mechanics was founded in 1853 as a fraternal and political secret society for American citizens of both sexes. Insurance was added later. If the order is still extant, it is probably only at a local lodge level. The full title of the governing body, incidentally, was even longer than the version at the head of this entry: the National Council of the Junior Order of United American Mechanics of the United States of North America, Inc.

The Union of Workers was founded in Philadelphia in 1845 by a group of working men; their aims were to stop immigration, especially Catholic immigration, and (almost incidentally) to provide the usual mid-19th-century benefits of a sick fund and a funeral fund.

It changed its name to the Order of United American Mechanics shortly after its foundation (in those days, "mechanic" was closer in meaning to "artisan" rather than connoting a practical engineer). Membership was open only to native-born white Americans who professed belief in a supreme being, supported the separation of church and state, and were not engaged in the liquor trade.

In 1853, the O.U.A.M. authorized a junior lodge, to be called the J.O.U.A.M. The J.O.U.A.M. soon outgrew the parent organization, which it absorbed some time after declaring its independence from them in 1885. Age was no longer an issue, and eventually the organization also admitted women in their own right, though there was also a short-lived women's auxiliary, which was founded in 1875.

The J.O.U.A.M. originally wanted to prevent sectarian influence upon the public school system while upholding the reading of the Holy Bible. Its enthusiasm for Bible reading may have stemmed from the fact that Catholics objected strongly to the use of the Vulgate. Since the 1840s and 1850s, which were the high point of xenophobic nativist parties in the United States, the J.O.U.A.M. settled down more and more into a conventional fraternal benefit society.

The nature of the RITUALS AND CEREMONIES is unclear, but they apparently contain no prayers in the name of Jesus Christ, and there seems to have been only a single degree (see DEGREES), complete with an oath of initiation. There is a form of burial service sanctioned by the J.O.U.A.M.

At some point, racial and religious restrictions were removed, but membership was still open only to American citizens, though they might be "of both sexes and all ages from the cradle onward." In addition to very modest fraternal benefits and dues, the J.O.U.A.M. also operated a legal reserve insurance department, which had been in operation since 1899.

There were 200,000 members at the organization's height in 1900; 35,172 members (15,000 social, the rest insured) in 1,000 Councils (LODGES) in 27 states in 1965; 8,500 members in 1979; and the subsequent history of the order is unclear.

Kabbalah

Properly speaking, the Kabbalah or Qabbalah (also Caballa, Cabal, Qabal) is not a secret society, but a Hebrew mystical system, which seeks to link the infinite and the finite. It has, however, been a central part of countless mystically inclined secret societies, and the term *Kabballists* is sometimes used almost synonymously with "members of a secret society." Purely by accident, as described below, "cabal" also has significance as a political secret society.

Simplistically, the argument of the Kabbalah is this. The deity being transcendent and infinite, all of His creation (which is finite) must necessarily involve a voluntary limitation of His powers. For reasons not immediately clear to any but a student of the Kabbalah, God accomplishes this by putting forth a series of "emanations," principally the 10 Sephiroth (singular, Sephira), which form a web of associated qualities. In most graphic representations, sometimes called the "Tree of Life," the Sephiroth are ranked — with *Malkuth* (the Kingdom of Earth) at the bottom and *Kether* (the Crown or Spirit) at the top. The others exist in various relationships to one another, whether superior, inferior, or equal. The Sephiroth are:

Malkuth	Kingdom
Yesod	Foundation
Hod	Splendor
Netzach	Firmness or Victory
Tiphareth	Beauty or Harmony
Geburah	Justice, Strength or Might
Chesed	Love, Mercy, or Compassion
Binah	Understanding or Intelligence
Chokmah	Wisdom
Kether	Crown or Spirit

Kabbalism is divided into theoretical (*'Iyyunith*) and practical, called *Ma'asith*, with the following principal postulates:

1. Gematria or numerology
2. Ranking of angels and demiurges
3. *Qellipoth* and *Sodh has-Zwig*, dualism, which states that everything must have both a "light" and a "dark" side
4. *Merkabah*, the "Chariot," whereby man may ascend from imperfection and the finite to perfection and the infinite
5. Voluntary self-limitation by the Deity to allow the existence of the finite universe
6. Adam Kadmon, a primordial sexless intermediate being between man and the Sephiroth
7. *Gilgulim* or the Transmigration of Souls

With at least 1,500 years of Kabbalistic literature to investigate, and an oral tradition reputed to be centuries or millennia older, the Kabbalah provides a fertile field for mystics of all varieties. Some people may attempt to stay within the traditional Jewish framework of Kabbalistic thought, while others (such as the Hermetic Order of the Golden Dawn; see GOLDEN DAWN, HERMETIC ORDER OF) have modified, synthesized, and extrapolated the old ideas to an extraordinary extent.

Cabal as a Secret Society

Since the 17th century, the word *cabal* has been used to mean an association of people with a secret quest or ambition (a "hidden agenda," in the parlance of the late 20th century); or, alternatively, to mean the secret into which they delve or the plot that they hatch. By one of those coincidences that delight the hearts of students of such matters, this meaning was reinforced just as it was coming into popularity by the fact that the names of five ministers who were said to exert undue influence over King Charles II were:

*C*lifford
*A*rlington
*B*uckingham
*A*shley
*L*auderdale

Cabal is a generic term for secret societies and not some supreme secret society in its own right.

Kadiriyya, Order of

This order of dervishes was named after Abd al-Kadir (d. 1166), the principal of a school in Baghdad, who preached to a growing group of followers. Kadirism developed in two distinct directions: as a religious sect, consisting of members who regarded Abd al-Kadir as the "Lord of Creation after God," and as a secret society, the rituals of which called to the minds of some 19th-century Western observers the FREEMASONS. Kadiriyya became politically active in the late 19th century, working with the French colonial invaders against ISAWA and many other groups that resisted French domination of Morocco and Algeria.

Initiation begins with the candidate's testimony that he has seen Abd al-Kadir in a dream. After a year elapses, the candidate brings to the order an *arakiyya,* a small felt cap. If he is accepted, a symbolic green rose consisting of 18 sections, with Solomon's seal in the center, is affixed to the cap. Members conduct festivals honoring the founder, and they make a variety of religious pilgrimages. They also engage in ecstatic dances and in quasihypnotic rituals that may last many days.

As a political and military force, the Kadiriyya were active in the French conquest of Algeria. In the 19th century, Mubyi 'l-Din was offered leadership in the war against the "infidel." He gave this responsibility to his son, Abd al-Kadir, who instead sporadically cooperated with the French in return for their promise that they would respect and support his sovereignty. With the fall of Abd al-Kadir late in the century, the Kadiriyya threw their wholehearted support behind the French and survived into the 12th century.

Kadosh

"Kadosh" is a Hebrew word meaning "holy" or "consecrated" and is used indiscriminately by a number of secret societies as the name of various DEGREES, such as Kadosh of the Hebrews (in the FRENCH RITE of the FREEMASONS);

Kadosh of the First Christians; Kadosh of the Crusades; Kadosh of the Templars; Kadosh of Cromwell or Kadosh of the Puritans; Kadosh of the Jesuits; and the True Kadosh.

Kalastaasen Kagalanaglad Katipunan

It is probably no coincidence that the initials of the Very Exalted and Honorable Union, often known as the Katipunan League, are K.K.K. Originally a Malay derivative of a Chinese secret society in the Philippines, it became a blood-thirsty anti-Catholic secret society. It also functioned as a political movement, originally anti-Spanish and later anti-American. It is unclear whether the "K.K.K." still exists under its original name in the Philippines, but there is no doubt of its continuity with other Filipino resistance movements.

Kamelia

Founded in March 1923, the short-lived Kamelia was perhaps the most important of several competing KU KLUX KLAN female auxiliaries that came into being before the Klan officially admitted women. In addition to Kamelia, these groups included Ladies of the Invisible Eye, Dixie Protestant Women's League, Grand League of Protestant Women, White American Protestants (W.A.P.), and Ladies of the Invisible Empire (L.O.T.I.E.), the immediate predecessor to a national women's Klan.

Kamelia's founding came just three months before a scheduled "Klonvokation" (KKK convocation) set to create an official women's Klan. Kamelia members wore white robes and scarlet capes and quickly spawned three chapters in 20 states. In the Midwest, yet another female Klan group, the Queens of the Golden Mask, was established, but quickly faded.

In June 1923, the KKK leadership founded the Women of the Ku Klux Klan (WKKK). A propaganda and courtroom battle began between it and Kamelia, with WKKK seeking an injunction against Kamelia and all other competing Klan organizations. W. J. Simmons, founder of Kamelia, unsuccessfully countersued and was ordered to relinquish all rights to Kamelia and to resign from the Klan itself in return for a $145,000 cash settlement. Kamelia henceforth yielded to WKKK as *the* official women's Klan organization. Judge R. M. Mann, of the second circuit court in Little Rock, Arkansas, officially chartered the WKKK on June 10, 1923.

Karpokratians

The Karpokratians were a religious society founded by Karpokrates, or Carpocrates, who lived in Alexandria at the time of Emperor Adrian. He taught that the soul must rise above the superstition of popular creeds and the laws of society, and, through contemplation, to unite with the "Monas," or supreme deity.

Carpocrates has been accused of teaching that the only way to purge oneself of impurity is to throw oneself into every vice with abandon, until one has seen the hollowness of vicious pleasure.

Khaki Shirts

The 1920s and 1930s saw a proliferation of "shirt" societies and movements: BLACK SHIRTS, BLUE SHIRTS and BROWN SHIRTS. The Khaki Shirts were a small remnant of the so-called Bonus Army of U.S. World War I veterans, who had marched on Washington, D.C., in 1932 demanding payment of a promised veterans' "bonus." President Herbert Hoover ordered troops under Douglas MacArthur to disperse the Bonus Army, but the diehards, calling themselves Khaki Shirts, found a leader in one Art J. Smith and vowed to raise an army of 1,500,000 in order to secure payment of the elusive bonus, abolish Congress, revalue silver at the Populist rate of 16 to one, and generally rearm the nation. The group was pro-Nazi and anti-Semitic.

Khaki Shirt leader Smith proposed setting up a dictatorship under Franklin D. Roosevelt (presumably without consulting the President-elect on the matter). From his Philadelphia headquarters, Smith planned a massive veterans' march on Washington for Columbus Day 1933. It never materialized, and the group's single rally, in New York during July, provoked a riot in which one man died and 24 persons were injured. Smith was subsequently arrested, tried, and convicted of perjury. After he was sentenced to six years in prison, his leaderless Khaki Shirts dissolved.

Khlysty

This sect of flagellants was founded in 17th-century Russia and based its painful rituals on a belief in the perpetual rebirth and reincarnation of Christ. Its name derives from *Khylstovschchina*—"The Faith of Christ."

It is known that members of the sect practiced various forms of self-flagellation as part of their ritual of worship. However, the order was also accused of ritual cannibalism, in which an illegitimate boy child was supposedly sacrificed so that his blood and heart could be mixed with honey to make a blasphemous Host. While there is much evidence to suggest that the Khlysty were ascetics, who abstained from meat, tobacco, and alcohol, engaging in fasts and performing harsh acts of penance, it was also alleged that they engaged in orgiastic hetero- and homosexual acts. It is believed that another Russian religious sect, the Skoptsi, developed from the Khlysty about 1757. The Skoptsi added ritual self-castration and the amputation of breasts to the self-flagellation practiced by the Khlysty. Reportedly, castration was performed using a

bewildering variety of instruments, including razors, knives, and broken glass, as well as crushing the testicles between bricks or heavy stones.

The most famous adherent of the Khlysty sect was Grigory Yefimovich Rasputin, the so-called "Mad Monk" who was the favorite of Russia's last tsar and tsarina, Nicholas II and Alexandra. Rasputin interpreted—or deliberately distorted—Khlysty teachings into a doctrine of what he called "holy passionlessness," a state of union with God, which was attained only through the sexual exhaustion that came after prolonged debauchery. By all accounts, Rasputin enthusiastically practiced what he preached.

Some authorities report that the Khlysty sect died out by the mid-18th century. Others bring it into the 1860s. Still others credit Rasputin with reviving his narrowly orgiastic version of it. It is by no means certain that the sect has died out in Russia today. Skoptsism may also still exist, as references to it are to be found in Soviet periodicals and in reports originating from Romania as late as the 1950s.

Kiwanis Club International

3636 Woodview Trace
Indianapolis, IN 46268-3196
(317) 875-8755; Fax: (317) 879-0204

The Kiwanis (the word itself is meaningless) was founded in Detroit in January 1915 as a businessmen's luncheon club dedicated to "close fellowship among its members, both in social and business activities, and active cooperation for civic improvement."

In 1994, the organization had 330,000 members in 8,900 local groups. Although largely a North American organization, there are local chapters in 83 countries.

Kiwanis sponsor the Key Club International, for high school students; the Circle K International, for college students; Builders Clubs, for junior high students; and the Ki-Wives International, an organization made up of the wives and widows of Kiwanis members. (Kiwani membership is open to men and women, however.) Ki-Wives sponsors Keyette International, an organization for high school girls (though Key Club International is open to male and female high school students).

Knife and Fork Degree

One Townsite Plaza, Ste 315
Topeka, KS 66603
(913) 232-0892

The "Knife and Fork Degree" is a sarcastic term used by traditionalist FREEMASONS in the United States to describe those Master Masons who (according to the traditionalists) see the Craft as no more than a social club.

There is, however, a Knife and Fork Club International, listed by the ENCYCLOPEDIA OF ASSOCIATIONS as a social dinner club with 29,000 members in 1989, founded in 1898.

Knighthood

Large numbers of organizations call themselves "Knights" of this or that—so many, in fact, that a brief examination of knighthood and knightly behavior is appropriate.

In most languages, the status of the knight as a mounted (and hence wealthy) warrior is confirmed in the word: *chevalier* in French, *Ritter* in German, *caballero* in Spanish. In English, the word *ridere* or *rider* was essayed in the 11th century, but "knight" prevailed.

Knighthood probably arose first as the rite of passage (see RITES OF PASSAGE) into adulthood for Frankish boys in the Dark Ages, but as feudalism evolved in early medieval times, it became both an honor and a form of feudal service. A knight was required to serve his lord in time of war, in return for which he was accorded certain feudal rights over lower ranks.

Knighthood was also essential in the feudal system. The feudal system is strictly hierarchical, with the king at the top; next a number of barons, the most powerful of whom might rival the king, but who owe their allegiance to him; and below them the knights, who were pledged to render knightly service to the barons. "Knightly service" meant, in the main, military service.

After the Crusades, and with the decay of the feudal system, when taxes replaced knight service, raising someone to knighthood became to an increasing extent a means of granting honor and prestige. Although military men were made knights, not all knights were military men; and it was only a few of the supranational orders, such as the Knights HOSPITALLERS, that remained as fighting orders.

The basic ritual of conferring knighthood (see RITUALS AND CEREMONIES) is sufficiently well known to need little explanation here. The sovereign taps the candidate on both shoulders and says "Arise, Sir [Name]." Such simple dubbing is, however, an appointment such as might be made "in the field." There are many far more complex rituals, including ritual bathing, presentation of a sword (and possibly spurs, decorations, and robes), feasting, and much else. In strict feudal theory (and practice), the sovereign is not the only person who can confer knighthood: Anyone can be feudally empowered to do so, though this has not been usual for some time.

The oldest regularly constituted British Order of Knighthood is almost certainly the Order of the Garter, dating back to the 1340s. Although other orders were founded as early as the 11th century, the oldest for which the rules of admission and a formal constitution survive is this one.

The other eight historic British orders are the Thistle (1687), St. Patrick (1788), the Bath (1725), St. Michael and St. George (1818), the Star of India (1861), the Indian Empire (1878), the Royal Victorian Order (1896), and the Order of the British Empire (1917).

The astute reader will notice that more than half of these Orders were instituted between the beginning of the 19th century and near the end of World War I, the heyday of secret societies. Nor do the parallels between secret societies and knightly orders end there. The Order of the Garter is widely believed to have its origins in nothing more profound than a tourney or joust (records prior to 1416 have been lost).

The various orders have different DEGREES, though they are hardly "worked" in the same way as in a secret society. The Order of the British Empire, for example, has five classes:

Knight (or Dame) Grand Cross of the Order of the British Empire: G.B.E.
Knight (or Dame) Commander of the Order of the British Empire: K.B.E./D.B.E.
Commander of the Order of the British Empire: C.B.E.
Officer of the Order of the British Empire: O.B.E.
Member of the Order of the British Empire: M.B.E.

In the higher ranks, the numbers of knights in an order are usually formally limited.

Other leading orders of knighthood established before the end of World War I include the following, many of which are no longer awarded. Dates in brackets indicate the legendary foundation, if the date of formal or recorded foundation is later.

Orders marked with a single asterisk were for women; those with two asterisks were open to both sexes. In some cases, orders were renamed or reestablished; in others, orders were first founded in one nation and then adopted by another.

Orders of Chivilary

1156	Spain	Order of Knights of Alcantara
1158	Spain	Order of Knights of Calatrava
1162	Portugal	Order of St. Benedict of Evora
1175	Spain	Order of Knights of St. James of Compostella
1318	Portugal/Papal	Order of Christ
1336	Sweden	Order of Seraphim (1280)
1362	Savoy	Order of the Collar
1429	Austria and Spain	Order of the Golden Fleece (see GOLDEN FLEECE, NOBLE ORDER OF THE)
1434	Savoy	Order of St. Maurice
1444	Bavaria	Order of St. Hubert
1459	Portugal	Order of the Sword
1469	France	Order of St. Michael
1496	Papal State	Order of the Holy Sepulchre (see HOLY SEPULCHRE OF JERUSALEM, EQUESTRIAN ORDER OF THE)
1518	Savoy	Order of the Annunziata

Year	Country	Order
1522	Portugal	Order of Christ
1522	Sweden	Order of the Sword
1559	Papal State	Order of the Golden Spur
1573	Savoy	Order of St. Michael and St. Lazarus
1578	France	Order of the Holy Ghost
1580	Netherlands	TEUTONIC ORDER
1667	Prussia	Order of Generosity
1668	Austria-Hungary	Order of the Starry Cross*
1671	Denmark	Order of the Dannebrog (1219)
1690	Saxe Gotha	Order of German Integrity
1693	Bavaria	Civil Orders of Merit of St. Michael
1693	Denmark	Order of the Dannebrog (1462)
1693	France	Order of St. Louis
1698	Russia	Order of St. Andrew
1701	Prussia	Order of the Black Eagle
1705	Prussia	Order of Sincerity
1713	Poland	Order of the White Eagle
1714	Russia	Order of Rescue (later St. Catherine)
1715	Baden (Germany)	Order of Fidelity
1725	Russia	Order of St. Alexandr Nevsky
1729	Bavaria	Order of St. George
1732	Saxe Weimar	Order of the White Falcon
1734	Prussia	Order of the Brandenburg Red Eagle
1735	Poland	Order of St. Anne
1740	Prussia	Order for Merit (*Pour le Mérite*)
1748	Sweden	Order of the Pole Star
1750	Austria-Hungary	Order of Elizabeth Theresa
1757	Austria-Hungary	Order of Maria Theresa
1759	France	Order of Military Merit
1759	Württemburg	Order of Merit
1764	Austria-Hungary	Order of St. Stephen of Hungary
1765	Poland	Order of St. Stanislaus
1766	Bavaria	Order of Elizabeth*
1770	Hesse (Germany)	Order of the Golden Lion
1771	Spain	Royal and Illustrious Order of Charles III
1772	Sweden	Order of Vasa
1782	Russia	Order of Vladimir
1792	Spain	Order of Maria Louisa*
1797	Russia	Order of St. Anne
1801	Portugal	Order of St. Isabella*
1802	France	Legion of Honour
1806	Bavaria	Military Order of Maximilian Joseph
1807	Baden (Germany)	Order of Charles Frederick
1807	Hesse (Germany)	Order of Louis
1807	Saxony	Order of the Crown of Rue
1808	Austria-Hungary	Order of Leopold
1808	Bavaria	Order of the Bavarian Crown
1808	Persia	Order of the Sun and the Lion
1808	Portugal (Brazil)	Order of the Tower and the Sword
1809	Spain	Royal Order of the Knights of Spain
1811	Spain	Order of St. Ferdinand
1811	Sweden	Order of Charles XIII[1]
1812	Baden (Germany)	Order of the Zaehringen Lion
1814	Prussia	Order of Service*
1815	Hanover	Royal Guelphic Order
1815	Netherlands	Order of William
1815	Sardinia	Order of Savoy
1815	Saxony	Order of Civil Merit
1815	Spain	Order of Isabella the Catholic
1815	Spain	Order of St. Hermenegildo
1816	Austria-Hungary	Order of the Iron Crown
1818	Netherlands	Order of the Netherlands Lion
1818	Württemberg	Order of the Crown of Württemberg
1819	Portugal	Order of Our Lady of Villa Vicosa**
1822	Brazil	Order of the Southern Cross
1826	Brazil	Order of Dom Pedro I
1827	Bavaria	Order of Theresa*
1829	Brazil	Order of the Rose
1830	Württemberg	Order of Frederick
1831	Papal State	Order of St. Gergory the Great
1831	Russia	Order of St. Stanislaus
1831	Russia	Order of the White Eagle
1831	Sardinia	Order of Savoy
1831	Turkey	Order of Glory
1832	Belgium	Order of Leopold
1833	Greece	Order of the Redeemer
1833	Saxe Altenburg / Saxe Coburg Gotha / Saxe Meiningen	Order of Ernest
1834	Brunswick	Order of Henry the Lion
1836	Anhalt (Germany)	Order of Albert the Bear
1838	Oldenberg (Germany)	Order of Duke Peter Frederick Louis
1839	Hanover	Order of St. George
1840	Hesse (Germany)	Order of Philip the Magnanimous
1841	Luxembourg	Order of the Oak Crown
1847	Norway	Order of St. Olaf
1847	Papal State	Order of Pius
1849	Austria-Hungary	Order of Francis Joseph
1851	Prussia	Order of the House of Hollenzollern
1852	Montenegro	Order of St. Peter
1852	Montenegro	Order of Danilo
1852	Turkey	Order of Mejidi
1853	Mexico	Order of Our Lady of Guadalupe
1854	Venezuela	Order of the Bust of Bolivar
1856	Spain	Order of Beneficencia
1857	Nicaragua	American Order of San Juan
1858	Luxembourg	Order of Adolphus of Nassau
1858	Monaco	Order of St. Charles
1861	Prussia	Order of the Crown
1861	Thailand	Order of the White Elephant
1862	Turkey	Order of Osmanie
1863	Yugoslavia	Order of Takovo
1864	Mecklenburg	Order of Wendish Crown
1865	Mexico	Order of the Mexican Eagle
1866	Spain	Order of Naval Merit
1866	Spain	Order of Military Merit
1867	Belgium	Order of the Iron Cross
1868	Italy	Order of the Crown of Italy
1869	Thailand	Order of the Nine Precious Stones
1869	Thailand	Order of the Siamese Crown
1870	Saxony	Order of Civil Merit*
1871	Württemberg	Order of Olga**
1875	Japan	Order of the Rising Sun
1877	Japan	Order of the Chrysanthemum

1877	Romania	Order of the Star of Romania
1878	Turkey	Order of Schefakat*
1879	Turkey	Order of Privilege (*Nischan-i-Imtiaz*)
1881	Bulgaria	Order of St. Alexander
1881	Romania	Order of the Crown of Romania
1882	China	Order of the Imperial Double Dragon[2]
1882	Yugoslavia	Order of the White Eagle
1883	Yugoslavia	Order of St. Sava
1884	Mecklenburg	Order of the Griffin
1888	Belgium	Order of the African Star
1888	Japan	Order of the Crown*
1888	Japan	Order of the Mirror[3]
1889	Belgium	Congo Star
1890	Brazil	Order of Columbus
1890	Japan	Order of the Golden Kite
1890	Spain	Order of Maria Christina
1891	Belgium	Royal Order of the Lion
1892	Netherlands	Order of Orange-Nassau
1893	Prussia	Johanniter Orden
1893	Turkey	*Haledani-Ali-Osman*
1896	Baden (Germany)	Order of Berthold I
1896	Prussia	Order of William
1898	Austria-Hungary	Order of Elizabeth
1898	Yugoslavia	Order of Milosch the Great
1900	Württemberg	Silver Cross of Merit
1902	Spain	Order of Alfonso XII
1902	Spain	Civil Order of Alfonso II
1903	Turkey	Ertogroul
1904	Norway	Order of the Norwegian Lion
1904	Yugoslavia	Order of the Star of Karageorgevich
1906	Saxony	Maria Anna Order*
1907	Prussia	Verdienst-Kreuz*
1909	Bulgaria	Order of SS Cyril and Methodius
1912	Greece	Order of George I
1912	Egypt	Order of Mohammed Ali
1915	Egypt	Order of the Nile
1915	Egypt	Order of Al Kamal*
1915	Egypt	Order of Agriculture
1919	Egypt	Order of the Military Star of King Fuad

Notes:
1. Awarded only to FREEMASONS
2. Awarded only to foreigners
3. Or "Order of the Happy Sacred Treasure"

It is remarkable how many of these Orders—about 60 percent—were founded in the 19th and early 20th centuries. While secret societies were flourishing in America, something similar seems to have prompted an efflorescence of orders of knighthood among the grand and petty nobility of Europe and elsewhere. One obvious conclusion is that in an increasingly industrial and "modern" world, old-world orders of knighthood and American secret societies both fulfilled a similar purpose: a way of holding on to the old order, without delaying to any significant degree the advance of the new order.

False Orders of Knighthood

One of the best statements on the nature of modern chivalry has appeared repeatedly in *L'Osservatore Romano* in the form of an Official Statement by the Holy See. The main point that is made is that a true order of chivalry must be founded by a sovereign as a recognition of merit, but the student of the subject will be wearily sympathetic with the following statement: "Thus, with a terminology which is almost monotonous these alleged Orders claim for themselves—in differing degrees—such titles as *Sacred, Military, Equestrian, Chivalric, Constantinian, Capitular, Sovereign, Nobiliary, Religious, Angelical, Celestial, Ladcaris, Imperial, Royal, Delcassian,* etc."

The Belgian Ministry of Foreign Affairs has pointed out that "the creators of these decorations pretend to foster . . . a spirit of loyalty and generosity. In reality, their main end appears to be . . . vanity." The ministry also declared that those who had been duped were unlikely to protest too loudly, for fear of being seen for what they were, and that financial gain was at least conceivable as a motive for the founding of these so-called orders.

In Germany, there is a maximum penalty of three months in prison or a heavy fine, or both, for deceiving the public with decorations that might be mistaken for recognized legitimate national or foreign decorations.

For an entertaining account of pseudo-orders, read *Ordres et Contre-Ordres de Chevalerie,* by A. Cheffanjou and B. G. Flavigny (Paris 1982). The authors list 16 orders purporting to derive from the Knights of Jerusalem, Rhodes, and Malta, all founded between 1960 and 1975, together with lists of the fees charged for initiation.

Knight Masons, Order of

One of many masonic affiliates, the Knight Masons were founded in Ireland in 1923 to confer the Green DEGREES, which were allegedly in the gift of the Irish Knights Templar. These degrees are Knight of the Sword, Knight of the East, Knight of the East and West, and Installed Excellent Chief.

Knights, Masonic

The powerful fascination exercised by the word *knight* on the founders of secret societies is evident from even a cursory glance at this encyclopedia, or at any other book dealing with secret societies. There are, however, so many "Knights" connected with the FREEMASONS that a list is in order. Anyone seeking to learn where these titles fit into the order of the Craft is referred to any of the standard Masonic encyclopedias. Many are used in more than one rite; for example, the Knight Elect of Fifteen may be the 16th degree (see DEGREES) of the Ancient and Accepted Rite, the 10th degree of the Council of Emperors of the East and West (see EMPERORS OF THE EAST AND WEST, COUNCIL OF), or the 11th degree of the Rite of Mizraim. Many of these "Knights" are of French origin.

Although some of these "orders" bear titles similar to

(or even identical with) those of real orders of chivalry, the reader should not be misled; every single one of those listed below is also a Masonic ornament with no lineal relationship with the original, and there are about 120 in the list.

Knight Commander
Knight Commander of the White and Black Eagle
Knight Crusader
Knight Elect of Fifteen
Knight Elect of Twelve, Sublime
Knight Evangelist
Knight, Illustrious or Illustrious Elect
Knight Jupiter
Knight Kadosh
Knight Kadosh of Cromwell
Knight Levite
Knight Mahadon
Knight of Asia, Initiated
Knight of Athens
Knight of Aurora
Knight of Beneficence
Knight of Brightness
Knight of Constantinople
Knight of Hope
Knight of Isis
Knight of Jerusalem
Knight of Justice
Knight of Malta
Knight of Masonry, Terrible
Knight of Palestine
Knight of Patmos
Knight of Perfumes
Knight of Purity and Light
Knight of Rhodes
Knight of Rose Croix
Knight of St. Andrew, Grand Scottish
Knight of St. Andrew, Free
Knight of St. Andrew of the Thistle
Knight of St. John of Jerusalem
Knight of St. John of Palestine
Knight of the Altar
Knight of the American Eagle
Knight of the Anchor
Knight of the Ape and Lion
Knight of the Arch
Knight of the Argonauts
Knight of the Banqueting Table of the Seven Sages
Knight of the Black Eagle
Knight of the Brazen Serpent
Knight of the Burning Bush
Knight of the Chanuca
Knight of the Christian Mark
Knight of the Columns
Knight of the Comet

Knight of the Courts
Knight of the Crown
Knight of the Door
Knight of the Eagle
Knight of the Eagle and Pelican
Knight of the Eagle Reversed
Knight of the East
Knight of the East and West
Knight of the Eastern Star
Knight of the East, Victorious
Knight of the East, White
Knight of the Election
Knight of the Election, Sublime
Knight of the Golden Eagle
Knight of the Golden Fleece
Knight of the Golden Key
Knight of the Golden Star
Knight of the Grand Arch
Knight of the Holy Sepulchre
Knight of the Inextinguishable Lamp
Knight of the Interior
Knight of the Kabbalah
Knight of the Lilies of the Valley
Knight of the Lion
Knight of the Mediterranean Pass
Knight of the Morning Star
Knight of the Ninth Arch
Knight of the North
Knight of the Phoenix
Knight of the Prussian Eagle
Knight of the Purificatory
Knight of the Pyramid
Knight of the Rainbow
Knight of the Red Cross
Knight of the Red Eagle
Knight of the Rose
Knight of the Rose and Triple Cross
Knight of the Rosy Cross
Knight of the Round Table
Knight of the Round Table of King Arthur
Knight of the Royal Axe
Knight of the Sacred Mountain
Knight of the Sanctuary
Knight of the Sepulchre
Knight of the South
Knight of the Star
Knight of the Sun
Knight of the Sword
Knight of the Tabernacle
Knight of the Tabernacle of the Divine Truths
Knight of the Temple
Knight of the Three Kings
Knight of the Throne
Knight of the Triple Cross
Knight of the Triple Period

Knight of the Triple Sword
Knight of the Two Crowned Eagles
Knight of the West
Knight of the White and Black Eagle
Knight of the White Eagle
Knight of Unction
Knight, Perfect
Knight, Professed
Knight, Prussian
Knight, Royal Victorious
Knight, Sacrificing
Knight, Victorious
Knight of the East, Council of
Knights Templar
Knights of the True Light

Knights, Order of

The Order of Knights was founded in the late 18th century at Wetzlar, Germany, as a parody of the orders and pseudo-orders that were then becoming so fashionable, and especially as a parody of the FREEMASONS. They worked four DEGREES, as follows:

1. Transition
2. Transition's Transition
3. Transition's Transition to Transition
4. Transition's Transition to Transition of Transition

The Order attracted some well-known names of the time, including Johann Wolfgang von Goethe (Goetz von Berlichingen, to give him the name he adopted in the order). The order itself did not survive for long.

Knights and Daughters of Tabor, International Order of Twelve

This was a black fraternal beneficiary society, allegedly founded originally as the International Order of Twelve in 1846 as an antislavery society. In this incarnation, it was founded in 1872 in Independence, Missouri, by Moses Dickson, a clergyman of the African Methodist Episcopal Church. Now apparently extinct, in the 1890s and early 1900s it claimed 100,000 members in England, Africa, and the West Indies as well as in 30 of the United States of America. The relationship of the various organizations that purported to be part of the order is confusing, but included the delightfully named Princes and Princesses of the Royal House of Media, who gathered in "Palatiums" for "literary and social entertainment." Men's LODGES were called Temples; women met separately in Tabernacles.

Knights and Ladies of Honor

The Knights and Ladies of Honor, formed out of the Knights of Honor in 1877, affords a classic example of the blithe disregard for actuarial soundness that afflicted (and brought low) so many fraternal beneficiary societies.

The simple ASSESSMENT plan, for many years set at $1.80 a month, at first paid maximum death benefits of $1,000; but in 1881, this was raised to $5,000. Although this brought in many new members (there were more than 72,000 Knights and Ladies in 1898), it also invited a skeleton to the feast. As the members aged and died, the assessment had to be raised repeatedly, beginning in 1901. By 1916, the assessment was $18.40 per month *per $1,000* of income coverage, a hair-raising increase, which drove many out of the society and led others to appeal for state intervention. Eventually, this devil-may-care attitude to actuarial certainties killed the organization.

The *Loyal Knights and Ladies* was an offshoot of the Knights and Ladies of Honor, founded in 1881 in Boston, Massachusetts; they are long gone.

Knights Beneficent of the Holy City, Holy Order of

The Holy Order of Knights Beneficent of the Holy City is a Masonic organization founded in 1754 in Germany and exported to the United States in 1934, where it still exists. Membership, which is restricted to Master Masons, is by invitation only and is limited to a total of 81 individuals divided into three preceptories of 27 members each. The chief executive is the Great Chancellor, and, as of 1980, headquarters was in Syracuse, New York. No more recent information is available.

The order is dedicated to maintaining and strengthening among its members—as well as among Masons and Masonic groups generally—attachment to the spirit of Christianity, patriotism, "individual perfection" through the subduing of one's own passions, and the practice of enlightened charity to all humankind.

Knights of Columbus

1275 Pennsylvania Avenue N.W.
Washington, D.C. 20004-2404
(202) 628-2355

The Knights of Columbus was founded in 1882 in New Haven, Connecticut, as a fraternal, insurance, religious, and patriotic organization for Catholic men over 18. Young men aged 12–18 may join the Columbian Squires. Although the order is international, it is concentrated mostly in North and Central America. There were 1,495,251 members in 1994.

On March 29, 1882, a new fraternal insurance organization called the Knights of Columbus was chartered by the state of Connecticut, under the leadership of the 29-year-old curate of St. Mary's Parish, Connecticut, Rev. Michael J. McGivney. The title was chosen over the alternative "Sons of Columbus." The original intention was to provide a measure of security for widows and orphans of the parish. Since then, the Knights of Columbus has become the largest fraternal benefit society of Roman Catholic men in the world.

The charter defined four aims, as follows:

Rendering pecuniary aid to its members and beneficiaries of its members

Rendering mutual aid and assistance to its sick and disabled members

Promoting such social and cultural intercourse as shall be desirable and proper

Promoting and conducting educational, charitable, religious, social welfare, war relief, and welfare and public relief work.

The description often applied to the Knights of Columbus, "Catholic Masons," is fairly accurate. Denied the opportunity to join the FREEMASONS by papal edict, many Catholic men have used the Knights of Columbus in much the same way as their Protestant brethren have used the Masons. The fraternal assistance is as often unofficial as official, as Knights do business with friends whom they meet at the lodge.

A more important similarity between the Knights of Columbus and Freemasonry is that the Knights of Columbus lodges work a number of DEGREES. The first three correspond more or less to the Entered Apprentice, Fellow-Craft, and Master Mason, and were introduced when the order was set up.

The fourth degree, corresponding to the Higher Degrees of Masonry, was introduced in 1900. Its theme is patriotism; its existence seems to have been inspired equally by a desire to dress up after the manner of other secret societies, and by an attempt to show that Catholics are not some sort of subversive heathen, but Americans much like any others. Initiates wear somewhat florid pseudomilitary costumes, rather like those of a 19th-century U.S. Navy admiral.

In contrast to the Masons, Knights of Columbus members swear no oaths, as this would be contrary to the wishes of the Church. They do, however, agree not to divulge the "secrets" of the order. Another important difference between the Masons and the Knights of Columbus is that many people join the Knights of Columbus mainly for the insurance. This is one of the factors that accounts for the low attendance at many lodges, where 20 percent of the enrolled members would be regarded as a good turnout. There are no attendance requirements for a member who wishes to remain in good standing, unlike some other organizations. Those who cannot pass the physical examination necessary for health insurance, or who want to join only for social purposes, are admitted as Associate Members. They can then share in the considerable number of social, family, and athletic events organized by the Knights.

Like most Catholic organizations, the Knights' faith tends to be sturdy. Virgil C. Dechant, the Supreme Knight, stated: "Knights of Columbus are very Church-oriented people. They don't second guess the magister-ium. But they do accept the challenge of the Second Vatican Council to be more active and involved in the Church." This attitude means that members can devote their energies to practical works. They raise—and spend—a great deal of money to support and promote the Catholic Church. Some of their projects are temporal, such as the restoration of St. Peter's Basilica in Rome, while others are more intimately connected with the spiritual: The *Vicarius Christi* fund of $10 million places its interest at the disposal of the Pope, and R.S.V.P. (the Refund Support Vocations Program) provides "moral and financial support to seminaries and postulants pursuing religious vocations." Since 1948, the order has funded advertisements in a wide variety of periodicals, with the intention of interesting non-Catholics in the faith. Yet other projects are divided nicely between the spiritual and the temporal, as in the Vatican Microfilm Library at St. Louis University.

The Knights contributed the $1 million campanile at the National Shrine in Washington, D.C. and have promoted less spectacular forms of devotion, as in their campaign of giving away as many as 10,000 rosaries a *month*.

In addition to raising money and support for the church, the Knights also supports a number of secular or community causes. Within a few years of the initial charter, the order contributed $50,000 toward a Chair of American History at the Catholic University of America, and in 1907 it raised half a million dollars toward scholarships at the same university.

During World War I it lived up to the promise embodied in their fourth head, by operating five Knights of Columbus huts in London and 45 in France. Many grateful servicemen joined the organization when they were demobilized and returned home. In World War II, the Knights of Columbus was less than pleased when the work that it regarded as its own was placed in the hands of the National Catholic Community Service by American Catholic Bishops.

More recently, the Knights of Columbus is noted for working to organize blood drives; running shelters for the homeless; delivering Meals on Wheels; and other good works—an aspect of the order that has become more important since about 1970, when the organization became less inward-looking under Virgil C. Dechant, the most influential Supreme Knight of recent times.

Some of recent K of C activities have been political, including support for the phrase "under God" in the U.S. Pledge of Allegiance, opposing Communism, and participating in such moral/political causes as fighting pornography and opposing the right to abortion.

Cheese Clubs

These were apparently social clubs for Knights of Columbus; the leader of the order was called the Head Cheese. It was probably a short-lived aberration.

Knights of Equity

c/o Patrick P. Costello
363 Dalebrook Lane
Bloomfield Hills, MI 48301
(313) 646-6071

Founded in 1895 in Cleveland, Ohio, for Americans of Irish ancestry who are practicing Catholics, the Knights of Equity currently has 10,000 members in the Northeast, Midwest, and Middle South. It seeks to advance members spiritually, materially, and socially, and also to teach Irish history and culture. It is concerned about furthering the cause of liberty for the people of Ireland.

The order sponsors Celtic courses at universities (for members only) and awards high school and university scholarships, with particular emphasis on assisting young men interested in the priesthood. The Knights of Equity assists orphan homes and homes for the aged and bestows the annual Celtic Culture Award to deserving members.

Knights of Jubilation

This secret society was formed in the early 18th century by French Protestant exiles in the Netherlands. Its first recorded meeting was at Leyden in 1710, and seems to have prefigured modern FREEMASONS. Some authorities call this radical Whig order "proto-Masonic."

The original members of the Knights of Jubilation, largely French refugees, were all involved in the book trade as publishers and members of the publishing guild. The Knights adopted mock-aristocratic titles and engaged in serious political and philosophical discussion of a distinctly radical stamp, leavening this with good fellowship, good food and drink, and a downright Rabelaisian sense of humor.

The Knights chose the figures of Minerva and Mercury as its standard bearers—Minerva signifying wisdom, and Mercury the god of commerce as well as a representation of HERMES TRISMEGISTUS, the great ancient Egyptian teacher of theology. In effect, the Knights sought to revive ancient wisdom as the cornerstone of a radical version of the Enlightenment, promoting a Newtonian vision of the universe along with the spirit of pagan pantheism.

The Knights of Jubilation seems to have disbanded some time after 1720.

Knights of Khorassan, Dramatic Order

110 Wabash Avenue, P.O. Box 332
Marion, IN 46952
(317) 664-7925

The Dramatic Order, Knights of Khorassan was founded in 1894 as a "fun" division of the KNIGHTS OF PYTHIAS. In 1994 there were 10,000 members. The order publishes the *Dokey-Nomad Herald* quarterly.

The "Dokies" or "Dokkies" is clearly modeled after the SHRINERS (which was established more than 20 years earlier), but is rather less than one-eightieth of the size, and its repu-

tation for rowdiness is proportionately less. The RITUALS AND CEREMONIES are predictable for a late 19th-century American order; it consists of Persian or Arabic imagery, and the Knights meet in "Temples." The Knights used to be noted for its torchlight pageants and fantastical costumed processions between sessions of the Supreme Lodge of the Knights of Pythias.

Knights of Liberty

The Knights of Liberty is a fairly obvious name for a secret society, and it is no surprise to learn that there have been at least two different and unrelated organizations under this banner.

First, it was the title adopted in 1820 by one of the French anti-Bourbon secret societies, which soon merged with the CARBONARI.

Then, a century later and on the other side of the Atlantic, the Knights of Liberty was one of the many groups that arose in the 1920s to counter the renascent KU KLUX KLAN. Unlike most of the others, it was founded by an ex-Klansman, who had been a Grand Goblin, no less. Andrew J. Padon founded the order in New York in 1923 and assembled a distinguished advisory board of clergymen, judges, and politicians.

Knights of Luther

The Knights of Luther was organized as an anti-Catholic society, in Des Moines, Iowa, in 1912. It was one of many *anti-Papish* and nativist organizations that flourished during the early part of the century. Dedicated to disseminating the "truth" about the "Catholic menace," it reportedly had 128,000 members in 1915. It is apparently extinct.

Knights of Malta

See HOSPITALLERS.

Knights of Peter Claver

1825 Orleans Avenue
New Orleans, LA 70116
(504) 821-4225

The Knights of Peter Claver is an order founded in 1909 as a fraternal religious (lay) organization for Catholic men aged 18 and over. It operates principally in North America and publishes *The Claverite* monthly. There were 35,000 members in 1994.

The Knights of Peter Claver is a strongly Roman Catholic order founded for blacks by four Josephite priests and three laymen. The order was incorporated in 1911 at Mobile, Alabama, two years after it was first founded. The purpose of the Knights is summed up in the preamble to the constitution:

> For the purpose of rendering service to God and His Holy Church; of recognizing the Fatherhood of God and the brotherhood of man; particularly as these attributes are

defined in the spiritual and corporal works of mercy; of assisting the Hierarchy and clergy of the Roman Catholic Church. . . .

St. Peter Claver (1581–1654) was a Jesuit canonized in 1888 for his work with slaves in Carthagena in the West Indies. The founders were inspired by the parallels between the ostracism St. Peter Claver endured in his work with the unhappy slaves of the Middle Passage, and the ostracism blacks faced in white society at the time they founded the new order. To this day, most Knights of Peter Claver are black.

Originally, men had to be under 55 in order to join, but since 1964 it has been possible for older men to join as associate (social or uninsured) members.

The Knights works two DEGREES, somewhat confusingly called the Third Degree and the Fourth Degree; the latter was added in 1917. Since 1980, there has also been a Ladies of Grace, Fourth Degree Division. The RITUALS AND CEREMONIES are Roman Catholic and fully approved by the Church. Indeed, the organization is blessed annually by the Pope. Local Courts (male LODGES) and Councils (their female equivalent) usually meet in church halls, though they may also meet in the church itself, or at a private individual's home. There are also state and national meetings.

The order's religious work includes fund raising for the Roman Catholic Church; Holy Communion in a body; uniformed participation in religious ceremonies; and masses for the souls of departed members, every Sunday. There is a long litany in honor of St. Peter Claver.

The Knights is, however, much more than a pietist and fund-raising organization. In the 1960s, it encouraged African Americans to register for voting and introduced a group insurance program. In 1970, it organized the Sickle Cell program to assist research into a disease that affects blacks, and it awards scholarships, promotes sport and recreation, and participates in civic action.

The effectiveness and relevance of the Knights of Peter Claver are shown by the fact that, in a world where memberships of most fraternal organizations are falling, their roles are growing: in round numbers, from 13,000 in 1959 to 18,000 in 1969 to 25,000 in 1979 and 35,000 in 1994.

Associated organizations include the Junior Knights (7–17 years of age), founded in 1917 and with a membership of 1,800 in 1994; the Ladies' Auxiliary (1922); and the Junior Daughters (the female equivalent of the Junior Knights), founded in 1930, and with a 1994 membership of 3,600.

Knights of Pythias

2785 Desert Inn Rd., Ste. 150
Las Vegas, NV 89121
(702) 735-3302

The Knights of Pythias was founded in 1864 in Washington, D.C., as a secret society for government clerks,

but admission and goals have both broadened since. The order now functions as a fraternal organization with service aspects, in the United States and Canada. It publishes the *Pythian International* quarterly. There were 80,000 members in 1994.

The story of Damon and Phintias, as reported by Diodorus Siculus and Cicero, is given below. It is worth noting that "Pythias" is a widespread misreading for Phintias.

In Syracuse in the fourth century B.C., Phintias was condemned to death for opposing the tyrant Dionysius. His friend and fellow member of the PYTHAGOREANS, Damon, offered himself as hostage so that Phintias could go make his farewells.

When the time for the execution of Phintias drew near and he had not returned, Damon offered himself in Phintias' stead. At the last minute, Phintias reappeared and embraced his friend. Dionysus was so impressed that he released both men and begged to be admitted to their friendship.

Justus H. Rathbone was so taken with this story that he organized the Knights of Pythias on February 19, 1864. Initially, he had intended to limit membership to government clerks like himself and his six cofounders, but membership was soon broadened. Even so, in its original form, the Knights of Pythias lasted less than six months, and the Venerable Patriarch Rathbone resigned from the wreckage. Then he rejoined, and with the help of a new ritual that he devised, he managed to attract about 3,000 members by 1868. The lodges were called "Castles," though they are now commonly called "Subordinate Lodges"; the usual three-tiered structure went on to Grand Lodges (state level) and the Supreme Lodge.

Rathbone then invented a new higher degree, the Supreme Order of the Pythian Knighthood; this would have added a fourth degree to the three described above. The Supreme Lodge not only rejected the new degree in 1869; it also forbade anyone to take the degree under pain of expulsion. The founder was out again, but was allowed to rejoin (after some debate within the organization) in 1874. Hired by the Knights as a lecturer, he was in serious financial trouble by 1884 and was bailed out by a collection that raised some $5,085. He died in late 1889.

With a fine disregard for the remote antiquity of its inspiration, there is a medieval flavor to the general terminology. Lodge buildings are called Castles, and officials include the Chancellor Commander, Vice Chancellor, Prelate, Master of the Work, Keeper of the Records and Seal, Master of Finance, Master of the Exchequer, Master at Arms, Inner Guard, and Outer Guard.

The RITUALS AND CEREMONIES are unusual in that they have been *officially* published in full, as distinct from being "pirated." They follow a pattern typical of DEISM, with three DEGREES, Page, Esquire, and Knight. The ritual has some rough-house qualities; for example, candidates were led to believe that they would have to jump barefoot onto a spiked board, though the spikes were removed (or rubber spikes were substituted) before the jump. It is unlikely that these aspects of the ritual survive.

For the Page degree, postulants are asked if they believe in a supreme being and are of sound bodily health; they must also answer in the affirmative the question:

Are you willing to take upon yourself a solemn obligation to keep forever secret all that you may hear, see or be instructed in — an obligation that will in no way conflict with your creed or your conscience.

The paraphernalia includes the following:

On two trestles, twelve inches high, covered by a black pall reaching to the floor shall be placed an open coffin which shall contain a skeleton. On the coffin shall be two crossed swords, with the hilts towards the Prelate, and on these the open book of law.

This is the usual sort of symbolism for DEATH AND RESURRECTION; and, again in typical Masonic fashion, the candidate is blindfolded for part of the ceremony.

The Esquire degree is similar, except that there is a trick in it. The candidate specifically promises not to commit to writing any of the secret work of the order, nor to permit this to be done by another if it be within his power to prevent. The ritual then requires him to do just that, by filling in the motto in the blank space provided. If the candidate remembers his oath and refuses to fill it in himself, the Keeper of Records volunteers to do it for him. If he still protests, he is congratulated and installed; if he fills in the blank space, proceedings are delayed for a while during a mock trial. When the trial is over, he is inducted as an Esquire.

For the Knight degree, he is equipped with a shield on his left arm and a helm on his head; the visor serves as a blindfold. In another merry jump through space and time, his admission is publicly debated by other lodge members who take the part of "Senators," whose job it is to keep unworthy candidates from becoming Knights. This is where the bit about jumping on spikes comes in.

In addition to all this, pietist "historians" of the order invented all kinds of wonderful symbolism, quite unsupported by Rathbone's mish-mash of ritual; the number of Pythian symbols was variously placed at 10,000 and 20,000. Predictably, Pythagorean philosophy (as interpreted by said pietists) plays no small part in this symbolism.

In 1887, the Knights founded an Endowment Rank to provide insurance coverage, which no doubt helped growth; the insurance department financially separated from the Knights proper in 1931, and the United Mutual Life Insurance Company took over its role in due course, leaving the Knights where it started as a fraternal organization.

By 1900, the Knights of Pythias had more than half a million members, despite the fact that in 1894 the Holy Office forbade membership to Catholics. In 1896, the Catholic Church did, however, make a few concessions: A Catholic might remain in the organization if he had joined in good faith; and if he would suffer severe temporal loss (i.e. of insurance) if he quit; and if he were in no danger of loss of faith.

The Uniform Rank, open only to Knights, is entitled to wear a pseudomilitary marching costume and was founded in 1877–78, while the Endowment Rank (again introduced in 1877) provided insurance benefits. In 1930 the Endowment Rank became a separate organization; it now calls itself the *American United Insurance Company,* with headquarters in Indianapolis, Indiana.

At its peak, in 1923, the Knights claimed 908,000 members. It lost tens of thousands a year during the Depression, however, and never really recovered despite the initiation of President Franklin D. Roosevelt in 1936. By the 1960s, it was down to about 200,000, where it apparently remained in the 1970s, and matters have not improved since: 80,000 (1994) is a fraction of the membership the group once enjoyed. Many lodges have closed, as have some of the 22 original Knights of Pythias retirement homes.

From a service/community viewpoint, the Knights sponsors an annual international public speaking contest.

Colored Knights of Pythias

This is a small black order, formed when blacks discovered that they would not be admitted to the Knights proper. It is less significant than the Knights of Pythias of North and South America, etc., below.

Improved Order of Knights of Pythias

This was a German-speaking version of the Knights of Pythias, which seceded from the determinedly English-speaking parent organization in 1895 and disappeared at the time of World War I.

Knights of Pythias of North and South America, Europe, Asia and Africa

Although the membership requirement that candidates be white males was not introduced until after 1871, blacks had never been admitted. The K of P of N and S America, etc., is a duplicate of the Knights of Pythias for blacks, and was founded in 1869.

Knights of the Orient, Ancient Order of

This was a side degree (see SIDE DEGREES), which was full of mock-serious ritual.

Princes of Syracuse, Junior Order of

This is or was the junior or "farm" order for the Knights of Pythias. It has probably vanished altogether, though there may be a few odd local pockets still holding out.

Pythian Sisterhood

This was an unusual auxiliary (see AUXILIARIES), which admitted women only, though the women had to be relatives of the Knights of Pythias.

Rathbone Sisters of the World

The Pythian Sisters of the World became the Rathbone Sisters of the World in 1894, and was the other female auxiliary of the Knights of Pythias. It permitted members of the masculine parent order to join, in the usual fashion.

Knights of Reciprocity

The Knights of Reciprocity organized itself in 1890 as a political secret society to oppose the Farmers' Alliance, a movement with ideological ties to the Populist Party (see FREEMEN'S PROTECTIVE SILVER ASSOCIATION for more on the Populist Party). The founders were mostly recidivist joiners, including FREEMASONS, ODD FELLOWS, and KNIGHTS OF PYTHIAS. Like many American political societies, the career of the Knights was meteoric. It claimed 126,000 members in the Midwest in 1895, but effectively disappeared a few years later.

Knights of the Ancient Essenic Order

The Knights of the Ancient Essenic Order were organized in 1888 in Olympia, Washington. The order appears to have been a social and benevolent society, without beneficiary or insurance features. Despite the fact that the order had 35,000 members in the late 1890s, there is no visible trace of the organization today.

Knights of the Ancient Order of the Mystic Chain

The Knights of the (Ancient Order of the) Mystic Chain were founded in 1887 by a locomotive engineer and a merchant in Reading, Pennsylvania. Both founders were FREEMASONS, and 21 of the candidates at the first initiation were Knights of Pythias; it was a joiners' order from the start.

The RITUALS AND CEREMONIES were based on the legend of the Knights of the Round Table, and the organization was complex, as follows.

Under the Supreme Castle, there were the Civic Branch with its Select Castles (state level) and subordinate Castles (LODGES); the Military Rank, introduced in 1880; the insurance benefit fund, started in 1889; and the

Daughters of Ruth, the women's branch, dating from 1890.

The subordinate Castles could award the White or Esquire Degree; the Blue or Sir Knight's Degree; and the Red or Round Table Degree (see DEGREES). A fourth degree was available for those who fancied the military branch. Past officers received a Past Commander's or Mark degree, a prerequisite for serving in a Select Castle (which also conferred the degree), and the Supreme Castle conferred a Supreme Degree, which made the recipient a non-voting member of the Supreme Castle; only elected officers had a vote. The Degree of Naomi, also known as the Degree of the Daughters of Ruth, was introduced as a female auxiliary (see AUXILIARIES) in 1890.

During the initiation degree, the candidate (divested of all metallic possessions, in the Masonic fashion) was asked to put a coin in the cup of a "beggar" who came into the room after being "set upon by highwaymen, wounded and robbed." The candidate was, of course, unable to comply; but when he was searched, the searcher would "find" money and impose on him a penance for his deception and want of charity. In at least some lodges, the candidate was then asked to wash his hands in an electrified mystical bowl. Despite the Arthurian references, the robes of the officers during the initiation were apparently Egyptian, complete with fez.

In 1899 the Ancient Order decided to introduce an insurance feature called the Funeral Benefit Relief Fund, and the order continued for many years after that. There were 13,167 members as of January 1, 1923. It is not clear when the order disappeared (or merged with some other organization), but it seems to have been some time ago.

Knights of the Apocalypse

The Knights of the Apocalypse were founded in 1693 in Italy, ostensibly to defend the Church against the imminent Antichrist. Shortly afterwards, the founder, Augustine Gabrino, was confined to a madhouse. Gabrino called himself Monarch of the Holy Trinity, and he wanted to introduce polygamy. After Gabrino's demise, the organization seems to have perished during the Inquisition.

Knights of the Cork

A very obscure group. All that is known about it is that it was established in Italy after a papal bull excommunicated the Freemasons, and it was intended by its founders to take the place of the Masonic institution. It was open to men and women.

Knights of the Flaming Circle

The "Flaming Circle" worn on the left breast of the robe of the Knights of the Flaming Circle symbolized truth;

the organization was formed in 1923 in Pennsylvania to counter the KU KLUX KLAN. They admitted blacks, Jews, and Catholics—but excluded Protestants.

Knights of the Globe

The Knights of the Globe, organized in Chicago in 1889, was a blend of the organizations to which its founders belonged: FREEMASONS, OLD FELLOWS, members of the United Workmen (see UNITED WORKMEN, ANCIENT ORDER OF), ROYAL ARCANUM, AMERICAN LEGION OF HONOR, WOODMEN of the World, Grand Army of the Republic and other secret societies. The organization was strongly patriotic in its orientation, and there were four DEGREES: Volunteer, Militant, Knight, and Valiant Knight.

The Knights of the Globe appear to have become extinct in the first decade of the 20th century.

Knights of the Golden Circle

The Knights of the Golden Circle was a prosecessionist movement, apparently formed some time before the American Civil War out of the Order of the Lone Star, itself founded in 1852 as a manifestation of the KNOW-NOTHINGS. The order was also known as the American Knights, the Knights of the Mighty Host, the Mutual Protection Society, the Circle of Honor and the Sons of Liberty, among other names. There was also an auxiliary, the Ladies of the Golden Circle (see AUXILIARIES). This organization seems to have done everything in its power to promote the Confederacy, and when that cause was lost, it advocated the annexation or at least "Americanization and Southernization" of Mexico. The movement died with the end of the Civil War.

The origin of its name is obscure, but may have signified the claimed extent of the order—the circumference of its influence touching the Mason-Dixon Line to the north and the Isthmus of Panama to the south. The order was much talked about during the Civil War and may have served to organize southern sympathizers in the north (the so-called Copperheads).

Knights of the Golden Horn

The Knights of the Golden Horn was a social and benevolent order founded in Hull, England, in about 1872. It operated in the United Kingdom and is probably extinct.

The founders and many of the subsequent leading lights were apparently prominent members of the Royal Antediluvian Order of Buffalo (R.A.O.B.; see BUFFALO, ROYAL ANTEDILUVIAN ORDER OF), though the order was not a subsidiary or inner group, and non-Buffaloes seem to have been welcome to join the organization. The Knights appear to have had much the same aims and RITUALS AND CEREMONIES as the older organization, from whom they obtained a charter in 1902. Then, between 1919 and 1925, there was an outbreak of bickering over the wearing of regalia, and in 1925, the Grand Scribe of the Knights gave notice to the R.A.O.B. (G.L.E., or Grand Lodge of England) that his organization wished to sever all links with the "parent" organization, though without ruling out the possibility of dual membership.

There are (or were) three DEGREES, of Companion, Knight Commander, and Order of the Shield, and the LODGE is (or was) called an Encampment. The history of the organization ends in 1925.

Knights of the Invisible Colored Kingdom

The Knights of the Invisible Colored Kingdom, now defunct, was founded in August 1923 to counter the renascent KU KLUX KLAN. Headquartered in Chattanooga, Tennessee, the avowed purpose of the order was to organize "male members of the Negro race into grand and subordinate organizations and [teach] them the principles of good citizenship and their political duties and possibilities."

Knights of the Mystic Circle

The Knights of the Mystic Circle was founded in 1861 as a political secret society in the United States, and was operative principally in the Middle West. It was the first incarnation of a society of "Peace Democrats," who were opposed to the way that Lincoln was prosecuting the Civil War. It sought to restore the Union as it had been before Lincoln's election, and, to this end, encouraged desertion, draft dodging, and the obstruction of places of enlistment. Some encouraged armed rebellion.

Widely reviled as "copperheads" (members wore a copper penny as a token of their political views), the group was perforce a secret society. Civil rights were virtually nonexistent in the North during the Civil War, and federal courts sentenced three of the ringleaders to death, though it was never proved that they were actually engaged in illegal acts. They were pardoned in 1866 as a result of a Supreme Court battle.

In 1863, the organization changed its name to the Order of American Knights, and in 1864 the order changed it again to the Sons of Liberty.

Knights of the Red Cross of Constantine

P.O. Box 579
Springfield, IL 62705
(217) 788-5090; Fax (217) 523-0013

The Knights of the Red Cross of Constantine constitutes one of the myriad organizations of the FREEMASONS. The relationship between the Masonic organization and the original Knights of the Red Cross of Constantine, an order of chivalry instituted by the Emperor Constantine in A.D. 312, is entirely fanciful; this is a division of the YORK RITE of Freemasonry, open only to those who are

Royal Arch Masons. The organization is also known as the Knights of Rome.

The DEGREES are as follows:

Knight of the Red Cross of Constantine
Knight of the Holy Sepulchre
Knight of St. John the Evangelist
Chapter of Knights Grand Cross
Grand Senate of Sovereigns (limited to Coroneted Sovereigns)
Grand College of Viceroys (limited to Coroneted Sovereigns and Consecrated Viceroys)

In 1994 there were 6,000 members, compared with 5,800 a decade previously and 5,000 a decade before that.

Knights of the York Cross of Honour

6832 44th Place N.E.
Seattle, WA 98115
(206) 523-1050

The Convent General of the Knights of the York Cross of Honour is another group representing FREEMASONS and is dedicated to promoting friendship and helpfulness among its members. Conceived in 1930 by John Raymond Shute II as an association of those who had held the four highest offices of the YORK RITE of Freemasonry, it had 1,300 members in 1994 and works two degrees: the Initiatory or Reception of the Candidate, and the Knight York Grand Cross.

Knights Templar, Grand Encampment of the United States

5097 North Elston Avenue, Ste. 101
Chicago, IL 60630-2460
(312) 777-3300

The (Masonic) Knights Templar was founded in 1816 as a fraternal service organization for Master Masons. The order flourishes in the United States, where there were 300,000 members in 1994.

As with other organizations using the word "Templar," the connection between these FREEMASONS and the actual TEMPLARS is wishful rather than actual. The first recorded reference to the Knight Templar degree (see DEGREES) is in 1769, when it was conferred upon one William Davis at Boston; and in 1780 an Encampment of Knights Templar was organized in Charleston, South Carolina. The organization as currently constituted traces its formal establishment to 1816, from which year the modern constitution dates.

The Knight Templar is the 10th degree and highest rank of the YORK RITE. Candidates must be in good standing in their own BLUE LODGE, as well as being holders of the Royal Arch Degree, the seventh of the York Rite. Confusingly, there are two routes to the Knight Templar degree. In one, the eighth and ninth degrees are awarded via the Council of Royal and Select Masters, while in the other, the Order of the Red Cross is the eighth degree and the Knights of Malta constitute the ninth. These two orders (Red Cross and Malta) are commonly referred to in the United States as the two "Appendant" degrees of the Masonic Knights Templar.

The RITUALS AND CEREMONIES and their trappings are based on the original Templars: part of the oath (see OATHS) is, "I furthermore promise and vow, that I will wield my sword in defense of innocent maidens, destitute widows, helpless orphans and the Christian religion." There are the usual penalties for breaking the oath, including having one's head struck off and placed "on the highest spire in Christendom."

LODGES are called Commanderies; states with three or more lodges form Grand Commanderies; and the leading body is the Supreme Encampment. Inside the Craft, the Knights Templars are frequently referred to simply as a "Commandery." The officers of a Commandery are as follows: Eminent Commander, Generalisimo (spelled thusly), Captain-General, Prelate, Senior Warden, Junior Warden, Treasurer, Recorder, Warden, Standard-Bearer, Sword-Bearer, and Sentinel. In a Grand Commandery, they are Grand Eminent Commander and so on to General Sentinel.

The order has drawn criticism from some Christians as well as Masons. Several Christian churches, notably Catholic and Lutheran, forbid membership of the Masons, while the specifically Christian orientation of the Knights Templar has led more than one deistic Masonic author, to describe the order as less than strictly Masonic. Membership appears to be dropping slowly but steadily: 398,000 in 1968, 368,000 in 1978, and 300,000 in 1994 — about 7.5 percent per decade.

The Social Order of the Beauceant is the female auxiliary (see AUXILIARIES) to the Masonic Knights Templar; it was formed in 1889 with the same initials ("S.O.O.B."), but this was said to stand for "Some Of Our Business" until the present style was adopted in 1913. The "Beauceant" was the Templar banner of the Crusades.

Knothole Clubs

The Knothole or Knot-Hole Clubs was a juvenile order organized by ROTARY INTERNATIONAL, originally in Bristol, Tennessee, and probably in the early 20th century.

The arrangement was this. The local Rotarians would make a deal with the management of a local baseball park, which would agree to admit members of the Knothole Club for only a dime instead of a quarter, subject to the following conditions:

1. The boy (it was a male-only club) had to be under 14
2. He had to be wearing short trousers

3. He had to be carrying his Knothole card

In order to get the card, he had to sign an obligation, which said, "I will attend Sunday School every Sunday except in case of sickness. I will not use curse words, and will lead a clean life. I will be a rooter for the home baseball team. I have read or have had read to me this obligation and I promise that I will always obey."

Knots

The "Knots" is not a secret society in its own right, but rather comprises the LODGES of the Ancient and Benevolent Order of the Friendly Brothers of St. Patrick. This notwithstanding, P.B. Rear Admiral Ronald f Portlock (the "f" seems to be a part of the club's RITUALS AND CEREMONIES, inserted before the surname) wrote a *History of the London Knots 1775 to 1973* in about 1973, concentrating on the four London Knots of this originally Irish society.

The London Knots existed in about 1775–85 ("None of its records exist today, and we know nothing about its members"), 1808–36, 1854–60 and 1870 onward. There is also information on the Marching Knots of the First Foot, 1757 and 1784, which apparently transferred their allegiance to the FREEMASONS when that became fashionable. Unfortunately, Admiral Portlock's book is remarkably uninformative, consisting mainly of accounts of what various brethren of the Knot did in history.

Know-Nothings

The Know-Nothing Party was an American isolationist and nativist movement, which rose to national prominence in 1852 and disappeared in official form as the new Republican Party gained strength after 1856. The sentiments of Know-Nothing politics existed long before 1852 and continue to exist to this day, and the Know-Nothings lent its name to this school of political belief. The improbable name of the Know-Nothings came from its members' ritual answer to questions about their party: "I know nothing about it."

Its nucleus before 1852 was a coalition of secret societies, and when the movement lost momentum as a legitimate political party, it returned to its secret-society roots. Many of these societies, which were often even shorter-lived than the Know-Nothing party, were pseudo-PATRIOTIC ORGANIZATIONS of the most virulent kind. Several of the larger ones, such as the AMERICAN PROTECTIVE ASSOCIATION, have their own entries; the organizations listed below are smaller societies, here consolidated for ease of reference.

The thrust of all these societies was primarily negative, directed *against* immigration, Catholicism, and the Irish (the three were, in the 1840s, all but synonymous). Others who bore the brunt of these organizations' opposition were the Germans and the Jews.

Bereans, Benevolent Order of

The Order of Bereans was more malevolent than benevolent, a product of "nativist" and anti-Catholic sentiment prevalent in the late 1840s. It has been extinct for over a century.

Daughters of Columbia

The Daughters of Columbia was founded in 1888 as a female auxiliary (see AUXILIARIES) to the American Patriot League and is long extinct.

Daughters of Liberty

The Daughters of Liberty was an offshoot of the JUNIOR ORDER OF UNITED AMERICAN MECHANICS, founded in 1877. As so often, the presence of the word "Liberty" in the name is a warning that the members were at least as interest in restricting the liberties of others as in promoting their own. In 1915, it changed its name to the Sons and Daughters of Liberty, while retaining the same goals. It purported to stand for the American public school system, which it wished to commandeer as a vehicle for Protestant evangelism and simplistic nationalism. The order was also anti-immigration and anti-Catholic. There were over 100,000 members as late as the 1920s, but there are none today.

Hindoos

This was actually a name given to the Know-Nothings themselves—according to one authority, this was "in consequence of their candidate for the presidency, David Ullman, having been charged with being a native of Calcutta."

Loyal Knights of America

Patriotism was the favorite, if not the last, refuge of this particular band of scoundrels. It was an anti-Catholic group that first convened in Wilkes-Barre, Pennsylvania, in 1890; it disappeared within a decade or two.

Kravez Kelt

Kravez Kelt was a tightly closed religious order with RITUALS AND CEREMONIES based on a Celtic calendar discovered at Coligny near Boug-en-Bresse, France, in 1897. The calendar is a bronze tablet written in Gaulish in the first century B.C. It is not only the oldest surviving specimen of written Celtic language, but is often seen as an ancient Druidical relic, which suggests that Kravez Kelt was a neo-Druidical order. Its membership was under 100.

Ku Klux Klan

The Ku Klux Klan was founded in about 1866; died, and rose again in 1915; then died a second time, only to be reborn yet again, in the 1950s. It is a "fraternal, patriotic, and religious" society of white Protestant American-born men, which is notorious for violence against anyone who is not a white Protestant (see PATRIOTIC ORGANIZATIONS). The size cannot be accurately estimated.

In the aftermath of the Civil War, treatment of the South by the North was often vengeful and capricious; those were the days of disenfranchised taxpayers, bought votes, carpetbaggers, and radical Republicans. President Ulysses S. Grant was an honest man, but his administration was notoriously corrupt; he was apparently better able to control his soldiers than his subordinate politicians.

In such a climate, secret societies of all kinds flourished. The very first members of the Ku Klux Klan probably did not see themselves as a political movement. Their earliest activities seem to have been dressing up as ghosts (the origin of the white robes) and terrorizing former slaves. The Klan was but one of many similar groups, but it rapidly expanded into a very large, popular, and ill-defined organization. The name reputedly came from the Greek kuklos or kyklos, a circle, though it has also been suggested (almost certainly inaccurately) that the name was in imitation of "the sound of an old-fashioned rifle being cocked."

Members of the original Klan have been portrayed both as murderous racists and as heroes fighting against corruption and the breakdown of law and order. The two views are not necessarily mutually exclusive; in some cases, the same person may have answered both descriptions.

Under the former Confederate General Nathan Bedford Forrest, who became Grand Wizard in 1869, the ideals of a "good" Klan probably came closest to being realized. Unfortunately for all concerned, the Klansman's mask could as readily hide a looter, murderer, or rapist as a fighter against corruption; and it could also hide a black face as well as a white one. Criminals of many kinds hid behind the white sheets.

Federal investigations by a congressional committee predictably confirmed all the worst accusations against the Klan, but it is important to remember that radical Republican and Reconstructionist committees were far from unbiased. In all fairness to the Congressional Committee, on the other hand, there was no doubt that at least some Klan members, and quite possibly the majority, were guilty of all the crimes of which the organization was accused: tarring and feathering, flogging, castration, and lynching.

As a result of the investigation, General Forrest agreed to disband the organization, though not all Klaverns (LODGEs) followed his orders. Congressional Acts of 1871 and 1873 failed to destroy the Klan completely, despite the use of federal troops against the Klansmen. Pro-Southern historians date the final collapse of this first

version of the Klan to 1876–77; Northern historians prefer to believe that the federal government had succeeded by 1873.

For a pro-Southern, wildly romanticized view of the early Klan, see Thomas Dixon's novel The Klansman, which inspired David Wark Griffiths's motion picture Birth of a Nation. Although the opposite view is popular today, The Klansman did much to prepare the popular white imagination for the resurgence of the Klan. It downplayed all the unpleasant truths and emphasized those rare good qualities, which could almost certainly have been found, albeit with difficulty, among at least some early Klansmen.

The second version of the Klan was chartered in Georgia on December 4, 1915, but did not really take off until 1919, when the Southern Publicity Association (E. Y. Clarke and Mrs. E. Tyler) took over recruitment from the founder, William J. Simmons. A member of the FREEMASONS, Knights Templar (see KNIGHTS TEMPLAR, GRAND ENCAMPMENT OF THE UNITED STATES), KNIGHTS OF PYTHIAS and ODD FELLOWS, Simmons also worked on salary for the WOODMEN of the World.

Simmons devised RITUALS AND CEREMONIES for the Klan while recuperating from an automobile accident, then placed newspaper advertisements inviting people to join "a classy order of the highest Class." This alone would almost certainly have proved insufficient to attract even the worst white trash, but Clark and Tyler were professional fund raisers, who had previously worked for the Salvation Army, the Y.M.C.A. and the Red Cross. They saw a golden opportunity in the revised Klan to do well at the financial expense of various bigots, and devil take the bigots' victims. It did not matter what they called their enemies—Jews, commies, niggers, child molesters, adulterers, drug-dealers, liberals—there were always plenty of simmering resentment against some classes of people, and Tyler and Clark tapped right into it.

Essentially, they franchised Klan membership to those who shared the sentiments of the KNOW-NOTHINGS, but they also promoted the fraternal aspect of the organization, with robes, rituals, and a campaign that urged Klansmen to trade with one another. And they did it at a handsome profit.

In 1921, the initiation fee was $10. Of this, $4 went to the recruiting Kleagle (see below), $1 to his superintending King Kleagle, and $0.50 to the district Grand Goblin, $1.50 to the Klan coffers, and the remaining $3 to the Southern Publicity Association.

Active recruiting, often from the ranks of Masons, resulted in explosive growth for the revised Klan. By 1923, there were half a million Klansmen who were also Masons, quite apart from the two million or so who were not Masons. Even the Southern Protestant churches supported the Invisible Empire, as the Klan was sometimes known. The Baptists, the Methodists, and the

Disciples of Christ were said to be particularly enthusiastic.

This was the golden age of the Klan, and it seems that the manic list of words beginning with a "K" dates from this period. A brief glossary includes:

Klabee	Treasurer
Klecktoken	Initiation fee
Kligrapp	Secretary
Klonvocation	Gathering or convention
Kloran	Book of rituals
Kloreroe	Delegate at state convention
Kludd	Chaplain

There were also non-"K" offices, including

Exalted Cyclops	Head of Klan chapter
Grand Dragon	State head of Klan
Grand Goblin	Other state head
Imperial Wizard	Head of the Klan

The ritual was loosely based on the Masonic model, with an altar bearing an American flag, an unsheathed sword, and a Bible open at the 12th chapter of Romans. The oath (see OATHS) had no particularly blood-curdling penalties, though candidates promised to keep the secrets and added, "I will die rather than divulge same."

Almost as fast as it had mushroomed, the new Klan faded. In 1924, an estimated 40,000 robed members marched in Washington, D.C.; by 1930, the total membership of the organization was estimated at about 35,000. The Depression depleted the ranks still further, and a federal back tax bill for $685,000 in 1944 ended the second Klan.

In the 1950s, the Klan was reborn again, this time in opposition to the nascent Civil Rights movement. This third Klan was more political, and therefore more like its 1860 grandfather than its 1915 father, but this time there was next to no question of fighting against graft and corruption. The third incarnation of the Klan was reactionary and racist. Furthermore, the new Klan lacked the unity of the old and came in several varieties. Several Klan organizations were actually chartered in Southern states.

The United Klans of America, Knights of the Ku Klux Klan Inc. was the biggest, run by a former rubber-worker named Robert Shelton. The Nation Knights of the Ku Klux Klan, Inc. was the next largest, and between the two of them they could probably boast many tens of thousands of members in the 1960s. Membership in the 1980s and 1990s is unknown.

Although the crosses still burn, and the Klan still does its best to dominate by terror anyone who is not a white Anglo-Saxon Protestant, the heyday of the hooded riders is gone; but it would be a brave person who said that they would never return.

Throughout its history, the Klan has been accused of the crimes already mentioned: tarring and feathering, beatings, torture, castration, lynchings, and much else. Many of these accusations are unquestionably true. The atrocities of the 1950s are too well documented to warrant repetition here; nor did they stop with that decade. On balance, the judgment of history must be overwhelmingly against the Klan. Pro-Southern apologists for the first version of the Klan are almost uniformly overenthusiastic in their attempts to show that the Klan was not all bad.

Ladies Oriental Shrine of North America

1111 East 54th Street, Ste. 111
Indianapolis, IN 46220
(317) 259-1996

The Ladies Oriental Shrine of North America was founded in 1914 in Wheeling, West Virginia, as a ladies auxiliary (see AUXILIARIES) to the SHRINERS. There were 32,000 members in 1994.

The wives of Shriners had been holding their own social meetings for at least a decade before they organized the Ladies Oriental Shrine of North America on June 24, 1914. They did not get around to legally incorporating their organization until 1954.

Like their husbands, the lady members aim at enjoying themselves as well as promoting good works. As has been the case with a number of the better-run women's organizations, their numbers have been increasing while all-male organizations have mostly declined or remained stagnant. From 24,000 in the mid-1960s they had risen to 30,000 in the mid-1970s and 32,000 by 1994.

Ladies Pennsylvania Slovak Catholic Union

69 Public Square, Ste. 922
Wilkes-Barre, PA 18701
(717) 823-3513

A fraternal benefit insurance society founded in 1898, now open to both sexes but still with a strong Slovak appeal. It publishes *Zornicka,* monthly. There were 14,600 members in 1994.

The Slovaks seem much given to fraternal benefit societies, and this is one of the larger and more successful ones. Membership has fluctuated around the 16,000 mark—sometimes higher, rarely lower—for several decades, which is indicative of the fundamental health and soundness of the organization. In operation, it is a typical ethnic fraternal benefit society, with a strong Catholic interest. It is noted for supporting seminaries, churches, and related institutions as well as providing scholarships and doing good works, including community-based projects.

Land and Liberty

Land and Liberty—in Russian, *Zemlia i volia*—was a name applied to two secret revolutionary societies. The first was founded toward the end of 1861, and the second in 1876.

The first organization, which was headquartered in St. Petersburg and Moscow, with satellite cells throughout Russia, was primarily educational, covertly publishing leaflets and manifestos for distribution to workers, soldiers, and the "educated classes." The basic platform of the group consisted of the propositions that the peasants be allotted all the land they formerly used, that the army be cut to half its present size, that bureaucracy be slashed, and that peasant self-government be established. The organization went further, advocating government by a classless National Assembly or "Assembly of the Land."

Revolutionary fervor died down in Russia by 1863, and many members of the first Land and Liberty were compelled to emigrate or were arrested. The order dissolved in 1864.

The second Land and Liberty was founded in 1876 in St. Petersburg, although the name "Land and Liberty" was not officially adopted until 1878, with the publication of the organization's newspaper of that name. At its founding, the organization had been called (less euphoniously) the Northern Revolutionary Populist Group and also the Society of Populists.

Like its predecessor, the second organization advocated a radical redistribution of land among the peasantry. Members saw the peasants as the source of revolution, relegating the urban workers to a subordinate role. Although this contrasted with the later policies of Vladimir I. Lenin, architect of the Bolshevik Revolution of 1917, which concentrated on radicalizing urban workers, Lenin later acknowledged the role of Land and Liberty in their attempt "to enlist all the discontented into the organization and to direct this organization to the decisive struggle against the autocracy."

The second Land and Liberty took their program well beyond propaganda, assassinating the chief of the gendarmerie, N. V. Mezentsov, in 1878. The order deemed terrorism a valid means of self-defense and vengeance, though not as the primary means of revolution.

In August 1879, Land and Liberty splintered into two independent organizations, People's Will and Black Repartition.

Legion of Honor

The original French Legion of Honor is a state-conferred nonchivalric dignity. The name was borrowed by the American Legion of Honor (1878), a fraternal, social, and beneficiary ASSESSMENT society; by the Iowa Legion of Honor (1879), a similar organization; and by the Northwestern Legion of Honor (1884). None of the American namesakes seems still to exist.

Lenhadores e Lenhadoras, Ordem dos

Despite its Portuguese name, the order was founded in Paris, on August 17, 1747. The plural nouns of the order's name are the masculine and feminine forms of the word for "wood cutters," denoting that this was an androgynous society. Modeled on the COMPAGNONNAGE, it was a fraternal and social society, probably created at the behest of women who were unhappy about being excluded from the FREEMASONS. Contemporaries saw it—and similar organizations, such as the Order of the Knights and Nymphs of the Rose, the Society of the Companions of Penelope, and the Order of Felicity—as frivolous and even degenerate alternatives to Freemasonry.

The meeting places of the Ordem dos Lenhadores e Lenhadoras bore such Arcadian names as "groves," "re-treats," and "temples of love." Female members were referred to as "lady friends" or "cousins." The society seems to have attracted prominent men in search of diversion and those who had grown tired of the stiff formalities of the Masonic lodge.

Leopard Societies

See HUMAN LEOPARDS.

Lichtseher

The Lichtseher, also known as the *Erleuchtete,* was a mystical sect or secret society founded in Schlettstadt by Küper Martin Steinbach in the 16th century. It may or may not have had connections with the ILLUMINATI; one translation of "Erleuchtete" is "Enlightened," or "Illuminati." The order's chief activity was arcane Scriptural interpretation. The only mention of the order appears in the 1566 *Handbuch* of Pastor Reinhard Lutz.

Lions International

Lions Clubs International
300 22nd Street
Oak Brook, IL 60570-0001
(312) 571-5466; Fax: (312) 571-8890

Lions International was founded on June 17, 1917, in Chicago as a service organization for businessmen (not businesswomen) who were of the age of majority and interested in community service. It has since expanded internationally and now admits women. There were about 1.4 million members in 1994. It publishes *The Lion,* a periodical.

The avowed purpose of the Lions is for members to serve those less fortunate than themselves; discussion of business is expressly forbidden at meetings. The founder was a Chicago businessman named Melvin Jones. However, the organization differs from a charity in two ways. It disburses money to good causes, rather than applying it directly to the beneficiaries, and Lions members expect to enjoy the club. It channels a steady stream of money raised on an almost daily basis by its membership. The effect of giving relatively slowly, but very steadily, means that the Lions are first-class fundraisers.

It is also noteworthy that they are *genuinely* international, instead of being an American organization that calls itself "international" because there are a few token branches overseas.

One of its main charitable projects is assisting the visually handicapped, worldwide; this arose from a challenge from Helen Keller at the International Convention in 1925. It also contributes to diabetes education and research, drug awareness, and many civic causes.

Although women have been eligible for full membership of the Lions since July 1987, the Lioness Clubs program still flourishes with over 150,000 members; the

Leo Clubs, the youth side of the organization, boasts more than 100,000 members in over 100 countries.

Lions, Royal Order of

The Royal Order of Lions was founded by a doctor from Evansville, Indiana, in 1911. It was presumably intended to emulate the ELKS, the Moose (see MOOSE, INTERNATIONAL) and the EAGLES, and enjoyed a good deal of success at first, with 300,000 members in 23 states in the early 1920s. Its disappearance since then may perhaps be attributed (at least in part) to its elaborate and lengthy RITUALS AND CEREMONIES, and its six DEGREES. Such things may flourish in the FREEMASONS, but among other fraternal orders, the more successful ones seem mostly to keep such matters to a minimum.

Lithuanian Alliance of America

307 W. 30th Street
New York, NY 10001
(212) 563-2210

This fraternal benefit life insurance society was founded in 1886 in Shenandoah, Pennsylvania for those of Lithuanian ancestry. There were 5,000 members in 1994. The alliance publishes *Tevyne* (directory) monthly, and publishes *Susivienijimas Lietuviu Amerikoje 1886–1976* (1976).

The idea of a *Susivienijimas Lietuviu Amerikoje* was canvassed in the *Lietuwizka Gazieta* of August 16, 1879. As the author of the article pointed out, everyone else had organized fraternal benefit societies, so why not the Lithuanians?

From 1886–88 there was a joint Polish-Lithuanian organization, but they fell out and separated, and there have been political upheavals since.

Membership has declined greatly from the 22,000 or so of 1930. There were about 10,000 members in the mid-1960s, and 6,563 in 1978, so 1994 membership represented a considerable drop.

It is a typical fraternal benefit society with insurance, cultural events, scholarships, and a library of books on Lithuanian studies.

Lithuanian Catholic Alliance

P.O. Box 32
Wilkes-Barre, PA 18703
(717) 823-8876

The Lithuanian Catholic Alliance was founded in 1886 as a fraternal benefit life insurance society. Today it is open to both sexes, with no restrictions on religion. There were 3,069 members in 1994. The Alliance publishes *Garsas* 10 times a year.

Until 1975, called the Lithuanian Catholic Alliance of America, this is a typical fraternal benefit society with slowly falling rolls.

Lithuanian Workers, Association of

26 North Street, Room 42
Middletown, NY 10940
(914) 343-3774

The Association of Lithuanian Workers was founded in the United States in 1930 as a fraternal benefit society for Lithuanians or those of Lithuanian descent. There were 1,800 members in 1994. The Association publishes *Tiesa* (monthly).

The *Lietuviu Darbininku Susivienijimas* is a relatively recently founded fraternal benefit society, which is fairly typical in its activities, sponsoring college scholarships, golf and bowling tournaments, cultural events, charitable donations, and fraternal and social activities. It has never been large, though its present membership is greater than the 1,000 reported as recently as 1979.

Little Red Schoolhouse, Order of the

The Order of the Little Red Schoolhouse, long extinct, was a patriotic fraternal organization founded in 1895 in Boston by members of the AMERICAN PROTECTIVE ASSOCIATION and others. Unusually for a 19th-century order calling itself an American patriotic organization, it appears to have been genuinely patriotic. Membership was open to all Americans, regardless of race, color, or creed. Most so-called "patriotic" organizations of the period were (for example) anti-Catholic or anti-black.

The order sought to instill a greater love of "Old Glory" and a reverence for public observation—the principle of the "Little Red Schoolhouse." LODGEs were called Schools, and the superior levels (state lodges) were called Seminaries.

Locomotive Engineers Mutual Life

The Locomotive Engineers Mutual Life and Accident Insurance Association, to give it its full title, was organized in 1867 to provide insurance for the practitioners of a traditionally almost uninsurable trade; in writing of the First Battle of Manassas (Bull Run), the London *Times* correspondent Billy Russell said that an American battle was very little more dangerous than an American locomotive, and significantly less dangerous than an American steamboat. His irony was based in reality.

Membership in the Brotherhood of Locomotive Engineers, effectively a TRADE UNION, was always a prerequisite for membership. It is chiefly of interest as an illustration of the overlap between fraternal orders, trade unions and insurance companies.

Lodge

The lodge is the basic unit of fraternal orders and secret societies. In the remote past, "lodges" were just that—places where a member might lodge while traveling, while looking for work, or even while working locally.

Today, few lodges offer any kind of overnight accommodation. The main features, instead, are the lodge room or altar room, where initiations and other rituals are conducted; the club rooms, which may include dining facilities; libraries; card rooms; rooms for playing billiards, snooker or pool (depending on social class); and even gymnasia, swimming pools, and other facilities. In most lodges, the bar is one of the central gathering places, though the American FREEMASONS is a "dry" organization.

The lodge is, however, a state of mind rather than a state of place. Many wealthy lodges own extensive premises, sometimes of modest antiquity, but other, poorer, or more footloose lodges may rent a couple of rooms, meet in a pub, or even meet on an *ad hoc* basis whenever they can afford the space.

The lodge room or altar room is theoretically sacrosanct and should never be open to the "profane," but some lodges take a more relaxed view and argue that when the lodge is not in session, the lodge room is just another room. In Fredericksburg, Virginia, there is even a Museum of Freemasonry, and visitors may enter the lodge room.

In the lodge room, the positions of the various officials for the various rituals are carefully laid out in the handbook, and they take up their stations with great seriousness.

Lodges have been known by a bewildering variety of titles, according to the fancy of the founder or his successors. Not all of these terms are still in use, even if the organization that coined them still survives. Some organizations have followed the lead of their older and more dignified counterparts and changed to the word "Lodge" instead. Alternatives include:

Aerie	Fraternal Order of EAGLES
Bethel	Job's Daughters (see JOB'S DAUGHTERS, INTERNATIONAL ORDER OF)
Bughouse	Order of Bugs (see BUGS, ORDER OF)
Caldron	GROTTO
Camp	WOODMEN
Caravan	Order of the Alhambra (and others; see ALHAMBRA, INTERNATIONAL ORDER OF)
Castle	Knights of the Golden Eagle (and others)
Colony	NATIONAL MUTUAL BENEFIT
Court	Catholic Order of FORESTERS (and others)
Encampment	Knight Masons (and others; see KNIGHT MASONS, ORDER OF)
Forest	TALL CEDARS OF LEBANON OF NORTH AMERICA
Grange	GRANGE
Grove	DRUIDS
Homestead	HOMESTEADERS
Jungle	Benevolent Order of Monkeys (see MONKEYS, BENEVOLENT ORDER OF)
Kennel	Houn' Dawgs (see HOUN' DOGS, ORDER OF)
Klonklave	KU KLUX KLAN
Nest	Fraternal Order of OWLS (and others)

School	Order of the Little Red Schoolhouse (see LITTLE RED SCHOOLHOUSE, ORDER OF THE)
Shrine	Mystic Shrine (and others)
Temple	Several
Vendita	CARBONARI
Watering Place	Loyal Order of Moose (see MOOSE, INTERNATIONAL)
Wigwam	Improved order of RED MEN

Loyal Christian Benefit Association

700 Peace Street, P.O. Box 13005
Erie, PA 16514-1305
(814) 453-4331

The Loyal Christian Benefit Association was founded in the United States in 1890 as a fraternal benefit life insurance society for practicing Christian men, women, and children. There were 46,000 members in 1994. It publishes the *Fraternal Leader,* a periodical.

When it was founded, the Ladies' Catholic Benevolent Association was extremely unusual in that it was *only* for Catholic women; in 1890, few women were insured. The association succeeded, though, and deservedly prospered. In 1927, sons and daughters were also accepted for insurance; in 1960, husbands, brothers, and nephews, too. The current name was adopted in 1969.

Today, the order is essentially a typical fraternal benefit life insurance society, declining slowly in numbers. The decline in the '80s was only about 10 percent, compared with 30–40 percent in the previous decade, so perhaps it is stabilizing in numbers. One would like to think so; it has given millions and perhaps 10s of millions to charity.

Perhaps surprisingly, in view of the Catholic roots of the organization, there is a ritual of initiation for both insured ("benefit") members and uninsured (social) members (see RITUALS AND CEREMONIES).

Loyal Knights of the Round Table

The Loyal Knights of the Round Table is the full name of the Round Table service/luncheon clubs, the first of which was founded in Oakland, California, in March, 1922. The four-minute ritual or "Ceremony of Reception into Knighthood" (see RITUALS AND CEREMONIES) was based around the legend of the Sword in the Stone, and, therefore, qualifies the organization for mention in the present work.

Loyal Sons of America

Charles Herbert Walker created this organization in 1920 in Newark, New Jersey, as a "non-sectarian and non-political patriotic, ritualistic fraternal Order . . . founded upon dependable character." Membership was restricted to "picked" men and "loyal American citizens who take pride in being such." It paid sick, disability, and funeral benefits to members and emphasized "absolute protection of, and a continuous vigilance over, our free public schools."

Early literature for the order announced that "the Loyal Sons of America, like a great tidal wave, is sweeping through all the avenues of modern life" and set a membership goal of 5 million. By 1923, it boasted a grand total of 515 members coordinated from a "Supreme Lodge" in Newark's Iroquois Building.

The Loyal Sons of America is extinct and unrelated to the still-active Patriotic Order of Sons of America, founded in 1847 and based in Valley Forge, Pennsylvania.

Luncheon Clubs

Luncheon clubs, where local worthies gather at a set time each week or month to eat together, have long flourished in many countries, though arguably nowhere so well as in America.

Originally, luncheon clubs were motivated almost entirely by self-interest: They provided a forum for businessmen to meet and reinforce their mutual ties. Many of these clubs were divided by occupation, so that (for example) there would be one seat for the local furniture store owner, one for the local steel stock holder, one for the owner of the automobile dealership, and so forth. If there were more than one representative of each business in town, joining the "right" luncheon club became a matter of considerable importance. And if one man wore more than one hat—for example, if he were both the furniture store proprietor *and* the manufacturer of coffins—it would be a matter of no small importance which he chose to represent himself as at the luncheon club.

Sometime in the first or second decade of the 20th century, this idea was gradually supplanted by the concept of the *service club,* where instead of overtly boosting one another, the local businessmen ostensibly worked for the good of their community; the LIONS INTERNATIONAL is the paradigm example.

Luso-American Life Insurance Society

Luso-American Plaza, 7080 Donion Way
Dublin, CA 94568
(510) 828-4884

The Luso-American Life Insurance Society was formed by merger in 1957 as a fraternal benefit life insurance society for Americans of Portuguese birth or descent. There were 15,000 members in 1995. The Society publishes *The Luso-American* (periodical).

The Portuguese Protective and Benevolent Association of the City and County of San Francisco was formed in 1868 and reincorporated in 1875. It was an ethnic fraternal benefit association of a familiar type, founded a little earlier than most, which combined fraternal benefits with a regard for the culture of the homeland and general charitable works. A Grand Council was formed in 1872, a Supreme Council in 1921. Women were not admitted until 1945; three years later, the society changed its name to the Benevolent Society of California.

Meanwhile, in 1917, the *União Portuguesa Continental do Estado da California* had been formed and had gone its own way. In 1957 the two societies merged, and the new organization took the name of the United National Life Insurance Society, essentially continuing the aims of the previous societies, and continuing to operate mainly in California. Later, the name was changed to its present form. Membership has been stable for a quarter of a century or so.

Luso-American Fraternal Federation

The Luso-American Fraternal Federation is a division of the Luso-American Life Insurance Society. It was founded in 1957 to administer the fraternal aspect of the former societies and also administers the Luso-American Education Foundation, founded in 1963, which provides summer-school scholarships to qualified California high school students of all races and creeds to help them understand Portuguese history and culture.

Maccabees

25800 Northwestern Highway
Southfield, MI 48037
(313) 746-6216

The Maccabees was founded in 1878 in London, Ontario, as a fraternal order with mutual ASSESSMENT fraternal benefits. There were 3,500 members in the United States and Canada in 1994. The quarterly magazine, *The Maccabees Bee Hive,* is no longer published.

The Maccabeans or Maccabees were a Jewish tribe of the second century B.C., which revolted against Antiochus IV of Syria in the name of freedom of religion. Judas Maccabeus was a leader of military genius who secured a Jewish state, Judaea, in 143–42 B.C. The exploits of the tribe are recorded in two eponymous books of the Apocrypha.

The aspects of Maccabeus's feats that appealed to the founders of the modern Maccabees were steadfastness and persistence; his wisdom in the use of power; and (perhaps most relevantly) the fact that he seems to have been the first recorded military leader to order his soldiers to reserve a part of their spoils for the widows and orphans of their fallen colleagues.

Under the original title of the Knights of the Maccabees (the name was changed in 1914), each member of the society pledged to contribute 10 cents to the widow of a deceased "brother," with a ceiling of $1,000 on the widow's portion; any surplus was to be deposited with the treasurer. A constitution and RITUALS AND CEREMONIES had been devised by the time of the first grand convention on August 7, 1878.

The organization grew very rapidly—there were 10,000 members by 1880—but the leadership was marred by the kinds of factional struggles familiar in the history of fraternal societies, and actuarial soundness was still a dream; essentially, the Maccabees functioned by a well-ordered and institutionalized form of passing the hat. Under a Major Boynton, there were extensive reorganizations in both 1881 and 1883, so that by 1900 there were about a quarter of a million members, and by 1915 there were almost a third of a million.

The insurance aspect of the Maccabees has always been paramount. In 1921, the organization adopted the American Mortuary Table of Rates, and in 1961 it became a mutual life insurance company but retained the lodge structure for the benefit of those who had joined before the change and preferred to cling to the past. The LODGES were called Subordinate Camps, with Great Camps at the district level and the Supreme Tent at the top. There are no more lodge publications, and the fraternal aspect of the society is probably on the way out, though the society apparently changed little in size in the whole of the 1980s.

In the middle of the Great Depression, in 1935, the Maccabees quietly absorbed the Brotherhood of America, an unremarkable society founded in 1890 in Philadelphia to provide fraternal insurance benefits for men and women on equal terms. By the 1920s almost four-fifths of the 14,000 or so members of the Brotherhood were "social" (uninsured), and this no doubt contributed to the end of the order. Then, in 1937, the Maccabees also absorbed the Slavic Progressive Beneficial Union, followed by the Michigan Union Life Association in 1941.

Moving in the other direction, the Western Bees seceded from the Maccabees in 1905, but merged with the Highland Nobles by 1911.

Ladies of the Maccabees of the World

This auxiliary (see AUXILIARIES) was founded in Muskegon, Michigan, and merged with the Maccabees proper in 1926. It began in about 1885 as a local auxiliary; expanded to statewide status in 1888; and became a national auxiliary in 1892. The Supreme Hive of the Ladies of the Maccabees of the World seem to have been the first fraternal benefit group to have been managed by women. A splinter group, which split off in the very year of foundation (1892), first called itself the Ladies of the Modern Maccabees and then went on to become the NORTH AMERICAN BENEFIT ASSOCIATION.

Mackey, Albert G.

Albert Mackey's *Encyclopedia of Freemasonry* is one of the standard works in the field. Published during the zenith of fraternalism in the United States, its coverage of the minutiae of the FREEMASONS is unparalleled.

Originally published in 1873, it was revised several times. The edition consulted in the preparation of the present encyclopedia was the "New and Revised Edition, prepared under the direction, and with the assistance, of the late William J. Hughan, 32° . . . by Edward L. Hawkins, M.A., 30°," published in two volumes ("profusely illustrated" with engravings) by the Masonic History Company, New York and London, 1916; copyright, The Masonic History Company, 1912. It has been reprinted many times.

Mad Councillors

This was a comical order founded in 1809 by a Doctor Ehrmann of Frankfurt-am-Main. Mock diplomas in Latin and bearing an outsized seal, were granted to members, who included the likes of Jean Paul and Johann Wolfgang von Goethe. The order was also open to women. On the granting of the 100th diploma, in 1820, the joke was dropped, and the Mad Councillors disbanded.

Mafia

The date of foundation of the Mafia is uncertain, as is its extent, but no one seriously doubts that this criminal fraternity exists, principally in the United States and Italy but also in England and possibly elsewhere.

One version of the origins of the Mafia traces the name to *Morte alla Francia Italia Anela* ("Death to the French [is] Italy's cry"), which was supposed to have been the slogan of a 13th-century organization dedicated to opposing the Angevin oppressors. Another dates to the same period, but has the mother of a Sicilian girl who was raped by French soldiers on her wedding day screaming *"Ma fia! Ma fia!"* ("My daughter! My daughter!") as she ran through the streets.

The Mafia did not come to prominence until after Napoleon's invasion of Italy, when they rather resembled the scalawags and carpetbaggers of the Reconstruction period after the American Civil War: men with an eye to the main chance, who ran things to their own advantage while keeping a semblance of order to satisfy a corrupt national government. Repeated attempts were made to break their power, but they survive both in Sicily and in the United States. The most important attempts to break them were made in 1892, and under Mussolini in the 1920s; although he believed that he had succeeded, the main thing he had done was to drive them out of the less lucrative "dirty hands" crimes like cattle rustling and into white-collar or at least blue-collar management of crime.

The presence of dangerous Sicilian criminals in the United States was first reported in a New Orleans paper as early as 1869, and it was on October 15, 1890 that the New Orleans chief of police, David Peter Hennessey, was murdered by the Mafia, which he was trying to suppress in that city. The following year 11 Italian immigrants, acquitted of the murder, were lynched by outraged citizens of New Orleans, and Italy broke off diplomatic relations with the United States over the incident.

The Mafia active in New Orleans at the time was organized along the same lines as the Sicilian originals. Inter-gang rivalry among Mafia groups was fierce, and real or even imagined insults (especially to women) gave rise to blood feuds. The code of *omerta*—literally "manliness," but effectively silence when questioned by outsiders—was more important than mere personal gain.

It was with the arrival of Prohibition in 1919 and the rise of ORGANIZED CRIME that the Mafia became important in the United States. This period was a halcyon time for well-organized criminals, and after struggles with other illegal organizations, including the CAMORRA and the few remnants of Irish gangs such as Chicago's O'Bannion Gang, the Mafia either slaughtered the opposition or joined forces with them.

Few people realize that the Mafia was by no means the sole provence of the Sicilian "Mustache Petes." One of the principal architects of the modern Mafia was, for example, Meyer Lansky (Maier Suchowljanski, 1902–1983), a Polish-Jewish immigrant. Although the great Mafia "families" are Italian and interrelated, and although the Italian term "Cosa Nostra" ("Our Thing") is habitually used to describe the Mafia, it is a remarkably racially mixed organization; however, the highest levels of the Mafia are populated by individuals of Italian—specifically Sicilian—extraction.

The Mafia may have enjoyed a degree of United

States government patronage. The invasion of Sicily during World War II was assisted by Mafia contacts though kingpin Charles "Lucky" Luciano, and the story of the C.I.A. enlisting Mafia help to "hit" Fidel Castro has been confirmed by numerous sources close to one-time Mafia boss Sam Giancana, who was also implicated in a scheme of payoffs to secure the election of John F. Kennedy as president. The real genius of the contemporary Mafia in the United States, however, is the degree to which it infiltrates and controls legitimate businesses and many aspects of organized labor. The policy of racketeering—gaining control of legitimate commerce through coercive and criminal means—and of simply investing the financial proceeds of crime in legitimate enterprise was masterminded by Lansky and Luciano beginning in the late 1920s. If organized crime—aka the Mafia—in the United States has a single visible monument, its it the gambling paradise of Las Vegas, Nevada, which was funded by the Mafia beginning in the late 1940s, when Lansky-Luciano associate Benjamin "Bugsy" Siegel built the Flamingo hotel and casino. Although gambling was legal in Nevada, no bank or conventional financial institution would back resort development associated with it. The Mafia, in part through manipulation of Teamster Union pension funds it controlled, bankrolled the Vegas startup and profited handsomely.

The workings of the Mafia are necessarily shadowy, but it would seem that the only formal DEGREE was one of admission, worked with a RITUAL involving a Bible, a pistol and a knife. With the Bible, the initiate swore obedience, often to the accompaniment of symbolic bloodletting (a nick or pin-prick). Some writers describe making a bloody hand-print on either a photograph, or a lithograph of a saint—a fine piece of sympathetic magic—but this smacks somewhat of the BLACK HAND and may be an embroidery of the truth or an account of something that did not invariably happen. Certainly, the celebrated accounts of the Mafia by hitman-turned-informant Joseph Valachi are not always in agreement with other accounts by leading *mafiosi*.

To make things still more shadowy, the F.B.I. for many years denied that there was any such thing as the Mafia—a conceit in which the mafiosi were only too happy to acquiesce. J. Edgar Hoover seems to have feared failure if he took on an opponent of this magnitude, and so (by default) he let it grow. There are those who argue that "Cosa Nostra" as a name is almost entirely an invention of the F.B.I., who were forced to come up with some sort of criminal organization when the evidence of gang warfare could be ignored no longer; the Kefauver congressional commission of 1951 and the later McClellan Committee served to rub the nose of the F.B.I. in the Bureau's past incompetence.

Rather than calling the Mafia the Mafia, the F.B.I. took an old but little-used name and adopted that, then fought this "new" organization. In any case, it was not until Robert F. Kennedy became U.S. Attorney General in 1961 that the F.B.I. and Justice Department vigorously pursued the Mafia.

To this day, the Mafia retains characteristics of the old Sicilian lifestyle. Many members are ostensibly devout Catholics and make heavy contributions to the Church: The spectacle of a Mafia funeral is, of course, legendary, though many parishes have now refused to conduct such services for "public sinners." In an area that is run by the Mafia, the public may actually be safer than in a conventionally policed locality or neighborhood: Small-time criminals and muggers are summarily dealt with, while the Honored Society gets on with the serious business of "organized" crime.

It must be noted, however, that in Sicily, where the order is still very much active as well, the Mafia is rarely perceived as a boon to the community. It is virtually a shadow government, holding sway through terror and vendetta. Government attempts to prosecute Mafia figures in Italy often result in the assassination of prosecutors and judges.

Magi

The word "Magi" derives from the same root as "magic and imagination"—ultimately, from the Sanskrit "Maya," the world of illusion. It is, therefore, no great surprise to find the Magi referred to as a "secret society," especially by devotees of conspiracy theories. In fact, it is only such devotees who can sustain a case, because there is absolutely no evidence of any large or enduring secret society of this name. To the true believer, all this means is that the Magi is so secret that no one has ever heard of it outside its circle of initiates.

There are innumerable references in antiquity to the Magi, the best known in Christian cultures probably being the Wise Men who visited the infant Jesus. Incidentally, nowhere is it written in scripture that there were three of them; it was three *gifts* that they brought. The term "magus" was originally used to refer to the priest-kings of the Medes and Persians—whom even Aristotle (384–322 B.C.) described as being of the utmost antiquity—and then it was adopted as a term for the priests of Zoroastrianism, a pre-Islamic Persian religion, which ante-dated Christianity. Today it also bears the meaning of one skilled in arcane wisdom, astrology, and the occult arts.

Although the Magi as such was never an organized secret society, there was an Order of the Magi, which was mentioned in the Chicago *Times-Herald* of July 26, 1896. Its secret was summarized as "the instrument by which Religion is taught in its different degrees of conformity with the universal law of evolution," and its program was said to be identical to that of the Masonic lodge of the Quatuor Coronati in London.

There was also an Order of the Magian Masters, purporting to be the oldest secret society in existence and guarding secrets entrusted to its founders by no less a luminary than the Holy Ghost, several thousands years before Christianity. The Grand Registrar in 1896 was Ada Bartoni of Bloomington, Illinois, but no subsequent record of the society is readily discoverable.

Magic and Secrets

A number of secret societies have either been based on, or have had the reputation of being based on, magic. It is therefore worth considering exactly what is meant by "magic," and it may be useful to look at the relationship between "magic" and "secrets."

Every generation recasts magic in its own likeness. To the Romans, famous for their religious tolerance but frequently hard pressed politically, it was treated in the same way as any other political risk, such as poisoning, rebellion, and so on. To Christians, during their period of expansion, it was treated as a religious threat: Anything that did not fit in with their world picture was "magic" and therefore to be extirpated with the utmost vehemence and brutality. With the Age of Reason, this attitude diminished, at least in those areas that subscribed to reason, and magic took a back seat for some time. Where it was noticed at all, it was often treated as a joke (see, for example, HELL FIRE CLUB). Then, in the 19th century, as in our own time, an interest in magic resurfaced as an antidote to the materialism and scientific reductionism of the period.

The 19th-century view of magic was, however, both utilitarian and mechanistic. Most 19th-century mages saw magic in terms of power—over people, over the material world, over the spirit world, or whatever—and set about its accomplishment in an extremely pedestrian manner, following medieval (and pseudomedieval) *grimoires* in the most slavish fashion.

Today, with still fewer constraints set by the Christian church and its fellow travelers, magic is even more popular than in the 19th century, though for much the same reasons.

The science-fiction writer Arthur C. Clarke said that any sufficiently advanced technology is indistinguishable from magic. To this assertion might be added the rider that the average person feels as powerless to control technology and "progress" as he or she feels to control fate. A 20th-century school of magic has therefore grown up, which is concerned with individual empowerment, an antidote to the supertechnological world.

In what follows, the assumption has been made that magic works. There are two reasons for this. First, if magic had no validity, why should so many people be so frightened of it, and why should so many religions (especially those of the Judaeo-Christian-Islamic tradi-

tion) have condemned so many people accused of practicing it to such unpleasant deaths? Second, even the greatest skeptic must agree that magic *can* work, if only by the power of suggestion; if the victim of magic believes that he has been ensorcelled, then he has been, and the sorcerer has power over him.

Whether magic is objective or subjective is not of great importance to the magician; his aim is to bring the world within his domain. In order to do so, he first seeks to expand his domain, and, second, he attempts to bring himself into tune with the world. Being "in tune with the world" is part scientific, part philosophical, part empathic; and the proportions of the parts can vary. All magical traditions agree, though, on the need for the magician to perform a more or less rigorous program of self-preparation. This involves ridding oneself of distraction, in order to concentrate full attentions on the task in hand, and liberating one's inner energy, in order to have the maximum possible power to devote to the job.

It is at least arguable that the performance of the program of self-preparation is more important than the form of the program itself. In other words, the approach may be hermetic, or Islamic, or Kabbalistic, or almost anything else. The path is merely a tool. The elaborate rituals and improbable ingredients of medieval magic—the pentacles, the incantations, the finger of a hanged man—all these things are merely a way of preparing the magician.

Three possibilities now present themselves concerning the "secrets" of secret societies. The first is that genuine magical paths are being taught, though the definition of "genuine" must remain open to dispute. An example of this sort of society is the Hermetic Order of the Golden Dawn (see GOLDEN DAWN, HERMETIC ORDER OF). The second possibility is that the "secrets" are a mere sham, a mumbo-jumbo appealing to the same need as "real" magic, but which has been sanitized and pasteurized so that it cannot possibly offend or harm anyone. The "initiate" is taking on the world in the same way that the sorcerer does, but only symbolically. This is probably the root of the vast majority of "secrets" in the secret society in this book.

The third and final possibility is that the superficial "secrets" described in the last paragraph are no more than a cover for real secrets; that is, the sham secrets disguise the "genuine magical paths" from recognition by outsiders. This is of course the stock in trade of adherents of the conspiracy theory of history.

Mala Vita

The *Mala Vita* or "Evil Life" was apparently derived from the CAMORRA and exercised itself mainly with petty extortion. The three DEGREES were *Giovanotti* (boys), *Piccotti* (youths) and *Cammoristi*. The head of the order was known as the Wise Master. The initiation RITUALS AND CEREMONIES involved standing in an open grave with chains on one foot and vowing to give up even the closest family ties for the sake of the order. The organization is probably extinct.

Mannekeh

Mannekeh is (or was) one of the WEST AFRICAN SECRET SOCIETIES. Each degree (see DEGREES) carries a different-shaped horn, called *aneke,* which members use to speak to one another. As a member rises in the order, he retains the already acquired horn and gets an additional one. The men of the higher degrees are known by their collection of horns.

Mannekeh is or was a prohibitory society, enforcing taboos. Membership was male, with admission at puberty.

Mantra

A *mantra* is a word, phrase, or longer passage, which is chanted repeatedly with the purpose of altering the chanter's mental or spiritual state. The word *mantra* is sometimes translated as "spell."

There are three theories on how mantras may work. One is the "gibberish" theory, which points out that if you recite *anything* often enough, you will start to hear "hidden meanings." The second is the "right mindfulness" theory, which says that mantras are an aid to concentration, and that without the concentration, they are worthless. The third theory says that mantras evoke cosmic resonances, and that there are some (such as the Great Mantra, below) which, even if said mechanically, will benefit all sentient beings.

The Great Manta is not (as many think) *Om, mani padme hum* ("Om" [the cosmic syllable], the jewel in the lotus, Hum! [exclamation of recognition or surprise]), but *Om, Gate, Gate, Paragate, Parasamgate, Bodhi Sowha!* This loosely translates as "om!" (the cosmic syllable), "Gone, gone, gone beyond, gone utterly beyond, what freedom!"

Mariel, Pierre

Pierre Mariel edited the *Dictionnaire des Sociétés Secrètes,* published in 1971 by Culture, Art, Loisirs in Paris as a part of the series *Histoire des idées, des héros, des sociétés de la France Secrète et de L'Occident,* under the direction of Louis Pauwels. It is French in its orientation, so that English or American orders are scarcely treated, unless they are (or have been) well established in France.

Marras, A. P.

Americo Palfrey Marras, B.A., wrote the Arnold Prize Essay of 1865, which was published in London and Oxford by the Oxford University Press as *The Secret Fraternities of the Middle Ages.*

The subjects covered in detail are the Ancient Mysteries (Chapter II), the Gnostics, and the sects connected with them (III), the Ismailites and Assassins (IV), the Vehmgerichte (V), the Knights Templars (VI), the Origin of Freemasonry (VI) and Rosicrucianism, the Parent of Freemasonry (VII). Marras's closing words are well worth repeating as evidence of his overall stance:

> When civilization was rude and imperfect, Secret Fraternities may have fostered justice, and may have protected the weak; but the evils which are inseparable from such associations have scarcely been outweighed by their advantages; and if we find in them the germs of progress and freedom, we also perceive that the instances are rare in which they have not rapidly degenerated from their original purpose.

Martinism

"Martinism" is a term often used by writers on the subject of secret societies, but little defined. It refers to at least two varieties of Christian spiritual teaching, usually but not always inseparable from the FREEMASONS. Mariel (see MARIEL, PIERRE) suggests that the ELECT COHENS were Martinists, named after Martinez Paschales, along with the *Ordre des Chevaliers Bienfaisants de la Cité Sainte,* which is the highest of the DEGREES of the Revised SCOTTISH RITE. Paschales is presumably the same person as Martin de Pasqually, a name that also appears in Masonic literature.

Then there are the devotees of Louis-Claude de Saint-Martin (b. 1743, and in his turn a follower of Paschales). The Friends of St-Martin were organized in 1882 by two of his pupils, who discovered that there were both his students when talking over the lunch they habitually took (with others) each Tuesday in a small restaurant on the Rive Gauche. RITUALS AND CEREMONIES were hastily gotten up, grades were invented, and Martinism has trundled on to this day. It has survived the occasional schism and reunification, but (as in many branches of Freemasonry), no one appears to be quite sure what the teachings are, other than the fact that they are Christian.

In what little literature appears in print, specifically in Mariel and Bayard (see BAYARD, JEAN-PIERRE), they sound like born-again Christians with a Roman Catholic spin.

Masonic Life Association

This was an insurance association organized by American FREEMASONS in 1872, in order to arrange formal fraternal benefits similar to those enjoyed by members of other organizations. The association was extinct by the 1970s.

Masonic Relief Association

32613 Seidel Drive
Burlington, WI 53105
(414) 534-2159

The Masonic Relief Association was founded in 1885 in Baltimore, Maryland, with the object of being a central clearing house for Masonic disputes or cooperative ventures, and also to uncover (and publish in their *Bulletin*) "unworthy Masons and impostors preying upon the Fraternity." It continues in its original purpose today, publishing *The Bulletin* quarterly. There were 15,000 members in 1994.

Mellor, Alec

Alec Mellor's numerous titles on the FREEMASONS include those given below. Even his "exposés" are tempered with a pro-Masonic bias. Mellor's works are of somewhat limited interest to anyone not obsessed with Masonic anecdotes and minutiae. All were published in Paris.

Nos Frères séparés, Les Francs-Maçons (Mame, 1961)

La Franc-Maçonnerie a l'heure du choix (Mame, 1963)

La Charte inconnu de la Franc-Maçonnerie chrétienne (Mame, 1965)

La vie quotidienne de la Franc-Maçonnerie (Hachette, 1973)

Les Myths maçonniques (Payot, 1974)

Les Grands problemes de la Franc-Maçonnerie aujourd'hui (Belfond, 1976)

La Grande Loge nationale française (Belfond, 1980)

Dictionnaire de la Franc-Maçonnerie et des Francs-Maçons (Belfond, 1979)

Histoire des scandales Maçonniques (Belfond, 1982)

Mennonite Mutual Aid Association

The Mennonite Mutual Aid Association was founded in 1966 as a fraternal benefit insurance society in the United States for members of Mennonite churches, of either sex, age 16 or older. It is based in Goshen, Indiana, and publishes *Sharing* quarterly.

The date of founding of the Mennonite Mutual Aid Association, 1966, is astonishingly late; the church was founded in Zürich in 1525. For many years before 1966, however, the Mennonite General Conference had acted in many ways as a beneficiary society. In 1945, Mennonite Mutual Aid was formed to help returnees from World War II (who were not soldiers; Mennonites do not join armies); in 1961, Mennonite Aid Insurance was founded; and in 1966 the form of a fraternal benefit society, without ritual, was adopted.

Mercelots

For want of a better collective noun, a number of vagabonds' organizations are included in this heading. They mostly had their origin in the wars between the French and English in the years 1336 and 1452; these disrupted the economies of both countries and, by destroying old certainties, allowed to flourish as outlaws many who might otherwise have remained within the normal bounds of society. By the end of these wars, five groups or tribes of wandering malefactors were recognized: Soldiers, Peddlers (or Packmen: *Mercelots*), Beggars, Gypsies, and Robbers.

Soldiering has, of course, always had its own traditions and ranks, but it is worth remembering that in those days there were effectively two classes of fighting men. There were those of noble birth, for whom soldiering was a combination of sport and *noblesse oblige*, and the brutal and licentious soldiery who (if they professed the trade of arms rather than being impressed for a season) were for the most part misfits, mercenaries, or psychopaths.

The Mercelots were closely allied with the Beggars, and the two are dealt with together in what follows. The Gypsies (so called from the wide belief that they were "Egyptians") were already separate, with their own language and customs, and hardly constituted a secret society, while the Robbers (from the very nature of their trade) were inclined to be of a solitary persuasion.

The French Mercelots

According to tradition, the Mercelots were founded in 1455; today, it is extremely difficult to separate them from the Beggars, with whom they coexisted. They borrowed their RITUALS AND CEREMONIES from the guild (see GUILDS) of Merciers, with considerable modification, and worked the following DEGREES:

1. *Pechon* (Little Child): Apprentice
2. *Blesche* or *Mercelot*: Retailer
3. *Coesme* or *Cosmelotier Hure*: Wholesale Merchant
4. *Cagou* or *Pasquelin*: Provincial Officer
5. *Archi-Suppots*: Higher Officer
6. *Le Grand Coestre* or *Roi des Thunes*

The *Pechon* would be initiated at a country fair, where he had successfully sold his first bundle of goods. He would buy drinks for the other *Gueux* or members; be subjected to a homily on the rights and duties of the fraternity; and then be given a stick and a pack. He had to load the pack on his back while fending off a dog with the stick—an admirably practical ordeal (see ORDEALS) for such an organization—and if he succeeded, he was given a fencing lesson with the stick and then passed to the degree of *Blesche*.

Victor Hugo's novel *Notre Dame* contains a great deal of information about the French orders; harder to find, but possibly more interesting so far as members are concerned, is a book called *Pechon du Ruby*, published in 1596.

English Vagabonds

A Caveat or Warening for Comen Cursetors Vulgarly Called Vagabones was published in 1576; its author was Thomas Harman. Together with Henry Mayhew's *London Life and the London Poor*, published almost three centuries later, it gives an excellent introduction to "vagabones," thieves' cant, and much more.

The "vagabones" of the 16th century were organized regionally under "Upright Men," petty lords of crime who held sway over beggars, highwaymen, horse stealers, sham madmen, strumpets, and others and (of course) extracted dues from them. The dues were for the most part probably spent on drinking with cronies.

Installation of a beggar was colorfully known as "stalling to the rogue," with "stalling" presumably a form of "installing." Harman says that "a gage of bowse" was poured over the "peeled pate" (bare head) of the hitherto uninitiated rogue, and "the man obeyeth for fear of beating."

An interesting point is that "gage" (in the sense of a legal measure of beer, a quart according to Harman) is cognate with "gauge," while "bowse" must surely be cognate with the Dutch "bousen" from which we get "booze." Thus the cant is not a made-up language based on weak classical roots, as are many of the terms used by (for example) FREEMASONS, but is a more genuine process of etymology.

By the 19th century, these secret societies had withered almost to nothing—not that crime had been reduced, but increasing population and prosperity, which created vastly greater opportunities for crime, had led to greater fragmentation and a "freelance" approach. Mayhew makes no mention of formal organizations of this kind, though he does describe *ad hoc* gangs' and brothel owners' loose connections, along with beggars' and thieves' cant and more.

Mesmerism

Mesmerism was a system of healing founded by Friedrich Anton Mesmer (1733–1815), a German physician educated in Vienna. His principal theory, which he called "animal magnetism," exerted great influence on many devotees of the occult, including those who organized or joined secret societies. As set forth in his *De Planetarum Influxu,* Mesmer's doctrine can be summarized as follows:

1. There is a mutual influence among the celestial bodies, the earth, and "animated bodies."
2. The vehicle of this influence is a universal fluid.
3. The reciprocal action of mutual influence is subject to mechanical laws as yet unknown.
4. The results of the reciprocal action are evidenced as fluxes and refluxes.
5. The effects of the fluxes and refluxes are particularly evident in the human body and in animal bodies.

The practical application of Mesmer's theory of animal magnetism was the attempt to effect cures for various disorders through the application of magnetic plates to the limbs of sufferers of illness. Later treatment methods involved the *baquet,* a large circular tub filled with bottles that were dipped into water. Iron rods projected from holes in the lid of the tub. The rods could be applied to any part of the bodies of the patients who were gathered—roped or chained together—around the tub. While music was played, a practitioner walked around the patients, touching them with an iron wand he held in his hand. At his touch, patients fell into convulsions and trances, sweating profusely and vomiting—then, Mesmer claimed, emerged from the ordeal cured of what had ailed them.

In the course of Mesmer's career, he turned progressively away from any pretense to science and increasingly embraced a combination of spiritualism and out-and-out charlatanry. Later followers of Mesmer found that they were able to induce a variety of trancelike and hypnotic states in their "patients." The term "mesmerism" and the expression "to mesmerize" were applied to these precursor phenomena of hypnosis.

Mithraism

The worship of Mithra or Mithras is a religion rather than a secret society, but it clearly shows the overlap: There were several DEGREES of initiation and a strong fraternal spirit. In the latter, as well as in many points of ritual (see RITUALS AND CEREMONIES), it had a lot in common with its contemporary rivals in Rome, the Christians.

Mithraism is an offshoot of Zoroastrianism, somewhat as Christianity is an offshoot of Judiasm and Buddhism is an offshoot of Hinduism. Mithras was a *yazada* in the older religion, an assistant of Ahura Mazda in his fight against the powers of darkness. From Assyria to Persia to Greece and thence to Rome the cult of Mithra spread. Early in the Christian era, it found considerable favor with merchants, businessmen, and slaves, all of whom were outside the Patrician tradition. For almost two centuries, Mithraism seriously rivaled Christianity, but the fall of Dacia (roughly corresponding to modern Romania and Transylvania) in A.D. 275 removed the power base of Mithraism. It had all but vanished by the fifth century.

There were seven degrees, as follows:

Corax	(Raven)
Cryphius	(Hidden)
Miles	(Soldier)
Leo	(Lion)
Perses	(Persian)
Heliodromus	(Courier of the Sun)
Pater	(Father)

The first to third degrees were not in full communion; after the fourth degree, the initiate could partake of the sacred bread and water (or maybe wine—this is no longer clear). Numerous other similarities with the cult of the Galilean also exist; the legend of the shepherds and their adoration at the birth of the god, the use of bell and candle, the idea of abstinence and self-control, the doctrine of Heaven and Hell, the immortality of the soul, the final judgment and even the reservation as sacred of Sundays and December 25th.

Modern Knights of St. Paul

The Modern Knights of St. Paul was a Christian group for young men who were "converted" by the tremendously popular evangelist Billy Sunday—forerunner of another Billy (Graham) half a century later. The three DEGREES (Order of Jerusalem, Order of Damascus, Order of Rome) bore some resemblance to the first three degrees of the FREEMASONS. The society was formed in Detroit, Michigan, in 1917 by a Methodist clergyman; what happened to it since is unknown.

Modern Knights Templar

The Modern Knights Templar was one of the various Polish nationalist secret societies that arose in the 19th century to combat Russian domination of Poland. Founded by students about 1820, it was either suppressed or driven into complete secrecy within a very few years. Reportedly, Russian authorities acted with such brutality against this and other secret societies that numerous members committed suicide rather than face the consequences of discovery. The Modern Knights Templar are related neither to the Knights Templar (see KNIGHTS TEMPLAR, GRAND ENCAMPMENT OF THE UNITED STATES) nor to the MODERN TEMPLARS.

Modern Templars

The Modern Templars were a Polish group who, like the NATIONAL FREEMASONS, used the symbolism of the FREEMASONS in their patriotic secret society, which was devoted to independence for their country. It was founded by a Captain Maiewski some time before 1822, and to the three traditional DEGREES of Freemasonry they added a fourth in which the initiate swore to do all in his power to bring about a free Poland.

Monkeys, Benevolent Order of

The Benevolent Order of Monkeys was founded in St. Paul, Minnesota, in 1911; the LODGEs were called "jungles." It was presumably intended to ape the better-established animal orders such as the Moose (see MOOSE, INTERNATIONAL, the ELKS and the EAGLES), but was extinct by the early 1920s.

Moose, International

Mooseheart, IL 60539
(708) 859-2000

The Loyal Order of Moose was founded in 1888 in Louisville, Kentucky, as a social and drinking club. It has since spread to Bermuda, Canada, Guam, and England but remains primarily a U.S. organization, though it changed its name to International Moose in 1991. It is open to men who believe in a supreme being, and publishes *Moose Magazine* monthly. There were 1,010,000 members in 1994.

The Moose and the ELKS are the two biggest American "animal" fraternities, but in their early days the Moose came close to collapse. In the words of their own publicity department, "The Loyal Order of Moose began on a spring day in 1888 in Louisville, Ky., apparently for no better reason than that Dr. John Henry Wilson, a 52-year-old physician, wanted to organize a group of his friends into a fraternal order." He was apparently inspired by "another recently organized benevolent order," probably the Elks. Unfortunately, Dr. Wilson was unable to provide strong leadership, and within half a decade of the founding of the order, there were 1,000 members meeting in 15 "Watering Places" (LODGEs). But in another half decade, three-quarters of the members had left. At the turn of the century, one authority, Stevens, dismissed the Moose in his *Cyclopaedia of Fraternities* as follows:

> Loyal Order of Moose of the World—Cincinnati is credited with having given birth to the fraternity with this title, but no-one communicated with at that city has been able to vouch for its continued existence. It is a mere conjecture that attempted rivalry to the Benevolent and Protective Order of Elks may have been responsible for the name of the society.

Matters got worse before they got better. By 1906, there were only three lodges with a total of 246 members, and at the National Moose Convention in that year, only seven delegates were accredited. This convention of 1906 was, however, an important one for the Moose, for it was there that James J. Davis was initiated. When he addressed the handful of Moose who were there with him, they were so stirred by his words that they appointed him Supreme Organizer then and there.

And Supreme Organizer he certainly turned out to be. For more than 20 years, he traveled all over the United States setting up lodges and canvassing for members. By 1928 there were 650,000 members in 1,709 lodges, to say nothing of 59,000 in the ladies' auxiliary.

He profited well from this activity. The former miner and steelworker, who was far from a rich man when he joined the Moose, received a commission on every Moose inducted—a commission that was sufficiently valuable that when his financial agent and secretary bought the rights to it in 1930, they paid $600,000. What was more, he was accused in 1932 of improperly receiving $173,000 from a lottery, which brought in $2,200,000 in ticket sales. He was acquitted after an initial mistrial.

The basic unit is the Lodge, which follows the usual plan: a club room or rooms, plus the lodge room with an altar. The orientation is also the usual approach based on

DEISM, with strong Christian overtones. Apparently, the Catholic church has no objection to anyone becoming a Moose, but the Lutheran Church has objected.

The ritual (see RITUALS AND CEREMONIES) for the first degree (see DEGREES) was composed by James Davis and is relatively simple and straightforward, without any regalia. It is conducted in the evening, before nine o'clock, and it is administered by the Sergeant at Arms, upon the formal request of the Governor (the senior lodge official).

The candidates must (as usual) affirm belief in a supreme being and express their willingness to assume the obligation. The oath, taken with left hand over heart and right hand raised, is as follows:

> I, [Name], solemnly promise that I will not in any manner communicate or disclose or give any information concerning anything I may hereafter hear, see or experience in this lodge or in any other lodge of the Loyal Order of Moose unless it be to one whom I know to be a Loyal Moose in good standing. By this vow I bind myself for all time. Amen.

The initiate is then welcomed and instructed in the secrets of the Moose, including passwords and similar matters. At nine o'clock, all Moose turn toward Mooseheart and silently pray. The Governor leads them in a prayer, which goes, "Suffer little children to come unto me and forbid them not, for such is the Kingdom of Heaven. God bless Mooseheart."

After this Nine O'Clock Ceremony, which is observed by all Moose, the Junior Governor addresses the new members. The Prelate then delivers the 10 "Thou Shalts," which begin: "Thou shalt believe in God, and worship Him as they conscience dictates. Thou shalt be tolerant to let others worship each in his own way." The Governor now shakes hands with each of the new members, and "Blest Be the Tie That Binds" is sung. Yet another official—the Orator—says his piece, and the Governor then administers the Obligation. This begins:

> I, [Name], in the presence of Almighty God and those here assembled, do most solemnly promise that I will obey the Laws of the Supreme Lodge of the World— Loyal Order of Moose, and of the Lodge of which I am a member as well as all orders of the Supreme Council or of the executive officers of the Supreme Lodge or of the officers of the Lodge of which I am a member.

It continues with pledges to support Mooseheart, to spurn unauthorized Moose lodges, to try to keep disputes within the Loyal Order of Moose, and of course to help their brethren. The Obligation is followed by a prayer offered at the altar by the Prelate, after which all sing "Friendship We Now Extend," and the Governor closes by exhorting the newcomers to be loyal members. The whole ritual takes about three-quarters of an hour.

After six months' membership in good standing, Moose are eligible for the second degree, Legion of the Moose. A Legionnaire may wear a "tah" with purple tassel, and a Legion jacket, tie, and lapel pin. The third or Fellowship degree is awarded for service to the fraternity; regalia include a white shirt, lapel pin, tie, and Alice-blue blazer, and the right to wear an Alice-blue tassel on the "tah."

The fourth and highest degree, that of Pilgrim, is again honorific and is awarded to perhaps one Moose in 5,000: Pilgrims wear a black and gold Pilgrim cape and tie, a gold tassel on their "tah," and a Pilgrim lapel pin. It is conferred at the House of God (otherwise known as the "Children's Cathedral") at Mooseheart.

Mooseheart in Illinois and Moosehaven in Florida are the best-known charitable/fraternal activities of the Moose. Sometimes known as the "City of Children," Mooseheart is something between an orphanage and a town, with its own hospital, church, sports stadium, and schools at all levels, as well as both Catholic and Protestant ministers—according to the publicity sheets, more than 20 denominations of Protestant are to be found in Mooseheart, where children are brought up in the faith of their parents.

Initially conceived in 1911, Mooseheart began as a circus tent in a field in 1913, when it was dedicated by the then Vice President of the United States, Thomas R. Marshall. Since then, it has grown to almost 100 buildings on more than 1,000 acres and caters to the children of deceased Moose, their mothers, and other fatherless or motherless children. The population varies considerably, but there are typically 300–500 children at the Village, and perhaps a tenth as many mothers. Children may stay at Mooseheart until they are 18.

Mooseheart is vocational rather than academic in its orientation: It runs a very fine dairy farm, and pupils at the school are required to learn at least one of a dozen or so trades. When they graduate, they receive not only a high school diploma but also a vocational education certificate. The regime is based on old-fashioned values and timetables: rising at 6:30, breakfast at 6:50, school from 8:00 to 11:30 and 1:00 to 3:30, sports after school, and supper at 6:00. Younger pupils start later: 8:30 for elementary school, 8:45 for primary school.

The Supreme Lodge of the World is also located at Mooseheart, in a two-story colonial-style brick building.

Moosehaven, a retirement home for Moose and their wives, was founded in 1922 on the banks of the St. John's River at Orange Park, 14 miles south of Jacksonville, Florida. There are more than 30 buildings on about 60 acres of land, with more than a third of a mile of river frontage. "Every resident whose physical condition will permit is assigned to some daily duty usually not to exceed three hours," and everyone receives a monthly allowance. Those no longer able to work are called

"Sunshiners." Their job is to sit in rocking chairs in the sun, and smile at passers-by. There is a well-equipped 150-bed hospital, in addition to many other facilities.

Aside from Mooseheart and Moosehaven, Moose lodges also support a number of health-oriented charities, such as the March of Dimes, Muscular Dystrophy, Heart Fund, Cancer Crusade, Cerebral Palsy, and much more. Many lodges are also active in highway safety, Boy and Girl Scouting, civil defense cooperation, and local community activities of all kinds.

Membership of the Loyal Order of Moose has grown steadily since the 1960s: There were just over 1 million members in 1965, 1,323,240 members in 1979, and 1,765,333 members in 1988—a remarkable accomplishment. It seems likely that it is the "service" element of the organization that tips the balance in the organization's favor, though it must be admitted that Moose lodges provide a convivial and very economical place to eat and drink.

Women of the Moose

The Women of the Moose had its informal origins in "Women's Circles," associations of wives, mothers, daughters, and sisters of Moose. These "Women's Circles" were formally recognized by the 1912 International Convention, and in 1913 the name was changed to "Women's Moose Circles." In 1916 the Circles were unified into the "Women of the Mooseheart Legion," organized in chartered Chapters; and in 1933, the name changed yet again to its present form.

The Women of the Moose works two DEGREES: the Academy of Friendship and the College of Regents. As with the two highest degrees of the Moose proper, these are earned honors. The Friendship Degree originated in 1927; changed its name to Academy of Friendship in 1935; and was joined in 1935 by the College of Regents Degree. The "Star Recorder" is not a degree, but an honor first awarded in 1946 to women who keep perfect records.

In addition to practical work in Mooseheart, Moosehaven, and elsewhere, Women of the Moose fund scholarships for Mooseheart graduates in music, nursing, and business and raise money for building and other one-off projects. For example, the Mooseheart Health Center had cost about $1 million when it was dedicated in 1974, and the Women of the Moose made a substantial contribution to this. The Women of the Moose is also active in community work of many kinds.

Mopses, Ordem dos

The Ordem dos Mopses, or Order of Mopses (the word appears to have no meaning), arose in response to the bull *Eminente Apostolatus Specula* (Clement XII, April 28, 1738), which effectively banned the FREEMASONS. Ordem dos Mopses was a diluted version of the Craft, designed to be acceptable to the Church while still providing many of the benefits of Freemasonry. It was founded in Cologne on September 22, 1738, under the protection of Clement Augustus, Duke of Bavaria, and apparently spread to Austria, throughout Germany, to Holland, and to France.

In some ways, Ordem dos Mopses was an improvement on the Masonic original. It was androgynous, and it was avowedly beneficial. In due course, the order lost its identity as a secret society and became a social club. It appears to be long extinct.

Moral Re-Armament

1156 15th Street NW, Ste. 910
Washington, D.C. 20005–1704
(202) 872-9077

Moral Re-Armament was founded in 1938 by an American, Frank Buchman, as a forum outside formal government in which ambassadors, religious and civil leaders, politicians, and others could meet and exchange views. It is based on "fundamental Christian values." Estimates of its importance and efficacy vary widely, but several leading politicians have confirmed that it has been useful to them. It was formerly called Oxford Group—Moral Re-Armament.

Morgan Affair

The Morgan Affair is now all but forgotten except among FREEMASONS and students of secret societies, but it was for many years a *cause célèbre*, and it affected the development of secret societies in the United States for most of the second quarter of the 19th century.

Captain William Morgan of Batavia, New York, published at least some of the Secrets of Freemasonry in *Illustrations of Masonry* in about 1825. In an attempt to suppress the book, other Masons sought to bribe him to leave the country, offering him money and the prospect of a farm in Canada. But Morgan never made it to Canada. More than a year later, a body was found on the shores of Lake Ontario. Although it was badly decayed, it was identified by Morgan's wife, his publisher and others as Morgan's mortal remains. The Masons were accused of having done away with the unfortunate man, and the next 10 or 15 years were the heyday of anti-Masonry in the United States.

Anti-Masonic feeling was extraordinary during this period. Many Masons burned their aprons, or, less demonstrably, stopped attending their lodges. Masons were denounced from the pulpit and in the press. There was even an Anti-Masonic Party, which nominated a candidate for president in 1832, author and one-time U.S. Attorney General, William Wirt. The party carried only one state, Vermont.

By the end of the 1830s, the hysteria had died down and American Freemasonry began its long, slow, but ultimately very effective recovery. Even so, a massive statue of Morgan was apparently erected in Batavia, with the legend of the pedestal, "MURDERED BY THE MASONS." It was paid for by public subscription, and was raised as late as 1882.

As a footnote, in the 1930s, a Masonic investigator wrote to all the surviving immediate descendants of the principals, and concluded that Morgan, a sometime brewer and connoisseur of good whisky, had not died at all, but took a boat for Smyrna and became a Moslem.

Mormons

The Church of Jesus Christ of Latter Day Saints (normally abbreviated simply to LDS) purports to be the only true Christian church, the result of new revelations made by God to Joseph Smith, a New York farm boy. The Angel Moroni marked Smith out for greatness when he was still 14, in the early to mid-1820s. In 1827, Moroni showed Smith the whereabouts of the Book of Mormon. Buried in a hillside, it was inscribed on plates of gold, which Smith translated from a hitherto unknown language with the aid of the *Urim* and *Thummin* (see Exodus 38:30), another gift of the Angel. The original plates disappeared shortly afterward. The Book of Mormon was published in 1830 (Mormonism is regarded as having been founded on April 6, 1830, at Fayette, New York), and subsequent revelations were made public in the *Pearl of Great Price* (P.O.G.P.) and the *Doctrines and Covenants* (D&C), as well as in later publications.

In 1844, the 39-year-old Smith was lynched on June 27, in Carthage, Illinois, but the church was sustained by Smith's lieutenant Brigham Young, who led the Mormons from their principal settlement in Nauvoo, Illinois, to Utah in 1847.

The LDS meets many of the criteria for a secret society, including exclusiveness, unusual regalia, the ownership of special "secrets," and a strong inclination for members to favor their own. There are several sects within the religion, with the Reorganized Church of Jesus Christ of Latter Day Saints as the second largest; it was formed in 1844 by those who rejected the leadership of Brigham Young.

Regardless of sect, the religion is strongly paternalist. Men constitute the "Priesthood," and may receive revelations. These may be on a wide range of subjects, but the higher the hierarchical standing of the recipient, the more credibility the revelations have. One of Smith's later (and by far most controversial) revelations, a year or so before his death, concerned the advantages of polygamy. This doctrine has now been forsworn by all by a few sects. There is also deep interest in genealogy, particularly because ancestors may be posthumously received into the Church.

Theological analysis is complex and often bears little resemblance to that found in other forms of Christianity. In addition to the Celestial, Telestial, and Terrestrial Realms, there is also a Spirit World and an Outer Darkness. Access to the Celestial Kingdom is available only to those who are married; those who are fortunate enough to be admitted are permitted to create their own universes. Priests have been known to debate such matters as whether Adam and Eve could have conceived any children *without* eating of the fruit of the tree of knowledge.

Men receive titles of steadily increasing rank as they progress through the church. An unusual aspect of the regalia is that the basic garment (which is very widely worn) is an item of underwear closely resembling an old-fashioned "Union Suit," but with short sleeves and short legs. This was formerly worn by both sexes after they had been admitted to the temple ("received their temple recommends," in LDS parlance), but at the time of writing it is apparently worn only by women. Within the temple, all-white clothing—even down to the soles of the shoes—forms part of the regalia.

Women, who all share the same rank of "Sister," are apparently denied revelations. Their child-bearing status exalts them so far in the eyes of Mormon men that they are reckoned to need nothing more. A few sects permit women to join the priesthood, however.

A Mormon in trouble can rely on strong support from his coreligionists: House-cleaning, gardening, and many other chores are undertaken for the sick or incapacitated, while the poor are never permitted to starve.

One of the most remarkable aspects of the LDS, at least to an outsider, is the one that most strongly emphasizes its nature as a secret society. In order to get into heaven, the applicant is required to know a series of passwords, which are given to the various ranks of angels guarding the Celestial Kingdom. These passwords are learned in the temple. It may be from this custom that the alleged links with the FREEMASONS arose. Unfortunately, although there are plenty of Mormons who are willing to talk about their church, and a good number of Masonic sources, Mormon Freemasons seem to be a rare breed. As it is, neither party admits to recognizing very much in the rituals of the other, and the resemblances (such as they are) seem to be a result of convergent evolution.

Mosel Club

The Mosel Club was a German political secret society founded in Weimar in 1762, dedicated to uniting Germany under Prussian leadership. An inner circle of the Mosel Club, called the Order of Friendship, was formed in 1771. Branches were formed in various university cities; the original Moseler Tavern, after which the club was named, was a students' haunt. After investigation by various university authorities in 1779, the club was suppressed, but reappeared as the Black Order, except at Halle, where it became the Unionists. It appears to have disappeared in the 1780s or 1790s.

Mount Tabor, Dames of
This was an androgynous Masonic society, founded about 1818 under the auspices of the Grand Orient of France. It was dedicated to providing charitable relief to "destitute females." It is extinct.

Mumbo-Jumbo
The name of this organization, one of the WEST AFRICAN SECRET SOCIETIES, is also transliterated as Mahammah-Jamboh.

The English term *mumbo-jumbo* derives from the activities of a Mandingo secret society, which apparently served chiefly to settle disputes between men and women. When a dispute arose, the society would convene, and the "mumbo-jumbo" would be sent for. This was an image, eight or nine feet high, made from the bark of trees, dressed in a long coat, and crowned with a wisp of straw. A man would conceal himself beneath the mumbo-jumbo's coat and pronounce judgment in the dispute. Since the society was exclusively male—with no one under age 16 admitted—these judgments were almost always in favor of the man.

The Mumbo-Jumbo society was not a benign organization. Women summoned to judgment were not left to come voluntarily. If they failed to answer the call, they were brought by force and whipped. Moreover, members of the society were sworn to absolute secrecy. About 1727, the king of Jagra disclosed his membership to his wife, resulting in his death at the hands of other members of the order.

Muscovites, Imperial Order of
The Imperial Order of Muscovites was a "fun" organization for the ODD FELLOWS; at least the founders, who organized the Order in Cincinnati, Ohio, in 1894 had the originality to deviate from the standard Islamic-parody path. Lodges were called "Kremlins" and the Lord High Poobah was known as the Supreme Czar.

In 1924 they merged with the Veiled Prophets of Baghdad, the Oriental Order of Humility and Perfection, the Knights of the Oriental Splendor, and the Ancient Order of Cabirians to form the Ancient Mystic Order of Samaritans (see SAMARITANS, ANCIENT MYSTIC ORDER OF).

Muts, Ancient Order of
The name of the Ancient Order of Muts comes from Mut, the sister, spouse, and divine consort of the sun in the ancient Egyptian pantheon. The name is also said to come from "Men United to Serve." The order was organized at Portland, Oregon, in 1914, and relied on the presumed inherent funniness of all things Near Eastern. Officers of the LODGE, apart from the Imperial Chief Mut, included Ras Ma Taz, Neffer Kara Dam, Tol Et Yuh, Heiro Glyph (the secretary), and Koph Uptha Kash (treasurer). The order may be presumed dead.

Mutual Guild of Grand Secretaries
This organization was founded in 1900 as the Masonic Grand Secretaries Guild, which adequately describes it. It changed its name to the present form in 1948.

Myriam
Myriam was founded (or revived) in Italy in about 1910 by a magician who went under the name of Ciro Formisano and was still extant in 1971, with "ramifications" in the south of France and in California.

The society seems to be based on its inventor's understanding of TANTRA. Under the influence of incense and possibly of hallucinogenic drugs, a man and a woman go into the *sanctum sanctorum* and undress completely. They face one another, a few feet apart, contemplating one another ardently. Eventually, their astral bodies detach themselves from the gross shells and throw themselves upon each other. When satisfied, they return to the bodies.

Myriam is (or was) a small organization, working two unspecified DEGREES, transmitted orally. It enjoyed some following among hippies of the 1960s and possibly 1970s.

Mysteries
A great deal of what has been written about "mysteries" derives (whether deliberately or not) from a confusion with the homophone *mistery*, an uncommon word today. "Mystery" derives from the Greek word mysterion and refers to something secret, while "mistery" (the spelling of which has now been completely abandoned) comes from the Latin word *ministerium* and means nothing more than a trade or craft, or the guild (see GUILDS) of that craft. Hence, for example, a "Mystery Play" (in the sense of a religious play about biblical events) does not derive from the "mysteries" of Christianity, but is a play that was originally put on by a trade guild; and the "Mystery of Painting" is nothing more (or less) than the artist's craft.

This alone explains a great deal. But what is a "mystery" as distinct from a "mistery?"

In the original Greek sense, we do not know: The heyday of the Mysteries of Dionysius and ELEUSIS is now millennia in the past. It seems extremely likely, though, that the initiation of the *mystai* or *menyimenoi* in ancient Greece did *not* involve anything that would be regarded as "knowledge" in the modern sense. That is, there were no rigorous scientific explanations of the workings of the universe, or of human relationships, or of anything else.

Rather, the initiation was a transcendental or *mystical* experience.

In this sense, the Age of Mysteries is not past: the elevation of the Host at a Catholic mass, or the cry of "He is Risen!" at an Orthodox Easter vigil, is a mystical or emotional experience that, in the final analysis, does nothing other than make the true believer feel good. The parallel between these Christian services and the Greek mysteries may be very close. Both are (or in the case of the Mysteries, were) open to all, though not all will wish to attend and not all will be in full communion unless they have been initiated. The initiations are different (but what are baptism and confirmation or first mass if not initiations?), and the doors of the Catholic Church are not literally locked to exclude non-Catholics (though they may be locked in a figurative sense, in that a non-Catholic cannot experience the same depth of feeling at, say, the elevation of the Host as will be felt by the devout).

Almost by definition, these Mysteries are of value only to the believer, devotee, or sincere initiate; there are individuals who become figures of fun because they collect initiations like butterflies, or like stamps in their passports, without ever really taking on board the true meaning of the initiation. Different Mysteries will appear to noninitiates to have different inherent values, both spiritually and intellectually. No matter how sincerely any belief may be held, it is profoundly unlikely that any one person will believe equally in the efficacy, spiritual merit, or intellectual credibility of the E-Meter in Scientology, the Four Noble Truths in Buddhism, and the Transubstantiation of the Host in Christianity—to say nothing of the merit of purified bulls' urine in the Parsee religion.

Most modern secret societies and fraternal orders (and many from the past) are firmly based either on the confusion between "mystery" and "mistery," as already noted, or on a deliberately constructed "Mystery," which often degenerates into bathos even when it is not deliberately a burlesque of some earlier ritual. To an outsider, the three basic DEGREES of the FREEMASONS present an apparently perfect example of the confusion between "mystery" and "mistery," while those societies that are based on novels (such as the BEN HUR LIFE ASSOCIATION and the VRIL SOCIETY) illustrate the concocted "Mystery."

In some cases, fabricated "Mysteries" may teach some genuine moral or ethical lesson; in others, they strike one as patently childish nonsense. Even so, most of them are based (however loosely) on the traditional stages of initiation into the ancient Greek Mysteries:

1. Purification (*katharmos*)
2. Communication of mystic knowledge (*teletis paradosis*)
3. Revelation or demonstration of the central mystery (*epopteia*). This was always something done (*dromenon*) rather than something said; Lucian (c. A.D. 125–c. 190) writes in *De Saltatione* that all mysteries included dancing.
4. Garlanding of the initiate. This was historically done with flowers or sashes; now, a Masonic apron or chain of office suffices.

With the exception of the purification, now much abbreviated or reduced to a mere affirmation, the elements of initiation into Mysteries look remarkably like the initiation into a modern secret society.

Mystical Seven

The Mystical Seven was a college fraternity (see COLLEGE FRATERNITIES AND SORORITIES) founded in 1837, without the customary Greek letters. It was an ambitious effort at creating a college secret society with a good ritual, now lost. The fraternity was absorbed by Beta Theta Phi. See also the Order of the HEPTASOPHS.

Mystic Star, Order of the

The Order of the Mystic Star, founded in New York City in about 1872 or 1873, was a short-lived attempt to rival the Order of the Eastern Star (see EASTERN STAR, ORDER OF), which was at the time rapidly growing. It is not clear why the inventors, A. J. Duganne and others, felt the need to challenge the existing order. Like the Eastern Star, the Mystic Star was open to Master Masons and their female relatives.

National Defenders

The National Defenders was founded in 1919 as a fraternal benefit and patriotic/anti-Bolshevist order during the height of the "Red Scare" in the United States. The order enrolled white males aged 18 or older. Although nothing survives of the ritual, it has been described as "ornate and secret" (see RITUALS AND CEREMONIES). There was also a women's auxiliary (see AUXILIARIES) called the National Co-Defenders.

National Federated Craft

1003 Pendle Hill Avenue
Pendleton, IN 46064
(317) 778-2356

The National Federated Craft, as suggested by the word "craft" in the title, is a part of the FREEMASONS. It is a club for Master Masons who work or have worked in United States government service — a civilian equivalent of the NATIONAL SOJOURNERS, INC. It has a conservative political agenda.

The order was founded on June 3, 1929, and had 952 members in 1993. It publishes the quarterly *National Federated Craft News*.

National Fraternal Congress of America

1300 Iroquois Drive, Ste. 260
P.O. Box 3087
Naperville, FL 60566-7087
(708) 355-6633

The National Fraternal Congress of America, an umbrella organization for American fraternal societies, was formed in 1913 in Chicago by the merger of the ASSOCIATED FRATERNITIES OF AMERICA and its natural parent, the National Fraternal Congress. With 97 members distributed across 37 states in 1993, it offers life, accident, and health insurance. The order publishes three annual reports.

National Fraternal Society of the Deaf

1300 West Northwest Highway
Mt. Prospect, IL 60056
(312) 392-2982

The National Fraternal Society for the Deaf was founded in 1901 as a fraternal benefit insurance society. There were 11,000 members in 1994. It publishes *The Frat* monthly.

The National Fraternal Society for the Deaf was founded at a time when deaf people in the United States and Canada found it difficult to get insurance. From 1901 to 1907, it was known as the Fraternal Society for the Deaf, but "National" was added in 1907. Non-hearing-impaired persons who work in the field of deafness are also eligible.

In many ways, it is a typical "ethnic"-style fraternal benefit society, except that instead of representing a nationality, it represents a disability. In addition to providing the insurance benefits, it acts as a pressure group to oppose discrimination against deaf people, promotes education for the deaf, and maintains a library on deafness.

It is remarkable in that the DEGREES were adopted only in 1947, though they are not quite the same as in other organizations. The second degree is known as the fifth degree, and requires that the initiate have held office or already served on committees; the third (10th) degree requires longer service; and the same is true of the fourth (15th), fifth (20th), sixth (25th), and seventh (30th) degrees. The 34th degree—an indicator of the remote links with FREEMASONS, from which it derived via the COMING MEN OF AMERICA—requires in addition a written examination on the laws and history of the society.

National Freemasons

The National Freemasons were a Polish secret society, formed in 1818 with the object of gaining Polish independence. Whether they were actually FREEMASONS or not is open to dispute, but they used the RITES OF PASSAGE, DEGREES, and other paraphernalia of Freemasonry. After a year or two they reconstituted themselves as the Scythers, commemorating the Polish uprising of 1794 when scythes had been a principal weapon, and then in 1821 they changed their name again to the Patriotic Society before combining with the MODERN KNIGHTS TEMPLAR in 1822.

National Mutual Benefit

119 Martin Luther King Jr. Boulevard
Madison, WI 53707
(608) 257-1031

The National Mutual Benefit was founded in the United States in 1902 as a typical fraternal benefit life insurance society for men and women. There were 60,000 members in 1994. The organization publishes *Benefit News* quarterly.

Originally named the Beavers' Reserve Fund Fraternity, in 1916 it became known as Beavers' National Mutual Benefit, and was reorganized on sounder actuarial lines (previously, it had been a flat-rate ASSESSMENT society). In 1931 it abandoned the Beavers designation, though the LODGEs are still known as "colonies."

The organization absorbed the Farmers' Life Insurance Association in 1931, and the United Danish Society of America in 1945. The organization is in decline, having lost about one-quarter of its members through the 1980s.

National Order of America

The National Order of America was a short-lived operation halted by police officials in Connecticut in 1923. The promoters charged members $17 to join what they represented as a fraternal benefit society, holding out the promise of various benefits and giving members a magnificent colored membership certificate with an enormous seal and ribbons (this at a time when a loaf of bread went for eight cents). The cost, and the suspicion that these

promises might be too good to be true, did not seem to deter people; at Waterbury, a LODGE of 300 members was established, representing a gross income of $5,100 from one city alone. The fact is that the proceeds were appropriated by the order's officers, and law enforcement was called in.

The chief interest of the National Order of America is that such a scam should have been possible at all. It shows the extraordinary extent to which fraternal orders were a part of American society in comparatively recent history.

National Slovak Society of the United States of America

2325 East Carson Street
Pittsburgh, PA 15203
(412) 488-1890

The National Slovak Society was founded in 1890 as a fraternal benefit life insurance society for men and women of Slovak descent and their families and friends, aged 16–65, in the United States. There were 18,000 members in 1994. The Society publishes *Narody Noviny* (monthly), *Juvenile YFC Magazine* (semiannual), and *Kalendar* (annual).

The National Slovak Society of the U.S.A. is doubly unusual in that it is not heavily religious (in its early days, it was even opposed by the Catholic church), yet it was founded by a sometime theology student, Peter P. Rovianek. Otherwise, it is a typical ethnic fraternal benefit society, with the usual insurances, charitable and educational works, a Slovak Hall of Fame, and a commitment to Slavic culture. There is also a political element of helping European kinsmen to free their countries—a matter of some interest and considerable accomplishment in the wake of the breakup of the Soviet empire in 1989–90.

National Sojourners, Inc.

8301 East Boulevard Drive
Alexandria, VA 22308-1399
(703) 765-5000

The National Sojourners was founded in 1918 as a fraternal order for American military FREEMASONS—past or present commissioned officers and warrant officers of the uniformed services of the United States who are Master Masons. There were 10,000 members in 1994. The organization publishes *The Sojourner* bimonthly.

The Heroes of '76 is a subsidiary organization of the National Sojourners, based at the same headquarters and apparently sharing in the parent group's membership.

National Union Assurance Society

The National Union Assurance Society was a fairly typical fraternal benefit society of the late 19th century (founded as the National Union at Mansfield, Ohio, in 1881). The order was distinguished chiefly by its early adoption of a graded ASSESSMENT plan. At 20 (the minimum age), each $1,000 certificate was $0.40, rising through $0.60 at 30 years of age and $0.80 at 40, but jumping fairly steeply thereafter: $1.00 at 45, $2.00 at 60 and $2.80 (the maximum) at 65. No one could join after 50, and the maximum benefit was $5,000.

The RITUALS AND CEREMONIES were heavily nationalistic, with an American flag at the center and the LODGES called "Councils" (local); "Assemblies" or "Legislatures" (State); and "Senate" (national). It is extinct.

Native Sons of the Golden West

414 Mason Street
San Francisco, CA 94102
(415) 392-1223
Native Daughters of the Golden West
543 Baker Street
San Francisco, CA 94117
(415) 563-9091

The Native Sons of the Golden West is a fraternal and service society founded in California in 1875. Eligibility is confined to native-born Californian men and boys; the Native Daughters of the Golden West (see below) is the female auxiliary (see AUXILIARIES). There were 13,500 Native Sons and 13,500 Native Daughters in 1994.

General Albert Maver Winn, a native of Virginia, who first came to California in the Gold Rush days of 1849, was the Grand Marshal of San Francisco's Independence Day Parade in 1869. In that year he made an attempt to found an organization for native-born Californian boys over 10 years of age; he got as far as organizing a marching unit of about 125 boys in the parade, recruited via newspaper advertisements.

The N.S.G.W. was not, however, formally founded until 1875, when General Winn ran another advertisement in the *Daily Alta* of June 19. This time, the idea took off. The youngest of the 21 charter members was just shy of his 16th birthday; the oldest was 23. Winn, an Odd Fellow and Mason, was born in 1810 and was elected an honorary member. His generalship had been gained in the California Militia, though he had also served (at a less exalted rank) in the regular army.

The declared purpose of the Native Sons was "for the mutual benefit, mutual improvement and social intercourse of its members; to perpetuate in the minds of all Native Californians the Memories of one of the most wonderful epochs in the world's history, the Days of '49; to unite them in one harmonious body throughout the state by ties of friendship mutually beneficial to all."

Since their foundation, the Native Sons have always taken a lively interest in the history of California and have raised money for the restoration and marking of various historic places in the state. They also sponsor public speaking competitions to encourage schoolchildren in grades 9–12 "to learn and tell others about the fascinating history of California, while mastering the skills of self-expression, communication and confidence."

The N.S.G.W. has made generous contributions to St. John's Hospital in Santa Monica, California, and to the Cleft Palate Clinic at the University of California Medical Center. It also remains true to its origins as a marching unit, especially at an annual parade on September 9 to mark the admission of California to statehood in 1850. Most of the active members are rather older than the original 15- to 23-year-olds. The organization publishes *The Native Son* (bimonthly).

The Native Daughters of the Golden West was founded in 1886 and publishes the *California Star* (bimonthly) as well as the *Annual Proceedings*. Both organizations are described in the N.S.G.W. publication *The Origin and Purposes of the Native Sons and Native Daughters of the Golden West* (1966).

Neguiti

Neguiti is (or was) a WEST AFRICAN SECRET SOCIETY among Bakongo farmers. The following list of officials and their duties gives some idea of the order's scope:

Metambola	"Raising the dead": persuading the dry, dead-looking seeds to grow, by magical means or otherwise
Molongo	Weather forecasting (by astrological means) and weather control
Neconzi	Charming disease away from the crops
Negodi	"Curing the deafness" of the guardian deities, so that they can listen to the farmers' prayers
Nesambi	"Cleanser of lepers"; as leprosy was thought to be caused by an insufficiency of moisture, this is a Bakongo euphemism for a rain-bringer

The order has or had ritual passwords, secret speech, and signs, all designed to exclude outsiders from its business.

New French Liberals

In the 1820s, a modest number of well-to-do and influential French citizens—prominent under Napoleon I and who wanted the new monarchy overthrown—banded together under the name of the New French Liberals. Some idea of their bourgeois status may be gauged from the regalia: a small black ribbon attached to their watches, bearing a gold seal (symbolizing the money needed for the revolution), an iron ring (the means of revolution), and a piece of coral (emblematic of their hope that America would help them from across the sea, just as France had helped the Americans in their revolution).

Nkimba

Derived from SI'MO and PORO, Nkimba is a WEST AFRICAN SECRET SOCIETY and the greatest of the Bakongo societies.

Its influence extends some 300 miles inland along both shores of the Congo River. Membership is male, with admission at puberty, but there is a corresponding women's society called Nkamba.

Candidates for admission to Nkimba and Mkamba must be tutored, for which they traditionally pay a certain value in cloth and two fowls. They also pay five strings of blue pipe beads to officials of the order, food or money to the counselors of the order, and a pair of goats to its head. For these payments, the candidate, if he is accepted following a six-month period of initiation, is initiated into mysteries that include magic and augury of all kinds. Nkimba also fashion a variety of charms, especially to improve and enhance love and lovemaking. Members of Mkimba enjoy the services of physicians, who specialize in magic potions to cure a range of ills.

See also WEST AFRICAN SECRET SOCIETES.

New Reform of France, Society for the

The Society for the New Reform of France was one of the many anti-Napoleonic secret societies of the 1820s that formed a rallying point for the Paris insurrection of July 1830. It disappeared along with that abortive revolution, later to resurface as the Union of the Rights of Man. It admitted only members of such other secret societies such as the FREEMASONS, the CARBONARI, the European Patriots or the Greeks in Solitude.

Nihilism

Nihilism was originally (about 1860) a literary movement, which later became political. It operated mostly in Russia and the Slavic lands. It was never a formal secret society, but it did inform the philosophy of other revolutionary organizations and terrorist groups.

Although it is a word little heard since World War II, *nihilism* was a term that struck fear into the hearts of many. Whenever dark deeds, especially of political secret societies, were afoot, the words *nihilist* and *anarchist* would be muttered or barked. It therefore warrants coverage sufficient to show just *why* it was so feared.

In its original incarnation, the society of Nihilists was more philosophical than practical—though even then it was by Western standards revolutionary. As Arkady says in Ivan Turgenev's *Fathers and Sons* (1862), a Nihilist is "a man who bows to no authority, who accepts no principle without examination, however high this principle may stand in the opinion of men." Once accepted, this viewpoint necessarily led to a reaction against the excesses of government—especially tsarist government—and an attempt to transform the state of Russia. There had already been some such transformation in 1860, with the liberation of the serfs, and some political progress, but the tsar's regime remained autocratic and his servants unaccountable.

The Nihilists of the 1860s were partly anarchists—Mikhail Bakunin was a leading light—partly socialists, and partly anarcho-syndicalists; but they were not, for the most part, men of action. There were exceptions, such as Sergei Nechayev, who was so feared by the tsar's men that he was extracted from Switzerland (where he took refuge in about 1871) in what amounted to a judicial kidnapping. Twenty thousand francs was paid to the Zürich prefect of police to ensure his "extradition," and he died in a tsarist prison.

Nihilism also attracted popular disapproval because of the attire and attitudes of the early Nihilists, who dressed like 19th-century punks with unconventional haircuts, slovenly attire, and sometimes the additional badge of blue spectacles. The original Nihilist approach was, however, more "hippie" than "punk," advocating free love and socialism. Hundreds of thousands of rubles were given away or spent by the anarchist philosopher Pyotr Aleseyevich Kropotkin and other high-minded individuals, but despite the nonviolent nature of the original movement, it was stamped out with the utmost viciousness by the government in the early 1870s.

As so often happens, this had precisely the opposite effect of what was intended, and the movement became radical and violent. The process was exemplified by the case of Sophia Bardina, 23 years old, who was held in close confinement for two years without trial. Her crime was espousing the beliefs of nihilism. At her trial, in 1879, she made a speech that was both stirring and prophetic:

> I am convinced that our country, now asleep, will awake; and its awakening will be terrible . . . It will no longer allow its rights to be trampled under foot, and its children to be buried alive in the mines of Siberia . . . Society will shake off its infamous yoke, and avenge us; and this revenge will be terrible . . . Persecute us, assassinate us, Judges and Executioners, [but] as long as you command material force, we shall resist you with moral force- . . . for we have with us the ideas of liberty and equality, and your bayonets cannot pierce them.

She was sentenced to nine years penal servitude in Siberia.

The Will of the People

In 1878, a section of the Nihilists (who published the revolutionary journal *Land and Liberty*) split off from the original movement and called themselves "The Will of the People." Whether its members ever called themselves "The Party of Terror," or whether that was a name applied to them by others, is disputable. Unlike the other nihilists, who seem to have wanted a constitutional monarchy (or constitutional tsarism) and professed themselves as being against the tsar's corrupt coterie only, the Will of the People wanted to overthrow the tsar, and it was prepared to go to any lengths to do it. It was not, however, given to random violence. The celebrated case of Vera Zassulic, who in

January 1878 shot one man she had never met for the sake of another man she had never met, was widely presented as the act of a madwoman; but in fact, the 26-year-old Zassulic had been in and out of tsarist prisons for suspected revolutionary activities (without ever having given any very good cause for her imprisonment) since she was 17.

The facts of the case are these. General Trepov, the chief of police in St. Petersburg, had ordered another political prisoner, one Bogolinbov, to be flogged for a slight infringement of prison regulations. Zassulic managed to get into Trepov's presence and presented him with a document to read. As he was reading it, she drew a revolver and shot him. She then surrendered to the police without a struggle. At her trial, where she did not deny the murder attempt, she was found not guilty *and released.* The Russian justice system was more open and honest, at least, than the Russian police system. She managed to escape to Switzerland before the tsar's men could react, but Trepov recovered and was made a Councillor of State. This marked the beginning of a new phase of Nihilist activity, with assassination a professed weapon. General Mesentsov, another hated police chief, was gunned down in August 1878. In February 1879, it was the turn of Prince Alexis Kropotkin; in March, an unsuccessful attempt was made on the life of General Drenteln; and in April, a revolutionary called Soloviev fired four shots at the tsar himself. In December of the same year, an attempt to blow up the tsar's railway train succeeded only in blowing up his baggage. In February 1880, the tsar escaped destruction by a hundredweight of dynamite, because he was late for a dinner. At last, in March 1881, the tsar was assassinated by Ignatius Grinevizki.

The Nihilists petitioned the new tsar, Alexander III, for a more constitutional rule, but were unsuccessful. Their campaign was therefore renewed. An attempt on the life of General Tcsheverin of the state police was made in November 1882, the assassination of General Sudeikin of the secret police in December 1883, an attempt on the life of the new tsar in January 1884, and so forth. Between July 1, 1881, and January 1, 1886, 1,500 Nihilist "affairs" were examined by the police, and 3,046 individuals were punished, as follows:

Death	20
Penal servitude	28
Exile to Siberia	681
Internal exile under police supervision in European Russia	1,500
Lesser punishments	717

A private report prepared for the tsar in 1902 showed 39 people assassinated, but by then the glory days of the Nihilists were long over. The group continued its operations into the 1890s, and even the early 1900s; and no less a person than Oliver Wendell Holmes said in a speech at Harvard University in the 1890s that "Nihilism is the righteous and honorable resistance of a people crushed under an iron foe. Nihilism is evidence of life. . . . Nihilism is crushed humanity's only means of making the oppressor tremble."

Nihilism is now long dead and gone, but its emotional appeal for revolutionaries remains, as does its sinister threat for lovers of the Establishment. Thus, modern terrorist movements such as the Red Brigades, the Angry Brigade, and so forth, are still occasionally labeled "nihilist" by their detractors.

Nine Unknown Men

Many people believe that there is a small group of people who "really" run the world. The Nine Unknown Men rank alongside the GREAT WHITE LODGE as leading contenders for this secret government; they are discussed at length in *The Morning of the Magicians* (English translation, c. 1960, of *Le Matin des Magiciens,* Paris, 1959) by Louis Pauwels and Jacques Bergier. See also ILLUMINATI and ROSICRUCIANS. It is highly possible that the order is entirely mythical.

North American Benefit Association

P.O. Box 5020, 1338 Military Street
Port Huron, MI 48061
(313) 985-5191 or (800) 521-9292

The North American Benefit Association was founded in 1892 as a fraternal benefit life insurance society for women. There were 80,000 members in 1994. It publishes *the Log* monthly and a *Review* quarterly.

The beginnings of the North American Benefit Association were unpromising: a schism in the ranks of the Ladies of the Maccabees of the World (see MACCABEES). The Association was formerly known as Women's Benefit Association (1915–66), and before that as the Ladies of the Modern Maccabees (1892–1915). The Ladies of the Maccabees of the World was founded in 1885.

Bina M. West, a young schoolteacher, wanted to establish a fraternal benefit insurance society for women and was *very* successful. In the first years of the 19th century, membership hit 150,000, while by the late 1920s it had exceeded the quarter-million mark easily. In 1931, men were admitted, and sound administration kept the organization prosperous.

Like many such societies, it has declined since its glory days, and is still declining. Between 1979 and 1989, the organization lost something like 40,000 members, and the number of LODGES dropped from 700 to 447. This notwithstanding, the North American Benefit Association is still a force to be reckoned with. In addition to insurance benefits (including aid to orphans, education benefits, retraining after blindness, cancer support, and assistance in cases of natural disaster), local lodges organize and support charitable works to their own tastes. A lodge is called a "Review" when it consists only of female members, or a "Club" if men are also members.

North American Swiss Alliance

7650 Chippewa Road, Room 214
Brecksville, OH 44141
(216) 526-2257

The North American Swiss Alliance was founded as a fraternal benefit life insurance society for persons of Swiss birth or ancestry. There were 3,350 members in 1994. The Alliance publishes the *Swiss-American* monthly.

The *Gruetli Bund der Vereinigten Staaten von Nord Amerika* was founded on June 14, 1865, in Cincinnati, Ohio, and thereafter followed a peripatetic existence with the head office moving frequently. In 1911, the name of the society changed to the *Nordamerikanischer Schweizerbund,* before finally settling on the present style (usually abbreviated to N.A.S.A.) in 1940.

It is a typical ethnic fraternal benefit society with the usual mix of fraternal jollifications and straightforward insurance. "Social" members (without insurance) account for 10 to 15 percent of the membership. The size of the organization has fluctuated over the years, from about 2,000 in 1965 to about 4,000 in 1978 and just over 3,500 by 1994.

North American Union Life Assurance Society

70 East Lake Street, Ste. 1018
Chicago, IL 60601
(312) 782-5350

The North American Union Life Insurance Society was founded in 1893 (incorporated 1895) as a fraternal benefit insurance society for men. There were 6,200 members in 1994. The society publishes *North American Union News* monthly.

Originally called simply the North American Union, the Society changed its name to the present style in 1925. It was a typical late 19th-century fraternal benefit society, initially open only to white males, now open to both sexes without regard to race. The moneys raised by its charitable activities are directed toward good causes, especially those promoted by FREEMASONS.

Oaths

In order to preserve their secrets, almost all secret societies have an oath that is sworn by initiates. The few that do not have oaths, usually because of religious objections, are likely to have solemn agreements, which have the moral force of an oath, though without the spiritual overtones.

A number of oaths are reproduced in this book, either in whole or in part. Although they differ in detail, they share common underlying principles. The main ones are as follows:

1. Oath of secrecy. The initiate promises not to disclose the secrets of the organization to outsiders.
2. Oath against schism. Given the factionalism that has been rampant in so many secret societies, many oaths require the initiate to promise that he (or she) will not attend any "clandestine" meetings or meetings that are not "duly constituted."
3. Oath of obedience. The initiate promises to obey the rules of the organization and possibly also the following: the orders of his superiors within the organization, the laws of affiliated organizations, and (sometimes) the laws of the state or country.
4. Oath of honesty. The initiate promises not to defraud the lodge or any member of the lodge.
5. Oath of mutual support. The initiate promises to aid fellow members of the organization. This may be extended to include an obligation to warn them of present danger.
6. Penalties. These range from drastic measures—often described in the most blood-curdling detail— to mild. The SHRINERS' penalty (for example) *begins* with having "my eyeballs pierced to the center with a three-edge blade, my feet flayed," and goes on from there. Milder penalties are, typically, being "shunned as an outcast by all decent people."
7. An appeal to honor or to God: "I swear upon my honor" or "May God help me keep these vows."

In a surprising number of oaths, there are also provisions dealing with the chastity of maidens and pledges to respect the wives (and sometimes daughters) of fellow members.

Odd Fellows

The Odd Fellows or Oddfellows are second only to the FREEMASONS as a long-established and still reasonably healthy fraternal organization or secret society. They have, however, been subject to many schisms, and the number of members today is unclear. The date of foundation is likewise unclear, but it was presumably prior to 1745 when the first recorded LODGE of Odd Fellows, "Loyal Aristarchus, No. 9," met at various London taverns, including the Oakley Arms in Southwark; the Globe in Hatton Garden; and the Boar's Head in Smithfield. Dues were a penny per visit. The purpose is as obscure as the origin of the name, but the society seems to have combined the functions of a modern working men's club or Moose lodge (see MOOSE, INTERNATIONAL)—that is, offering a place for reliable food and drink at a good price—with a degree of self-help. The members, who were mostly working men, would pass the hat to help a fellow in distress and would provide an out-of-work member with a card that entitled him to accommodation at other lodges until he found work. Because of this emphasis on formal and informal self-help, and because of the antiquity of Odd Fellowship, the society is sometimes called "the poor man's Freemasonry." Most members were originally mechanics and artisans, though it seems that anyone who could afford a penny for the dues was admitted.

In the late 18th century, many individual lodges were prosecuted by the Crown on the grounds of potential sedition and were closed (this was the period of the French Revolution and the rebellion of the American colonies), but the order as a whole survived. Some Odd Fellows lodges seem to have arisen at around this time as a result of disaffected Freemasons seceding from their parent order; these coalesced into the Ancient and Honorable Loyal Order of Odd Fellows. It is a common belief of Freemasons that this was the *only* origin of Odd Fellowship. At the same time, most other Odd Fellows' lodges amalgamated into the Patriotic Order of Odd Fellows, which later became known as the United or Union Order of Odd Fellows. London remained the seat of the order.

The first great schism came in 1813. Odd Fellows at that time were notoriously fond of a dram, and a group of unusually sober-minded northerners took exception to this bibulousness and formed the Independent Order of Odd Fellows, Manchester Unity (or Union). This is the root order of most subsequent Odd Fellows foundations, including the American Independent Order of Odd Fellows (see below). In some countries (notably Australia), the term "Manchester Unity" is used interchangeably with "Odd Fellows."

There have been some 20 English orders of Odd Fellows, most of which were small and short-lived. They arose for various reasons, some to meet local prejudices, some out of disputes over temperance (i.e. abstinence from alcohol), and some out of the conflicts that seem always to characterize fraternal societies. Yet others had never joined either the Union Order or the Ancient and Honorable Loyal Order. The English orders are as follows:

Albion Order of Odd Fellows
Ancient Independent Order of Odd Fellows, Kent Unity
Ancient Independent Order of Odd Fellows, Bolton Unity
Ancient, True Order of Odd Fellows
Auxiliary Order of Odd Fellows
British Order of Odd Fellows
Derby Midland United Order of Odd Fellows
Economical Order of Odd Fellows

Enrolled Order of Odd Fellows
Handsworth Order of Odd Fellows
Ilkstone Unity Order of Odd Fellows
Improved Independent Order of Odd Fellows, S.L. Unity
Kingston Unity Order of Odd Fellows
Leeds United Order of Odd Fellows
Leicester Unity Order of Odd Fellows
National Independent Order of Odd Fellows
Norfolk and Norwich Order of Odd Fellows
Nottingham Imperial Order of Odd Fellows
Staffordshire Order of Odd Fellows
West Bromwich Order of Odd Fellows

It is worth noting that where a place name is incorporated in the name of the order, it is usually a place in the industrial Midlands and North, areas that, historically, have always lagged behind the Southeast both financially and culturally.

In what follows, the Independent Order of Odd Fellows (I.O.O.F.) in the United States is taken as the paradigm of Odd Fellowship, though lodges of Odd Fellows operate worldwide.

Independent Order of Odd Fellows

Sovereign Grand Lodge, I.O.O.F., 422 North Trade Street, Winston-Salem, NC 27101-2830; (919) 725-5955

The Independent Order of Odd Fellows (I.O.O.F.) was founded either in 1819 or 1843 as a fraternal order in North America. Insurance was added later. The I.O.O.F. publishes the *International Odd Fellow*, monthly, and boasted 462,780 members in 1994.

The I.O.O.F. had its roots in Washington Lodge No. 1, organized on April 26, 1819, by an expatriate Englishman named Thomas Wildey and a few fellow Odd Fellows. Other lodges were founded in Boston in 1820 and Philadelphia in 1821. The Grand Lodge of Odd Fellows of the United States was organized in 1825 under the auspices of the Manchester Unity, though other Odd Fellows organizations also supplied members to the new order. This lodge, now the Sovereign Grand Lodge, oversees Canadian as well as American Grand Lodges.

The reasons for the split from the English parent(s) are by no means clear. It is possible that it was provoked by the 1843 chartering of a black lodge, the Grand United Order of Odd Fellows, under the jurisdiction of the old United or Union Order of Odd Fellows in England. Whatever the reason, the split came in 1843, and the I.O.O.F. became the American Branch of Odd Fellowship. As in England, it attracted many of the artisan class; in California's gold country, for example, I.O.O.F. halls still stand as testimony to their attractions for miners who did not want to spend all their money in the saloons. By the time of Wildey's death in 1861, there were over 200,000 members of the I.O.O.F. and during the Civil

War the seats of secessionist members were kept vacant, and their dues were remitted.

The peak membership was probably in 1915, when there were 3,400,000 members; the Great Depression halved that number, and by the late 1970s membership had fallen below the quarter-million mark. Astonishingly, this figure had nearly doubled by 1994, though this number may reflect the inclusion of AUXILIARIES.

The lodges work four basic degrees (the number of degrees was stabilized in 1880), but there are three additional degrees in the Encampment Lodge, which maintains a pseudomilitarily uniformed marching society called the Patriarchs Militant. There is also one honorary degree.

Lodge degrees:
Initiatory
Friendship
Love
Truth
Patriarchs Militant degrees:
Patriarchal
Golden Rule
Royal Purple
Honorary degree:
Grand Decoration of Chivalry

All degrees are based on the customary rituals. William J. Whalen, in his *Handbook of Secret Organizations,* mentions skull and crossbones, scythe, scales, hourglass, coffin, and more. Many other Masonic symbols are also used, such as the all-seeing eye, the three links, and so forth. The rituals are rooted in DEISM; the postulant is required to believe in a Supreme Being who is described as the Creator and Preserver of the Universe, and the Bible is used, but according to a Sovereign Grand Lodge statement of 1963, "Odd Fellowship is not a religious institution."

Masonic influence and terminology are clearly evident. The first-degree ceremony, for example, involves putting the blindfolded candidate in chains and forming a mock funeral procession. When the blindfold is removed, the candidate is brought face to face with a skeleton illuminated by two torches and is invited to mediate upon death. Various instructions in the secrets of the order are given by different lodge worthies, the Chaplain offers prayers, and with his right hand on his left breast the candidate vows:

I, [Name], in the presence of the members of the Order here assembled, do solemnly promise that I will never communicate to anyone, unless directed to do so by a legal lodge, the signs, tokens or grips, the term, travelling or other passwords belonging to the Independent Order of Odd Fellows. Nor will I expose or lend any of the books or papers, relating to the records or secret works of the Order, to any person or persons, except one specifi-

cally authorized to receive them. That I will never reveal any private business which may be transacted in my presence in this or any other Lodge. I also promise that I will abide by the laws rules and regulations of this Lodge, of the Grand Lodge of Odd Fellows, of [the State] or any other Grand or working Lodge to which I may be attached.

I further promise that I will never wrong a Subordinate or Grand Lodge to the value of anything. Nor will I take part or share, directly or indirectly, in any illegal distribution of the funds or other property of the Lodge; but will, to the best of my ability, endeavor to prevent the same. Nor will I wrong a brother or see him wronged without apprising him of impending danger, if in my power to do so. Should I be expelled or voluntarily leave the Order, I will consider this promise as binding out of it as in. To the faithful performance of all of which I pledge my sacred honor.

He then receives the passwords, the signs of distress and recognition, the grip, and so forth from the Noble Grand performing the initiation, and brief homilies from the Chaplain and Past Grand. He is told that the organization "studiously avoids all affinity with systems of faith or sects," while the "moral precepts which govern us, and according to which we would have all men regulate their conduct, are the laws of God."

The essentially Judeo-Christian nature of the I.O.O.F. is made all the more clear in the next three degrees. The Degree of Fellowship is based on the story of the friendship of Jonathan and David. The Degree of Brotherly Love casts the candidate in the role of a traveler going from Jerusalem to Jericho and recites the parable of the Good Samaritan. The Degree of Truth uses a variety of Christian and Masonic symbols, and confers full membership of the lodge.

The I.O.O.F. is not viewed with favor by the Roman Catholic Church, though Catholics may belong under the same sufferance as to the KNIGHTS OF PYTHIAS: They are traditionally denied the sacraments, but are not excommunicated. The order is similarly discouraged by a number of other churches.

Odd Fellows, Junior Lodge

Formerly known as the Loyal Sons of the Junior Order of Odd Fellows, the Junior Lodge was founded in 1923 and in 1994 reported only 556 members. It still publishes *Youth Reporter* quarterly.

Grand United Order of Odd Fellows

262 South 12th Street, Philadelphia, PA 19107; (215) 735-8774

The Grand United Order of Odd Fellows was founded in 1843 in the United States. There were 108,000 members in 1994.

Peter Ogden, an African-American sailor, obtained the charter for the first lodge of this order from an

English Grand Lodge; it was possibly because of the English willingness to admit blacks that the white American order decided to split. The Grand United Order of Odd Fellows continues to this day.

Odwira

Odwira is or was a West African purification and protective secret society among the Ga-speaking peoples of Ghana, with many resemblances to Oyeni. It seems to have been founded in 1642 by one Nee Wetse Kojo, who landed with the man for whom James Town, Accra, is named.

Purification was accomplished by pouring rum and other liquids on the ground, followed by a ritual cleansing of the stool or throne of the order's head. The throne is smeared with gold dust, frankincense, and myrrh—a triple emblem of omnipotence. During colonial days, the order also performed a public purification ceremony at James Town, in which a log of wood was presented to a British official.

See also WEST AFRICAN SECRET SOCIETIES.

Old Religion

"The Old Religion" is a phrase frequently encountered among mystical secret societies, and sometimes found among political ones, especially German political societies, which seem often to have had a mystical bent. It can signify almost any pre-Christian survival in a Christian country, or those forms of Christianity embraced by HERETICS or believers in GNOSTICISM, or virtually whatever the user means to import from some other tradition or to make up from whole cloth. Most commonly, it refers to "Wicca," an ill-defined 19th-century "revival" (actually, more of a reconstruction) of the religion of "White Witches" as it might have existed in areas untouched by Christianity. As there are very nearly as many survivals and interpretations of those survivals as there are scholars, it has not been difficult to reconstruct any number or variations on a central theme. The central theme usually involves a vague but nonetheless genuine respect for the earth, and a belief that we are stewards of the earth rather than "having dominion" over it; a high regard for the feminine, earth, dark, or moon principle (all are much the same); and the introduction of fertility themes, which may range from the intellectualized to the physical. As interpreted in the late 20th century, the Old Religion is inclined to be gentle; whether it was gentle 2,000 years ago is not known, because the formal guardians of the Old Religion, the Druids, did not believe in writing anything down on the grounds that it impaired the memory and the understanding, and because the folk practitioners of the Old Religion were until one or two centuries ago illiterate.

Overlaid upon or coexisting with this Wicca-type religion are entire pantheons of Norse, Teutonic, Old English, and occasionally even Celtic deities, some benevolent, some wrathful, together with a variety of demons. It is therefore extremely easy for almost anyone to make whatever they like out of the "Old Religion." Nor does it end here. There are many mystics who believe that their tradition is the guardian of some even older religion. To some, the Greek MYSTERIES are regarded almost as contemporary degenerations of genuinely antique understandings, so Egypt is a favored source of True Knowledge (as it has been since the time of the Greeks themselves); but Egypt was not averse to importing deities from Akkad, Sumer, or Assyria, so some enthusiasts go back even further. The Himalayas are another prime hunting ground for would-be Masters of the Old Religion. Some individuals and orders have managed to combine two or more of these traditions, as in the origin of the GREAT WHITE LODGE (or Great White Brotherhood) or as in the pronouncements of Madame Blavatsky (see BLAVATSKY, HELENE PETROVNA). Still others have added ideas of their own invention to any or all of the religious traditions just mentioned, often supplementing them because they seem insufficiently antique. Finally, few if any of the "Old Religions" are allowed to stand as a spiritual system. Instead, they are tied to ethical and (often) political theses, usually well out of the mainstream.

Omah Language, Order of the

The Order of the Omah Language purported to be based upon the ancient primal language "which allied man to Yahweh." Yahweh is the tetragrammaton or "unknowable name" of God, spelled conventionally with the Hebrew letters *yod, he, vau, he.* It is interesting to speculate whether the founders of the order also had certain MANTRAS in mind. "Om," sometimes spelled "Aum," is the Cosmic Syllable of Buddhism, and "Om-Ah" is a common combination; for instance, a well-known Guru Rinpoche mantra runs, *"Om Ah Hung Vajra Guru Pema Siddhi Hung."*

Omladina

The Omladina ("Youth" in Serbian) was a pan-Slavonic secret society founded in the mid-19th century, which dreamed of a Slavonic nation embracing the Balkan nations, Bohemia, and parts of Poland, as well as Moravia, Silesia, and Romania. It was the first pan-Slavic secret society of note. The order was funded by the Russian tsar as a means of terrorizing Serbia. Members shot Serbian Prince Michael in 1868; kidnapped Serbian Prince Alexander a short time later, taking him to Russia for indoctrination (he abdicated on his return); organized an unsuccessful rebellion on behalf of the Karageorgevich faction to attempt to overthrow King Milan (who finally abdicated in 1889); murdered the 27-year-old

King Alexander Obrenovič and his young queen in 1903; and gave rise to the Serbian BLACK HAND.

Tsrnogorska Omladina, "Montenegrin Youth," was a continuation or possibly a splinter of Omlandina. Narodna Obrana, or National Defence Society, was another splinter or descendant, formed in about 1909 as a forerunner of the Black Hand or Ujedinjenje ili Smrt ("Unity or Death").

The Bohemian Omladina

The Bohemian Omladina may or may not have been separate from the pan-Slavic Omladina. It was founded in 1891. It was organized into basic units called "Hands," each consisting of five members, one of whom was elected "Thumb." The superior, or Upper Hand, was literally all Thumbs; five Thumbs would elect their own leader, again a Thumb.

The organization came to grief in massive government trials during early 1894. There were 77 accused, many or all of whom seem to have been convicted — though the Bohemian Omladina (whose aim was political self-determination) nevertheless survived until the foundation of Czechoslovakia after World War I.

Opus Dei

Prelature of the Holy Cross and Opus Dei
Viale Bruno Buozzi 73
1-00197, Rome, Italy
(396) 808 961

Opus Dei was founded as a Catholic religious fraternity in Spain in 1928 and is now worldwide, though about 40 percent of the members are in Spain. The order is also strong in South America. There are about 70,000 members.

Opus Dei means "[the] Work of God." In traditional Catholicism, it refers to the prayers that monks sing in common at the beginning and ending of the day. Today, it also signifies a powerful group of indeterminate size within the Catholic Church.

Opus Dei was founded on October 2, 1928, by José Maria Escriba de Balaguer, a Spaniard. (In 1940 "Escriba" became "Escriva," which is apparently more distinguished, and in 1960 the two first names were elided to Iosemaria or Josemaria; in 1968, Iosemaria Escriva petitioned for and received the title of Marques de Peralta.) For technical reasons difficult for the layman to follow, Opus Dei is unique within the Catholic Church as a personal prelature. This gives it a high degree of independence from local control by parishes or bishops, and, according to some writers, this degree of control has made Opus Dei in effect a secret society. The agenda of the society, according to its critics, is the reimposition of an almost medieval form of Christianity and the support of reactionary governments and regimes, so long as they

are nominally Catholic. The organization includes both clergy and lay people and is strongly committed to proselytizing, especially youths. Adherents are discouraged from making their affiliations known to outsiders.

Formally, there are two DEGREES or Grades within Opus Dei: "supernumerary" (normally living outside the residences of the Work) and "numerary" (normally living inside a residence, and a potential candidate for eventual ordination). Priests hold an anomalous position, being part of the Sacerdotal Society of the Holy Cross, which is intimately intertwined with Opus Dei. Within the numeraries, there are also "inscribed" members (part of the administration and allowed to vote for their superiors) and "elect" numeraries, who are eligible for election to office. At first there is a probation, followed by a five-year oblation, followed by the "fidelity," which (for numeraries) involves the monastic vows of poverty, chastity, and obedience.

The most probing critical analysis of Opus Dei is *The Secret World of Opus Dei* by Michael Walsh (London, 1989), who links Opus Dei with right-wing political movements and with the Vatican banking scandals of the 1980s. He suggests that the organization may have tried to buy respectability by pumping money into the Vatican and also implicates Opus Dei in a number of other financial scandals.

A distinguishing feature of the organization is its emphasis on recruiting those of high academic ability or potential. From all but the most reactionary viewpoints, it appears that Opus Dei goes beyond religion's traditional regard for family values and preaches the inferiority and subjugation of women; the value of unquestioning obedience (very useful to totalitarian governments); and a high degree of regulatory power for the Church. It is worth noting that in Australia, the Archbishop of Melbourne was in 1985 advised by his priests not to permit Opus Dei to open a house in the diocese.

Orangemen

Orangemen usually refers to a group of militant anti-Catholic organizations first formed as the Loyal Orange Lodge in Armagh, Ireland, in 1795. The precise number of Orangemen today is hard to determine, because some organizations are called "Orange" by their detractors while denying any such affiliation themselves, and some so-called Loyal Orange LODGES are not really exceptionable or even traditionally "Orange." The *Orange* in the word *Orangemen* refers to William of Orange, who led Protestant troops to victory against the Catholic forces of James II at the Battle of the Boyne in 1690. William of Orange, or William III, is also the hero of the Orangemen's song, "In Good King Billy's Golden Day."

By 1797, two years after the founding of the first Orange Lodge, there were about 200,000 Orangemen, who fought Catholicism with a will. Particularly bloody fighting took place in 1828 and 1829, and the order was officially dissolved in Ireland in 1836. Meanwhile, it had spread to England in 1808. Headquarters was initially in Manchester, but moved to London in 1821. In 1827, the Duke of Cumberland lent the movement some respectability, and by 1845 the Loyal Orange Lodges were re-formed in Ireland.

The movement refuses to die, and while it does undertake some good works, it is hard to deny that its main driving force is anti-Catholicism. To this day, Orange parades to commemorate the Battle of the Boyne are held in many countries, including Ireland, and violent clashes with Catholic counterprotesters are by no means unusual. In Ireland, the Loyal Irish Lodges can claim that they are Unionists—in other words, that they support the Union of the Six Counties with the United Kingdom.

Loyal Orange Lodge of British America

This was founded in 1830 as a religious, fraternal, political order in the United States and Canada for Protestant men over the age of 18 who met a number of religious and patriotic requirements including belief in the Trinity. They publish *The Sentinel* 10 times a year.

In Canada ("British America"), there were army Orange lodges as early as 1812, though the Grand Lodge of British America was not formed until 1830. Loyal Orange Lodges were formed throughout the British Empire and elsewhere throughout the 19th century. The first United States Lodge was founded in 1867, and the United States Grand Lodge was founded in 1870. On July 12, 1871, Orangemen marching in New York City were attacked by Catholics of Irish ancestry or sympathy. Sixty perished in the riot that followed. In 1891, the Loyal Orange Lodge Association of Canada took on fraternal insurance functions. It also maintains a number of children's homes and a senior citizens' home.

Lodges work five DEGREES, which are Protestant in orientation. The lowest is the Orange Degree, and the highest is the Scarlet Degree, members of which are eligible to become Royal Black Knights of the Camp of Israel. Unusually, the lodge hierarchy is fourfold, though the lowest level (Primary Lodge) may be omitted in some areas. The superior lodges are County Lodge, Provincial Grand Lodge (in Canada), and Grand Lodge. The overall leader is the Most Worshipful Master; there is clear borrowing from FREEMASONS in the structure.

While the organization is fairly small in the United States, it is strong in Canada, where it is both anti-Catholic and anti-French Canadian.

Ordeals

Ordeals are very much a part of primitive societies, and (by extension) of secret societies. The function of an ordeal is simple: It is to make sure that the initiate does not forget what he or she is being told, and to impress the importance of the occasion on everyone present. Ordeals are primitive versions of RITUALS AND CEREMONIES and are commonly associated with RITES OF PASSAGE.

The most extreme ordeals can be very dangerous and painful and are often associated with mutilation of the sexual organs: circumcision, clitoridectomy, and (among at least some tribes of Australian aborigines) subincision of the penis. The ordeals of some North American tribes are also legendary; one of the most famous is hanging suspended by hooks through the flesh. The YAKUZA or Japanese criminal fraternities lop off parts of their fingers.

In most modern secret societies, the "ordeal" falls into one of three groups. The first is the "nonevent," in which the candidate is made to believe that something unpleasant is to happen, but it does not. Such non-events include touching an ice cube to the face to simulate a red-hot iron, or jumping barefoot onto a spiked board, which is either removed before the jump or replaced with a board where the "spikes" are made of rubber. Sometimes, these ordeals go wrong, as in "hazing" in COLLEGE FRATERNITIES AND SORORITIES.

The second type of ordeal is even more of a non-event. The candidate acts out a little playlet (as in the HOMESTEADERS) or is merely told about the awful things that will happen if he breaks his oath. Masonic initiations are of this type. Thirdly, there are the "ugly sight" ordeals, in which the initiate is asked to contemplate a skull or some other symbol of death. Some ordeals may combine elements from two or more of these traditions.

Curiously enough, the only ordeals that inflict real discomfort are likely to be those of "joke" orders, for example, E CLAMPUS VITUS and SONS OF MALTA. There are, however, periodic reports of people bringing lawsuits against LODGE officers after they have been injured by some form of initiation ordeal.

Order Hounds, Exalted Society of

The Exalted Society of Order Hounds was a semisecret and fraternal salesmen's club founded in Chicago (a hotbed of fraternalism) in 1919, to develop "scientific" selling methods and "higher ideals" in the lives of the members. It is likely that the order is now long extinct.

Order of the Bath of the United States of America

The original name of this organization of FREEMASONS (they used to be called the Wahoo Band and were founded in 1921 in Red Bank, New Jersey) is perhaps more appropriate than the pirated name of a well-known English order of chivalry, which they adopted in 1930. If the organization is not now defunct, it is either wholly dormant or very small. There were only 217 Wahoos in 1950, the only year for which any source appears to have figures.

Ordo Novi Templi

The Ordo Novi Templi or Order of New Templars was founded in 1907 by Lanz von Liebenfels, and was one of numerous right-wing mystical German orders of the period. Its relationship to the original TEMPLARS was spurious, and its political ambitions seem to have been greater than its mysticism. The order is alleged to have supported the Serbian BLACK HAND in 1914 and the Austrian National Socialist Party in the 1930s. Despite its obvious fascism, it was banned by the Third Reich in 1941. Either that was the end of it, or it was later reconstituted in such secrecy as to remain invisible to this day.

Ordo Templi Orientis

Characteristically abbreviated O.T.O. or O∴T∴O∴ (using the magical arrangement of dots), the Ordo Templi Orientis may be translated as the Order of Templars of the East. It was an occult society founded in Germany at the beginning of the 20th century, primarily by Karl Kellner, Heinrich Klein, and Franz Hartmann. Kellner was a student of Tantric yoga, and with his associates created an order that combined Masonic ritual with Eastern sex magic. Indeed, the title of the order alludes to the sexual practices that supposedly led to the downfall of the original Templars in the 1300s. Members of the order worshiped the Templar idol Baphomet at O.T.O. functions.

The English magician and Satanist Aleister Crowley (later branded by the popular press as the "wickedest man in the world"; see CROWLEY, ALEISTER) became an enthusiastic adherent and subsequently founded a British branch of the O.T.O., proclaiming himself Baphomet. Rudolf Steiner, founder of the ANTHROPOSOPHICAL SOCIETY IN AMERICA, was also a member for a time.

The O.T.O. seems to have perished in Germany with the ascension of Naziism. It continued in England, however, though diminished in significance following the death of Crowley in 1947.

Ordre Christique Fraternel

3 bid, rue Clairaut
75017 Paris

This "very closed" order sought unity with the universe by means of sacred homosexuality. It may be associated with the Forum des Groupes Chrétiens Gais d'Europe (the Forum of Christian Gays of Europe), which apparently embraces the Centre du Christ Libérateur, the Chevaliers de l'Horloge and Arcadic.

Ordre Vert Celtique

c/o René Lixon
B.P. 75
4000 Liège 1, Belgium

The Ordre Vert Celtique, or Green Celtic Order, takes its name from Ireland, the "Green Isles" or "Emerald Isle," but also embraces the Holy Grail, which according to some traditions is carved of a single emerald. The founder was the Archdruid Pierre-Marie Beauvy de Kergaelec, who also founded a Masonic and revised Druidical order of "the occidental Rosy-Cross and of the Hyperborean Grail," according to Bayard (see BAYARD, JEAN-PIERRE).

Oriental Rite of Memphis and Mizraim

The original Oriental Rite of Memphis and Mizraim was an Italian manifestation of FREEMASONS, organized in Venice in 1788 by Count Cagliostro (see CAGLIOSTRO, ALESSANDRO). After the Count's heretical practices earned him a life sentence in 1791, the rite was restarted in Milan in 1805 and introduced into France in 1814 or 1815, where the Grand Orient Lodge failed to recognize it. The Supreme Council of the Rite was dissolved in 1817. The Rite had worked 87 (later 90) DEGREES in four series and 17 classes.

Periodical attempts at reviving the Rite, which was an admixture of Egyptian mystic lore and SCOTTISH RITE Freemasonry, met with limited success. A Rite of Memphis, devised by an M. Marconis, who was initiated into a Memphis lodge in 1833, survives in the United States today, and (as may be seen in the list that follows) there are several French branches. Giuseppe Garibaldi (1807–82) was elected Grand Master of yet another branch in 1881. The worst schisms apparently came after 1934, giving rise to at least the following:

Echelle de Naples
Grande Sanctuaire Adriatique
La Lodge Audiart
Ordre Maçonnique Oriental de Misraïm d'Egypte
Ordre Maçonnique Egyptien de Belgique
Order Maçonnique Universel du Rite Oriental Ancien et Primitif de Memphis et Misraïm Réunis
Rite Ancien et Primitif de Memphis-Misraïm
Souverain Sanctuaire du Rite de Memphis-Misraïm

Orioles, Fraternal Order of

c/o Peason S. Slough
48 East Seventh Avenue
York, PA 17404
(717) 854-1671

The Fraternal Order of Orioles was founded in 1910 in Rochester, New York, as a fraternal order. There were 10,000 members in 1994. The order publishes *Oriole Life,* formerly *The Oriole Bulletin,* quarterly.

This is a traditional fraternal benefit society, in which individual members in good standing are helped on an *ad hoc* basis rather than having insurance rights. Social members receive no benefits, but attend "Nest" (LODGE) social events; honorary members live in places where there is no Nest. Grand Nests and a Supreme Nest, presided over by the Supreme Worthy President, complete the lodge hierarchy. The order works three DEGREES, the Initiatory, the Supreme and Invincible, which is above the Supreme. The RITUALS AND CEREMONIES are basically Christian and involve the use of a Bible.

One of the stated objectives of the order is to "assist our members who are candidates for public office," though it is unclear whether Orioles are particularly active in this field. In fact, they are decreasingly active in all fields: From a high of more than 140,000 members in the early 1920s, they had declined to 12,649 in 1979 and to about 10,000 a decade later.

Orphic Mysteries

The Orphic Mysteries of ancient Greece centered around Dionysus (in the Roman pantheon, Bacchus), God of Growth, Spring, and (above all) the Grape. As with the Gods of most ancient Mysteries, there are elements of DEATH AND RESURRECTION about him; he is also a god of fertility.

Even less is known about the rites of Dionysus than about other ancient Mysteries, and much of what is known is even more confused and corrupted than usual by those who reported it. Briefly, the celebrations of the rites of Dionysus or Bacchus were matters of wild abandon, usually involving drunkenness and sexual profligacy and sometimes self-mutilation and flagellation. Celebrants might tear apart animal sacrifices with their hands and teeth, the flesh and blood devoured as part of the communion.

The rites originally came from Thrace and Phrygia, to the northwest of modern Greece, and were apparently diluted as they moved into the more civilized parts of the region. The *Dionysias* (festivals) were as follows:

1. December (month of Poseidon): Rust Dionysia
2. January (month of Gamelion): Lenea or "Festival of Maenads"
3. February (month of Anthesterion): Anthesteria
4. March (month of Elaphebolion): City Dionysia
5. October (month of Pyanepsion): Oschophoria or "Carrying of Grape Clusters"

The fourth of these festivals was the most famous; the second was (by repute) the most abandoned. Women were heavily identified with the Orphic Mysteries.

Osiris, Ancient Order of

Founded somewhere in the United States during the 19th century (sources neither specify precisely where or when), the Ancient Order of Osiris was governed by a Supreme Tribunal and posed as its objectives "to clothe the naked, feed the hungry, educate the orphan, and 'to know each other and ourselves.' " Its watchwords were "Truth, Justice, and Equity." It is certainly extinct.

Owls

There have been at least two varieties of owls, the Independent Order of Owls and the Order of Owls. The Independent Order came first.

Independent Order of Owls

The Independent Order of Owls was founded in 1890 in St. Louis, as a "fun" organization within the FREEMASONS, open to Master Masons. It is long extinct, along with its "Nest" (LODGEs), which were headed by a "Sapient Screecher."

Owls, Order of

P.O. Box 17278, Bishops Corner Bridge, West Hartford, CT 06117; (203) 236-0049

The Order of Owls was founded in 1904 in South Bend, Indiana, as a fraternal order. There were 5,100 members in 1994. The order publishes a magazine, *The Owl.*

The order of Owls has declined from its heyday in the early 1920s, when it had 600,000 members in 2,148 "Nests" (lodges), to about 200,000 in the late 1950s; 40,000 in 1979; and about 5,000 a decade later. It is a fraternal society, not an insurance society, and it seems to have a strong social bent.

The Owls works four DEGREES, the RITUALS AND CEREMONIES of which are rooted in DEISM. The oath says "may God keep me steadfast," but the order's own literature says "We have a beautiful ritual but no religious observance." The forms of the rituals are typical; for example, the candidate for admission says:

> I swear in the presence of these Owls that I will abide by and obey all laws and regulations of this order. I will never commit to writing or reveal any of its signs, grips or other secrets, except within the body of a duly and regularly constituted and sitting nest of Owls. I further swear I will not cheat, wrong or defraud a nest of Owls or any Owl, or allow the same to be done if within my power to prevent. I will give an Owl due and timely notice of any threatening danger and will if able render assistance.

Despite such noble promises, the founder of the order, John W. Talbot, was sentenced to five years at Leavenworth in 1921 as a result of a morals charge involving a nurse at the Owls' hospital.

P2

P2 was founded in Italy in 1966 as a part of the FREEMASONS and had a brief but eventful career in Italian politics. Although now probably extinct, it had about 953 members in the early 1980s.

Raggruppamente Gelli Propaganda Due, better known simply as P2 (*Propaganda Due*) was founded by a Tuscan Freemason called Licio Gelli, at the behest of Giordano Gamberini, Grand Master of the Grand Orient [Masonic LODGE] of Italy. It is debatable whether Gamberini ever foresaw what P2 would become, but there are at least two reasons why he might have wanted to see it founded. One was to have as many Masons as possible in positions of power in Italy, where Freemasonry has frequently been the subject of attacks both religious and secular. The other is that if Masons could help get the nascent United States up and running in the late 18th century, maybe Masons could accomplish the same for the divisive Italian government in the late 20th century.

Although frequently referred to as a LODGE, P2 was never officially constituted as such. It was called "Propaganda Due" (*due* is Italian for "two") in honor of the old "Propaganda" lodge of Turin, an elite lodge numbering among its members the king himself.

It is an excellent modern example of how the Craft may be adapted for many ends. Gelli recruited large numbers of extremely influential Masons, sometimes using blackmail to do so, and infiltrated the very highest corridors of power in Italy. P2 is also grist for the mill of lovers of conspiracy theories, since it really *was* a conspiracy—arranged in 17 cells with extremely limited contact between each other, all information being funneled to Gelli. Indeed, the sheer scale of the operations of P2 was staggering, and it may be that Gelli was either knowingly or unknowingly a tool of the KGB; or he may have accepted KGB help in the belief (probably well founded) that he could get more from them than they could ever get from him. The P2 scandal blew up in 1981, in a complex network of subscandals including financial chicanery, espionage, and apparently even the attempted assassination of the Pope.

Palladium, Order of the

The Order of the Palladium is or was one of the many American organizations offering "higher" DEGREES in the FREEMASONS—in this case, "Adelphos" and "Companion of Ulysses" for men, and "Penelope" for women. Allegedly instituted in 1770, it remained dormant after its introduction in the United States until 1884; and then, in 1886, it was revived as the new and reformed Palladium, also known as the Free and Regenerated Palladium.

Panacea Society

The Panacea Society was founded about 1909 in Bedford, England, by Alice Seymour, publisher of *The Express,* a pamphlet that expounded the religious doctrine of an 18-century diary maid-turned-prophetess, Joanna Southcott.

Southcott became a Methodist in 1791, but the following year became convinced that she was the "woman clothed with the sun" mentioned in Revelation, chapter 12. In 1801, Rev. T. P. Foley, an Anglican rector in the

Exeter area, attested to his conviction that Southcott indeed had prophetic powers. Southcott taught that as man had first been led astray by a woman, so a second woman would save mankind, and she identified herself as this "Second Eve." Southcott set about gathering followers—144,000 of the elect mentioned in Revelation, chapter 7—calling upon her adherents to observe the Jewish laws as set forth in the Old Testament. When one of her followers was hanged for murder in 1809, the sect fell into some disrepute; however, Southcott continued to produce and circulate a large number of religious pamphlets and, in particular, bombarded the House of Commons and officials of the Church of England with documents relating to her views. It is nevertheless likely that the "Southcotties" would have disbanded shortly after her death in 1814 had she not left behind a sealed box, which was to be opened only by the bishops of the Church of England. Southcott said that the box was an "ark" containing the means by which the world might be saved from plagues of war, disease, and crime, which would otherwise engulf humankind.

The bishops did not open the box, which, nevertheless, was faithfully preserved by a handful of adherents. Then, in 1902, one Alice Seymour encountered Southcott's writings, published *The Express* in 1909, established the Panacea Society, and, with its members, concentrated her efforts on persuading the Archbishop of Canterbury to open the box. He refused. Finally, in 1927, the box was opened unofficially—with no bishops present. It was found to contain a lottery ticket and a woman's nightcap.

Panacea Society members claimed that it was, after all, the *wrong* box and that they retained the *true* box, which they would surrender only when the bishops agreed to open it. As of this writing, the Panacea Society still exists, and the bishops have yet to open the box.

Papal Awards

Papal Awards may be distinguished from PONTIFICAL ORDERS OF KNIGHTHOOD by the fact that they do not ennoble the recipient, nor have they ever done so. The principal awards are the Golden Rose, which is described as "well-known" in a document dating from the reign of Leo IX in 1049; the cross *Pro Ecclesia et Pontifice,* inaugurated in 1887 to mark the golden priestly jubilee of Leo XIII; the *Benemerenti* modal, first awarded during the reign of Pius V (1566–72); and annual Papal or Pontifical medals.

None of them has any particular connection with fraternal orders or secret societies, except that proponents of One World Government and other conspiracy theories repeatedly assert connections.

Passwords

Typically, a fraternal order requires a password before admitting a member to a LODGE. There may also be a countersign, a brief sequence of exchanged passwords, by which the initiates recognize one another. The FREEMASONS' password of "Boaz" is well known, sometimes split with the other person, so one says "Bo" and the other says "Az." One KU KLUX KLAN sequence is said to being. "Ayak?" which elicits the reply "Akia": "Are You A Klansman?" and "A Klansman I Am." See CRUSADERS for an example of a particularly long and involved sequence of passwords and countersigns.

Many organizations retain passwords, which may be the last vestige of ritual in some fraternal insurance organizations. Secret society passwords are commonly changed annually or half-yearly.

Patriarchal Circle of America

The concept of patriarchy held a peculiar fascination for 19th-century men, and the word appears in the names of a number of secret societies.

The Patriarchal Circle was apparently conceived as a military-flavored add-on to the already existing Uniformed Patriarchs of the ODD FELLOWS. The order worked three DEGREES, Preparatory, Perfection and Patriarchal Feast, and Knighthood, but in 1885 the parent organization rejected the Patriarchs of the Circle as illegitimate, and the small band became independent.

Sick and funeral benefits were established on a local basis, at the option of the Temples (LODGEs). The Circle appears to have broken long since, probably in the first decade or two of the 20th century, along with its auxiliary (see AUXILIARIES), the Circle of the Golden Band.

Patriotica

Patriotica was a Polish patriotic society dedicated to the liberation of Poland. It was founded on May Day, 1821, in Potok, near Warsaw. In 1830, Adam Czortoryski (one of the chiefs of Patriotica) attempted to form a national government, but as with those of so many other Polish national movements, the hopes of Patriotica were crushed at the Battle of Ostrolenka in 1831.

Patriotic Order, Sons of America

The Patriotic Order, Sons of America (the name appears with and without the comma) was, like many organizations with "Patriotic" in their title, an anti-Catholic, anti-immigration Know-Nothing society (see KNOW-NOTHINGS). It originated as the Patriotic Order, United Sons of America at some time prior to 1847 in Philadelphia. The order disappeared with the collapse of the Know-Nothing Party, but was resuscitated in 1868, this time minus the epithet "United." The DEGREES were Red, White, and Blue, and the women's auxiliary was the (Patriotic) Daughters of America. The Patriotic Order, Junior Sons of America was founded as the junior branch in 1847, and the Patriotic Order of True Americans was the result of a merger between the Patriotic Order of Americans (another auxiliary) and the Daughters of America. There was even (according to the Philadelphia *Public Ledger* of September 1, 1923) a "fun" or "mummers" division of the Patriotic Order, Sons of America, called the Rough Riders.

The order is defunct, as are its offspring.

Patriotic Organizations

Organizations describe themselves as "patriotic" for various reasons. The noblest motive is true patriotism, an altruistic desire that one's country should be the best possible country for everyone who lives in it, including even nonnatives. A more common motive, especially in Europe, has been for organizations to use the words "patriotic" or sometimes "loyal" as a means of reassuring other people that they are not revolutionary or threatening to the established order. But possibly the most common usage, especially in the United States, is to denote organizations such as the KU KLUX KLAN and the KNOW-NOTHINGS, whose aims are generally bigoted, repressive, and reactionary. Traditionally, in the United States, the term *patriotic* was commonly hijacked by white Protestant xenophobic patriarchs, who preached "the Faith or the Sword" to anyone who opposed them, especially African Americans, Catholics, socialists, or immigrants.

Several "patriotic" (in the negative sense) and some truly patriotic organizations have their own entries in the book; others include:

American Rangers, Inc.

The American Rangers was an anti-Catholic secret society based in Macon, Georgia, in the 1920s. The name of its official organ—*The Menace*—suggests the nature of its point of view.

American Union, Order of the

The American Union was nativist and anti-Catholic, and was founded in New York in 1873. It suffered a severe decline after being "exposed" in the press during the late 1870s, but regrouped in 1881 and turned the adverse publicity to its own advantage; by 1890, the Union boasted one and a half *million* members. The population of the United States, according to the census of 1890, was just under sixty-three million, so more than one American in fifty was a member. The Union was eventually swallowed by the AMERICAN PROTECTIVE ASSOCIATION.

Ladies of Abraham Lincoln

The Ladies of Abraham Lincoln were a typical anti-Catholic "patriotic" society formed just after the Civil War, with some influence from the ORANGEMEN. The

order was moribund or extinct by the end of the 19th century.

Loyal Women of American Liberty

This anti-Catholic association pledged "not to assist the Roman Catholic clergy or their institutions." It was founded in Boston, in 1888 and apparently lasted for some 20 years.

Red, White, and Blue

Suspicions about this organization are confirmed when one learns that the first, or Red, degree taught protection of the Protestant religion against Catholicism. The second, or White, degree inculcated "purity," and the Blue degree was "strictly American." Applicants had to be the *grandchildren* as well as the children of native-born Americans. It was organized in Rochester, New York, at the end of the 19th century.

Templars of Liberty

Ironically, the Templars of Liberty were specifically *against* liberty for Catholics—the faith of the original Templars. The order combined this stance with graded ASSESSMENT death benefit insurance. Its RITUALS AND CEREMONIES were based on scenes and incidents from the Reformation: The Templars of Liberty was formed in Newark, New Jersey, in 1881 and disappeared long ago.

Patriotic Reformers

The Patriotic Reformers was one of the many Italian secret societies of the early 19th century, akin to the CARBONARI, dedicated to securing its country's independence from Austria. It was founded in Messina, and corresponded with lodges on the mainland by the unlikely medium of coded musical scores.

Pednosophers

The Pednosophers, or "Children of Wisdom" (the etymology is uncertain), is alleged to have arisen in the 17th century from the Pythagorean schools, which had been suppressed in the 530s by Justinian I because they would not pay court to the Empress Theodora. The Pythagoreans, inspired by the Greek philosopher who lived from about 560 to 480 B.C., held a belief in the transmigration of souls and, like Pythagoras himself, cherished the clandestine.

There were different degrees among the Pednosophers, which perpetuated itself until 1672 in various European countries, England included. In 1672, Charles II of England prohibited all secret societies, and the Pednosophers changed its name to Tobaccologers. The order declined in England by the end of the 18th century, and its records and mysteries fell into the hands of a certain Frenchman, whose heirs reconstituted the society at Poitiers, France, in 1806. It continued as a French secret society until about 1846.

It is quite possibly that the Tobaccologers was a real secret society, and that it invented the Pednosophers as part of a specious history of its origin.

P.E.O. Sisterhood

3700 Grand Avenue
Des Moines, Iowa
(515) 255-3153

P.E.O. was founded at Iowa Wesleyan University (Mount Pleasant, Iowa), on January 21, 1869, and has survived as a remarkably secretive society ever since, with 247,600 members reported in 1994. It owns and administers Cottey College for Women in Nevada, Missouri, and is active in the field of education.

P.E.O. may or may not stand for "protect each other."' No one is quite sure. The organization was founded by seven teenager girls, apparently because some of them had not been asked to join the new chapter of I.C. Sorosis, a sorority that had been established about a month previously in Mount Pleasant. As the order's official history says, the founders wrote vivid accounts of their brainchild, which "did not always agree in all details." They key was Hattie Brigg's statement, "Let's have a society of our own."

The seven founders remained friends when they grew up, maintained P.E.O., and other women joined the organization. It evolved into a well-run society with considerable funds, administered by middle-aged ladies. In addition to the college and scholarship funds already mentioned, P.E.O. also established an International Peace Scholarship Fund.

Peter Pan Club

The Peter Pan Club was founded in the late 1960s or early 1970s in Plymouth, England, as a society for those who had not yet made up their minds what they were going to do when they "grew up" (whatever their chronological age). It has two levels of membership, Junior (*over* 21) and Full (*under* 21).

There are no formal LODGES; the club normally meets at private houses or in pubs, and the headquarters moves with the senior officers. The RITUALS AND CEREMONIES center around Wendy and Tinkerbell (inspired by the characters in Sir James Barrie's story), normally the youngest (12 years old or over) girls present at a gathering, though the age limits are far from strict. The DEGREES are Vertical and Horizontal.

Philadelphes

The Philadelphes was a short-lived society founded in France in about 1800 as a social club. The name comes from the Greek and means "brother-lovers," the same root as "Philadelphia" ("brotherly love"). Shortly after the order was founded, it was taken over by Colonel Jacques Josephe Oudet (1775–1809) as an implement of revolution against Napoleon I; Oudet's intention was the restoration of the Bourbons, and he was an enthusiastic infiltrator of secret societies. In about 1805, the authorities learned of the Philadelphes' new activities, so the society changed its name to *Les Olympiens,* "The Olympians."

After Oudet's death at the battle of Wagram in 1809, the Olympians (which had been directionless for some time) apparently reverted to its original name, and chapters appeared in a number of American cities, notably Boston and Philadelphia. Its aims also reverted to the philanthropic and amicable nature of the original foundation.

Philadelphian Society

The Philadelphians were a late 17th-century religious society, which was founded on the mystic theology of the Christian esotericist Jakob Boehme as interpreted by John Pordage (1607–81), rector of the church in Bradfield, England. Although Pordage was removed from his living during 1655–60 by the Triers (commissioners appointed by Oliver Cromwell "for the approbation of all public preachers"), he accumulated a large following, chief among whom was Jane Leade (or Lead), who had experienced visions, which she recorded in her diary and subsequently published as *A Fountain of Gardens* in 1670. It was in 1670 that the Philadelphia Society was formally established.

Philadelphians were nature pantheists, much imbued by mysticism and believing that their souls were immediately illuminated by the Holy Spirit. The order declined rapidly after Leade's death in 1704.

Philanthropic Assembly

709 4th Street
North Bergen, NJ 07047
Europe: L'Ange de l'Eternal, Le Chateau
1236 Cartigny, Switzerland

The Philanthropic Assembly was founded by a Swiss named F. L. Alexander Freytag (1870–1947) in 1921. Freytag had been in charge of the Swiss Bureau of the International Bible Students Association, which was founded on the theology of the American evangelical leader Charles Taze Russell, publisher of the *Watch Tower* religious periodical. Freytag became increasingly disenchanted with Russell's teachings and finally published in 1920 an attack on them entitled *Message of Laodicea.* The following year, Freytag withdrew from the Swiss Bureau and established the Church of the Kingdom of God, also known as the Philanthropic Assembly of the Friends of

Man, consisting of many Swiss, German, and French Bible students. (In France, the organization is known as the Amis de l'homme.)

Freytag's organization is based on his belief that one overcomes death by conforming to the form of Jesus, eschewing sin to escape the wages of sin. Moreover—and in contrast to Russell—Freytag believed that God set eternal happiness as the goal of all mankind, not the prospect of eternal punishment in hell.

The Philanthropic Assembly is now concentrated mainly in Switzerland, Germany, France, Spain, Austria, Belgium, and Italy. While no precise membership figures are available, its periodical, *The Monitor of the Reign of Justice*, circulates to 120,000. There are at least several hundred members of the Assembly in the United States.

Philareten

The "Philareten of Wilna" was one of many Polish secret societies of the early 1820s. As with the others, it was dedicated to the overthrow of Russian rule.

Philiker

The Philiker was a Greek political secret society, a successor to the HETAIRA. It was founded in 1812 as the Friends of the Muses, and, like a number of other European political societies, was an ostensibly literary and artistic organization with an underlying political motivation. It worked seven DEGREES, using the forms of FREEMASONS and (at least outwardly) studying alchemy; the RITUALS AND CEREMONIES seem to have emphasized the Christian struggle against Islam, the religion of the Greek's Turkish masters. After 1818, the headquarters was in Istanbul, but the Philiker came to an end when the leader of the movement, Alexander Ypsilanti (of Byzantine ancestry and in sympathy with the Russian tsar, who may have contributed funds to the organization) led an ill-considered rebellion, which was wiped out at Dragatshau on June 19, 1821.

The spirit of the rebels, however, lived on, and numerous other Greek secret societies, whose names are now long forgotten, continued the struggle. The savagery of the Turks in repressing the rebellion evoked revulsion throughout the civilized world. When Chios was burnt, for example, 20,000 men, women, and children were slaughtered and 50,000 were carried off as slaves. Greek independence was finally achieved after the destruction of the Turkish fleet in Navarino Bay in 1827 by combined English, French, and Russian forces.

Pilgrims

The Pilgrims was a society discovered in Lyons, France, in 1825 after a member, a Prussian shoemaker, was arrested. The order's printed "catechism" was in his possession. It was modeled on the tenets of the FREEMA-SONS. The Pilgrims were activists in the cause of religious freedom. Beyond these spare facts, nothing more is known of them.

Pink Goats, Order of

Very little is known about this society, other than what is contained in the *Christian Cynosure* of November 1919 (vol. 52, no. 7). It was founded in 1919 "in an Eastern city," and its members "appear in public in pink pajamas and gowns, carrying goats of all kinds of descriptions." The supreme officer was dubbed He Goat, and other officers included Little White Goat, Chief Bleater Goat, Chief Billy Goat, Chief Wise Goat, Goat Getter, Inner Angora Goat, Ball Goat, and Musical Goat. The order has absolutely no connection with the 18th-century GOATS active in and around Limburg.

Platonic Academy

The Platonic Academy is reputed to have been founded in 1480 in Florence under the patronage of Lorenzo de Medici, and to have been part of the FREEMASONS. The Hall of the Platonic Academy contained symbols later claimed as Masonic. It is possible that the Academy was a society of Masons who had abandoned Masonic forms for Masonically inspired mysticism. If this is the case, the Platonic Academy would figure as one of the earliest instances of the separation of speculative from operative Masonry.

Polaires, Fraternité des

The Fraternité des Polaires ("Polar Fraternity") was a secret society based on a method of divination using "a special arithmetic" acquired from a hermit called Père Julian by Mario Fille in Bagnaia, near Rome, in 1908. Shortly afterward, Père Julian apparently returned to the Himalayas, home of all good Masters, but the fraternity was established in Montmartre.

The mission of the fraternity is a little hazy—"The time has come [or "the times are near"] . . . we must reconstruct on fraternal basis"—but some members had a more concrete goal and made an attempt to find the Treasure of the Albigeois (see HERETICS) near Montségur. They used the oracle, but prudently took up a handsome subscription first. This resulted in accusations of fraud, and the organization fell apart.

Police, Fraternal Order of

Grand Lodge, F.O.P.
2100 Gardiner Lane
Louisville, KY 40205
(502) 451-2700 or (800) 451-2711

The Fraternal Order of Police was founded in 1915 in Pittsburgh, Pennsylvania, for American police officers of all ranks. There were 215,500 members in 1994, and the quarterly magazine is the *National FOP Journal*.

The F.O.P. is effectively a fraternal TRADE UNION, though strikes are theoretically forbidden. It is limited to the single profession of police work, and it is the only national organization for the working policeman or policewoman.

The original constitution, even before the order went national in 1918, contained the admirable provision that "Race, Creed or Color shall be no bar," and furthermore stated that the F.O.P. should be strictly "non-political, non-sectarian, and shall have no affiliation, directly or indirectly, with any labor union, congress, federation or . . . similar organization by whatever name known." The original antistrike provisions, which called for expulsion from the order if they were contravened, have not had the same force since 1967, when the F.O.P. Lodge in Youngstown, Ohio, refused to let its members work during a salary dispute. Each lodge is fully autonomous, requiring a minimum of only 10 policemen or policewomen, and some lodges have actively adopted a strike stance. There is only one degree (see DEGREES), and while the RITUALS AND CEREMONIES have a distinctly Christian flavor ("Our father, which art in Heaven, we ask Thee to bless this meeting . . ."), there is no altar or open Bible. The founders had more respect for Latin than skill in it, for the motto *"Jus, Fidus, Liberatum"* does not translate as the usual rendition of "Justice, Friendship, Equality" but rather as Jus (right, law, or justice), fidus (safe, trustworthy; conceivably "faithful"), liberatum (of freedom).

In addition to its fraternal work, the F.O.P. furthers its original aims of "bettering existing conditions for Policemen" and "advancing Social, Benevolent and Educational Undertakings among Policemen by publishing an annual survey of police pay and working conditions; conducting seminars, sponsoring competitions and awards and maintaining a speakers' bureau." The F.O.P. also sponsors such things as anti–car theft drives, and other projects to inform the public how to safeguard their property.

Polish Falcons of America

615 Iron City Drive
Pittsburgh, PA 15205
(412) 922-2244 or (800) 535-2071

The Polish Falcons of America was founded in 1887, but was not chartered until 1894; it reincorporated again in 1924. It is an ethnic fraternal benefit life insurance society for persons of Polish or Slavic descent and their spouses. There were 30,000 members in 1994. The organization publishes *Sokol Polski* monthly.

The Alliance of Polish Turners of the United States of America founded its first "nest" in 1887, with a strong emphasis on physical fitness, but in 1914 the name was changed to the Polish Falcons Alliance of America, and a specifically political tinge was added: the independence of Poland. The 1924 reincorporation saw a renewal of emphasis on physical culture, and on March 30, 1928, the order changed to the present name and added new objectives of accumulating and maintaining a fund for sickness, accident, and death benefits.

Like many similar societies, the Falcons offers beneficial (insured) and social (noninsured) membership, the former accounting for about nine-tenths of the adherents. The Falcons is still strongly oriented toward physical fitness, and it organizes many athletic events.

Polish National Alliance of Brooklyn, U.S.A.

155 Noble Street
Brooklyn, NY 11222
(718) 389-4704

The Polish National Alliance of Brooklyn, U.S.A. was founded in 1903 as an ethnic fraternal benefit life insurance society. The Alliance publishes the *Polish American Journal*, monthly. There were 9,713 members in 1995.

The Polish National Alliance of Brooklyn, New York, is a typical fraternal benefit life insurance society, which (despite its name) spreads across several states in the northeastern United States. It offers the usual range of ethnic fraternal group services and is particularly strong in its support of the Catholic church. In 1960, it absorbed the Polish American Workmen's Aid Fund, but although a marked drop in membership in the late 1960s and 1970s (from 21,413 in 1965 to about 12,000 in 1979) slowed slightly in the mid-1980s, it dropped from 11,135 in 1995 to 9,713 the following year.

Polish National Alliance of The United States of North America

6100 North Cicero Avenue
Chicago, IL 60646
(312) 286-0500 or (800) 621-3723

The Polish National Alliance of the United States of North America was founded on St. Valentine's Day, 1880. It is an ethnic fraternal benefit life insurance society open to people of either sex, over 16, who are of good moral character, physically and mentally sound, who by birth, descent, or sanguinity, are of Polish, Lithuanian, Ruthenian, or Slovak nationality, and their husbands and wives. Membership was 256,997 in 1994. It publishes *Polish Daily Zgoda, Zgoda* (semimonthly), and *Promien Youth Magazine,* stated to be quadrennial but more probably quarterly.

The Polish National Alliance of the United States of North America is a typical ethnic fraternal benefit insurance society, originally designed to provide both financial and moral support and to meet the twin aims of making immigrants into better U.S. citizens while still preserving their pride in their national heritage. It has had a long history, has avoided religious ties, admitted women early (1900), and in 1912 founded Alliance College, a four-year liberal arts college. It has always been active in civic, cultural, educational, and charitable work.

Polish National Union

1002 Pittstown Avenue
Scranton, PA 18505
(717) 344-9051

The Polish National Union (*Sponjnia*) is an ethnic fraternal benefit insurance society, founded in 1908, and operating in the United States. Membership is open to men and women over 16, and it mainly attracts persons of Polish ancestry. In 1994 there were 30,000 members. The union publishes *Polish Weekly Straz* (The Guard).

Sponjnia was founded in 1908 in the parish hall of St. Stanislaus Cathedral in Scranton, Pennsylvania. It has always been closely linked with the Polish Catholic Church, though it does not bar or even discourage non-Catholics. It is a typical ethnic/religious fraternal benefit society, very slightly declining (losing about 1,000 members a decade between 1960 and 1990), but still healthy withal. It maintains a home for the aged and disabled, sponsors sporting and cultural events, and has always contributed generously to disaster relief funds, especially in Poland.

Polish Roman Catholic Union of America

984 Milwaukee Avenue
Chicago, IL 60622
(312) 278-3210

The Polish Roman Catholic Union of America was founded in 1873 as an ethnic fraternal benefit life insurance society. There were 90,000 members in 1994. It publishes *Narod Polski* monthly.

The union is a large, successful ethnic fraternal benefit organization, with the usual fringe benefits of Polish cultural events, sports and youth activities, and language and dance classes. It maintains the large and estimable Polish Museum of America and its associated library of 25,000 volumes. Membership is now open, but remains mostly Polish.

Polish Union of America

P.U.A. Building
P.O. Box 684, 4191 North Buffalo Street
Orchard Park, NY 14127-0684
(716) 667-9782

The Polish Union of America was founded in 1890 as an ethnic fraternal benefit life insurance society. There were 9,000 members in 1994. The organization publishes the periodical *PUA Parade*.

The Polish Union of America is a typical, successful ethnic fraternal benefit life insurance society. In the decade of the 1980s, membership rose about 20 percent. This is attributable, in part, to responsive management and the provision of useful, relevant services such as ethnic awareness programs and a vocational placement service, as well as a library, museum, and speakers' bureau. The Union also runs the White Eagle Young Adults Club.

Polish Women's Alliance of America

205 South Northwest Highway
Parkridge, IL 60068
(708) 692-2247

The Polish Women's Alliance of America was founded in 1898 in Chicago as a fraternal benefit insurance company for women of Polish extraction "and/or conviction." There were 65,000 members in 1994. The order publishes *Glos Polek* bimonthly.

The Polish Women's Alliance of America owes its success to two factors. The first is a strong national identity, which is nevertheless flexible enough to remain relevant to modern Americans of Polish descent—*Glos Polek* is published in both English and Polish. The second is that it is a women's organization. Although the glory days of fraternal orders are long over, it seems that women's organizations in general are better run, healthier, and less mired in obsolete RITUALS AND CEREMONIES. Otherwise, it is a typical ethnic fraternal benefit insurance society, contributing to charitable and relief foundations in the United States and elsewhere, as well as looking after its own members and promoting Polish culture and traditions. An example of the scope of its good works was the establishment of a home for blind children in Laski, Poland.

Pontifical Orders of Knighthood

Chivalry—literally, noblemen soldiering on horses—originally had a strong religious connection. The Pope recognized several European orders and even became patron of some of them. With the slow disappearance of medieval courtliness and medieval battles, the term *knight* became more and more an honor, and less and less a description of military obligation: "Knights" were created who might or might not be called upon to fight. Originally, too, the word *order* meant much the same as a monastic *rule*, such as the Rule of St. Benedict, which was intended to govern the lives of those under it. But with the passage of time, *order* came to mean an organization or even the insignia and decorations of that organization.

The process of change can be clearly seen in the *Collegia Militum* (Colleges of Militia) founded by the papacy in the 16th century. All were short-lived, but they included the College of St. Peter (Leo X, 1520); the

College of St. Paul's Militiamen (Paul III, 1540); the Knights of the Lily (Paul III, 1546); the Pian Nights (Pius IV, 1559); and the Lauretan Knights (Sixtus V, 1586). The concept of a military order, fighting for Christendom, was preserved, but the reality grew further and further from mace and sword. It was the lack of direction that killed these orders.

By the late 18th or early 19th century, the military aspect had all but vanished, and abuses were rampant. Papal titles were handed out thoughtlessly, often by ecclesiastics or minor princelings, to whom the Pope had delegated the right to do so. The value of the titles was accordingly diminished. Pius VIII made an attempt at reform, not least by abolishing the most frequently— almost casually—awarded title, that of "count Palatine," but his success was limited.

Pope Gregory XVI effected real reforms in 1841 with *Cum hominem mentes,* reserving still more closely the right to bestow honors, and in 1905 Pope Pius X again reformed the whole field of Papal titles and ranks with the Apostolic Letter *Multum ad Excitandos.* Pius XII (1939–58) further reformed matters, including abolishing hereditary ennoblement, and led by example, cutting down the number of people on whom Pontifical Orders of Chivalry were bestowed. In 1966, Paul VI formalized many of these restrictions in *Equestres Ordines.* As a result of all these reforms, interest in (and respect for) pontifical orders has grown considerably.

In 1990, there were five Pontifical Orders of Knighthood extant. In order of seniority, they were the Supreme Order of Christ, the Order of the Golden Spur, the Order of Pius IX, the Order of St. Gregory the Great, and the Order of Pope St. Sylvester. All five are called "pontifical" because they are awarded by the Holy Father himself, *motu proprio,* or indirectly as a result of a request submitted via the Vatican Secretariat of State.

They are mentioned here (and detailed below) in order to provide a contrast with those self-styled "Orders of Knighthood," which are particularly popular in the United States and which are no more than clubs where the DEGREES are conferred by the peers of the "knight."

The Supreme Order of Christ

The Supreme Order of Christ was founded on August 14, 1318, as the Militia of Jesus Christ, by King Denis I of Portugal and his consort, Queen St. Isabella. The original aim of the order was the reconquest of Portugal and defense against the Moors, after the suppression of the TEMPLARS in 1312. A few months later, Pope John XXII approved the new order (March 14, 1319), gave it the rule of the Cistercians, and confirmed its endowment with some of the property of the Templars, as well as becoming its patron. It spread through Spain, France, Italy, and Germany, though the Pope always appointed the Portuguese sovereign as his administrator of the order in Portugal.

In 1499 it lost its monastic character, and in 1522 the *de facto* division of the order into a papal, religious order and a Portuguese civil order was recognized *de jure* by both parties. The religious order was widely conferred— so widely, after about 1789, that it became almost meaningless—while the civil order all but vanished. The papal order was, however, reformed in 1878 and again in 1905 (the latter by Pius X); a notable 19th-century recipient was Otto von Bismarck. In 1966, Paul VI decreed in *Equestres Ordines* that, henceforth, the order would be given only to Christian heads of state, and then only on extraordinary occasions when the pontiff would normally be present in person. It is the highest of the five Pontifical Orders of Knighthood and has only the one degree.

Golden Spur, Order of the

The origins of the Order of the Golden Spur, also known as the Order of the Golden Militia, are genuinely lost in the mists of antiquity. The order apparently predates the Crusades, and some believe that it dates back to the fourth century, when Pope St. Sylvester gave the Rule of St. Basilius to the Knights of the Emperor Constantine.

From the time of Pius IV (1559–65) to Benedict XIV (1740–58) the Order of the Golden Spur was normally bestowed together with the title of Count Palatine, a hereditary ennoblement, which had become honorary in the early 16th century and was conferred generously by both the Holy Father and the Holy Roman Empire. So widely was the title of Count Palatine available that it could even be conferred by papal legates, nuncios and patriarchs; by archbishops and bishops assistant at the papal throne; by the College of Abbreviators; and even by the occasional marquis and duke. In 1815, Pius VII abolished the title altogether, while continuing to bestow the Order of the Golden Spur.

In 1841, Gregory XVI reserved the power of conferment to the pontiff and changed the name of the order to the "Order of Pope St. Sylvester and of the Golden Militia." As with many of the other reforms introduced by Gregory XVI in *Cum hominem mentes,* October 31, 1841, Pius X made further changes with *Multum ad excitandos* in 1905: The Order of Pope St. Sylvester was separated and made an order in its own right, while the Order of the Golden Spur was renamed as the Order of the Golden Militia and placed under the patronage of the Blessed Virgin to mark the 50th anniversary of the proclamation of the Dogma of the Immaculate Conception.

There were to be a maximum of 100 knights, in a single degree, and the order was to be second only to the Supreme Order of Christ. After 1966 (Paul VI, *Equestres Ordines*), it was to be awarded only to heads of state and

Christian sovereigns—though previously it had been awarded to those prominent in the arts, including Wolfgang Amadeus Mozart, and to such non-Christian recipients as Amanullah, King of Afghanistan, who received the order in 1928. King Hussein of Jordan received the order in 1964.

Pius IX, Order of

The Pian Order has seen three manifestations. The first was founded by Pius IV in 1560 and did not long survive his death. The second was founded by Pius IX on June 17, 1847; it was unique among papal orders of knighthood since the Gregorian Reform in that it conferred hereditary nobility on its recipients. Then, in 1939, Pius XII made it a personal honor for life, removing hereditary nobility.

There are four orders or degrees: Knights Commander, Knights Commander with Star, Knights Grand Cross, and Gold Collar. The last is reserved for heads of state, while the others are bestowed for civil or religious merit. Both Catholics and non-Catholics are eligible.

St. Gregory the Great, Order of

The Order of St. Gregory the Great was founded on September 1, 1831, by Pope Gregory XVI as a means of honoring citizens of the Papal States. There were originally four orders, which were reduced to three in 1834. They are Knight Commander, Knight Commander with Star, and Knight Grand Cross; awards may be either civil or military. Today, these honors may be bestowed by the Holy Father upon citizens of any nation, for religious or civil merit. The order is even open to non-Catholics.

Pope St. Sylvester, Order of

The Order of Pope St. Sylvester, which ranks fifth among the Pontifical Orders of Knighthood, was instituted by Pope Gregory XVI on October 31, 1841. It was originally intended to absorb the Order of the Golden Spur, but it effectively remained separate; it owes its present form to Pius X, who revised it in 1905. It is used as a means of recognizing laymen who have distinguished themselves in religion, the professions, and the arts; it is named after Pope St. Sylvester (d. 335), who drew up the Nicene Creed. Catholics and non-Catholics alike may be honored.

There are three civil Orders or degrees, namely Knight, Knight Commander (with or without star), and Knight Grand Cross. There are no military orders.

Poor Conrads

The Poor Conrads, like the BUNDSCHUH, was a German peasants' society of the late 15th and early 16th centuries and contributed leaders and followers to the Peasants' War of 1524.

Poro

Poro is one of the WEST AFRICAN SECRET SOCIETIES and is of considerable antiquity, going back at least to the 16th century, based in what are now Liberia, Sierra Leone, and Guinea. It may or may not survive.

It furnishes an excellent example of a primitive secret society in which the initiation is really an ORDEAL, not a recital of symbolic or quasisymbolic oaths. Like many tribal secret societies, or many modern ones for that matter, it is open to all male members of a tribe. The initiation involves circumcision, along with other RITES OF PASSAGE, which mark the end of childhood and the acquisition of manly status. Girls, who are or were admitted to Sande, the female equivalent of Poro, were (or are) subjected to clitoridectomy. The boys were (or are) fed the excised clitorises and the girls, the removed foreskins.

Portuguese Continental Union of the United States of America

899 Boylston Street
Boston, MA 02115
(617) 536-2916

The Portuguese Continental Union of the United States of America was founded in 1925 as a fraternal benefit life insurance society for persons of Portuguese birth or descent (and later for individuals interested in Portuguese culture). There were 8,688 members in 1994.

The Portuguese Continental Union of the United States is a typical ethnic fraternal benefit society. The fraternal or benevolent side of its work includes sponsoring student exchange programs between Portugal and the United States, sponsoring nine scholarships per year for students of Portuguese descent, maintaining a library, and more.

Prevention of Calling Sleeping-Car Porters George, Society for the

Older readers will guess the origins of this society immediately; others will be puzzled. It owes its origin to the fact that George Mortimer Pullman (1831–97) founded the sleeping-car company that bore his name. Would-be wits therefore habitually addressed the porters on these cars as "Mr. Pullman," and, later, took to calling them "George."

The S.P.C.S.P.G. was founded around the time of World War I by a Chicago banker named George W. Dulany, Jr., who traveled frequently by train and grew understandably tired of this usage; he found himself looking around every time someone called "George! Oh George!" to attract the porter's attention. His diligent research proved that only 326 of 12,558 Pullman porters were actually named George, a mere 2.6 percent of the total. Most members of the S.P.C.S.P.G. were called George (first, middle, or last name), but exceptions were made for persons "actively sympathetic" to the cause.

In the 1930s, there were reportedly 30,000 members. As a formal organization, it is very probably extinct today.

The Process

The Process was founded in about 1966 in London as a religious/mystical secret society open to all. It is probably now extinct, though it apparently moved to Chicago in the mid-1970s, where it may yet survive.

Although The Process was apparently short-lived, it was briefly a very influential secret society. Its full name was the Process Church of the Final Judgement, and it was a curious blend of Manichaeism (see HERETICS), the ORDO TEMPLI ORIENTIS, and Scientology, assembled by a Robert de Grimstone and his wife Mary-Ann.

The basic thesis of the church was that equal reverence was due to three coequal deities: Jehovah, Satan, and Lucifer (the distinctions between the latter two were not always easy to understand). This is the Manichaean aspect of the order. The members of the Process were much given to sexual magic (see MAGIC AND SECRETS), which they preached in a number of books and in their elaborately produced magazine, which enjoyed wide circulation in rebellious circles. This magical aspect was derived from the Ordo Templi Orientis. Finally, The Process cloaked it all in a pseudoscientific or pseudopsychiatric language, and made a great deal of money by charging people to be "processed" and by appealing to admirers for yet more money. In this one may discern the influence of Scientology. (At least one student of cults, Dr. Christopher Evans, identifies The Process as a direct offshoot of scientology.)

To return to the deities, in the theology of The Process it did not matter much which of the three deities one followed. One could even choose more than one aspect. The important thing was to be wholehearted in one's devotion. Life is either black or white: failing to choose—becoming a gray by default—is the sole mortal sin of The Process. Members of The Process wore black trousers and black turtlenecks, usually devoid of ornament, though the Chicago group apparently added a red triangle (the symbol of The Process) to their uniform. The latter also devoted itself to worthy causes, such as raising money for sick children—something the British founders would never have done.

At first sight, The Process appears to have been fairly harmless—all talk, and no magic—but reports of more sinister attempts at Satanic ritual have surfaced.

Providence Association of Ukrainian Catholics in America

817 North Franklin Street
Philadelphia, PA 19123
(215) 627-4984

The Providence Association of Ukrainian Catholics in America was founded in 1912 as a fraternal benefit life insurance society for Catholics, especially those of Ukrainian ancestry. There were 17,927 members in 1994. The organization publishes the periodical *America*.

The Provident Association of Ukrainian Catholics in America is a typical ethnic fraternal insurance benefit society, with four stated objectives: moral, material, religious, and civic. The Association is strongly Ukrainian, and many of its publications are in the Ukrainian language.

Prudent Patricians of Pompeii of the USA

The name of this whites-only organization might lead one to suspect a spoof, if it were not for the fact that it was the first fraternal beneficiary society to be incorporated by an Act of Congress in 1897. The order issued sickness and death policies and an annuity plan. Any member who reached 70 years of age received an annual 10 percent of his (or her) certificates' face value, without paying any further ASSESSMENTS. The founders of this organization included ELKS, ODD FELLOWS, and members of the ROYAL ARCANUM. The head LODGE, or "Prothonotary," was in Saginaw, Michigan. No trace of the organization remains.

Pythagoreans

The ancient Greek philosopher Pythagoras (fl. 530 B.C.) is now remembered chiefly for his famous geometric theorem that the square of the hypotenuse is equal to the sum of the squares of the other two sides of a right triangle. His original followers were, however, essentially mystics, and were known as such. The big difference between the Pythagorean MYSTERIES and others was that doctrine and logic replaced direct experience of divine power. Of course, the doctrines that Pythagoras actually taught were kept secret by initiates. By combining intellectual inquiry with the traditional asceticism and food taboos of previous mystery sects, Pythagoras and his followers hoped to unravel the secrets of the universe. Various secret societies of medieval, Renaissance, and modern times have identified themselves as Pythagoreans.

Pythian Sisters, Supreme Temple Order

c/o Wenonah Jones
P.O. Box 1257
Anaconda, MT 59711
(406) 563-6433

The Pythian Sisters was founded in 1888 in Concord, New Hampshire, as the female auxiliary (see AUXILIARIES) of the KNIGHTS OF PYTHIAS. There were 22,000 members in 1994. The order publishes the *Pythian International* four times a year.

The Pythian Sisters was set up as a classic auxiliary, admitting women relatives of the Knights of Pythias provided they were over 16 years of age. However, the organization became divided over the admission of men. One faction wanted to admit only women, while the other wanted to include men after the fashion of the Order of the Eastern Star (see EASTERN STAR, ORDER OF THE). The faction that wanted to admit men split some time before 1894, becoming the Pythian Sisters of the World, but changed its name in that year to the Rathbone Sisters of the World. That faction is extinct, and the all-female Supreme Temple order remains.

The Sunshine Girls is the children's division.

Qaïrowan

This is a secret society that was or is active among the Tunisians and Berbers of Algeria, Tekna, Rio de Oro, and Senegal. It was allegedly founded by Ogbar-ben-Nagi in the first century A.D.; however, one Ben Aïssa, by whose name the society is sometimes known, was its most influential early leader.

Qaïrowan is an ascetic society, its members gaining merit by eschewing all fleshly comforts and pleasures that bar the way to spiritual purity. Members do not practice simply passive self-denial; they actively inflict pain on themselves, often in public displays. The object is to create indifference to physical suffering and thereby transcend it. Members recognize one another through passwords and pledge adherence to a stringent code of conduct, the violation of which entails severe penalties.

Membership in Qaïrowan is limited to men and is highly selective — so prestigious that the order maintains a long waiting list of those desiring admission.

Rainbow for Girls, Order of

P.O. Box 788
McAlester, OK 74501
(918) 423-1328

The Order of Rainbow for Girls was founded in 1922 in McAlester, Oklahoma as a fraternal and social club for girls, aged 13-20, related to members of Masonic lodges (see FREEMASONS) or to members of the Order of the Eastern Star (see EASTERN STAR, ORDER OF THE). It operates principally in the United States, but also in Australia, Canada, Guam, Mexico, and the Philippines. There were 1.1 million members in 1994.

The Order of Rainbow for Girls clearly illustrates the extent to which Christianity influences ADOPTIVE MASONRY. It was founded by a clergyman, the Reverend Mark W. Sexton, the RITUALS AND CEREMONIES are based on the ninth chapter of Genesis, and Sister Faith, one of the officers, advises candidates that "The Altar is the most sacred place in our Assembly Room. Upon it rests the Holy Bible, symbol of white light, from which we derive strength to sustain us through life." During the initiation ritual, the Bible is opened so that "its White Light may penetrate the heart of every member of this Assembly." A hymn entitled "Have Thine Own Way, Lord," is sung, and three girls are chosen to represent Faith, Hope, and Charity.

There are two DEGREES, the Initiatory and the Grand Cross of Color. The colors of the rainbow are said to symbolize life, religion, nature, immortality, fidelity, patriotism, and virtue, and to derive from the White Light of the Bible. Introducing a more worldly note, the

initiate is portrayed as traveling to find the pot of gold at the end of the rainbow, as she progresses around the seven stations that symbolize the colors and their attributes. At the station of Charity, she is shown a pot of gold, which also contains a Bible and a miniature lambskin Masonic apron. Reverting to Christianity, the Mother Advisor counsels the initiate to keep a Bible beside her bed at night, open to the ninth chapter of Genesis, which contains the story of the Flood, and the rainbow.

Randolph, P. B.

Paschal Beverly Randolph (1825-75) was a celebrated magician of his day. He was sometime head of the Fraternatis Rosae Crucis, one of the more magically inclined groups of the ROSICRUCIANS. He was also a great proponent of sexual magic (see MAGIC AND SECRETS).

Rebeccaites

The Rebeccaites was a secret society, formed about 1843 in Wales and dedicated to the goal of removing toll booths or toll gates from the turnpikes of the day. In this way it was similar to the Irish White-Boys, and, like them, performed its anti-toll gate activities at night while members were dressed in white. Also as with the White-Boys, the order was ultimately suppressed by the government.

The name is derived from Genesis 24:60: "And they blessed Rebekah, and said unto her . . . Let thy seed possess the gate of those which hate thee."

Rechabites

227 Rayleigh Road
Hutton, Brentwood CM13 1PJ
England

The Rechabites—variously the Order of Rechabites, the Sons and Daughters of Rechab, and so on—were founded on August 25, 1835 in Salford, near Manchester, England, as a fraternal benefit total-abstinence society. It now operates worldwide, and will admit anyone willing to "sign the pledge." The size of the order is no longer clear, and the Rechabites are apparently not centralized; however, the *Rechabite News* is published by Richard Barton at the above address.

In Cornwall, well into the second half of the 20th century, a common description of extreme intoxication was "as drunk as a Rechabite on the annual outing." Such is the irreverent Cornish sense of humor; for the Rechabites are a strict Temperance movement (see TEMPERANCE SOCIETIES).

The Rechabites were the archetypal temperance society; their influence, once so great and popular, has now greatly waned. In the first decade of the 20th century, the (American) Independent Order of Rechabites alone was only 10,000 short of a million members—though this seems high in view of the 220,000 figure for worldwide Rechabitism given by Stevens at the beginning of the century. Probably no one ever knew precisely how many Rechabites there were.

The Salford Unity of Rechabites was founded in 1835 by a small group of abstainers who wanted to form a fraternal benefit secret society. They called their first LODGE "Tent Ebenezer, No. 1," because the Sons of Jonadab, the sons of Rechab, were apparently instructed by the Almighty not only to abstain from wine but also to live in tents. There were soon Tents for male adults (over 16) and female adults (over 12); for boys, aged 12–16; and for children of both sexes aged from 5 to 12. All who could write were required to "sign the pledge," saying (among many other things) that they would "abstain from all intoxicating liquors except in religious ordinances, or when prescribed by a legally qualified medical practitioners during sickness which renders one incapable of following any employment." If you lived in a temperance town or village, you might well have signed the pledge a dozen times before you reached your majority.

The sick fund originally paid half a crown a week (about 60 cents) in return for one penny per week subscription (about two cents at the then exchange rate). The funeral fund was approximately 10 cents for a £5 ($24) benefit, and you could buy up to six shares in either. Later, a grade ASSESSMENT plan was adopted, but the teetotalers argued that their health record was better than that of the drinkers, and that they therefore represented better value because they paid out less in sickness benefits or for premature deaths.

In the United States, the Independent Order of Rechabites in North American fared poorly, while the Independent Order of Rechabites (without the North American qualifier) did very well. There was also the Encamped Knights of Rechab of North America, which seem to have had a negligible impact, except locally in small areas. At the end of the 19th century the Independent Order had a $100 funeral benefit.

The RITUALS AND CEREMONIES seem to have varied from place to place, but generally worked three DEGREES: Knight of Temperance, Knight of Fortitude, and Covenanted Knight of Justice. The ritual also had elements of the FREEMASONS, and the governing body, at least in England, was (and continues to be) the Movable Committee, which meets in different cities every two years.

In the United States, the Rechabites collapsed with the repeal of Prohibition, and in Britain, the order diminished in size and influence after World War II.

Red Eagles, Order of

This was a benevolent, protective, and patriotic society incorporated in Michigan by H. R. Caulfield in 1912, as an American reincarnation of a society of the same name founded in Germany in 1705. It seems no longer to exist, though it claimed 13,612 members in the early to mid-1920s.

Redemption of Russia, Association for the

The Association for the Redemption of Russia was a constitutionalist secret society founded in 1816 by three officers of the Imperial Guard. A year or two later, after its suppression, it reappeared as the UNION OF PUBLIC WELFARE.

Red Front Line Fighters

The Red Front Line Fighters was one of the many militarily and politically oriented secret societies that flourished in Germany after World War I. Its left-wing political sympathies may be deduced from its name. It was communist groups like this that Adolf Hitler's S.A. (*Sturmabteilung*) was formed to fight.

Red Men

4521 Speight Avenue
Waco, TX 76711-1708
(817) 756-1221

The precise date of foundation of the Red Men is debatable; the Improved Order was founded in Baltimore in 1834. It is a fraternal, social, insurance, and political society in the United States for men over 18 who profess belief in a Supreme Being. The organization publishes *Red Man* three times a year. There were 38,000 members in 1995.

There are or have been several varieties of Red Men,

all of whom were by tradition white; until recently, American Indians were banned from admission. The original Society of Red Men, now apparently extinct, was founded in Pennsylvania about 1813, but dissolved in disrepute because of a reputation for drunkenness among its members. The anti-Freemasonry sentiments caused by the Morgan Affair (see FREEMASONS) did nothing to improve the Red Men's standing in the community, and the Improved Order of Red Men appears to have been a completely new organization.

The Red Men itself claims that the organization was founded not in 1813 or 1834, but in 1765, and that it is the oldest secret society in the United States, a continuation of the SONS OF LIBERTY, who antedated the Revolutionary War. There is, however, no good evidence for this, though the present order does share some rituals and terms with such early American secret societies as the Sons of Liberty.

The stated aim of the Red Men is "to perpetuate the beautiful legends and traditions of a vanishing race and to keep alive its customs, ceremonies and philosophies." Despite this, the order's ethnology is more patronizing and eclectic than accurate. In the Improved Order, the "Sachem" declares at the beginning of each meeting,

> The primitive Red Men ever recognized a Supreme Being controlling the destiny of their Tribes. No important matter was ever undertaken without an invocation for its guidance and protection. We, as improved Red Men, wisely follow their example and imitate their reverence. Therefore, Brothers, you will now rise while our beloved Prophet invokes the Great Spirit on our behalf.

He then offers a prayer to the Great Spirit of the Universe. A formal lodge meeting is opened with the lighting of the Sacred Fire, and closes with its extinction.

"Tribes" meet in "Wigwams" (LODGES) to initiate "palefaces" in return for "wampum," and officers include the following (the tribal names in parentheses denote the origins of the terms):

Great Inchonee	Supreme head of the order
Sachem	Tribe head (Algonquian/Narraganset)
Prophet	"Religious" leader
Senior Sagamore	Lesser chief (Algonquian/Penobscott)
Junior Sagamore	Lesser chief (Algonquian/Penobscott)
Chief of Records	
Collector of Wampum	(Wampum is an Algonquian word)
Keeper of Wampum	

The months of the year are also given Indian or pseudo-Indian names, but they do not work according to a lunar calendar; instead, they correspond to regular Gregorian months. They are:

Cold Moon	January
Snow Moon	February
Worm Moon	March
Plant Moon	April
Flower Moon	May
Hot Moon	June
Buck Moon	July
Sturgeon Moon	August
Corn Moon	September
Traveling Moon	October
Beaver Moon	November
Hunting Moon	December

Rather astonishingly, the Improved Order of Red Men uses alongside the Gregorian calendar its own system of reckoning, based on the "discovery" of the Americas by Columbus in 1492; 1992 was, therefore, the year 500 of the I.O.R.M. calendar.

The RITUALS AND CEREMONIES are based on white perceptions of some northeastern Native American tribes, especially those of the Algonquian linguistic group. There are three DEGREES, Adoptive, Warrior, and Chief. There is also a noninitiatory Beneficiary Degree for insurance. The Adoption and Warrior degrees illustrate the order's line of thought. For the Adoption degree, a hunting expedition (made up of Wigwam members) has stopped for the night, when a lost paleface comes upon their camp. He is captured, taken back to the main encampment, and tied to a stake to be killed. At the instigation of the Prophet, the tribe changes its mind and adopts him into the tribe, giving him a new tribal name based on an animal or bird, or on some trait of character. He takes the following oath:

> I, [Name], being desirous of becoming acquainted with the mysteries of the Improved Order of Red Men, do hereby solemnly promise and declare, that I will keep secret from all persons, except such as I shall prove to be Improved Red Men, all signs, passwords, and other matters that are to be kept secret.
>
> And I do further promise, that I will never attempt to kindle a council fire unless I am duly and regularly authorized to do so, or assist or participate in any council the fire of which has been kindled by a suspended or expelled brother, or any other person not authorized by the Great Council of the United States to kindle the same.
>
> To all this I promise and pledge my sacred honor, without intending any evasion whatever. So help me the Great Spirit.

For the Warrior degree, the familiar Masonic touches are employed: The coat is removed and a blindfold is applied. The candidate carries a bow and arrow, and the ritual is based upon a meeting between him and a Junior Sagamore, who asks for a sign of recognition and then, later in the ceremony, hands him a bundle of arrows tied in a snakeskin. At the advice of his guide, the candidate spits upon the arrows and throws them at the Sagamore's feet. This is the signal for the Junior Sagamore to say

Warriors, behold! he hurls them from him in
Contempt. Seize him, and with
Your clubs beat out his forfeit life.
First bind him fast, and my faithful knife shall
Let forth the purple current from his veins
And dry it quickly up. Seize him, I say,
And let the unpitying torture rack his limbs.

Once again, he is tied to a stake, and the Junior Sagamore is about to drive the knife into his heart just as he "notices" a token, which the candidate has earlier received from the Sachem.

The third or Chief's degree is an adaptation of the HIRAM ABIF legend in Indian guise — including the use of a pipe of peace.

Apart from its customary fraternal activities, the I.O.R.M. espouses a right-wing conservative political agenda.

In 1935 there were apparently well over half a million Improved Red Men and Pocahontases. By 1965, the number had dropped below 85,000. The Degree of Pocahontas is the female auxiliary (see AUXILIARIES): the Degree of Hiawatha is for boys; and the Degree of Anona is for girls.

Red Youth Storm Troops

Hitler was not the only German to organize a private army of stormtroopers (see BROWN SHIRTS, FASCIST ORGANIZATIONS) in the 1920s. The communists had their own as well, and Germany was very close to civil war during the days of the Weimar republic.

Reindeer, Fraternal Order of

The Fraternal Order of Reindeer was clearly intended to lock antlers with the Moose (see MOOSE, INTERNATIONAL) and the ELKS in the membership stakes; but despite rosy predictions by the Supreme Secretary in 1920 and a membership of 40,000 in 1921, by July 1923, no trace of the order remained.

Resistants

The Resistants was a German secret society dedicated to the overthrow of Adolf Hitler. It was led by Ernst Nikisch, who was arrested before World War II and disappeared, presumably executed.

Rhigas, Associations of

In the wake of the French Revolution, a Professor Rhigas, a teacher of history, consolidated a number of secret societies into the HETAIRA, working from headquarters in Vienna and Trieste. The combined orders agitated for Greek independence from Turkey. Rhigas was captured by the Austrians and handed over to the Turks, who shot him in 1798.

Ribbonmen

The Ribbonmen movement was founded in Ireland in the late 18th century as a fraternal and religious — later, political — society for Catholic men.

The term "Ribbonmen" has been applied to a number of Irish political secret societies, including the DEFENDERS and White-Boys. Its tangled lineage also embraces the Brotherhood of Saint Patrick, the Ancient Order of HIBERNIANS, the Fenians, the IRISH REPUBLIC BROTHERHOOD and much else. The "ribbons" in question were two in number: green for Ireland, red for the blood of her enemies.

The origins of the Ribbonmen were much the same as for other Irish Catholic self-help organizations formed at the same time: principally, a reaction against the ORANGEMEN and Protestant oppression. In the words of the novelist William Carleton (1794–1869), "The truth, however, is, if there can be an apology for Ribbonism, that it was nothing more or less than a reactive principle against Orangeism, of whose outrages it was the result."

The Ribbonmen were probably founded in or near Belfast during the last decade of the 18th century, and spread thereafter into the rest of Ireland. About 1809, Ribbonmen were in Donegal, for example. By 1811, there was a Grand Lodge at Derry, with over 90 lodges affiliated and a total membership in excess of 20,000. Membership in the north of Ireland probably peaked in the 1810s and 1820s, though in the south it survived much longer, especially in Connaught, with 1855 as the peak year. Ribbonism was declared illegal by the Westmeath Act in 1871, but as late as 1896, an Irish author was still able to say, "Connaught was (as indeed I fear it still is) the headquarters of Ribbonism" (O'Leary, *Fenians and Fenianism*).

The OATH was a blend of the practical and the ideal and is particularly revelatory. Article 1, expressly pledging allegiance to the King, makes strange reading when compared with the final paragraph of the Oath:

I, [Name], with the sign of the Cross do declare and promise, in the name and through the assistance of the Blessed Trinity, that I will keep inviolate all secrets of this Fraternal Society from all but those whom I know to be regular members of the same, and bound by the same solemn oath and fraternal ties:-

1st I declare and profess without any compulsion, allegiance to his present Majesty, George the Third, King of Great Britain and Ireland.

2nd That I will be true to the principles of this Society, dedicated to St. Patrick, the Holy Patron of Ireland, in all things lawful and not otherwise.

3rd That I will duly and regularly attend on the shortest possible notice, at any hour, whether by night or by day, to perform without fail or inquiry, such commands as my superior or superiors may lay upon me, under whatever penalty he or they may inflict for neglecting the same.

4th   I will not deliberately or willingly provoke, challenge or strike any of my brothers, knowing him to be such. If he or they should be ill-spoken of, ill-used, or otherwise treated unjustly, I will, according to circumstances and the best of my judgement, espouse his cause, give him the earliest information, and aid him with my friendship when in distress as a Ribbonman.

5th   I also declare and promise, that I will not admit or propose a Protestant or heretic of any description as a member of our Fraternal Society, knowing him to be such.

6th   That whether in fair or market, town or country, I will always give the preference in dealing to those who are attached to our national cause, and that I will not deal with a Protestant or a heretic—but above all with an Orangeman—so long as I can deal with one of my own faith on equal terms.

7th   That I will not withdraw myself from the Society without stating my reasons for the same, and giving due notice to my superior or superiors; and that I will not without permission join any other society of different principles or denominations, under God's judgement, and whatever penalty may be inflicted on me—not including in these the Masonic Institution, Trade Societies, or the profession of soldier or sailor.

8th   That I will always aid a brother in distress or danger by my person, purse and counsel so far as in me lies; and that I will not refuse to subscribe money, according to my means, for the general or particular purposes of this our Fraternal Society.

9th   That I will not, under the penalty inflicted by my superiors, give evidence in any Court of Law or Justice against a brother, when prosecuted by an Orangeman or heretic; and that I will aid him in his defence by any means in my power.

10th   That when forced to take refuge from the law in the house of a brother or of any person friendly to our national cause, I will not have any improper intercourse or foul freedom with his sister, daughter, wife or cousin, and thus give cause of scandal to our Society.

Having made the above solemn declaration and promise of my own free will and accord, I swear true and real allegiance to the cause of Ireland only, and no longer to be true as a subject nor to bear allegiance to George the Third, King of Great Britain and Ireland; and I now pray that God may assist me in my endeavours to fulfil the same; that He may protect me and prosper our Society and grant us to live and die in a state of grace! Amen.

There were GRIPS and words of recognition, and the usual paraphernalia, but the oath makes clear that this was not (by the standards of most political secret societies) particularly militant. And that seems precisely to have been its undoing; for its very diffuseness makes it difficult to trace a clear "Ribbonmen" strand in Irish history. Some Ribbon lodges probably joined the Irish Republican Brotherhood wholesale, others piecemeal, while yet others moved in the direction of religious and charitable works, such as the Brotherhood of St. Patrick.

At any rate, the term "Ribbonism" is now dead and (mostly) forgotten, except by a few who wear the Orange or the Green. For the former, it is a catch-all pejorative; for the latter, a fond folk memory.

Right Boys

The Right Boys was one of the many Irish secret societies that have, through the years, sought to make Ireland an independent nation. It was apparently founded in the late 18th century, perhaps in 1787. It lasted for many years.

Rite of Swedenborg

The Rite of Swedenborg is one of the innumerable invented Rites of the FREEMASONS, and is noteworthy not because of the illusory nature of the RITUALS AND CEREMONIES, but because Swedenborg himself was not actually a Freemason (see SWEDENBORG AND SWEDEN BORGIANS). The Rite appears to have been devised in France in about 1760, along with the Rite of the Illuminati, by Antoine Joseph Pernetti, the theologian who codified much of Masonic practice. At the beginning of the 20th century, the rite may still have been worked in Sweden, but it seemed to be declining, and it is not clear whether it has since undergone any significant revival. It involved six DEGREES: Apprentice, Fellow-Craft, Master Neophyte, Illumined Theosophite, Blue Brother, and Red Brother.

Rites of Passage

A rite of passage is a ritual marking the transition from one stage of life to another; in many ways, it is similar to the initiation ritual of a secret society, and in primitive secret societies the two were often synonymous (see RITUALS AND CEREMONIES). The best-known rite of passage in modern life is the Bar Mitzvah of Jewish tradition, marking the transition from boy to man. Bat Mitzvah, the feminine equivalent, is increasingly popular as the outer bastions of Jewish patriarchy are eroded. The Christian confirmation is much the same sort of ceremony, while graduation from high school or university may be regarded as a secular right of passage.

Rituals and Ceremonies

At its simplest, a ritual is no more than a formalized way of doing something. For example, a wedding may be conducted in any number of ways, but most religions and most civil proceedings have accompanying rituals. There are typical marriage vows (akin to OATHS), and there are frequently physical rituals, such as the exchange of rings.

In the world of fraternal orders and secret societies, rituals are used for initiation and to mark progress from one rank, grade, or degree to the next. Always, the "outsider" nature of the new candidate is emphasized. The "shock of entry" of the FREEMASONS is more dignified and coherent than the role assigned to the novice in some other organizations, where he is frequently "condemned to death" (often in an imaginatively horrible way) before one of the other members of the organization moves that he be "spared." Once the candidate has been admitted and is a member of the lowest rank, this aspect of ritual is toned down considerably.

For examples of the well-treated "outsider," the Mystic Shrine treats candidates as "poor sons of the desert, who are weary of the hot sands and the burning sun on the plains and humbly crave shelter and the protecting dome of the Temple," while the Grand United Order of Wise Sons and Daughters of America represents them as "wandering candidates from the plains of Judea, who want to be admitted to the mystic circle."

For examples of the badly treated outsider, the Improved Order of RED MEN was all in favor of killing the intruder; the bloodthirsty HOMESTEADERS wanted to tie him to the back of a horse, with burning brands tied to its heels; and the Ancient Order of FORESTERS are after hanging him.

Ceremonies are much the same as rituals; the distinction is made here largely for ease of description and to provide a way of distinguishing between rituals normally associated with lodge work and degrees, and ceremonies for special occasions, such as the dedication of a new temple, the installation of officers, the death of a member, and so on.

Types of Ritual

Rituals may be religious, patriotic, neutral, or dramatized. Many also incorporate elements of parody.

Religious rituals normally call for holy oaths sworn to help one another and to preserve the secrets of the order. In the organizations covered in this book, the most usual religion is Christianity. From time to time, various churches have forbidden their members to join specified organizations because the oath sworn does not fit in with the church's ideas of religious propriety. For example, there have been repeated papal bulls forbidding Roman Catholics to become Freemasons, and the Missouri Synod of the Lutherans in America has taken it upon itself to pronounce upon the acceptability of various organizations from a Protestant point of view.

Many religious rituals are not tied to any specific sect, but are based on a belief in a supreme being—so-called "DEISM." Freemasonry is one such; the Benevolent and Protective Order of ELKS is another. Buddhists and others who deny or are unsure about the existence of a supreme being are therefore prevented by their consciences from joining such organizations, unless they also deny the efficacy of oaths.

Patriotic rituals usually involve national flags and pledges of allegiance. These are very popular among American organizations. In the rituals of many organizations, patriotic and religious elements are combined.

"Neutral" rituals are arguably not rituals at all; for example, the swearing-in of a bank president would not normally be called a ritual. Even so, a number of organizations in this book say that their rituals are no more than consistent with the dignified and orderly induction of members and swearing-in of officers.

Dramatized rituals typically involve the candidate in a playlet, drawn from the Bible, from legend, or from the more or less fertile imagination of the person who devised the ritual. Typically, the candidate has to undertake some sort of symbolic journey—rescuing a pioneer's wife and daughter in the Homesteaders, or traveling the "rough and rugged" road to Jerusalem in Royal Arch Freemasonry (see ROYAL ARCH MASONRY, GENERAL GRAND CHAPTER OF). The "journey" is, of course, made around the lodge room; the candidate may or may not be blindfolded ("hoodwinked") for some or all of the journey.

Rough-house rituals—"hazing," or a special case of dramatization—are less common than they were, but a typical example is the "Ritual by Red-Hot Iron" practiced by a number of organizations in the past and possibly surviving to this day. The candidate is shown a red-hot poker, then blindfolded. An ice cube is then touched to his bare buttock. In September 1989, an association of college fraternities made a statement condemning hazing, in which candidates have been injured, sometimes seriously, or even killed (see COLLEGE FRATERNITIES AND SORORITIES).

Rituals with elements of parody usually mock either the solemnity of other orders or the Islamic religion; the extent to which the latter is parodied in the various "Arabic" or fez-wearing organizations is extraordinary.

Form of Rituals

Often, coffins, skeletons, skulls, and other types of *memento mori* are employed as part of initiation ceremonies. One view is that these props are to emphasize the primitive secret societies' concepts of being "born again" into the organization. Another is that the psychology is akin to that of small boys playing with unusual or repulsive objects for their imagined shock value. The shock value of having the point of a sword laid on your bare chest can also be considerable.

Normally, each degree (see DEGREES) conveys certain secrets and obligations upon the initiate, and, as token of these, he is taught a new password and often a new grip (see GRIPS). There may also be symbols that relate to the degree. If there are, they will be explained.

Each degree is usually sealed with an oath not to reveal the secrets, passwords, grips, and so forth. These oaths are not always taken too seriously, as witness the fact that most rituals have at one time or another been published either in part or in full; indeed, some organizations (such as the KNIGHTS OF PYTHIAS) have actually committed their ritual to book form.

The exact wording of the ritual varies and is usually based either on Masonic practice or upon whatever took the founders fancy. The story of Damon and Phintias, and the legends of Robin Hood and his Merrie Men, are but two examples. Often, the rituals are larded with fake archaisms and grammatical solecisms such as "thou doeth" for "thou dost."

The Purpose of Ritual

Rituals are designed to reinforce a sense of "belonging." To the initiate, the ritual is something new and out-of-the ordinary; it therefore helps impress on him (or her) the nature of the organization, the benefits and obligations of membership, and so forth. This is true whether the initiation is into the lowest grade of the organization or into the higher ranks, grades, or degrees. In many primitive societies, initiation rituals are bound up with the infliction of physical pain, such as circumcision or clitoridectomy—a powerful reinforcement of whatever tribal secrets are imparted at the same time; see ORDEALS. To the established member, ritual is a reminder that he or she is one of a privileged club.

To some extent, the clearer the objectives of an organization are, the less need there is of ritual. Thus the LIONS INTERNATIONAL has no real ritual, while some mystical organizations have very little else.

Ceremonies

When a new LODGE is dedicated, there is normally a ceremony to mark the event. For example, in San Antonio, Texas, the WOODMEN of the World dedicated a chapel in 1931. No fewer than eight local ministers presided, after which various officers placed the symbolic tools of the order on or beside the "Stump," the Woodmen's altar.

Installation ceremonies are more common. Normally, the various officers (who may be legion) are called forth individually by the principal officer, who delivers a short homily on their responsibilities, sometimes with a question-and-answer session.

Many organizations also have a funeral ceremony, which may be conducted at the graveside (or crematorium) or may be held separately in the lodge or even in the home of the deceased member, after the interment or cremation. Normally, the burial ceremony is a mixture of militarism, grips, and signals. For example, the Independent Order of Foresters specifies that if the dead man is a Royal Forester, the pall bearers must also be Royal Foresters. The pall bearers create an "arch of steel" over the grave with their swords, while the others adopt the "burial attitude," with their left hands over their hearts and their left feet slightly ahead of their right feet. This is maintained until the end of the funeral oration. If the dead man is not a Royal Forester, but merely an ordinary one, the pall bearers stand with their upper right arms at right angles to their bodies, and their forearms bent upwards so that the index finger points at the sky (the other fingers are curled). After the oration, the dead man's fellows circle the grave and throw in sprigs of evergreen (a common symbol of the afterlife in many religions and in Freemasonry), then re-form the "arch of steel," but tapping their swords together nine times, in three groups of three taps. Then comes the "circle of concord," with everyone crossing his arms in front of him, grasping his neighbor's hands, and raising the linked hands in the air.

Some organizations may also have memorial ceremonies, which are more restrained and normally cover all deceased lodge members. The Foresters apparently favored the second Sunday in October for this event.

Roberts, J. M.

J. M. Roberts wrote an excellent book titled *The Mythology of the Secret Societies* (London: Secker and Warburg, 1972), in which he addresses not the *actual* history and influence of the secret societies, but rather their *perceived* history and influence. His thesis is that for about a century and a half, from the middle of the 18th century to the end of the 19th, many—perhaps most—intelligent and rational people believed that secret societies were enormously powerful.

> What seems to be worth considering is the possibility that there exists always a readiness and perhaps even a need among many men to take a distorted, even paranoiac view of society, and that this is intensified at moments of great stress, though it may be impossible to delineate and measure it by historical methods.

Roberts, Marie

Marie Roberts wrote *British Poets and Secret Societies* (London: Croom Helm, n.d. [perhaps 1980s]). The title is self-explanatory, though the author deals with only a few poets: Christopher Smart (1722–71), Robert Burns (1759–96), Percy Bysshe Shelley (1792–1822), Rudyard Kipling (1865–1936), and William Butler Yeats (1865–1939). The book shows how various secret societies influenced these eminent figures, especially the FREEMASONS but also the ILLUMINATI, the ROSICRUCIANS and the Hermetic Order of the Golden Dawn (see GOLDEN DAWN, HERMETIC ORDER OF THE).

Rochester Brotherhood

The Rochester Brotherhood is a long-defunct religious, mystical society founded in Rochester, New York, in 1887, with the thesis that "the Perfect Man is the anthropomorphic God." It adopted as its symbol a triangle with R.B. in the center, L.L. at the upper point, S.S. at the left, and K.D. at the right, signifying "Live the

Life," "Search the *Scriptures*," and "*Know* the *Doctrine*." Membership was always small.

Roman Catholic Apostolic Congregation

The Roman Catholic Apostolic Congregation was an early 19th-century Italian secret society dedicated to the freedom of Italy, under Catholic rule. The order was contemporaneous with the CARBONARI, but both its goals and composition were very different, since the Carbonari were rationalists, at best indifferent to Catholicism. The order was formed at the turn of the 18th century when Pope Pius VII was being held prisoner by the forces of Napoleon (1799). Members wore a yellow ribbon with five knots, and while those initiated into the higher degrees occupied themselves with discussing the independence of their nation, those in the lower degrees were ignorant of the order's secrets and were concerned chiefly with charitable works. Lodges were composed of five members each. The password was "Eleutheria," and the secret word "Ode."

Rosheniah

The Rosheniah was founded in the 17th century by Bayezid Ansari, the son of Abdullah, a leader of the tribe of Vurmud in Afghanistan. Bayezid became attracted to the sect of the Ishmaelites and began proselytizing on their behalf among the Afghans of Gharihel. He developed the Rosheniah as an Ishmaelite secret society composed of eight degrees and attracted to it Afghans, Hindus, and Persians. Those followers who attained the eighth degree Bayezid declared perfected, telling them that they were beyond all prohibition and laws. With these individuals, Bayezid retreated into the mountains of Afghanistan, plundering merchants, extorting tribute money, and generally propagating his religious doctrine by force and coercion. Bayezid advised members that they had the right to dispose of the lives and property of any and all nonmembers as they saw fit. The Rosheniah attracted many female adherents, whom Bayezid employed to seduce potential members. Among the higher degrees of the Rosheniah, men and women engaged in what one chronicler calls "promiscuous assemblies."

After the Rosheniah was well established, Bayezid founded a city, Pir Roshan (meaning "Father of Light") in the Hashtnagar district of Afghanistan. From this base, Bayezid conceived plans of deliberate conquest. A Moghul government official, Mahsan Khan Ghazi, at one point took Bayezid into custody, bringing him to the capital city of Kabul, publicly humiliating him by exhibiting him with his hair shaven on one side only. Through means of bribery, however, Bayezid obtained his release and embarked on an expedition to conquer Khorasan and Hindustan, only to be checked in battle by Mahsan Khan Ghazi. Bayezid escaped capture, but died of exhaustion.

Bayezid's followers elevated his son, Omar, to leadership, but he was almost immediately killed in battle with the Yusefzei tribe, along with three of his four brothers. The remaining brother was killed soon after this battle, and leadership fell to his son, Ahdad, who died in battle about 1650. A succession of leaders followed, all of them short-lived. The last, Allah-da-Khani, died about 1730, and, with him, the Rosheniah ceased to exist.

Rosicrucians

The Rosicrucians are one of the most mysterious of all the major secret societies, at least in origin. When the public was first apprised of their existence—through the publication of the *Fama Fraternatis of the Meritorious Order of the Rosy Cross* in Germany in 1614—several leading savants, including René Descartes, came to the conclusion that there was no such order of brotherhood at all; the *Fama Fraternatis* was an intellectual manifesto, an attempt to start a society, even an elaborate hoax. The Rosicrucians still exist today, though the link between them and the original order is tenuous, at least in the eyes of non-Rosicrucians.

The Christian symbolism of the cross is well known, but it also symbolizes other things in other cultures. To alchemists, it denotes the four elements; in alchemical writing, it was sometimes the symbol for light; in Hinduism, it is the sign of creation. The rose is an Egyptian symbol of rebirth (see also ANKH); an attribute of the Hindu goddess Lakshmi; and a part of the Rosalia festivals associated with Dionysus, who was an important patron of the MYSTERIES at ELEUSIS. To this day, we use the expression "sub rosa" ("under the rose") to convey that what is said is secret, or at least, "off the record." (Indeed, the rose as such may not be involved in Rosicrucianism at all; dew—*ros* in Latin—was considered by alchemists to be a more powerful solvent than ordinary water.)

In all probability, the first stirrings of Rosicrucianism were a part of the same unrest that gave rise to the Renaissance; but instead of searching primarily in Greek and Roman sources, the forebears of the Rosicrucians went back to Near Eastern sources, the Jewish KABBALAH and the works attributed to HERMES TRISMEGISTUS. Increased awareness of Byzantium and the Arab world, dating back to the Crusades, had spurred learning; people were searching for the secrets of the universe wherever they might find them, blending many traditions, mysteries, sciences, and pseudosciences in a way that has its parallel in the "New Age" pursuits of the late 20th century. These two streams of thought, which might be called the Classical and the Semitic, probably came together in individuals as early as the 14th century, but it was not until the 15th century that there were enough people familiar with both traditions to start what seems to be the origins of Rosicrucianism. Paracelsus (1493–1541) was one such person.

The *Fama Fraternatis* itself traces the foundation of Rosicrucianism to Christian Rosenkreutz (1378–1484), which is considerably more recent than many modern Rosicrucians would claim—although Rosenkreutz himself was said to have studied ancient secrets in Damascus, Fez, and other places. There is more than a little doubt as to whether he ever actually existed; he may have been provided as a ready-made mythology to help start the Rosicrucians. The *Confessio Fraternatis Rosae Crucis* followed the *Fama Fraternatis* in 1615, and *The Chemical Wedding of Christian Rosenkreutz* was written in 1616. The latter is an elaborate allegory by Johann Valentin Andrea (1586–1654)—so elaborate, in fact, that some suspect it of being a parody, though others believe that Andrea was one of the authors of the *Fama Fraternatis* and, therefore, one of the founders of Rosicrucianism.

Various 17th-century individuals held themselves out as Rosicrucians and published Rosicrucian works: Robert Fludd (*A Compendious Apology for the Fraternity of the Rosy Cross, Pelted with the Mire of Suspicion and Infamy, but now Cleansed and Purged as by the Waters of Truth*, 1617?); Michael Maier (*Themis Aurea*, 1618); Irenaeus Agnostus (*Epitimia Fraternis Rosae Crucis*, 1619). Also, there were the anonymous posters, which appeared in the streets of Paris in August 1623, proclaiming, "We, deputies of the principle College of the Brethren of the Rosy Cross, are staying visibly and invisibly in this town by the Grace of the Most High, to whom the heart of the Just turns. We show and teach without books or masks how to speak the language of every country where we wish to be, to bring our fellow men out of the error of death." There were many, many more publications until about 1630, when general interest waned almost as sharply as it had begun. Many of the books, manifestos, and proclamations contradicted one another, and it is safe to say that even if there is (or was) an apostolic or even written teaching lineage among the Rosicrucians, not all of those who purported to belong to the brotherhood are likely to have been initiates.

According to Rosicrucian theory, the movement operates in 108-year cycles, alternating action and inaction. If we date these eras from the *Fama Fraternatis*, we therefore find 1614–1722, active; 1730–1838, secret; 1838–1946, active; 1948–2056, secret. This does not coincide well with the observed activities of the brotherhood, however, nor does any other 108-year cycle (unless calculated by someone within the Rosicrucians).

Throughout the 18th century, constitutions and sets of rules for the brotherhood were published, mostly in Germany, and groups were also active elsewhere. Catherine the Great suppressed the Russian orders, and they were also suppressed in Austria during the late 18th century. It seems, though, that these groups were little above the SHRINERS in the transmission of ancient wisdom, and akin to the modern FREEMASONS as a social/

fraternal organization with mystical overlays. They may have exercised some influence on the form of modern Freemasonry, as witness some of the degrees of that society. They were also connected with the ILLUMINATI.

The organized lodges of the 18th century had elaborate rituals of admission. There were many symbols, including a glass globe standing on a pedestal of seven steps and divided into two parts, representing light and darkness; three candelabra, placed triangularly; nine glasses, symbolizing male and female properties, the quintessence, and various other things; a brazier; a circle; and a napkin. The postulate faced the usual symbolic death-and-rebirth initiation procedure, and he agreed to support his brethren and lead a virtuous life.

In the later 19th century, the Rosicrucians experienced a considerable revival, but it was mostly in the form of groups that were unable to agree completely concerning the fundamental teachings of the brotherhood. ELIPHAS LEVI laid the groundwork for some, including his own Kabbalistic Order of the Rosy Cross (see the following) as well as the Hermetic Order of the Golden Dawn (see GOLDEN DAWN, HERMETIC ORDER OF). The roots of the THEOSOPHICAL SOCIETY, as defined by Madame Blavatsky (see BLAVATSKY, HELENA PETROVNA), grew in the same soil.

The organizations that follow are the principal Rosicrucian bodies still extant, though others may claim Rosicrucian ancestry. See also FREEMASONS for an account of Masonic Rosicrucian degrees.

A.M.O.R.C.

1342 Naglee Avenue, Rosicrucian Park, San Jose, California 95191; (408) 287-9171

The Ancient Mystical Order Rosae Crucis (almost always known as A.M.O.R.C. or just AMORC) was founded in 1915 in New York City. It is international, but operates principally in the United States and is open to all ages and both sexes. There were 120,000 members in the United States in 1994, maybe a total of 250,000 worldwide.

The large, modern American Rosicrucian movement of the A.M.O.R.C. sprang from the Kabbalistic Order of the Rosy Cross (see the following). The Ancient Mystical Order Rosae Crusis was founded in 1915 by H. Spencer Lewis, a New York advertising man who had become a Rosicrucian in Paris in 1909 (and the organization also gives this as the date of its founding). At first, the organization led a peripatetic existence, with headquarters in New York, then in San Francisco, then in Tampa, and then in San Jose, California, where it remains to this day. It describes itself as "the world's oldest fraternal organization" (similar claims are made by a number of secret societies).

When Lewis died in 1939, his son Ralph succeeded him as "Supreme Autocratic Authority," and "Imperator for North, Central and South America, the British Commonwealth and Empire, France, Switzerland,

Sweden and Africa." He died in 1987 and was replaced by Gary L. Stewart. The president as of 1995 was Kristie Knutson.

Elements of Buddhism, Cabalism, Christianity, Gnosticism, Hinduism, Masonry, Odd Fellowship, general pantheism, Theosophy, and vegetarianism are all present in the A.M.O.R.C. Among the "hundreds of fascinating subjects taught and thoroughly explained" is a "Discourse on Experiments in Creating Life out of Nonliving Matter." "Experiments on Thought Transmission" and "The Human Aura and its Vibratory Effect" are other topics similarly treated. Reincarnation is part of A.M.O.R.C. doctrine, and, on rising, the A.M.O.R.C. Rosicrucian faces east, takes seven deep breaths, and drinks a glass of water.

The A.M.O.R.C. advertises in many periodicals. Those who answer the advertisement receive a booklet promising to tell one how to change one's life. Spencer Lewis's *Rosicrucian Questions and Answers* presents a history stretching back for thousands of years to the GREAT WHITE LODGE of Egypt in the XVIII Dynasty—though the precise date when the brotherhood became Rosicrucians is by no means made clear.

Joining A.M.O.R.C. involves no oaths incompatible with Roman Catholicism or any other religion or sect. There are Lodges, where lectures are given and initiations performed, but home study is also possible; an hour to an hour and a half a week is recommended.

In the Lodge, a Master is seated at one end on a triangular dais; at the other end is his female counterpart, the Mater, while a Vestal Virgin sits before the Master and guards the Sacred Fire, which is used to light incense. The Vestal Virgin is an unmarried girl between 18 and 21. Between the Master and the Mater, in the center of the room, is the Sacred Triangle or Shekinah; the members line the walls along the sides, wearing aprons, which have a distinctly Masonic look to them.

In addition to home study (sometimes referred to as "The Lodge at Home") and convocations in a Lodge, local meetings are held at a "Pronaos." The word comes from the Greek (and not the Egyptian, as many Rosicrucians believe) and refers to the space in front of a temple, enclosed by the walls or colonnade, a sort of portico. Sexual differentiation of roles is less clear-cut in the Pronaos than in the Lodge; the Master may be a woman.

At the Vernal Equinox, the "fraters" and "sorors" eat corn and salt and drink grape juice, while at the Autumnal Equinox they hold their Outdoor Fete. This, like other aspects of the A.M.O.R.C. ritual, is almost entirely non-Christian (see RITUALS AND CEREMONIES).

Initiations for the first three DEGREES (beginning with the First Portal) can be administered by correspondence course. The candidate studies for six weeks. Subjects include "the mysteries of time and space; the human consciousness; the nature of matter; perfecting the phys-ical body; the effect of light, color and sound upon the mind and body; the ancient philosophies; development of will; human emotions and instincts; and the phenomena of intuition." The A.M.O.R.C. reckons its teachings are accessible to "anyone able to read and understand his daily newspaper."

Armed with a knowledge of the mysteries, the candidate sets up an altar in his home; darkens the room; and lights two candles, one after the other, to the accompaniment of incantations. The first candle, for instance, is lit with the prayer, "Blessed Light, Symbol of the Greater Light, cast thy rays in the midst of darkness and illuminate my path." The candles are also extinguished in turn, to the accompaniment of further incantations. The initiation is complete when the candidate extinguishes the second candle and says, "Into physical darkness do I walk and move and have material expression, but the Greater Light dwelleth now within." He then signs and returns the Great Oath, which binds him to secrecy.

Further study leads to the second and third degrees; each is more time-consuming than the last, and the third contains such passages as, "The divine essence which I breathe into my body brings with it an influx of the Soul of God; and I likewise breathe out of my body the exhausted essence which has given me life and maintained the Soul in my body. All evil influence surrounding my soul and contaminating my body went forth from my body with the passing of the exhausted and devitalized breath. With the newer breath, the sweet and holy air, I took into my body the purer essence, which is Divine and is God." This is the mystical part. The "scientific" part contains such passages as, "From a chemical or elemental viewpoint, water is composed of two kinds of atoms: those which manifest the nature of hydrogen and those which manifest the nature of oxygen. Therefore, water is a dual principal, and as such is truly in sympathy with the other principals, as we shall learn. . . ."

The oath is administered by copying. After copying each seventh word, the candidate stops and repeats the word seven times while looking in the mirror: "I shall strive forever to deserve the approbation of all good Souls on earth and to serve God silently and peacefully, not in fear of the future made, but in consideration of an unmade future, a realm for my greater development. So mote it be." "So mote it be" is a common usage among Freemasons, where an ordinary Christian would normally say, "Amen."

The nine temple degrees, which are available to the third-degree initiate, are slightly less widely publicized. Some Rosicrucians report that there are possibly more degrees.

In addition to monographs (teaching pamphlets), the A.M.O.R.C. subscriber also receives *The Rosicrucian*, which contains articles of a general, popular nature. Also available to members are Rosicrucian marriage ceremonies (to be held within three days of a civil ceremony); a Rosicrucian "Rite of Appellation," which replaces baptism for those under 18 months old; and funeral rites, in which the color of mourning is purple.

Despite A.M.O.R.C.'s claims to coexistence with all creeds and religions, established churches frown on the A.M.O.R.C., and it is proscribed by any church that proscribes any organization. Nor is A.M.O.R.C. the only version of Rosicrucianism presently available.

Rosicrucian Fraternity

Beverly Hall, P.O. Box 220, Quakertown, PA 18951; (215) 536-5168

The Rosicrucian Fraternity was founded in 1858, but no membership figures are available. It maintains a library of 10,000 "arcane books." Also known as the Fraternitas Rosae Crucis, it calls itself the United States descendant of the Rosicrucian Fraternity founded in Germany in 1614.

Kabbalistic Order of the Rosy Cross

The Kabbalistic Order of the Rosy Cross was founded in France in 1889. Its principal interest seems to have been in forming a Catholic version of Freemasonry, despite the Lutheran origins of Rosicrucianism itself. The order had a strong magical component (see also MAGIC AND SECRETS) in addition to the study of Cabalism and the Hermetic tradition, but it soon degenerated into a power struggle between strong-willed eccentrics. Joseph Peladan, a founder-member, expelled a number of other members, resulting in two moribund branches. Both lingered on well into the 20th century.

Rotary International

1 Rotary Center
1560 Sherman Avenue
Evanston, IL 60201
(708) 866-3000; fax, (708) 328-8554

A "Rotary Club" was founded in Chicago in 1905 by a group of four men: an attorney, a coal merchant, a mining operator, and a tailor. Because their organization originally met in rotation at each of their places of business, they dubbed the club Rotary. In 1908, a second Rotary Club was established in San Francisco, and more quickly followed. In 1910, the organization called itself the National Association of Rotary Clubs, and two years later it became the International Association of Rotary Clubs. Today, it is Rotary International, with clubs in every U.S. state and 172 countries. In 1995, its membership stood at 1,125,050.

Originally, Rotary was founded "to encourage and foster high ethical standards in business and professions" and to encourage the "ideal of service as the basis of all worthy enterprise." Today, the organization's objectives have been expanded to encompass the promotion of "international understanding, goodwill, and peace." While Rotarians support many community-oriented social projects and programs, also financing a scholarship program and public health programs such as polio immunization, the organization also functions as a *de facto* common ground for business people to meet, interact, and (presumably) create profitable relationships and generate opportunities.

Round Table

The "Round Table" has been used as a symbol for a number of organizations, but one of the more intriguing is the society allegedly founded by Cecil Rhodes, imperialist founder of Rhodesia. Rhodes is said to have been a disciple of John Ruskin at Oxford, himself reputedly a student of the ILLUMINATI. In Rhodes' will, he allegedly instructed Lor Rothschild to continue the work of the Round Table, the organization and structure of which were modeled upon that of the JESUITS and the FREEMASONS.

The basic premise was that, since Britain was better at ruling than anyone else, the British should rule the entire world. After World War I, the Round Table sought to extend its political influence on an international scale, and looked to the United States, including followers there to found a counterorganization to the League of Nations, the COUNCIL FOR FOREIGN RELATIONS, which corresponded to the ROYAL INSTITUTE OF INTERNATIONAL AFFAIRS in Britain. Thereafter, the Round Table may have ceased to exist, or it may have played a diminished role, or it may have continued to pull the strings of new organizations, becoming so secret that not even conspiracy theorists could ferret it out.

Royal

The word "Royal," like the words "Knight" and "Grand," exerts a peculiar fascination over the members of secret societies. This is especially true in republican lands, where there are no restrictions on the promiscuous use of the word, and where it carries no connotations of actually being associated with genuine royalty. The following is a comprehensive sample of "royal" coinages found in Freemasonry:

ROYAL AND SELECT MASTERS, INTERNATIONAL GENERAL COUNCIL OF
Royal Arch, Ancient
Royal Arch Badge
Royal Arch Banners
Royal Arch Captain
Royal Arch Clothing
Royal Arch Colors
Royal Arch Degree

Royal Arch, Grand
Royal Arch Grand Bodies in America
Royal Arch Jewel
Royal Arch Masonry (see ROYAL ARCH MASONS, GEN-
    ERAL GRAND CHAPTER OF)
Royal Arch Masonry, Massachusetts
Royal Arch of Enoch
Royal Arch of Solomon
Royal Arch of Zerubbabel
Royal Arch Robes
Royal Arch Tracing-Board
Royal Arch Word
Royal Arch Working-Tools
Royal Ark Mariners
Royal Art
Royal Ax
Royal Lodge
Royal Master
Royal Order of Scotland (see SCOTLAND, ROYAL ORDER
    OF)
Royal Priest
Royal Secret, Sublime Prince of the

Royal and Select Masters, International General Council of

This order of FREEMASONS is purely American; it was invented in June 1872 in New York City and is a part of the YORK RITE. It controls the three Cryptic DEGREES of Royal Master, Select Master, and Super-Excellent Master, and is headed by a Most Puissant Grand Master.

Royal Arcanum, Supreme Council of the

P.O. Box 392
Boston, MA 02101
(617) 426-4135

The Royal Arcanum is neither royal nor arcane; it is a fraternal benefit life insurance company founded in Massachusetts in 1877, and which still boasted 28,111 members in 1994. It publishes the *Royal Arcanum Bulletin* bimonthly.

The milk-and-water oath (see OATHS) of the Royal Arcanum carried the penalty that if it were broken, the members should be expelled from the fraternity. The Royal Arcanum is a tribute to the extraordinary predilection of 19th-century Americans for pasting all manner of curious rituals and restrictions upon an insurance organization. Members had to believe in a Supreme Being, and "Mongolians, whether of pure or of mixed blood, no matter what they believe, are ineligible." Today, this and other restrictions have been removed.

The present size of the Arcanum is almost 100,000 members smaller than it was its heyday of the early 1920s.

The Loyal Ladies of the Royal Arcanum is the female auxiliary (see AUXILIARIES), founded in 1909 and formally recognized by men in 1923.

Royal Arch Masonry, General Grand Chapter of

P.O. Box 489
Danville, KY 40423-0489
(606) 236-0757

Royal Arch Masonry is nearly as old as organized Accepted Freemasonry, established in the United Kingdom in the early to mid-18th century and brought to the United States in 1797, where it mainly flourishes. Any Master Mason may join, and there were some 295,000 Royal Arch Masons in 3,000 United States chapters alone in 1994. The order publishes the *Royal Arch Advance* and *Royal Arch Mason Magazine,* both quarterly; and the *Directory of Royal Arch Chapters,* every eight to 10 nears.

Royal Arch Masonry is part of the YORK RITE super-structure of Freemasonry and probably dates from about 1740, when the Craft was a veritable boom industry and innumerable people were inventing, "discovering," "reviving," and otherwise popularizing new DEGREES. The Chapter Degrees that constitute the Royal Arch as administered by the (American) International Grand Chapter are Mark Master Mason, Past Master Mason, Most Excellent Master Mason, and Royal Arch Mason.

Royal Fellows of Bagdad

The Royal Fellows of Bagdad were no relation to the BAGMEN OF BAGDAD, but rather were an organization of liquor salesmen, established in 1914 to lobby against license laws prohibiting the sale of intoxicating drinks on Sunday. It is unlikely that the organization survived Prohibition.

Royal League

The Royal League was founded in Chicago in 1883 as an offshoot of the ROYAL ARCANUM, as a fraternal benefit organization with a social aspect. It is chiefly noteworthy for being the first fraternal society to open a sanatorium, in Black Mountain, North Carolina. In 1923, it was on such shaky ground financially (despite having 22,000 benefit and social members) that all members were assessed $1 in an attempt to refill the coffers; those who brought in a new member were excused the levy. The stratagem presumably worked. In 1932 it absorbed the Order of MUTUAL PROTECTION, and in 1970 it merged with the EQUITABLE RESERVE ASSOCIATION.

Membership was originally open to white males only, with white females joining the Ladies of the Royal League. Local units were "Councils," state groups were "Advisory Councils," and the national headquarters in Chicago was the "Supreme Council."

Royal Institute of International Affairs

10 St. James Square
London, SW1Y 4LE
(071) 957-5700; fax (071) 957-5710

The Royal Institute of International Affairs, founded in 1920, is said to be the British counterpart of the COUNCIL FOR FOREIGN RELATIONS. It is supposedly a quasigovernmental body, which attracts prominent political figures and is financed by wealthy international bankers. It is cited by conspiracy theorists as a body dedicated to "one world government."

Royal Neighbors of America

230 Sixteenth Street
Rock Island, IL 61201
(309) 788-4561

The Royal Neighbors of America was originally founded in 1892 as a fraternal benefit insurance society for men and women aged 16–60. There were 159,982 members in 1994. The organization publishes *Field News, Office News,* and *Royal Neighbor,* all monthly.

The Royal Neighbors began as an auxiliary (see AUXILIARIES) of the Modern WOODMEN of the World and were then reorganized in 1895 as a separate benefit society. The RITUALS AND CEREMONIES are rooted in DEISM with heavy Christian overtones, and the overall head of the organization is a Supreme Oracle. In practice, this is a typical successful insurance society, in which the fraternal ritual is increasingly irrelevant. Its good works are directed toward orphans and the deaf.

Royal Riders of the Red Robe

The Royal Riders of the Red Robe was organized for naturalized American citizens who, because they had been born overseas, were denied the opportunity to join the KU KLUX KLAN, which accepted only native-born Americans. The Riders were dedicated to "Christian religion and Protestantism . . . absolute and unqualified allegiance to the government and Constitution of the United States . . . free press, free speech, the sanctity of womanhood, the supremacy of the white race . . . tolerance in religion . . . and a square deal for all, regardless of race, color, or religion." Needless to say, the last element of the order's credo is hardly compatible with its racial agenda.

The Royal Riders was separate and distinct from the Ku Klux Klan, but had its support. The Riders seem to be extinct, but were active during the mid-1920s.

Royal Tribe of Joseph

The Royal Tribe of Joseph, founded in 1894 in Sedalia, Missouri, was unusually logical in its RITUALS AND CEREMONIES. There was only one degree (see DEGREES), but it was based on the biblical Joseph's providence in storing up food against the Egyptian famine, which the founders maintained was the first life insurance company.

Membership was open to white men aged 21–60, and

excluded railroad brakemen and others engaged in extrahazardous occupations (however, railway engineers, firemen, freight conductors, express messengers, yardmasters, and postal clerks were admitted). The order is extinct.

Russian Brotherhood Organization of the U.S.A.

1733 Spring Garden Street
Philadelphia, PA 19130
(215) 563-2537

The Russian Brotherhood Organization of the United States of America was founded in 1900 (incorporated 1903) as a fraternal benefit life insurance society for people of Russian or Slavic descent. The organization publishes *The Truth* monthly. There were 7,832 members in 1995.

The Russian Brotherhood is typical of the various Russian fraternal benefit societies of the United States—larger than most, but still declining steadily. There were 12,000 members in the mid-1960s and fewer than 8,000 in 1995. It accomplishes more than its relatively small numbers might lead one to expect, however. Local groups have built sports and cultural centers, and the society has supported Russian culture and religion (many LODGES are intimately linked with parishes).

Russian Independent Mutual Aid Society

917 North Wood Street
Chicago, IL 60622-5005
(312) 421-2272

The Russian Independent Mutual Aid Society was founded in 1931 as a fraternal benefit life insurance society for Americans of Russian descent. Among the most recent of Russian fraternal benefit groups, the Russian Independent Mutual Aid Society had been shrinking slowly but steadily for many years. There were 1,475 members in 1965, fewer than 900 in 1978, 789 in 1989, but 825 in 1995. In addition to the fraternal benefit insurance, it still remains active in promoting Russian culture and supporting the Russian Orthodox church. It operates mainly in Illinois and Michigan.

Russian Orthodox Catholic Mutual Aid Society of the U.S.A.

100 Hazle Street
Wilkes-Barre, PA 18701
(717) 822-8591

The Russian Orthodox Catholic Mutual Aid Society of the United States of America was founded in 1895 as a fraternal benefit life insurance society for Americans of Russian descent. There were 1,510 members in 1995. The organization publishes *Svit,* bimonthly.

This organization has been about the same size for a decade or more; in the early 1960s, it was almost twice as large as it is now. In addition to its fraternal life insurance, it also contributes to Orthodox Catholic causes and to some other charities.

Russian Orthodox Catholic Women's Mutual Aid Society

975 Greentree Road
Pittsburgh, PA 15220
(412) 922-6664

The Russian Orthodox Catholic Women's Mutual Aid Society was founded in 1907 as a fraternal benefit life insurance society for women of the Russian Orthodox Catholic faith in the United States. There were 1,789 members in 1995.

This small organization, which has remained roughly constant in size for many years, makes handsome contributions to Russian Orthodox seminaries and civic and cultural charities, as well as offering fraternal benefit life insurance.

St. George, Sacred and Military Constantine Order of

The Sacred and Military Constantine Order of St. George is one of the DYNASTIC ORDERS OF CHIVALRY, now bestowed by the Royal House of Bourbon of the Two Sicilies, and is a legacy of the countless royal houses that once intrigued all over Europe.

It is historically interesting because it seems to derive from the Order of the Angelical Knights, founded by Isaac II Angel Cominus, Emperor of Byzantium, in 1190, and to have moved a great deal since. From Byzantium it moved to Venice, where it was in the gift of Marino Caracciolo, Prince of Avelino, and from there it moved again to the gift of John Andrew of Drivastus. Through his descendants, it went to the First Duke of Parma and Piacenza (Francis Farnese), and thence to Don Carlos of Bourbon, who became King of Naples in 1734. When Don Carlos became King of Spain in 1759, he renounced the Grand Mastership of the order along with his claim to the Throne of the Two Sicilies. In recent years, it has been in the gift of the Duke of Castro. The order is recognized by the Holy See and other authorities.

The same family has the right to confer the Royal and Illustrious Order of St. Januarius, which was originally founded in 1738 by Carlos, Infant of Spain.

Saint Germain, Comte de

The Comte de Saint Germain, a celebrated adventurer, is one of a select group including Roger Bacon (see BACON, ROGER), Sir Francis Bacon (see BACON, FRANCIS), ALBERTUS MAGNUS, and a few others, who is claimed as a member (and sometimes as a Past Master, or occasionally as a founder) by a large number of secret societies.

Although his dates are commonly given as c. 1710–80, believers have attributed to him immortality or, at least, a life spanning to centuries, if not millennia. The Comte himself fostered this belief, claiming to lived for 2,000 years. Saint Germain makes at least a passing appearance in almost every historical survey of the occult and of secret societies, and in a good number of more conventional histories.

It is likely that he was a Portuguese Jew and a universal genius, who spoke almost every language of Europe. A talented musician and painter, he had an encyclopedic knowledge of history. He was a chemist or alchemist, who claimed to be able to remove flaws from diamonds and to have mastered the transmutation of metals. His exploits were legendary in his own time. Horace Walpole wrote in a letter of 1743 (Saint Germain was in London at the time, where he had been arrested as a Jacobite spy and then released): "He called an Italian, a Spaniard, a Pole; a somebody that married a great fortune in Mexico and ran away with her jewels to Constantinople; a priest, a fiddler, a vast nobleman."

Saint Germain turned up at the French court in about 1748 and enjoyed such standing with Louis XV that he was employed on secret missions for France. After falling out with the Duke of Choiseul following involvement with a dispute between Austria and France, he fled to England in mid-1760, but was in St. Petersburg, Russia, by 1762. There, he was credited with a major role in the *coup* that brought Catherine II to the throne in place of Peter III. From Russia he went to Germany, where Cagliostro (see CAGLIOSTRO, ALESSANDRO) credited him as being the founder of the FREEMASONS, no less. Then he returned to Paris, living there from 1770–74, after which he stayed at various German courts until he settled upon that of the Landgrave Charles of Hesse in Schleswig-Holstein, where he and the landgrave pursued "secret sciences."

He is alleged to have died in Schleswig in about 1780–85, though he was reported as turning up in Paris in 1789, and the legend of his immortality has been enthusiastically perpetuated since. The more exotic accounts of his life make him a hermaphrodite (or, sometimes, a woman in disguise; though they may have been confusing him with the Chevalier D'Eon; see EON, CHEVALIER D'), and in *The Secret Teachings of All Ages* by Manly P. Hall the following ideas are canvassed:

That he may have been the same person as Christian Rosenkreutz (see ROSICRUCIANS)
That he was the codiscoverer, with Mesmer, of MESMERISM
That he was the same person as Sir Francis Bacon
That he was Hompesch, the Grand Master of the Knights of Malta at the time of Napoleon
That, as Peter Stuart Ney, he was a schoolteacher in North Carolina for 30 years in the 19th century
That he was Marshal Ney of France (who fled to North Carolina)
That he was a prophet (somewhat tactlessly telling Marie Antoinette of the future of the French monarchy)
That Clive knew him in India in 1745

Nor does this exhaust the list of extraordinary identities attributed to this man.

St. John, Companions of

The Companions of St. John was a secret society formed in Pembroke College, Cambridge, England, in 1886, ostensibly to inculcate the virtues of High Church (traditional Anglicanism) and confession. It may or may not still exist. Oxford and Cambridge have long been seats of High Church devotees.

Saint-Martin, Louis-Claude de

Louis-Claude de Saint-Martin (1743–1803) was a Christian mystic who believed that *"sophia"* (divine wisdom) was the key to union with God through Christ. His was a valiant attempt to bring to bear upon Christianity the kind of pantheistic DEISM that was popular at the time. In Saint-Martin's view, *sophia* was the feminine principle of the "Supreme Architect of the Universe," and man was the *logos* (word/act) of *sophia*.

Saint-Martin expounded his philosophy in numerous works including *Tableau Naturel* (1782) and the oddly titled *Le Crocodile* (1799).

St. Patrick's Alliance of America

The St. Patrick's Alliance of America was organized in 1868 as a benevolent and charitable secret society for men, principally Catholics and Irish. The order's ritual (see RITUALS AND CEREMONIES) specifically upheld the right of every man to worship God according to the dictates of his own conscience. At the turn of the century, there were some 50,000 members, but the Alliance is now extinct.

St. Stephen, Order of

The Order of St. Stephen was founded by Cosimo de'Medici, Duke of Florence, in 1562 for the purpose of fighting pirates, defending the Christian faith, and freeing Christian slaves. The order was suppressed in the French Revolution, but was revived in 1817 by Ferdinand III, Grand Duke of Tuscany, who had in 1807 revived the Order of St. Joseph, originally founded in 1514.

The Order of St. Stephen is recognized by the Holy See.

Saints Maurice and Lazarus, Order of

The Order of St. Lazarus was founded in about 1060 in Palestine, to help lepers who made the pilgrimage to the Holy Land. Its Master was always a leper, and so were many of its Knights. After the fall of Acre, the order was best known for the St. Lazarus Hospital in Capua, but after the 15th and 16th centuries the order declined. Several popes attempted to fuse it with other orders to ensure its survival.

The Order of St. Maurice was founded under Amadeus VIII of Savoy in 1434. Its aims were to serve God, to lead the monastic life, and to assist the state. In this form it was short-lived, but it was revived as a religious order in 1572 under Pope Gregory XIII, and it was amalgamated with the Order of St. Lazarus in the following year. No other orders of St. Lazarus are now recognized by the Holy See. The amalgamated order is now a dynastic order (see DYNASTIC ORDERS OF CHIVALRY) in the gift of the House of Savoy, the former Ruling House of Italy.

Saltpetriers

The Saltpetriers or Saltpeterers were a small, very local secret society opposed to the oppressive rule of the abbot of the Monastery of St. Blasius in the country of Hauenstein in the Duchy of Baden, Germany, formed about 1750. The society was suppressed in the late 1750s, but reestablished in the early 19th century to oppose reforms in church and school. It disappeared again in 1840, as the society and the authorities came to terms on the proposed reforms.

Samaritans, Ancient Mystic Order of

974 Willey Street
Morgantown, WV 26505
(304) 292-9635

The Ancient Mystic Order of Samaritans was founded in 1924 as the unofficial "fun" auxiliary (see AUXILIARIES) of the ODD FELLOWS in the United States and Canada. There were 3,953 members in 1995. The order publishes the *Amos Realm* (quarterly).

The Ancient Mystic Order of Samaritans was formed by the amalgamation of the Oriental Order of Humility and Perfection (see following), the Imperial Order of Muscovites (see following), the Veiled Prophets of Baghdad, Knights of Oriental Splendor, and the Ancient Mystic Order of Cabirians. It is to the Independent Order of Odd Fellows as the SHRINERS is to the FREEMASONS, or the Order of Alhambra (see ALHAMBRA, INTERNATIONAL ORDER OF) is to the KNIGHTS OF COLUMBUS: a "fun" side degree (see DEGREES) for men.

Like the Shriners and Alhambra, the Samaritans adopt many trappings associated with a Western vision of the Near East. For example, officers bear pseudo-Arabic names—Supreme Kalifah, Supreme Ali-Baba, and Supreme Muezzin.

The order is not officially recognized by the parent body, but it is certainly acknowledged unofficially. Members pride themselves on their support for the mentally retarded.

The Samaritans work two DEGREES, the lower being Humility and the upper (available only to those who have attended a supreme or divisional convention) being Perfection.

Imperial Order of Muscovites

This society was founded in Cincinnati, Ohio, in 1894. Its originators departed from the standard Islamic-parody model. Lodges were called "Kremlins," and the head of the organization was the Supreme Czar.

Oriental Order of Humility and Perfection

The "Oriental" side degree was introduced in the early 1880s, apparently originating in San Francisco but propagated through London, Ontario. In 1901, the Supreme Temple of the Oriental Order of Humility and Perfection was invented; all present at the meeting were designated "sheikhs," and near Eastern trappings adopted. The organization was incorporated in New York in 1919, becoming defunct within four years.

It is likely that the Oriental Order of Humility and the Oriental Haymakers were the same organization.

Sanfedisti

The Sanfedisti was an Italian Catholic secret society of the late 18th and early 19th centuries, devoted to expelling the Austrians from Italy but, in contrast to other Italian nationalist societies, not to unifying Italy. Like the CONSISTORIALS, they proposed to divide the country between the existing Italian princelings and the Pope. They were anti-Napoleonic, and also opposed the CARBONARI.

Sanhedrim, Order of the

The Order of the Sanhedrim was a beneficiary society consisting of members of the press as well as others. It was based mainly in Michigan, and is now extinct.

The Ancient Order of Sanhedrims was an unrelated fraternal benefit society founded in Richmond, Virginia, in 1895. Now long extinct, it was an outgrowth of the Orientals, a side degree (see DEGREES) of the KNIGHTS OF PYTHIAS.

Scald Miserable Masons

The Scald Miserable Masons were (according to a report in the London *Daily Post* of March 20, 1740) a group of parodists who purported to expose at a public parade the "secrets" of Freemasonry. Masonic authors then and since have been at pains to emphasize the parodic aspect and to deny that anyone took notice of the Scalds, but Sir John Hawkins, one of Samuel Johnson's biographers, observed that "it was not until thirty years afterward that the Fraternity [of Masons] recovered from the disgrace which so ludicrous a representation had brought upon it."

Scandinavian American Fraternity

The Scandinavian American Fraternity was organized in 1893 as a fraternal beneficiary insurance society for Christians of both sexes of Scandinavian descent. The *Christian Cynosure* of May 1921 condemned it as "a real tail-feather of Masonry." It is unclear whether it died, merged with another society, or converted itself into a conventional insurance company. It is unrelated to the SCANDINAVIAN FRATERNITY OF AMERICA.

Scandinavian Fraternity of America

1350 North Howard St., Apt. 505
Akron, OH 44310
(216) 923-0718

The Scandinavian Fraternity of America was founded in 1894 as the Scandinavian Brotherhood of America, but changed its name to the present form in 1915. With only 2,500 members in 1995, it is a small ethnic fraternal insurance organization, but its *Monitor* was still listed as a monthly publication in 1990.

Schlager

Schlager is the kind of sword play that was at one time popular in German universities and that is said to survive clandestinely to this day. Students' clubs that preserve it qualify as secret societies. It was the *Schlager* that produced the infamous and coveted "Prussian duelling scar."

Schlager was not as dangerous as it might seem. The eyes were protected with metal goggles and the neck with thick padding. Only the cheeks were really exposed, and the purpose was to inflict (or receive) a cut there. The traditional way to treat the cut was with white wine, which served both as an antiseptic and as a way of getting a better scar.

Fencing with "sharps"—sharpened *epées* or (academic) broadswords for "first blood"—has also been a feature of some student clubs, and it is considerably more dangerous.

Schmidt, Alvin J.

Alvin Schmidt wrote *Fraternal Organizations,* under the series heading *The Greenwood Encyclopedia of American Institutions* (Westport, Conn.: Greenwood Press, 1980). Dr. Schmidt, a sociologist, is a leading academic authority on fraternal orders and secret societies.

Schwarze Brüder

See BLACK BROTHERS, ORDER OF THE.

Schwarze Front

See BLACK FRONT.

Schwarzer Ritter, Deutscher Orden

The Deutscher Orden Schwarzer Ritter (German Order of Black Knights) was a secret, benevolent society in the United States from the 1870s to the end of the 19th century. Despite its modern origin, it claimed great antiquity. Beyond this, nothing is known of the order.

Sciots, Ancient Egyptian Order of

Sciots Supreme Pyramid
2372 Lloyd Lane
Sacramento, CA 95825
(916) 489-5822

The Sciots were founded in 1910 in San Francisco as a social club for FREEMASONS, and to this day the order operates chiefly in California and Arizona. It is open to all Master Masons in good standing; there were 1,700 members in 1995. The organization publishes a *Newsletter* and the *Supreme Pyramid Bulletin,* both 10 times a year.

The Ancient Egyptian Order of Sciots is not ancient, nor Egyptian, nor Sciot, and it is not even particularly Masonic—though it limits its membership to Masons. Founded in 1910, its origins may be traced five years earlier, to a 1905 organization called the "Boosters Club."

The Sciots' motto remains "Boost One Another." It declined drastically between the 1920s and the 1960s, a drop from 21,000 to 3,000, then down to 1,800 in the late 1970s. It still seems very active, however.

The RITUALS AND CEREMONIES are based on events that are supposed to have happened on the "isle of Scio," near Syria in 1124 B.C. The fraternal support that the Sciots afforded one another is said to have impressed the Egyptian Pharaoh so much that he invited them to his palace for feasting and merry-making every third moon. To commemorate this, the single degree (see DEGREES) is called the League of Neighbors. Would-be members must promise to attend their own BLUE LODGE once a month.

The structure consists of a relatively small number of "Subordinate Pyramids" (under 20 at the time of writing), ruled by a "Toparch" and a "Supreme Pyramid." The word "Toparch" derives from the Greek, and means "the ruler of a small district."

The Sciots preserved the old tradition of a formalized whip-round or impromptu ASSESSMENT on the death of a member; in 1979, this was $1.20 each, for a widow's benefit of $1,000. It is not clear whether this practice survived into the 1990s, but the Sciots now function as a fund-raising organization to help disadvantaged children.

Scotland, Royal Order of

P.O. Box 125
Annandale, VA 22003
(703) 683-2844

The Royal Order of Scotland was founded in London in 1872 as a division of the FREEMASONS, for Masons renowned for service to their fellow men. There were 8,400 members in the United States in 1995. The order publishes *Annual Proceedings.*

According to Masonic tradition, this order was founded by Robert Bruce after the Battle of Bannockburn on June 24, 1314, to honor the Scottish Freemasons who had fought at his side. By the same tradition, the "King over the Water" (Prince Charles Edward Stuart, better known as Bonnie Prince Charlie) asserted his Grand Mastership in 1747. The present Royal Order was established in London in 1872 and (more fruitfully) in the United States in 1878. Current international headquarters are at 96 George Street, Edinburgh. It is an unusually Christian branch of the Craft, but otherwise typically Masonic.

Scottish Clans, Order of

The Order of Scottish Clans, which merged with the Independent Order of FORESTERS in 1971, was founded in 1878 in St. Louis, Missouri, as a fraternal order for men of Scottish descent; later, women were also admitted. It provided death and sick-relief benefits, as well as preserving Scottish traditions. It suffered actuarial insolvency in Missouri in the 1920s, but temporarily recovered. At the time of its merger with the Foresters, there were some 16,000 members. The RITUALS AND CEREMONIES were based on Scottish history and legends, but the number of DEGREES worked is no longer clear.

The Daughters of Scotia were the auxiliary (see AUXILIARIES). The organization was founded in 1895 for women of Scottish descent or birth, and originally contained 23 women.

Scottish Rite

The Scottish Rite of the FREEMASONS appears first to have been organized in the United States in 1801, with a good deal of spurious history as underpinnings. It offers higher DEGREES to a Master Mason (the third and highest of the traditional degrees, and as far as he can go in his BLUE LODGE). Twenty-nine of these Higher Degrees (the 4th to the 32nd) are normally taken more-or-less simultaneously over the course of a few days. (It *is* possible to work each degree fully, in stages, but this is not usual.) The ritual (see RITUALS AND CEREMONIES) for these speeded-up degrees (called "communicated" degrees) normally consists of a short lecture on the degree, followed by a recitation of the appropriate oath (see OATHS). The 33rd degree is honorary and is conferred upon those who already hold the 32nd degree and have distinguished themselves in the Craft.

There are both Northern and Southern Jurisdictions of the Scottish Rite in the United States. Taking the Northern Lodge as an example, the Lodge of Perfection confers the 4th to 14th degrees; the Council, Princes of Jerusalem, confers the 15th and 16th; the Chapter of Rose Croix confers the 17th and 18th; and the Consistory confers the remainder.

Unlike the YORK RITE, which can be worked to the highest degree only by Christians, the Scottish Rite is open to Jews and others.

Scouting

The Boy Scouts was founded by Robert Stephenson Smyth Baden-Powell, 1st Baron Baden-Powell, in 1909, and has since spawned a number of imitations and female equivalents; in England, the female equivalent is the Girl Guides, and in the United States, the Girl Scouts.

Scouting does not spring to mind when secret societies and fraternal orders are mentioned, yet there are some resemblances (passwords and signs, in particular), and (incredible as it may seem), scouting has drawn some religious objections similar to those leveled against secret societies, especially from Catholics. In the United States, some priests rejected the movement entirely as a fad, and even as anti-Catholic. The *Catholic Transcript* (Hartford, Connecticut, May 4, 1911) observed that " 'non-sectarian' so often means 'non-Catholic'." The National Catholic

War Council did, however, recommend scouting with the proviso that exclusively Catholic troops be organized for Catholic boys, with Catholic leaders. The Catholic Boys' Brigade of the United States was established in New York City in 1916 as an alternative to The Boy Scouts.

Scrying

Scrying is the technique of foretelling the future, or of seeing events at a distance. The classic scryer's tool, at least in the popular imagination, is the crystal ball, but scryers have also used glass and metal mirrors (flat, convex, or concave) and pools of liquids; black ink is a traditional medium, though some have used mercury. In Tibet, there is an entire lake—Chokhorgyal—traditionally used for scrying. Whether the scryer only sees images or also hears words is unclear and seems to depend on the scryer and on the tradition in which he or she is working.

Needless to say, elements of scrying appear in a number of mystically oriented secret societies, and even in the nonmystical ones there are sometimes ritual implements that derive from scryer's tools (see RITUALS AND CEREMONIES). Most likely, the adoption of mirrors and similar reflective paraphernalia in rituals is a result of eclecticism rather than arcane knowledge.

Seal of Solomon

The "Seal of Solomon," referred to (and adopted as a talisman) by so many secret societies, is no more than the six-pointed Star of David that symbolizes Judaism.

Sembe

Sembe is or was a WEST AFRICAN SECRET SOCIETY, influential among the Vai, Gora and Gallinas of Sierra Leone and Liberia, and open to boys at puberty. Its schools also trained prospective members of Belli Paaro, Jamboi and Nanam.

It seems to have been akin to the FREEMASONS in its brotherhood, though Masonic hospitality was rarely if ever so comprehensive. For example, a dispute between a head porter and the villagers where the journeying party had stopped for the night was headed off when the village chief learned that the "head-boy" (chief porter) was a Sembe, who had joined in the same year as his own son. Not only was there a feast, the village chief exclaimed to the head-boy: "Wonderful! Wonderful! It is several years since I saw a Sembe! Welcome! Welcome! Be my guest! Be my son! Be my brother! Accept my home, my wives, my children! They are yours, for you are my blood relation!"

As was the case with all West African secret societies, members were charged a fee, but while many societies adopted to the colonial world by assessing fees in currency, the Sembe accepted payment in traditional cowry shells. The Sembe practice or practiced medicinal magic and hold or held group celebratory dances.

Senf Korn, Orden vom

Der Orden vom Senf Korn or Order of the Mustard Seed was founded in Germany and based on the New Testament verses in Mark, chapter 4, 30–32. The order's objective was propagation of morality. The Gospel verses in question liken the Kingdom of God to a grain of mustard seed, which grows up greater than all other herbs.

Serb National Federation

1 Fifth Avenue, 7th Fl.
Pittsburgh, PA 15222-3126
(412) 263-2875

The Serb National Federation was founded in the United States in 1901 (as *Srbobran-Sloga*) to be a fraternal benefit insurance society for Americans of Serb or Slav ancestry, aged 16–60. Those under 16 join the Junior Order. There were 15,200 members in 1995. The federation publishes *The American Srbobran* (weekly).

The Serb National Federation is a typical ethnic fraternal benefit society, with insurance, cultural and social events, as well as sports programs.

Serpent, Military Order of the

The Military Order of the Serpent was an American secret society for veterans of the Spanish-American War, founded in Cleveland, Ohio, in 1904. It was headed by a Supreme Gu-Gu, who was assisted by a Supreme Thrice Infamous Inferior Gu-Gu. The order illustrates the passion for spurious histories that informs many, if not most secret societies. It purported to be a continuation of the KALASTAASEN KAGALANAGLAD KATIPUNAN, which the founders of the society believed to be extinct.

Sexennial League

The Sexennial League was organized in Philadelphia under the laws of Pennsylvania on July 18, 1888, by David C. Reynolds "to enable all persistent members to have an opportunity to save small amounts periodically, which, merging in a common fund, would produce large increase from safe investments, the benefit to be shared by the persistent members in proportion to the certificates held by them." Membership was open to members of the Ancient Order of United Workmen, Royal Arcanum, AMERICAN LEGION OF HONOR, Order of Sparta, and to FREEMASONS, as well as ODD FELLOWS (see ROYAL ARCANUM, SUPREME COUNCIL OF THE; UNITED WORKMEN, ANCIENT ORDER OF THE). Its name derives from the six-year term of membership, after which the proceeds of one's investment could be collected or the membership renewed for another six-year term, *ad infinitum*.

The league survived into the early 20th century, but is now extinct.

Shirtless

The Shirtless were a short-lived French revolutionary group, with Samson as their emblem, formed in about 1820. The same shirtless symbolism (*Descamisados*) has been used in various South American political movements of the poor against the rich. Little of a specific nature is known about the Shirtless. It is not even clear what the group's original French name was—though *Sans-chemises* is a good guess.

Shriners

P.O. Box 31356
Tampa, FL 33631-3356
(813) 281-0300

The Imperial Council of the Ancient Arabic Order of Nobles of the Mystic Shrine, better known as the Shriners, was founded in 1871 in New York City as a "fun" side degree (see SIDE DEGREES) of the FREEMASONS. It is open to Master Masons of the 32nd degree, or Knights Templar. There were 720,000 members in 1995.

The "Shriners" are the archetypal "fun" auxiliary to a well-established secret society. They are also archetypically American; the Grand Lodge of England has in the past threatened English Masons with expulsion if they join the organization, believing that the Shrine brings Freemasonry into disrepute with childish antics, funny clothes, and ritual some find offensive. On the positive side, however, the Shriners raises a tremendous amount of money for a wide range of worthy causes, especially where children are concerned. The hospitals it funds for crippled and for badly burned children are state-of-the-art facilities and free to those in need.

Like a number of other secret societies, the Shrine was originally little more than a drinking club. In the United States, where teetotalism has always been popular, Masonic lodges are "dry." The Shrine was set up by a group of 13 Master Masons who had already been meeting for some time at a weekly luncheon club; the leading lights were a medical man, Dr. Walter M. Fleming, and a stage comedian named Billy Florence. The fact that there were 13 founding members commemorates the short-lived "13 craze" of 1870. In the aftermath of the Civil War, the craze was a (mostly Northern) attempt to deny superstition and bad luck. For example, 13 people for lunch or dinner was considered witty, invitations were issued for 13 minutes past the hour, and a number of short-lived games were invented wherein the winner acquired 13 points.

Florence and Fleming restricted membership to those who had attained the 32nd Degree or were (Masonic) KNIGHTS TEMPLAR. The LODGE is known as a Temple, and the officers have such names as Most Illustrious Grand Potentate, Illustrious Grand Chief Rabban, and Illustrious Grand High Priest and Prophet. Ornaments include both a Christian Bible and al-Quran; a foot-square Black Stone or Holy Stone (after the Qaaba in Mecca); a gavel and scimitar; crossed swords; an Altar of Incense; and a bier and coffin. The gaudy clothes and ornaments affected by Shriners are familiar to many, and as early as 1887 some Shriners were wearing fezzes decorated with gold and tiger claws—and valued at $1,000.

The RITUALS AND CEREMONIES are a loose parody of Islam and are offensive to followers of the religion. Like other Middle Eastern parody rituals, this ritual claims remote antiquity, supposedly dating back to the foundation of the Shriners by the son-in-law of the Prophet Mohammad, the Caliph Ali, in A.D. 644. In the 1890s, controversy raged within the organization as to its historical foundation, and many people argued that it was indeed the legitimate descendant of an Arabic vigilante organization.

The Shriners traditionally reveled in various pranks and ritualistic shenanigans, together with a great deal of drinking. This cast the Shrine into such disrepute by the 1910s, that some American Masonic Grand Lodges seriously considered following the course of the Grand Lodge of England and suspending any Mason who became a Shriner. Accordingly, at the 1920 convention, it was proposed that the Shrine organization divert some of its energies into good works—specifically, to financing a children's hospital that would be open to crippled children under 14, of any race or creed, whose parents could not afford to pay for medical care. (Somewhat improbably, the first chairman of the hospital committee was a Christian Scientist, who, however, proved to be an excellent choice.)

The emphasis was still on fun rather than charity, and the exploits of Shriners at conventions became legendary. Traffic was stopped, citizens were annoyed, and the peace was disturbed. Yet, because the hooligans were well-to-do citizens, the police routinely turned a blind eye to what was deemed harmless fun. The Shriners' tenuous image of respectability was reinforced in the 1950s, when the order enthusiastically joined in the near-hysterical denunciations of communism that swept the United States. On October 17, 1958, J. Edgar Hoover wrote an official laudatory letter headed "Shrine Versus Communism."

The wilder excesses both of anticommunism and bibulous conventioneering have declined, and the Shrine is now recognized at least as much for its network of children's hospitals as for its riotous merrymaking. Shrine drill motorcycle units are also a regular feature of many civic parades. And it is undeniable that the organization has had many prominent members, including several U.S. presidents (among them Harding, Roosevelt, and

Truman); J. Edgar Hoover; Thomas E. Dewey; Barry Goldwater; Chief Justice Earl Warren; and such noted comedians as Harold Lloyd (a sometime Imperial Potentate) and Red Skelton.

A related organization is the Shrine Directors Association of North America, headquartered at 1108 Arizona NE, Albuquerque, NM 87110, (505) 255-6538. Founded in 1919 for directors of every Shrine Temple of North America, the order had 188 members in 1995. The Ladies Oriental Shrine of North America is a female auxiliary (see AUXILIARIES) of the Shriners, with membership open to wives, mothers, daughters, and sisters of Shriners. The organization, which was established in 1914, had 32,000 members in 1995, and is headquartered at 1111 E. 54th Street, Suite 111, Indianapolis, IN 46220, (317) 259-1996.

Sicarii

The Sicarii or "dagger carriers" (a *sica* is a small dagger) was a radical Jewish sect of the first century A.D., alleged by Roman historians to have used assassination as a political tool. They are sometimes identified as synonymous with the Zealots, an anti-Roman resistance movement that arose just after the birth of Christ and endured for perhaps three-quarters of a century, but other authorities identify them as a specific subset of the Zealots. At a remove of almost 2,000 years, it is difficult to determine precisely who or what the Sicarii were, but they seem to have been a classic example of a secret society that was either political or criminal, depending on the sympathies of the reporter. Some recent commentators have suggested that Simon called Peter was probably a Zealot, that Judas Iscariot was really Judas Sicarius, and even that Jesus and his followers were members of a political secret society that (almost accidentally) founded a religion in passing.

Side Degrees

In the language of secret societies, a "side degree" is usually a social or other "fun" club within a society. It is called a side degree because it is not hierarchical, as are the 53 degrees of the Order of Zuzimites (see ZUZIMITES, ANCIENT ORDER OF) or the 33 degrees of some types of FREEMASONS. Rather, it exists beside them, and brethren in the main organization may join or not, as they feel inclined. In theory, a side degree may also be for a special interest group (such as those interested in history, or some other specialized aspect of a society), but the vast majority of side degrees are just for fun.

Signs

Signs, like PASSWORDS and GRIPS, are supposed to be a way for members of a secret society to recognize and communicate with one another. Normally, a sign is met with a countersign, which is somewhat different from the sign. Signs and countersigns must be unobtrusive, preferably mimicking everyday mannerisms. Obvious and bizarre gestures are likely to draw unwelcome attention to the person giving them. The ODD FELLOWS sign of recognition is, therefore, a good one: "First, when a Brother shall desire to be recognized as an Odd-Fellow, by a member of the Order, he shall grasp with his right hand the lapel of his coat, the hand being placed over the right nipple, the thumb extending upward." The countersign is, however, somewhat more awkward: "Second, an Odd-Fellow observing this sign, shall recognize and answer the same by taking hold of the right lapel of his coat with his left hand, the same being also placed over the nipple, thumb concealed beneath the coat."

The sign of recognition must not be too subtle, though, or it might easily be missed. To return to the Odd Fellows, the recognizing sign of Rebekah is as follows: "When a sister of the Rebekah Degree shall desire to be recognized as such by an Odd-Fellow, she shall give the Sign for Recognizing Brothers, which is made by placing the first three fingers of the right hand, extended, but closely touching each other (thumb and little finger concealed) on a table, chair or other object, or by placing them on a book, reticule, handkerchief, or other thing held in the left hand."

At the other extreme, the Sign of Bravery used by the KNIGHTS OF PYTHIAS may also be used as a sign of recognition: "Place your left hand upon your left breast, raise your right hand (fist) and raise it as high as your eye, and strike a downward blow. When used as a sign of recognition, the person making the sign, indicating, 'I am a Knight of Pythias;' then the person answering the sign, indicating, 'And so am I.' " The last sign is used chiefly in the Lodge (though it is hard to see why quite so many signs are needed in the Lodge, where there are no strangers.)

The Knights of Pythias had all kinds of curious signs, such as the Sign of Courtesy, Rank of Esquire: "Rest your chin in the cup of your left hand, touch with your right hand the elbow of your left. . . . This sign must be given by all who enter or retire while the lodge is open in this rank, except those acting under the orders of the Chancellor Commander, and will be answered by the Chancellor commander with a wave of the hand or gavel, which indicates permission to be seated or to retire as the case may be." The signs of the Eastern Star (see EASTERN STAR, ORDER OF THE) are curious, too. For the Widow's Sign, "take anything convenient, as a handkerchief or newspaper, in each hand, to represent handfuls of barley heads, filling the hand and sticking out a few inches. Then extend the hand in front as if to display their contents, and next cross the wrists on the breast, the contents of each hand pointing upwards toward the shoulders, also looking upward. The sign alludes to Ruth holding out two handfuls of barley to Boaz, and appealing mutely to God. A Mason seeing this sign, writes his name on one side of a card, and on the other writes, 'Who is this?' which is the pass of this degree. He then presents her the card."

Almost all secret societies have, or have had, such signs and countersigns. The Elks, for example, spread their arms to represent the antlers of their totem. The most peculiar signs, though, are the "signs of distress," by means of which brethren signal to one another that they need help. The person on the receiving end of the sign then makes another countersign. In the case of immediate *physical* danger, the only use is when the person in distress is unobtrusively seeking special attention when an outright appeal might alienate as many as it attracted. It has been reported that the captain of a ship in the 1930s escaped the clutches of a piratical Cuban by giving an appropriate Masonic sign; the pirate was a fellow Mason.

Silver Knights of America

The Silver Knights of America and their auxiliary (see AUXILIARIES), the Silver Ladies of America, were a product of the bimetallist movement of the 1890s, which was all a part of the "Sound Money" debate; see FREEMEN'S PROTECTIVE SILVER ASSOCIATION. The Silver Knights favored a joint silver and gold standard, and were founded in 1895. The defeat of the Free Silver movement in the 1896 elections marked their end.

Si'mo

Si'mo and Oro are the two oldest WEST AFRICAN SECRET SOCIETIES. Although much diminished in power, and somewhat diminished in size, Si'mo remains a respected institution. As an old saying on the West Coast of Africa had it, "Time and Si'mo are brothers," and one of the titles of the head of Si'mo was "The Ancient of Days."

Originally founded by a family, clan or sept of priest-warriors, Si'mo's philosophy was for centuries at the heart of the Baga war ethic. It was always mystic and religious, priestly and protective. Membership was (and presumably still is) male only, with admission at puberty and the right of membership jealously guarded.

A "law-god" association, its functions were traditionally mystic, religious, and protective. Warrior-priests belonging to the order often accompanied campaigning armies.

Of great antiquity—probably more than a thousand years old—Si'mo is more significant as the ancestor of various other West African Secret Societies than in its own right.

Sindungo

Sindungo is or was a WEST AFRICAN SECRET SOCIETY, apparently derived from Penda-Penda and influencing the Loanga of Angoy and the Kabinda of the Congo. There is also a language called Sindungo (usually spelled Si'ndungo) in Angola. The society preserves in its secret speech some of the archaic words of this language. The Ritual (see RITUALS AND CEREMONIES) is said to contain Egyptian and Masonic survivals. Part of the ritual includes a dance in which adult members arrange themselves in opposing lines and hold sticks. They strike at one another's sticks as they alternately advance and retire. Membership is (or was) adult, of both sexes, with occasional puberty schools to train young members, who are or were admitted to a minor, non-secret degree.

Sion, Priory of

The Priory of Sion—or, more accurately, the secret society underlying the Priory of Sion—may have been founded at any time between about A.D. 20 and 1956. It is or was a religious secret society, purportedly international, but based principally in France. The size (and all other information concerning the Priory) is unclear, but the order is a truly remarkable secret society, if we can credit accounts by Baigent, Leigh, and Lincoln, the authors of *Holy Blood, Holy Grail* (London, 1982) and *The Messianic Legacy* (New York, 1989). According to these books, Jesus did not die on the cross, but went on to marry (possibly Mary Magdalene) and to found a royal dynasty, the Merovingian kings of France. The *Saint Grael*, or "Holy Grail," is actually a mistranslation or mishearing of *Sang Real* or "Royal Blood." Briefly, the Merovingian dynasty ruled from the latter part of the fifth century to the middle of the eighth. Its foundation is traditionally taken from the victory of Clovis at Soissons in A.D. 486, though the name comes from his grandfather Merovech, and the dynasty ended in 751. The last Merovingian king of any consequence was Dagobert, who reigned from 628–38. The Priory of Sion is allegedly the organization that was entrusted with keeping the "treasure" of the Merovingian dynasty, not corporal riches, but the bloodline of Christ himself.

The Priory may have been founded in Jerusalem in 1099 by Godfrey de Bouillon as a precursor of the TEMPLARS, and Joan of Arc and Gilles de Rais were both members. However, it is impossible to date its founding with any certainty. The organization is alleged to have existed since at least the time of Dagobert, yet the first publicly recorded evidence of an independent Priory of Sion seems to be in 1956, when the *Prieuré de Sion* was legally registered and constituted under French law, only to wink out of existence again in 1958. According to internal records of the Priory, no less a person than Jean Cocteau was Grand Master from 1918–55, and Pierre Plantard de Saint-Clair was elected Grand Master in 1981. Plantard was the principal source of Baigent, Leigh, and Lincoln's books, and in the early 1940s published a magazine called *Vaincre*, which was the organ of an association called ALPHA GALATES, an organization similar to the Priory of Sion. Even the statutes or rules of the order, deposited with the French authorities when the Priory was registered in the *Journal Officiel*, are surrounded with a modest amount of mystery, with Baigent, Leigh, and Lincoln claiming those deposited to be spurious.

It is known that the Priory was divided into the Legion, charged with the Apostolate, and the Phalange, which was the Guardian of the Tradition. Little or no further explanation of Apostolate or Tradition can be found, but it is recorded that, as of 1956, there were no fewer than 729 Provinces, 27 Commanderies, and an Arch called Kyria. The division into Provinces and Commanderies is stock material from the Templars or other DYNASTIC ORDERS OF CHIVALRY, while the Arch is probably a Masonic inspiration. (A believer in the Priory of Sion could argue that the Masons took their Arch from the Priory.)

There are (or were) nine Grades: Novices, and Croises in the Provinces; Preux, Ecuyers, Chevaliers, and Commandeurs in the Commanderies; Connetables, Senechaux, and a sole Nautonier in the Arch. All of these ranks and chivalries apparently echo those of Alpha Galates, the major difference being that Alpha Galates was pagan in its orientation, while the Priory is avowedly Catholic.

Skoptsi

See KHYLSTY.

Slavonic Benefit Order of the State of Texas

P.O. Box 100
Temple, TX 76503
(017) 773-1575 or (800) 792-3024

The Slavonic Benefit Order of the State of Texas was founded in 1896 in La Grange, Texas, as a fraternal benefit life insurance society. It publishes *Vestnik* weekly. There were 60,000 members in 1995.

The *Slovanska Podporujici Jednota Statu Texas* or S.P.J.S.T. is a typical ethnic fraternal benefit society, with one major exception: It is big, and it is growing. From 35,000 in the late 1960s, to 54,000 in the late 1970s, and 60,000 in the late 1980s is impressive.

The benefits are of the usual kind: fraternal life insurance, social and cultural events, including youth clubs, and mutual assistance. In addition, there are two rest homes for the elderly, a large library (15,000 Czech volumes), a museum, and a computerized database. During World War II, the order funded a B-24 Liberator as part of the war effort.

Sleeping Lion

Formed in Paris in 1816, Sleeping Lion was one of several secret societies having as their object the restoration of Napoleon to the throne of France. The government suppressed it. Beyond these few facts, nothing more is known of Sleeping Lion.

Sloga Fraternal Life Insurance Society

2538 West National Avenue
Milwaukee, WI 53204
(414) 645-8922

The Sloga Fraternal Life Insurance Society was founded in 1897 as a fraternal benefit life insurance society. Membership is now open, though the Slavic appeal remains strong. There were 2,247 members in 1995.

Rather surprisingly, this typical small ethnic fraternal benefit society (formerly known as South Slavic Benevolent Union, "Sloga," until 1968) actually increased its membership by about 50 percent in the 1980s. In addition to selling insurance (principally in Wisconsin), it provides the usual fraternal benefits of scholarships, cultural events, and charitable contributions (including blood bank drives), together with social sporting events such as bowling, golf, and softball.

Slovak Catholic Sokol

205 Madison Street
Passaic, NJ 07055
(201) 777-2605

The Slovak Catholic Sokol was founded in 1905 as a fraternal benefit society with emphasis on physical fitness for Americans of Slovak or Slav descent. The order publishes *Katolicky Sokol* ("Catholic Falcon," periodically) and *Children's Friend* (weekly). There were 50,000 members in 1995.

For a brief history of the Sokol movement, see SOKOL U.S.A. The Slovak Catholic Sokol was originally founded as the Roman and Greek Catholic Gymnastic Union Sokol. It is a typical ethnic fraternal benefit society, with insurance, social and cultural events, scholarships, charitable works, and a library. There is also a lot of support for the Catholic Church (including financial assistance for missionaries and those preparing for the priesthood), and a strong Sokol emphasis on physical fitness. Among the many gymnastic and athletic activities sponsored by the organization is a biennial track and field event.

Slovak Societies

The Slovaks have always been very strong on fraternal aid societies, most of them typical ethnic fraternal aid societies, with programs of ethnic culture and education, often alongside insurance. A list of the leading organizations follows; those that offer insurance are denoted by "(INSURANCE)" following the entry.

American Council of the Slovak World Congress. Founded 1975, 100,000 members in 1995.

First Catholic Slovak Ladies Association. Founded 1892 (formerly First Catholic Slovak Ladies Union), 87,000 members in 1995. (INSURANCE)

First Catholic Slovak Union of the U.S.A. and Canada. Founded 1890, 80,000 members in 1995. (INSURANCE)

National Slovak Society of the United States of America. Founded 1890, 18,000 members in 1995. (INSURANCE)

Slovak-American National Council. Founded 1982, 500,000 members in 1995.

Slovak Catholic Federation. Founded 1911, formerly Slovak Catholic Federation of America. No membership figures available.

Slovak Catholic Sokol. Founded 1905, 50,000 members in 1995. Strong gymnastic influence.

Slovak League of America. Founded 1907, 5,000 members in 1995, but claims to represent 500,000 individuals.

Sokol U.S.A. Founded 1896, 12,000 members in 1995. Strong gymnastic influence.

Slovene National Benefit Society

166 Shore Drive
Burr Ridge, IL 60521
(708) 887-7660 or (800) 445-2693

The Slovene National Benefit Society was founded in the United States in 1904 as a fraternal benefit society. It now functions mostly as an insurance society, with open membership and a Slovenian bias. The order publishes *Voice of Youth* (monthly) and *Provesta* (a newspaper). There were 47,764 members in 1995.

The Slovene National Benefit Society is a typical ethnic fraternal benefit society, formed in 1904 and incorporated in 1907 as a flat ASSESSMENT benefit society ($1) with a single rate of death benefit ($500). One unusual feature is that it is bound by its constitution to a foundation "on a free-thought basis," and it "grants to its members personal freedom of religious philosophical, ethnical and political creeds." This reflects the founders' reaction against the close ties that many ethnic fraternal benefit societies maintained with the predominant church of their forefathers.

In addition to providing insurance, the society funds scholarships, sporting activities, and Slovene cultural programs. There is also a museum, with biographical archives and even an on-line computer data service, as well as an Ethnic Heritage and Recreation Center in Enon Valley, Pennsylvania.

Sociedade do Espirito Santo

The Society of the Holy Spirit is a Portuguese ethnic fraternal benefit society founded in 1895 in Santa Clara,

California. Membership is open, and the organization is active in California. Its current address is unavailable.

The full name of this society, commonly known as S.E.S., is the *Conselho Supremo da Sociedade do Espirito Santo*. It is a typical ethnic fraternal benefit society, with the usual mix of insurance, help in time of trouble, visitation to the sick, scholarships, and charitable and social activities. It is also dedicated to preserving Portuguese culture and the Portuguese heritage.

Sociedade Portuguesa Rainha Santa Isabel

3031 Telegraph Avenue
Oakland, CA 94609
(415) 658-0983

The Portuguese Society of Queen St. Isabel was founded in 1898 in Oakland, California, as a fraternal benefit society for women aged 15 years and 5 months to 55 years and 5 months. The society publishes the *Boletim da S.P.R.S.I.* monthly. There were 12,000 members in 1995.

The Sociedade Portuguesa Rainha Santa Isabel was formed as an altar society at the Catholic Church of St. Joseph in Oakland in 1898, but two years later became a fraternal benefit society while retaining a very strong religious flavor. Its activities include fraternal benefits, a Portuguese cultural bias, promotion of Catholicism, award of scholarships to eligible members, and other good works.

Societas Rosicruciana in Anglia

The Soc. Ros. in Anglia (its usual abbreviation) was (and probably still is) a secret literary or research society claiming descent from the ROSICRUCIANS. While it is not a Masonic order, many prominent Freemasons have belonged to it or taken an interest in it. Almost certainly, it was founded in the 19th century, freighted with a fictitious story of ancient lineage.

Sokol U.S.A.

276 Prospect Street, P.O. Box 189
East Orange, NJ 07017
(201) 676-0280

Sokol U.S.A. was founded in 1896 as a fraternal benefit life insurance society for persons of Slovak descent or married to same. It publishes the *Sokol Times* (monthly). There were 12,000 members in 1995.

In the Czech language, a *sokol* is a falcon, a bird of great grace, bravery, strength, and agility. It is also the name of a kind of organization, first founded in 1862 in Prague, dedicated to physical fitness and health, as suggested by the long and compendious alternative name for Sokol U.S.A.: the Slovak Gymnastic Union Sokol of the United States of America.

The earliest American Sokol seems to have been founded in St. Louis, Missouri, as early as 1865; the first Slovak Sokol fraternal lodge appeared in Chicago in 1892; and the S.G.U.S. of the U.S.A. was founded four years later.

Sokol U.S.A. offers the usual fraternal benefits, such as insurance, scholarships, and social or cultural events, together with its original inspiration of gymnastic competitions called *Slets*, which also involve dance, calisthenics, and other physical activities. It also maintains "camps and halls" in several states. The society has declined from 23,000 in 1979 to about half that a decade later. This despite the fact that the Tatran Slovak Union and the Slovak Evangelical Society were both absorbed in 1944.

Sonderbare Gesellen

The Sonderbare Gesellen is a German version of the ODD FELLOWS, dating from about 1870. The name is a literal translation of the English term, though the organization is also known as Freie Gesellen (Free Brethren) or Helfende Gesellen (Helping Brothers). The order apparently possesses much closer links with the FREEMASONS than its English or American counterparts, which are more inclined to view members of the Craft as rivals.

Sons of Adam

In the United States, the Sons of Adam was organized in Parsons, Kansas, in 1879 by prominent business and professional men, many of whom were Masons. As far as can be ascertained, the main purpose of the order was the initiation ritual, which was harrowing and similar to that of the SONS OF MALTA, involving a life-threatening ride in a basket down a homemade shoot-the-chute. The Sons of Adam was a short-lived organization.

Sons of Hermann, Grand Lodge Order of the

P.O. Box 1941
San Antonio, TX 78297
(512) 226-9261

The Sons of Hermann was founded in 1890 in New York City as a mutual protection league and fraternal benefit society for persons of German extraction. There were 80,000 members in 1995. The order publishes *Hermann Sons News* monthly.

Hermann, more widely known as Armenius, was a German hero who wiped out three Roman legions (XVII, XVIII, and XIX) at the Battle of the Teutoburger Wald in A.D. 9. He therefore seemed a natural choice as a symbol for those Germans in the United States who, in the 1830s, were already feeling the brunt of xenophobic attacks. In 1840, the Sons of Hermann banded together as a measure of self-protection.

With the decline of the KNOW-NOTHINGS, the fraternal benefit aspect of the Sons of Hermann moved to the fore, including the usual burial benefits, care of the sick and needs of widows and orphans, and so forth. The Orden flourished throughout the 19th and early 20th centuries, but in 1921 the Grand Lodge in in Texas seceded because it was bigger and richer than all the rest of the lodges together. It now seems to be the only major representative of the old order, and the figure of 80,000 members refers to the order in Texas. Since 1937, meetings have been conducted in English rather than in German, and nationalities other than Germans have been admitted.

Although the RITUALS AND CEREMONIES survive (without DEGREES; there have never been any), members may join the organization merely by buying insurance. As with so many similar societies, it is essentially a provider of insurance, though the organization does include an old people's home, children's camps, athletic events, and so on.

Sons of Idle Rest

The Sons of Idle Rest was an organization within the ELKS, primarily a side degree. It seems to have been organized just after the turn of the century. Shortly thereafter, the Elks banned auxiliaries and side degrees.

Sons of Italy in America, Order of

219 E Street NE
Washington, DC 20002
(202) 547-2900

The Order of the Sons of Italy in America was founded in 1905 in New York City as an ethnic fraternal society for American men and women of Italian descent. The order publishes *OSIA News* monthly; *State Newspapers* monthly; a national directory; *Italian-American Characters in Television and Entertainment;* and a *Survey of Italian-American Representation.* There were 500,000 members in 1995.

The Sons of Italy was founded at the time of many other ethnic fraternal organizations, but instead of evolving into an insurance society, it remained more involved with cultural, educational, and charitable work, as well as establishing a Commission for Social Justice, the anti-defamation arm of the organization. The Sons also fund scholarships; civic programs; its own Garibaldi-Meucci Museum; and general charities such as the March of Dimes. Many of its members are apparently not Italian-Americans, but people of other ancestry who support the goals and works of the Sons of Italy.

The ritual (see RITUALS AND CEREMONIES) is of peripheral interest only, but the Sons do don uniforms for parades. The structure is the familiar three-level arrangement of LODGE, State Lodge (formerly Grand Lodge) and Supreme Lodge (national).

Sons of Liberty

The Sons of Liberty was an American intercolonial secret society organized to oppose the Stamp Act, one of the taxes imposed upon the British colonies by the government of King George III. The term "sons of liberty" was at first loosely applied to any group proclaiming themselves defenders of civil liberties, but it became more formally associated with secret political organizations after John Lamb and Isaac Sears formed the Sons of Liberty in New York City in November 1765. Chapters soon appeared throughout the colonies, mainly in cities and larger towns. The Sons welcomed all members, but most were tradesmen, laborers, and shopkeepers.

The various Sons of Liberty chapters closely communicated with one another and resisted implementation of the Stamp Act through a variety of means, including political eloquence, economic pressure, and violence. In New York and Connecticut, the Sons of Liberty were effectively a paramilitary association. After the Stamp Act was repealed in March 1766, the Sons of Liberty officially disbanded. However, the phrase persisted as a generic term for those who supported the independence movement.

The Sons of St. Tamina (after an Indian chief the order claimed as a patron "saint") was formed in New York City following the Revolution and claimed descent from the original Sons of Liberty. Ironically, this new organization furnished the model for the Tammany Society, which controlled the notorious New York City party machine called Tammany Hall, which rigged elections by a combination of vote-buying, intimidation, and political patronage.

The Sons and Daughters of Liberty, an unrelated organization, was founded in 1877 as a "patriotic and nationalist" (that is, Know-Nothing; see KNOW-NOTHINGS) fraternal benefit society in the United States. It was open to white Protestants only and excluded those who manufactured or sold intoxicating liquor. Based in Philadelphia, the order is long extinct.

Sons of Malta

The Sons of Malta was a short-lived secret society that parodied the American craze for secret societies on the eve of the Civil War. As far as can be determined, it existed principally to initiate new members. The technique was as follows:

First, word of a new and highly prestigious secret society would be circulated in town. Only men of standing might be enrolled, and then only if they passed the demanding criteria set by the existing members. When enough men had been lured, the organizers would take them to an initiation ceremony, in which they were subjected to an outrageous cross-examination. Candidates were next placed in a large basket and hauled up to the ceiling to rest there while the organizers ate a large, leisurely, and luxurious banquet on tables beneath. Another common feature of initiation was "shooting the chute." One Boston LODGE constructed a chute, which began on the third floor and ended in the basement. Candidates were sent hurling down it.

Many initiates remained in the organization so that they could do to others what had been done to them. It should be noted, however, that the Sons of Malta did often turn over to charity the considerable sums gathered as initiation fees, after deducting their costs.

Sons of Norway

1455 West Lake Street
Minneapolis, MN 55408
(612) 827-3611

The Sons of Norway was founded in 1895 as an ethnic fraternal benefit society for (mostly American) persons of Norwegian birth, descent, or affiliation by marriage. There were 90,000 members in 1995. The order publishes *Resource* monthly, *Viking* monthly, an annual directory, and a biennial convention directory.

The Sons of Norway is a large, successful ethnic fraternal benefit organization, offering the usual mix of insurance, cultural events and facilities, and general good works. In particular, the Sons can boast two features found only in the larger organizations; a good-sized library and a retirement home. There is also a strong publication program, not just for printed material, but also for Norse-oriented film strips and motion pictures.

The society was incorporated as the Independent Order of the Sons of Norway in 1898, three years after its foundation. After union with the Grand Lodge of the Sons of Norway of the Pacific Coast in 1912, it adopted a new constitution, which reflected a growth in ethnic self-esteem. Members talked about giving their adopted land the benefits of their "social and political consciousness," while in the earlier document the organization had hoped merely that "the Norwegian people in this country may be properly recognized and respected."

The Sons of Norway began as an all-male adult club, but as early as 1916 women could be admitted to male LODGES where there was no branch of the female auxiliary (see AUXILIARIES), the Daughters of Norway. The male and female branches united in 1950, and in 1956 a system of junior lodges was introduced. The Sons also merged with or absorbed the Knights of the White Cross in 1940.

The original RITUALS AND CEREMONIES attracted some adverse comment from conservative churchmen for being somewhat paganistic, drawing on Norse heritage and deities. As a result, they have been heavily modified over the decades; for example, the burial trial was abandoned completely as early as 1909.

The insurance aspect of the society has also been through a number of iterations. At first, life, sickness, and accident were offered, then (in 1934) life only, then a gradual expansion of the insurance offerings to include

mortgage protection, pension plans, and automobile insurance.

The Sons of Norway have never permitted the consumption of alcohol in lodge halls, picnics, or other functions.

Sons of Poland, Association of the

333 Hackensack Street
Carlstadt, NJ 07072
(201) 935-2807

The Sons of Poland was formed in 1903 as an ethnic fraternal benefit society for persons aged 16–60 "of good character, by birth, descent and relationship of Polish or Slovanic nationality." The Sons publishes the *Polish American Journal* monthly. There were 7,000 members in 1995.

The Sons of Poland are a typical ethnic fraternal benefit society with the usual mix of life insurance, scholarships, social and cultural events, and so forth. The Sons has also sent relief of all kinds to needy Poles in Poland.

Sons of St. George, Order of

The Sons of St. George banded together in 1871 in Scranton, Pennsylvania, for the purpose of resisting attacks by the Molly Maguires (see UNITED IRISHMEN), but soon settled down into an ethnic fraternal benefit society for Englishmen in America and their sons and grandsons, with sick benefits, funeral benefits, and so forth. The society ceased to exist a long time ago. Eligibility was limited to first-, second-, and third-generation Englishmen. There was also a female auxiliary (see AUXILIARIES), the Daughters of St. George.

Sons of Scotland Benevolent Association

90 Eglinton Avenue East, 7th Fl.
Toronto, ON, Canada M4P 2Y3
(416) 482-1250

The Sons of Scotland was formed in 1876 in Toronto, Ontario, as an ethnic fraternal benefit society for Scots, their families, and descendants living in Canada. The Sons publish *The Scotian* quarterly and an annual directory. There were about 9,000 members in 1995.

The Sons of Scotland is a typical ethnic fraternal benefit society, offering the usual mix of life insurance, cultural and social activities, and good works, including contributions to such charities as the Kidney Foundation and the Alzheimer's Foundation. The organization seems to be lively, despite losing about a third of its members in the decade 1980–90.

Sophisiens

The Sacred Order of the Sophisiens ("Followers of Wisdom") was founded in 1788–89 by French generals who participated in Napoleon's Egyptian expedition. Little is known about it, beyond the possibility that a book dealing with it, entitled *Mélanges relatifs a l'ordre sacrée des Sophisiens, établi dans les Pyramides de la République Français* ("Miscellany concerning the Sacred Order of Sophisiens established in the Pyramids of the Republic of France"), partially printed and partially in manuscript, once existed but is now lost without any surviving copies.

Spartacists

The German Spartacist movement, one of the many political secret societies that arose immediately after World War I, has been unconvincingly linked to the ILLUMINATI (Illuminist founder Adam Weishaupt was alleged to have borne the Masonic pseudonym of "Spartacus"). The Spartacists was a left-wing organization opposed to the developing Nazi party. The Nazis carried out a campaign of assassination against key Spartacist members.

Spectres Meeting in a Tomb

The Spectres Meeting in a Tomb was a short-lived French political secret society, founded in 1822, and dedicated to the overthrow of the Bourbons. The choice of name suggests a love of intrigue for its own sake, and the organization is so obscure that no additional information is available concerning it.

S.S.S. and Brotherhood of the Z.Z.R.R.Z.Z., Order of

This was a mystical organization derived in part from the THEOSOPHICAL SOCIETY. Its motto was "All things come from within," and one of its relics was "a large cube of cream-white stone," of great antiquity, presented to the society by "a Mexican chief." Membership was always very small, and the order is now extinct.

It was headquartered in Boston, Massachusetts, and members believed that love with wisdom is the secret of life and that the "Torch of Life is fed by the Oil of Love." The meaning of the initials in the name of the order was lost with the order's passing.

Stags of the World, Patriotic and Protective Order of

As the ELKS and the Moose (see MOOSE, INTERNATIONAL) were enjoying some success with clubs bearing the names of large horned ruminants, the Stags formed on New Year's Eve 1911 in Chicago. The "Droves" (LODGES) never prospered as much as those of the older organizations, however, and the order is long extinct. It vanished during the Depression.

Star of Bethlehem, Ancient and Illustrious Order of the

The Knights of the Star of Bethlehem, an American secret society "reintroduced" in 1869, changed its name to the Ancient and Illustrious Order of the Star of Bethlehem after a substantial reorganization in 1884. It claimed ancestry from an order founded in the first century A.D. via the 13th-century Bethlehemite order of monks and various subsequent bodies. Reputedly it was *first* introduced into America by Giles Cory in 1681, but it was driven from the continent because of its fanaticism by about 1694, when the order's grand commander was publicly executed. The "reintroduced" society described itself as a "high-class ceremonial order, its work being distinctly different from all other orders and peculiarly beautiful and impressive"—though it is entirely unclear just what that "work" was. As it turn-of-the-century peak, the Star of Bethlehem had 17,000 members in 250 lodges in the United States and the Canal Zone, in addition to some 20 lodges in the British West Indies. The Office of the Eminent Grand Scribe was at the Star of Bethlehem Temple, at 5004 Cass Avenue, Detroit, Michigan. It was still operating during the 1920s, but is now extinct.

Steinmetzen

The Steinmetzen was founded in Germany, probably in the 12th or 13th century, as a secret society of stonemasons. The organization is almost certainly extinct.

The order is interesting in that, like the COMPAGNON-NAGE, it represented a genuine tradition of operative masonry; that is, members actually worked stone. Despite attempts to link the group with modern FREEMASONS (especially by modern Freemasons), it was unrelated.

The first written records of the Steinmetzen—a copy of its statutes—date from 1459, though the group seems to have been well established by then. Unlike the Compagnonnage, however, they were genuine Master Masons, time-served apprentices who could themselves take apprentices. The actual word "Steinmetzen" has been derived both from *meitzel*, a chisel, or *messen*, to measure; *Stein* is "stone." Members specialized in the elaborate carving of stone and in drawing up (and working from) plans, which placed them above mere stone cutters in the hierarchy of trades.

The Steinmetzen provided a court for the settlement of grievances; enforced (or attempted to enforce) a monopoly for their members; administered a benevolent fund, paid for out of a weekly subscription; furnished PASSWORDS and GRIPS for recognition; and ran a central administration from the Head LODGE in Strasbourg. Apprentices were vouchsafed one word and one token for each year of their five-year apprenticeship, so that it was easy for any Master Mason to gauge the level of a prospective worker's skill. They were also taught a password corresponding to the borough or incorporated city in which they were apprenticed, and a word identifying their master—all of this made it easier to check up on them.

Like other guilds, the Steinmetzen declined greatly during the Reformation and the Thirty Years' War, and in 1731 it was officially suppressed by an Imperial edict banning all brotherhoods of journeymen and oaths of secrecy. Even so, it survived. As late as 1760, when Strasbourg lodge still claimed the customary contribution from the (German) Rochlitz lodge. It seems, however, to have become finally extinct in the 19th century.

Strict Observance, Clerks of the

The Clerks of the Strict Observance, also known as the Spiritual Branch of the Templars or the *Clerici Ordinis Templarii*, was a LODGE of FREEMASONS. Despite the name, it had no real connection to the original TEMPLARS.

Chief among the founders was Johann Augustus von Starck, who put the organization together in 1767. Claiming to be the only possessor both of the secrets of Masonry and of the knowledge as to the whereabouts of the treasures of the Templars, the order worked seven DEGREES: the three of ordinary Masonry, plus Junior Scottish Mason; Scottish Master or Knight of St. Andrew; Provincial Capitular of the Red Cross; and Magus, or Knight of Purity of Light. The last was further divided into Knight Novice of the Third Year; Knight Novice of the Fifth Year; Knight Notice of the Seventh Year; Levite; and Priest. The order seems to have been extinct by 1800.

Sublime Perfect Masters

The Sublime Perfect Masters—or Sublime Masters of Perfection, *Sublimi Maestri Perfecti*, and so on—referred to by a number of 19th-century writers on the subject of secret societies, and by some from the 20th century. It is commonly referred to as the supreme ruling body of all secret societies, much like the GREAT WHITE LODGE, though with even less consistency and detail. Indeed, the order is presumed to be so secret that nothing is known about it, except the fact of its existence. (The title "Sublime Perfect Master"—or a variant thereof—has been adopted by a number of different bodies, including officers of some branches of FREEMASONS.)

Sun of Mercy, Society of the

Little is known of this 18th-century society, except that Antoine Joseph Pernetty, the presumed author of the 28th Degree of the Masonic SCOTTISH RITE, became a member and induced Emanuel Swedenborg (see SWEDENBORG AND SWEDENBORGIANS) to join as well. It was centered in Avignon and Montpellier, France, and the nature of its beliefs was Hermetic (see HERMES TRISMEGISTUS).

Svithiod, Independent Order of

The Independent Order of Svithiod was a Swedish fraternal benefit society, founded in 1881, which in 1978 merged with Banker's Mutual Life Insurance of Freeport, Illinois. The RITUALS AND CEREMONIES referred to the Norse gods: Baldur, Thor, Odin, and so on.

Swedenborg and Swedenborgians

Emanuel Swedenborg (1688–1772) was a Swedish scientist, theosophist, and mystic. He was educated at the University of Uppsala, and was employed as a natural scientist and official by the Swedish board of mines from 1710–45. In 1734, he produced his most important works of natural science, the *Opera philosophica et mineralia (Philosophical and Mineralogical Works)*, which was published in three volumes in 1734. Increasingly, however, his study of mathematics, mechanics, and physics was motivated by his passion for cosmology and, ultimately, theology, which led to his evolution as a theosophical seer of divine wisdom. In 1745, Swedenborg reported having been visited by a divine apparition, which admitted him to a direct vision of the spiritual world underlying the natural one. He set about interpreting this vision, producing voluminous works in the guise of divinely revealed biblical interpretations.

The most central of his theological works, *Divine Love and Wisdom* (1763), presents Swedenborg's conception of three spheres: divine mind, spiritual world, and natural world. Each corresponds to a degree of being in God and in humankind: love, wisdom, and use (that is, end, cause, and effect). The object of life is to achieve unity with each degree in turn, thereby fulfilling the ultimate human destiny: union with creator and creation.

After receiving a vision of the "last judgment" and the "return of Christ," Swedenborg proclaimed a new church, that of the New Jerusalem, which is currently based in England. In addition to the Church of the New Jerusalem, Swedenborgian thought spawned a number of sects or secret societies, the most important of which follow:

The Illuminati of Avignon. Founded in 1760 and Masonic in nature, its members occupied themselves with philosophy and astronomy, as well as an examination of political society.

Illuminated Theosophists. An adaptation of the Avignon Illuminati by Parisian Freemasons, the order was founded in 1766.

Philosophic Scotch Rite. This Masonic adaptation of Swedenborgianism was French and dates from 1780. It incorporated the earlier Hermetic Rite (1770), which was a mixture of Freemasonry, Swedenborgianism, Alchemy, and more. The highest degree (of twelve; see DEGREES) was "Sublime Master of the Perfect Ring," and in 1780 an academy of Sublime Masters of the Perfect Ring was established in Paris.

Philalethes. This Masonic society has its own entry.

Rite of Swedenborg. This was another modification (by the Marquis de Thome, in 1783) of the Avignon Illuminati. The Masonic rite involved six degrees: Apprentice, Companion, Master Theosophite, Illuminated Theosophite, Blue Brother, Red Brother.

Universal Aurora. Count Cagliostro (see CAGLIOSTRO, ALESSANDRO) was involved in this group, which also supported MESMERISM.

Synarchie

Also known as Le Mouvement Synarchique d'Empire, Synarchie was a French political secret society begun in 1931 by one Jean Coutrot, who had founded a group he called "X-Crise." Its object was to bring about a "synarchic" order, first in France and then in the world, a form of government through which a perfect collective life could be achieved through the leadership of "technocrats," each of whom were specialists in a given field. Indeed, the term *technocrat* may have been coined in connection with Synarchie; for Coutrot, like the other charter members of the order, were alumni of The École Polytechnique in Paris. The order was particularly active in Vichy France during the early part of World War II.

While Synarchie was founded in 1931, its origins may be traced to the Marquis d'Alveydre, an 18th-century figure who had proposed a society to restore "the form of government instituted by Moses," which he described as "Synarchy, that is to say three social powers, none of which is political."

Synarchie apparently disappeared some time before the end of World War II.

Tall Cedars of Lebanon of North America

2609 North Front Street
Harrisburg, PA 17110
(717) 232-5991

The Tall Cedars of Lebanon was founded in 1902 in Trenton, New Jersey, as a "fun" side degree (see SIDE DEGREES) for Master FREEMASONS. The organization is confined mainly to the northeastern United States and publishes *The Cedar Digest* twice yearly. There were 25,000 members in 1995.

The Tall Cedars of Lebanon is one of the smaller "fun" organizations within the Freemasons, though, even at that, it is still larger than many independent secret societies. Admission is open to all Master Masons in good standing in their BLUE LODGE. The name comes from the trees supposed to have been used in the construction of the Temple of Solomon. The watchwords of the order are "Fun, Frolic and Friendship."

The original side degree of the Tall Cedars of Lebanon was apparently conferred well before the formal foundation of the organization; some trace it to the 1840s. It apparently involved a certain amount of rough-housing; the extent to which it has since been toned down is not clear. The modern LODGES are called Forests and offer two further side degrees, the Royal Court and the Sidonian. There is also a marching division, the Royal Rangers. The chief officer is the Supreme Tall Cedar.

Tall Cedars are much given to comical-seeming attire. All Tall Cedars wear triangular, pyramidal hats, in different colors for officers, past officers, and nonoffi-

cers. The Royal Rangers march in a military outfit, while the Tuxedo Units march in white tuxedos.

In addition to the usual social activities and support for Masonic youth organizations, the Tall Cedars operate the Tall Cedar Foundation, which funds research into muscular dystrophy.

Until 1972, when the current style was adopted, the Tall Cedars were known as the Tall Cedars of the U.S.A.

Tantra

Tantra, like MESMERISM, is a term often casually used, and many who use the term are either members or students of secret societies. Even those who have studied Tantra dispute the precise meaning of the term. It may, however, be defined as an esoteric inner teaching found in Hinduism, Buddhism, Bonpo, and possibly in some of the other old religions that originated in the Indian subcontinent and on the Tibetan plateau. The inner teachings of Tantra are extremely secret, and even the traveler in the Himalayas will meet very few true adepts, which means that many writers and others have seized upon the term as one they can use to mean almost anything, especially if it has a sexual dimension.

For some Westerners, especially for would-be gurus, sex is the major attraction of Tantra. The sexual aspect of the teachings is typically represented as the *yab-yum* sexual union of male deities and their *shaktis*, though the altogether less formal and ritualistic representations of carnal high spirits that are to be found at temples such as Khajuraho in central India have also been claimed (with no scholarly basis) as being Tantric in origin. By a convenient theological short cut, the initiation into Tantric mysteries is therefore assumed to be sexual intercourse. (The number of unscrupulous male teachers who have performed such "initiations" probably runs into the thousands or tens of thousands; the Hermetic Brotherhood of the Light for an example.)

The rarity with which the higher reaches of Tantra are actually taught by those who have mastered them may be gauged from an anecdote current in Dharamsala (seat in exile of the Dalai Lama, and of Tibetan Buddhist teaching) in the 1980s. An *inji* (Westerner) asked his teacher when he would be able to start studying the sexual magic (see MAGIC AND SECRETS) of Tantra. His teacher pointed to a heap of *tsampa* (barley flour). "When you have learned to blow a hole through that by mind-power alone; then, you will be ready to begin the study of that part of Tantra."

Taverns and Pubs

The tavern or public house warrants attention here for two reasons. The first is that innumerable secret societies were either founded or have met in such places, and the second is that the institution of the British pub may illustrate why fraternal orders, and especially the Moose (see MOOSE, INTERNATIONAL) and ELKS are vastly more successful in the United States than in Great Britain. The average pub is a social center, rather than just a place to get drunk on your own. Unlike the typical American bar, which is dark and unwelcoming, the typical British pub is reasonably well lit, and provides a home away from home, where friends frequently arrange to meet. At lunchtime, it often provides food, and "lunch at the pub" is a British institution. In the evening, it provides a neutral ground for conversation. Each person at the pub is free to eat, or not, as he or she feels inclined; and because each person traditionally "stands his round," buying a drink for each person in the party (and later being bought a drink by the other members of the party), everyone can drink what they want, when they want. What is more, different pubs attract different clienteles, an older or younger crowd, persons with special interests, and so on. Traditionally, there are also several different rooms within the pub. At the very least, there are normally two: a Public Bar, where a working man could stop off in his working clothes, and a Saloon Bar, where slightly higher standards of dress are seen, the chairs are more comfortable, and the beer is more expensive. There might also be a Smoking Room, a Lounge Bar (a more genteel Saloon Bar), a Back Bar (traditionally a meeting place for clubs, or the home of the skittles alley), a Select Bar or Snug (a small bar for close friends to meet), and more.

Many open clubs meet at pubs. For example, many pubs run a "folk club" (for singers and musicians) or a darts club. Dues, if there are any, may be payable only on the evening of the event, or the dues may be more organized. In any event, club members and non-club members share the same premises, unlike the American Moose or the Elks, where you have to join the club in order to get in.

A very important point about the pub is its continuity. There are pubs whose origins are lost in history, but which are at least five centuries old. More important than age alone, though, is the fact that Britain never experienced prohibition, which killed the American tavern. The end of the Prohibition era coincides with the beginning of the decline of most fraternal orders and secret societies, but if the American people had not lost the habit of going to taverns, and the taverns had not in many cases been irrevocably closed, the decline would have been even faster. By the time of the repeal of Prohibition, the Moose or Elks Lodge already provided a substitute for the tavern, at least for many, so the American tavern never recovered as anything like the equivalent of the English pub.

Temperance Societies

The roots of temperance go deep: The Order of Temperance, founded by the Duke of Hesse in 1600, restricted its knights to no more than "seven goblets of wine at a meal, and not more than twice a day." The modern temperance movements began to gather force in the United States at the beginning of the 19th century. By 1828 there were 11 major temperance societies with a total membership of more than 100,000, though the first to advocate total abstinence was apparently the Sons of Temperance in 1842. The International Order of Good Templars (see GOOD TEMPLARS, INTERNATIONAL ORDER OF) followed in 1851 and then the Knights of Jericho (1853). Next came the Women's Christian Temperance Crusade of 1873, which became the Women's Christian Temperance Union, and the Anti-Saloon League of America was united from various local bodies in 1895.

The culmination of political pressure brought to bear by temperance societies was the 24th Amendment to the United States Constitution and the accompanying Volstead Act, which instituted and enforced prohibition.

Templars (Poor Knights of Christ and the Temple of Solomon)

For such a relatively short-lived organization—it was operative for less than 200 years—the Knights Templar or *Pauperes Commilitones Christi Templique Salomonici* have exercised a powerful fascination on the popular imagination. The Poor Knights of Christ and the Temple of Solomon were founded in A.D. 1119 by the knights Hughes de Paynes of Burgundy and Goddefroi de St.

Omer of Northern France. Its aim was to protect pilgrims visiting the Holy Land after the First Crusade, and it took the "Temple" part of its name from its quarters, which were in a part of the palace of Baldwin II that was believed to be on the site of Solomon's Temple. After its foundation, the order grew steadily in power until it was conclusively (and ruthlessly) suppressed between 1307 and 1314, largely on the basis of manufactured evidence. Since then, a large number of organizations that have no historical connection with the original Poor Knights have also adopted the name "Templar," including Masonic and TEMPERANCE SOCIETIES, among others.

At first, the Templars seems to have been genuinely humble and poor. The order was not exclusive, its members wore old clothes given to them by the charitable, and it sought out excommunicated knights with two objects: first, to return them to the bosom of the church; and second, to recruit them to the order. St. Bernard's support was instrumental in obtaining recognition for the new order at the Council of Troyes in 1128.

The Grand Master was the Master of the Temple in Jerusalem (or Cyprus, after the fall of the Latin Kingdom in 1290), and the structure of the organization is described in the Rule of the Temple, which was jealously kept secret by the chief officers of the Templars. This secrecy was to prove its downfall. The group was accused of having a blasphemous "Secret Rule" in addition to the Rule of the Temple. The Grand Master was elected by an electoral college of 12 (plus an appointed chaplain), which worked in an unusual way. Two Templars would be selected by their brethren. After prayer and meditation, these two would select two more, who would join in the process. These four would select two more, then the six would select two more, and so forth, until there were 12. Although the Grand Master's power was very great, and in many respects absolute, there were some reserved areas (such as the declaration of war and the admission of a new brother) in which he had to consult the Chapter and was bound by a simple majority vote.

The Brethren were often noble and were either admitted for life or oath-bound to a term of years. Married brethren had to bequeath one-half of their property to the order, which was not chaste. At first the order had no priests of its own, though after about 1200 it had its own clergy owing allegiance only to the Pope and, because of the bull *Omne Datum Optimum* (1163), to the Grand Master. An extraordinary privilege enjoyed by the Templars, partly as a consequence of its original methods of recruitment, was immunity from excommunication by bishops and parish priests.

The slow destruction of the Latin Kingdom was resisted heroically, if not always effectively, by the Templars, and its power in other lands reflected the high esteem in which it was held. It also rose to preeminence in banking, circumventing the laws against usury (loans with interest) by a fine distinction between "real" rent and "nominal" rent. This, even more than the trumped-up charges of religious deviance, was among the three main circumstances that led to its downfall. The other two were straightforward political resentment of the power of the order, and the fall of the Latin Kingdom with the loss of Acre. When the Templars left the Holy Land and moved to Cyprus, its prestige was inevitably dimmed, and in the absence of daily conflict with the *paynim,* the order's thoughts turned to power elsewhere.

A carefully orchestrated attack on the Templars began in France, where Philip IV was deeply in the group's debt and where the order was so powerful that it constituted a virtual state-within-a-state. Moreover, there had long been rumors of extraordinary goings-on in the Temple: of ritual desecration of the Cross, of worship of BAPHO-MET, and more. In order to overthrow the Templars, Philip turned these rumors into a whispering campaign. Once this had been done, it was a simple matter to accuse the Templars of heresy, apostasy, and other outrages. Since both Pope Clement V and the Grand Inquisitor of France owed their positions principally to Philip's patronage, convictions were not difficult to obtain.

To the credit of the Pope, he was at first unwilling to accept Philip's allegations, but William of Paris (the Grand Inquisitor of France) was Philip's personal confessor. The Inquisition was, of course, able to act without the consent of the Holy Father, and on Friday, October 13, 1907, the Grand Master of the Templars and sixty of his companions were seized. Under torture from Philip's men and the Inquisition alike, confessions to all manner of abomination were obtained; spitting on the Cross was a favorite. In Paris alone, 36 Templars died under torture, either before or after making confessions. Jacques de Molay, the Grand Master, succumbed to the mere threat of torture, however, not only confessing but publicly acknowledging his confession in a letter sent to all Temples.

Philip next enlisted the help of other princes, knowing that they would be eager to loot the Templars' coffers and to break the temporal power of the order in their own kingdoms. James of Aragon, Edward of England, and others were solicited by Philip. On October 27, 1308, the Pope took the extraordinary step of suspending the powers of the Inquisition in France, but less than a month later (November 22, 1308) he issued a bull calling for the general arrest of Templars. The fall of the Templars thereafter was rapid. In England and Sicily, members were arrested in January 1309; in Cyprus, in May 1309; and so on. The Templars of Aragon and Castile resisted with military force, and the group's last stronghold (Castellat) did not fall until November 2, 1308. In 1312, the Bull *Ad providam* transferred the property of the order to the Knights of St. John.

The next few years are poorly documented. No doubt,

many Templars perished or disappeared. On March 14, 1314, Jacques de Molay was burned alive in the square before Notre Dame in Paris. Immediately before his death, he delivered a stirring speech recanting his confession, and saying that he was guilty of the greatest sin of all, that of lying about the order under fear of torture and thereby bringing about its downfall. It is on the story of this man that the Masonic Order of De Molay is based (see DE MOLAY, ORDER OF).

Modern Pseudo-Templar Orders

Many secret organizations claim descent from the Templars. Among these are the following, in addition to those discussed in their own entries throughout this book.

Association Française des Chevaliers du Christ. Founded in 1970 and apparently enjoying good relations with the Vatican, this society numbers among its members one Canon Ledit, who is the author of various works on numerology and the Golden Number (11 rue du Paon, 10000 Troyes).

Les Chevaliers de L'Alliance Templière. Fights against modern life and against drugs; works in harmony with the *Ordre des Veilleurs du Temple* (Jean-Luc Verger, 4 rue du Cietiere-Saint-Cyprien, 31000 Toulouse).

Fraternité Johannite pour la Résurgence Templière. The directors of the GREAT WHITE LODGE are alleged to have decided in 1962 to begin a 14-year spell of preparation ("Putrefaction," in alchemical parlance) before founding the society in 1978 and passing three more years in Purification before moving on to Sublimation in 1981. This antimaterialistic, anticommercial organization has Brothers Servant, Brothers Equerry, and Brothers Cavalier, and involves vows of poverty, chastity and obedience (B.P. 25, 59670 Cassel).

Ordo Militiae Crucis Templi. This widely established order fights "modern paganism" and operates in 35 countries. It is open to all Christians "of knightly disposition," provided their character is irreproachable and they are over 20 years old. The Master of the Order is Horst Frischmuth (Hildesheimer Strasse 119D, 3000 Hannover 1).

Ordre Sovereian et Militaire de Temple de Jérysalem. Founded in 1945 by a Portuguese diplomat, Antonio Campello Pinto Pereira de Sousa Fontès, this order suffered a schism in 1970, when the son of the founder lost the election for the new Grand Master and founded the *Ordo Supremus Militaris Templi Hierosoly Militair* with a seat in Portugal. The "rump" group continued under General Count Antoine Daniel Zdrojewski, who dissolved the Grand Prior of France of the 1945 order in 1973.

Nouvel Observance Templière. Also known as the Order of the Rose, this is a "personal growth" movement with solstice observances (B.P. 11, 06701 Saint-Laurent-du-Var, Cedex).

Ordre d'Alibert. Founded in 1957 by Alibert de Brandicourt, this order promotes chivalric values and admits Christians, Jews, and Muslims alike (Raoul Alibert de la Vallée, résidence Les Mourinoux, 11 avenue de la Redoute [esc. 5], 92600 Asnières).

Ordre des Chevaliers de France. To join this order, one must have been born into a monoitheistic religion, believe in God, and be 21 or over. After a year as a Postulant, a doctrinal thesis has to be produced. The motto of this group is "Etre La," or "To Be There" (B.P. 54, 54139 San-Max, Meurthe-et-Moselle).

Ordre des Chevaliers du Saint-Temple. Aims to revive chivalrous ideas via prayer and a strictly controlled diet (Résidence Pont-Cardinal, 19100 Brive).

Ordre des Chevaliers du Temple, du Christ et de Notre-Dame. This is another innovation from the Great White Lodge, which decided at its convocation on February 5, 1962, to refound the Templars in 1984, this being 648 years (6 × 108 years) from 1314. They believe in the perfectibility of man (B.P. 12, 78430 Louveciennes).

Templiers de Chypre. This order purports to be derived from the original Templars via knights who escaped to Scotland at the time of the suppression of the original order, and has a heavy admixture of Rosicrucianism (see ROSUCRICIANS).

Ordre Equestre et Hospitalier de Chypre, ou Ordre Templier de Chypre. This order appears to have confused the Templars and the Hospitallers, but its intentions are philanthropy and charity. There are two degrees (8 allée Mozart, 93270 Sevran).

Ordre de la Massenie du Saint-Graal. Combines Templars and the Holy Grail in an esoteric organization dedicated to helping its adepts along the road of knowledge (B.P. 13, 95509 Gonesse Cedex).

Ordre Renové du Temple. Open to men and women of the legal age of majority, this is a mystical and esoteric school (Julien Orago [Grand Master], La Cammaderie-Roais, 84110 Vaisons-la-Romaine).

Ordre Souverain du Temple Solaire. This is apparently a Masonic order founded in 1952 and made public in 1967. It demands the rehabilitation of the Templars (20 boulevard Princesse-Charlotte, Monte-Carlo).

Ordre du Temple Cosmique. This order was formed by a schism in the previous order (the *Temple Solaire*) and was founded in 1978. It publishes *La Lettre d'Helios,* formerly just *Helios,* and is more mystically inclined than its parent (9 bis rue de Liège, 92140 Clamart).

Ordre des Vielleurs du Temple. Open to "all serious seekers" in the Templar tradition. No address is available.

Templars of Fraternity

The Templars of Fraternity was a short-lived society, founded in Syracuse, New York, in 1896. Members were given to studying occult and psychic matters; they also worked a ritual (see RITUALS AND CEREMONIES) with no fewer than 11 DEGREES. Seven of these constituted the "White Fraternity," while the four highest degrees were the "Temple." The order probably lasted less than a quarter of a century.

Templars of Honor and Temperance

As one might expect from the title of the society, this was a mixture of Christianity, FREEMASONS, and the legends of the TEMPLARS; the eclectic RITUALS AND CEREMONIES also incorporated elements from the Old Testament stories of David and Jonathan, plus more from the Greek myths of Damon and Phintias (see KNIGHTS OF PYTHIAS), as well as mandating total abstinence from alcohol. There were six DEGREES.

The chronology of its evolution is as follows: The Sons of Temperance (1842) did not have an elaborate enough ritual for some of its members, who in 1845 seceded to form the Marshall Temperance Fraternity and then, later in the same year, changed the organizations name first to Marshall Temple, No. 1, Sons of Honor, and then to Marshall Temple of Honor, No. 1, Sons of Temperance. In 1846, the National Temple of the Templars of Honor and Temperance of the United States organized itself in New York City. The organization is long extinct.

Teutonic Order

The *Fratres domus hospitalis sanctae Mariae Teutonicorum in Jerusalem* ("Brothers of the hospital of Holy Mary of the Germans in Jerusalem") was founded in 1190 as a hospital order for pilgrims visiting the Holy Land. It later became a military order, and, much later, in 1929, was transformed into a purely clerical order.

The military rule of the Teutonic Order was modeled on the TEMPLARS, and the hospital rule was modeled on the Hospital of St. John of Jerusalem. After a relatively brief period as a hospital order, the main object of the Teutonic Order seems to have been fighting fellow Christians, especially the King of Poland. When medieval warmongering diminished, the order fell into quiescence, but was eventually reformed as a nonmilitary clerical order with an abbot for a High Master.

In the 20th century, the reformed order was grievously persecuted by the Nazis, who set up a rival—and totally spurious—Teutonic Order of their own, complete with a magnificent and almost completely fictitious history.

Clerical brothers (priests of the order) make solemn perpetual vows; lay brothers and the Sisters of the German Hospital make simple vows; and members of the Institute of Familiars may be either secular priests or lay people who can advance the cause of the Church because of their positions in public life. A few Familiars are made Knights of Honor.

Theosophical Society

The term *theosophy* derives from the Greek *theos* ("god") and *sophia* ("wisdom") and literally signifies wisdom of or about God. In practice, theosophy refers to a broad range of occult or mystical philosophies, usually pantheistic. The Western theosophical tradition is derived from the Hermetic tradition of the Renaissance and post-Renaissance and is characterized by an emphasis on secret traditions passed down from the ancients. These traditions are believed to be a universal key to nature and humankind's role in nature.

In contemporary use, the term "theosophy" often refers specifically to the Theosophical Society and all that is associated with it.

The Theosophical Society was founded in 1875 and is now spread throughout the world. There seems to be no clear overall headquarters, nor is the number of adherents clear.

Helena Blavatsky (1831–91; see BLAVATSKY, HELENA PETROVNA) founded the first manifestation of the Theosophical Society in New York on November 17, 1875. Colonel H. S. Olcott (a U.S. government official) and others were also involved. Its premise was that secret wisdom has been transmitted through the ages by or through the medium of "Mahatmas" (Hindi for "Great Souls"), and Madame Blavatsky claimed to be in touch with them. In 1879—by which time she was already a popular figure—she and Col. Olcott moved to Adayr, a suburb of Madras, and directed the Theosophical Society from India. The stated aims of the Society were (and continue to be) threefold: to establish a nucleus of the Universal Brotherhood of Humanity; to promote the study of comparative religion and philosophy; and to make a systematic investigation into the mystic potentialities of life and matter.

In 1891, shortly after Mme. Blavatsky's death, a schism arose, and a separate organization was founded in the United States by William P. Judge. The original Theosophical Society was taken over by Col. Olcott, who continued to run it until his death in 1907, when Annie Besant (see BESANT, ANNIE) took over.

The religious teaching of the Theosophical Society centers on the Mahatmas and on the doctrines of *karma* and rebirth or reincarnation (many Theosophists do not or are unaware of a distinction). *Karma* may be thought of as "merit," though it can be both good and bad, and the accumulation of *karma* is what determines the quality of the rebirth (of the bundle of desires) or reincarnation (of the personality).

Thuggee

Thuggee was founded in remote antiquity and was suppressed after 1830. It was a religious/criminal fraternity of Hindu men over the age of 10. Membership was by birth or—rarely—by initiation.

The word *thug* has entered the English language as meaning ruffian, bully, or criminal strong-arm man; but the original Thugs were much more sinister. It was an Indian sect whose members lived by waylaying and killing travelers, strangling them with a *rumal,* or knotted handkerchief. Their legendary beginning was thus:

When mankind was created, there was a vast demon who devoured each human as he or she came into being. The goddess Kali killed the demon, but from each drop of his blood another demon arose, and as these were killed, their blood gave rise to still more demons. Orthodox Hindus believe that Kali solved the problem by licking up the blood as it fell. She is a "wrathful" or "terrible" deity. According to Thug legend, though, Kali created the first two Thugs from the sweat on her arms and gave them a knotted kerchief with which to strangle demons, which shed no blood. As a reward, their descendants were to be allowed to earn their living by strangling and robbing travelers.

Strangulation was normally carried out by three Thugs working together: one at each end of the *rumal,* and a third to hold the victim's legs and kick him in the crotch, which rendered resistance unlikely. Originally, the Thugs' choice of victims was severely circumscribed; they were not allowed to kill washermen, potmakers, untouchables, shoemakers, lepers, the blind or mutilated, or a man driving a cow or female goat. In addition, they were reluctant to kill women, metalsmiths, carpenters, and stone cutters. All members of a traveling party had to be killed and the bodies ritually mutilated—though young boys might be spared and initiated into the brotherhood. By the 18th century, few (if any) of these rules were observed by the majority of Thugs. Female children were often spared in order to sell them into prostitution.

Despite the lapse of ancient rules, the Thugs maintained a mystical system of belief. The sacred pickax (used for burying the victims) was supposed to have been made from one of Kali's ribs; the knife used to mutilate the body, from one of her teeth; and the *rumal* from the hem of her sari. The consecration of the pickax involved passing it through fire seven times; an oath sworn upon it was sacred. There was a Thuggee feast with similarities to a Christian Mass: *Gur* or *jaggery* (raw sugar) was the sacramental food, and holy water was sprinkled around. Initiation was normally by participation in a ritual murder. If anyone who had not murdered a traveler ate the *gur,* he was obliged to go out and commit a murder forthwith.

When the British took over India, a young British army officer, William Sleeman (1788–1856) became interested in Thuggee beginning about 1815. By 1830, the Governor-General, Lord William Bentinck, appointed him to suppress Thuggee throughout central India. In 1840, Sleeman's courts had tried 3,689 Thugs, hanging 466, pardoning 56 as "approvers" (informers), and sentencing the rest to penal transportation or imprisonment for life. In the decade 1840–50, only 651 more were tried, and by 1850 the cult had effectively ceased to exist.

An interesting theory suggests that the Thugs might be lineal descendants of the ASSASSINS. After the older order was defeated, the surviving Assassins made their way from the Near East to India. This is not impossible—though it must be observed that there is a lot of ground to cover between the Near East and Central or Southern India, which is where Thuggee flourished.

Thule Gesellschaft

The Thule Gesellschaft or Thule Society was founded in Munich toward the end of World War I by the self-styled Baron Rudolf von Sebottendorf, allegedly the son of a railway worker. It drew upon members of a secret society founded some years earlier, a society based on a combination of Sufi mysticism, Freemasonry, Alchemy, and right-wing, anti-Bolshevik and anti-Semitic politics. Von Sebottendorf was a steamship stoker and electrician who had visited various ports in the Near East and had been initiated into an order of FREEMASONS that came under the aegis of the French Grand Orient. The mere fact of his Near Eastern travels was sufficient qualification for mystic leadership in the eyes of many who gathered around him.

The Thule Gesellschaft supported the N.D.S.A.P. or National Democratic Socialist Workers' Party, better known later as the Nazis. A Thule Gesellschaft member (identified as F. Kohn) is said to have supplied Hitler with the design of the Nazi flag. Another National Socialist who had been a member of Thule Gesellschaft was Wilhelm Frick, Minister of the Interior under the Third Reich. Von Sebottendorf himself was arrested by the Gestapo in 1934, the year after secret societies, other than those invented or sanctioned by the Nazis, were banned. He was later released and settled in Istanbul, where he committed suicide in 1945 after learning of the German surrender. He claimed to be working for the *Sicherheitdienst* (the S.D., or German Secret Society) at the time.

Members of the Thule Gesellschaft also translated the Protocols of the Elders of Zion, which allegedly influenced Hitler while he was writing *Mein Kampf.* The Protocols are rabidly anti-Semitic, probably invented in Russia during the 19th century, and purporting to be the blueprint for world denomination drawn up by unspecified but incredibly evil Jews. Hitler was an occultist himself, and in *Mein Kampf* he argued that, because the myths of Freemasonry were based on the legends of the Temple of Solomon and HIRAM ABIF, the Masons were themselves part of a Jewish conspiracy.

Tobaccologers

See PEDNOSOPHIERS.

Tontine

A tontine is an unusual form of benevolent association in which a number of people agree that a piece of property or a fund established by all the members of the group shall go to the last surviving member of that group or (sometimes) to the last surviving child of any member of the group. Tontines were popular among many groups of ethnic immigrants to the United States during the 19th and early 20th century. The word is French and derived from the name of an Indian-born French banker, Lorenzo Tonti, who was born in 1635 and died about 1690.

Trade Unions

Trade unions are fraternal, and they have also functioned as secret societies from time to time, although their modern role and structure is rarely secret and their methods of working are a matter of constant examination in the newspapers.

In most capitalist countries, trade unions have been through five main stages to date. Britain is a good example, because it was the first country to industrialize.

1. Combinations of tradesmen. These first appeared in significant numbers in Britain, the first country to industrialize, as early as the 18th century. They were mostly small and local, organized on an *ad hoc* basis to help bring pressure upon employers, and they attracted skilled workers such as printers, tailors, or weavers. Under the Statute of Artificers and Apprentices, an Elizabethan Act of Parliament, Justices of the Peace had the power to fix wages, and trade combinations were often formed to petition them to do so; at a higher level, of course.

Toward the end of the 18th century, with the spirit of revolution in the air, some people began to see that trade and other associations had political implications. What is more, increasing industrialization and the urbanization of the working class meant that factories were dependent on semiskilled labor as never before. A strike of millhands meant that a factory stopped, which was for more consequential than a few days' delay suffered when an agricultural laborer walked off the job.

2. Outright Prohibition. As working-class groups began to organize, whether as "straight" trade unions or as associations with more overtly political ambitions, the ruling classes acted to counter them. Initially, existing laws were adapted (especially those relating to "conspiracy"), but soon new laws were passed forbidding the combination or banding together of workmen. In pro-gressive France, newly liberated by the Revolution, the Le Chapelier law banned all combinations as early as 1791; in backward England, still afflicted with royalty, it took until 1799–1800 for the Combination Acts to be passed. During this period, which was usually fairly short in most countries (about a quarter of a century in England), the unions almost inevitably became politicized, even if they had not been so before.

3. Relaxation of Controls. In England, 1824 saw the passage of a remarkably forward-looking act, which recognized the impossibility of destroying associations of labor and repealed the Combination Acts. The next year, however, a reactionary law removed much of what had been granted in 1824. A number of additional laws were passed or adapted to restrict the right of assembly. Despite such setbacks, the Trade Union movement grew steadily.

4. Acceptance. Mere acceptance is always grudging—management and labor see one another as class enemies, rather than as people with a common goal—but it signals a new era in industrial relations. Often, it was not a question of major changes in statute law that ushered in the change; it was change in the way the law was administered. This is the stage at which the unions realize their basic social demands: shorter working weeks, higher (or merely adequate) wages, banning of child labor, and so forth.

5. Cooperation or Decline. After acceptance, and after achieving its original goals (which are based on conflict), a unionized industry can do one of two things. Management and unions can work together to increase productivity and hence the standard of living of the workers in that industry, or they can remain in the fourth phase *after* the unions have achieved their basic demands. In the latter case, either the *industry* is likely to decline, as "feather bedding" sets in and the union's demands become unrealistic, or the *union* will decline as the workers cease to perceive a need for it.

Unions as Secret Societies

It is during the first and second of these five stages that unions are most likely to function as secret societies. They do so in the first stage because that is the only model available to them. They imitate the old GUILDS and journeyman's associations, such as the STEINMETZEN or the COMPAGNONNAGE. In the second stage, they are secret out of necessity, as any banned political society must be.

They may also appear to function as secret societies in the third stage, but this is not so much a matter of their being true secret societies as it is a function of a class struggle, in which the ruling class uses the few remaining weapons in its armory to fight a rearguard action. Having failed to throw the unions out of the front door, the courts may attempt to use conspiracy laws and the like as a means of throwing them out the back.

Given that these three stages are now well in the past in advanced capitalist countries, there is little more to say about unions as secret societies.

Unions as Fraternal Orders

Although unions are undoubtedly fraternal, and although many of them were founded around the same time as many of the nonunion fraternal orders that are still strong to this day—the Elks, Moose, and so on—there are three major differences between them.

The first is that, unlike a social club, a trade union has a business purpose, and everything else is subordinated to that business purpose. This means that there is not the scope for the paraphernalia associated with so many fraternal orders. Instead of a multiplication of DEGREES and RITUALS AND CEREMONIES, an increasingly specialized and professional class of union officials begins to emerge.

The second major difference is that there is much less of an element of free association in a union than there is in a fraternal order. In some industries, in some countries, there is a "closed shop," so that a worker *must* join a union if he is to work in a particular job in a particular place. Even where this is not the case, union membership may be so much the norm that nonmembership must be a conscious (and sometimes inconvenient or personally costly) decision. Also, a union has the power (whether *de jure* or *de facto*) to compel a strike, which may or may not be in the best interests of an individual worker; there is, therefore, a good deal of ambivalence of feeling among the members of the union.

The third major difference is political. There is a distinction between the *inevitable political effect* of unions, and the *concomitant political ambitions* of unions. The inevitable political effect of the existence of unions is the injection of a degree of socialism into the society in which they exist. Any organization that is for "the workers" and their rights can hardly fail to have a political impact in terms of redistribution of wealth, regulation of working hours and conditions, and so forth. The concomitant political ambitions are normally a result of the way in which unions attract a certain kind of people as organizers. Drawn from the proletariat, union leaders may be of a utopian bent or of a ruthless disposition—or sometimes both. Those of a utopian bent will try to engineer political ends that are a long way from the original, practical purposes of the union. The ruthless faction normally enjoys personal power for its own sake, and, frequently, they also enjoy the normal corollary of power, wealth. Either type of leader may be easy prey for outside political influences.

Unions in Totalitarian States

In a totalitarian state, whether of the left or of the right, unions are seen and manipulated as part of the state apparatus of control. Independent trade unions are, therefore, illegal, and their success marks the failure of totalitarianism. The early history of Solidarity in Poland affords an example of an independent union that was both symptomatic of and instrumental in the downfall of late Stalinist Marxism.

Transcendental Meditation ("TM")

See WORLD PLAN EXECUTIVE COUNCIL—U.S.

Travelers' Protective Association of America

3755 Lindell Boulevard
St. Louis, MO 63108
(314) 371-0533

The Travelers' Protective Association of America was founded as a fraternal benefit insurance society for traveling salesmen aged 18–60. There were 161,000 members in 1995. The association publishes a monthly bulletin, a quarterly magazine, and an annual report.

The Travelers' Protective Association of the United States was founded in Chicago in January 1882 by a group of traveling salesmen, principally to seek discounts from railroads, hotels, and the like, and to assist its members. It was not particularly successful until 1890, when it moved to St. Louis, changed its name slightly, and started to offer accident insurance. Since then, it has functioned as a combination fraternal benefit insurance society and pressure group. Causes espoused have included sanitary regulations in hotels, driver training, and more. Membership is no longer restricted—as it was until at least the late 1970s—to commercial travelers. The RITUALS AND CEREMONIES are vestigial and devoid of oaths and pseudohistory, but still exist. There is even a Ritual Committee.

Triangle, The

Probably founded in the late 19th century, The Triangle, also called the Triangle Club, was a very secret organization consisting of members of New York City's Socialist Labor Party who were also members of the Knights of Labor and of the Central Labor Federation of New York. The majority of members of the Knights of Labor were opposed to The Triangle, emphasizing that it bore no official connection to the organization and that it was "a small cabal . . . having for its object the subordination of labor organizations . . . to the principles of socialism." The order was also accused of advocating anarchy.

Since members of The Triangle were so secretive, very little more is known about the organization, including the date of its demise. It is known that Daniel De Leon, a Columbia University lecturer and editor of the socialist newspaper *The People,* was among its most prominent (and one of its few visible) members.

Note that the U.S. Census of 1890 listed an "Order of

the Triangle." This was a New York City–based fraternal benefit organization, which apparently had no connection with The Triangle—although nothing is known about the organization beyond its mention in the census.

Trilateral Commission

The Trilateralists or Trilateral Commission is a group of political, economic, and industrial leaders, whose aim is variously described as creating a new community of nations centered on North America, but including Western Europe and Japan and supporting One World Government. Zbigniew Brzezinski, national security adviser to President Jimmy Carter, was the director of the commission from 1973–77. Some have seen the commission as a kind of high-level secret society, a form of political Freemasonry and shadow government, in which world leaders and national insiders can secretly plot the destiny of the globe. The Trilateral Commission is also commonly linked with the BILDERBURG GROUP, the United World Federalists, the ROYAL INSTITUTE FOR INTERNATIONAL AFFAIRS, and the COUNCIL FOR FOREIGN RELATIONS. However, all such connections as well as the imputations of conspiracy are highly speculative.

Troubadours

According to some authorities, the medieval troubadours or minstrels constituted a secret society, working four DEGREES. Heckethorn (see HECKETHORN, CHARLES WILLIAM) derives the word *minstrel* from the troubadours being "ministers" of a secret religion, allied to the Albigensian HERETICS. However, etymologists generally derive the word *minstrel* from the Latin *ministerium* ("servant"). It is, all in all, unlikely that the medieval troubadours were organized into any coherent body, secret or otherwise.

Trowel, Society of the

Despite the best efforts of some Masonic apologists to fit it into their capacious and flexible histories, the Society of the Trowel cannot easily be incorporated in the history of the FREEMASONS. What is known is that it was an Italian dining club, formed by a number of Florentine artisans in about 1512. It may have lasted for a decade or two.

True Kindred, Supreme Conclave

The True Kindred, Supreme Conclave, is a division of ADOPTIVE (female) MASONRY, incorporated in the United States in 1905. There are four DEGREES: True Kindred, Heroine of Jericho, Good Samaritan, and Daughter of Bethany.

True Masons, Academy of

The Academy of True Masons was founded in France in 1778 by Dom Antoine de Pernetty in Montpelier. It was concerned with "hermetic science" and worked the six DEGREES of the Philosophic Scotch Rite:

1. True Mason
2. True Mason in the Right Way
3. Knight of the Golden Key
4. Knight of Isis
5. Knight of the Argonauts
6. Knight of the Golden Fleece

The Academy seems to have ceased to exist long ago.

True Sisters Inc., United Order,

212 Fifth Avenue
New York, NY 10010
(212) 679-6790

The True Sisters was founded in New York City as a fraternal and service organization for Jewish women. It publishes the quarterly *Echo*. There were 12,000 members in 1995.

The United Order, True Sisters, Inc., may well be the oldest national fraternal organization for women in the United States, having been founded on April 12, 1846.

There are no OATHS in the initiation, and the main cause espoused by the United Order, True Sisters is a Cancer Service. A somewhat smaller, but still substantial, amount is spent on Jewish and community charities and on projects such as summer camps and youth work.

Tugendbund

The Tugendbund, or Union of Virtue, was an anti-Napoleonic German secret society founded in 1812, though its roots (in the sense of an informal association of those who joined the Bund) went back to about 1807. It seems to have functioned as an "inner lodge" of FREEMASONS, though it was not a Masonic organization as such. The order's exact political ambitions were unclear. Some members wanted a new German Empire, modeled on the Holy Roman Empire, while others wanted a republic, and yet others favored a northern and a southern kingdom. The Tugendbund dissolved into a welter of other German-nationalist societies, including the following:

> Burschenschaft
> CONCORDISTS
> Knights of the Queen of Prussia
> Order of Charlottenburg
> SCHWARZER RITTER, DEUTSCHER ORDEN

The last of these to disintegrate was the Bursenschaft, which disappeared in the 1820s and was briefly revived in 1830, before being suppressed for good in 1833.

Although the Tugendverein is frequently mentioned in literature on secret societies, it seems that the society is identical with the Tugendbund; *bund* and *verein* can both mean "union" or "club."

Tugendverein

See TUGENDBUND.

Turf, Society of the

Compagnia della Teppa, or Society of the Turf, was founded in Milan, Italy, in 1818 following the suppression of popular movements to evict the Austrians from Italy. Certain well-to-do youths refused to give up the fight and organized the society, which resembled the Mohocks of London or the HELL FIRE CLUB. Members swore to beat every man they met in the streets after dark—though, apparently, they tended to confine themselves to men whose wives they wished to abduct (often, it seems, with the permission of the wives!). The Austrian police largely turned a blind eye to the Turfists, feeling that it was better that they should vent their energies on individuals than turn them against the government.

Turfists recognized each other by a secret salute. A member would clasp his hands together, and the other member would respond by putting his right hand to his side, as if to place it on a sword hilt. The order worked two degrees—brother and captain—the latter attaining his rank after initiating four new members.

The order's name derived either from the fact that members wore plush hats, with the plush specified to be cut as short and smooth as turf, or from their early meeting place on the lawns of beautiful turf in Milan's Piazzo Castello. The order was suppressed by 1821.

Ukrainian Fraternal Association

440 Wyoming Avenue
Scranton, PA 18503
(717) 342-0937

The Ruthenian National Union was founded in Scranton, Pennsylvania, in 1910 as a mutual support group for Ukrainian immigrants to the United States, who saw themselves as particularly discriminated against. The name was changed to the Ukrainian Workingmen's Association in 1918 and to the present name in 1978. There were 20,000 members in 1995.

Originally, insurance policies issued by this fraternal benefit association were intended to cover funeral expenses only (providing $500 to $1,000 for men; $200 to $400 for their wives), but today the organization is a full-benefit ethnic fraternal insurance society.

Ukrainian National Aid Association of America

925 North Western Avenue
Chicago, IL 60622
(312) 342-5102

The Ukrainian National Aid Association of America was founded in 1914 as an ethnic fraternal benefit society open to persons of Ukrainian descent and their relatives. It operates mainly in the northeastern United States. There were 8,710 members in 1995. The Association publishes the quarterly magazine *Ukrainian National Word.*

The Ukrainian National Aid Association of America is one of the smaller Ukrainian ethnic fraternal benefit

societies, though its membership appears to have undergone a slow but significant growth in the latter half of the 20th century: from almost 7,000 in 1965 to over 8,000 in 1978 to almost 9,000 a decade later.

The organization seems to be more politicized than the UKRAINIAN NATIONAL ASSOCIATION, its much larger (and significantly older) brother, and because of its relatively small size, its activities are less extensive. It is a typical, modestly successful, ethnic fraternal benefit association.

Ukrainian National Association

30 Montgomery Street, 3rd Fl.
Jersey City, NJ 07303
(201) 451-2200 or (800) 253-9862

The Ukrainian National Association was founded in 1894 in Shamokin, Pennsylvania, as a fraternal benefit society for those of Ukrainian or Slavic ancestry and their relatives. There is a junior division for those under sixteen. There were 69,000 members in 1995, and the Association publishes *Svoboda* (daily), *Ukrainian Weekly,* and *Veselka* (monthly).

The Ukrainian National Association is a typical successful ethnic fraternal benefit life insurance society, with charitable works, summer schools, cultural events, athletics, folk dances, and so forth. Like so many others, it was formed as a very modest self-help group "for the relief of destitute families and to cover funeral expenses of members," and, like many others, it was at first actuarially unsound and survived only because of the good faith and hard work of its early members. Now, it offers substantial scholarships, promotes major Ukrainian cultural events, and runs a 400-acre resort in the Catskills called Soyushiva.

Ulieach Druidh Braithreachas, An

An Ulieach Druidh Braithreachas (the spelling is Celtic) literally means "The Universal Druid Bond" and was founded in 1717 to restore the old Celtic religion. The poet William Blake served as Chief Druid from 1799–1827, and Francis, Earl of Dashwood, was a member before he founded the HELL FIRE CLUB. An Ulieach was apparently not too keen on the Earl of Dashwood's brand of sexual magic (or sex without the magic), so it withdrew its charter from his group in 1743. Thereafter, An Ulieach, declined more or less gracefully. It is not clear when it finally petered out, and there may yet be a California or Pennsylvania chapter based on some 19th-century revival; but it is likelier that the order is long gone. The link (if any) with the various orders of DRUIDS cannot be readily proven.

Union Fraternal League

The Union Fraternal league was first formed, by members of the Knights of Honor, the Royal Society of Good Fellows, the PILGRIMS, and others, in 1889 as a beneficiary society, but was dissolved and refounded in 1893–95, and then became the Catholic Fraternal League in 1916. It is now long extinct, but it is noteworthy because of its unusual, possibly unique, metamorphosis from a regular secret society into a Catholic organization.

Union League of America

According to the *Century Magazine* of July 1884, the Union League of America consisted of "disorderly elements of the negro population . . . led by white men of the basest and meanest type . . . [who] met frequently . . . armed to the teeth." They " 'breathed out threatening and slaughter' . . . against [those] whose sole crime was that they had been in the Confederate army." Apologists for the KU KLUX KLAN have declared that the organization was established explicitly to counter Union League violence and threats. Beyond the *Century* article, however, no information on the Union League of America exists.

The Union League Club, an organization founded in New York City about 1919 by a lawyer named Archibald E. Stevenson, is unrelated to the Union League of America. The Union League Club was dedicated to unearthing conspiracies to overthrow the U.S. government and was a product of the "Red Scare" that swept the nation in the wake of the Bolshevik Revolution in Russia.

Union of Polish Women of America

2636-38 East Allegheny Avenue
Philadelphia, PA 19134-5185
(215) 425-3807

The Union of Polish Women of America was founded in 1920 as a fraternal benefit life insurance organization for those of Polish extraction or married to someone of Polish extraction. Both sexes are admitted: Adult members must be 15½ years old; younger members join the youth division. There were 9,379 members in 1995. The union publishes the weekly *Gwiazda*.

The surprisingly late date of foundation of the Union of Polish Women in America—1920—is because its genesis effectively lay in World War I. When the war was over, Polish women who had worked together for the war effort decided that they could also work together for peace. Otherwise, it is a standard (though more than usually active) ethnic fraternal benefit society, with programs of fraternal insurance and other benefits; cultural events; programs to assist and educate the young; and programs to promote the Catholic church.

Union of Public Welfare

The Union of Public Welfare was a Russian secret society dedicated to a more constitutional government. It arose in about 1817–19 out of the former Association for the Redemption of Russia and may have had Decembrist sympathies, though it seems actually to have been more moderate. It never accomplished anything in the face of increasingly severe Tsarist rule.

Union of Safety

The Union of Safety was a Russian patriotic secret society that vowed to work toward constitutional rule. It was founded at about the time that the Czar banned secret societies in 1822.

The union borrowed much from the FREEMASONS, whose furniture had been sold in the street when the lodges were closed down, and worked three DEGREES: Brethren, Men, and Boyards. *Boyard* is a Russian term for a variety of aristocrat.

The Russian Knights were an offshoot of the Union of Safety, with the dual aim of promoting constitutional rule in Russia and thwarting the Polish secret societies, which wanted independent constitutional rule for Poland. The Russian Knights and the Union of Safety coalesced into the Union for the Public Weal, which promptly dissolved and then reappeared as the Union of the Boyards—a body now in favor of Polish independence *and* constitutional rule. In 1824, this new incarnation merged with the UNITED SLAVONIANS.

Union Saint-Jean-Baptiste

P.O. Box F, One Social Street
Woonsocket, RI 02895
(401) 769-0520 or (800) 225-USJB

The Union Saint-Jean-Baptiste was founded in the United States in 1900 as a fraternal benefit life insurance society for Roman Catholics of French origin. There were 40,000 members in 1995. The union publishes

L'Union and *Communiqué,* both bimonthly, and *Fun and Games,* quarterly.

Originally the Union Saint-Jean-Baptiste d'Amérique, this was founded in the familiar pattern of an ethnic fraternal benefit society "to unite in a common spirit of brotherhood persons of French origin living in the United States and to promote their collective welfare." The "d'Amérique" was dropped in 1968.

Perhaps surprisingly for a Catholic organization, there is a ritual (see RITUALS AND CEREMONIES), and new members have to be initiated. In addition to the usual life insurance and other fraternal benefits, the union's activities include or have included Meals-on-Wheels, hospital volunteer work, and parish work.

United Americans, Order of

The Order of United Americans, in its first incarnation, was a nativist secret society, a precursor of the KNOW-NOTHINGS, founded in about 1843. It may also have drawn upon Tammany Hall for members. It effectively ceased to exist by the end of the century. The name "Order of United Americans" was recycled in 1896 for a patriotic and beneficiary society, open to both sexes, probably established in Pennsylvania. It was still current in the 1920s, but is now probably extinct.

United Brothers of Friendship

The United Brothers of Friendship, now apparently extinct, was an African-American fraternal order formed in 1861 to care for the sick and bury the dead. It was reorganized in 1868, and a National Grand Lodge was formed in 1879. Whites were also eligible for membership. The Sisters of the Mysterious Ten constituted the female auxiliary (see AUXILIARIES) and was founded in 1878. Members of the Grand United Order of ODD FELLOWS, another African-American society, may have instigated the formation of the United Brothers.

United Commercial Travelers of America, Order of

632 North Park Street
P.O. Box 159019
Columbus, OH 43215
(614) 228-3276

The United Commercial Travelers of America banded together as an order in 1890 in Columbus, Ohio, as a fraternal and insurance society for traveling salesmen. Members must be 18–55 for insurance benefits. There were 175,000 members in 1995.

The Order of United Commercial Travelers (OUCTA) is mainly a provider of insurance for salesmen, businessmen, and professional men. Membership is no longer limited to commercial travelers; the criteria for admission were relaxed in 1948.

The objectives of the OUCTA were originally seven-fold:

1. To unite fraternally all commercial travelers
2. To aid all members and their dependents, financially and materially
3. To establish death and disability funds
4. To obtain just and equitable favors for its members
5. To raise its members both morally and socially
6. To operate as a secret society
7. To establish a reserve fund for widows and orphans

Members pledge not merely to defend the character of woman, but never to violate the chastity of womanhood. The original RITUALS AND CEREMONIES were based on the "secrets" of commercial travelers, much as those of the FREEMASONS were based upon the secrets of stone workers; but they are said to have been much modified through the years.

The "fun" side of the order is represented by the BAGMEN OF BAGDAD, and the Sunday nearest April 9 is observed as a memorial day for departed brethren.

United Friars, Fraternity of

The Fraternity of United Friars was a society established in 1785, apparently as a social/charitable organization along the lines of the modern LIONS INTERNATIONAL or KIWANIS CLUB INTERNATIONAL. It is now long extinct.

United Irishmen, Society of

The United Irishmen was founded in Belfast on October 14, 1791, as a political society. It has the distinction of having been founded as an open society with public meetings, and then being reconstituted three years later as a secret society after it was suppressed by the authorities. It is one of the best known of the Irish secret societies.

Its original aims were fourfold:

1. Parliamentary reform
2. Catholic emancipation
3. The disestablishment of the Church of Ireland
4. The abolition of pensions granted on the Irish Establishment

Nor was this the only reasonable part of the organization. The "test" or oath (see OATHS) was eminently constitutional:

> I, [Name], in the presence of God, do pledge myself to my Country that I will use all my abilities and influence the attainment of an impartial and adequate representation of the Irish Nation in Parliament; and as a means of absolute and immediate necessity in the establishment of

this chief good of Ireland, I will endeavour as much as lies in my ability to forward a brotherhood of affection, an identity of interests, a communion of rights, and a union of power among Irishmen of all religious persuasions, without which every reform in Ireland must be partial, not National, inadequate to the wants, delusive to the wishes, and insufficient for the freedom and happiness of this Country.

The founder, Theobald Wolfe Tone, was a Protestant barrister from Dublin, and when the organization was reconstituted as a secret society on May 10, 1794, its leaders were mainly Belfast Presbyterians and Republicans. It soon transpired, though, that the aims of the United Irishmen were considerably less constitutional than they had initially appeared. This might well have been a reaction to the suppression of the original, carefully legal society. The oath of the second society no longer referred to "adequate representation . . . in Parliament," but instead was phrased as follows:

In the awful presence of God

I, [Name], do voluntarily declare, that I will persevere in endeavouring to form a brotherhood of affection among Irishmen of every religious persuasion, and that I will also persevere in my endeavours to obtain an equal, full and adequate representation of the people of Ireland.

I do further declare that neither hopes, fears, rewards nor punishments, shall ever induce me, directly or indirectly, to inform on or give evidence against any member of this or similar societies, for any act or expression of theirs done or made, collectively or individually, in or out of this society, in pursuance of the spirit of this obligation.

The Test was administered either on a Bible or a prayer book, together with an eight-page Constitution, which was held in the right hand. The signs of recognition began with "I know U," to which the appropriate reply was "I know N" and so forth, through "UNITED." "You" for "U" is of course easy; and "I know N" sounds (in a Belfast accent) much like "I known 'un," so it was quite a safe code. There was another, which ran:

Are you straight?
—I am.
How straight?
—As straight as a rush.
Go on then?
—In truth, in trust, in unity and liberty.
What have you got in your hand?
—A green bough.
Where did it first grow?
—In America.
Where did it bud?
—In France.
Where are you going to plant it?
—In the Crown of Great Britain.

Members also wore a green neckerchief or neck cloth, depending on their station, and wore their hair short—hence the epithet "croppies" commemorated in the ORANGEMEN's song, "Croppies lie down." Both of these external signs soon became known to friend and foe alike and could be an invitation to a beating. Their symbols were the harp, the shamrock, and the crossed hands.

The FREEMASONS also figured in the society. Many Irishmen were members of the Craft, and the Masonic lodges would have been an excellent cover for the United Irishmen. Unlike their counterparts in continental Europe, though, the Masters of the various Lodges were disinclined to unite in support of any one political cause, and the association between Freemasonry and the United Irishmen (where it existed at all) was mostly a local affair.

Wolfe Tone himself, charged with the task by the Ulster Directory of the United Irishmen, sought an alliance with France—still in the throes of its own drawn-out revolution—and a revolution in Ireland. When the English authorities caught up with him, he proposed voluntary exile. In May, 1795, when he returned to Belfast before leaving his country for good, he was again asked by his countrymen to secure a French invasion in support of an Irish uprising, and he began negotiations for this a year later in May 1796. Meanwhile, back in Ireland, the United Irishmen took on an increasingly military air. The old organizational hierarchy had consisted of Societies (of 12 men), Lower-Baronial Committees (secretaries of five Societies), Upper-Baronial Committees (delegates from 10 Lower-Baronial Committees), County Committees and the Provincial Committee, while the National Directorate drew its members from County Committees and the Provincial Committee. Now there were Sergeants (of Societies), Captains, and (from the old Upper-Baronial Committees), Colonels. Adjutants-General for the several countries were selected by the Directorate from names put forward by the Colonels. The Directorate also selected generals.

Fortunately for the English and unfortunately for the Irish, the French invasion miscarried when a storm drove their fleet into Bantry Bay, where no provision had been made to aid them. Had their 43 ships landed their 15,000 troops in Ulster, the French would have found 100,000 Irishmen waiting to support them. As it was, the fleet returned to Brest and no more was heard of the Irish-French alliance.

The aftermath of the attempted invasion was predictable: increased suspicion, recrimination, revenge. The English infiltrated the organization. Given the size of the Society of United Irishmen, there were always informers who could be bought. The United Irishmen faded away, though many individual members remained as threads in the broad green ribbon of Irish nationalist history.

United Patriots

The United Patriots was a short-lived secret society, based in the south of France, which conspired against Napoleon. It was quickly suppressed.

United Slovanians

The United Slavonians were founded in about 1820 by a group of young Russian army officers who had been with the Army of Occupation in France, where they had absorbed revolutionary ideas. Initially, they were pro-Tsarist. Their four aims were to discover and report abuses of government charity; to watch over educational matters; to observe the administration of law; and to study political economy. The Grand Master was Prince Troubetzkoi, and many of Russia's finest young aristocrats were members.

Perhaps inevitably, their speculations led them into discontent. They were involved in the Decembrist palace revolution to substitute the Grand Duke Constantine (who had renounced his claim to the throne in 1822) for the Grand Duke Nicholas, on the death of Tsar Alexander in 1825. They believed that Constantine might more easily be persuaded to grant constitutional rule, while Nicholas would be another autocrat.

They were right—at least in their assessment of Nicholas. The revolution failed, the conspirators were tried, and 36 were sentenced to death—though 31 of those sentences were commuted. One hundred thirty others were also imprisoned.

United Societies of the U.S.A.

613 Sinclair Street
McKeesport, PA 15132
(412) 672-3196

The United Societies of the U.S.A. was founded in 1903 as a fraternal benefit life insurance society for persons of both sexes who are members of the "One, Holy, Catholic and Apostolic Church of the Greek Catholic or Latin Rite of which His Holiness, Pope of Rome, is the Visible Head." There were 3,875 members in 1995. The organization publishes *Enlightenment* monthly.

Despite its somewhat grandiose title, the United Societies of the United States of America is modestly sized and declining in membership. The organization was formerly called The United Societies of the Greek Catholic Religion of the United States.

Originally, the organization was founded as a local group to promote Greek Catholicism and Ruthenian culture as well as visiting the sick and offering *ad hoc* material assistance, but it metamorphosed into a fraternal benefit group having two forms of membership: beneficiary (with insurance) and social (without). Charitable work is mostly on a local parish level, though external good works such as children's hospitals are also the recipients of contributions.

United States of the Earth

The ambitiously named United States of the Earth, also known as the Universal Republic, was a utopian society projected by Iowa enthusiasts in 1896. It proposed to establish a universal brotherhood, where love, truth, and purity should prevail to the utter exclusion of ignorance, want, and crime. Unfortunately, little came of this organization, which was very short-lived.

United Workmen, Ancient Order Of

The Ancient Order of United Workmen was founded on October 27, 1868, in Meadville, Pennsylvania, as a fraternal beneficiary society for white males. It was dissolved in 1952.

The Ancient Order of United Workmen is historically significant for two reasons. First, it was the first fraternal group to sell insurance, though for the first 11 months or so of its existence (until October 6, 1869) it was at least as much concerned with workmen's conditions and rights, and the maximum that could be paid to the legal heirs of a deceased member was $500. After October 1869, the benefit was upped to $2,000 on an *ad hoc* ASSESSMENT. Offering insurance to working men—then called "mechanics"—was a novel idea, though it must be added that within a very short time, the rules were broadened so that almost all white males could be admitted. Eventually, non-whites were admitted as well—despite the founders' stipulation that the white-only rule could never be "altered, amended or expunged." Secondly, the United Workmen were the instigators of the NATIONAL FRATERNAL CONGRESS OF AMERICA in 1886.

Originally there were four DEGREES in a ritual (see RITUALS AND CEREMONIES) that owed a great deal to the FREEMASONS, but the ritual was revised in 1871 to give only three degrees, and in 1929 the Supreme Lodge structure was dissolved, with a "congress" in place of the Supreme Lodge. In 1932, the religious aspect of the lodge ritual was deleted, and in 1952, the United Workmen dissolved still further. Some state lodges simply ceased to exist, others converted to regular mutual insurance societies or merged with them, and some (such as the Texas branch of the order) went into receivership or liquidation.

As recently as 1989 the Washington branch still existed, but a telephone call to the Supreme Workman in 1990 elicited no more than a recorded announcement that the number had been disconnected. No new listing was reported.

Universal Aurora, Society of the

Founded in Paris, in 1783, the Universal Aurora practiced and promoted MESMERISM. Cagliostro, "the Divine

Charlatan," participated in its establishment. Beyond this, nothing is known of the society. (See CAGLIOSTRO, ALESSANDRO.)

Universal Craftsman Council of Engineers

The Universal Craftsman Council of Engineers is a branch of the FREEMASONS organized in Chicago in 1894 by a group of engineers who were also Freemasons. The order was incorporated in 1903 in Cleveland, Ohio. Beyond this, very little is known about the order. The Masonic degree bestowed upon members was intended to accent the "dignity of labor," and its governing body was called the Grand Council. The order was listed in a 1978 unpublished manuscript prepared by the Masonic Service Association as an "allied Masonic group." The most recent ENCYCLOPEDIA OF ASSOCIATIONS also mentions the order, but provides no other information and notes that its address is unknown.

Universalists, Order of

All that is known of the order is that it was related to the FREEMASONS and was founded by one Retif de la Bretonne in Paris about 1841. It worked a single degree and is long extinct.

Universal Regeneration, Society of

The Society of Universal Regeneration was a precursor of YOUNG EUROPE, consisting of nationalist patriots of various countries in exile in Switzerland between 1815 and 1820.

Unknown Superiors

The Unknown Superiors, or *Superiores Incogniti,* were the (probably mythical) high-ranking FREEMASONS who were supposed to direct the clerks of Strict Observance (see STRICT OBSERVANCE, CLERKS OF). Adherents of conspiracy theories point out that the initials of the Superiores Incogniti are the same as those of the Societas Iesu, or JESUITS. This connection is almost certainly coincidental and spurious.

Ustaša

Also spelled Ustashi, this organization started out as a secret society formed in Italy by a Croatian exile and dedicated to Croatian independence. It became the brutal ruling force of Croatia during World War II. The order was founded by Ante Pavelic in 1929 in response to King Alexander I's establishment of a Serbian-dominated dictatorship in Yugoslavia. Operating from Italy, Ustaša worked to foment a peasant rebellion in Croatia and participated in the assassination of Alexander in 1934.

Ustaša failed to establish an independent Croatian state until the outbreak of World War II, when Germany invaded and partitioned Yugoslavia, sanctioning the terrorist fascism of Ustaša and allowing it to establish a Croatian puppet government. Ustaša functioned to combat anti-German resistance in Croatia and practiced a program of ethnic cleansing, slaughtering Serbian and other non-Croatian people, especially the Jews. Bolstered by Germany, Ustaša remained in power until May 1945, when Ustaša constituents fled before the onslaught of Communist partisans.

Utopia

"Utopia" (from the philosophical protonovel written by Sir Thomas More in 1516) was founded in Prague in the 1850s and by 1885 boasted 85 lodges in Germany, Austria, Hungary, Switzerland, and elsewhere. It was a feasting-and-fun society, which did not take itself seriously. The DEGREES were Squires, Younkers, and Knights. Guests were called Pilgrims. The president or Master of the LODGE was known as Uhu (Screech Owl), and the members of the society were wont to display joy with cries of "Aha!" and to condemn transgressions of the Laws of Utopia with "Oho!"

V.A.S.

Vera amicitia sempiterna, "true friendship lasts forever," was the full name of this society, which was always known by its initials. It was a graded ASSESSMENT fraternal benefit society founded in Grinnell, Iowa, in 1897. It merged with the Security Life Association of Clinton, Iowa, in 1897.

Vasa Order of America

65 Bryant Road
Cranston, RI 02910
(401) 461-0016

The Vasa Order of America was founded in 1896 in New Haven, Connecticut, as a fraternal and insurance society for men aged 16-50; women were later admitted. There were 35,000 members in 1995. The order publishes the *Vasa Star* magazine.

The "Vasa Order" of America was founded in 1896 as a confederation of several Swedish sick benefit societies. Fraternal RITUALS AND CEREMONIES were overlaid on the original purpose of the member societies, and a LODGE structure of Lodge, District Lodge, and Grand Lodge was instituted. The DEGREES corresponded strictly to the lodge structure. The original ritual was revised in 1915, and a whole new ritual was circulated in 1923, at which time the entry requirements were changed to admit "male and female persons of the Caucasian race," aged 16–50, in good health, who could also speak and understand Swedish, or who were the descendants of Swedish parents.

The high point of membership was in 1929, with 72,261 members; half a century later, there were fewer than half as many members, and a decade later again membership had fallen to 32,000. The traditional "secret society" fraternal aspect of the situation also declined steadily, and the $10 initiation fee was waived in 1966.

Veilleurs, Fraternity of

The *Fraternité de Veilleurs* was founded just after World War I as a mystical society constituting of two "circles:" the outer circle and the inner, or esoteric circle. The guiding lights, René Schwaller and Jeanne le Vailleur, called Aor and Isha, first visited Switzerland, near St.-Moritz, where they established a *monastaire initiatique* ("initiatory monastery") called Suhalia. Next, they went on to Palme de Majorca, then Luxor, then back to France. Like Aleister Crowley (see CROWLEY, ALEISTER), they were "magicians," who did not consider themselves subject to the rules of the common crowd. Their fraternity was quite small and no longer exists.

Vehmgericht

The Vehmgericht, Vehm, or Veme (often called "Holy Veme") was founded in the 13th century as a secret society to control crime in Westphalia and neighboring areas. Now extinct, there were perhaps 100,000 members at its peak.

In 1180, Henry the Lion, Duke of Saxony and Bavaria, was placed under interdict by the Holy Roman Emperor, Frederick I. The result was an effective collapse of law and order in those areas that Henry had ruled; and the Vehm was constituted as a vigilante force to make good the deficiency. The members of the Vehm, called *Die Wissenden* ("The Knowing Ones") came from all walks of life and were bound to administer the code of the Vehm by the following oath (see OATHS):

I swear by my sacred honor that I will hold and conceal
   the Secrets of the Holy Veme
From Sun and from Moon,
From Man and from Woman,
From Wife and from Child,
From Village and from Field,
From Grass and from Beast,
From Great and from Small,
Except from the Man
Who can serve the Holy Veme.
I will leave nothing undone
For Love or for Fear
For Silver or Gold
Or for any wife's scold.

The precise nature of the Code is unclear. At the very least, the Vehmgericht (the Court of the Vehm) tried cases of theft, with only one penalty possible: hanging from the nearest tree. At some times, in some places, the jurisdiction of these self-constituted courts was even greater than this, but the underlying principle was that the Code was administered with the consent of all. In the absence of imperial or other law, the law of the Vehm was democratic, rapid, and efficient.

There were three DEGREES. The highest was that of the *Stuhlherren*, the "Seated Gentlemen" or judges. Next came the *Freischoeffen*, the "Free Jurymen." Third was the *Frohnboten*, the nearest literal translation might be "willing assistants," but "honest workers" might be more appropriate.

The Courts of the Vehm were held in public places. At Nordkirchen, for instance, they were held in the churchyard, and in Dortmund in the marketplace. They sat in the morning, like any other court, and the accused had 45 days in which to appear. Both sides were allowed to call up to 30 witnesses and to be represented by their lawyers. There was even an appeals procedure, to the *Heimliche Acht*, who normally sat at Dortmund. Nonappearance could result in outlawry (*Vehmbar*), and an outlaw could be hanged by a posse of three or more *Wissenden;* but the accuser who sought such a hanging had to produce seven witnesses to swear that he was an honest man.

In 1371, a decree of Emperor Karl IV specifically recognized the powers of the Vehm, which marked the beginning of the end of the "secret society" aspect of the organization, as it began to be assimilated into the mainstream. Improvements in imperial civil justice made the Vehmgericht increasingly irrelevant thereafter, and the last regular Vehm court was held in Celle in 1568. Irregular courts were held long after that, however, and the last officially recognized "Free Court" (at Gemen, in Muenster) was abolished by the French in 1811, after they had invaded the area. The *idea* of the Vehm persisted long after that. It was sometimes used as a bogeyman to frighten children, while the Nazis pointed to it as a sort of "popular court," which justified their own murderous activities against opponents of the Nazi state.

Vendicatori

The Vendicatori was formed about 1186 in Sicily to avenge public wrongs. It was modeled on the VEHMGE-RICHT and the BEATI PAOLI. Adiorolphus of Ponte Corvo, grand master of the sect, was hanged by order of King William II the Norman. Many members of the Vendicatori were branded with hot irons.

Verhovay Fraternal Insurance Association

The Verhovay Aid Association (after 1935, the Fraternal Insurance Association) was founded in 1886 in Pennsylvania as a fraternal beneficiary society. In 1955 it merged with the Racoczi Aid Association to form the WILLIAM PENN ASSOCIATION.

Veterans of Future Wars

The Veterans of Future Wars was founded by a group of upperclassmen at Princeton in late 1935 or early 1936. A proposal for a similar society had been made in the *Daily Iowan* (of the University of Iowa) for April 9, 1935, but it apparently never came to anything.

Much taken with the idea of bonuses for veterans of World War I, Lewis J. Corin (the society's chief instigator) and his friends reasoned that they would inevitably be the veterans of the next war, so they might as well have their bonus while they were young enough to enjoy it. The basis of their calculations was an immediate $1,000 bonus to all male citizens aged 18–36, *plus* interest compounded annually and retrospectively from June 1, 1965 (when they decided it should fall due), to June 1, 1935. June 15, 1936, was set as the date for the disbursement, accompanied (according to the official invitation that was printed up) by "dancing in the streets from four to six."

The idea was received with good humor in some quarters, and with extreme distaste in others. The press seized the idea with enthusiasm, and chapters were rapidly formed at Georgia Tech, Harvard, New York, North Carolina, Stanford, and many more colleges and universities. Within 10 days of the first article's appearance, there were said to be posts on 120 campuses, with over 6,000 members. The veterans also invented the Association of Future War Propagandists (dedicated to writing only atrocity stories), the Profiteers of Future Wars, and the female auxiliary (see AUXILIARIES), the Homefire Division. Their parodies of regalia, RITUALS

AND CEREMONIES, and everything else were carefully thought out. The salute, for example, was with the right arm held up and out in almost a Nazi style, but with the palm outstretched for money.

Videttes, Order of

A vidette is, in military terms, a mounted forward sentry or scout. The Order of Videttes (also called the Order of Thirteen) was organized in Texas during the summer of 1886 and appealed to the same nativist principles as the earlier KNOW-NOTHINGS and the later AMERICAN PROTECTIVE ASSOCIATION, into which it was absorbed by about 1890—though it survived in name alone until about 1900. The order claimed half a million members within 18 months of its founding, though that number may be, at least in part, the product of wishful thinking.

Vikings, Independent Order of

2200 East Devon Avenue, Ste. 257
Des Plaines, IL 60018
(708) 298-3550

The Independent Order of Vikings was founded in 1896 in Chicago as an ethnic fraternal insurance benefit association. Eligibility was restricted to Swedes, those of Swedish descent, and those married to Swedes or persons of Swedish descent. In 1995 there were over 9,300 members. The order publishes the *Viking Journal* monthly.

The Independent Order of Vikings is another typical "old country" fraternal benefit organization founded in the late 19th century to provide insurance coverage and to promote the culture of the founders. It provides scholarships to high school seniors and makes charitable donations as well as providing (at the local lodge level) a variety of activities, such as language classes, folk dance classes, and the like.

Vivian, Herbert

Herbert Vivian, M A , wrote *Secret Societies Old and Now* (London: Thornton Butterworth, 1927). His book is the work of an advocate of conspiracy theories and is informed by a strong monarchist and right-wing bias. However, he was a thorough researcher, and *Secrets Societies Old and New* includes a copious and detailed bibliography.

VMRO

See IMRO (INTERNAL MACEDONIAN REVOLUTIONARY ORGANIZATION).

Vril Society

The Vril Society (sometimes mistakenly known as Viril Society) was first invented by the novelist Edward Bulwer-Lytton in his 1871 novel *The Coming Race*. The novel concerns a people that has mastered *"Vril,"* the Life Force, and this mystical term, with its suggestion of the *Ubermensch*, spurred the formation of an actual Vril Society in Germany shortly after the novel's publication. It may originally have been called the Luminous Lodge, and it reportedly combined the political ideals of the ILLUMINATI with Hindu mysticism, the THEOSOPHICAL SOCIETY and the KABBALAH.

Although the original society is long gone, there was for some time a French society called the *Grande Loge du Vril, Religion des Druides* (GLDV), founded in 1969 by one Jean-Claude Monet, also known as Karl Thor. Monet claimed to be the illegitimate son of Adolf Hitler and a Norman girl. Monet also founded the *Ordre Maçonnique de l'Himalaya, Karlburg,* or *"Communauté Ahrimanique du Reich Luciférien"* and Breuriezh an Hevoud.

Wanka

Wanka is or was a WEST AFRICAN SECRET SOCIETY in northern Sierra Leone, with connections with Gbangbani. It is or was open to both sexes, admission at puberty. It is most remarkable for one of its explicit aims: In addition to teaching crafts and domestic skills to young people, it also taught girls to curb their sexual desires and trained them in the duties of wife and mother. Wanka members enjoyed the assurance that their graves would be protected.

Washington, George

George Washington was initiated into the ranks of the FREEMASONS on November 4, 1752, in Fredericksburg, Virginia, for a fee of 2 pounds 3 shillings. He was passed as a Fellow-Craft on March 3, 1753, and was made Master Mason on August 4 of the same year. It is possible to visit the lodge today, which is a Masonic museum open to the "profane."

Subsequently, Washington was prominent in the Craft, and he and his Masonic cronies and descendants must surely be responsible for the extraordinary proliferation of Masonic symbolism on American money. He was far from alone in being a military Freemason: Both the British army and the Patriots had traveling field lodges, and if one were accidentally overrun by the enemy it would be returned under flags of truce. Another eminent soldier who belonged to the Craft was the Duke of Wellington, who was initiated in 1790.

There is a George Washington Masonic National Memorial Association, located at 101 Culhan Drive, Alexandria, VA 22301, (703) 683-2007, organized in 1910.

Water Rats

The Water Rats is a British theatrical fraternity combining self-celebratory dinners with charitable and benevolent work among retired actors and the public at large, especially for children. The name comes from a horse, which an association of actors was hoping to train to race. After a particularly wet day's training, someone remarked that it looked like a water rat—and the name was adopted.

The American equivalent of the British order is called the White Rats, in honor of the white hair of one of the founders.

Wehrschaft

The Wehrschaft was a militaristic secret society founded in Jena, Germany, in 1814. It was a pan-Germanic movement, which probably influenced or gave rise to other German political secret societies such as the JUNGLINGSBUND, the Arminia Society, and others.

West African Secret Societies

In West Africa, until the incursion of Europeans, secret societies were central to the culture. They regulated innumerable aspects of day-to-day life, and they epitomized the values of the societies in which they existed. The foremost European student of West African secret societies was Captain F. W. Butt-Thompson (see BUTT-THOMPSON, CAPT. F. W.), who summarized their essentially conservative purpose:

> They were instituted to enforce and maintain tribal traditions, customs, and beliefs that were in danger of changing or becoming obsolete. The organizers were the champions of the old against the new, as some of their descendants still are. They were the restrictors of mental advance and punishers of the heretic and the unorthodox. They were clever enough to know that prohibition alone was not sufficient foundation for any organization desiring longevity, and, therefore, made their societies the repositories of the folklore, myths and history and the conceptions of art and culture and learning and wisdom the tribes possessed. Moreover, they became the teachers of these things. The only teachers.

Following Butt-Thompson's nomenclature, West African secret societies may be divided three ways—into Islamic, Pagan, and Pagan-Islamic. The Islamic societies include Sirri, JAVIA KARTAS, QAIROWAN, Masubori, Mori, MUMBO-JUMBO (Mahammah-Jamboh), Kongkorong, and Bori. The Pagan derive from Si'mo, a secret society of French Guinea, and Oro, from Nigeria. They include: Poro (Sierra Leone); Egbo (Nigeria), Bundu (Sierra Leone); Dyoro (Ivory Coast); Nkimba Nkamba (Congo); Mungi (Cameroon); Butwa (Angola); Ogboni, Orisha and Eluku (Nigeria); Ampora (Sierra Leone); and Nkanda (Congo). The Pagan-Islamic group derives in part from these societies via Penda-Penda, which developed in French Guinea. Later, Penda-Penda gave rise to Dou (Senegal); Afa (Dahomey); Belli-Paaro (Liberia); Katahwira (Senegal); Naferi (Senegal); Boviowah (Liberia); Sindungo (Congo); Kwaga (Bornu); and Jamboi, Sembe, and Nanam (Sierra Leone and Liberia).

West African secret societies include those of essentially mystic and religious content, including law-god societies, priestly associations, prohibition societies, protective societies, and purification societies; democratic and patriotic purposes, including agricultural associations, cooperative societies, dance, play, and sports clubs, political societies, social organizations, trade guilds, and war clubs; and subversive and criminal organizations.

The following is a list of the major West African secret societies Butt-Thompson catalogued. Those treated in separate entries in this book are given here as cross-references only. Because the continued existence of many of these societies is uncertain, all entries should be taken to read "is or was."

Abam. Originally founded as a militia among the Aro of Nigeria, but after the British occupation it became a social organization. It is a traditional rival of Eku-Meku. Membership was male.

Adamu. This agriculturally based society was originally a lodge of Orisha, using some EGBO ritual. The links

among fertility, religion, agriculture, and secret societies is typical of West Africa.

Afa. Found among the Ewe-speaking Yoruba in what is now Ghana, Togo, and Benin, Afa, like Dou, evolved from Penda-Penda, but (like other West African secret societies) it adapted itself to fit local conditions. For example, it may or may not originally have been a cult of one of the two Yoruba gods, Ifa or Aramfe. Its influence, together with that of SINDUNGO was seen among Liberian, Sierra Leonian, and Senegalese tribes. Membership was male, with admission at puberty, and associate membership for women.

Agbaia. A society of the Sanda-Temne of Sierra Leone, Agbaia was originally founded to help the tribe to entertain strangers. Like ethnic associations in the United States, the society broadened its purpose to include general fund raising for community projects. The committee consists of six couples, usually recently married.

Aiyasa. This society was found among the Temne of Sierra Leone and apparently served the chief purpose of executing melodramatic dances.

ALLIGATOR SOCIETIES

Ampora. Restricted to the Mende people of Sierra Leone, Ampora may have been the first separate society to split off from PORO. There is an associated women's organization called Yassi; although membership of Ampora is male (with admission at puberty), there is also a woman on the council.

Andomba. Found among the Koranko of Sierra Leone, Andomba was derived from Ampora, but was transformed into a primarily social society with an emphasis on dance displays. Membership was mainly male, with selected women as well.

Ankoi. This society consisted of women of the Sherbro-Bullom people of Sierra Leone and was derived from Bundu, but claimed a separate development and history. It was primarily a social club, a friendly rival of Kinki. Admission was at puberty.

Ankumunko. Among the Temne of Sierra Leone, Ankumuko involves a long and complicated ritual centered on dances performed in honor of the after-death spit (*krifi*) of past members.

Apowa. A religious secret society of the coastal Ahanta people of Ghana, Apowa is essentially a purification and fertility cult. Membership was open to male and female adults.

Ayaka. This society may have derived either from Okonko or from a trade GUILD of blacksmiths. Its chief influence was among the Ibo of Nigeria.

Baboon Societies. Baboons fight viciously when cornered, which may have inspired their adoption as a symbol by some West African criminal societies of Sierra Leone, Liberia, the Ivory Coast, and the

Volta River. Typically, the victims of such societies would be mutilated with weapons that emulated the bite of a large ape. These societies are also known as Ape Societies or Chimpanzee Societies. Cannibalism was imputed to a number of them.

Bakelebroa. A trade guild of blacksmiths, Bakelebroa offered selective hereditary membership and honorary membership for the sons of chiefs.

BAMILEKE SECRET SOCIETIES

Banban. Concerned mainly with the enforcement of taboos, Banban also functioned as a social organization among the Limba people of Sierra Leone. Membership consisted of male and female adults, with occasional puberty schools.

Baya-Gbunde. The name literally means "Traitor-Catchers," though the "traitor" in question seems to have been a malignant deity who caused an epidemic of disease among children at the time the society was founded. The "evil eye" of the deity in question could be spotted by looking at villages from the surrounding bush. This society consisted of youths banded together for the purpose of doing daring deeds. It was found among the Mende boys of Sierra Leone.

Bebere. Among the women of the Akuna-kuna of Nigeria, Bebere functioned as a female branch of Ekene. Members practiced protective and purification rites, though the organization also functioned as a friendly society. Admission was to adults and to girls.

Belli Paaro. Derived from Penda-Penda, Belli Paaro figured in the cultures of various tribes of Liberia, including the Gbandi and Kpwesi. It contained elements of Si'mo and Mumbo-Jumbo (Mahammah-Jamboh). Membership was open only to adult males, though the sons of members might also be admitted to a low, nonsecret degree after passing through the SEMBE puberty school.

Bena-Riamba. Although assisting foreign trade and promoting dealings with the white man was the ostensible aim of this society, which was founded in the Belgian Congo about 1870, the name literally means "The Sons of Hemp." The initiation ritual involved smoking the five-lobed weed through a ceremonial hash pipe, a device so large that two men were required to carry it. From its inception, the society admitted adults of both sexes, who were charged handsomely for the privilege of joining and who were expected already to be marijuana smokers.

Boa Societies. Like the Alligator Societies and Baboon Societies, Boa Societies were criminal organizations and reputedly cannibalistic. They existed among the Mende of Sierra Leone.

Boibente. This protective secret society influenced the

Temne peoples in some parts of Sierra Leone. The members were the spirits of their own ancestors. They kept as much as possible in darkness and silence. Admission was exclusively to youth, who were charged admission fees.

Bori. The name means "Ghosts" or "After-Death Spirits." Ostensibly Islamic, this society of the Nupe, Igbiri, and other Hausa tribes of the southern Sudan and northern Nigeria was not even recognized as Islamic by the more orthodox Islamic communities where it flourished. Membership was open to adults of both sexes, with branch lodges for children. The head of the organization (the *Sarakin Bori*) was always male, but the deputy (*Ayenge*) could be either male or female. There were numerous offices in the organization, including the *Magajia* or Marshal and the *Uban Mufane* or Deputy Marshal. There was also a Chief Musician, a Drummer, and a Chief Dancer (*Maikiddan Kwaria, Maikwaria,* and *Karua*). Other offices included *Dan Maiaba* ("Little Flatterer," or messenger), *Uwar Tuo* ("Mother of Porridge," or caterer), *Maigoge* (Shaver or rubber).

Borro-Mia-Gundu. Among the Pendembu of Sierra Leone, this organization functioned as a friendly society or a kind of "savings and loan," and also as a dance club. In 1919, it tried to corner the cassava market during the famine of that year.

Boviowah. Influencing a number of Liberian tribes, including the Basa, De, Gibi, Grebo, Nifu, Putu, Sikon, and related Kru tribes, Boviowah was originally a war band. It had two official heads, the *Worabanh,* or War King, and the *Bovio,* or Peace King. It was a masculine society, with admission between the ages of 14 and 20.

Bundu. This was a women's secret society in Sierra Leone, derived from Porro and itself the mother of Ankoi, Sande, and Yassi. Legends concerning its founding are widely varied. One refers to a country far to the east of Sierra Leone, inhabited only by women, called Beled-el-Mia. The ritual was long and elaborate, centered on purification (see RITUALS AND CEREMONIES).

Butwa. Butwa ranged from Angola through Zimbabwe (formerly Rhodesia), with a strong political structure and completely open admission for both sexes at all ages, even babies. The name may derive either from "the hidden mystery" or from "the people who beat [those who pry into their mysteries]."

Bweti. Found among the Bakele of the Belgian Congo, Bweti was an important social organization for males, with admission at puberty. Selected women served as honorary members.

Chibados. This purification society influenced the Western Balunda and other Lunda-Lunda peoples in Angola and the Belgian Congo. Because some

LODGES were open only to girls at puberty, while others admitted adults of both sexes, it may be that Chibados resulted from a merging of two or more older traditions, possibly SIMO, PORO, KNIMBA, and Mukanda.

Dou (in some places, "Lou"). Appealing mostly to the Bambara and Bobo tribes of Upper Senegal, with headquarters south of Timbuktu, the society was an offshoot of Penda-Penda. Unlike the older society, it was open to adults of both sexes.

Dubaia. An offshoot of Ampora, Dubaia was founded by Ampora officers who had migrated to the upper lands of the River Rokel. It may also have been a personal protective society founded by a European slaver, who was trying to use the power of a Poro-like organization for his own purposes. Admission was male, either by payment as an adult or via neighboring puberty schools.

DUK-DUK

Dus. This protective secret society was prevalent among the Mossi and other tribes of the Upper Volta (now Burkina Faso) and the Ivory Coast. The symbolism was phallic, and there was reputed to be an oracle at one time. Membership was open to men and women, with heavy fees for the higher degrees.

Dyoro. Centered on a phallic ritual, Dyoro was derived from Oro and was active among the Lobi and Dinla peoples of the Upper Volta (now Burkina Faso). It admitted both sexes at puberty.

Ebomici. Probably derived from Omia but claiming a separate history, Ebomici was open to adults of both sexes, with admission at puberty. The center of influence was the Ugo district of Nigeria.

EGBO

Egugu. "Egugu" means "disembodied spirits," those who have risen from the dead. The society was influential among the Kukuruku of southern Nigeria, and membership was male, with admission at puberty.

Egungun. "Egungun" may be translated as "skeleton" and was a protective secret society among the Yoruba of Sierra Leone, the Gold Coast (Ghana), the Ivory Coast, and Nigeria. Originally religious, it became mostly social and protective and was noted for *Agugu* parties, similar to the parties of American COLLEGE FRATERNITIES AND SORORITIES.

Ekene. Among the Akuna-Kuna of Nigeria and among the Kwa of the Cross River district of Nigeria, the Ekene once wielded great political power, but it had evolved into a primarily social society by the 1920s. The officials of Ekene also serve as officials in Ebere. Membership was male, with admission as adults or via periodical puberty schools for the sons of members.

Ekkpo-Njawhaw. Founded by a woman chief who had enslaved her "subjects," Ekkpo-Njawhaw was a protective secret society, at one time riotous and disruptive. By the 1920s, it was mainly a social club, with protective powers. It was open to men and women and influenced the Ibibio people of southern Nigeria.

EKKPE

Ekongola. Founded as a war club, Ekongola was later transformed into a protective and social club. Although membership was male (with women admitted to an honorary branch), the head of the society was known as the Mother of Ekong, and the processional dress was female.

Eku-Meku. Founded as a war society for young warriors of the Ibo in southern Nigeria, Eku-Meku included a severe penalty for breaking its oath: execution by the oath breaker's closest friend. After the British occupation of the region, Eku-Meku became a criminal society devoted to robbery and intimidation, which led to conflict with white authorities. After this, the organization was transformed into a social club. Membership was open to both sexes.

Eluku. Derived from Oro via Egbo, Eluku was open to males admitted at puberty—though the leader of the society might be either a woman or a man. It strongly influenced the Gold Coast and some parts of the Congo, but by the 1920s was little more than a social organization, with protective rights.

Elung. Elung figured among the Quolla or Dualla peoples of the Cameroons and was possibly derived from Ikung. It was a rival to Ekongola, with membership restricted to men, though there was an honorary women's branch as well.

Epe. Among the Aro around Lagos in Nigeria, Epe was derived from Ngbe and had a primarily political thrust. Membership was open to men and women.

Eshorbo. This West African protective secret society influenced the Yoruba peoples of Nigeria and nearby states, especially the Ife people, who were the guardians of the headquarters. It probably derived from Oro, perhaps via the Egbo or the Ogboni. Membership was male, with admission at puberty.

Eturi. Found among the Ibibio of southern Nigeria, Eturi claimed to be a branch of the original Egbo, but by the 1920s was little more than a social organization. Membership was open to men and women, who paid heavy fees.

Eyo. This society with a protective ritual was found among the Awori of Nigeria. Admission, at puberty, was exclusively male.

Gbangbani. The taboos of Gbangbani were reputed to

be very powerful. Their *kotongi* fetish either had the power to drive sharks away, or to render them harmless. Membership was open to both sexes at any adult age.

Gelede. Originally a phallic religious cult, Gelede metamorphosed into a social organization holding large festivals. It was open to adults of both sexes, who paid large fees.

Homowo. Among the Ga-speaking peoples of West Africa, the Homowo was a society honoring the gods Nai, Sakumo, Korle, and their servants Dantu, Afieye, Guan, and Oyiadu. It was open to adults of both sexes, with high fees levied for higher degrees. Homowo used to cause famines during the Great Festival at Accra in August. The concentration of people and the limited numbers who ermained at work in the countryside contributed to the problem.

HUMAN LEOPARDS

Human Panthers. Like the Baboon, Boa and Alligator societies, the Human Panthers was a cannibalistic secret society. Members mutilated their victims' bodies with weapons that emulated the slash of a big cat's paw. The order existed in French Guinea and Sierra Leone and was sometimes known as N'Kee.

Humoi. This purification secret society for the women of the Mende and Sherbro-Bullom of Sierra Leone was, like a number of other women's secret societies in West Africa, apparently designed at least as much for the entertainment of men as for the edification of women. The religious underpinnings were phallic and fertility rites, and the society supervised the public whipping and washing of offending women—or, in some cases, of her entire family. Offenses included those against tribal morality, including marriage within prohibited degrees of kindred and affinity. Admission was restricted to marriageable females, with an honorary lodge for selected men, two of whom acted as officials.

JAVIA KARTAS

KADIRIYYA, ORDER OF

Kaloko. Dedicated to dance and play and appealing mostly to young people among the Temne of Sierra Leone, Kaloko was named for a minor deity. A member acted the part of Kaloko in a dance, and his movements were copied by all the other dancers. As part of the ritual, a man or woman would be "captured" from the crowd, ritually bound, then symbolically "killed" and "eaten" by Kaloko. Before they could be untied, a ransom had to be paid. The person so "devoured" was often a candidate for membership.

Kambonbonke. This was a guild of Temne blacksmiths of Sierra Leone.

Kangar. With its female counterpart Kemah, Kangar

was dedicated to enforcing prohibitions and taboos. Bearing similarities to Poro, it admitted males at puberty.

Katahwira and Katahwiriba. Derived from Penda-Penda and popular among the Aku (Yorub) of the Gold Coast (modern Ghana), this was a phallic cult with an elaborate ritual and a host of officers. Initiates, known as *baba-alawo,* underwent purification rites. Membership was exclusively male, with admission at puberty, and a women's branch of Katahwira, possibly modeled on an Ashanti (Asante) association, was Katahwiriba.

Kimpasi. A protective secret society for women in the Zombo district of the Belgian Congo, Kimpasi admitted adult women and had an honorary branch for girls who passed through puberty schools.

Kinki. Open to the women of the Kafu-Bullom of Sierra Leone, Kinki derived from Bundu and enjoyed considerable political power.

Kofoo. This was a protective secret society for women of the Limba and Sanda-Temne peoples of Sierra Leone. The guardian deity or spirit that attended each member could (in spirit form) pass through walls, loosen bonds, and perform other useful tricks. Admission was at puberty.

Koliumbo. Among the Koranko of Sierra Leone, Koliumbo was an agricultural society with a ritual concerned with the growing and harvesting of crops. In addition, members staged plays about famous past members and about deities relevant to the harvest. The society was open to men, who paid substantial fees.

Kongkorong. Active chiefly around the sound and west of the Sudan, Kongkorong traced its roots to al-Moqanna, conqueror of the Sudan in the ninth or 10th century A.D. Like many such societies, its Islamic veneer is transparently thin in places. Membership was restricted to adults, and sons of members were eligible for training schools organized by the society. Most adherents were Susu, with some Mandingos also joining.

Kongold. This was originally a phallic religious cult, but it later functioned as a protective and social society among the Abo and Bakundu of the French Congo as well as in Nigeria and the Cameroons. As with many other West African protective societies, the members represent after-death spirits; the head man's mask is a black-and-white death's head. Membership was male, with admission at puberty. There was an honorary lodge for selected women.

Kono. Among the Koranko of Sierra Leone, Kono was a branch of Tilang, affiliated with Segere. Men were admitted.

Kufong. Kufong was a protective secret society among the Limba, Temne, Koranko, Mende, and Sherbro of Sierra Leone. Claiming equality of age with Ampora, and using the same ritual as Poro, it is said to have been founded by a *djinn,* who granted the members the gift of "invisible levitation." Once political, it evolved into a protective and social society. Membership was male, with admission at any adult age. Boys who have passed through Poro were also admitted. The society was also known as Kofo, Kofoo, and Kufo. Branches (which may also be claimed by Ampora) include Banban and Dubaia.

Kure. Active in Sierra Leone, Kure was formed as a dancing club to perform ancient tribal dances, but retained some links with Poro and Bundu. Membership was open to both sexes, with candidates admitted as young as five before progressing through junior and then senior degrees.

Kwaga. An exclusive, expensive West African secret society deriving from Penda-Penda, possibly via Dou, Kwaga influenced the Kanuri of Bornu and other districts.

Lubuku. This West African secret society among the Bashilange of the Belgian Congo practiced purification and fertility rituals. Lubuku may be translated as "The place where friendship dwells." Membership was open to men and women.

Malanda. Among the Batanga of the French Congo and other tribes in the Cameroons, Malanda was a great organization in power and membership, though there was little secret about it. It was largely social and protective, and had purification rites. Males were admitted at puberty.

MANNEKEH

Masubori. The Masubori, or "Spirit-Possessed," had many adherents among the Hausa people. The members were assumed to be possessed by the spirits of either humans or animals, and the head of the lodge was female and was known as *Arifa* (Priestess) or *Sarauniya* (Chieftainess). Adults of both sexes joined, and there were separate lodges for children.

Mawungu. This women's West African secret society in the French Congo influenced the Mpangwe, or Fang people. It is unclear whether it was a women's auxiliary to Ngi (see below), but it had its own separate organization and officials. The symbolism was phallic, and the initiates traditionally dressed as men. Admission was at puberty.

Mborko. Among the Aro of Nigeria and based on Ogboni (see below), Mborko emphasized mutual cooperation and support and included such benefits as legal advice and a funeral club. Membership was mostly adult male, but included some women as well, usually the wives of officials of the organization.

Miweyeti. Found among the Shekani of Nigeria, this was a guild of ironworkers. It used the ritual of Malanda. Membership was adult, of both sexes.

Mori. Among the Fula, Mandingo, and Susu peoples, Mori had a strong priestly component. In some areas, adults of both sexes were admitted; in others, women were eligible to join only as honorary members. Like a number of other West African secret societies, it wore an Islamic cloak, but its beliefs were scarcely compatible with Islam, which it probably antedates.

Muemba and Mukuku. This purification secret society among the Duala of the Cameroons featured a phallic ritual concerned with fertility and owing a great deal to Mungi (see below). Membership was male, with admission at puberty. Mukuku was the female equivalent, again with admission at puberty.

Mukanda. A protective secret society among the Western Balunda of Angola and the Belgian Congo, the Mukunda featured a ritual derived from Mungi, of which the society may originally have been a branch or degree. The head of the society is also the head of Chibados (see above). Membership was male, and admission was at puberty.

MUMBO JUMBO

Mungi. Mungi was derived partly from Si'mo and Oro, but had an Islamic tinge; the High Priest was traditionally supposed to be chosen from a family that had long professed Islam. Membership was male, with admission at puberty. As with Egbo, Mungi had a strong antiwar influence. Derivatives from Mungi include the Congolese Ndembo and, in Angola, the Mukanda and Chibados.

Naferi. This derivative of Penda-Penda influenced the Wakore and Wngara, Mandingo tribes of upper Senegal. Open to adults of both sexes, it developed a strong rivalry with Dou at around the end of the 19th century.

Nanam. Derived from Penda-Penda, Nanam enjoyed influence among the Kru tribes of Liberia and Sierra Leone. It claimed an ancient origin and jealously guarded its secrets. It was strongly protective in function. Not only adults of either sex were eligible for admission, it also ran training schools, and accepted Poro youths and postpubescent girls from the Bundu and Yassi schools.

Nda. Influencing the Bakongo of the Belgian Congo, Nda claimed to be the most sacred and secret of secret societies. Some of its branches became powerful societies in their own right, such as Muemba and Njembe. Males were admitted at puberty.

Ndembo. The fetish power of this protective secret society, influencing the Bakongo of the Belgian Congo as well as being known in Angola and the

Cameroons, could ward off sickness and check the violence of unjust chiefs. The members were known as *Nkita*, "the Knowing Ones," and included such officials as the Player (*Nembimbi*) and both male and female doctors (*Lubwiku* and *Kumbi*); the *Kumbi* was also an official of Kimpasi. The penalty for breaking the oath was originally perpetual slavery for the traitor and his family, but was later reduced to the threat of a twisted neck, a broken leg, or a crooked spine. Both sexes were admitted as adults, but with honorary membership for children who completed retreats.

Ndito-Iban. A purification secret society among the Efik and Ibibio of Nigeria, possibly derived from Oro, with which it claims equal antiquity, Ndito-Iban was effectively a social club, with an underlying ritual of phallic fertility and purification. Some officials of Ndito-Iban also hold office in Iban-Isong. Membership was male, with admission at puberty.

NEGUITI

Ngbe. Among the Ekoi of southern Niberia, Ngbe claimed (as did a number of others) to be the original Egbo. Males were admitted at puberty. The legend of the society (again like many others) claims that it was founded by a woman, but that it was changed to a masculine society after a man learned its secrets and had to be initiated.

Ngi. This society features a phallic ritual, concerned mostly with purifications and prohibitions. It is associated with Mawungu, and membership is male, with admission at puberty.

Nimm. This society, found in Nigeria (among the Ekoi) and also in Liberia, Sierra Leone, the Ivory Coast, and the French Congo, was particularly interesting because it is sometimes held up as the origin of Voodoo. The degrees represented the time before birth; baby; child; youth or maiden; adult; and ancient. Membership was open to both sexes and all ages, and there was a dual leadership consisting of the Royal Father and the Royal Mother.

Njembe. A purification secret society among the Mpongwe of the Ogowe district of French Guinea, Njembe may have started as a female lodge of Izayoga, its great rival. Although membership was open to both sexes (adults by payment, children through puberty schools), by the 1920s, most of the officers were women. The underlying ritual is phallic.

Nkanda. Derived from Ogboni, and influential among the Bakuba of the Congo Bend district, or Bushongo, Nkanda membership is exclusively male, with admission at puberty.

N'KIMBA

Nri. Among the Ibo of southern Nigeria, Nri functions as a priestly caste in a sort of "established church." Nri must be present at a coronation, for example. Membership is hereditary and male, with admission at puberty, but the members take no part in public ritual until 10 years after their admission.

Oduwa. This was a protective secret society among the Nkoranza and other Ashanti-related peoples of the Gold Coast (Ghana). It was open to men and women.

ODWIRA

Ofiokpo. Found among the Andoni of Nigeria, Ofiokpo was possibly derived from Oshorbo and Egbo, but it was transformed into a dance society for men, with an honorary lodge for women.

Ogboni. Derived from Oro via Egbo, Ogboni was an influential political and social secret society restricted to men, with admission at puberty. Several of the degrees became strong societies in their own right. Its influence was among the Yoruba of the west coast. In addition to the Ogboni, or chief, the other officers included *Alafiu* (deputy leader), *Alakatu* (arbitrator), and the ominously named *Awaijate* (Executioner, or "He Who Shows Mercy in Death").

Okonko. Found among the Ibo in Nigeria, Okonko claimed in the 1920s that more than half of the four million Ibo people were members. Membership was open to both sexes, admitting adults by payment and juniors via puberty schools. The women's side of Okonko made its own laws for women, disregarding men, and (male) judges were required to consult with the women's committees before passing judgment in any case involving women. The leader of a senior committee was called *Amwu* or "Queen," with the privilege (alone among women) of wearing a man's hat.

Olokemeji. This society illustrates the difference between "operative" and "accepted" farmers. Mostly, the officials of the Olokemeji are responsible for weather control, intercession with weather and crop deities, and so on, but a few "accepted" or honorary members are not farmers. An interesting feature of the organization is that there is no human headman; a vacant seat represents the head of the organization, and remarks are addressed literally to the chair. Speeches are made in order of seniority, with the most senior member present having the privilege of speaking last. There are also honorary women members, subject to handsome admission fees.

Olugumbu. In the Bihe district of Angola, Olugumbu was originally conceived as a "police" society (like Babende) to punish those who broke tribal law, but it later functioned more as a social club. Membership was open to adults of both sexes.

Orisha. Derived from Oro via Egbo and influencing the Ekita, Ijebu, Awori, and Egbado peoples of southern Nigeria, Orisha was open to males, with admission at puberty.

Oro. Oro was the oldest of the pagan secret societies of West Africa, and the oldest secret society indigenous to Nigeria. As old as Si'mo, its remnants are to be found among the Egba and Oyo peoples. Like Si'mo, it has for many decades been more important as the root of other societies, especially Egbo. The Head of Oro was the greatest high priest of his land. By the 1920s, however, Oro was little more than an inner council of Egbo. Oro was probably a phallic cult in honor of Oloron, the thunder-voiced, Oke, the ruler of mountains and hills, and Olokun, the ruler of the sea. As in Si'mo, membership was limited to a few specially selected male adults. The sons of members might, however, attend puberty schools run by Egbo.

Ovato. Ovato was found in the Geduma district of Nigeria, possibly derived from Egugu. It functioned as a social club for adults of both sexes.

Ovia. This was a purification secret society among the Ede of Nigeria, in the Kukuruku country. Membership was for male adults, with honorary membership for a few women.

Owo. Among the Ekita of Nigeria, Owo was a branch of Ayaka, with primarily political aims. Membership was male, with admission at puberty.

Owu-Ogbo. Found among the Ibani of the Lower Niger, Owu-Ogbo was primarily a dramatic and dancing society, but also included purification and fertility rites. Membership was open to men and women, who paid heavy fees.

Oyeni. On the Gold Coast, Oyeni influenced the Sempe and Ga-speaking peoples. Its political power derived from its members renown for victories over the Awuna tribe. It was also protective against certain diseases. The signs of the group were connected with fishing. Oyeni was open to men and women.

Penda-Penda. Penda-Penda drew many adherents among the Baga and Susu people in the area of what is now Guinea. It was shaped both by Islamic secret societies such as Sirri (see below) and by societies that had not abandoned their pre-Islamic roots, such as Si'mo. Its Islamic features were patchy, and were syncretic rather than orthodox. The lowest two of the society's numerous degrees were not secret. Some of the officials in Penda-Penda held their position by heredity. Membership was reserved for adult men, though women might (at the discretion of the men) be admitted to honorary lodges. Training schools were provided for youths.

PORO
QAÏROWAN

Ramena. This purification secret society among the marriageable women of the Temne of Sierra Leone was heavily influenced by Ankoi and Kinki, and affiliated with Poro. Any men admitted to the honorary lodge had to be members of Poro. The members paid high fees, which resulted in an exclusive membership. The underlying religious symbolism is phallic, connected with fertility.

Raruba. A West African secret society among the women of the Temne in Sierra Leone, Raruba possibly derived from Bundu (see above). The word *Ruba* may be translated as "blessing," and the "Ruba Women" of the organization commanded high fees for blessing anything and everything. The ritual emphasized the cycle of life and death. The medicine or magic of the society was noted for its power to promote fertility, while the care and maintenance of graves was another high priority of the society. Membership was limited to certain families, with the eldest daughter of a member being selected for initiation soon after her marriage.

Sande. This women's society among the Vai and Gallinas of Sierra Leone conducted a puberty school, where girls were taught household duties, the law affecting women, respect for their future husbands, and fishing and agriculture. Sande was affiliated with Ampora (see above), and used the ritual of the Bundu (above).

Segere. A women's purification secret society, among the Ijebu of southern Nigeria, Segere included a ritual derived from Bundu and Sande (see both above). Membership was female, with admission as adults by fee or as girls through its own schools or those of Bundu and Sande.

Shopono. Shopono was a protective secret society among the Egba and other peoples in Nigeria. Its origins were religious, mainly phallic/fertility, but the chief attraction was the medicine or magic for warding off smallpox and other diseases. It was banned at the beginning of the 20th century, but continued to survive well into the 1920s and may still exist in places to this day. Membership was open to adults of both sexes.

SI'MO
SINDUNGO

Sirri. The "Society of the Magicians" appears to be genuinely ancient, perhaps having originated as early as 1600 B.C. Sirri was found all along the north and west coasts of Africa, "mostly among the Fula, Hausa, Mandingo, and Susu peoples." Although generally regarded as an Islamic society, its roots obviously extended far beyond the origins of Islam. Like other Islamic societies, it was mainly male-oriented, but in some cultures, women were admitted.

Tilang. This protective secret society among the Mende and Sherbro of Sierra Leone offered honorary membership to members of the Temne people. The medicine or fetish was supposed to be able to counteract all diseases. The ritual shows evidence of ancient Poro links. Membership was male, with admission at puberty.

Tongo Players. This criminal secret society was founded in the 1880s in Sierra Leone. Its was originally formed to hunt HUMAN LEOPARDS, but with the decline of that cannibalistic order, the Tongo Players turned to less discriminating violence.

Tormai. Tormai was a protective and social secret society among the Ebo of Benin, admitting adults of both sexes.

Tuntu. Tuntu was a "prohibitive" society; that is, it prescribed certain behavior and prohibited the rest. In case of Tuntu, the prohibition concerned the seemingly improbable subject of fishing nets. The death of Paramount Chief Kai Ngabi, who used a seine net rather than the traditional forms, is said to have been due to breaking this taboo. Meetings were traditionally held only in the dry season, as the medicine used must not be touched by rain. Area of influence included Sierra Leone, especially the Sherbro people, and membership was open to men and women.

WANKA

Wunde. Among the Gpa-Mende of Sierra Leone, the Wunde held fertility dances at sowing time, harvest time, coronations, marriages, births, and birthdays. Members also gave athletic displays. The ritual and organization echoed those of Poro, with an initiation based on DEATH AND RESURRECTION.

Yasi. Yasi, found among the Igalwa and Mpongwe of the Congo, apparently related to Izyoga, with which it shared officials. Its principal activity was organizing fairs, at which members competed for dancing prizes.

Yassi. Attracting the women of the Mende in Sierra Leone, Yassi originally derived from Bundu, but by the early 20th century it was Bundu's greatest rival. It was affiliated with Ampora, which supplied three men as chief drummers, and was rich and influential, possessing many permanent buildings. Admission was via puberty school.

Yugu. Yugu was found among the Duala of the Cameroons and was also known in Angola and the Belgian Congo. Members held festivals at sowing time and at harvest. Fees were steep, and membership was exclusively male, with admission at puberty.

Zangbeto. Found among the Ewe-speaking peoples of what used to be French Dahomey—roughly, the modern Benin—*Zangbeto* may be translated as "the Voice Heard in the Night." The foundation legend was similar to that of Babende (above). It was a sort of "sheriff's posse," but at some time after its foundation it changed sides, and members became robbers instead of police. Finally, it was transformed into a friendly society, with a funeral benefit aspect.

Western Catholic Union

506 Maine Street
Quincy, IL 62301
(217) 223-9721

The Western Catholic Union was founded on October 16, 1877, in Quincy, Illinois, as a fraternal benefit life and health insurance company. It is open to Catholics of both sexes, and there were 27,730 members in 1995. The union publishes the *Western Catholic Union Records* bimonthly.

When the Western Catholic Union was established, it worked on a simple ASSESSMENT basis to provide help to the widows and orphans of deceased members. In 1881, juvenile members were admitted; in 1912, women were allowed to join in their own right; and the organization has flourished ever since.

There is no ritual (see RITUALS AND CEREMONIES), as this is contrary to Catholic doctrine, and there are no DEGREES. Each branch (or LODGE) is affiliated with a Catholic parish, bears the name of that parish, and contributes to the good works of both the parish in particular and the Catholic Church in general. There are also fraternal gatherings, including outings, social nights, and so forth, as well as more serious activities such as organized pilgrimages to Catholic shrines.

Construction of a Western Catholic Union retirement home did not begin until 1976. It now occupies an entire city block in Quincy, Illinois, where the 10-story headquarters of the organization is still the largest building.

Western Fraternal Life Association

1900 First Avenue N.E.
Cedar Rapids, IA 52402
(319) 363-2653

The Western Fraternal Life Association was founded in 1897 as a fraternal benefit society, primarily for Czechs, but open to all over the age of 15. In 1995 there were 51,030 members. The association publishes the *Fraternal Herald* monthly.

The Western Fraternal Life Association (until 1971, the Western Bohemian Fraternal Association) was formed as a splinter group from the western lodges of the Czecho-Slovak Protective Society. Part of the organization's longevity and success is probably due to the fact that the organizers recognized at an early stage that Czech immigrants would learn English and would want to conduct lodge meetings in that language rather than Czech. The association has an active tradition of externally oriented works. In World War II, for example, it bought three bombers, and in more recent years it has run a home for the aged and has supported such general fund raisers as the March of Dimes, American Cancer Society, and so forth. The organization retains elements of ritual (see RITUALS AND CEREMONIES).

Western Slavonic Association

9025 Grant Street, Ste. 201
Denver, CO 80229
(303) 451-1494

The Western Slavonic Association was founded in the United States in 1908 as a fraternal benefit life insurance association with a mainly Yugoslav appeal. There were 9,500 members in 1995. The association publishes the monthly *Fraternal Voice*.

In 1990, the Western Slavonic Association changed its name to W.S.A. Fraternal Life. It was licensed to sell insurance in Colorado, Utah, Minnesota, Pennsylvania, and Ohio, and had a staff of four. Activities apart from insurance are the usual ones: Visiting the sick and bereaved, college scholarships, and organized trips, including trips to Yugoslavia—before the break-up of that country. In the LODGES, Slavic culture is traditionally promoted, and a ritual is worked (see RITUALS AND CEREMONIES). There are still some trappings of fraternalism, including membership in the Fraternal Congress.

White Rabbits, Supreme Order of

The Supreme Order of White Rabbits was incorporated in St. Louis, Missouri, in 1921 by former members of the Order of OWLS. Little has been heard about it since, and no information was available on its RITUALS AND CEREMONIES or other details of its operation and membership.

White Shrine of Jerusalem, Supreme Shrine of the Order of the

107 East New Haven Avenue
Melbourne, FL 32901
(407) 952-5323

The White Shrine of Jerusalem was founded as a Christian auxiliary (see AUXILIARIES) to FREEMASONS in the United States. There were 69,000 members in 1995.

The White Shrine of Jerusalem is yet another variety of Christianized ADOPTIVE MASONRY—that is, Freemasonry for women. It is perhaps more congenial to evangelically minded Protestant women than the Order of the EASTERN STAR, though, until 1953, members of the White Shrine of Jerusalem were required to be members of the Eastern Star.

The original White Shrine of Jerusalem was founded by Charles D. Magee in Chicago on October 23, 1894, but three years later he founded a rival organization of the same name in Grand Rapids, Michigan. The two Supreme Shrines managed to reconcile their differences by 1909, and in that year they were united in Chicago. Membership is open to Master Masons as well as their wives, mothers, daughters, widows, and sisters. Members are known as Sojourners; the head of the organization is the Supreme Worthy High Priestess.

William Penn Association

709 Brighton Road
Pittsburgh, PA 15233
(412) 231-2979

The William Penn Association was founded in 1886 as a fraternal benefit life insurance society in the United States. In 1995 there were 70,000 members. The association publishes *William Penn Life* monthly.

The William Penn Fraternal Association was typical of the fraternal benefit assessment societies that mushroomed in the United States in the last part of the 19th century. The founders were coal miners of Hungarian extraction, so a secondary purpose was to encourage Hungarian culture and retain the Hungarian heritage. Not until 1924 was the insurance placed on a sound actuarial basis, a year after a juvenile department had been formed to insure those under 16. There is a ritual (see RITUALS AND CEREMONIES), but it does not play a major part in the working of the modern organization.

In 1955, the William Penn Fraternal Association absorbed the Verhovay Fraternal Insurance Association and the Rakoczi Aid Organization, and in 1971 it dropped the "Fraternal" from its title and took the present name. In 1980, it absorbed the American Hungarian Catholic Society, and, in 1983, the CATHOLIC KNIGHTS OF ST. GEORGE. In addition to enrolled members, there are social members (without insurance benefits), of whose numbers no central records are kept.

In addition to the usual fraternal insurance benefits, the association also makes donations to worthy causes, provides scholarships, and organizes summer camps, Christmas parties for underprivileged children, and so on. Local branches organized visits to the ailing and infirm.

Verhovay Fraternal Insurance Association

The Verhovay Aid Association was founded in 1886 in Pennsylvania as a fraternal beneficiary society. It changed its name to the Verhovay Fraternal Insurance Association in 1935.

Wissahickon Pietists

Pietism was a movement among 17th- and 18th-century Protestants that emphasized good works and the spiritual necessity of leading a holy life. The leader of the Pietist revival was Philipp Jakob Spencer, but the movement was also greatly influenced by the mystical teachings of Jakob Boehme.

Pietism was a religious movement rather than a secret society; however, one American Pietist group, the so-called Wissahickon Pietists, bears mention here because some believe that the group functioned as a secret society by serving as a quasipolitical organization advocating American independence from Great Britain. This may or may not have been the case, but the fact is that Johann Kelpius, a student of Boehme, settled in the Philadelphia area (the present-day Germantown neighborhood) and established a colony of Pietists on nearby Wissahickon Creek. Whatever political activities they may have engaged in, they were devoted to holiness and good works as well as mysticism, drawing in particular on Hermetic (see HERMES TRIMEGISTUS) traditions. They also produced beautiful sacred music based on Baroque German sources.

The Wissahickon Pietists died out within a generation of the death of Kelpius (1708); however, Hermit Spring and Hermit Lane in Philadelphia's Fairmount Park remain today as mute testament to the order's existence along the creek.

Woodcutters, Order of

See LENHADORES E LENHADORAS, ORDEM DOS.

Woodmen

The attraction of the forest seems to be strong for founders of secret societies. In addition to the FENDEURS, the FORESTERS, and even the CARBONARI, there have been several varieties of "Woodmen." There have also been Woodchoppers (the Woodchoppers Association was a small beneficiary society founded as a derivative of the Foresters in Philadelphia in 1890) and an Order of Wood Cutters, which was a short-lived Masonic group of about 1847.

Modern Woodmen of America

1701 First Avenue, Rock Island, IL 61201; (309) 786-6481

The Modern Woodmen of America was founded in 1883 at Lyons, Iowa, as a life insurance and fraternal benefit society for white men aged 18–45. The racial criterion was later abandoned. There were 704,800 members in 1995, and the group published *The Modern Woodman* quarterly.

Joseph Cullen Root, who founded the Modern Woodmen of America, was an enthusiastic joiner; he was or had been a member of the FREEMASONS, KNIGHTS OF PYTHIAS, ODD FELLOWS and United Worker (see UNITED WORKMEN, ANCIENT ORDER OF), to say nothing of being the rector of V.A.S. His new organization was founded as a fraternal benefit life insurance society, with rigorous limits on who might be admitted. Candidates had to be

white males aged 18–45, from the 12 "healthiest" states (the Dakotas, Illinois, Indiana, Iowa, Kansas, Michigan, Missouri, Minnesota, Nebraska, Ohio, and Wisconsin), and not inhabitants of large cities, even in these "healthy" states. Also excluded were "railway brakeman, railway engineer, fireman, and switchman, miner employed underground, mine inspector, pit boss, professional rider and driver in races, employee in gunpowder factory, wholesaler or manufacturer of liquors, saloon keeper, saloon bartender, aeronaut, sailor on the lakes and seas, plough polisher, brass finisher, professional baseball player, professional fireman, submarine operator, or soldier in regular army in time of war." Anyone who took up one (or more) of these hazardous professions lost all coverage, but, provided he gave up anything to do with the sale of intoxicating liquors, he could regain some protection by filing with the Head Clerk an affidavit waving all rights to benefits in case of death or injury arising from the prohibited activity. Religion—or lack thereof—was *not* a bar to membership. The organization accepted "Jew and Gentile, the Catholic and Protestant, the agnostic and atheist."

Life insurance was always the principal focus of the group, and the main reason that there was a secret-society overlay seems to have been that Root liked writing rituals (see RITUALS AND CEREMONIES). The LODGES worked four DEGREES, in which forests and Roman courts figured as symbols in the proceedings.

After the schism that led to the founding of the Sovereign Camp of the Woodmen of the World (see the following), the Modern Woodmen disposed of much of Root's ritual, though local organizations are to this day called Camps and regional lodges are called Districts.

The Royal Neighbors of America was the female auxiliary (see AUXILIARIES), which was long ago absorbed by the parent organization.

Supreme Camp of the American Woodmen

P.O. Box 504, Denver, CO 80201; (303) 280-9013

This group was founded on April 4, 1901, in Colorado as a fraternal insurance company. The fraternal veneer seems to be thin over this insurance company, which until 1970 published a magazine, *The American Woodmen Informer*. No membership figures were available in 1995.

Woodmen Circle

This was the former female auxiliary of the Woodmen of the World. It was absorbed in 1965 by the Woodmen of the World Life Insurance Company.

Woodmen of the World

97775 South Yosemite, P.O. Box 8005, Littleton, CO 80124; (303) 792-9777

The Woodmen of the World was founded in 1890 as a fraternal insurance society for those over 16. It publishes the *Pacific Woodman,* bimonthly, and boasted 22,000 members in 1995.

The Woodmen of the World was founded by three members of the original Modern Woodmen of America. Its precise relationship to the earlier body is unclear, but it may well be a result of the same schism that gave rise to the Woodmen of the World Life Insurance Society (see following). It was known initially as the Head Camp, Pacific Jurisdiction, Woodmen of the World; in 1916, it became simply Woodmen of the World, though it was also known as Woodmen of the World (of Colorado). Its fraternal character, in the sense of ritual and the like, was stronger than that of the original society. In 1962 it absorbed the Christians' Mutual Benefit Association, followed in 1965 by the Pike's Peak Mutual Benefit Association.

The society organizes social and recreational events, awards scholarships, supports orphans, and donates lifesaving equipment to hospitals.

Woodmen of the World Life Insurance Society

Woodmen Tower, 1700 Farnam Street, Omaha, NE 68102; (402) 342-1890

This organization was founded in 1890 as an insurance society for those over 16. It publishes several magazines: the monthly *Chips* and *Woodmen of the World Magazine,* as well as *Shavings,* which appears 11 times a year. There were 975,000 members in 1995.

In 1890 the stability of the Modern Woodmen of America was threatened by a conflict between Mr. Root and the chief physician of the organization, Dr. P. L. McKinnie. The Woodmen solved their problems by simply ejecting both men from the organization. Root then set up another organization in Omaha, Nebraska, which was almost identical to the one from which he had been expelled. Like his earlier organization, the new one prospered as a life insurance society—though the fraternal side still exists, complete with initiation ritual, and beneficiary members are still given an annual password. Only the initiatory degree, that of Obligation, is compulsory, however, though Root also provided three further degrees (Morning, Noon, and Night) to "Camps desiring to elaborate fraternal work." Masonic influences are evident, though the implements are woodworking tools rather than stoneworking ones. There is the mallet or beetle, the wedge, and the ax.

This is the strongest of all the Woodmen organizations, with almost 150,000 more members in 1989 than a decade previously, though it has boosted its numbers over the years by absorbing a number of smaller fraternal benefit insurance groups: the United Order of the Golden Cross (1962); Order of Railroad Telegraphers (1964); Supreme Forest Woodmen Circle (1965); and the New England Order of Protection (1969).

Woodmen Rangers and Rangerettes

1700 Farnam Street, Omaha, NE 68102; (402) 271-7258

The Woodmen Rangers and Rangerettes were founded in 1903 as the youth auxiliary of the Woodmen of the World Life Insurance Company. Boys and girls, 8–15 years of age, may join. There were 139,000 members in 1995.

Workmen's Benefit Fund of the United States of America

99 North Broadway
Hicksville, NY 11801-2905
(516) 938-6060

The Workmen's Benefit Fund of the United States of America was founded in 1884 (and incorporated in 1899) as a fraternal benefit society, originally for the benefit of German Americans; since 1976, membership has been open. There were 15,000 members in 1995. The fund publishes a bimonthly magazine, *Solidarity.*

The Workmen's Benefit Fund of the United States of America is typical of the ethnic self-help organizations founded by various immigrant groups in the United States in the late 19th century. For the first 15 years of its existence it was unincorporated; in 1899 it incorporated in the state of New York.

Like other such organizations, its activities went beyond mere insurance to embrace recreational camps, old people's accommodation, charitable donations, and so on, but these activities declined in scale as the organization itself declined in size: 53,000 in 1965 to 15,000 in 1995.

Workmen's Circle

45 East 33rd Street
New York, NY 10016
(212) 889-6800

The Workmen's Circle was founded in 1900 as a fraternal and insurance society, principally for Jews in the United States and Canada. It publishes two quarterly magazines, *Kultur und Leben* and *Workmen's Circle Call.*

The Workmen's Circle dates back to the days of massive Jewish immigration from the ghettos and *shtetls* of Europe, when many Jews were at or close to the bottom of the economic heap; earlier self-help Workmen's Circles began in the 1890s. When the original Central Farband of Workmen's Circle Branches was formed, the stated premise was that "continuous poverty and frequent illness, which are especially burdensome for the worker, have brought us together within the Workmen's Circle so that through our unity we may be of mutual assistance to each other." Within a decade, the organization had almost 37,000 members; at its highest point, in 1925, it had some 85,000. In 1995, membership stood at 37,000.

The basic LODGE is the Branch; above that is the Convention Territory or Territorial Conference and the National Convention (which includes Canada).

Long a supporter of social causes and "progressive" legislation such as the New Deal, *Der Arbeter Reng* (to use the Yiddish title) also maintains Jewish schools and homes for the elderly. The "workers" currently enrolled include physicians and surgeons. The Workmen's Circle League absorbed the Young Circle League at some uncertain time in the past.

World Federalist Association

P.O. Box 15250
Washington, DC 20003
(202) 546-3950

Founded as the United World Federalists in 1947 and subsequently called World Federalists U.S.A., the World Federalist Association works to transform the United Nations into what it calls a "democratic world federation capable of ensuring peace, economic progress, and environmental protection." It had 10,000 members in 1995, and it warrants mention here only because conspiracy theory advocates have described it as a possible "front" for the ILLUMINATI with the aim of creating a one-world government by subverting the ideologies of left and right alike.

Whether this is the case or not, the organization is hardly secret, but quite visible, maintaining a speakers' bureau, organizing study groups, conducting seminars and conferences, and publishing the *World Federalist* quarterly, in addition to occasional reports. The association also bestows the Norman Cousins Global Governance Award annually.

World Masons, International Supreme Council of

This is another of the organizations within the FREEMASONS. It is a part of the SCOTTISH RITE; it exists in some forty countries; and membership automatically confers the Thirty-Third Degree of the Scottish Rite. The order conducts classes in foreign languages, electronics, mathematics and automobile maintenance.

There were 40,000 members in 1988, compared with only 31,000 in 1979. No more recent statistics are available, and the *Encyclopedia of Associations* reports that the order's address has been "unknown since 1986."

World Plan Executive Council – U.S.

P.O. Box 370, Lake Shandelee Road
Livingston Manor, NY 12758

The World Plan Executive Council was founded in 1972 pursuant to the announcement of a "World Plan" by Maharishi Mahesh Yogi, the modern exponent and popularizer of Transcendental Meditation (TM). Many

have claimed that Transcendental Meditation is a religion and that, therefore, the World Plan Executive Council is a religious organization. The U.S. District Court in Newark, New Jersey, ruled that TM was indeed religious by nature (and, therefore, the teaching of TM was banned in the public schools of New Jersey), but adherents of TM have steadfastly asserted that it was established on a theoretical base called the Science of Creative Intelligence and that, therefore, it is the practical product of scientific theory rather than religion. However one ultimately defines Transcendental Meditation, the World Plan Executive Council sufficiently resembles a secret society to merit inclusion here.

Maharishi Mahesh Yogi, who was born about 1911, studied for 13 years with Guru Dev, the modern founder (or rediscoverer) of Transcendental Meditation. Following Guru Dev's death in 1958, Maharishi (a highly educated man, who held a physics degree from Allahabad University) began to share the teachings of his master with the world. He made his first world tour in 1959, and the movement gathered momentum throughout the 1960s, gaining popularity in the "mind-expanding" context of the era's vast "counterculture" movement, but really taking off when high-profile celebrities, including the Beatles, Mia Farrow, Jane Fonda, and others, identified with it and sought direct counsel from Maharishi.

The "World Plan" Maharishi announced in 1972 called for the establishment of 3,600 World Plan centers (one for each million people on earth) in order to broadcast to the world the Science of Creative Intelligence and, ultimately, to bring about a new Age of Enlightenment. Five major structures were created by the World Plan Executive Council: the International Meditation Society, the Spiritual Regeneration Movement, the Student International Meditation Society, and Maharishi International University, a four-year university in Fairfield, Iowa, offering a mix of traditional curriculum with a TM slant. Finally, the American Foundation for the Science of Creative Intelligence works within the business community.

While all of this would seem very public, TM ultimately rests on an initiation into the "secrets" of meditation (based on ancient japa yoga meditation techniques), which includes the performance of quasi-religious ritual, and the repetition of a specially conferred mantra, a constantly repeated sound, which bears a strong resemblance to the kind of secret words found in many secret societies. In 1983, Maharishi offered the services of World Government to the world's more conventional governments to assist them in solving their problems.

Maharishi currently has no legal ties to the World Plan Executive Council, but he is regarded by the society as its founder, the founder of TM, and the founder of the Science of Creative Intelligence.

The organization currently does not report its membership, but by 1984, more than a million people had taken TM courses offered by World Plan Executive Council bodies. During the late 1980s, the council sponsored a genuine political party, the Natural Law Party, which is active in the United States and in Europe.

Wren, Sir Christopher

Sir Christopher Wren (1632–1723), the eminent architect most noted for St. Paul's Cathedral in London, is claimed as a member of the FREEMASONS — a rare example of a major figure who links operative Masonry (albeit at a much higher level than anyone but a Freemason would call "masonry") with speculative masonry. It is, however, unclear whether he actually *was* a Freemason. If he was a member of the Craft, he was probably initiated in 1691.

Xerophagists

The Xerophagists was a transformation of the Italian FREEMASONS, which changed its name to escape the punishments to which Freemasons were liable after the Bull of Pope Clement XII in 1738. The curious word is alleged to derive from its being a temperance society. The first half of the word comes from the Greek word for "dry," and the second half from a Greek word meaning "to eat"; hence, "eaters of dry food."

Yakuza

The Yakuza is to Japan roughly what the MAFIA is to the United States: the Mob, the core of organized crime. The word means "useless" or "good-for-nothing" and is derived from a gambling term denoting a losing—"useless"—card combination.

The modern Yakuza is structured very much as a secret society. There are rituals of initiation and rituals of conduct (resembling those of the ancient samurai warriors), oaths of secrecy (violations of which are punishable by death or by the amputation of a finger), and a very special sign of recognition: elaborate tattoos, often covering large parts of the body. Rank-and-file Yakuza (corresponding to the "soldiers" of the American Mafia) also are known for wearing very flashy clothing that strikes Western observers as a parody of American gangster movies. However, there is very little comic about the conduct of the Yakuza. Yakuza members account for 30 percent of the Japanese prison population and are involved in all manner of organized crime activity: gambling, drugs, prostitution, protection rackets, and the like.

The origin of the Yakuza is not clear, although it probably originated in the Tokugawa period (1600–1868). It is possible that the modern Yakuza derives from mid-17th-century urban merchant and labor groups, which protected their interests and the interests of their communities against marauding bands known as *hatamoto yakko*. In this early incarnation, the Yakuza were held in esteem, as knights or as Robin Hood–like defenders of the defenseless. It is also possible that the Yakuza descended from gangs of wandering gamblers.

Yellow Dogs, Order of

Little is known about this apparently long-extinct order. It was apparently Southern in origin, introduced to the North in 1923. LODGES were called Kennels, Masonic symbolism abounded, and the presiding officer was the Grand High Cur. By 1923, there were 45 "kennels" in Columbus, Ohio, alone; Kennel No. 15 had 710 members.

The Improved Order of Yellow Dogs was a fraternal order that, by 1915, had branches in many large cities. It is unclear whether this was the same as the Order of Yellow Dogs. Neither organization exists today.

Yeomen, Brotherhood of American

The Brotherhood of American Yeomen, founded in 1897, was one of a vast number of fraternal benefit assessment societies established toward the end of the 19th century. The LODGES were called Homesteads, and there was a strong Christian element to the RITUALS AND CEREMONIES, which also praised the Magna Carta and the English language. The HOMESTEADERS was the result of a schism within the Yeomen.

In 1917, the Yeomen changed its financial footing to assure greater stability, and in 1932 it transformed itself into the Mutual Life Insurance Company. The order is now extinct.

York Rite

The so-called York Rite, also known as the American Rite, confers DEGREES above that of Master Mason in Freemasonry. Unlike the SCOTTISH RITE, where the degrees are merely numbered and are commonly worked somewhat perfunctorily, the degrees of the York Rite have names and can be worked more fully. The degrees (starting with the fourth, because Master Mason is the third) are:

Mark Master (4th)
Past Master (5th)
Most Excellent Master (6th)
ROYAL ARCH Mason (7th)

Superposed on the Royal Arch are the "Cryptic" Degrees:

Royal Master (8th)
Select Master (9th)
Super Excellent Master (10th)

Otherwise—or *after* taking these—a Royal Arch (7th Degree) Mason may proceed via the following:

Order of the Red Cross (8th)
Order of the Knights of Malta (9th)
KNIGHT TEMPLARS (10th)

The Knight Templar degree is closed to non-Christians. See also RED CROSS OF CONSTANTINE, and ROYAL ORDER OF SCOTLAND.

The York Rite is currently administered by the Most Worshipful National Grand Lodge Free and Accepted Ancient York Masons, P.O. Box 2789, Orangeburg, SC 29116-2789; (803) 531-1985. The Grand Lodge has 50,000 members in 38 state and 96 local groups.

Young Europe

"Young Europe" was an international revolutionary secret society founded in Berne, Switzerland, in 1834; each country was to have its own branch. The stated aims were "Liberty, Equality, and Fraternity for all Mankind."

Young Italy

The most successful of the organizations was Young Italy, *La Giovine Italia,* under the direction of Giuseppe Mazzini (1805–72). This society was dedicated to the unification of Italy, and its flag was the tricolor now in use. A former member of the CARBONARI who had escaped in 1833 from a sentence of death for his part in the revolt of the Sardinian army, Mazzini was thrown out of Switzerland in 1836 and moved to England.

Young Italy took only as many of the trappings of a secret society as were necessary. There were no PASSWORDS, but the tokens of recognition were a grip (see GRIPS) and a piece of paper cut into a distinctive shape. Both the grip and the shape of the paper were changed every three months. The Carbonari and Young Italy joined forces in 1852 to create Reunited Italy.

Young Germany

In 1837, as a result of a schism, many members of the Young Germany movement became Communists, but by 1845, Young Germany had recovered to the point of mustering more than 25,000 members. The order was represented in Berlin in 1848, but in the uprising of June 1849, Young Germany was quashed by the Prussians. It was relatively inactive thereafter.

Young Poland

Young Poland was founded by Simon Konarski in about 1835 or 1836. It died with him in 1839, after his prolonged imprisonment and torture by the Russian forces then occupying Poland.

Young Turkey

The expression "Young Turks" has passed into the English language to mean a radical group dedicated to the overthrow of the old order, but the Young Turks was once a discrete secret society, originally called Young Turkey. It was founded contemporaneously with the other revolutionary groups of Young Europe, but it never amounted to much. The second incarnation—called the Young Turks—was founded in 1867, simultaneously in London, Paris, and Constantinople (Istambul). Extremely well funded and unusually well organized, it gradually built power, ultimately spearheading a full-scale revolution in 1908, which was almost immediately successful, and which led to a major redrawing of the map of Europe.

Young Switzerland

Young Switzerland was an electoral reform society, but despite changing its name to the Association of the Gruetli, it was declared illegal in the Canton of Zürich in 1844. The Swiss Civil War of 1845 was fought largely over the principles of the Gruetli. When the Progressives won, the Young Swiss/Gruetli decided to dissolve the society.

Zonta International

557 West Randolph Street
Chicago, IL 60661-2206
(312) 930-5848

Founded in 1919 in Buffalo, New York, as Zonta and then expanded in 1930 into the Confederation of Zonta Clubs, Zonta International is an organization of 36,000 (1995) business and professional executive women "dedicated to improving the status of women and encouraging high ethical standards in business." Conceived as a female equivalent of LIONS INTERNATIONAL, it now sponsors cooperative projects with the United Nations, conducts programs to assist women in the fields of public affairs and policy making, and has consultive status with the Council of Europe, the International Labor Organization, and several U.N. agencies. It awards the Amelia Earhardt Fellowship annually to women doing graduate work in aerospace sciences. *The Zontian* is its quarterly publication.

Zoroaster, Oriental Order of

The Independent Order of Zoroaster united in 1897 with the Oriental Order of Zouaves to create the Oriental Order of Zoroaster. Unfortunately, nothing beyond this is known about the order or its antecedents.

Zuzimites, Ancient Order of

The Ancient Order of Zuzimites was a secret society resembling the FREEMASONS, which was imported from England to the United States some time before the 1920s. Members claimed that the order had been founded about 1903 B.C.

The order worked no fewer than 53 DEGREES. LODGES were called "Tents," and the headquarters of this society was in Liverpool, England. By the 1920s, however, the whereabouts of the headquarters was unknown, and the order may have disappeared.

Bibliography

Alba, Victor. *Transition in Spain: From Franco to Democracy.* New Brunswick, N.J.: Rutgers University Press, 1978.

Albuquerque, A. Tenorio d'. *A Maçonaria e a Independencia do Brasil.* Rio de Janeiro: Editora Espiritualista, n.d.

Artisans' Order of Mutual Protection. *A Century of Fraternalism: 1873–1973.* Philadelphia: By the Order, 1973.

Bacon, Francis. *Novum Organum* (1620) in *Works,* 15 vols. New York: Scholarly Press, 1987.

Bagon, Michael. *Withstanding Hitler in Germany, 1933–45.* London: Routledge, 1988.

Baigent, Michael, *et al. Holy Blood, Holy Grail.* New York: Dell, 1983.

–––––– . *The Messianic Legacy.* New York: Dell, 1989.

Beatty, Sir Kenneth James. *Human Leopards: An Account of the Trials of Human Leopards before the Special Commission Court* (1915; reprint ed.). New York: AMS Press, 1978.

Beck, Carl R. *A Time of Triumph and Sorrow: Spanish Politics during the Reign of Alfonso XII (1874–1885).* Carbondale: University of Southern Illinois Press, 1979.

Besant, Annie. *Autobiographical Sketches* (1893; reprint ed.). New York: Gordon Press, 1972.

Bibliotheca Estoerica: Catalogue Annoté et Illustré de 6707 Ouvrages Anciens et Modernes qui traitent des Sciences Occultes . . . comme aussi des Sociétés Secrètes . . . en vente a Librarie Dorbon-Aine (reprint ed.). Paris: Editions du Vexin Français, 1975.

Bishop, Peter, and Michael Darton, eds. *Encyclopedia of World Faiths.* New York: Facts On File, 1987.

Blavatsky, Helena Petrovna. *Complete Works,* 10 vols. New York: Gordon Press, 1972.

–––––– . *Isis Unveiled,* 2 vols. (1877; reprint ed.). New York: Theosophy, 1931.

–––––– . *The Voice of Silence* (1889; reprint ed.). New York: Theosophy, 1928.

Boorstin, Daniel. *Revolution without Dogma: Hidden History.* New York: Macmillan, 1987.

Bowben, Henry Warner. *Dictionary of American Religious Biography.* Westport, Conn.: Greenwood Press, 1993.

Brooks, Charles H. *The Official History and Manual of the Grand United Order of Odd Fellows.* Philadelphia: Privately printed, 1902.

Brownstone, David M. *The Irish-American Heritage.* New York: Facts On File, 1989.

Buloz, Herr A. (Jean De Witt). *Les Sociétés secrètes de France et d'Italie.* Paris, 1830.

Bulwer-Lytton, Lord Edward. *The Coming Race* (1847; reprint ed.). New York: Philosophical Publishers, 1973.

–––––– . *The Last Days of Pompeii* (1834; reprint ed.). New York: Buccaneer, 1983.

–––––– . *Zanoni: A Rosicrucian Tale* (1848; reprint ed.). New York: Spiritualist, 1990.

Burkert, Walter. *Ancient Mystery Cults.* Cambridge: Harvard University Press, 1987.

Butt-Thompson, Captain F. W. *West African Secret Societies.* London: H. F. & G. Witherby, 1929.

Cagliostro, Count Alessandro. *Memoires pour servir a l'histoire du comte de Cagliostro.* Paris, 1786.

Carnes, Marck C. *Secret Ritual and Manhood in Victorian America.* New Haven: Yale University Press, 1989.

Carr, Raymond. *Spain: 1808–1975.* Oxford: Clarendon Press, 1982.

Casey, Robert J., and W. A. S. Douglas. *The World's Biggest Doors: The Story of the Lions.* Chicago: Willcox and Follet, 1949.

Catholic Daughters of the Americas. *A History of the Catholic Daughters of the Americas, 1903–1986.* New York: Catholic Daughters of the Americas, 1986.

Catholic Knights of Ohio. *The Fullness of Fraternalism: A History of the Catholic Knights of Ohio.* Hamilton, Ohio: Catholic Knights of Ohio, n.d.

Cavendish, Marshall, ed. *Illustrated Encyclopedia of Mankind.* New York: Marshall Cavendish, 1990.

Cavendish, Richard. *Man, Myth, and Magic: The Illustrated Encyclopedia of Mythology, Religion, and the Unknown.* New York: Marshall Cavendish, 1985.

———, ed. *Encyclopedia of the Unexplained, Magic, Occultism, and Parapsychology.* New York: McGraw-Hill, 1974.

Central Office of Information. *Britain 1994: An Official Handbook.* London: Central Office of Information, 1993.

Chalmers, David M. *Hooded Americanism: The First Century of the Ku Klux Klan, 1865-1965.* Westport, Conn.: Greenwood Press, 1965.

Chang, Maria Hsia. *The Chinese Blue Shirt Society: Fascism and Developmental Nationalism.* Berkeley: University of California Press, 1985.

Chesneaux, Jean. *Mouvements populaires et sociétés en Chine aus XIXᵉ et Xᵡ siècles.* Paris: Maspero, 1970. Abridged English-language ed., Palo Alto, Calif.: Stanford University Press, 1972.

Clapp, Stella. *Out of the Heart: A Century of P.E.O., 1869-1969.* Mount Pleasant, Iowa: P.E.O., 1969.

Clave, Abbé F. T. Begue. *Histoire pittoresque de la Franc-Maçonnerie et des sociétés secrètes anciennes et modernes.* Paris, 1842.

Clifton, Charles S. *Encyclopedia of Heresies and Heretics.* Santa Barbara, Calif.: ABC-CLIO, 1992.

Colombo, John R. *Colombo's Canadian References.* Toronto: Oxford University Press, 1976.

Conway, David. *Secret Wisdom: The Occult Universe Explored.* London: Jonathan Cape, 1985.

Crow, John A. *Spain: The Root and the Flower.* New York: Harper and Row, 1965.

Crowley, Aleister. *Magick in Theory and Practice* (1919; reprint ed.). New York: Weiser, 1992.

Cumont, F. *Textes et Monuments figures relattifs aux Mystérès de Mithra.* Brussels, 1896 and 1899.

Daraul, Arkon. *A History of Secret Societies* (1962; reprint ed.). New York: Pocket Books, 1983.

Demott, Bobby J. *Freemasonry in American Culture and Society.* New York: University Press of America, 1986.

Dillon, Richard H. *The Hatchet Men: The Story of the Tong Wars in San Franciscos Chinatown.* New York: Coward-McCann, 1962.

Douglas, J. D., ed. *New Zion Twentieth Century Encyclopedia of Religious Knowledge.* Grand Rapids, Mich.: Baker Book House, 1991.

DuMenil, Lynn. *Freemasonry and American Culture, 1880-1930.* Princeton, N.J.: Princeton University Press, 1976.

Dyer, Colin. *William Preston and His Work.* Shepperton, Eng.: Lewis Masonic, 1987.

Eco, Umberto. *Foucault's Pendulum.* London: Picador/Pan, 1990.

Editors of Time-Life Books. *Ancient Wisdom and Secret Sects.* Alexandria, Virginia: Time-Life, 1989.

Eliade, Mircea. *History of Religious Ideas.* 3 vols. Chicago: University of Chicago Press, 1981-85.

Elliott, J. H. *Imperial Spain: 1469-1716.* New York: St. Martin's, 1969.

Emerson, A. Ralph. *New World Order.* Tucson, Ariz.: Publius, 1990.

Encyclopedia of Associations. Detroit: Gale Research, 1993.

Erbstoesser, Martin. *Heretics in the Middle Ages.* Leipzig, 1984.

Federation Life Insurance of America. *A Brief History of Federation Life Insurance of America, 1913-1976.* Milwaukee, Wisc.: Federation Life Insurance of America, ca. 1976.

Ferguson, Charles W. *Fifty Million Brothers: A Panorama of American Lodges and Clubs.* New York: Farrar and Rinehart, 1937.

Fong, Mak Lau. *The Sociology of Secret Societies: Chinese Secret Societies in Singapore and Peninsular Malaysia.* London: Oxford University Press, 1981.

Foucar, G. *Les Mystères d'Eleusis.* Paris, 1914.

Fraternal Order of Police. *The Fraternal Order of Police 1915-1976.* Pittsburgh: Fraternal Order of Police, 1977.

Frost, Thomas. *Secret Societies of the European Revolution, 1776-1876.* London, 1876.

Funchion, Michael F. *Irish American Voluntary Organizations.* Westport, Conn.: Greenwood Press, 1983.

George, John, and Laird Wilcox. *Nazis, Communists, Klansmen, and Others on the Fringe.* New York. Prometheus, 1992.

Gist, Noel P. *Secret Societies: A Cultural Study of Fraternalism in the United States.* Columbia: University of Missouri Press, 1940.

Gray, Tony. *The Orange Order.* London: The Bodley Head, 1972.

Green, Miranda. *Dictionary of Celtic Myths and Legends.* New York and London: Thames and Hudson, 1992.

Griffin, William D. *The Irish in America, 550-1972.* Dobbs Ferry, N.Y.: Oceania, 1973.

Guiley, Rosemary E. *Encyclopedia of Witches and Witchcraft.* New York: Facts On File, 1989.

Gurdjieff, George I. *Beelzebub's Tales to His Grandson.* New York: Viking Penguin, 1992.

———. *Meetings with Remarkable Men.* New York: Viking Penguin, 1991.

Hall, Manly Parker. *An Encyclopedic Outline of Masonic, Hermetic, Cabbalistic, and Rosicrucian Symbolical Philosophy: Being an Interpretation of the Secret Teachings Concealed within the Rituals, Allegories, and Mysteries of All Ages.* New York: Philosophical Research Society, 1977.

Hanson, Carol G. O. *History of the Sons of Norway*. Minneapolis: Sons of Norway, 1944.

Hapgood, Norman, ed. *Professional Patriots*. New York: Albert and Charles Boni, 1927.

Headings, Mildred J. *French Freemasonry Under the Third Republic*. Baltimore: Johns Hopkins University Press, 1949.

Heckethorn, Charles William. *The Secret Societies of All Ages and Countries* (reprint ed.). New Hyde Park, N.Y.: University Books, 1965.

Hickey, D. J., and J. E. Doherty. *A Dictionary of Irish History Since 1800*. Dublin: Gill and Macmillan, 1980.

Hilgarth, J. N. *The Spanish Kingdoms: 1250–1516*. Oxford: Clarendon Press, 1978.

Hine, Darlene Clark, ed. *Black Women in America: An Historical Encyclopedia*. Brooklyn, N.Y.: Carlson, 1993.

Hodde, Lucien de la. *Hastier des sociétés secrètes et du Parti Républicain de 1830–1848*. Paris, 1850.

Hoffman, Peter. *The German Resistance to Hitler*. Berkeley: University of California Press, 1970.

Howard, Michael. *The Occult Conspiracy*. Merrimac, Mass.: Destiny, 1989.

Howe, Ellie. *Magicians of the Golden Dawn*. New York: Weiser, 1978.

Johnston, Robert M. *The Napoleonic Empire in Southern Italy and the Rise of Secret Societies*. London: Macmillan, 1904.

Kalous, Milan. *Cannibals and Tongo Players of Sierra Leone*. London: M. Kalous, 1974.

Katz, Jakob. *Jews and Freemasons*. Cambridge: Harvard University Press, 1970.

Kibbe, P. C. *Damon and Pythias*. Washington, D.C.: Knights of Pythias, 1930.

Krebs, Albert. *The Infamy of Nazism*. New York: Franklin Watts, 1976.

La Fontaine, Jean Sybil. *Initiation*. New York: Penguin, 1985.

Large, David Clay. *Contending with Hitler: Varieties of German Resistance in the Third Reich*. Cambridge: Cambridge University Press, 1991.

Laukhard, F. C. *Orden nach seiner Entstehung, innern Verfassung und Verbeitung auf den deutschen Universitaten, usw*. Halle, 1799.

Leemon, Thomas A. *The Rites of Passage in a Student Culture: A Study of the Dynamics of Transition*. New York: Teachers College Press, Columbia University, 1972.

Lejeune, Anthony. *The Gentlemens Clubs of London*. London: Dorset Press, 1984.

Lepper, John Heron. *Famous Secret Societies*. London: Simpon, 1932.

———. *Famous Secret Societies*. London: Sampson, Low, Markston, 1932.

Lewis, H. Spencer. *Rosicrucian Questions and Answers, with a Complete History of the Rosicrucian Movement* (1929; reprint ed.). San Jose, Calif.: Rosicrucian Press Ltd., 1981.

Lindner, Theodor. *Die Veme*. Muenster, 1888.

Little, J. P., ed. *Encyclopedia of Heraldry*. New York: Pergamon, 1970.

Lovett, A. W. *Early Haspburg Spain: 1517–1598*. Oxford: Oxford University Press, 1986.

Low, W. Augustus, and Virgil A. Clift, eds. *Encyclopedia of Black America*. New York: McGraw-Hill, 1981.

Mackey, Albert G. *An Encyclopedia of Freemasonry and its Kindred Sciences*. New York: Masonic History Co., 1920.

Madden, Richard Robert. *United Irishmen*. London, 1843.

Mariel, Pierre. *Dictionnaire des sociétés secrètes*. Paris: Culture, Art, Loisirs, 1971.

———. *L'Europe parisienne au Xx^e siècle*. Paris and Geneva, 1964.

———. *Nicholas Flamel et l'Alchemie*. Paris: Culture, Art, Loisirs, 1971.

Marras, Americo Palfrey. *The Secret Fraternities of the Middle Ages*. London and Oxford: Oxford University Press, 1865.

Mather, George A. *Dictionary of Cults, Sects, Religions and the Occult*. Grand Rapids, Mich.: Zondervan, 1993.

Matossian, Mary K., "Armenia and the Armenians," in *Handbook of Major Soviet Nationalities*. New York: Free Press, 1975.

Mazrui, Ali A. *The Africans: A Triple Heritage*. Boston: Little, Brown, 1986.

Melton, J. Gordon. *Biographical Dictionary of American Cult and Sect Leaders*. New York: Garland, 1986.

———, ed. *The Encyclopedia of American Religions*. Detroit: Gale, 1989.

———. *Handbook of Cults in America*. New York: Garland, 1986.

———. *Religious Bodies in the U.S.: A Directory*. New York: Garland, 1992.

———. *Religious Leaders of America*. Detroit: Gale, 1991.

Merson, Allan. *Communist Resistance in Nazi Germany*. London: Lawrence and Wishart, 1951.

Miller, Timothy. *American Communes, 1860–1960: A Bibliography*. New York: Garland, 1990.

Morely, H. *Life of H. C. Agrippa*. London, 1856.

Murray, Jocelyn, ed. *The Cultural Atlas of the World: Africa*. Alexandria, Va.: Stonehenge, 1990.

Newland, H. Osman. *Sierra Leone: Its People, Products, and Secret Societies*. New York: Negro Universities Press, 1969.

Newman, Peter R. *Companion to Irish History: 1603–1921*. New York: Facts On File, 1991.

Norborg, C. Sverre. *An American Saga*. Minneapolis: Sons of Norway, 1970.

O'Donaghue, David J. *The Life of William Carlson, Being His Autobiography*. London, 1896.

O'Donnell, Elliott. *Strange Cults and Secret Societies of Modern London*. New York: Dutton, 1933.

O'Leary, John. *Recollections of Fabians and Fabianism*. London, 1896.

Oliver, Roland. *The African Experience*. New York: HarperCollins, 1991.

Parker, Derek, and Julia Parker. *The Power of Magic: Secrets and Mysteries Ancient and Modern*. New York: Simon and Schuster, 1992.

Pauwels, Louis, and Jacques Bergier. *Le Matin des magiciens*. Paris, 1959.

Payne, W. W. *Origin and Development of the Royal Antediluvian Order of Buffalo*. London: R.A.O.B., 1973.

Ploski, Harry, and James Williams, eds. *The Negro Almanac: A Reference Work on the African American*. New York: Gale, 1989.

Pollard, Captain H. B. C. *The Secret Societies of Ireland: Their Rise and Progress*. London: Philip Allan, 1922.

Pope-Hennessy, Una. *Secret Societies and the French Revolution, Together with Some Kindred Studies*. London, 1911.

Portlock, Ronald. *History of the London Knots 1775 to 1973*. London: Privately printed, ca. 1973.

Potter, Warren, and Robert Oliver. *Fraternally Yours*. London, Ontario: Independent Order of Foresters, 1967.

Presto, Douglas J. *Cities of Gold: A Journey Across the American Southwest in Pursuit of Coronado*. New York: Simon & Schuster, 1992.

Preuss, Arthur. *A Dictionary of Secret and Other Societies*. St. Louis: Herder Book Co., 1924.

Ragon, J. M. *Rituel de la Maçonnerie Forestière*. Paris: n.d.

Ratner, Lorman. *Antimasonry: The Crusade and the Party*. Englewood Cliffs, N.J.: Prentice-Hall, 1969.

Regardie, Israel. *The Golden Dawn* (6th rev. ed.). St. Paul, Minn.: Llewellyn Publications, 1986.

Roberts, J. M. *The Mythology of the S.S.* New York: Scribner's, 1972.

Robinson, John J. *Born in Blood: The Lost Secrets of Freemasonry*. New York: M. Evans, 1989.

Roller, David C., and Robert W. Twyman. *The Encyclopedia of Southern History*. Baton Rouge: Louisiana State University Press, 1979.

Ronayne, Edmond. *Ronayne's Hand-book of Freemasonry*. London, 1832.

Sackett, M. W. *Early History of Fraternal Beneficiary Societies*. New York: Scribner's, 1914.

Schmidt, Alvin J. *Fraternal Organizations*. Westport, Conn.: Greenwood Press, 1980.

Scott, Samuel F., and Barry Rothaus, eds. *Historical Dictionary of the French Revolution, 1789–1799*. Westport, Conn.: Greenwood Press, 1985.

Shannon, William V. *The American Irish*. New York: Macmillan, 1966.

Shapiro, J. J. *The Friendly Society: A History of the Workmen's Circle*. New York: Workmen's Circle, 1975.

Shepard, Leslie, ed. *Encyclopedia of Occultism and Parapsychology*. Detroit: Gale Research, 1978.

Snyder, Leslie, ed. *Encyclopedia of the Third Reich*. New York: McGraw-Hill, 1976.

Snyder, Louis L. *Louis L. Snyder's Historical Guide to World War II*. Westport, Conn.: Greenwood Press, 1982.

Stevens, Albert Clark. *The Cyclopedia of Fraternities: A Compilation of Existing Authentic Information and the Results of Original Investigation* (1907; reprint ed.). Detroit: Gale Research, 1966.

Swanton, John R. *The Indian Tribes of North America*. Washington, D.C.: Smithsonian Institution Press, 1952.

Symonds, John, and Kenneth Grant, eds. *Confessions of Aleister Crowley*. New York: Viking Penguin, 1989.

Thornton, Sister Mary Crescentia. *The Church and Freemasonry in Brazil, 1872–1875: A Study in Regalism*. Westport, Conn.: Greenwood Press, n.d.

Tiger, Lionel. *Man in Groups*. New York: Kampmann and Company, 1969.

Tihany, Leslie C. *A History of Middle Europe*. New Brunswick, N.J.: Rutgers University Press, 1976.

Train, A. C. *Courts, Criminals and the Camorra*. London, 1912.

Ukrainian National Association. *The U.N.A.: Its Past and Present*. Jersey City, N.J.: Ukrainian National Association, 1964.

Union Saint-Jean-Baptiste. *A Beautiful Dream Come True*. Woonsocket, R.I.: Union Saint-Jean-Baptiste, n.d.

United Societies of the U.S.A. *The United Societies of the U.S.A.* McKeesport, Pa.: United Societies of the U.S.A., 1978.

Van Dusen, Wilson. *The Presence of Other Worlds: The Findings of Emanuel Swedenborg*. Bryn Athyn, Pa.: Swedenborg Scientific Association, 1975.

Vasa Order of America. *Historical Review of Vasa Order of America 1896–1971*. Cranston, R.I.: Vasa Order of America, ca. 1971.

Vaughn, William Preston. *The Antimasonic Party in the United States, 1826–1843*. Lexington: University Press of Kentucky, 1983.

Vivian, Herbert. *Secret Societies Old and New*. London: Thornton Butterworth, 1927.

Webster, Nesta Helen. *Secret Societies and Subversive Movements*. London: Boswell Printing and Publishing Co., 1924.

Werlich, Robert. *Orders and Decorations of All Nations*. Washington, D.C.: Quaker, 1965.

Whalen, William. *Handbook of Secret Organizations*. Milwaukee, Wisc.: Bruce Publishing Co., 1966.

Wilson, Charles R., ed. *Encyclopedia of Southern Culture*. Chapel Hill: University of North Carolina Press, 1989.

Yarker, John. *The Arcane Schools: A Review of Their Origin and Antiquity*. Belfast: William Tait, 1909.

Yates, K. L. *A Brief History of the A.O.U.W.* St. Paul, Minn.: Ancient Order of United Workmen, 1966.

Yearbook of American and Canadian Churches. Nashville, Tenn.: Abingdon, 1994.

$\mathcal{I}$ndex

Page numbers in **boldface** refer to a major discussion of the topic.